THE POLITICS OF THE POST

THE POLITICS OF THE POST

Canada's Postal System from Public Service to Privatization

Robert M. Campbell

broadview press 1994

Canadian Cataloguing in Publication Data

Campbell, Robert Malcolm
The politics of the post : Canada's postal system from public service to
privatization

Includes bibliographical references and index.
ISBN 1-55111-034-2
1. Canada Post Corporation — History.
2. Postal service — Canada — History. I. Title.
HE6655.C35 1994   383'.4971   C94-931405-6

Broadview Press
Post Office Box 1243, Peterborough, Ontario, Canada, K9J 7H5

in the United States of America
3576 California Road, Orchard Park, NY 14127

in the United Kingdom
c/o Drake Marketing, Saint Fagan's Road, Fairwater, Cardiff, CF53AE

Broadview Press gratefully acknowledges the support of the Canada Council,
the Ontario Arts Council, the Ontario Publishing Centre,
and the Ministry of National Heritage.

PRINTED IN CANADA
5 4 3 2 1   94 95 96

Contents

PREFACE

My interest in postal matters likely has unconscious family roots, my mother having single-handedly kept the greeting card and postal industries afloat since her children left home. And, I am — perhaps — a distant relative of Sir Alexander Campbell, Canada's first post-Confederation Postmaster General (Canada Post is headquartered at the Sir Alexander Campbell building in Ottawa).

On a more professional note, I listened with scepticism to my collaborator Les Pal at the Canadian Political Science Association meetings in 1987 as he reported our friend Jim Struthers' observation that no book had yet been written about the Canadian postal experience. Predictably, a library check confirmed Struthers' observation. It also revealed a considerable and interesting British and American literature on postal matters.[1] This literature suggested to me that an examination of contemporary postal matters would reveal much about the Canadian state, its Crown corporations and its public policy, particularly in the transition from the Keynesian social welfare period to the neoconservative era. This hunch appeared to be confirmed in the summer of 1987, as Canada Post endured two bitter strikes; the labour situation in the Post Office appeared to be a metaphor for industrial relations in the post-Keynesian period. Even though I had no particular academic or professional experience in the area, I was drawn to explore the Canadian postal scene as a way of examining in a 'micro' and concrete fashion the political economy of the transition from Keynesianism to neoconservatism.

In earlier times, the Post Office was considered an uncompelling area for investigation and analysis, like the routine worlds of Public Works and Supply and Services. Postal matters were not subject to federal-provincial jurisdictional disputes and tensions, which may also explain the lack of Canadian academic interest in the area. Interest in postal policy has been stimulated recently by the remarkable transformation of government and postal management strategies in Canada, particularly since the 1986 corporate plan. The lacuna in the Canadian literature on the Post Office has been, to an extent, filled before the publication of this book.[2] A number of recent postal studies have reflected various approaches, from journalistic and historical accounts to studies informed by economic or cost-benefit concerns. Nonetheless, some key issues and broad themes remain unaddressed, and there remains a need to examine the Post Office in its government or political setting. This is the purpose of the present volume.

The Post Office Department was transformed into a Crown corporation in 1981. The original strategy of this study was to assess Canada Post's first decade as a Crown corporation and to analyze the evolution of its relationship with the government. A contribution could then be made to the literature on Crown corporations in Canada, an issue area as enduring and thoroughly Canadian as the Post Office itself.[3] This approach has been more or less sustained, with a few unanticipated detours. First, it became clear that the *raison d'etre* for the 1981 transformation, as well as an analysis of the Corporation's subsequent performance, could not be addressed realistically or effectively without a thorough examination and appreciation of the contours of the postal setting. An investigation of the Canadian postal experience before 1981 was absolutely imperative. However, this proved to be no small concern, given the absence of an academic study or history of the Post Office Department.[4] Thus, this study includes a substantial presentation of the pre-1981, pre-Crown corporation experience as a way of exploring the logic and implications of the transition to a postal Crown and its aftermath. Second, the Post Office's evolution as a Crown corporation coincided broadly with an extended period of Conservative governments (1984-88, 1988-93). The Conservatives turned out to be remarkably persistent in pursuing their neoconservative agenda, which included the goal of privatizing many of Canada's Crown corporations. As the Conservatives privatized de Havilland, PetroCanada, Air Canada and so on, it appeared at various moments that there would not be a decade's worth of postal Crown corporation experience to evaluate. Given the neoconservative and privatization context, the study came increasingly to focus on the *de facto* 'practice' as well as *de jure* 'idea' of the privatization of Canada Post.

The effort to research and write this book received considerable financial support. An award from the Social Sciences and Humanities Research Council (410-88-1158) allowed me to be relieved of some teaching responsibilities in 1988-89 and 1989-90, as well as to travel for research and interview purposes. The Trent University Research Committee provided seed money for projects on neoconservative economic policies and Crown corporations in Canada. Trent University approved my sabbaticals in 1990-91 and 1991-92, which allowed me to complete the research and write early drafts of the book. This study benefitted immensely from my association with the Centre for the Study of Regulated Industries at McGill University in 1991-92, and I appreciated greatly the support extended by Bob Cairns and Richard Shultz.

Many politicians, officials and individuals agreed to be interviewed for this study: past Postmaster Generals Jean-Pierre Cote (1965-68, 1971-2), Eric Kierans (1968-71), Andre Ouellet (1972-74, 1980-1, and 1981-4 as Minister Responsible for Canada Post), J.J. Blais (1976-8), Gilles Lamontagne (1978-79); David Collenette (Parliamentary Secretary to Gilles Lamontagne); Deputy Postmaster General John Corkery (1977-81); Hugh Mullington, co-author of the Arnott-Mullington study of the post office (1975); Alan Marchment, Chairman of the Marchment Committee (1985) and the Postal Services Review Committee, PSRC (1989-90), and Helen Hardy, his executive assistant at the PSRC; Michael Bourque, executive assistant to Perrin Beatty, Minister Responsible for Canada Post 1984-5; Bill Domm Parliamentary Secretary to Michel Cote, Minister Responsible for Canada Post Corporation 1985-6; Gary Billyard, Special Assistant to Harvie Andre, Minister Responsible for Canada Post Corporation 1986-1992; Michael Warren, Canada Post's first

President (1981-85); Rene Marin, Canada Post's first Chairman of the Board (1981-86); Roger Beaulieu, third Chairman of the Board (1991-3); Canada Post Vice-Presidents William Kennedy (Group Vice-President), Leo Blanchette (Mail Operations), and Kenneth Tucker (Information Technology and Strategic Development); other Canada Post Officials, including Jack Van Dusen (Media Relations), David Newman (Business and Community Affairs), Bob Labelle (Government Relations), Gregoire Crevier (Environmental Affairs), Steve Cameron (Director, Mail Operations Support), and David Smith (Marketing Research); David Salie, Crown Corporations Directorate of the Department of Finance and Treasury Board; Felix Holtmann, Chairman, Standing Committee on Consumer and Corporate Affairs; union officials including Shirley Carr (past-President of the Canadian Labour Congress), Bob McGarry (past head of the Letter Carriers Union of Canada, LCUC), Jean-Claude Parrot (past leader of the Canadian Union of Postal Workers, CUPW), and Geoff Bickerton (research director of CUPW); Cynthia Patterson, head of Rural Dignity of Canada. I have also corresponded with many others, including past Postmaster-Generals William Hamilton (1957-62) and John Fraser (1979-80); Liberal parliamentary critics Don Boudria and Robert Nault; John Gustafson of the Canadian Direct Marketing Association; Ralph Hancox and Kathleen Rowe of the National Association of Major Mail Users; and the Coalition of Canada Post Competitors.

Jean-Maurice Filion at Canada Post was particularly and cheerfully helpful in providing information and organizing interviews. Steve Cameron kindly provided a tour and explanation of the St. Laurent plant in Montreal. Bruce Moreland acted above and beyond the call of duty at the Corporate Library of Canada Post. I received assistance from John Bell, Thomas Hillman, Ian McClymont and John Smith at the National Archives. The Inter-Library Loan Offices at Trent University and McGill University were especially helpful and tolerant.

I benefitted from discussions and correspondence with others who are working in the postal area, including Julie White, Judy Fudge, Thomas Langford, Brian Osborne and Robert Pike. Caroline Porter, Marc Vincent and Joelle Favreau were exemplary research assistants at various stages in the project. This study has been stimulated by many analysts who have examined the role of Crown corporations in Canadian life: Allan Tupper, Bruce Doern, John Langford and Garth Stevenson, whose book on Canada's airlines was particularly influential.[5]

This book is dedicated to Christl Verduyn, who as an academic and scholar is only too familiar with the perpetual and often frustrating challenge of maintaining a healthy equilibrium between professsional and personal lives. With our children Malcolm, Lachlan, Colin and Frances (the latter two born since this project was first mooted), a lively and happy family life has sustained the effort and concentration required to research and write this book.

INTRODUCTION

In an article published in 1982, John Langford challenged political analysts to progress from the rhetoric about Crown corporations to a study of their reality. He criticized analysts' fixation on narrow and legalistic issues, such as political control and accountability, and recommended that they deal with the broader political and economic worlds in which Crown corporations function.[1] This work is a response to Langford's challenge, as well as to the examples set by a number of studies subsequently carried out in this spirit.[2] It moves beyond simple description of Canada Post as Crown corporation to examine it from broad historical and political economic perspectives.

The Post Office has been one of Canada's most visible and widely discussed political institutions. To paraphrase Garth Stevenson, no other public institution, not even the railroad, has had so pervasive a presence in so many communities.[3] It has not been as substantively or symbolically important in Canadian history as the railroads, but the Post Office's nation-building role has nonetheless been considerable.[4] Present in hundreds and thousands of cities, towns, villages, and rural communities across the vast Canadian landscape, the Post Office served an integrating function for the young country. It offered Canadians an inexpensive, accessible, and reasonably effective system of communication, reinforcing both the psychic and the physical bounds of the emerging Canadian nation.

Until the 1970s, the Post Office was widely perceived to have both economic and social responsibilities. It "subsidized" transportation and communication costs in this large and unwieldy country, by discounting the costs of mailing newspapers, books, and information and by establishing a postal presence in rural and isolated areas. In Canada's early days, communities vied to receive a postal outlet, as a means of ensuring their economic and social connection with the rest of the country. In the early twentieth century, there were over thirteen thousand post offices in Canada; in 1901 there was a post office for every 554 people.[5] Despite recent rationalizations and closings, and the advent of alternative modes of communication, Canada Post retains a tremendous physical presence today. It remains one of Canada's biggest real estate holders. It operates five thousand postal outlets (out of over eighteen thousand points of sale). It employs about the same number of people as Bell Canada (fifty-seven thousand), generates revenues at a level similar to CNR and Air Canada ($3.8 billion; thirtieth in Canada in operating revenue), and has more assets than Consumers Gas or Loblaws ($2.7 billion). Overall, Canada Post resembles a company like Sears: with $3.8 billion in revenue compared to Sears' $4.1 billion; each with $2.7 billion in assets; and Canada Post with nine thousand more employees than Sears' forty-eight thousand.[6]

Formed in 1867

The Post Office was one of the first federal departments formed in 1867, and it has been in the political spotlight ever since. Other governmental departments may be inefficient, make mistakes, take controversial decisions, and have labour problems, but in perhaps no other area are these decisions and results so visible and obvious, and their political consequences so immediate and brutal, as even a casual glance at Hansard or newspaper headlines will attest. The Post Office Department's transformation into a Crown corporation in 1981 was intended to take the "politics" out of the Post Office; but Canada Post remains a subject of persistent and near voyeuristic media scrutiny as well as regular discussion and debate in the House of Commons.[7]

This persistent attention to postal matters reflects Canada Post's visibility. Unlike other governmental actors, the Post Office operates primarily and directly in the daily life of the marketplace, where it retails products and services, transports letters and parcels, and communicates data and information within all parts of the country. Its activities touch the lives of Canadians daily, as checking for and sending mail is part of the ritual of life even in the age of fax machines and celluar telephones. The Post Office remains an important instrument of communications choice for thousands of businesses, organizations, and individuals, who sent 10 billion pieces of mail in 1992 to 11.4 million home and business addresses. The sheer volume and extent of its activity generates intense scrutiny. For example, at its average processing rate of forty million articles per working day, an error rate of 0.1 per cent will generate forty thousand problems or over one million potential complaints a year. When public expectations of reliable and speedy service are not met, there are complaints and demands that the government do something. Political debate and controversy is also generated by the periodic need to increase postal rates as well as by decisions over the location and closing of post offices.

Political matters are thus never long out of Canadians' consciousness. First, because the Post Office is one of Canada's largest employers, most Canadians are related to or friends with a postal employee. For example, the brother of Liberal postal critic Robert Nault is a Winnipeg letter carrier; the father of former postmaster general Jean-Pierre Côté was a postal clerk, as was the father of Jean-Claude Parrot, the long-time head of the Canadian Union of Postal Workers. Second, there have been numerous postal unions, which have been strong and active. Labour-management relations are scrutinized more closely, intensely, and persistently in the Post Office than in other areas of economic activity. Until recently, the large number of postal unions generated perpetual negotiations, which gave the permanent impression that a postal strike was imminent. This kept postal labour relations and the Post Office in the public spotlight.

The Post Office has not had the prestige of certain other departments, such as Finance or External Affairs, or other agencies, such as the CBC. As an "operational" (as opposed to "policy") department, it has not had much political sex appeal. It was associated in people's minds with "blue collar" departments, such as Public Works. It was, therefore, a ministerial assignment to be avoided or to be endured for as short a period as possible. This had important consequences for the Post Office's place in the political and budgetary pecking order, as well as for the quality of its political management. The Post Office's status has also declined, relative to other departments and agencies responsible for nation-building and communications (such as the CBC). Therein possibly lies the reason for the underdeveloped state of postal studies in Canada. For, despite the Post Office's size and impact, political scientists have neglected to study it as much as politicians have avoided thinking creatively about managing it.

Postal matters have always been closely identified with governments, in Canada as elsewhere. Since pre-Confederation times, the Post Office has enjoyed a state-sanctioned "exclusive privilege" in the transportation and delivery of letter mail, until recently called first-class mail. Broadly speaking, this monopoly has reflected the view that only the state could and would provide a postal service that would be both national and universal in scope. The private sector has been judged to be unwilling to make the large, expensive infrastructural investments and commitments required to service all areas, including outlying and low-density ones, and to provide a full range of services at equitable prices. As a result of the state monopoly, there has been a single charge levied for letter mail service in Canada since Confederation — regardless of the distance a letter travelled or the complication of its route. This principle of state monopoly has been adopted in most other countries, for practical reasons as well as reasons of equity. By far the greatest proportion of costs lies in handling, sorting, retailing, delivering, and administering the mail; transportation expenses account for a low proportion of postal costs (about 12 per cent in Canada, 7 per cent in the United States). Moreover, a system of distance-based rate differentials would be difficult and costly to administer.

The monopoly over letter mail has never extended to other categories of mail, such as newspapers and periodicals, addressed or unaddressed advertising mail and notices, or parcels. The relative importance of letter mail has varied; such mail presently comprises about 45 per cent of Canada Post's volume and 52 per cent of its revenue (see Tables 1 and 2). The remaining volumes and revenues are generated in the competitive market realm, images of a postal monopoly notwithstanding. Even within the domain of letter mail, the Post Office has competed increasingly with substitute products and services: the telephone and telegraph; fax machines; e-mail; fund transfer networks; computer-assisted communications; parcel shipping by truck, bus, air, and rail; and private courier services. There was some consideration given, when the Post Office was "Crowned" to extending the postal monopoly into the time-sensitive (courier) and telecommunications areas, but this was never seriously countenanced.

The nuances and practical implications of the Post Office's exclusive privilege will be analyzed below; here it suffices to say that, until recently, the state enjoyed a near-monopoly on the delivery of letter mail. This has been a political issue unto itself, and has encouraged the exceptional political scrutiny that the Post Office receives. The state has been held accountable for all features of postal functioning, from the location and closing of post offices to delivery standards and lost mail, from the price of a stamp and related postal services to postal labour relations and the security of the mail. Since Confederation, the site of this monopoly and political activity in Canada has been at the *federal* level of government. Along with national defence, the Post Office has been one of the few areas where Canadian federalism has not generated jurisdictional disputes.[9] This has simplified postal analysis considerably, and is likely another reason why political scientists have not found the Post Office an appealing subject of study.

Popular conceptions of postal functioning cluster around the image of personal letters delivered to one's doorstep during a raging blizzard, or birthday or Christmas parcels from distant friends and relatives arriving at the local post office . The reality is far less romantic: 80–85 per cent of postal volume and revenues is generated by business mail, and about 50 per cent of that by a handful of large postal users. A piece of mail is seven times more likely to be "business" rather than "personal" mail. Typically, Canadians *receive* business-related mail and *send* mail related to this business mail. They receive and send very little "personal" mail. This suggests how and why the post office has been transformed recently. At one time it was considered to be a "social" service, oriented to nation-building and national integration, and the provision of a social product in a universal and accessible way. The predominant postal vision has become more hard-nosed of late. The Post Office is now seen — by the state and business, if not by the population at large — as a part of the communications *business*, contributing in a vital way to the health of the capitalist economy. This postal vision has been shaped by, and in tune with, the requirements of increasing efficiency and competitiveness associated with the theme of "globalization." As a result, the Post Office has increasingly been directed to accord priority to market issues rather than social or political concerns.

Popular conceptions of the mechanics of the postal system also tend to the benign, the innocent, and the pre-industrial. This has been shaped by the familiar sights of the mail deliverer walking on his or her rounds, and postal clerks selling stamps or searching for registered letters in a local post office. The postal business may be simpler than, say, the nuclear industry, but it is far more complex than this vision suggests. Post-war economic expansion, population growth, and suburbanization have complicated immensely the collection, sorting, and delivery of mail. Daily postal volumes in the tens of millions and the expansion to over eleven million postal addresses have made it necessary to substitute machines for simple human memory and energy. Increasingly complex sorting equipment "read" addresses and process thousands upon thousands of pieces of mail an hour. The new generation of machines can sort mail into 1,150 different categories of regions, sites, addresses and so on. The processing and sorting of letters takes place in 150 mechanical facilities, 25 of which are major postal plants, some the size of multiple football fields. A half a billion kilometres are travelled each year moving the mail. Canada Post is the largest corporate user of transportation services in Canada. The postal distribution network connects with 600 airline flights every day, as well as with 5,400 vehicles (which drive more than 300,000 kilometres each day), and 100 Post Office trucks run twenty-four hours a day. Over 750,000 points of mailing and 11.4 million home and business addresses must be integrated into the transportation, sorting, and delivery systems.[10] All of this is engineered from a high-tech central control centre in Ottawa, which seems more suitable for launching rockets to the moon than to delivering the mail. There has been a technological revolution in postal processing since the 1970s, and another one is currently unfolding. These technological changes have had far-reaching implications for the Post Office, its customers, and its workers.

Nowhere have the implications of mechanization and modernization been more dramatic than with respect to labour. The Post Office has always been a labour-intensive business; an army of workers has been required to pick up, transport, sort, and deliver the mail, as well as to sell stamps and services. Handling of mail has always been more expensive than its transportation. Labour costs have typically comprised 70–75 per cent of costs,[11] while transportation has comprised about 11–12 per cent. By the late 1960s, there were fifty thousand postal employees processing five billion pieces of mail a year, using techniques and facilities not terribly different from those used in the nineteenth century. The advent of postal modernization in the late 1960s and 1970s coincided with a second critical development. Public servants were given the right to unionize in 1967, under the Public Service Staff Relations Act. The labour-intensive Post Office quickly became a union-intensive operation. There followed a pitched battle between labour and management/government over mechanization and its implications for job security, rates of remuneration, and working conditions. These and other labour-management issues comprise one of the most important features of the Canadian postal experience. Presently, there are nearly sixty thousand full- and part-time workers, a considerable, powerful, and expensive workforce. The centralization of mail processing and sorting, the high profile of postal operations and their unions, and the state's monopoly over letter mail have given postal unions an unusually high degree of bargaining strength, which has been used to considerable effect.

As in other policy areas, in the postal arena the Canadian state has had to juggle the various roles of the system, such as nation-building, national integration, and public service on the one hand (and extension of the market economy, provision of cheap and efficient communications, and balancing of postal costs and revenues on the other. The Post Office played a number of important economic roles in the hundred years after Confederation. On balance, it served social goals at least in equal measure to economic ones. For example, post offices were opened in most towns and villages across the country, with only marginal concern for their capacity to generate sufficient revenue to cover costs. A system of home delivery of mail was established free of charge, even in rural areas. Newspapers and periodicals were delivered free, or at a subsidized price, in order to build up a literate and well-informed society. A number of other postal items were subsidized, such as material for the blind, charitable organizations' mail, and food and perishables being transported to the North. The Post Office bore the economic burden of high transportation charges when the Canadian rail and air systems were being extended. Postal prices were kept low for this hundred-year period, as a deliberate matter of public policy (see Table 6). The price of a first-class stamp fell from eighteen cents per half ounce in 1851 to three cents in 1867, to three cents per *ounce* in 1889, to two cents an ounce in 1899. Postal prices were then increased from time to time, but at times of war and depression in order to raise governmental revenues, and not to serve postal purposes. Even so, the price of a first-class stamp was still only three cents in 1931 and four cents in 1951. As Canada celebrated its centenary in 1967, the price of mailing a letter was five cents an ounce (compared to six cents an ounce in 1867). Low postal prices were financed to a considerable extent by a low-wage policy; this policy became anachronistic when postal workers unionized and pressed for improved rights (e.g., job security), wages, and working conditions. Postal deficits appeared and increased, to be carried out of general revenues and absorbed in the state budget as an infrastructural socio-economic charge. In broad terms, then, postal policies were determined to a great extent by governments' values, which leaned to the social side of the social/economic equation.

The mix in the state's postal goals has altered in recent years, transforming the environment in which the Post Office functions. Governments' political and social orientations have changed, influenced by two interrelated developments. First, the post-war economic boom ended and a new generation of technology emerged. Second, the post-war consensus in support of the Keynesian welfare state collapsed and neo-conservatism emerged as the new ideological paradigm.[12]

The long post-war economic expansion slowed down in the late 1960s, weakening the growth in demand for postal products. Simultaneously, new technological developments emerged and produced a number of new communications alternatives to letter mail, which further weakened the Post

Office's economic position. Earlier in the century, the telephone and tele-graph had generated competition; but mail volumes managed to keep pace with economic and population growth (postal volumes did not keep pace with the expansion of these new services — see Tables 1 and 10). The latest generation of technological advances — telecommunications, fax machines, e-mail, and so on — was far more ominous for the Post Office. Overall growth in first-class mail volumes was halved; postal volumes rose 56 per cent between 1949 and 1959, but only 27 per cent between 1959 and 1969 (see Table 1). The Post Office faced an even more precipitous decline, because the major source of its activity — business mail — was easily adaptable to these new technologies and mechanisms. As will be seen in Chapter 4, the modernization and mechanization of the postal system in the 1970s seemed only to exacerbate matters. Productivity rises were not forthcoming, costs rose, and labour relations were disrupted. The Post Office did not increase its competitiveness, and its deficit grew. The new technology created inten-sified price and competitive pressures, thereby increasing the Post Office's need for capital and fiscal subsidies from the state. All of this created a highly uncertain economic context, and led the Post Office to adopt an increasingly defensive and protective posture. It appeared to face the prospect of long-term economic decline.

The transformation in economic and technological circumstances in turn generated far-reaching changes in the political environment. These political changes were equally consequential for the Post Office. The post-war Post Office had been insulated politically by the acceptance of Keynesian welfare economics. A service-oriented Post Office, extension of labour rights and improvements in working conditions, acceptance of postal deficits in the service of social and economic goals, maximization of employment possi-bilities, validation of postal practices as social "rights" — these were all very much in tune with the economic and social-democratic ethos of the post-war Keynesian era.

The economic decline of the late 1960s and early 1970s changed all this. Because governments failed to stem the economic decline, Keynesian eco-nomic strategy and the principle of state economic involvement were dis-credited. Neo-conservatism emerged triumphantly as the alternative political-economic paradigm; it articulated a radical strategy for encouraging eco-nomic regeneration and the flourishing of the new technological revolution. Simply put, this strategy required the liberation of the market economy from government involvement: dismantling of the welfare state, elimination of the deficit, deregulation, privatization, and withdrawal of the state from economic life. The Post Office took on a very different complexion within this rigorous market orientation. The postal deficit was considered as part of the larger public deficit, which had to be eliminated. The Post Office had to be weaned from government subsidy, if it was to become more efficient and competitive. Its labour practices and wage rates were seen as overly generous and totally out of synch with practice in the private sector. Its service functions in turn were thought to be indulgent, and to stifle economic growth and efficiency. The overall posture of the Post Office was seen as too "political" and not sufficiently commercial or competitive. Its monopoly position became suspect and its record of inefficiency an insult to economic and business sense. The Post Office appeared to be just another inefficient and uncompetitive firm or industry travelling along the path of economic decline, and looking to be propped up by a spendthrift government.

In this changed economic, political, and ideological context, the Post Office Department was transformed into a Crown corporation. Canada had had a grand tradition of using the Crown corporation as a policy instrument, particularly in the communication and transportation sectors in which the Post Office operated. The idea of a postal Crown corporation had long been mooted, and was given momentum after the strategy was embraced in the United Kingdom in 1969 and in the United States in 1971. But the Canadian government did not cross this Rubicon until 1981, and the extended delay revealed much about the politics of policy-instrument choice during this period. Moreover, by the time the Post Office took on its new status, the economic and ideological context had changed dramatically from that which fed the British and American initiatives. So too had the *raison d'etre* for the transformation. The postal Crowning in Canada occurred at a doubly inauspicious historical juncture. On the one hand, the triumph of neo-conservatism brought Crown corporations under exceptionally heavy political and ideological scrutiny. Indeed, many were privatized in the 1980s. On the other hand, competitive pressures in the communications sector at this time were extremely intense, as a result of a series of remarkable technological innovations. Thus, the new postal Crown corporation would live in very constrained circumstances in its first decade.

The transformation to Crown corporate status was the first significant institutional change at the Post Office in 114 years — and the first time a department of government had become a Crown corporation. The immediate economic and ideological context points to commercial and competitive factors as the determining causes of this change. Indeed, Canada Post was deliberately distanced from the government, and given the opportunity and direction to act more like a private-sector corporation. Although elimination of the deficit was only one of three priorities in the transformative legislation, it quickly became the dominant postal goal specified.[13] The Post Office was directed firmly by the government to put its operations on a pay-as-you-go footing and to follow the user-pay principle so politically popular in the 1980s. Henceforth, the Post Office would no longer be supported as a public good through general tax revenues.

These economic and ideological concerns were powerful, but they were not the only considerations that shaped the purposes of the new Crown

corporation. The Post Office's social role was not de-legitimized in the political and economic transformation of the 1970s. Indeed, it showed remarkable staying power. Canada Post was directed to maintain and improve customary postal standards (and) to repair labour-management relations. These
two goals were to be pursued even as it was transforming itself into an
innovative, competitive commercial operation. As will be seen in detail later,
the Crowning of the Post Office reflected the varied expectations of each
of its constituencies: business (which expected elimination of the deficit and
a commercial, business-like Post Office); labour (improved labour relations
under the Canada Labour Code); the public and general users (maintenance
and improvement of customary services); and postal bureaucrats (freedom
from both the department form and the control of other departments).
Although the form of the Crown corporation was an innovation, its original
substance or goals did not really change: the traditional and uneasy balance
between the social and economic goals of the Post Office was reproduced
within Canada Post. This was an unstable equilibrium that could not — and
did not — last for long.

This precarious balance reflected the state's continuing ambivalence in
postal matters. For the government, Crowning the Post Office was an attractive proposition, for that department had long been a political irritant
— labour, business, and the public complained constantly about deteriorating
service standards, the growth of the deficit, post office closings, and inadequate wages. Crowning would liberate the government from these complaints
and demands. The prospect of eliminating postal deficits and cutting the
size of the bureaucracy was also attractive. At the same time, though, the
state was reluctant to place the Post Office completely outside its reach. The
continuing legitimacy of the Post Office's social functions required that the
government retain some authority over postal matters, lest it be criticized
for political issues over which it no longer wielded control. Postal deficits
would continue for some time, so the government wanted some postal influence in return for paying this debt. Moreover, the state had to exercise
limits on what the Crown corporation could do in the market: the operation
of a "free" postal monopoly could not be allowed to interfere with capitalist
market activity. The Liberal government of the early 1980s thus established
a hybrid business operation: the Crown corporate form promised to shelter
the government from criticism, and the more commercial orientation promised to reduce the fiscal, labour, and competitive problems that the Post
Office traditionally had dumped in the government's lap. At the same time,
the postal Crown corporation would remain subject to the government's
broad policy orientations.

This introductory account of the Post Office's metamorphosis into a Crown
corporation suggests that the relevant state actions followed the pluralist
model of balancing all interests, including those of business, labour, bureau-

crats, and users. This ostensible balance or equilibrium was distinctly asymmetrical in practice and implication. The creation and subsequent actions of the new Canada Post and its state patron were informed more by business concerns than by those of, for example, Rural Dignity, the pressure group that aimed to maintain the postal presence in rural Canada. There were a number of reasons for this state of affairs. Technological change had given business a privileged position on the postal scene, inasmuch as it was better placed to take advantage of the technologies of machine-readable mail than, say, the ordinary private user. The Post Office was increasingly geared to business mail. At the same time, competitive pressures were increasing, political directives insisted on commercial behaviour, a political deadline was set for the elimination of the postal deficit, and the major postal users themselves became exceptionally well organized. The balance between social and economic concerns tilted towards the latter. Unless the government intervened to ensure the representation of social or public interests in the traditional balancing act, the commercialization of postal matters would result in the elimination of the Post Office's public functions. Privatization would then be but a short step away.

The evolution of the Post Office and postal policies has taken place in a complex environment, comprising many and varying elements and pressures. The geography of the country, Canada's historical inheritance, competitive changes in the capitalist economic system, technological innovations, labourmanagement relations, bureaucrats' and politicians' interests and biases, electoral results, institutional transformation, ideological considerations, interest group competition, and the character of postal activities themselves have all affected the direction and shape of the Post Office and its operations. One of the purposes of this study is to establish the relative importance of these factors. Have postal policies reflected the broad interests of all groups in society, or the dominant business interests, or the autonomous interests of the state? What has been the relative influence of labour, business, and user groups? What has been the impact of the various political institutions, including Parliament, cabinet, the postal Minister, and the bureaucracy? Has the state been able to act autonomously and with effect, or has it been constrained by socio-economic forces?

I also consider how the transformation of the Post Office into a Crown corporation affected these issues. Who were the political winners and losers at the time of this transformation? Who have been the winners during the first decade of Canada Post and why? A study of a single case provides at best limited insight into the nature of its object, but it will expose the state's orientation to economic and political matters and its capacity or incapacity to act autonomously and effectively, as well as whether its character has altered in the transition from Keynesianism to neo-conservatism. Finally, I draw conclusions about the character of Crown corporations as a policy instrument, their capacity to juggle economic and social goals, and their role under the new neo-conservative circumstances. The relevant question here is, to what extent has Canada Post been able to act autonomously of the government, and why?

My thoughts on these matters are organized as follows. Part 1 outlines and analyzes the broad setting for postal matters in Canada. Chapter 1 focuses on the social characteristics of the postal environment, including the geographic, historical, technical, and economic contexts in which the Canadian postal system has evolved. Chapter 2 explains the political and institutional contexts in which the Post Office functions. These chapters illustrate the relationship between society and the state as it has been played out in Canadian postal matters, and provide an account of the evolution of the Canadian postal system up to the beginning of the post-war period.

In Part 2 I analyze the Post Office's experience as a department of government between 1945 and 1980 using a case study method to illustrate the range of political issues, events and themes, major players, prevailing processes, and significant outcomes in the postal domain. Each of chapters 3-5 provides detailed historical background, a setting of the range of issues and possibilities, an account of competing players and interests, a description and evaluation of the political and policy process and its outcomes, and an assessment of the future implications of these outcomes. Chapter 3 sets out and evaluates the politics of the traditional Post Office in the immediate post-war era, a period that culminated in 1965 in an illegal postal strike which led the government to initiate a royal commission on the Post Office. Chapter 4 tracks and evaluates the government's attempts to pursue the recommendations proposed by this royal commission, and analyzes Postmaster General Eric Kierans' failed attempt to modernize and commercialize the Post Office and turn it into a Crown corporation. Chapter 5 reviews the tumultuous postal decade of the 1970s, which was marked by the mechanization process and intense labour struggles. The chapter suggests how traditional departmental forms and processes were incapable of dealing with the new realities of increasing competition and a unionized work force. The policy failures of the 1970s set the stage for the transformation of the Post Office Department into a Crown corporation.

Part 3 examines the *raison d'être*, mechanics, and results of that transformation. I again employ the case study format. Chapter 6 presents the historical background and evolution of this policy option, a discussion of the Crown corporation as a policy instrument, a description of the political context of the decision, an account of the key political and interest group players and their considerations, and a presentation of the political and policy process and outcome. The chapter also presents a detailed analysis of the result — the act itself — including an assessment of what the major players thought they were getting and who the winners and losers appeared to be. The chapter also evaluates the particular possibilities, problems, and constraints established by the act.

Subsequent chapters focus on the experience of the Post Office as a Crown corporation. Chapter 7 examines the debut of Canada Post under a Liberal government with Michael Warren as president of the Corporation, construing this period as an exercise in maintaining an equilibrium between social and economic goals. The period was marked by a relatively high degree of political intervention in postal matters, owing to continuing postal deficits (which perpetuated the Post Office's dependence on the government) and the persisting legitimacy of social goals. The period's strategic approach ended in 1984 with the defeat of the Liberal government and the advent of the neo-conservatively inclined Mulroney government. Chapter 8 tracks how the very idea of Canada Post was reconceptualized between 1984 and 1986. In rapid order, CPC President Warren resigned, a private-sector postal investigation (Marchment Committee) concluded that Canada Post had not been acting in a sufficiently commercial or business-like way, and the Conservative government directed the postal Crown to concentrate exclusively on economic as opposed to social concerns. This orientation was given concrete form in the corporation's 1986 five-year plan, whose rationale and strategy has continued to this day. The second period of Canada Post's existence was more commercially oriented; it focused its attention on reaching a profitable position and becoming increasingly competitive in the communications market. Two chapters examine the operationalization of the 1986 plan through 1992. Chapter 9 details the various initiatives pursued by Canada Post in its efforts to become more commercial and competitive, ranging from rationalizing and eliminating many of its services and operations, to increasing prices and eliminating the deficit, to contracting out activities and confronting the unions in bitter disputes over remuneration and jobs. These activities brought about a kind of "incremental privatization," as Canada Post came to act increasingly like a private corporation. These actions were consistent with — indeed, fulfilled — the aims of the 1986 corporate plan; but the policies had immensely controversial social and political consequences and generated considerable public controversy and scrutiny. Chapter 10 examines how the Conservative government gave active political support to Canada Post's actions. This period saw an effective and comfortable partnership between Canada Post President Donald Lander and the minister responsible for Canada Post Harvie Andre. Chapters 9 and 10 detail how the corporation gained increasing autonomy from the state: the Post Office's fiscal dependence was eliminated by balancing the budget and making profits, and its political constraints were lessened by the increasing delegitimization of its traditional social goals.

In the conclusion to this study, I sum up and evaluate the Canadian postal experience to 1992, suggesting what it illustrates about how the state acts and how policy is made. I also consider the experience of the Post

Office as a Crown corporation, both to contrast it with the pre-1981 experience and to generate some insights into the nature of Crown corporations. I conclude by evaluating who the winners, losers, and most effective players have been, and why; I characterize the Canadian postal experience and offer some predictions and suggestions for the future.

Chapter One

THE SOCIAL AND TECHNOLOGICAL SETTING

The Canadian Post Office functions in a highly complex socio-economic environment. Canada's geography and demography, competition and technological change, and union and nation building pressures have created a matrix of social and economic goals that have been difficult to pursue and balance.

Geography

Nowhere has the saying "Canada has too much geography" been more apposite than with regard to the Post Office's physical setting. Canada is the world's second-largest land mass, comprising almost ten million square kilometres, eight million excluding the Arctic Archipelago. Its coastline is ninety thousand kilometres long — over twice the circumference of the world. St. John's is as far east of Victoria as it is west of Warsaw or Algiers. Point Pelee on Lake Erie is as far south of the top of Ellesmere Island as it is north of Quito. Although 80 per cent of its population lives within 150 kilometres of the U.S. border, Canada includes thousands of communities flung from coast to coast and into its northern reaches.

Canada's immense geography has combined with a modest population to create an idiosyncratic demographic reality for its postal system. Canada's population density is 10 per cent of that of the United States and 1 per cent of that of the United Kingdom. As a result, there are 12 times more points of call per square kilometre in the United States and 120 times more in the United Kingdom (see Figure 1).

This low postal density has tended to conspire against postal efficiency and the benefits of economies of scale. Other factors have conspired as well. Postal transportation logistics are complicated by Canada's immense breadth, which comprises six time zones. A letter posted in Vancouver at 4 p.m. is being posted at 8:30 p.m. St. John's time. Canada's northern climate produces half a year of disobliging weather for the Post Office, from November through April. The country has no North Atlantic drift to ameliorate its northern climate, so that even its most southerly waters are ice-bound in winter. It is bounded on the west, east, and northeast by mountains. These geographic factors were especially constraining in earlier times; technology has, to an extent, speeded up time, neutralized the elements, and overcome physical obstacles. But none of these geographic realities has, for postal purposes, been totally neutralized.

FIGURE 1

	Population per square kilometre	Points of call per square kilometre
Canada	2.6	1.1
United States	26.3	12.3
United Kingdom	285.5	120.0

Source: Canada Post Corporation, *The Corporate Plan, 1990-91 to 1994-95*, Table 5. Ottawa, 1990

In its early days, the postal system met these physical challenges in thrilling and dramatic ways.[1] In the sixteenth century, the *coureurs de bois* were the first letter carriers, transporting messages by canoe between settlements along the St. Lawrence. Tavern keepers and ships' captains in turn provided the first post office services. Postal routes such as the widely used Temiscouata Trail from Quebec to Louisbourg had an epic quality:

> Leaving Quebec, the courier paddled his canoe across the St. Lawrence, walked until he reached the portage between the Kamouraska and Rivière-du-Loup and crossed 37 miles of mountains and swamps. He then paddled a total of 280 miles across Lake Temiscouata and down the Madawaska and Saint John Rivers. From there he crossed the Bay of Fundy to Annapolis, walked to Windsor and Halifax, and finally sailed to Louisburg. The trip took him about 14 days each way.[2]

The postal system was first established on a regular basis in 1734, with the opening of a road between Montreal and Quebec City. A special messenger was appointed to carry official dispatches on a system connecting Montreal, Three Rivers, and Quebec City. Private messages were also carried for a fee. At intervals along the route, post houses were set up to receive messages and fees and to provide conveyance to the next post. The extensive French network was then expanded considerably by the first deputy postmaster general in British North America, Hugh Finlay (1784-99). He hired a courier, Pierre Durand, to open a Canadian route to Halifax from Quebec City, through one thousand kilometres of forest. The round trip with mail took fifteen weeks. Post offices were established in Halifax in 1755; Quebec, Three Rivers, and Montreal in 1763; Kingston in 1789; and York (Toronto) in 1800. Post offices were also opened in New Brunswick in 1783 and in P.E.I. in 1801. In the late eighteenth century, mail travelled from Montreal to New

York via Lake Champlain and the portage to the Hudson, then down the Hudson to New York to connect with the monthly packet ship sailing to Britain. In the early nineteenth century, couriers left Montreal and Quebec on Monday and Thursday mornings, met at Three Rivers to exchange mail, and returned two days later. Mail between Quebec and Fredericton was exchanged fortnightly in summer, monthly in winter. The Post Office also followed the opening of the West. In the 1850s, mail was sent to the Red River settlements and regions of the northwest via Sault Ste. Marie and the *voyageur* route to Lake Winnipeg and Red River. On the upper lakes, mail was carried twice a month in summer between Collingwood and Fort William, and from there by canoe to and from the Red River. When navigation closed in winter, snowshoes and dog teams provided a monthly service.[3]

Geography was an important reason why early postal progress was slow. As Table 6 indicates, there were less than two dozen post offices at the end of the eighteenth century, rising to 25 in 1817, 151 in 1828, and 601 in 1851. When Manitoba entered Confederation in 1870, there were only six post offices between the Great Lakes and the Rockies. By this time volumes had reached only two million pieces of mail a year (Table 11). Postal costs were prohibitive and the population base was small, with the result that prices remained relatively high. Rates were graduated for distance, and averaged eighteen cents a half ounce. At the same time, though, postal speed and regularity began to improve. There was fortnightly delivery between Montreal and Kingston by 1810, and five-day delivery between Montreal and Quebec by 1812. The overland route from Halifax to Quebec took but ten days in 1821, and mail from Montreal to New York took three days (five in winter). By 1853, the Quebec-Toronto route took only forty hours, and the Quebec City-Windsor route, which originally took ten days, in 1857 took only forty-nine hours. There were nonetheless three mail deliveries a year in the West before 1853.

Nation Building

The early Post Office in Canada faced a human constraint as substantial as the physical one, in the form of colonialism. The logic of the French and British colonial postal systems was determined by the interests of the mother countries. This inhibited the expansion of the postal system as well as the economic development of the young nation.

The French postal system in Canada was designed exclusively for administrative and official purposes: the road opened between Montreal and Quebec in 1734 was intended to transport official messages. Private individuals could use the system, however, by paying messengers a fee to have their letters conveyed.

Following the Conquest and the signing of the Treaty of Paris, the postal system was the first government institution to be put on a settled basis in

British Canada. The postal system was controlled by the British postmaster general until 1851, and was used for Britain's military and economic ends. Ian Lee has argued convincingly that British interest in the Post Office was also mainly military; it was used primarily to transmit intelligence and to communicate with the home country. Its development was thus limited, and reflected the state's institutional needs for military, political, and legal communication into the interior of the nation.[4] The postal system was also directed to make money for the mother country. Postal surpluses were sent overseas for British purposes, and could not be used to extend or improve the local postal network. Local officials had no postal policy authority: they could not open new postal routes until they had convinced the authorities in London that the proposed routes would be self-financing.[5]

The upshot of these colonial military and economic priorities was that postal developments in Canada were sluggish. Even by 1800, there was limited postal contact between Upper and Lower Canada. When the navigation system was closed in the winter, the Montreal-Niagara round-trip took three months. By 1817, the Halifax to Quebec route continued to take a month, with an additional two days to get to Montreal and eight more days to reach York.[6] Overseas mail was slow and expensive: a sheet weighing less than one ounce sent from Montreal to London cost ninety-six cents and took seventy days. Rates were cheaper by Confederation, but still expensive in comparison to American rates: a letter weighing more than one ounce mailed from New York cost $1.52, but mailed from Halifax cost $4.48.[7] All of this inhibited socio-economic development.

High postal rates, slow service, and British appropriation of surplus revenue made the Post Office a target for reform in the 1830s and 1840s. Postal rates were outrageously high, far beyond the means of the mass of people. An 1840 study estimated that very little mail actually went through the "official" post offices; in some areas the amount was less than 10 per cent, and it was generally well below half. During the period 1818-1825, average annual surpluses of £15,970 were directed to the British Treasury, much to the displeasure of local residents. This mood of pique was fed by the disclosure that the deputy postmaster general for the Canadas was making as much money as the governor. One of his more substantial income sources was the postal revenue on newspapers, which was considered to be a perk. British authorities prospered, while studies suggested that in 1835, two to three hundred communities had inadequate postal facilities. During the Rebellion of 1837, many postmasters were sympathizers and thirty to forty of them were implicated after the Rebellion was quashed.[8]

Before he made his famous report, Lord Durham was instructed to comment on conditions in the Post Office in Canada. He recommended that if the provinces of Canada were united, the control of the Post Office should be handed over to them. On the basis of this recommendation, a commission of investigation was appointed and dealt with the matter, and the reorganization of the Post Office took place after the union of 1841.[9]

As Osborne and Pike have commented, the birth of the Canadian Post Office took place in 1851, at which time the postal system was placed formally under domestic control. The Province of Canada Post Office Department (POD) was the second department to receive independence from Britain (Customs and Excise had led the way in 1844).[10] Canadian postage stamps were first issued in 1851, including the famous red threepence beaver designed by Sir Sandford Fleming. The postal system was placed in the hands of the provinces, who had campaigned for this power, so that four postal systems operated until 1867.[11] As a national concern — like currency and customs — postal authority was assigned exclusively to the federal government at Confederation. The POD was one of the first federal departments formed, which suggests the importance of postal matters at the time. Indeed, one of the main conditions of entry for Prince Edward Island was the promise of improved postal service, including guaranteed boat service to transport passengers and mail during both the summer and winter months.[12]

Over and above these formal changes, the direction and purpose of the postal system was completely transformed after 1851, and especially after 1867. Instead of serving the communications and military needs of colonial administrators or the revenue goals of the mother country, the postal system took on a nation-building responsibility. It was directed to aid in the economic and social development of the young nation.[13]

The ensuing postal transformation had both commercial and social dimensions, which are difficult to untangle. As Osborne and Pike have noted, there was a distinct democratic or populist dimension: the Post Office was transformed from an elite to a mass system. This contributed to, and followed, an increase in literacy and improvement of the educational system. It provided an accessible and inexpensive means for personal mail and information to be communicated, which connected rural areas to urban ones, the frontier with settled areas, and immigrants with their home countries. These developments were encouraged by a number of innovative postal policies, such as subsidized mailing of newspapers and periodicals, the establishment of rural mail routes, and the general policy of low postal rates, each of which will be examined below.

Conversely, the postal system supported and subsidized the extension of the market and commercialization in Canada. The Canadian state extended the postal system to areas of new settlement, the key motive force in the evolution of the modern postal system. As the postal historian William Smith noted, this experience differed from the postal experiences of "settled" countries: "In a new country, a postal system was expected to afford the means of *extending* civilization, and to advance with equal step with settlement," as opposed to following civilization.[14] This was to be done even if postal activities did not pay for themselves. Hence arose the widespread view in the late nineteenth century that

> Post Offices are not established for the purpose of providing a revenue, but for the convenience of the people. They have been established on the same principle as that which has guided us in undertaking public works, not with the hope of obtaining a revenue but in the view that the general business of the community will be promoted by them.[15]

The Postmaster General's Annual Report of 1856 argued that

> with the progressive growth of the Provinces these requirements are constantly developing, as well as in the commercial centres as in the rural districts and newly opened settlements, and they cannot be administered to in a parsimonious spirit without cramping in this important element of progress, the commercial prosperity and social advancement of the community.[16]

Communities petitioned to be included in the postal network, so as to become integrated into the regional economy and with the rest of the country. Governments obliged them, "recogniz[ing] that the national welfare was enhanced by cheaper, more accessible and more efficient postal services."[17]

An important feature of the Post Office as nation builder was its symbiotic relationship with the Canadian transportation system. The Post Office encouraged and benefitted from improvements in roads, stagecoach routes, and steamboats in the 1850s, railroads in the late nineteenth and early twentieth centuries, and air travel in the twentieth century. The changing quantitative dimension of its relationship with the transportation system can be seen in Figure 2. The Post Office encouraged the development of better roads and increased business opportunities locally, regionally, and nationally. Railway development was stimulated by the Post Office's need for improved communications. It was also subsidized by the costly mail contracts that the Post Office purchased.[18] The extension of the Post Office contributed to the opening of the West and the linking of Canada from coast to coast. The railway brought regular postal service on the Brandon-Winnipeg route in 1882, and continuous daily mail service from Atlantic to Pacific was realized in 1886. Only twenty years earlier, a letter from New Brunswick to Vancouver travelled via Great Britain.

The Canadian airline system was similarly encouraged and its development accelerated under postal stimulation. Mail was first flown in June 1918 by military aircraft. In the 1920s, it was delivered by air to northern mining camps. Mail was taken from the trans-Atlantic ships arriving in Rimouski, and flown to Quebec City, Ottawa, and Montreal, thereby saving fourteen to ninety-six hours. The world's most northerly air service was established

FIGURE 2
Distribution of Postal Transportation Costs (%)

	Land	Water	Rail	Air
1860	83.2	6.1	10.7	—
1863	55.7	4.2	40.0	—
1866	41.9	5.7	52.4	—
1904	34.1	4.0	61.9	—
1931	41.1	2.9	47.4	8.6
1940	39.7	1.8	47.4	14.6
1946	31.5	8.2	28.7	31.5
1975	49.1	1.2	15.0	34.2
1981	48.8	0.3	13.5	37.4

Source: I. Lee, *The Canadian Postal System: Origins, Growth and Decay of the State Postal Function, 1765-1981.* (Ottawa: Carleton University, 1989), 482-85.

in December 1929, on a route between Fort McMurray in Alberta and Aklavik in the Northwest Territories. By 1928, there was six-days-a-week service between Montreal and Toronto. The Depression brought these developments to a halt; they did not get under way again until after World War II, when, anxious to get into air mail services and frustrated by the lack of a national air service, the postal system supported the public-sector approach to the development of an air transportation system. This encouragement was significant. The Post Office, the biggest purchaser of contracts in the air system's early days, in effect subsidized the air system, as the Post Office paid "above market" rates to support that system's development.[19]

The Post Office thus played a vital role in Canadian economic development and in encouraging the improvement and expansion of the transportation system. This extended "civilization" and the market into new areas in a variety of ways. The Post Office provided a network for distributing retail goods and acted as a medium for mail-order cataloguing.[20] It provided a commercial link with the outside world through money orders, parcel post, and COD services. It assisted the development of the newspaper and periodicals industry via free or cheap circulation and free rural delivery. As Osborne and Pike conclude,

Without the spreading postal network, the development of large-scale bureaucracy, of wide-spread commercial and industrial activity, and of the mass circulation of the news would have been severely hampered. Without efficient postal services, the policy of opening up areas of new settlement, and the financial health of business enterprises in log-settled country towns, would have been severely at risk.[21]

There were three other broad and deliberate policy initiatives that illustrate the Post Office's economic and social role in national development: universal home delivery, low prices, and an extensive network of post offices.

Free home delivery was first introduced in Halifax in 1851, before a national postal system was established. The practice was adopted in Montreal in 1874 and nationally thereafter. This policy revolutionized the postal system and extended its economic and social contribution to national development, making it more accessible to all Canadians and increasing considerably its commercial possibilities. The system was made universal in 1908 with the introduction of free mail delivery in rural areas, also a tremendous fillip for the national integration of the young country. Business activities and financial transactions were facilitated by the creation of a universal delivery system, particularly one that initiated a number of useful services: registered mail (1852), postal money orders (1855), parcel post (1859), the post office savings bank (1868), post cards (1871), special delivery (1898), COD services (1922), and business reply envelopes and cards (1929).

National social and economic development was also stimulated via the creation and maintenance of a uniform, universal, and inexpensive pricing system. This price system had a populist or mass element to it that was also of immense benefit to business users. Prices were kept deliberately low in order to increase the system's accessibility (see Table 5). This policy was founded on a policy change made in 1851, which had immensely far-reaching consequences for national economic development. Before 1851, the charge for a first-class stamp was prorated for distance; the average price was eighteen cents per half ounce. This approach constrained the extension of the communications market. A universal or uniform postal rate was introduced in 1851, following the earlier British introduction of the penny post, and was based on the view that, at high mail volumes, transportation costs declined to marginal levels. At five cents per half ounce, the 1851 rate was less than 30 per cent of the colonial charge. After Confederation, the rate was cut again, to three cents. In 1889, the charge was lowered to three cents per *full* ounce, a rate cut again in 1899 to two cents. This rate remained for the next three decades (save for during World War I).

The price cuts at first resulted in the creation of postal deficits (see Table 11). These deficits were related to other policy decisions as well: the speeding up of mail delivery through the use of quicker but more expensive rail services[22] and the rapid expansion of post offices in outlying areas.[23] Further price cuts were introduced in 1868 and 1889. Postal deficits totalled $17 million between 1869 and 1901. This amounted to about a half a million dollars a year and represented about 27 per cent of total postal revenues. In effect, the state was subsidizing mail services. These deficits were accepted without great controversy by taxpayers and politicians alike. They were seen not as evidence of operating inefficiencies or policy irrationalities, but as an assertion of the national values realized by postal expansion.[24]

It had, however, been anticipated that price cuts would so increase volumes that postal accounts would balance out over the long run. This did indeed happen eventually: despite a third price cut in 1899, the budget deficit was later replaced by a surplus. Between 1902 and 1926, the Post Office experienced only three deficit years. The net surplus was $25 million, which was greater than the accumulated deficits of the previous period. The positive fiscal balance attested to the success of the strategy to increase popular usage of the postal system through lowering of prices. At the birth of the Canadian postal system in 1851, the volume of mail in Upper and Lower Canada was a bit over two million; this rose sevenfold to over fourteen million by Confederation (see Table 11). The figures increased to 54 million by 1871, tripled again to 154 million over the next two decades, and reached nearly 700 million by 1911. This represented volume growth far in excess of population growth. Each Canadian sent five times as many letters by the end of the nineteenth century as at Confederation (twenty-four versus five).

The increases in postal volumes reflected both the state's low price policy and its rapid expansion of the postal network. There was a fourfold increase in the number of post offices from 1851 to Confederation (Table 6), by which time there were 2,333 post offices. By the turn of the century the number had quadrupled again, to 9,834. Extension of the postal network peaked in 1911, at 13,324 post offices. This increase was complemented by the extension and improvement of postal routes. Their reach tripled from 7,595 miles in 1851 to 18,100 miles in 1867 to 23,475 miles in 1875. The introduction of street letterboxes in 1859 encouraged use of the system as did a variety of other service improvements, such as free home delivery in 1874 (urban) and 1908 (rural) and multiple deliveries in urban areas. The speed of the system was also increased. For example, the Toronto-Winnipeg route declined to less than three days by 1880; the Quebec-Windsor route took but twenty-four hours in 1866. Even remote areas received weekly delivery.

The Post Office thus played a key role in opening up the Canadian nation and in aiding Canada's social and economic development. Similar to the railroad, the Post Office became a symbol of the state's positive role in nation-building. This has had important long-term policy consequences. This symbolic inheritance has given history a role in recent formulation of postal policy. Admittedly, the Post Office's nation-building role has diminished, if not ended, in the modern era. Many of its integrating and national functions have been replaced by cultural agencies such as the CBC and the Secretary of State. Its communication functions have been rivalled, if not displaced, by the telegraph, the telephone, and telecommunications. Yet postal services continue to be identified as a metaphor for national development, integration, and identity. The Post Office also retains a popular and democratic image of providing easy access to inexpensive and effective communications. Its historical role and accomplishments have made it a compelling feature of Canadian political culture.

Social vs. Economic Goals

The early Canadian postal service synthesized commercial and social objectives in a non-antagonistic manner. Three policy examples will illustrate this point: low postal prices, free rural delivery, and second-class mail.

Price cuts in the late nineteenth century had negative medium-term consequences for the Post Office's accounts (see Table 11), but "the colonists bore the resultant deficits without too much complaint."[25] The Post Office's budget balance — whether positive or negative — was not a substantial part of the political discourse of the late nineteenth and early twentieth centuries, and had no symbolic value. Instead, postal discussions centred on the need for rapid strenthening, extension, and accessibility of the system. Thus, the budgetary situation did not create a postal constraint. Taxpayers subsidized postal users and the development of the postal system. Furthermore, one part of the country subsidized the other parts: a study in 1880 revealed that the Ontario postal region was the only one operating in a surplus situation. This was accepted in sanguine fashion.[26]

A second example of the early identity between social and economic goals was the introduction of rural route mail delivery. This was not a particularly rational economic decision at the time, as it was clear that the policy would not pay for itself.[27] Indeed, for a considerable time governments resisted popular demands for extended free home delivery in rural areas. As late as 1908, Postmaster General Lemieux refused to support its introduction on the grounds that it was impractical. Interest group pressure persisted, however, and the opposition made free rural mail delivery an election issue in 1908. The government then rushed an informal system into place in October of that year, starting in Hamilton-Ancaster. The system was expanded when Borden took power in 1911. The legal basis for rural mail delivery was finally established by the Post Office Act of 1913, at which time 1,385 routes served almost 72,000 boxes.[28] By the end of World War II, there were nearly 5,000 rural routes in place. This policy ensured that rural Canada would be integrated socially and economically into the mainstream of Canadian life. The Post Office's public-service orientation was also exhibited in the introduction of a uniform first-class rate in 1851, the introduction of free home delivery in 1874, and the creation of over 13,000 post offices in Canada by 1911. None of these decisions could be considered "economic," in narrow or formal terms; they were motivated by a political sense of how the Post Office could best serve economic and social development.

FIGURE 3

Rural Routes in Canada

	No. of Routes	Households Served
1912	900	
1913	1385	72,000
1947	4887	
1955	5322	531,000
1965	5561	654,653
1979	4991	1,031,221
1981	5072	1,074,186

On January 1, 1991, there were 11,416,444 points of delivery as follows: urban households 8,028,582; rural households 2,435,721; urban business 746,914; rural business 205,222.

Source: Post Office Department, *Annual Report,* Ottawa: various years.

The second-class mail system (publications mail) was a third policy area that synthesized commercial and social goals. The origins of the "concessionary" postal tariff on newspapers and periodicals lie in the pre-Confederation period. After the transfer of postal authority to the provinces, each province abolished postal rates on newspapers. Free distribution was provided for periodicals devoted to science, agriculture, education, and temperance. This suggested "the extent to which the policy makers viewed the Post Office as a medium for the spread of 'civilization,' through education communicated via the postal system."[29] After Confederation, the national postal authorities attempted to impose a substantial postal tariff on newspapers, but backed down in the face of considerable press and public opposition. Newspapers circulated at a cost of a half cent a copy, an extremely economical rate relative to the three-cent cost of a first-class stamp. The price was lowered in 1875 to one cent a *pound*, effectively in the range of one eighth to one fifteenth of a cent per copy. In 1882, the charge was removed altogether on religious, educational, and temperance periodicals as well as on those addressed specifically to a subscriber. These changes were affected without political controversy, despite the fact that low second-class rates contributed substantially to the growing postal deficit in the late nineteenth century. The policy and charges were given an administrative fine-tuning over the next half century, in response to the explosion in second-class volumes (from five million to twenty-seven million pounds between 1882 and 1898) and the emergence of "phoney" newspapers (containing only advertisements), both of which required changes in eligibility requirements.[30] Publications produced and distributed in smaller communities were targeted for support. For over a century, there was no challenge to, or weakening of, the principle of subsidized distribution of newspapers and periodicals with educational content. Postal policy was informed by social objectives, such as the dissemination of ideas and information, the pursuit of mass literacy, the creation of a politically well-informed population, and the integration of smaller communities into larger Canadian life.

As the Canadian postal system expanded rapidly, these socially informed policies appeared to be compatible with budgetary realities. As Table 3 indicates, the postal budgetary situation seemed reasonably healthy through to the early 1960s. This fiscal picture was seriously misleading, though, as a result of two factors that understated postal expenditures. First, the Post Office kept its costs at an unusually low level. As will be seen in Part 2, below, it did not carry out capital investments to upgrade and modernize its equipment and facilities, and it suppressed the wage level at an unreasonable level. These were chickens that would eventually come home to roost. Second, a number of peculiar accounting practices understated postal costs by assigning them to other departments (e.g., retirement benefits, building maintenance). These factors persisted throughout the post-war period, but could not continue indefinitely: postal unionization resulted in wage increases from the late 1960s through the 1970s, and the decision in the 1970s to modernize and mechanize the postal system also raised costs. Finally, alteration of the accounting system in 1964, to give a truer picture of the Post Office's budgetary status, immediately transformed its budgetary balance into an enormous deficit, even though it had as yet done nothing to raise its expenditures or lower its revenues (see Table 3). Increasing costs associated with unionization and modernization would then exacerbate the "new" deficit.

Up to the early 1960s, then, it *appeared* that the Post Office was in good fiscal shape, and that its social-service orientation was more or less affordable. However, the advent of serious deficits in the late 1960s altered the perception of the postal situation and changed forever the character of political discussion of the Post Office. This perception and subsequent discussion locked the Post Office's social and economic goals into an antagonistic relationship. The need to balance the postal books became part of the postal discourse, and the deficit took on a symbolic quality previously reserved for postal questions of economic development and national unity. A conflict in postal policy then developed: between national development and social- and public-service goals on the one hand, and efficiency and fiscal matters on the other. This has been a key axis around which the discussion and formulation of modern postal policy in Canada has revolved.

This policy conflict played out awkwardly at first because of the century-long tradition of low postal charges. As Table 5 shows, there were but four first-class price increases between 1867 and 1967, three of which were part of exceptional revenue-raising efforts in wartime and during the Depression. There was, thus, only one "normal" first-class price increase during the Post Office's first century. The postal deficit, low wages, and pre-modern postal conditions essentially followed on the heels of this low-price policy, which had been pursued for competitive and political reasons, as will be seen shortly, but also pursued under the illusion that the budget was in balance. Even after the appearance of the deficit, it was exceedingly difficult for policy makers to raise prices quickly and substantially; price increases would have predictable and negative political consequences, in the highly visible and political postal environment.

The tension between the Post Office's social and economic goals also reflected changes in the wider world of communications, from the solidification of the rail system to the advent of the telegraph from World War I onwards.[31] The emergence of the telephone, airline transportation, and other modes of communication accelerated the development of alternatives to postal communications. In the process, the Post Office began to lose its privileged position as an essential policy instrument of national development. The perception of the Post Office's social function weakened, replaced by a sense that a narrower economic mandate was required.[32] Governments' economic concerns about the Post Office then waxed while its social concerns waned. There was a perceptible lag between these developments and public perception of the issue. The tension between social and economic goals did not appear on the political agenda or get public airing until the 1960s. A "crisis of identity" developed in the Post Office in the 1960s and 1970s, as postal administrators became uncertain of the postal mission: was it to pursue social goals or to balance the postal books? This question, a fundamental one, required a political answer; but politicians were reluctant to give wholehearted assent to either side, economic or social, given the highly visible and political character of the Post Office and its well-established and entrenched traditions. Instead, the postal policy pendulum swung according to the rhythms of elections and deficit figures, sometimes directing the Post Office to a stricter economic orientation and other times to a more social one. Interest-group and public pressure was split, with those who benefitted from the Post Office's social orientation not being inclined to support its transformation into a strictly economic concern. Governments initiated a rash of studies and presented various institutional proposals, to be detailed below.

The transformation of the POD into a Crown corporation apparently resolved the question of purpose, for it was based on the view that the Post Office was a commercial operation, and required commercial values to be given substantial if not exclusive consideration in postal policy making. Simultaneously, however, the new Crown corporation was directed to maintain customary social-service goals. The tension between social and economic goals was thus reproduced within the mandate of Canada Post Corporation. The politics of the Post Office have since been played out in symbolic terms. Balancing the budget, improving productivity and efficiency, and creating postal profits has become the political mantra of those supporting an economically sound and commercial Post Office, whereas advocates of a socially oriented Post Office have portrayed these strictly economic values as destructive of the Post Office's traditional customary services — as leading to rural post office closings, limits on home mail delivery, and elimination of subsidies for second-class mail. The elimination or perpetuation of postal jobs has also become part of this debate. These have been some of the key symbolic issues in the 1970s and 1980s postal debate, an expression of the competitition between two different visions of the Post Office's role in Canadian life.

Technology: Problems of Scale and Complexity

By the end of World War II, the modern Canadian postal system was well in place. A network of twelve thousand post offices and over two million points of call stretched across Canada, with forty thousand employees processing and delivering over two billion pieces of mail annually via a complex and regular coast-to-coast rail and air mail service.

Ironically, the very size, scale, and impact of the Post Office became an issue. On the one hand, the Post Office became one of Canada's most visible institutions. As the Marchment Report put it, "Its operations touch on the lives of Canadians virtually every working day and [are] the most frequent evidence of federal presence in every community in this country."[33] This visibility and service were a source of pride and a sense of accomplishment well through the 1960s, but created very high expectations for the postal service. On the other hand, the increasing size and scale of the postal operation presented a substantial technical challenge. Postal volumes doubled from 1947 to 1968, to five *billion* pieces a year — about twenty million each working day.[34] Short of doubling the work force — with the concomitant problems of housing, organizing, and paying this expanded postal army — there was no option but to increase postal productivity. But there were limits to how much productivity could be increased via increased effort or improved memory. Postal clerks or sorters could sort letters only so quickly, and there were physical limits to the weight of mail that could be carried on routes. But this was only one part of the problem: economic growth, urbanization, and suburbanization had led to an explosion in addresses and points of call. By 1968, there were five million points of call and four million addresses serviced, more than double the immediate post-war level. Postal sorters were legendary for their capacity to memorize addresses and street locations and sort mail quickly. They were tested each year on their accuracy, and many practised at home in their spare time. *La crème de la crème* of postal sorters were the railway clerks, who sorted mail on overnight

FIGURE 4

Delivering the Mail

		(in millions)
	Delivery Addresses	Points of Call
1944-5	1.7	2.3
1957-8	2.8	3.7
1967-8	3.9	4.9
1980-1	6.3	8.4
1990-1	8.5	11.4

On January 1, 1991, there were 11,416,444 points of delivery as follows: urban households 8,028,582; rural households 2,435,721; urban business 746,914; rural business 205,227

Source: Post Office Department/Canada Post, *Annual Report,* Ottawa: various years.

trains, shunning labelled sorting boxes in favour of exclusive reliance on their memory and capacity. The explosion of volumes and points of call overwhelmed the human brain's capacity for recall; the postal system, previously based on memory and muscle, would have to be replaced by one based on technology. This switch to technology would have enormous consequences for all facets of postal functioning.

A postal system is different in several respects from most other economic entities.[35] For example, the notion of holding an "inventory" is anathema within the Post Office: the mail has to be processed quickly to avoid complaints. In earlier times, it was possible for all of the mail to be sorted the day it arrived, at which time everyone in the sorting plant simply went home. But, increased volumes mean the bottom of the sorting barrel tends not to be reached. This created a series of related problems for worker morale as well as for the organization of sorting. Inventories grew to over thirty million pieces a day (this has subsequently been cut, to twelve to thirteen million in 1990 and to seven million in 1991).[36] Unfortunately, the Post Office has no control over the volumes it receives on any given day. If the system is clogged or working to capacity, it cannot refuse business; it has to accept the stamped letter however busy it is. This situation is, in turn, exacerbated by pattern of input to the postal system. There are over seven hundred thousand places within Canada for mail to enter the system, but the flow is uneven. More mail arrives on Monday than on Tuesday (because of the weekend), less mail in the first two weeks of the month than the last two (because of government cheques), and mail flows are uneven from month to month (e.g., the summer months are slower than the Christmas period). Further, businesses and individuals typically dump mail into the system at the end of the work day and expect it to be received at the beginning of the work day. These various factors generate enormously complicated logistical, planning, and staffing challenges. Moreover, these challenges must be met at a quality-control rate that most operations cannot even dream of. A 4 to 5 per cent error rate on an assembly line is not uncommon or unacceptable and is factored into the product's cost. But a million letters a day cannot be thrown away or delayed without enormous public outcry.

The Post Office's experience with technology has been an enduring element of the Canadian postal history, and a central challenge for postal policy makers. The Post Office has had a symbiotic relationship with technological change, similar to its relationship with the transportation system: it created a demand for new technologies, and new technologies themselves transformed its character. Indeed, Canada Post is presently the most technologically sophisticated postal operation in the world. It is studied by other national postal systems, and it sells its technology and systems to other post offices around the world.

Through to the mid-1960s, though, the Post Office was technologically relatively backward. Electrical mail-marking machines were introduced in Montreal and Ottawa in 1896, but there were few significant developments until the 1920s. In 1925, a POD report noted that

> the growth of the postal business brings with it the necessity of considering mechanical appliances for the handling of mail ... It will be necessary to introduce equipment ... in the near future ... [which] will result in a more efficient and economical treatment of the mail.[37]

Some mechanical innovations appeared at this time,[38] and mechanical installations were introduced in some of the larger post offices in 1929. The Post Office itself organized for this purpose in 1930, when a Postal Engineering Unit was established. A mechanical engineer was employed in 1934 to investigate and develop equipment that would assist in mail processing.[39] These developments were halted during the Depression, and thereafter the Post Office administration "seem[ed] to have done nothing to offset the technical backwardness of postal operations."[40] This state of affairs continued through to the mid-1960s. Hard-pressed postal employees worked feverishly and competently to keep up with mushrooming volumes and an increasingly complex network of addresses — in physical and mechanical conditions almost unchanged from the nineteenth century. Indeed, it was postal workers who kept the postal system afloat, albeit precariously.

As we will see in Chapter 3, the 1965 postal strike forced the government to consider modernizing the Post Office. This move was perhaps a generation too late. The Post Office was the last government department and one of the last sectors of the economy to upgrade its technological capacity to the standards of post-war economic activity. The mechanization process of the 1970s — elaborated upon in Chapter 5 — was a case of the pent-up demand for modernization meeting an oversupply of technological developments. Modernization arrived too suddenly and without adequate consideration of its implications. The program was carried out with the fervour of the religiously converted, and suscribed to that era's faith in the healing qualities of technology. It was fired by the fond belief that mechanization would solve the Post Office's commercial and fiscal problems. Mechanization decisions were optimistic if not naive, with their potential benefits exaggerated and the problems of implementation not fully thought through.

The Post Office's love affair with modern technology was played out on two levels. The first was the need to respond to the challenges of increasing volumes and complexity and to remain economically competitive with new technologies (see below). The second involved the equally consequential implications of embracing these technological innovations. Adoption of the new technology affected working conditions and the character of postal work, the size of sorting plants, and the role of labour. These issues are discussed in detail in Chapter 5; for now, it is worth noting that modernization of the Post Office led to substantial "de-skilling" of work and a decline in postal job satisfaction, particularly for inside workers. Immense, noisy, and de-humanizing sorting plants were constructed to centralize mail volumes and their processing via "smart" machines, which could handle, "read," and sort mail. These working conditions increased stress and absenteeism, radicalized the work force, soured labour management relations, and strengthened labour unions. Ironically, the new set-up brought no obvious short-term benefits. The first decade-long wave of technological change resulted in a medium-term decline in postal productivity. The machines did not work as well as expected, or at anywhere near full capacity for years. A parallel manual system had to be kept operating until the mechanical system was fully in place across the country. As the 1970s concluded and a new generation of studies and leaders took stock of the mechanization program, there was near universal consensus that modernization had been mishandled: that the sorting plants were too big, that job satisfaction had been obliterated, that labour militancy had substantial cause, that management had been inadequately consultative and overly ambitious, and that the anticipated productivity pay-off had not been forthcoming.

The modernization process also had important consequences for users of the mail system and for their relationship with the post office. The large, major mailers were best situated to use the new technologies, with postal codes and machine-readable capacity. The result was that the new postal system became skewed to the needs and interests of the large-volume (business) users. This in turn directed the Post Office's gaze to economic as opposed to social concerns. At present, the postal system has become extraordinarily technological, with 87 per cent of the mail using the postal code and 83 per cent of the mail being machine processed. The machines can process tens of thousands of pieces of mail an hour, and the new generation of machines can do up to 1,152 different sortings.[41]

Ironically, the pattern of delayed technological change and the consequences of playing catch-up reproduced itself in the 1980s. As we will see in Part 3, Canada Post underspent on capital equipment in the drive to balance the budget in the early 1980s. As the decade came to a close, an enormous capital outlay was required to replace what was by then fifteen to twenty-year-old equipment and technology. As opposed to the situation in the 1970s, here the government was disinclined to pay for these capital expenses, given its own budget deficit. Canada Post was thus directed to generate higher levels of postal profits to finance this new generation of technological improvements. This intensified search for profits in turn had consequences for labour and postal services as serious as those of the earlier modernization decisions (it should be noted that Canada Post is far more in control of shaping the development of this technology than it was in the 1970s, at which time it essentially accepted what the market produced). In this and many other ways, the reaction to technological imperatives has had greatly affected the evolution of the postal system. Technology has offered possibilities, created constraints, and required postal and political decisions of critical consequence. These, in turn, have had enormous implications for the functioning of the postal system.

Competition

The Post Office's technological push was also driven by increasing competitive pressures in the market. Indeed, the Post Office has faced competitive pressures since the nineteenth century; response to those pressures has been a central feature of its political economy.

On the political level, the Post Office has had to convince governments of its continuing national importance. The advent of new communications and transportation technologies created both market and political competition for the Post Office. Governments became increasingly tempted to pursue national goals via these other technologies. As Ian Lee points out, the telegraph surpassed the Post Office in the state's vision of how to integrate the country and connect it to the outside world. Radio and television, particularly the CBC, subsequently joined the Post Office as instruments of nation building. This had serious budgetary and financial implications for the Post Office, which became increasingly poorly placed to press its case, and so became extremely cautious about the financial demands it made (which was a substantial factor in the Post Office's adherence to a low-price, low-wage policy).[42]

On the economic level, the Post Office is popularly perceived to be a monopoly. However, it has never enjoyed a complete monopoly over all of its activities. It has always had an exclusive privilege to pick up and deliver letters, or first-class mail. Governments and the public have always accepted the view that, in the absence of this exclusive privilege, a national or universal postal system would be all but impossible to construct or maintain: private operators would be apt to concentrate the dense and lucrative urban markets and be uninterested in the more far-flung and less densely populated rural, outlying, and frontier areas.[43] A postal system could be devised that employed a matrix of differential tariffs covering the entire market; but this would be an administrative headache, and would complicate what should be a speedy, simple, and accessible service. Hence, even during the neo-conservatively inclined 1980s, most large private-sector mail users insisted on the maintenance of the state postal monopoly, in order to ensure the existence of a national postal system to serve their needs.[44]

First-class postal activity has been the most important activity for the Post Office, in terms of both volume and, particularly, revenue, but it has never been its sole activity, and its other postal activities have not been assigned exclusive privilege. For example, its fourth-class mail service (parcel post) has always competed with rail, air, trucking and, later, courier operators. During the post-war period, around 50 per cent of the Post Office's revenue was derived from first-class mail activity (see Table 2); the other half came from business generated in a competitive environment.

This other half of its business faced different degrees of competition at different times. Some areas were not terribly competitive, as the Post Office's size gave it a competitive advantage over other participants, who were scared away. Nonetheless, there is evidence that early postal policies reflected these competitive pressures. For example, the decline in charges for newspaper delivery in 1875 was the Post Office's response to increasing competitive pressures from express companies and local deliverymen.[45] Similarly, the late 1920s price cuts in third-class mail (circulars) reflected increasing competition from individuals delivering advertising circulars at a cheaper rate.[46] As will be seen in Chapter 3, there was continuing post-war concern about the increasing competitive pressures in the market. For example, the 1944-45 POD report expressed anxiety about a post-war postal business collapse, as a result of competition from telephone, telegraph, private wire services, and private delivery firms as well as from rising wage and transportation costs.[47] (The relative positions of mail, telephone, and telegraph can be seen from Table 9.) Anxiety about competition led to internal postal debates about whether to diversify postal products and services, how to react to emerging telecommunication technologies, whether to go deeper into the communications market or pull back, whether the Post Office should act like a private or public player, and so on. Perhaps the most obvious impact of competitive concerns was in the area of pricing policy. The persistently low price of a first-class stamp and other services was thought to be a way of maintaining the Post Office's competitiveness (this was also the *raison dê'tre* for the low-wage policy, which will be examined below).

At the end of the post-war boom in the late 1960s, the reality of competition hit home with even greater force. The rate of growth of postal volumes went increasingly flat, reflecting sluggish economic conditions as the post-war cycle wound down. This naturally generated increasing market competition. Equally if not more daunting was the emergence of new electronic and telecommunications technologies. The Post Office's scale and universal presence, low prices, and hard-working, efficient, and cheap workforce had previously given it a competitive advantage in the market; with the advent of these technologies, this advantage was now lost. For example, in the early days of the telephone, the Post Office remained price-competitive as a populist or cheap communications option; long-distance telephone calls remained an expensive option for elites. But as the telephone system spread, as household telephones became as common as running water, and as long-distance telephone charges declined, first-class mail confronted a grave competitive threat. In 1989, the cost of a five-minute business call from Montreal to Toronto was thirty-nine cents, exactly the price of a first class stamp. Subsequent adaptations of telephone usage — from fax machines to computer-based electronic transmissions, from electronic bill paying to telephone ordering — would increase this competition intensely. By the early 1990s, the number of annual fax transmissions had grown to two billion — about half the volume of first-class mail. Hand delivery of circulars continued to threaten third-class mail, as did weekly and daily newspaper delivery of advertising inserts. The parcel delivery business became stagnant, and was subsequently lost to bus, trucking, and other transportation alternatives. In the age of the Reagan and Thatcher revolutions, competitive alternatives sprung up daily, fired with profit-seeking enthusiasm and staffed by cheaper, non-union labour. The hard reality was that the Post Office confronted stagnancy in its first-class mail operations, the only area where it enjoyed a monopoly; and in non-monopoly situations, it was losing business.

This competitive reality had varying implications at different stages of postal history. In the late 1960s and early 1970s, the strategic response of political and postal authorities was to modernize and mechanize the postal system. This move was designed to keep costs down and to improve postal service; its various implications have been noted above and will be explored fully in Chapter 5.

The failure of mechanization to neutralize competitive pressures was then followed by another critical strategic decision: the Post Office's assumption of a more commercial posture. Its transformation into a Crown corporation was motivated by the practical concern that an uncommercial, sluggish Post Office was in danger of being overwhelmed by its communications competitors. As Table 1 indicates, first-class mail volumes grew by only 4 per cent in *total* in the second half of the 1970s; the parcel post business was cut almost in half to fifty-four million parcels a year; and second-class mail was declining in importance. In short, volume growth was sluggish or declining and competition was increasing in unexpected ways. For example, the labour disruptions of the 1970s simultaneously inhibited postal volumes and generated a competitive alternative to first-class mail in the form of private courier services. As the proportion of first-class mail that was generated by business grew to 80 per cent, the core of postal volumes and revenues became susceptible to the application of new technologies, such as electronic financial transactions, and credit card bill payments.

The political factors motivating the transformation into a Crown corporation were various and interrelated, and included a concern over competition. Postal deficits appeared to be increasing alarmingly and the state, facing its own budgetary crisis, wanted to distance itself fiscally from the Post Office. Moreover, it appeared highly unlikely that the Post Office could come to grips with its deficit unless it was able to perform competitively. Hence, the objective of creating a commercially oriented, customer-driven postal Crown corporation.

Competition and the Post Office's reaction to it has been another enduring theme in Canada's postal history. The Post Office's monopoly has always been a matter for political discussion, one that increased in intensity in the 1970s and after. The transformation into a Crown corporation seemed only to increase public suspicions about the Post Office's monopoly position, and this had serious policy consequences. As we will see in Part 3, Canada Post was constrained from acting like a commercial, competitive business for political and ideological reasons. It was limited in its authority to enter the telecommunications industry; it was forced to accept a limitation on its first-class monopoly when the Crown corporation legitimized the use of private couriers for time-sensitive material; it would see the definition of a letter narrowed to limit its exclusive privilege; it would be forbidden to diversify and compete in a variety of areas. In short, Canada Post faced increasing competitive pressures with a limited range of strategies at its disposal. In this context, it pushed the commercial orientation to its logical conclusion, in the form of a quasi-privatization strategy of franchising, contracting out, and cutting of services, all designed to increase productivity and competitiveness by cutting total and relative wages and costs. As had technological imperatives, inexorable competition led the post office to adopt an increasingly commercial and diminishingly social orientation. This took place in the broad context of a decline in post-war economic growth, the state's fiscal crisis, and the replacement of the Keynesian social welfare orientation by the neo-conservative one.

Labour

The early technology of the Canadian postal system made postal operations a labour-intensive activity. A moment's reflection will suggest the size of the labour force required to collect, sort, and deliver tens of millions of pieces of mail a day from hundreds of thousands of entry points to millions of addresses; to staff thousands of post offices; and to work the countless machines, trucks, and service vehicles required to make the postal system operate. After the war, the Post Office employed over forty thousand full- and part-time workers, a figure that would rise to over sixty thousand from the mid-1970s to the late 1980s. This labour intensity continued even after the 1970s mechanization program (see Table 4): despite a billion-dollar modernization and mechanization program, the level of employment rose from under fifty thousand in 1968 to over sixty thousand throughout the 1970s. The level of employment grew more or less at the same rate as postal volumes in this period, about 33 per cent. The lack of labour savings can be attributed to a number of factors. A parallel manual sorting system had to be maintained until the full mechanical system was in position at the end of the decade. Population growth and suburbanization forced the expansion of postal routes and points of call, automatically requiring more and more people to deliver the mail — regardless of mechanization. Hence arose the continuous questioning of the economics of home delivery and the advent in the 1980s of the community mailbox. Similarly, mechanization did little to affect the staffing of the more than ten thousand post offices in Canada; hence also the subsequent advent of postal closings, "conversions," and franchising of post offices, particularly in rural areas.

The postal labour force has always ranked among the largest in the economy. Unlike most government departments, it has employed predominantly "blue-collar" workers. The labour-management situation in the Post Office has thus had an idiosyncratic quality to it: the postal workforce has been as "industrial" in its composition, orientation, and needs as industrial concerns in the private sector, yet its employer was the federal government, which had neither the experience nor the sensibilities of private-sector industrial managers. Indeed, early governments attempted to segregate postal "labourers" from white-collar civil servants.[48] Nonetheless, over the last thirty years postal workers have had an unusually high and effective degree of bargaining strength. First, they are employed in a quasi-monopoly industry, where a large proportion of the population does not have access to alternate services. Second, they are employed in a highly visible public service, where they can articulate their concerns effectively to a national audience. Third, given the concentration of labour and processing activity in and around centralized plants, it has been easy to organize and to shut down the national system in the event of a dispute.

Labour-management relations in the Post Office have almost always been strained. This is a legacy that informs all postal discourse and discussion. Indeed, it is part of the "political culture" of the Post Office, in as fundamental a way as French-English relations affect constitutional discussions or regionalism affects transportation or industrial policy. These strained relations can be traced back to early postal eras. Post Office management was highly paternalistic in its behaviour and fundamentally anti-union and anti-worker in attitude. During the late nineteenth century, the Post Office was belligerent in restraining wage levels, both for class reasons and to limit postal demands on the government budget. In this we can already see the declining political status of the Post Office. Postal clerks went two decades, from 1882 to 1902, without a salary increase; and letter carriers went from 1872 to 1909 without a real increase, with predictable impact on worker morale.[49] Frosty relations between management and labour were also partly owing to the fact that much of management had a military background and orientation, and organized its workforce much like an army operating to move supplies. Later, the bitter struggles over the implementation of technology established opposed "paradigms" for ways of viewing the world, which further extended labour and management's mutual antagonism and distrust.

The so-called labour problem thus very much pre-dates the more familiar postal battles of the 1970s and 1980s. Postal workers were among the first public-sector workers in Canada to organize themselves: the Canadian Railway Mail Clerks Federation in 1889; the letter carriers in 1891 (subsequently called the Federated Association of Letter Carriers [FALC] the precursor to the LCUC, the Letter Carriers Union of Canada, formed in 1966); the Canadian Postmasters Association in 1902; and the Dominion Postal Clerks Association in 1911 (which later merged with the Mail Porters Association in 1928 as the Canadian Postal Employees Association, the forerunner of CUPW, the Canadian Union of Postal Workers, formed in 1965). These developments were not met with enthusiasm by postal management. A Post Office study noted that "Department attitudes toward staff associations in the early 1900s were generally hostile and consistent with the expressed sentiments of the Deputy Postmaster General at the time, who referred to one of the associations as 'malcontents.'"[50]

Two early strikes set the tone for postal relations over the following generations. The 1918 strike centred on the government's failure to honour promises it had made in Parliament for increased wages and bonuses. Lasting one month, strike activity was concentrated in the West, although there was some activity in Toronto and Hamilton. Many workers were fired and replaced by returning soldiers. The illegal 1924 strike was a reaction to cuts in salaries. Postal clerks in most major cities were involved, although for varying periods of time. When conditions returned to normal, strikers were replaced in Montreal, Toronto, and Windsor, and returning workers were demoted in other centres. Two years of intense and persistent labour pressures finally led to the rescinding of these punitive measures, and compensation for lost earnings. This was a bitter strike and result; it intensified anti-management militancy and deepened support for and loyalty to the workers' organizations for decades to come.

On management's side, there was little in the way of creative or intelligent response to these events and developments. A National Joint Council was established two decades later, in 1944, as a forum for consultation on wages and working conditions. But the government's attitude continued to be paternalistic, and this initiative had no positive impact and may even have exacerbated relations. In 1945 the postal unions joined together into a Postal Workers Brotherhood.[51]

The two decades after the end of World War II saw the *status quo* remain virtually unchanged. A paternalistic, militarily trained and oriented management ran a tight and efficient postal operation, basically on the backs of the workers, as Postmaster General Eric Kierans commented.[52] Management was "effective" inasmuch as it kept the postal system going with little political or fiscal support. But in the process it ran a repressive operation, and working conditions were abysmal. Wages continued to be pitifully low, with the hoary myth perpetuated that postal workers were happy with their lot, having traded away the right to decent wages in return for job security.[53] The hard fact was that the post-war postal system, balanced budgets, low prices, and decent service were all being attained at the expense of underpaid and overworked postal employees. Indeed, as will be seen in Chapter 3, postal employees enjoyed a remarkable level of public esteem if not of monetary remuneration, even during the 1965 strike. The post-war years comprised a kind of dream world of balanced budgets and contented and secure workers dedicated to public service. But Canadians were abruptly woken by the 1965 strike, which was induced by continued deterioration in working conditions brought on by increasing postal activity. The strike had as much to do with working conditions and self-respect as it did with wages.

Postal workers have been in the advance guard of labour accomplishments in the public sector. The 1965 strike — illegal, as the postal associations had no formal position from which to bargain or take action — was a substantial contributing factor to the passing of the Public Service Staff Relations Act, which gave public-sector organizations the opportunity to unionize. The postal associations quickly grasped the opportunity. The act, however, limited the terrain on which public-sector unions could bargain. A variety of critical areas remained outside bargaining, including technological change, job classification, and the use of part-time and casual labour. These were areas where the postal unions were desperate to bargain. The act also provided the option of using the threat to strike as a negotiating tool. This was a tactic adopted in principle by the newly formed postal unions, such as CUPW and LCUC, and used frequently and to effect in the 1960s and 1970s, mainly by CUPW.

Postal workers made path-breaking advances in a variety of areas: a guaranteed cost-of-living allowance, paid maternity leave, paid lunch hours, job protection from technological change, job security and pensions for part-time staff, the right to refuse dangerous work, the principle of time off to recuperate from night shift, and so on. The postal unions have been a kind of bellwether for the state of the Canadian union movement in the post-war period. In the more propitious Keynesian social welfare setting, they were able to acquire rights and make gains that set the standards for other labour unions to emulate. In the less propitious neo-conservative era, they have been in the foreground of the fighting to retain post-war rights and gains, facing back-to-work legislation, replacement by scabs, and even jail terms for their efforts. The 1987 strike over franchising was an especially symbolic event.

There have been three stages to labour-management relations in the Post Office. In advance of 1965, unions were not allowed in the public sector. This was followed by a period, spanning 1965 to 1981, when the Public Service Staff Relations Act (PSSRA) allowed unionization but limited the range of negotiable issues (excluding crucial areas such as technological change). Postal unions did not negotiate directly with postal management in this period, but rather bargained with the goverment's negotiating agent, the Treasury Board. Finally, during the post-1981 era postal unions have negotiated directly with postal management on the full range of issues of interest and importance. This was one reason why the postal unions supported the transformation of the POD into a Crown corporation. Released from the restrictions of the PSSRA, the unions would finally be allowed to bargain directly with postal management and, under the more expansive territory of the Canada Labour Code, would be allowed to bargain over the full range of issues critical to postal workers. However, postal unions found themselves continuing to negotiate with governments, particularly after 1984. The bargaining process has turned out to be far more constrained than had been anticipated. Indeed, the government has frequently resorted to back-to-work legislation to settle disputes. This has seriously pre-empted the bargaining progress. Ironically, although Crowning the Post Office was designed to ensure direct bargaining relations outside the political arena, it has perpetuated direct relations between postal workers and the state.

There were no strikes in the new Crown corporation before 1987, but this, as Part 3 will demonstrate, was the result of the government's anti-inflation program, which made public sector strikes illegal. Once negotiations proceeded openly again, the violent 1987 postal strikes erupted. Even the LCUC — which normally opted for shrewd negotiation — went on strike in a long and bitter dispute. Industrial relations have subsequently focused on a number of symbolic issues and themes, centring on management's attempt to increase productivity and make postal workers' conditions comparable to those in the non-unionized private sector. There have been intense battles over the level of absenteeism, contracting out, and franchising; the introduction of new technology; and new organizations of processing — all with the aim of cutting the size of the workforce and the wage bill. Wage-cutting initiatives generated an enormous number of grievances, stalemated negotiations, and increased the tendency of the government to use back-to-work legislation.

Labour, then, has been central to the history of the Canadian postal system. Its organizational and political strength has been an autonomous force affecting the way in which the postal system has evolved, and it has posed challenges to governments and postal officials as they have formulated postal policy, particularly in response to technological imperatives and competitive pressures.

The Post Office in Canada has existed within a particular, highly complex setting. Geographic and demographic realities have posed great challenges. The Post Office has functioned in an increasingly competitive market environment and has also competed for political attention and support. It carries with it a historical and nation-building tradition, which has created public expectations about its role. It has combined an uneasy mix of social and economic roles, which often collide. The business of moving and delivering the mail has its own peculiar logic and challenges. The Post Office's success in building up a high-volume business and an extensive communications system created problems of scale and complexity, requiring it to enter the uncertain and eventful world of technological change. The Post Office has operated in the context of a well-organized, highly motivated, and often fearless union movement. All the while, postal activities have remained highly visible and personal for the vast proportion of Canadians, who have developed high expectations of postal service.

These environmental influences have not simply been left to take their own course. The Post Office is a state-owned and state-operated entity, one that has been persistently in the public eye and which has enjoyed a certain degree of public notoriety. A laissez-faire postal attitude on the part of the state was not really possible, nor was it — until recently — a desired approach. The Post Office has functioned in a political setting, in which governments have had to respond to and shape these environmental conditions while directing the Post Office to desired goals and objectives. This political setting is the subject of the following chapter.

Chapter Two

THE POLITICAL AND INSTITUTIONAL SETTING

Postal policy has been one of the few Canadian political issues that failed to ignite federal-provincial conflict; perhaps only defence policy shares this charmed existence. The Post Office has not been subject to Canada's intense federal-provincial jurisdictional disputes and the associated complications of policy making in a federal setting. Indeed, it has functioned in an essentially unitary setting; only municipalities, and rarely provinces, have been involved in the politics of the Post Office.[1]

Within the national level of government, though, the Post Office enjoyed a less blissful situation. Postal policy was complicated by an internal tangle of overlapping departmental jurisdictions, rival authorities, and shared responsibilities. A variety of other departments contributed to and shaped postal policy, from Public Works, Transportation, and Labour to Treasury Board, Finance, and Supply and Services. The result was a policy process that was neither smooth nor rational; as a result, postal policy was not particularly effective. This disobliging situation was finally remedied in 1981, when the Post Office was given a considerable degree of autonomy as a Crown corporation.

All Canadians are affected by the activities of the Post Office – perhaps more than by the activities of most departments of government. Moreover, the discussion, formulation, and impact of postal policy has been far more open and visible than in most other policy areas. The Post Office's relationship with the public has had a mass or universal character because of the department's ubiquitousness and accessibility; its sheer size and scale in matters of employment, activities, service, and economic impact; its retail or commercial character; and its public and monopoly status. Like the weather, the Post Office is the subject of incessant Canadian attention and complaint. But there the analogy ends: Canadians have felt that they should be able to do something about postal matters. Recent governments have taken a hands-off attitude to the Post Office. Nonetheless, Hansard continues to present a regular litany of petitions, ministerial questions, and backbench statements that demand, plead, criticize, scrutinize, implore, and lament postal conditions and decisions. The media provided similar attention. Since the Post Office was "nationalized" in 1851, the public has insisted that it provide a public service and be held politically accountable to the people. This placed the Post Office under stronger day-to-day democratic scrutiny than most departments and areas of government.

The organization of the Post Office in this political setting has undergone two stages. From 1867 to 1981, the Post Office was organized as a department of government, despite its essentially retail and commercial character. The

Hansard

POD was unique in Canadian government: its institutional setting and character was the same as that of External Affairs or Finance, neither of which provided a retail service. This was an odd state of affairs, and one that was increasingly questioned in the post-war period. Nonetheless, the departmental form lasted over a century. And there was a rough and ready equilibrium between the *form* of the Post Office and democratic and public *expectations.* Its departmental setting made it intensely accountable to Parliament, which was a scene of exquisitely well developed political influences on its decisions and policies. Eventually, however, a consensus emerged that the Post Office was too "politicized" and needed political autonomy to pursue its retail responsibilities in a commercial way. This was a primary objective of the Post Office Department's transformation into a Crown corporation in 1981.

consensus re too political

Post Office Department

The Post Office *Department* bore the same formal relationship to Parliament as other departments of government, and it had the same formal place in cabinet. The POD was headed by a minister, the postmaster general (PMG), who was a member of cabinet. The PMG was answerable for the Post Office in Parliament. Apart from a short time in the late 1960s and early 1970s,[2] the POD was always a unique and separate department with its own minister. Its purpose, authority, and responsibilities were set out in the Post Office Act of 1867, which changed but in technical detail thereafter. The act repealed the laws of the previous provincial post offices, created the POD, and outlined the PMG's powers. The PMG was given the authority to open and close post offices and routes, appoint local postmasters, make postal regulations, and set rates on non-letter mail. The act established the principle of the POD's exclusive privilege and defined what was meant by first-class mail. The PMG in turn was given the authority to decide what qualified as first-class mail. In addition, the act set new first-class postal rates, which established the precedent that changes in letter rates had to be approved by Parliament, as a matter of legislative amendment to the Act. Other price changes and regulatory matters were simply to be gazetted. The act also established the principle of cheaper postal rates for newspapers, books, and periodicals. It was quite general in setting sweeping goals, general procedures, and non-specific guidelines for the POD. For example, it made no statements on service standards, the logic of price increases, or the relationship among the prices of different categories of mail, the jurisdictional relations with other departments, or the fiscal goals of the Post Office. In this it was no different from the operationalizing legislation of other departments. Political practice and experience would give more concrete form to these policy objectives.

The act required that the POD submit an annual report to Parliament, which would then evaluate the extent to which its activities conformed to the act. There were also formal supply debates in the House of Commons, when the minister would seek approval of the department's annual budget. This provided an opportunity for members of Parliament to hold the Post Office accountable for its actions, hear about the past year's performance, listen to future plans, and comment on and criticize postal operations. During the 1970s, the venue for parliamentary scrutiny shifted to parliamentary committee, where the minister would make a presentation, committee members would question and criticize, and the committee would issue a report to Parliament.

The Post Office's traditional relationship with Parliament extended to price and service matters. In order to increase the price of a first-class stamp, Parliament had to pass legislation amending the Post Office Act, complete with a full-scale parliamentary debate through the various reading, committee, and report stages. This was an exceedingly cumbersome and politically dangerous device, akin to requiring parliamentary approval to change the price of a loaf of bread: it was an invitation to political assault. Not surprisingly, there were few attempts to raise prices, and even fewer successes. The approach was challenged to effect in 1977, when PMG J.J. Blais concluded that the act allowed price changes to be effected by order-in-council as a simple regulatory change.[3] Howls of protest arose from parliamentarians, Opposition spokesmen, editorialists, and government committees; nonetheless, Blais and the government persisted. By the time the legislative committees concluded that this action was illegal,[4] the department was poised to become a Crown corporation.

The POD's traditional organizational form also extended to its operational structure and strategy. Despite its far-flung transportation, sorting, delivery, and retail operations, its management was extremely centralized. Operational decisions were made in Ottawa, regardless of how small or un important. There are legions of examples, from the bureaucratic steps required to purchase a new desk for a local post office to the dozen or so steps required to have a new postal route approved.[5] Expert studies and commissions — from the Woods and Gordon study (1951) to the Glassco (1963) and Lambert (1979) royal commissions — decried the POD's overcentralization and inadequate delegation of authority to the field. Some institutional tinkering ensued after these studies, but the basic, centralized approach persisted. The Post Office was traditionally plagued by tension between headquarters and the field.[6] One serious consequence was that senior postal management spent most of its energy and imagination on *operational* as opposed to *policy* matters. Swamped by the minutiae of postal operations, it lacked the time or staff to scan the forest instead of continuously worrying about the trees. This was especially evident in the area of research and forward-looking policy considerations: the POD had a poor record of innovation and response to technological change. Deputy ministers were con-

[handwritten margin notes: "dep't mgmt centralized" and "critical studies"]

cerned more about delivery routes in Saskatoon than the Post Office's future position in the communications market.

This focus on operational details was reinforced by the character of postal management. Most postal managers were recruited from within the organization. They worked their way up through the ranks, bringing their operational foci with them into the higher managerial levels. Deputy PMG W.H. Wilson was not untypical. He started as a temporary postal helper in Vancouver in 1929 and worked his way through the ranks, rising to postmaster in 1955, Pacific director in 1958, and director of operations in 1959. A specialist in the planning and operation of mail-handling techniques, he became deputy PMG in 1961, a position he held until 1968. Wilson's entire working career was spent in the Post Office, and he had no management or financial training. Consultancy studies in the late 1960s noted that postal management had little education — 70 per cent had no more than high school. The POD itself offered no training in areas such as personnel relations or business management, and spent only $35,000 on management training annually.[7] Management had neither financial or managerial training nor private-sector commercial experience to complement their operational experience and concerns. This condition was exacerbated by the recruitment of a disproportionate number of ex-servicemen into the ranks, as a matter of government post-war policy, which added a decidedly military cast to the Post Office's nuts-and-bolts tunnel vision. PMG Eric Kierans attempted to inject outside policy expertise and values in the late 1960s, in order to provide a broader postal vision and more modern tools and approaches. This strategy was pursued again by Canada Post president Michael Warren in 1981. Both experiments had mixed results, as will be seen.

The POD functioned within a complicated interdepartmental web. Areas of direct and indirect postal concern were managed and operated by other departments and so a substantial part of postal policy was made or considered by personnel outside of the department. For example, postal buildings and space were leased from the Department of Public Works, which also had the responsibility of maintaining the buildings. Decisions regarding the creation and location of new post offices, their character and construction, and their cleaning and maintainence were either taken or substantially influenced by Public Works. But Public Works had its own goals and priorities, which were not always in tune those of the Post Office. This situation prevailed in a variety of other areas. Purchasing was done by other Departments, such as Supply and Services. Transportation matters had to be dealt with via the Department of Transportation. And wages, salaries, working conditions, and job descriptions and classifications were processed and set by Finance and then by Treasury Board, whose thinking reflected less the needs and considerations of a blue-collar operation than the government's cash concerns and the white-collar contours of other departments. This dissonance caused considerable disruption when new technology was introduced in the 1970s. Moreover, Treasury Board was in the habit of settling contracts at the eleventh hour via concessions on non-monetary items, which would not affect their bottom-line cash position. But, knowing little about postal operations, it often approved principles that tied management's hands on operational matters, at considerable cost to the Post Office.[8]

Postal managers thus had remarkably little decision-making authority: wages and salaries, purchasing, building and maintenance, and various transportation matters were not part of their policy domain. This caused both operational and political problems. The Post Office had to wait for others in order to accomplish certain things, like making building repairs; or it had to accept decisions made by others, like changes in salaries and working conditions. In short, the Post Office was held politically accountable for many issues and conditions over which it had no control. Moreover, postal management had no power to determine the price of its product, which was a parliamentary matter.

The absence of effective Post Office authority also reflected the character of the cabinet system. Postal policy was set in cabinet, where the PMG attempted to sell postal policy ideas and innovations to the other members. But the PMG had little room for independent initiative. Ministers were happy to extend the PMG a free hand in operational matters — as long as their constituencies had home delivery and loads of post offices. However, cabinet took all the key pricing and regulation decisions. There was a surprisingly and disproportionately large amount of time spent on postal discussions in cabinet up through the early 1960s, centred mainly on issues of political concern, such as patronage jobs, post office locations, service issues, and rural route contracts. The PMG's task was to keep colleagues and the government out of trouble. Most importantly, the PMG was instructed to restrain postal spending and prices. Not surprisingly, there were almost never any price rises, as they were not in cabinet's interest. There were four first-class price increases between 1900 and 1967, only one of which (1954) took place in "normal" circumstances, and only after a vicious parliamentary debate (the other three were taken in wartime or during the Depression). Other price rises were either mooted and rejected in cabinet, defeated in Parliament, or withdrawn by the government for political reasons. The most fundamental postal policy issues were determined by the cabinet, by senior public servants in the central agencies, or by the prime minister. For example, the decision to restyle the POD as a Crown corporation was put off by the cabinet in 1970; the idea was embraced by the prime minister in 1978; but in both cases, the decision was taken against the wishes of the PMG. And between 1970 and 1978, senior civil servants outside the POD ensured that the issue was not placed on the policy agenda.[9]

Postal matters waned in importance throughout the post-war era. Canadian governments became increasingly concerned with welfare-state matters, technological change, and the nation-building possibilities of the new communications technologies. The PMG was given a free hand—as long as cabinet colleagues were kept out of trouble.[10] But the Post Office was still not given very much political space, opportunity, or resources with which to take initiatives. This reflected the fact that the Post Office did not carry much weight in cabinet or in the high reaches of the civil service. Despite its size, political visibility, and extensive activity, the POD had little political prestige. It was typically headed by a junior minister en route to another political assignment, or by a minister with limited possibilities for career advancement. Some ministers referred to it as a "political graveyard,"[11] a reflection of a number of political factors. The Post Office was considered to be a blue-collar or operational department much like Public Works, an anomaly in Ottawa's sea of white-collar departments and activities. It was a department in which one got one's hands dirty but where there was little opportunity for policy development or making one's political mark. Thus, the position of PMG was a quick pit stop, to be visited briefly, taking care to avoid an overlong stay. There were some extremely effective and imaginative PMGs, like André Ouellet and J.J. Blais. They found the POD to be an interesting challenge and wanted to remain longer in their position to pursue their policy ideas. Both recall being informed by the prime minister that staying would be considered political misjudgement.[12] A scan of the list of PMGs indicates that few took on top ministerial assignments, even fewer emerged as major leadership candidates, and none went on to become prime minister. At an earlier time, soft and unimportant portfolios were traditionally assigned to French Canadians to fill out their quota in the cabinet; hence twenty of forty-one post-confederation PMGs were French Canadians, and nine of sixteen since World War II.

The Post Office's low status and prestige extended to the deputy ministerial level as well. Deputy PMGs were not regulars on the civil service cocktail circuit. They were very much outside the policy making and discussion in-group of deputy ministers.[13] As a result, the Post Office's political bargaining power was always rather low and its needs were relegated to the end of the queue. The rapid turnover of ministers exacerbated what was an inherently bad political situation for the Post Office. From 1867 to 1945, there were *thirty* PMGs (one every 2.6 years), compared to *five* deputy PMGs (whose average tenure was 15.6 years). The comparable figures for 1945-68 were ten PMGs versus three DPMGs (7.7 years), and for 1968-1981 eight PMGs (1.6 years) and three deputy PMGs (4.3 years). Over the 124-year history of the POD, there were forty-eight PMGs who spent an average of 2.4 years in the position, and eleven deputy PMGs who spent an average of 10.3 years. During the four- to five-year life of a government, it would have at least two different PMGs; governments in the 1960s and 1970s had three PMGs every five years. This state of affairs did not afford the minister much opportunity to become familiar with the basic contours of the Post Office, never mind thinking through, selling, and implementing policy innovations.

FIGURE 1

Canada's Postmaster Generals, 1940-1981

William Pate Mulock	1940-45	Jean-Pierre Côté	1965-68
Ernest Bertrand	1945-49	Eric Kierans	1968-71
G.E. Rinfret	1949-52	Jean-Pierre Côté	1971-72
Alcide Côté	1952-55	André Ouellet	1972-74
Hughes Lapointe	1955-57	Bryce Mackasey	1974-76
William Hamilton	1957-62	J.J.Blais	1976-78
Ellen Fairclough	1962-63	Gilles Lamontagne	1978-79
Azellus Denis	1963-64	John Fraser	1979-80
John Nicholson	1964-65	André Ouellet	1980-81
René Tremblay	1965		

FIGURE 2

Deputy Postmaster Generals, 1935-81

John A. Sullivan	1935-45	Paul-André Faguy	1968-70
Walter J. Turnball	1945-57	John A.H. Mackay	1970-77
George A. Boyle	1957-61	James C. Corkery	1977-81
William H. Wilson	1961-68		

A typical deputy PMG would see four to five ministers come and go in his[14] far longer tenure. This was not a situation in which a deputy minister would feel inclined to take risks in responding to a minister's preliminary, usually highly political, and distinctly amateur policy musings. His top priority was to ensure that the PMG stayed out of political hot water until he or she received the prime ministerial call to a more prestigous position. The result was lethargic policy and the departmental *status quo*, particularly in the POD's persistent focus on operational rather than policy concerns and its perpetual distrust of labour.[15]

The POD continuously lost interdepartmental budgetary and political battles. More often than not, its interests were subsumed within other governmental objectives, often with catastrophic consequences. It was not the POD's decision to keep postal prices at ludicrously low levels in the post-war period. Whether for anti-inflationary purposes in the 1970s or political reasons in the 1950s and early 1960s, its economic and organizational needs were sacrificed to other policy goals. The government and other departments saw their needs met to varying degrees, while the Post Office remained desperately underfunded, undercapitalized, pre-modern, with an underpaid, overworked labour force. The unimaginative, undertrained, and militarily oriented postal management accepted this pricing and fiscal situation stoically, and turned the screws a bit harder to save dollars and cents and to keep the mail moving. The legacy of labour antagonism and strife of the late 1960s and 1970s, as well as the Post Office's technological and managerial backwardness, can be traced to this condition: the inadequate political and managerial concern assigned to the Post Office in the post-war period. This, in turn, reflected the structural or institutional realities of political life in Canada at the time.

Parliament's role in postal matters shifted and changed over the POD's history. Ironically, while the Post Office was of intense daily interest — given its ubiquitousness, visibility, and universal impact — it enjoyed a low level of prestige and importance within the government. Exactly the reverse was true of, for example, External Affairs. Members of Parliament, subjected to constituency pressures on postal matters, attempted to remedy this asymmetry and had a relatively high degree of influence within the Post Office's departmental setting. They could lobby the PMG directly for new routes, jobs for workers and party loyalists, contracts for rural route workers, and construction of new post offices. Governments tended to be politically sensitive to the "postal needs" of MPs. Postal decisions provided a relatively cheap and easy way to score political points at the riding level. For the local MP, they were an effective way of showing that he or she was "delivering the goods," (compare, for example, foreign policy, which could hardly be changed to suit riding opinion). Political influences played a substantial role in postal affairs up through the 1960s, with regard to hiring, opening of post offices and routes, and individual cases: PMGs and deputy PMGs had sensitive political antennae. Governmental reforms brought these patronage and political practices to an end in the late 1960s.

At higher policy levels, Parliament itself was influential on matters of price and regulation changes. Annual supply debates provided an opportunity for MPs to question and criticize postal policy. These debates were extremely thorough, informed, lively, and effective. And price and major regulation changes required legislative amendments to the Post Office Act, which gave Parliament real power. It could scrutinize and embarrass a government politically for taking a too cavalier attitude to such changes. It periodically defeated a governmment proposal for price increases, or caused its withdrawal, or deterred a government from even contemplating a price rise. Hence, only four price rises were carried out from 1900 to 1967, three of them under extraordinary circumstances. In this political setting, the Post Office's nineteenth century nation-building role persisted well into the late twentieth century. Commercial concerns continued to be subservient to social goals. MPs insisted that the POD extend door-to-door delivery, maintain and improve rural services, support various categories of mail, and subsidize postal activities as a public service.

It is no coincidence that this traditional public service orientation weakened when Parliament's postal role declined. In the 1970s, the postal supply debates shifted to parliamentary committee, a much less visible and intense venue. In 1977, PMG Blais increased prices through an order-in-council, without parliamentary debate. For good or for bad, this neutralized Parliament's and MPs' leverage over the Post Office. The result was that price and other postal issues increasingly became a matter of administrative routine rather than political struggle and controversy. Economic matters then came to take pride of place over social or public-service considerations.

This was precisely the government's aim. In the 1970s, the Post Office became a matter of increasing policy concern, if not of policy importance. Unionization and its aftermath, technological change and its consequences, and the emergence of the government's own fiscal crisis were critical policy issues needing careful attention. The government's lack of interest in matters postal had become a dangerous habit. Though they continued to be a low policy priority in the 1970s, postal matters were constantly causing political trouble for governments. Their shift away from parliamentary scrutiny was a strategic decision designed to ensure that the Post Office was given more careful and primarily adminstrative treatment. Parliament's role became that of a "sounding board" or "complaint" agency, where such issues as declining service, labour strife, rural route contracts, patronage, and the postal deficit were raised. These debates were marked by extensive all-party participation, reflecting the fact that postal matters continued to be one of the most prominent issues in MPs' mail. Despite this continuing parliamentary sound and fury, however, postal policy had become distanced from politics, a development that would be extended in 1981 with the transformation of the Post Office Department into Canada Post Corporation.

Canada Post Corporation

The POD was one of Canada's most studied and explored government institutions. Beginning with Durham's study of the post in the Canadas in the nineteenth century, there was no shortage of information or analysis on which to base proposed postal policy or institutional improvements. Major post-war studies included the Woods and Gordon study (1952), the Glassco Royal Commission on Governmental Organization (1962), the Anderson Report (1965), the 1965 Royal Commission on Wages, the Montpetit Royal Commission on Working Conditions (1966), the "Blueprint for Change" report and its fifteen consultancy studies (1969), the Goldenberg Report (1970), the Arnot-Mullington Report (1975), the Hay environmental study (1975), the Darling, Ubering, Kelly Report (1978), the Ritchie Report (1978), the Marin Royal Commission (1981), and an auditor-general's study (1980-81). There was also substantial analysis done in numerous internal POD and

parliamentary committee reports as well as postal union studies and conciliation reports.[16]

These studies had various purposes and settings, covered a variety of
subjects, and made numerous recommendations; a frequent one was to transform the POD into a Crown corporation. Indeed, the idea of Crowning the
Post Office was on the policy agenda for over fifteen years, from the mid-
1960s onward, and enjoyed a high degree of public and institutional support.
The postal unions supported the idea from the early post-war years onward.
Postal management also was sympathetic to the idea. Nonetheless, the recommendation was pursued only after an extended political "delay," which
was an interesting political issue in itself, examined in Part 3.

The setting for, and logic of, the POD's transformation into Canada Post
Corporation will also be explored in more detail in Chapter 6. This transformation reflected two sets of changes. First, the POD confronted a set of
disobliging environmental conditions: industrial relations were constrained
by bargaining under the PSSRA; commercial and competitive pressures im-
perilled its future; postal deficits were rising at an alarming rate; the increasing scale and complexity of postal operations and its technological imperatives seemed to have escaped control; social and economic objectives seemed
at war with each other. As a result of all this, the Post Ofice had lost its
sense of identity. Second, the POD existed in an uncongenial political setting:
it seemed institutionally incapable of dealing with these issues. Postal management didn't bargain with labour, Treasury Board did; postal authority
was shared and limited; postal management was not sufficiently motivated
commercially, tied too closely to departmental (and political) behaviour and
thinking; ministerial turnover inhibited policy formulation and development;
the political setting complicated simple issues like raising the price of a
stamp.

problems pre Crown

reasons to Crown

The move to Crown corporate form seemed compelling at the time. There
was broad consensus that the Post Office needed to act in a more commercial
way to meet competive pressures, and that it required an apolitical context
to improve labour-management relations, neutralize the deficit, and provide
better postal service. All of this seemed possible — or at least *more* possible
— under a Crown corporate regime. The change was supported by all political
parties and in most social and economic quarters. Government officials
seemed exasperated by the Post Office and wanted to rid themselves of postal
embarrassments and deficits. The transformation is a suggestive example of
the Doern-Wilson hypothesis that use of the Crown corporation as a policy
instrument is a tool of last resort, after all other instruments have been tried
and found wanting.[17] Ironically, but not untypically, the decision was made
unilaterally by Prime Minister Trudeau in 1978. There was no cabinet discussion and no forewarning given to even the PMG, Gilles Lamontagne, who
was generally not in favour of the idea.[18] This illustrated the absurdity of
the way in which key postal decisions were made outside of the Post Office.

Canada has a long, albeit weakening, tradition of using the Crown corporation, particularly in the areas of utilities, resources, transportation, and communication. An extensive geography conspired with a smallish population to make infrastructural economic development projects expensive and financially unattractive for private investors. Hence, the long state involvement in Canadian economic development, an involvement that combined elements of economic necessity and political and ideological preference.[19] The attraction of the Crown corporation has been its "mixed" logic: organized on a corporate as opposed to a departmental basis, the public institution adopts a commercial rather than a bureaucratic vision and values, which allows it to be efficient and rational in what is, after all, its commercial activity. But it will not be exclusively capitalist in its motives and functions. It is defined as a public institution acting in an area of the public good and so it will be motivated by the Crown, by governments' social and political values and goals. Thus, the Crown corporation uses a commercial instrument for public purposes.

Balancing corporate/commercial values with Crown/social ones is an optimistic goal, if not a utopian one, a claim often confirmed in recent experience of Crown corporations.[20] And the internal tension of the idea has been parallelled by governmental ambivalence. As Langford notes, Canadian governments have rushed to adopt the Crown corporation as a tool, but at the same time have always feared that its use would diminish their political authority.[21]

The Post Office was an obvious candidate for Crowning, given its essentially commercial and retail character and the need to ensure market and technological competitiveness. Crown corporations already abounded in the transportation and communication fields, in which postal activity took place. At the same time, postal activities embodied a Canadian tradition of social service and national economic development, and were a substantial part of the Canadian political culture. These social and commercial dimensions had co-existed — sometimes uneasily — within the Post Office since 1867. Thus, the Crown corporate form seemed an ideal structure for postal activity.

Chapter 6 will analyze the character of the new postal corporation in some detail. We can briefly sketch that character here: Canada Post Corporation (CPC), as a Crown corporation, was created with a president, chairman and board of directors. A minister of the cabinet was assigned responsibility for CPC and is answerable in Parliament for its actions and performance. Bill C-42, An Act to Establish the Canada Post Corporation, repealed the old Post Office Act and set out CPC's mandate and the objectives it was to pursue. The act authorized CPC to organize itself and to carry out its daily operational functions on its own, outside the structure and daily process of government. It was to be uninhibited by governments, save in its pursuit of the public objectives set out in the legislation.

CPC's responsibilities are similar to those of the POD. Bill C-42 gives CPC the responsibility to pick up, process, and deliver mail under relatively similar legal conditions and definitions. For example, the principle of the universal rate for postage, regardless of distance travelled, was reproduced. CPC was also given exclusive privilege over first-class mail. However, a number of categories were exempted from the postal monopoly. For example, "time-sensitive" mail could be delivered by private courier services (at a price at least three times the first-class rate). The legislation spelled out a number of general goals, which were quickly distilled and interpreted to mean the following:

- repair labour-management relations
- maintain and improve customary postal services
- control the deficit and move to a balanced budget

The setting, interpretation, and implementation of these objectives are matters of deep political interest and controversy, to be explored in Part 4. The point to notice here is that the new corporation would have the autonomy it needed to perform its commercial duties, as long as the government considered that it was meeting the above objectives. This autonomy would allow it to do things previously carried out by government departments. For example, it, not the Treasury Board, would now bargain directly with trade unions; it, not Supply and Services, would purchase and contract for supplies; it, not Public Works, would own, lease, and maintain its buildings; and it, not Finance and other economic departments, would organize its personnel, budgets, pension arrangements, and so on.

Although the legislation ostensibly assigned CPC independence and commercial autonomy, the government managed to retain a considerable amount of postal authority. It set the objectives of the corporation in the legislation, and assigned itself the responsibility of defining what the objectives meant and of judging whether they were being met. If in its eyes those objectives were not being met, it had the authority to intervene. Indeed, it can be argued that governments have subsequently set CPC's policy orientations. The 1981 budget (which dictated a deficit reduction schedule), the vetoing of CPC's re-definition of a letter in 1982, the abandonment of the Consumer's Post and diversification plan, the rejection of Michael Warren's last corporate plan, the crucial 1986 corporate plan (which directed CPC onto an exclusively commercial and privatization course), labour negotiations (where the government has used back-to-work legislation to shape the bargaining process), the 1989 corporate plan (which set profit targets) — these are but a few significant examples of governments' enormous influence since 1981 in setting the course of postal activity.

There were a number of other ways in which the government could direct and influence postal matters. First, it gave itself the power to appoint senior corporation officials, including the president, vice presidents, chair and board of directors. The character and orientation of Canada Post could be influenced considerably by these appointments. Second, the corporation was to submit annual reports to Parliament. It would thus be open to annual political scrutiny and comment, at which time it could face pressures to conform to alternative plans and ideas. The Financial Administration Act was subsequently amended to require commercial Crown corporations like CPC to submit for governmental approval annual updates of a five-year corporate plan; this extended considerably the government's influence over CPC's direction. Third, the government's "directive power" (section 20) could be used to establish policy guidelines and objectives for the corporation. Fourth, Canada Post's capital borrowing requirements were subject to government authority. The government could exercise even further policy leverage by means of the *quid pro quos* to be exacted in picking up the corporation's deficit for as long as it persisted. Finally, the legislation provided for a system of public notification or gazetting of price increases and regulatory changes. The public could convey criticism of CPC's price or regulatory proposals to the minister, who retained final power of approval or rejection.

The government, although committed to giving the new Canada Post enough space to act like a commercial operation, thus retained substantial postal powers under the new Crown corporation regime. This belied the widespread impression that the postal service was being "liberated" from political influence and interference. It provides another example of government ambivalence in the use of the Crown corporation as a policy instrument. The government's retention of postal powers did not necessarily imply that these powers would be exercised automatically or frequently. The powers existed on legislative paper, in the abstract, as a democratic check to ensure Crown corporation accountability. Only time, experience, and political decisions would establish the extent to which these powers would actually be exercised, if at all.

For reasons to be explored later, the chair and board of directors of CPC have not played a substantial role in the new institutional setting. The chair has been a formal figurehead. The first three were French Canadians, in the spirit of the long-standing Canadian political tradition of balancing French and English appointments to Crown corporations (the first two CPC presidents were English Canadians). The first two chairs did not have the kind of private- or public-sector background or experience to make an impact on either the business or the political side of the postal operation. René Marin was a judge and Sylvain Cloutier an accountant, both with public-service careers. Roger Beaulieu had a private sector background in business and law, but no postal or communications expertise or experience.[22] The Liberal government of the early 1980s made token attempts to make the board "representative," in contrast to a typical private-sector board. After discussions with the CLC and the postal unions, the minister responsible for CPC, André Ouellet, assigned two board seats (of ten) to labour.[23] This low-level experiment in worker participation greatly unsettled CPC's first president Michael Warren, even though it gave labour little real clout. The practice — promised informally but never written into the legislation — ended with the election of a Conservative government in 1984. The board's representative quality has subsequently extended only to regional and corporate considerations. The board is constructed on the basis of representation from each of CPC's operating divisions in the West, central Canada, and the Maritimes. This produces a fine regional balance recognizable, perhaps, only to researchers. At the same time, an exclusively corporate representation resulted, giving the board a decidedly private-sector flavour. However, there has been no noticeable attempt to professionalize the board or to integrate CPC into the wider Canadian business and communications communities through board appointments. Retired bankers and company presidents have been the most substantial appointments, who have joined executives from mid-size companies in the service, insurance, and other sectors. The board has not included presidents and directors from the major mail users, such as heads of direct mailing firms, periodical and newspaper associations, or the utility and banking sectors. Nor have board members been drawn from the transportation, communications, and telecommunications sectors. The CPC board is not integrated into the Canadian capitalist interlocking directorship network. Its members can be characterized as earnest and diligent, but comprised of neither business and political high-flyers nor individuals with strong postal, communication, or transportation experience. This suggests strongly the extent to which governments have wanted to give CPC management a relatively free hand — which would certainly not have been the case if the board were packed with the corporate elite of these sectors. Further, the chair's position has now been cut back to a part-time one.[24]

An important reason why the board and its chair have played such an insubstantial role is that the president of the CPC is also a member of the board. The president has been first among equals, and the board, while a source of ideas, morale, and support, has effectively backed and legitimized senior management's and the president's initiatives. The assymetry of interest and expertise built into the composition and appointments of the board has been reinforced in the fact that neither the chair nor the board has had a close or privileged position with the minister responsible for Canada Post. For example, Roger Beaulieu had no personal or close working relationship with the minister, Harvie Andre. Indeed, Beaulieu was not "recruited" for the position by Andre, but was chosen by Benôit Bouchard, the Conservatives' Quebec lieutenant, on the basis of being a Quebec Conservative.[25] In contrast, the CPC president has occupied a position of privilege and access to the minister. In this, the corporation has functioned politically much like

FIGURE 3
Leadership of Canada Post

Minister	President	Chairman
André Ouellet (1981-84)	Michael Warren (1981-85)	René Marin (1981-86)
Perrin Beatty (1984-85)		
Michel Côté (1985-86)	Donald Lander (1985-92)	Sylvain Cloutier (1986-91)
Harvie Andre (1986-93)		Roger Beaulieu (1991-92)
	Georges Clermont (1992-)	Donald Lander (1992-)

a department, with the president playing the role of the powerful deputy minister. But there have been some noticeable changes from the departmental era. There have been four ministers over the first decade or so of CPC's existence, for an average term of appointment of around three years. But the sample size is small and misleading. Two of the ministers did short stints (Perrin Beatty 1984-85, Michel Côté 1985-86), and the other two have held the appointment for substantial stretches (André Ouellet 1981-84, Harvie Andre 1986-93). At the same time, there have been only three presidents: Michael Warren (who overlapped primarily with André Ouellet), Donald Lander, and Georges Clermont (who overlapped with Harvie Andre). The relations between the minister and the president have been personable and—in contrast to those of the departmental era—have created an extremely stable management situation. Each of these relationships has also provided a rough-and-ready political/bureaucratic match. The pragmatic and socially concerned André Ouellet was a workable complement to the progressive and humane Michael Warren. The neo-conservatively inclined and combative Harvie Andre was a perfect match for the tenacious, commercially oriented, profit- and efficiency-driven Donald Lander. The relationship between the minister and the president has been one of the key determining factors to this point in CPC's experience: all political processes have revolved around it. The crucial issue of the degree of autonomy assigned to the president and the corporation is a central example. The pattern followed has been a function of the extent to which the minister has judged that the corporation is delivering the goods. As a broad and early generalization, Michael Warren and the corporation were given constrained autonomy in the early years, reflecting the continuation of the postal deficit, uncertainty about CPC's capacity to attain its objectives, and the government's insistence on balancing social and economic goals. The little autonomy that Warren enjoyed was quickly eliminated with the election of the Conservative government. The government's judgement was that the corporation had not moved fast enough to a commercial and balanced-budget footing. Under Donald Lander, though, it was given increasing autonomy, because it delivered precisely what its minister expected: elimination of the deficit, rising profits, and a degree of efficiency and commercialism that has made privatization a realistic possibility. This postal record has been aided considerably by the government's own willingness to decrease, if not destroy, the Post Office's social functions. The government declined to use its political authority in postal matters to the extent that the corporation attained its postal objectives. As will be seen, what looks like a "free" or unregulated corporation is in fact a corporation carefully following the strict and well-defined goals of the government.

The minister responsible for CPC does not have a large bureaucracy overseeing the corporation. He or she has three bureaucratic resources: senior CPC management, his or her own staff, and Treasury Board. The minister uses senior CPC management as "bureaucracy," giving them ideas of what he or she might like to see happen. Policy positions are then developed, which may be taken to cabinet. This relationship functions much like that within a traditional department. The minister's own postal staff is quite small, at present comprising only one person, who acts as the political liaison between the Minister's office and MPs, CPC, and Treasury Board. The issue with the highest political profile is whether to raise the price of a first-class stamp. CPC proposals for price or regulation changes are presented to the minister, then gazetted to stimulate public response. These and other political reactions are submitted to the minister, who makes a recommendation to the Special Committee of Cabinet, which deals with regulatory matters. Price increases in the early 1980s generated thousands of letters to the minister. The most recent proposals, however, have generated but dozens of submissions — and mainly from institutions.[26] The corporate plan has also to be approved by the minister as well as by Treasury Board, a procedure discussed below. These processes afford the minister considerable influence in postal matters. In the first half-dozen years of CPC's existence, the minister was under considerable pressure from backbench Members of Parliament. For example, in 1987 the minister's office received two to three calls a day and loads of mail each week asking the minister to take up local postal matters. Presently, the minister might get one or two calls a month, as he or she no longer responds substantively to MPs' enquiries. These are directed to CPC, which has organized an office to deal with the MPs.[27]

On technical matters, the minister and his or her assistant rely on Treasury Board for information and expertise. This is especially the case in the process surrounding the corporate plan. The amendments to the Financial Administration Act in June 1984 required most commercial Crown corporations to submit annually a five-year plan to the government for approval. A Crown Corporations Directorate (CCD) oversees this process and reports to the Department of Finance and Treasury Board. This gives CPC a window of access to the central agencies of government, to gather information on the government's thinking on postal and related matters. The government, in turn, has the opportunity to evaluate and direct CPC's progress through the prism of its wider policies and objectives. This procedure is designed to ensure adequate political accountability and control.

Legally, Treasury Board approves CPC's capital and operating budgets and, on its recommendation, the governor-in-council approves the corporate plan. The process is as follows. CPC constructs its corporate plan, which is to be submitted to the minister for approval sixty days before the fiscal year begins (i.e., by the first week of February). After he or she signs it, the plan is passed along to Treasury Board, which reviews it and makes recommendations. These are substantial opportunities for political evaluation of CPC. The process is informed by the previous year's experience, as the CCD analyst sends to CPC his or her comments and observations about last year's plan, its formulation, and its impact. This informal communication connects CCD, CPC, and the minister's office. The corporation follows its own planning process, and produces a planning framework for its board's approval in principle. A final version is submitted to the board early in the new year, to allow CPC to present its corporate plan to the minister in early February. The plan is then passed on to Treasury Board.

The planning process is a formal one, but it is enveloped in a variety of informal processes and discussions. The result is that there are few surprises along the way. Where CCD and CPC disagree, the issue is passed up the chain of command to Treasury Board, which resolves the issue. Any disagreements between the minister and CPC or CCD are resolved through communications and discussions before the plan is submitted formally. The CPC plan is considered by CCD to be one of the best it receives from all of the commercial Crowns. This is because the CPC plan tends to comply with the Financial Administration Act (FAA) requirements in stating objectives, laying out strategies to meet them, tying in the financial plan with the operational one, and giving operations and performance indicators. This undoubtedly reflects the continuity in CCD's evaluation of CPC. CCD analysts typically rotate in their responsibilities from one Crown corporation to another every two to three years; but the CCD analyst assigned to CPC in February 1985 has retained this responsibility ever since.[28]

Parliament has played a steadily less important role since the Post Office became a Crown corporation. Parliament had already lost much of its political leverage in 1977, when PMG Blais enacted a price increase without parliamentary approval. The act creating CPC gave Parliament no direct authority or role in price and regulation changes. A gazetting system was established, in which a proposed price increase is published in the *Canada Gazette* to allow for a period of public scrutiny. Public reactions are directed to the minister who, within a certain time period, listens, gauges the political mood, and decides whether to approve or reject the increase. Parliament and MPs have no more influence in this process than an interest group, lobby, or private citizen. One of Parliament's few postal responsibilities is to review CPC's annual report. This is done in a parliamentary committee, which can hold hearings and issue a report to the House of Commons. The government is obliged to respond to this report. On occasion, the minister takes this parliamentary report under advisement. This was the case in 1985, when a backbench Tory revolt over closing of rural post offices resulted in a scathing committee review of the CPC's 1986 plan.[29] The minister, Michel Côté, subsequently directed the Corporation to alter this feature of its plan, which it ostensibly did, albeit for but a short period of time. There were one or two other similar examples, as in 1982 over the revised definition of a letter. Conversely a substantial committee report like Garth Turner's 1990 Consumer and Corporate Affairs report was all but ignored.[30]

The postal influence of caucus and individual MPs has diminished considerably since 1986. MPs have been directed to bring their complaints and concerns to CPC, not to the minister's office. Representations to the minister's office are redirected to the CPC's Government Relations office, which attempts to keep MPs informed on postal matters and to sell them on the merits of CPC's policies. The corporation has tried to take a pro-active role in explaining policies to MPs before they are announced. Government Relations mails four to six information packages a year to all MPs. It also sends extra or detailed material to the opposition parties' postal critics and to all MPs when controversial issues arise. MPs appear to be phoning and writing CPC far less than in the past, partially because of this proactive strategy.[31]

Parliament continues to perform the function of postal sounding board, particularly in the absence of a regulatory agency or other site for public involvement (the reasons for this lacuna will be examined in Part 3). After a short-lived experience with third-party regulation in 1989, the corporation has been effectively unregulated in any formal sense. This is an interesting and unique situation for a state monopoly. Parliament offers a soap box for hundreds of annual petitions, statements, and periodic opposition day debates, where MPs voice constituents' concerns. But even this limited legitimizing role has declined in importance, to the extent that Canada Post has been assigned increased political autonomy by the government. As Conservative MP Greg Thompson recently commented in the House of Commons, "Members of Parliament have just about zero clout when it comes to Canada Post."[32] Members direct pointed questions and demands to the minister, who replies that it is not his business to interfere in the management of the corporation. The decline in influence of Parliament in general, and individual MPs in particular, has been noted by some labour leaders, who rue this feature of the operation of the Crown corporation.[33]

special interest groups

As in most other policy areas, interest group politics has supplanted the parliamentary process as the site of effective postal politics. Organized postal pressures and groups have emerged as the third corner of the postal policy triangle, complementing the equally critical emergence of the minister–president relationship. In the earlier departmental era, organized pressure politics was a low-key and relatively informal affair. There was considerable *community* pressure, via the local MP to the department and the minister, to gain a post office or door-to-door mail delivery or a job. The department and the minister were politically sensitive to these requests, for reasons noted above. This tradition waned for two reasons: first, Eric Kierans' reforms in the late 1960s curtailed patronage; second, parliamentary authority declined substantially in the 1970s. Mailers with a "technical" relationship to the Post Office made suggestions on procedures, rates, and service, and the Post Office organized periodic conferences with major mail users. These were informal and *ad hoc* affairs and processes. The Post Office enjoyed a friendly working relationship with its customers in the operationally driven environment of the 1950s and 1960s. The relationship between the department and society at large was benign and paternalistic, and shaped primarily from the top down. There were groups and organizations with special needs and concerns, like the direct mailers, periodical publishers, and community newspaper organizations. They worked with the Post Office to satisfactory ends. Labour was essentially the major organized pressure group during this period, but it had limited influence until the passage of the PSSRA in 1967, and thereafter had a fundamentally antagonistic and ineffective relationship with the Post Office.

The interest-group setting changed dramatically after 1981. The relationship between the Post Office and individual constituents and ridings declined, because Crowning the Post Office diminished the role of Parliament and MPs. At the same time, the organization of postal pressure groups in the private sector improved. The committee hearings on the Crown corporation legislation indicated the range of groups that were interested in the postal situation. These included telecommunications companies, which wanted to limit the postal presence in this sector; private courier services, which wanted to hold on to the business they had gained through the perpetual strikes of the 1970s; small business associations, which felt abused by strikes; consumer groups, which were price and service sensitive; competitors like trucking firms and weekly newspaper groups; representatives of big users in the retail and commercial sectors; labour unions and workers associations; and farm groups and pensioners. The 1980s was the era of interest-group politics, a feature made obvious at these postal hearings.

Three other events galvanized interest-group activity: the 1981 price increase, controversy over the definition of a letter, and the introduction of the 1986 corporate plan. The first two of these incidents generated an enormous amount of business reaction. The prevailing feeling was that CPC was exploiting its privileged position to increase prices and extend its monopoly. This stimulated the formation of the National Association of Major Mail Users (NAMMU) in 1983. NAMMU included business, government, and public groups that mailed at least one million units a year. It grew to over one hundred members by 1990. Under the leadership of its first chair, Ralph Hancox of *Reader's Digest*, NAMMU became a formidable lobbying group with a high degree of influence with both the minister and the CPC president. Indeed, given that business provided 80-90 per cent of postal volumes and revenues, it was perhaps inevitable that it would develop disproportionate postal influence. And as a small number of businesses — about a thousand users — generated about 50 per cent of postal business, it was no surprise that the major mailers developed a special, privileged relationship with the corporation. Indeed, postal politics in the Crown corporate era followed the pattern of policy communities and elite accommodation pointed out by political scientists.[34] Major postal issues were resolved outside of both Parliament and public scrutiny as the minister and president dealt exclusively with what they perceived to be the authentic representatives of the national postal interest (the major mail users). For example, the issue over the definition of a letter was played out with the major users and the corporation in the minister's office, as were requests for price increases and the development of the corporate plans. The large organized postal interests have thus enjoyed a privileged policy position.

As we will see in Part 3, NAMMU had its own vision of the relationship between the Post Office and the major mail users: a non-regulatory one in which each of the major users would individually bargain for their own postal deals and relationships — outside of rates, regulations, and so on. At the same time, CPC's social and economic balancing act was tilted towards the latter, for reasons of political economy as well as of ideology. The sheer force and presence of the big users, the simplified institutional setting that allowed them to deal directly with postal management and the minister, and the absence of parliamentary or regulatory authority and scrutiny made this orientation possible.

The increasingly commercial orientation of CPC's plans from 1986 onward was lauded profusely by NAMMU and other business groups. But the plans were being castigated in other corners. Indeed, the 1986 plan saw the emergence of another matrix of interest groups, whose *raison d'etre* was to stop the corporation from emphasizing economic issues to the neglect of

social ones. For example, limited home delivery and the introduction of the
supermailbox led to the creation of pressure groups such as Residents against
Mailboxes (RAM) and Citizens United for Equitable Postal Service. Neither
of these groups had tremendous staying power: their defining issue was too
narrowly focused to catalyze participation in their urban constituencies. A
far more enduring group has been Rural Dignity of Canada (RDC), which
emerged in protest over rural post office closings in 1985 and afterward.
Funded mainly by the Canadian Postmasters and Postmistresses Association
(CPPA), Rural Dignity has acted as an umbrella group on postal matters for
rural communities, farm groups, municipalities, the handicapped, pensioners,
and rural women. It has enjoyed successes, but the group never gained legitimacy in the eyes of senior CPC officials or government ministers, who
consider Rural Dignity to be a self-interested pressure group, a characterization they did not apply to NAMMU. Since the introduction of the
1986 plan, there has been a broad popular sector front against CPC initiatives
such as franchising, contracting out, and post office closings. Postal unions
have joined with church groups, anti-poverty associations, and women's
groups to fight CPC's plans. But these groups have also lacked legitimacy
and have not had access to the site of postal policy formation. Lacking
direct access to the policy-making process, these groups have fought their
battles as outsiders and have tried to influence the government through
influencing public opinion — often using dramatic, colourful, and passionate
means. The corporation from time to time found itself engaged in a kind
of guerrilla warfare with these groups. This has exasperated CPC, which finds
these groups' claims to be misleading and unconstructive. The Corporation
has refused to battle these groups directly or on their own ground; instead,
it has sought to maintain its government support via influencing public
opinion through extensive and expensive advertising campaigns. As will be
seen, it has been effective in neutralizing a number of controversial policy
issues, which no longer enjoy political resonance. (Rural postal closings are
a case in point.) New issues have emerged in their place, predominantly
environmental concerns over increasing volumes of third-class mail (termed
"ad mail" by CPC and "junk mail" by its opponents). There has been no
"general public" interest group to represent the broad interests of non-busi-
ness users. The Consumers Association of Canada has played a relatively
small role in this regard. Indeed, the postal unions have felt obliged to take
on this public interest role, pursuing it either directly (with limited effect,
given the inevitable charge of self-interest) or indirectly, through the financing of postal interest groups and public relations campaigns.

The Crown corporation setting has afforded the Post Office a certain
amount of autonomous space for its functioning. Institutionally, the two
main axes for postal matters are the relationship between the president and
the minister, and the corporation's interaction with NAMMU. The two main

postal policy processes are ministerial and Treasury Board approval of the five-year plan, and ministerial approval of price and regulation changes. Oddly enough, for a government and an era suspicious of unchecked monopoly power, Canada Post functions in an environment relatively free of formal regulation. Its actions are limited only by market competition, major mail users' expectations, and ministerial judgement that the corporation is heading in the right direction. As will be seen in Part 3, the Mulroney government's unease over the latter led it to introduce a form of regulation in 1988, the Postal Services Review Committee (PSRC). This move was unsuccessful from the government's and CPC's perspectives, for the PSRC was far more aggressive than the government had anticipated. It was highly critical of the corporation, and expressed particular concern that social and public goals were being sacrificed in CPC's effort to make a profit. Since he thought that the corporation was heading in the right direction, the minister declined to pursue the PSRC's recommendations, and the government allowed the corporation to take the initiatives that the PSRC was proposing to deny. It subsequently disbanded the PSRC in the next budget. Canada Post Corporation thus entered its second decade as an unregulated monopoly, a situation unique in the industrialized world. It is effectively insulated from public scrutiny and governmental criticism. And the government gives the impression that it will continue to provide this protection so long as the corporation continues to realize the government's objectives.

Chapter Three

THE POLITICS OF THE TRADITIONAL POST OFFICE:

THE POST-WAR PERIOD, 1945-68

The political and administrative contours of the post-war postal scene remained substantially unchanged from those of the late nineteenth and early twentieth centuries. The organizational structure of the POD was essentially the same one created in 1867. Its range of tasks, the manner in which these tasks were pursued, and the postal political agenda also remained relatively unchanged. The postal world seemed very much to be business as usual.

Beneath this facade, though, a number of critical social and economic developments were unfolding, pushing the Canadian postal system into a state of crisis. First, Canada's aging postal plant and the increase in competition brought about by technological innovations generated significant departmental anxiety after the war. However, these concerns were buried in the avalanche of rising postal volumes, brought on by the long post-war economic boom. Second, this volume growth itself presented a daunting challenge. Considerable capital investment and far-reaching technological innovation were required to process efficiently rising volumes; instead, however, postal management simply pushed its labour force to increase productivity. Third, the Post Office's financial situation became increasingly shaky. This, too, was camouflaged by its remarkable restraining of costs and its equally remarkable but misleading postal accounting system.

The two decades after the war thus comprised a period of postal illusions. of rising volumes and efficient processing and delivery; of low postal prices and balanced budgets; of continued premium postal services delivered by a hard-working and much-admired postal "family." These illusions were rudely dispelled by the postal strike of 1965, which brutally exposed the weaknesses of the POD and the problems it was ignoring. This chapter considers *why* policy makers did not address the competitive, technological, and fiscal challenges faced by the Canadian postal system in the post-war period. Why was a postal strike required to recast the postal agenda? And how was this new agenda constrained as a result of policy inaction and the resulting postal crisis?

The chapter begins by delineating the challenges confronting the Canadian postal system in the post-war period. It then introduces the major postal policy actors and their worlds, and reviews their policy responses to these challenges, analyzing why postal policy took the particular and ineffective shape it did during this period. Third, the chapter investigates the results of these policy responses, particularly the 1965 strike. It concludes with an overview of the recast postal scene and the challenges faced by the POD at the end of the post-war period.

Post-war Postal Challenges

The Canadian postal system was a substantial and extensive communications operation at the end of World War II. Over twelve thousand post offices, nearly five thousand rural routes, and forty thousand postal workers served over two million points of call. The POD handled two billion pieces of mail a year and generated $66 million in revenue. Indeed, the POD was one of Canada's largest business operations. Postal volumes then doubled over the next two decades, from 2.5 billion pieces a year in 1947 to 5 billion pieces in 1968. First-class mail expanded even faster, by 125 per cent. This buoyant volume growth reflected the strength and persistence of post-war economic expansion. As Table 1 indicates, postal volume growth weakened only during recessions, as in 1950-51 and in 1961-62. This secular growth solidified the POD's fiscal picture, despite its maintenance of low postal prices. As Table 2 shows, revenues grew from $66 million in 1945 to over $300 million by 1967. The overall post-war postal budget was in surplus. But the period should be divided into two parts. There were deficits in only four years between 1946 and 1960, and most of these were negligible. From 1961 to 1968 there were surpluses only in 1963 and 1965. The overall budget balance for 1946 to 1968 was $8.7 million, mainly the result of the $69 million surplus generated from 1946 to 1960.

These healthy volume and budget figures masked the POD's deteriorating competitive and financial situation. POD activity barely kept pace with Canada's economic growth and did not keep pace with the expansion of the communications sector. Postal revenues grew only 70 per cent as fast as GDP between 1931 and 1951, by 247 per cent compared to the 348 per cent increase in GDP (see Table 10). This situation worsened over the following decades: postal revenues fell from .55 per cent of GDP in 1931 to .43 per cent in 1981. The growth of postal volumes and revenues also slowed in relationship to the growth of population, as Table 10 indicates, reflecting Canadians' use of alternative communications instruments such as the telephone. From Table 9 we see that telephone calls rose by 350 per cent from 3.2 billion calls in 1945 to 14.4 billion in 1968. In contrast, first-class postal volumes grew by only 57 per cent as much, merely doubling in this period. More importantly, long-distance telephone calls rose eleven-fold as the price of a call fell and the vast proportion of households acquired a telephone. As the table below illustrates, long-distance calls as a proportion of first-class mail rose from 5 per cent in 1945 to 14 per cent in 1968 to 64 per cent by the end of the 1980s. In general terms, postal activity represented a declining proportion of the communications sector. Postal revenue com-

FIGURE 1
Telephone Calls and First Class Mail

	Long-Distance Calls (1)	(billions) First-Class Mail (2)	Ratio 1:2
1949	0.105	1.342	0.078
1959	0.205	2.015	0.102
1969	0.434	2.532	0.170
1979	1.21	3.725	0.325
1989	2.847	4.471	0.640
		% Growth	
1949–59	95	50	1.9
1959–69	112	26	4.3
1969–79	179	47	3.8
1979–89	135	20	6.8
1949–89	2611	233	11.2

prised 62 per cent of the communications sector in 1945 but only 26 per cent by 1969.

The substantial absolute growth in mail volumes thus masked a weakening relative market position for the POD. Two factors created a similarly misleading budget situation. First, postal costs were restrained by a policy of ruthless expenditure control. As will be seen below, the government invested very little in modernizing the POD's aging and out-of-date mechanical plant and equipment. At the same time, the wages of postal workers were restrained to a remarkable degree. As Table 4 indicates, labour costs amounted to only 52 per cent of total postal expenditures. This figure was doubly impressive when one considers both the labour intensity of postal operations and the low level of capital expenditures on plant and equipment. Second, a number of peculiar accounting practices gave a misleading impression of the budget situation. The POD absorbed a number of governmental costs, such as franked mail, selling of licences and distribution of forms and applications.[1] However, a far larger number of postal costs were absorbed by other departments of government. These included the purchase and rental of buildings, as well as their heat and maintenance; recruiting of staff; auditing of the books; issuing of cheques; and provision of pensions. After years of criticism,[2] a new accounting system was finally introduced in 1964, and immediately transformed a marginal $6 million deficit (2.6 per cent of revenue) into a substantial $37 million one (15.6 per cent of revenue). Table 3 reconstructs the early post-war budgets using the new accounting system: the POD's $69 million surplus from 1946 to 1960 becomes a $137 million deficit, an average deficit of $9 million a year (6.5 per cent of revenue). Contrary to arguments advanced in ensuing decades, the POD had always run a deficit.

There was some recognition at this time that the Canadian postal situation was far from rosy. Nonetheless, the explosion of postal volumes, the restraining of costs, and a misleading accounting system shaped the dominant and benign postal vision of the time. Postal matters did not, therefore, command much media attention in the post-war period. For example, only eight entries in the *Financial Post* between 1956 and 1968 concerned postal matters. These focused narrowly on postal rate changes. Postal "controversies" were reported from time to time, but dealt with such crucial issues as the number of mail carriers bitten by dogs and complaints about the subject matter depicted on stamps.

Political Responses

The perpetuation of these postal illusions was a function of the POD's political and administrative setting, which had remained unchanged for nearly a century. The postal policy process focused primarily on the minutiae of administration and the management of day-to-day political pressures; in other words, the postal forest was obscured by concentrating on the postal trees.

Postal Policy Players

The POD was a classic pyramidal organization. At the top of the pyramid sat two chiefs: the titular political chief, the postmaster general, and the operations and administrative chief, the deputy postmaster general. Postal power and authority were centred exclusively in their hands. Their relationship was essentially an asymmetrical one. There were ten PMGs in the period 1945-68, including five from 1962-68. However, there were only three deputy PMGs in this period, who saw PMGs come and go every two or three years. PMGs were not recruited into the position on the basis of their background or expertise.[4] Moreover, in their short-term assignments, they acquired neither command of the postal portfolio nor understanding of the wider communications market in which the POD functioned. None of them commanded substantial personal political power or authority: Ernest Bertrand, G.E. Rinfret, Alcide Côté, Hughes Lapointe, William Hamilton, Ellen Fairclough, Azellus Denis, John Nicholson, René Tremblay, and Jean-Pierre Côté did not enter the top ministerial or prime ministerial ranks.[5] PMGs were directed by prime ministers and their political colleagues to ensure that cabinet was not bothered by trivial postal matters. Ministers had more important things to consider; the PMGs' main task was thus to keep the Post Office out of their hair.[6]

The deputy PMGs were, however, masters of their trade. All were long-serving postal officials, whose entire careers had been spent in the POD. Walter Turnbull was deputy PMG for twelve years and saw four PMGs come and go. G.A. Boyle had spent forty-two years in the POD by the time he was appointed deputy PMG. W.A. Wilson joined the POD in 1929 and was named deputy in 1961. He watched six PMGs come and go. It was thus relatively easy for the experienced, expert deputy PMGs to contain and direct their inexperienced, amateur political masters. The postal policy *status quo* was thus easily reproduced. The deputy PMGs were exclusively operations oriented; they had little to no training or experience outside of the POD and its immediate environment. Not surprisingly, the postal policy process concentrated on administrative and procedural details to the neglect of matters of wider policy and political concern. The deputy PMGs enjoyed as little status and clout among senior civil servants as their political masters had in cabinet. This was because the POD was considered to be a blue-collar, operations department and not a higher-status policy one. This low status and power also reflected the POD's diminishing importance, as its role as a political and nation-building instrument was weakened by developments in the communications market.[7]

The assymetrical relationship beteen the PMG and the deputy PMG, the narrow vision and experience of the latter, and the tentativeness and caution of the PMGs could not generate deep thinking about postal and communications matters or interesting policy innovations. Thus, the postal *status quo* was perpetuated.

Postal Organization

The predilection for the *status quo* was no less evident in the organization of the POD itself. The post-war POD remained unchanged from 1867. There was a minor departmental reorganization in 1922[8] and little change thereafter. It was recognized at the end of World War II that the POD was overcentralized, but the responses counted as more of a trickle than a tidal wave of changes, as the POD itself characterized it. The symptoms of this overcentralization were classic. Routine demands from the field swamped headquarters, which hung on to all authority. There was little real contact between headquarters and the field, "preventing an understanding and appreciation of their respective problems." Headquarters became a bottleneck for decisions.[9] This situation was recognized by the 1952 Woods Gordon organizational study, which recommended a policy of accelerated decentralization and proposed that many of the functions and responsibilities performed in Ottawa be directed to the field. This would liberate senior headquarters officials to study overall postal problems and plan for the future.[10]

Some of the Woods Gordon recommendations were pursued by the POD.[11] However, subsequent reports concluded that decentralization of postal functions "had not progressed satisfactorily."[12] Ironically, the deputy PMG was burdened as a result of the changes, as he carried responsibility for both operations and the new planning function.

A joint organization study group was established in 1962. It consisted of a representative from the Glassco Royal Commision on Government Organization, a member of the organizational division of the Civil Service Commission, and a representative of the POD. The study group concluded that it was "apparent that there was insufficient delegation of authority from Headquarters to the field." Officers in the field required headquarters' approval for most decisions, which delayed needed changes and made services ineffective. The numerous requests from the field in turn cluttered up operations at headquarters.[13] Some of the study group's recommendations were implemented,[14] but even so, by the mid-1960s it was evident that the POD remained too centralized. The ideas of delegation of authority, decentralization, and the separation of planning from operations had been given only lip service: the postal administration wanted to retain authority within its hands at headquarters, as it had since Confederation.[15] The resulting postal policy process concentrated on administrative details and procedures rather than on wider postal matters.

Postal Policy Activities

One can appreciate the extent to which the policy process centred on postal minutiae by examining the matters that commanded the PMG's attention. These were of two sorts: administrative details and day-to-day political pressures.

For example, PMG William Hamilton (1957-62) was fond of going on grand tours of post offices and facilities across the country. Upon returning to Ottawa, he would prepare a long state-of-the-postal-union memorandum, which he would send on to his deputy. After such a tour in the summer of 1958, he fired off two multi-page memos to deputy PMG Boyle, the highlights of which included:

- the need to purchase venetian blinds for the new Sydney, N.S., Post office;
- whether typewriter ribbons and adding machine rolls should be provided in semi-staff post offices, when the postmasters were using their own machines;
- why letter carrier uniforms had been changed from grey to navy blue;
- the use of stucco panels fronting new post offices;

- the purchase of a phone buzzer for the area superintendent in Sydney, to alert him when he was wanted on the phone in the local postmaster's office.

Boyle then tracked these issues, and memos flew back and forth between minister and deputy. Thus was policy made at the highest level of the postal administration in the late 1950s.

The administrative dimension of the POD focused primarily on operational details to the neglect of planning and policy matters. On the political side of things, the process was not terribly different. The PMG's postal environment was not within the cabinet; rather, his attention was turned to the caucus and to the floor of the House of Commons. The PMG's primary responsibility was not to develop policy innovations, but to process MPs' requests for improved postal services within their constituencies. These included demands for new mail routes, expansion of home delivery, service improvements, increased rural services and, particularly, appointments of local postmasters. For example, after the 1958 election, PMG Hamilton distributed a memo to government MPs who had made it clear to him what the government had not been doing on the postal front for them, reporting that "the Post Office Department is ... more sensitive than any other Government Department to the feeling on the part of the Members of Parliament that they should control Government activity and particularly personnel policy within their constituency." The memo explained how local (revenue) postmasters were appointed. Each riding was represented by the local MP, the defeated candidate, or a local Conservative activist, who interacted with the POD via the PMG's executive assistant: "Almost all his time is spent either in conversation with Members or in dealing with their correspondence and liaison on their behalf with the Department." Unlike the concerns pressed on other departments, he continued, most members' dealings with the Post Office "are not matters of policy but matters of administration concerning the detailed action in a particular case." He reminded MPs that there could not be a wholesale sacking of "Liberal" postmasters (in order to avoid raising the ire of thousands of postmasters, distributed in every corner of the country and well placed to mould public opinion). Rather, "every effort will be made when a position comes open through the normal course of events to fill it with a person satisfactory to the local Member." In a later memo, Hamilton wrote that "I am anxious that my department cooperates as closely as possible with our members and benefits from your knowledge of local conditions, because this can bring both increased satisfaction to you and improvements in postal service." Hamilton in turn was reminded of his political responsibilities in this regard; a survey of MPs on postal matters produced many responses in the spirit of MP C. Richard: "Ne jamais oublier que le patronage, dans les contes ruraux, est une chose nécessaire and très souvent importante. Les Libéraux s'en toujours servi et s'en servent encore contre nous. Nous leur avons laisé les armes."[17]

Organizing and managing postal patronage consumed a substantial amount of the PMG's time and energy, as well as that of the House of Commons, where it was a favorite issue.[18] Postal hiring was politically charged, value laden, and complicated by other government policies. For example, the Civil Service Act required that veterans be given first opportunity to apply for a postal vacancy. At times during the post-war period, 80 per cent of those hired were veterans, and the figure was still near 20 per cent in the early 1960s.[19] This large military constituency within the Post Office was not without its own implications: it encouraged the POD's top-down, centralized organization and its blinkered attention to detail.

An issue similar to patronage was the question of rural route carriers and their contracts. This issue commanded an extraordinary amount of political attention, and was perhaps the most widely discussed postal issue in Parliament during the 1940s and 1950s. The *Globe and Mail* described it as "the perennial question of pay of rural mail carriers."[20] Independent operators submitted competitive bids for mail-delivery contracts on rural routes. The winners often bid so low that they made little money or even lost it. This was dutifully reported by local MPs and the media, who accused the government of exploitation. Most governments sought authority to allocate funds to these carriers under certain conditions, but this policy left it open to charges of patronage. Numerous special committees were established to look at this issue, and various pieces of legislation were passed.[21] While not an earth-shattering issue — even within the postal domain — the question of rural postal service was a kind of metaphor for the Post Office in this period. It commanded and consumed an extraordinary amount of political attention and energy, and was a source of political controversy over hirings and service. It also raised the issue of the POD's role in national development, and any move to rationalize the rural postal system caused considerable political tension. The political setting of the Post Office was congenial to the argument that good rural mail delivery was necessary if rural communities were to survive.[22]

This political view prevailed with regard to construction of new post offices. As Table 6 indicates, the number of Canadian post offices peaked in 1913 at 14,178 and remained in the range of 12,000 to 13,000 from World War I until the 1950s. In any given year, some post offices would be closed and new ones would be opened. For example, in the period 1945-1965, 4,170 post offices closed and 3,200 opened. While the overall trend was downward (by 30 per cent from 1952 to 1972), the construction of post offices — particularly in small towns and rural areas — was a highly political issue, especially during the sluggish economic conditions of the late 1950s and early 1960s. The government initiated a Winter Works program to stimulate seasonal employment, which included the construction of local post offices during the winter in areas of high unemployment. This program stimulated the construction of a considerable number of highly visible, politically useful post offices. During the decade 1947/48 to 1956/57, 179 single-purpose post offices were constructed. During the following decade — spanning the start of Winter Works in 1957/58 and its peak in 1966/67 — 1,100 post offices were constructed. It appears that about three quarters of these were related to the Winter Works program.[23]

The PMG was also constantly besieged by MPs and constituents requesting improvements in postal services, including requests for new or upgraded post offices, expansion of door-to-door delivery (particularly into new suburbs), elevation of rural mail services to the standard reached in urban areas, and more efficient and faster mail delivery in general. The annual postal supply debates produced a remarkable array of requests and pleadings. For example, in the 1957 pre-election debate, sixty-five speakers presented a litany of requests for postal improvements. An extraordinary amount of ministerial time was directed to taking up all of the requests from MPs.[24]

Dominant Policy Issues

The day-to-day setting for postal matters conspired to ensure that policy or planning issues were not addressed. The POD administration was fixed firmly on operational details. The politics of the POD comprised local and constituency matters tilted particularly but not exclusively to the needs of government MPs. These perspectives shaped post-war postal discourse, which centred on two broad issues. First, the government and the Opposition were obsessed with issues of postal price and costs. This eventually evolved into a fixation on the postal deficit. Second, the relationship between the social and economic goals of the POD was perpetually debated, but never resolved.

There was substantial pessimism about postal matters, as about other areas of Canadian political life in the immediate post-war period.[25] Despite a healthy wartime budget surplus (see Table 3), authorities' post-war postal vision was negative: "It is difficult to estimate the effect of postwar conditions with any degree of accuracy. Undoubtedly much of postal revenue has derived from wartime businesses which will decline."[26] There were two other POD concerns: the rising costs of airmail and wages; and competition from telephone, teletype, wire services, and delivery firms. As Deputy PMG Turnbull put it,

The Service has rendered a good account of itself in spite of heavy odds, but our war weariness and operational difficulties are increasingly apparent in our seriously depleted and high average-age personnel, in our outworn equipment, and in our unsuitable and insufficient accommodation. If the people of Canada are to continue in the enjoyment of first class postal facilities, prompt and efficient remedial measures should be taken.[27]

These were pressing concerns that needed attention; however, they were smothered by the rising postal volumes. The 1945–46 POD report noted how increased domestic volumes neutralized declining overseas volumes; the 1946–47 report was even more optimistic; and the 1947–48 report noted the record volume of mail and increased postal revenues. By 1948-9, the POD breathed easier; it reported that the rapid expansion of postal volumes and revenues "reflects very accurately the greatly enhanced economic position of this country."[28] This revived optimism continued through to the mid-1950s; the 1954–55 report noted that the "continued buoyancy of the Canadian economy is again reflected in the demand made by the public on the Department's services."[29] PMG Hamilton waxed eloquent about the POD's accomplishments in the early 1960s, exclaiming that "while it may seem to be a sweeping statement, it is nevertheless true to say that never since Confederation has it been possible for a Postmaster General to record in one annual report ... such a wide range of new developments and progress ..." In 1961 he reported "the greatest volume of postal business ever, the highest revenues in history, the most sweeping expansions of service to the public since 1867, and the boldest and most effective economy moves within the operational records of the department."[30] Political hyperbole aside, the immediate postwar concerns about competition and deteriorating plant and equipment dissolved in the face of subsequent expansion. Although optimism prevailed, some concerns did persist in this period, the most prevalent of which being costs and prices. There was some consideration given to maintaining the competitiveness of postal products. This sort of strategic thinking was atypical, and reflected political anxiety about public reaction to rising postal prices. Particularly after the mid-1950s, there was extraordinary, almost irrational, governmental concern that postal expenditures and prices be kept as low as possible. For example, the 1956 POD report noted that postal costs rose automatically with the growth of postal activity, particularly with regard to service extension and labor costs, "areas over which the Department has little, or no, control." In the 1957 debate, Hamilton expressed concern that rising and uncontrollable transportation and wage costs would result in postal deficits, which would require price rises to cover the deficit. This concern persisted until the late 1960s, at which time a substantial deficit arose and was blamed on higher wages.[31]

Concern over rising postal costs was a function of the intensely political character of postal price increases. The price of a first-class stamp could rise only via amendment of the Post Office Act. This made the government a sitting target for opposition criticism. Indeed, the postal budgetary balance was a delicate issue. If the POD produced a surplus, then it was criticized for gouging the public and maintaining prices at too high a level.[32] But a postal deficit generated a variety of political controversies. First, the Opposition complained about waste, bad management, and costs let out of control. Second, defecits led to a debate about whether postal users or taxpayers should pay for postal services. (This point is examined below.) Third, a deficit forced the government to raise postal prices, a highly charged and politically dangerous act. Hence, it is small wonder that governments preferred to cut back or control costs rather than increase prices. Even a wartime price increase to generate war revenues resulted in bitter Opposition complaints. The government promised apologetically that the prices would soon come down.[33]

As Table 5 suggests, the price of a first-class stamp was increased infrequently in the post-war period.[34] In 1943, a one-cent wartax raised the price of a stamp to four cents. This price was maintained until 1951, when the government made the increase permanent. There was only one increase in the price of a first-class stamp between 1945 and 1968. PMG Côté proposed to raise the price of a first-class stamp to five cents in 1954. An incredibly bloody parliamentary debate ensued, and lasted for months. The price increase was defended on the grounds that costs had increased, as a result of the introduction of the five-day, forty–hour work week; expansion of rural services; and a salary increase. Côté maintained that postal services should be paid for by users, through higher prices, and not by taxpayers, through a tax-financed postal deficit. He cited the minister of finance in this regard: "It is the view of the government that the people of Canada expect the Post Office to pay for its operations out of postal revenue and not out of taxes." This policy reflected the POD's diminishing political stature; the government was less inclined to support postal activities where other policy instruments were available.[35] The opposition Conservatives fought bitterly against the action, which they characterized as a "monstrous increase in rates." What had happened to the $93 million in postal surpluses generated over the previous twenty years, they asked? They accused the POD of being "poorly organized, poorly run and inefficient." Moreover, they asserted that a deficit was not such a bad thing in itself, given the public service that the POD provided.[36] During committee hearings, the government intervened regularly throughout the debate. Most of the cabinet was brought out to give weight to the government's position.[37] The one-cent increase was finally approved on 9 February 1954. The $2.5 million postal deficit of 1954 was quickly transformed into surpluses of $7.7 million, $10.3 million, and $5.8 million over the following three years (see Table 3). This encouraged the Opposition to criticize the government for overcharging the Canadian people: "every time a Canadian citizen puts a postage stamp on a letter," thundered William Hamilton, "he is paying two cents more than the cost of carrying or transporting or handling this letter."[38]

The 1954 postal price increase was a political circus, an event that subsequent governments were keen to avoid. The absence of regular price increases did not lead to rising deficits, given rising postal costs. PMG Hamilton took the broad position that the postal budget should be in approximate balance.[39] This reflected the orthodox fiscal policies practised by Finance Minister Fleming in this period.[40] Political fear of price rises and the political unacceptability of postal deficits led to a policy of extreme wage restraint as well as low capital expenditures on plant and equipment. The consequences of this policy will be examined below.

A first-class mail increase was not given serious consideration for a decade. Other price changes were also avoided as much as possible, even though they did not require parliamentary approval. For example, in 1959 the POD requested a small increase in fourth-class rates, to cover a deficit on parcels. The backgrounder to cabinet noted the minor impact that this rate increase would have on individuals, who sent on average but three packages per year. Yet the request was turned down by cabinet on 3 April 1959, because it was "not an appropriate time to proceed." The POD tried again the next year, and the request was finally approved on 13 September 1960, but the increase would not go into effect until the following spring.[41]

The request for an increase involved only a few cents, and occurred outside the public domain deep within the administrative process. Even so, two years passed from first request to implementation of the increase; and all the while, the deficit on parcels grew. When the increase was announced it was, predictably, criticized by the Liberal opposition.[42] This incident was a metaphor for the politics and financing of the POD in this period. The government was paranoid about public reaction to higher prices and so did everything possible to keep the postal budget in balance without raising prices. When the POD requested increased government revenues or price increases, the minister of finance directed the PMG to cut costs to balance the books.[43] In this constrained fiscal setting, the deputy PMG looked at European examples of raising postal revenues through diversification of services and sales. This strategy was rejected by PMG Hamilton:

> I would personally be sympathetic to having our Canadian Post Office on the same basis but I am afraid that the increase in expenditures which would result if we had to provide our own facilities or pay for them would be so great that our rates would have to be substantially changed, and this has no appeal for me.[44]

This was the fiscal setting in which automation, planning, improved working conditions, postal diversification, and decent wages were not given adequate consideration.

Minority Liberal governments attempted in the mid-1960s to raise postal prices to cover rising costs. They had little success, and the political consequences were messy. In 1964, PMG Nicholson proposed five rate increases, only one of which required parliamentary approval (the drop rate on first-class mail). The others had already been announced (registered, third-class, second-class, and special delivery mail), and amounted to $8 million in increased revenues. These proposed changes were the culmination of an intensive POD study of rates and tariffs. But Nicholson was looking for $30 million more: "All we are trying to do is make each class of mail pay its own way," particularly first-class mail, which was then in a deficit situation. The Opposition opposed the proposed increases ferociously, and the initiative died when Parliament was dissolved for the 1965 election.[45]

The deficit then replaced price and cost concerns as the major postal concern, as a result of two developments. First, the change in the postal accounting system in 1964 transformed a small deficit into a large and persistent one (see Table 3). Second, a postal strike in 1965 (see below) brought substantial wage increases, which undermined the low-cost postal strategy. PMG Côté took the position that "if there is a department that should be run without a deficit, neither making money nor losing money on the revenues it collects, it is the Post Office Department."[46] Rates were raised on a number of items in 1967, including parcel post, registered mail, and special delivery. These were described by Opposition spokesperson McCutcheon as "unprecedented ... where is this escalation in the cost of living ever going to stop?" In fall 1967, the government introduced a bill to increase the price of a first-class stamp by one cent as well as to change the second-class schedule, the first increase in first-class rates in thirteen years and the first change in second-class rates in sixteen. The first-class change would raise the average Canadian's annual postal bill from $1.82 to $2.19.[48] Opposition assaulted Côté's proposals. "The poor defenceless public," McCutcheon thundered, "now have to face a 20 to 25 per cent increase in postal rates ... for curtailed services ... and chiefly because of government mismanagement." The Opposition claimed that business would simply raise prices to pass increased postal costs on to consumers, thereby exacerbating inflation.[49] The Conservatives caught the government unprepared in a snap vote in committee of the whole, and the legislation was killed on 28 November 1967.[50]

The government would not have another opportunity to raise postal prices until after the 1968 election, by which time the deficit had doubled from $30.7 million (in 1966) to $67.2 million.[51] Here we have another example of how the messy political process surrounding postal price increases constrained the POD's attempts to manage its financial situation.

The second ingredient of post-war postal discourse is an enduring theme of modern Canadian postal history: the relationship between the POD's social and economic goals. In an article in 1958, A.W. Currie wrote, "Governments since Confederation have emphasized social benefits rather than an existence of a 'surplus' in the postal service. In the last few years, the relative emphasis has tended to be reversed."[52] This reversal generated an important debate, which was enthusiastically carried on for decades in the political arena in which the POD functioned. However, the debate distracted political attention from the fundamental communications changes taking place, changes that threatened the very viability of the Canadian postal system.

There was a broad political consensus after the war that the Post Office did not have to "pay for itself." In the May 1947 budget debate, R.E. Drope made a typical and uncontroversial assertion: "I do not think that it was the intention that the Post Office should be a money-making concern; rather, it should be a service to the people." As Hatfield pointed out in a 1951 debate, "The CBC does not pay their way. Why should the Post Office Department and the postal services do so? I consider them a service to the country. I never expected that they would pay their own way." The view that the Post Office did not have to pay for itself was justified in five different, albeit related, ways. First, the POD carried out an expensive but important nation-building role; as Mackenzie maintained in 1952, "Do not forget that the Post Office Department goes hand in hand with the development and progress of our great nation." It was seen as playing a critical national role. The *Financial Post* declared that "the post office is the flagpole on which the nation hangs its ensign in hundreds of communities"; the Glassco Commission insisted that "the Post Office is more than a vast utility. It is a unifying force throughout the country." Second, the POD assisted Canada's economic development. Opposition leader Drew maintained that "in certain types of government service, efficiency must not be jeopardized by any attempt at false economy ... not only is the Post Office part of our whole social structure, but [it is] also a vital part of our economic structure." In the same 1951 debate Adamson said, "The delivery of mail transcends any dollars and cents considerations ... [it is] part of our economic and social life, and we cannot have it interfered with if the work of our country is to be carried on efficiently." Third, the POD was thought to have an important social role. PMG Rinfret reported in 1951 that the Post Office engaged in all sorts of uneconomic activities for social reasons: for example, "not one single rural route in Canada pays its own way." Fourth, postal deficits were defended on the grounds that the Post Office provided a public service. Future PMG Fairclough insisted in 1954 that "mail delivery is a service which the taxpaying public has a right to expect the government to provide ... the taxpaying public does not necessarily expect that the department which provides this service should be self-sustaining." This public service argument continued to be made even as the postal deficit grew substantially in the 1960s; Bigg argued that "our Post Office was designed to give service to the public. Their main function should not be to balance the books."[53]

These arguments were persistently, widely, and effectively put forth throughout the post-war period. Nonetheless, economic arguments crept into postal debates in the 1950s and 1960s. As early as the 1954 price debate,

PMG Côté introduced the pay-as-you-go approach to the Post Office: "I am convinced that as the Post Office Department is a service department, [it] should within reason pay its own way. In my opinion it is equitable that the increased costs should be paid by those who use the service."[54] This argument was rehearsed often over the next few decades. Who should pay for postal services: users, via higher prices for the services which only they use, or taxpayers, via taxes that support the postal deficit, as a general service or infrastructural cost?

This debate was played out in a number of concrete policy areas. For example, the POD eliminated twice-daily home delivery to cut its costs. This had been done during the war, as a result of labour shortages, but the service was reintroduced in 1946. However, it was cancelled again in 1950, in conjunction with the introduction of the five-day, forty-hour work week. It subsequently came to symbolize the tension between social and economic goals. The Conservatives, ironically, railed against the action, for it would lead to a decline in postal service. PMG Rinfret had readily admitted this: "We might as well face the cold facts. The service under the one-delivery system is not as good as that which was formerly given under the two-delivery system."[55] But the savings involved were not insubstantial: estimates ranged from $3 million in 1952 to $4–5 million in 1957. And once the Conservatives came to office, they changed their tune. PMG Hamilton did not reintroduce the service, despite his earlier criticism of its elimination, for it would cost $6 million. Again ironically, the Opposition assaulted him for this policy flip-flop.[56] More importantly, although the elimination of twice-daily delivery was extremely unpopular and politically controversial, the economic argument nonetheless triumphed over the social or service argument.

An issue with even greater political resonance was the second-class mail subsidy.[57] The POD had subsidized the postal distribution of newspapers and periodicals since Confederation. Second-class charges were maintained far below costs to give Canadians access to news and information, in order to create a literate, well-informed citizenry. This policy caused little controversy until after World War II, when the issue became politically confusing because it added two different ingredients to the debate.

On the one hand, the policy was expensive: its annual cost in 1947 was $7.3 million. The government, citing traditional arguments, declined to increase rates, and so the cost rose to $12 million by 1951 (rates generated only $4 million while costs were $16 million). The government then decided to increase second-class charges. Opposition leader Drew criticized the government's actions, asserting that this was "not just a question of dollars and cents," that the policy had its roots in Confederation. Raising rates would constrain citizens' access to newspapers and weaken democracy. As Conservative spokesperson Rowe put it, the price increase involved "imposing ... penalties on the dissemination of the news" and involved "a curtailment of the press."[58]

On the other hand, the policy seemed to benefit the large publishers to a disproportionate extent. The CCF/NDP criticized the subsidy as a hand-out to large magazines and newspapers that did not need assistance.[59] The main beneficiaries of the subsidy were advertisers, who occupied from 40 to 70 per cent of newspaper space.

Governments periodically moved to increase second-class charges to improve the POD's budgtetary situation, with predictable political reaction but to little fiscal effect. The Glassco Commission found that in 1958-59, the $35.5 million surplus on first-class mail was all but consumed by the $21.7 million deficit in second-class mail. The latter's charges generated $7.1 million in revenue, but $36.5 million in expenditures. Second-class policy was placing the POD in an impossible financial situation. It was widely thought that Parliament should make "an annual grant ... in amount sufficient to cover the costs of the Post Office in the handling of second class mail, to the extent that such exceeds the postal revenues arising from the rates set by Parliament"[60]; but this proposal was not adopted until the 1970s. By then there was also a growing feeling that the urgent need for the second-class subsidy had passed, given increased citizen access to information as a result of the emergence of alternative media.[61]

Nonetheless, by the mid-1960s PMG Nicholson asserted that the second-class subsidy remained a "political reality," which made it a policy very difficult to change or eliminate. Big publishers might benefit disproportionately, but they would not be inclined to accept stoically the elimination of the program. Indeed, whenever second-class rates were increased, the big publishers were the first to descend on the PMG's office. But, argued Nicholson, cutting the subsidy would also hurt smaller periodicals and newspapers as well as readers in outlying regions.[62] Thus, the second-class policy remained in place, despite continual buffetting and debate.

The furious postal debates of the 1940s, 1950s, and early 1960s, fixated on details, failed to deal with the general ailment. Administrative concentration on operational details was complemented by politicians' occupation with patronage, prices, and traditional themes and issues. The postal discourse thus centred on symbolic or metaphorical issues — like rural delivery and second-class mail — and managed to avoid confronting the looming crisis in the postal system. The political and administrative setting ensured that policy would be directed to short-term political and postal needs rather than to the long-term viability of the postal system itself.

It must be recalled, though, that there were few public or political pressures on the POD to act differently. Postal discussions and debates were enveloped in the warm cocoon of praise for the postal system emanating from all social and political quarters. This did not encourage postal authorities to reconsider their orientation or initiate radical changes. Given the low status to which the POD eventually fell, it is worth recounting the extent to which it and its workers were viewed positively in the post-war period.

Each year's postal supply debate was an occasion for the PMG and MPs to heap praise on the POD and its workers. Criticism of the Post Office was rare. Church's comments in 1948 were typical: "The post office is a magnificent public utility. It has the endorsement of ... practically all the people in the whole country." The 1952 Woods and Gordon study reported that "we have been impressed by the overall efficiency of the Department and the basic soundness of its organization and administration." PMG Hamilton's survey of MPs in 1958 found that the vast majority of Conservative MPs were content with the postal system and its functioning. Herrige referred to the Post Office as "a credit to the nation" and Regier suggested that it was "one of the most efficient institutions in Canada." The Glassco Commission found a "commendable degree of efficiency," with next-day first-class delivery "reached with impressive regularity." PMG Côté characterized the Canadian postal system as being "recognized as one of the best and most efficient in the world," and PMG Nicholson reported that "there have been remarkably few suggestions that our postal service is not doing a good job. For years the Post Office Department has been recognized as one that works hard and efficiently and does the best it can with the resources at its command." And the Montpetit Commission reported in 1965 that the POD "enjoys an excellent reputation ... Canadians recognize the good quality of our postal service."[63]

Praise was also heaped on postal workers. In the 1945 debate, MacNichol stated that "postal employees ... are as hard worked as any servants of the government ... There are no employees who work harder than these men ... They are poorly paid ... You rarely hear of any misdeliveries or mail troubles in this country." In 1950, Catherwood asserted that "I believe that every member of this house will agree that those 46,000 employees have done a marvellous job." Future PMG Fairclough referred to postal workers as "an institution" and Opposition leader Drew offered "nothing but praise for ... those who [carry] out the daily routine of the mail service." The Glassco Commission found that "the Post Office staff is conscientious, hard-working and dedicated ... This has enabled the service to function in a highly commendable manner." This praise for postal workers continued into the mid-1960s. PMG Hamilton characterized postal workers as "hardworking, conscientious people who are giving dedicated service to their country." In 1964, McBain claimed that the postal workers' "devotion to duty ... is a devotion of which Canadians can be justly proud." And in the 1967 supply debate both PMG Côté and the Opposition eulogized postal workers.[64]

Policy Results: Postal Crisis and the 1965 Strike

Despite public praise and POD optimism, the Canadian postal system was marching towards disaster. The emerging postal crisis had various causes, some beyond human control. The telephone and the television would have been invented no matter what the POD did. Rising postal volumes and the expansion of addresses were likewise phenomena beyond POD control. However, the human or political responses to these and other developments were uninspired. The POD's political setting constrained potential policy responses. Bolstered by praise from all quarters, blinkered by administrative details, and weighed down by day-to-day political concerns, it created policies that were passive, makeshift, and *ad hoc*. In fact, in two areas its policies contributed directly to the emerging postal crisis: its post-war technological strategy was inaedaquate, indeed almost non-existent, despite its awareness of technological competition and rising volumes; and it relied too heavily on the good nature and capacity of its workforce to deal with rising volumes. The postal workforce was driven and disciplined to this end without extra pay, using a plant and equipment from the previous technological era. These POD policies were overdetermined by governments' broader policies and priorities and the POD's place in the political pecking order. The POD's fixation on restraining costs and expenditures was related to the larger government fiscal agenda. Governments assigned insufficient resources to modernize the postal system or to pay decent wages and provide reasonable working conditions. They were more interested in balancing their budgets, or containing inflation, or being politically popular, or finding resources for other departments, than they were in ensuring the viability of the Canadian postal system. This in turn reflected the POD's low status in the budgetary queue and the postal system's diminishing importance — relative to other communications instruments and media — in the eyes of political decision makers. The POD managed to keep itself afloat and its operation on a fairly even financial keel; but restraining wages and avoiding capital investments were tactics that would tell in the end.

Technological Change

There was little technological development or discussion within the Canadian postal system through the post-war period. This is not to suggest that the POD or observers were unaware of the technological challenge facing that system. The 1957–58 POD Report declared it

had been apparent for some time that traditional methods for handling the mail are no longer adequate for present day needs. This is the common experience of all the larger postal administrations of the world which are endeavouring to apply the principles of electronics to mail-handling problems.[65]

Volumes had grown to 3.7 billion units a year, which, at on average of thirty handlings per piece, required 110 billion manual operations a year.[66] In an internal memo to postal supervisors, Deputy PMG Boyle noted that little had changed in the way mail was handled over the last forty years. He suggested that the time had come to "break through the barrier which has made the postal service, not only of Canada but generally throughout the world, one of the least mechanized of all mass handling operations," and promised that mechanization would not reduce postal jobs: "The purpose of the machinery is to allow us to handle a larger volume of mail more quickly and effectively with the same number of people."[67]

Early efforts to modernize the sorting system rested on mechanical innovations, like flat, incline, and vertical conveyors, skip hoists, and spiral chutes. There was some departmental reorganization: a new Engineering and Development Branch was created in 1958-59, with duties and authority separate from Operations. A Mechanization Development Division was established within this new branch. Prototypes of sorting machines were developed that, for the most part, were noisy, inefficient, and unsuccessful. The Transorma sorting machine was purchased from Holland and installed in Peterborough, Ontario, in the early 1950s. The POD reported in 1953-54 on the development of a new type of electronic sorter, "the only one in the world ... advanced to the stage where a pilot model will be in operation in the Ottawa Post Office within eight months." This experimentation continued through the rest of the decade, each year bringing reports of its imminent completion but also of rising costs. The electronic sorter and coding desk prototype was found not suitable and was scrapped in 1962. In 1960, a British segregating, facing, and cancelling machine called Safacan was purchased for installation in Winnipeg. None of these early efforts had any impact.[68]

Even this modest mechanical experimentation was politically controversial. The Opposition exploited workers' fears that they would lose their jobs to the machines. The Liberals' Denis argued that "unemployment is prevalent across the country and we should set an example. There is no hurry for those electronic machines to displace labour."[69] The Opposition also exploited anxiety about the costs of the new machinery. William Hamilton attacked the prototype, calling it the "million dollar monster," and this phrase was used against him when, as PMG, he defended the machine's development, with Denis characterizing the machine as the monster whose costs had risen past $3 million.[70]

The labour politics of postal mechanization would not unfold until the 1970s. At this point, the fiscal politics of mechanization were far more pressing. The penny-pinching environment within which the POD operated was a substantial constraint on mechanization. Starved for funds and prevented from raising revenues through price increases, the POD was obliged to squeeze more and more volume through an aging and out-of-date plant. Whenever possible, it cut costs to keep its budget in balance. Mechanization was lost in the financial shuffle. The Montpetit Commission in 1965 expressed amazement at the extent to which mechanization was not an issue and how little the idea had penetrated the consciousness of both postal staff and workers.

A second factor inhibited the appearance of mechanization on the postal agenda. The POD was operations oriented, and its senior management had neither the training nor the inclination to be speculative or innovative. Management was capable of running a tight, military operation and of using its labour force to ever greater effect. Indeed, the PMGs and postal observers of the era recount that the system was carried on the backs of postal workers. This had two implications. First, the POD was able to mitigate the volume crisis for a time. Rather than raising productivity through capital and technological expenditures and technological, it processed rising volumes more quickly and efficiently by disciplining and driving labour. The POD continued to use the techniques of memory and muscle, which delayed the postal crisis for a time. Second, despite its expanding labour force (see Table 4), the postal system remained financially solvent — even as postal prices remained low. This was the result of wage restraint and neutralized the incentive to substitute machinery for labour. Even given a labour-intensive operation, an expanding labour force, and little capital expenditures on plant and equipment, labour costs were only 60 per cent of postal costs in 1970.

This strategy of restraint had a limited life expectancy: postal volumes and addresses would eventually overwhelm the muscle-and-memory strategy. And there was a limit to postal workers' tolerance of deteriorating working conditions and poor wages.

The Labour Strategy

Despite the esteem of politicians and the public, workers suffered abysmal wages and working conditions. They were harshly disciplined to improve productivity as postal volumes exploded.

The working conditions at the POD were exhaustively rehearsed in the media and in the House of Commons. Postal facilities, particularly sorting plants, were aging and ill lit, dusty and poorly ventilated, and insufficiently insulated against seasonal extremes. Equipment was old and dangerous, and postal workers were encouraged to perform their duties in an unsafe way. The POD ranked second only to the Department of Defence in accidents and injuries. Postal sorters worked long and irregular hours under near-military discipline, with little to no regard for their physical comfort. Carriers delivered increasingly heavy loads. Loading docks were cramped and poorly ventilated. There were a number of particular sore points. Inadequate breaks were provided to use limited toilet facilities. Evening and week-end work was assigned thoughtlessly and unnecessarily. Vacations were ungenerous and distributed unfairly. Part-time workers were ruthlessly exploited; their increasing use undermined the conditions and privileges of full-time workers. Disciplinary measures were harsh. One-way mirrors and closed-circuit TVs were used for surveillance, even in washrooms. Clerks were penalized for shortages in their tills, and sorters were docked wages or suspended for making errors. Sorters were tested to standards annually and were penalized for less than adequate results. Favouritism was rampant, as was harassment, sexual and otherwise. The grievance procedure was inadequate and unfair. And the POD was grossly neglectful of worker welfare. For example, each Christmas season up to ten thousand extra workers were hired, yet no extra toilet facilities were provided.[71] The POD itself admitted that it had not done enough to improve working conditions. However, it maintained that improvements would require increased resources and suggested that the government had instead chosen to respond to other departments' demands.[72]

For all this, postal workers' remuneration was ungenerous. Wages increased moderately from World War II until 1965, despite productivity improvements and worsening conditions of work. Postal workers received a $120–180 salary increase in 1946; and wages were increased in 1954, when the forty-hour week was introduced. Neither wage increase was a matter of political controversy. Indeed, MPs reflected popular opinion when they insisted that postal wages be increased.[73] However, wages then stagnated, despite parliamentary and popular support. Between 1954 and 1965, postal workers received only one increase, at which time wages rose to $1.59 per hour. Postal wages were determined by other, non-postal concerns of the government. For example, they were caught in the Diefenbaker government's balanced budget strategy, which included a civil servants' wage freeze. Planned and promised postal wage hikes in 1958 and 1959 were cancelled, causing much bitterness. A twenty-cent-an-hour increase was finally awarded in mid-1960, under threat of a postal rebellion. A wage freeze again cancelled an expected pay increase in 1962; there was then no pay increase in 1963. After the election of the Liberals, a fifteen-cent-an-hour increase was granted; this was a modest sum after a three-year delay. The Liberals then delayed any further increase by creating a special study of postal wages. Former PMG Jean-Pierre Côté recounts how his father, an inside postal worker, had to work six nights a week and weekends to earn sufficient income to support his family. He also "sold" his Sunday days off to earn extra money. As a result, his children never saw him. He never made $2,000 a year in his career at the POD, and when a heart attack forced him to retire, his pension was $84 a month.[74]

Not surprisingly, labour relations within the POD were not ideal. Poor working conditions, low wages, and harsh discipline created an unhappy postal labour force. Postal management for its part had neither the capacity nor the wherewithal to improve labour relations. Recruited internally, and with either a military background or inclination, postal management did not possess industrial relations skills. Thus, poisonous labour-management relations developed in the POD — long before unionization and the mechanization battles of the 1970s.

Politicians and the media recognized these strained relations. As early as 1953, MP Noseworthy characterized the POD as "the most out-of-date, antiquated, arbitrary and reactionary employer in the country." Future PMG Fairclough reported in 1954 that "there has grown up in all parts of this country a most deplorable antagonism between the staff and management of the Post Office Department." In 1960, Regier claimed that "among all the civil servants, the employees of the Post Office have about the lowest morale." And a *Globe and Mail* article characterized postal management as "The Petty Tyrants of the Post Office," "holdovers from the Victorian era who exploit and mistreat their workers."[75]

The institutional context for labour-management relations was undeveloped and was outside the POD's control. This was a disastrous state of affairs, given the tens of thousands of workers and the industrial character of postal operations. First, the POD management did not negotiate directly with postal workers. Negotiation was the responsibility of other departments, such as the Department of Finance or Treasury Board. These departments were driven by a different political agenda and a different set of priorities. Their "white-collar" operations lacked relevance for the "blue-collar" postal scene. These departments were also wary of setting any sort of precedents that would be copied by the rest of the government bureaucracy. Once Treasury Board or Finance had made their decisions, POD management was left to pick up the pieces. Second, both labour and management had a low institutional capacity to negotiate with each other. There was little formal consultation between postal management and postal workers. A liaison body was not formed until 1961, when the Post Office-Canada Post Employees Committee was created. The POD did not have a separate assistant deputy minister (ADM) for personnel until 1963. The postal workers themselves were represented by associations that did not have full-time staff until 1951, at which time Treasury Board allowed dues check-off (which provided the associations with the financial security to hire staff). Postal workers' associations demanded collective bargaining rights, but these were refused outright. All major political parties committed themselves to public-sector collective bargaining in 1963, but this objective remained at least a few years away.

The 1965 Postal Strike

The post-war postal illusion was dispelled in the summer of 1965, when Canada experienced its first postal strike in over forty years. This followed hard on the heels of a British postal strike in 1964, whose success influenced Canadian postal workers' thinking and stategy. The proximate cause of the eleven-day strike was a dispute over wages. The Postal Workers Brotherhood (PWB) — the combined organization of three postal workers' associations — asked for a $660 wage increase. The Liberal government offered a $360 wage increase to mail handlers (inside workers) and a $300 increase to mail deliverers (outside workers). This offer was based on an "impartial" civil-service study of postal wages. Government and postal management were sympathetic to the postal workers' claims that their wages had been restrained unreasonably throughout the post-war period. However, the government was wary that a generous postal settlement would lead to equivalent demands in the rest of the civil service. Public and media opinion was very much on the side of the postal workers. The *Globe and Mail* suggested that "their demands for an increase ... are well-founded ... the salary range is miserably low for men who undertake an onerous, and at times, uncomfortable job ...[they have] the admiration and respect of the great mass of Canadians. There is evidence of substantial public sympathy for the postmen."[77]

Although money was an important consideration, the strike was not simply over a wage dispute; it was the inevitable conclusion of decades of government neglect of the postal system. This neglect had led to the horrendous postal working conditions, and prospects for change were not apparent.[78] Mounting postal volumes increased productivity pressure on postal workers, and this pressure was exercised in a militaristic and arbitrary way, exacerbating the postal workers' grim working and financial conditions. The strike had a double purpose and direction. It was directed at a postal management that exercised arbitrary power in a ruthless fashion, and against the government, the postal workers' real paymaster, whose neglect of the Post Office made it responsible for postal workers' conditions.

The strike was illegal, as postal workers — like other public-sector workers — did not enjoy collective bargaining rights. Even within this context, the strike was an extreme "wildcat" action. The national postal workers' associations did not initiate or authorize the strike, which was started and carried out by local postal units. The PWB had been uncertain as negotiations came to a standstill, and it appeared that postal workers' interests would once again be sacrificed to the wider governmental agenda: the PWB enjoyed minimal political leverage and its leadership was not inclined to rock the boat too hard. However, the PWB lost control of its postal membership when dissatisfied local groups decided to take the situation into their own hands. The Victoria and Vancouver locals took early strike votes, and a vote in Montreal set a strike deadline for 22 July 1965. After an emergency cabinet meeting, the government proposed to submit its offer to binding arbitration and an impartial commissioner. This proposal was rejected. On 22 July the strike began in Montreal, Hamilton, Vancouver, and Oshawa. Thirty-five other postal centres — including Toronto — went out the next day, bringing the total on strike to over ten thousand.

In an effort to stem the strike's momentum, the government appointed Judge J.C. Anderson as a one-person commission to investigate the dispute and recommend action. On 28 July the PWB executive urged its members to return to work and await the result of Anderson's report (which he had promised to deliver within a fortnight). Postal workers again ignored their leadership. Even after Anderson presented an interim report supporting the postal workers' claims, a number of locals remained out on strike. Urged by the Chamber of Commerce to send in the troops, the government hired three hundred non-unionized workers to help soldiers sort the backlog of mail, particularly in Montreal. On 4 August, Anderson issued his final report. He stated that the government's offer was comparable to wage settlements in the private sector, but the base salary level of postal workers had fallen below that of equivalent private-sector workers. He recommended a salary increase in the $510 to $550 a year range, $360 of it retroactive to October 1964. This amounted to a 10 per cent wage increase. Anderson also recommended that an impartial review be undertaken to examine working conditions in the Post Office, an idea already proposed by PMG Tremblay.[79] Cabinet accepted Anderson's wage and review recommendations. It also held out the promise of full collective bargaining to postal workers and the entire public sector. A postal referendum was held on the government's offer, and 80 per cent accepted (the Montreal local boycotted the election). Thus ended Canada's first national postal strike in over forty years. It cost the POD $2.3 million in revenue, a loss of $1 million.

The 1965 strike had numerous far-reaching consequences. It punctured a number of postal illusions, undermined the post-war postal strategy, and forced postal management and the government to bring the postal service into the modern age. It completely transformed the organization and situation of postal workers. To begin with, the strike accelerated the evolution of public-sector bargaining. The Public Sector Staff Relations Act was passed on 13 March 1967, at which time postal workers and other civil servants were assigned collective bargaining rights. As well, the leadership of the postal workers changed hands as a result of the strike. The moderate, not to suggest co-opted, PWB was completely delegitimized, and was replaced by a far more aggressive leadership, which learned in 1965 that striking could bring substantial benefits for postal workers. The 1965 strike forever changed the character of the relationship between postal workers and postal management/the government.

It also had important consequences for the organization of the postal system and for postal policy, by revealing how the postal system had been underfunded. The settlement increased postal costs, and the POD and the government were forced to consider new ways to balance the postal books, since the cheap-labour strategy was no longer viable. The strike also exposed the extent to which the POD was under-mechanized and under-capitalized, forcing postal management and the government to give postal mechanization more serious consideration. The strategy of increasing productivity through ruthless and military disciplining was exposed to considerable public and governmental scrutiny and could no longer be employed.

The 1965 strike undermined the logic and legitimacy of the POD's organization. Postal management was completely delegitimized, its approach and philosophy criticized and ridiculed. There were widespread calls for an infusion of new ideas and outside personnel. The strike laid bare the divided authority under which the POD functioned, and exactly how little authority it enjoyed. It was now clear to all observers that postal management did not negotiate with postal workers; other departments of government did. This was widely thought to be a recipe for disaster. Indeed, Judge Anderson urged the government to give serious consideration to the idea of transforming the POD into a Crown corporation.[80]

The Aftermath of the Strike

These themes and numerous labour grievances were examined by the Montpetit Commission, a one-person Royal Commission on Working Conditions in the Post Office established on 1 September 1965, a week after the government's offer had been accepted by the postal workers. The commission had been recommended by Judge Anderson and demanded by postal workers. It was the first in a series of external studies of the POD in the 1960s and 1970s, which made it one of the most-studied institutions in the country. Mr. Justice Andre Montpetit[81] was directed to enquire into postal workers' grievances regarding work rules, codes of discipline, and other work conditions, "keeping in mind both the welfare of employees and the efficient operation of the postal service." Montpetit and his staff travelled across Canada from September 1965 through March 1966, listening to presentations by national and local unions and talking to district postal directors and postmasters. They spent April through June 1966 at POD headquarters in Ottawa, interviewing management and distributing a questionnaire. A three-hundred-page report containing 282 recommendations was tabled in Parliament in October 1966.[82] In his concluding remarks, Montpetit speculated that "some will be surprised at the great number of recommendations which are favourable to the employees."[83] Indeed, the report was broadly critical of postal management's behaviour and attitudes and sympathetic to postal workers' conditions.[84]

The Montpetit report confirmed the horror stories about postal working conditions, which previously had been characterized as apocryphal or exaggerated. It catalogued an extensive list of substandard working conditions, including poor lighting, inadequate ventilation, problems with heat and dust, dangerous equipment and conditions, and bad transportation. It presented the POD's tally of 3,990 accidents in the period 1964-1966, a record second only to the Department of National Defence, and noted that six hundred mail carriers were bitten by dogs each year. Montpetit found that work schedules were inconsiderate and inhumane, over-reliant on night and weekend work. He also viewed summer and Christmas holidays as ungenerous, split shifts as exploitive, and lunch and coffee breaks and wash-up time as inadequate. Montpetit confirmed that workers were disciplined too harshly and unfairly by their superiors and had inadequate opportunities to launch grievances. Management was seen to be too ready to use part-time workers rather than employ full-time workers, which acted to keep wages low as well as to de-skill work.

Montpetit presented dozens of problems and recommendations, all of which were informed by two themes. First, POD management prioritized efficiency goals to the neglect of other considerations:

> From the moment a piece of mail arrives, every effort is made to deal with it speedily ... This preoccupation with speed, however, must not sweep aside every other consideration. Even though we are sure that the people of Canada want an excellent service, we are also sure that they do not want this at the expense of the employers' welfare.[85]

Second, POD management had "only a vague notion of the importance of maintaining good relations with staff"[86]:

> There are some senior employees in the higher groups in the Department who have been promoted from the ranks but still have the attitudes which were prevalent at the time. They did not keep up with the times and, consciously or unconsciously, they refused to do so. They are living in the past. They have a decided tendency to sacrifice the morale and welfare of the employees to their idea of an unequalled postal service.[87]

Less than half a million dollars had been spent on training in 1964–65. Montpetit recommended the development of human relations courses for supervisors, and the creation of a formal system of consultation and communications through the establishment of joint-management committees. This last recommendation was part of the 1966 postal settlement. He also urged that new external management be recruited, including a team of administrators to create a POD personnel department. The cabinet accepted the Montpetit report and its recommendations quickly and with little controversy and debate.[88] The recommendations were then put into practice and monitored, with the assistance of a joint labour-management committee that Montpetit helped establish in the course of the 1966 negotiations.[89]

Like the 1965 postal strike, the Montpetit report had numerous far-reaching consequences. It delegitimized the authority of postal management and its military, disciplinary approach. The post-war memory-and-muscle postal strategy was undermined; rising postal volumes would now have to be confronted in other ways. Postal workers were given increased authority and considerable political ammunition. The report gave their claims moral weight, and its cataloguing of abuses and problems provided labour with a valuable symbolic tool to be used long after the problems had been addressed. These consequences shaped the contours of political discourse and debate — and labour-management relations — over the next decade.

In conjunction with the 1965 strike, the Montpetit report also created an opportunity for postal reform and innovation. For example, both the Montpetit and Anderson reports put the Crown corporation option on to the postal policy agenda. Montpetit expressed sympathy for the POD's predicament of functioning with little authority, which limited its control over working conditions. The idea of transforming the POD into a Crown corporation picked up steam in the mid-1960s. The Glassco Commission mooted the notion of the Post Office's operating in a semi-autonomous way, with independent control of its financial resources.[90] Judge Anderson asked whether

> the needs of those who provide this service could best be met by organizing the postal service as a Crown corporation and giving the employees bargaining rights under the Industrial Relations and Disciplines Investigations Act. The reforms needed in working conditions and work rules in the postal service are not necessarily the same as those needed in other branches of the civil service. Under a Crown corporation organization, such matters ... could be best adjusted to meet the special character of the Post Office, un-restricted by an obligation to take into account needs of a quite different class of civil servants.[91]

Wages, working conditions, and negotiation matters appropriate to the "industrial" POD were of a different character from those in the rest of the civil service. Anderson's view was that they would always be constrained by the concern that the rest of the civil service would want whatever gains postal workers acquired.

Not surprisingly, postal unions supported the POD's becoming a Crown corporation. The CPEA (the earlier version of CUPW) proposed the idea in 1949. During the Montpetit hearings, most of the 217 union submissions advocated the Crown corporation option.[92] Montpetit's second recommendation was to transform the POD into a Crown corporation.[93]

During a parliamentary debate in 1987, PMG Côté stated that the Crown corporation strategy was being studied by the government. The reality was that the idea did not receive much attention: the government had other political priorities at this time. It was a minority government, and was inhibited by the fear of losing a vote on the issue or being stretched too thin politically in introducing such a change. The deputy PMG at this time — W.H. Wilson — had especially little political clout or authority to devote to such a substantial policy change. As always, political circumstances constrained the postal agenda, and the Crown corporation possibility was not seriously considered.[94]

Conclusion

Post-war Canadian governments pursued a postal policy of benign neglect. This policy was successful, inasmuch as the POD caused them few political embarrassments and they expended few resources on the postal system. This policy strategy did, however, have long-term consequences, among which were deterioration of the POD's plant and equipment and the estrangement of labour from management. These results may have been inevitable in the circumstances, given the POD's low political and administrative status and authority and the increase in postal volumes and competition. Moreover, they might have been "tolerable" if the government had been able to escape its postal responsibilities.

Governments had focused their attention on new and more exciting communications modes. However, the Canadian Post Office remained a substantial and growing concern. It employed tens of thousands of workers, delivered billions of pieces of mail annually, had the most extensive retail network in the country, and was one of Canada's largest commercial operations. It continued to play vital economic, social, and national roles. Regardless of the new communications technologies, regardless of the POD's declining status and authority, regardless of the existence of higher political priorities — the postal system remained an important national institution that required serious policy consideration. The 1965 strike and the Montpetit Commission reminded the government of this reality.

However, by the time the Canadian government recalled its attention to the Post Office in the late 1960s, it was late in the day. Industrial relations had been poisoned. Postal plant and equipment needed complete replacement, which would require an enormous investment. Management also needed replacement, as it lacked skills, imagination, and capacity. The POD's institutional setting required transformation. It had no control over its finances or resources, and most major postal decisions were made directly or indirectly by other government departments. Technological competition was well developed and well positioned to absorb an increasing proportion of the communications market. These factors combined to present an extraordinarily daunting postal policy agenda.

At the same time, the 1965 strike and the Montpetit Commission had created an opportunity for the pursuit of postal reform. This reform agenda, and the constraints created by the previous policy of neglect, are examined in the following chapter.

Chapter Four

THE POLITICS OF POSTAL REFORM:

THE ERIC KIERANS INTERREGNUM

The 1965 strike and the Montpetit report gave the POD central place on the political agenda of the late 1960s. Eric Kierans' appointment as PMG seemed to reflect the increased policy salience of postal matters. Kierans brought to the position exceptional credentials and an un-usually high political profile at both the federal and provincial levels. He had run for the leadership of the national Liberal party in 1968, and had been a cabinet minister in the Lesage government, which ushered in the Quiet Revolution in Quebec in the 1960s. A past president of the Montreal Stock Exchange, he had extensive business experience and professional cre-dentials as an academic economist. Gifted with a feisty temperament, great energy, and a thick skin, Kierans seemed an inspired choice to seize the moment and run with the new postal agenda.

This period was a reform interregnum between two business-as-usual eras: the traditional POD of the post-war period and the survivalist POD of the 1970s. The Kierans' period did alter the contours of the Canadian postal environment, and changed the character of the POD. But the reform agenda was not pursued to any great extent or with any ultimate success. Indeed, Kierans resigned prematurely after a turbulent and eventful stint as PMG. This chapter provides a case study in the rise and fall of this postal reform era. Starting with the ramifications of the 1965 strike and the Montpetit report, it presents the labour, financial, and political challenges faced by the POD at the end of the 1960s. It then outlines and explains the strategic response to these challenges and the specific policies this strategy generated. The implementation of these policies was constrained by the reactions of the major interests affected; this chapter illustrates how postal interests af-fected policy outcomes. The most significant casualty of the reform era was the cabinet decision to transform the POD into a Crown corporation, a commitment that was withdrawn as the reform process unravelled. The po-litical opportunity was lost, and the idea of a postal Crown corporation remained shelved for a decade. The postal strategy and policies of the Kierans era were quite similar to those pursued by Canada Post Corporation two decades later, in the mid-1980s; the chapter concludes by explaining why the policies could be pursued in the later but not in the earlier period.

Postal Challenges

The POD faced three major challenges in the late 1960s. First, the 1965 strike and the Montpetit Report transformed the status of postal workers, whose equanimity, commitment, and willingness to work for little pay in wretched conditions could no longer be taken for granted. Second, the POD's weak budgetary situation continued to deteriorate. Postal costs rose as wages and working conditions improved; postal revenues weakened as competition increased. Third, an extensive and contradictory array of postal pressures challenged the POD's limited managerial and political skills and resources.

The Labour Challenge

A postal strike was narrowly averted in 1966. Postal workers had been demanding a large "make-up" wage increase, but they settled for a twenty-five-cent-an-hour increase in a ten-month contract — about half of what they had asked for. After the 1965 strike fiasco, PMG Côté negotiated directly with the postal unions, with Treasury Board playing only a back-up role. Negotiations dealt primarily with working conditions; a joint labour-management committee was established to study the Montpetit report's recommendations. The government also promised to review rates of pay in various postal categories.[1]

This would be the last time that postal workers negotiated without collective bargaining rights, for the Public Service Staff Relations Act introduced collective bargaining into the civil service in 1967. As the Public Service Employment Act took effect, Treasury Board became the postal workers' employer. Public-sector unions were offered the choice of two negotiating processes, one that included binding arbitration and another that could involve conciliation and a strike. The postal unions opted for the latter process. The Public Sector Staff Relations Board certified the Council of Postal Unions (CPU) as the bargaining agent for all federal postal employees in non-supervisory categories (save for part-time workers and railway clerks). Postal workers were organized in two major unions: the Canadian Union of Postal Workers (CUPW) represented twelve thousand inside workers and the Letter Carriers Union of Canada (LCUC) represented ten thousand outside workers.

It was anticipated that postal bargaining would be more effective and peaceful under the PSSRA. This hope was quickly dashed. Postal negotiations in 1968 led to a twenty-two-day strike, from 18 July to 8 August. In contrast to negotiations in 1966, here Treasury Board took the management lead in bargaining; neither Jean-Pierre Côté nor Eric Kierans played a direct role in the process (Kierans was named PMG on 6 July 1968). There were two stumbling blocks to the negotiations: wages and job classification. The CPU aimed to bring postal wages back into parity with policemen and firemen.

It demanded a seventy-five-cent-an-hour increase over fourteen months, which represented a 29 per cent increase. Six months into negotiations, Treasury Board finally offered a 6 per cent increase. The more important issue, though, was the question of job assessments and promotions. The CPU feared that the government would neutralize wage increases by downgrading jobs. Thus, it asked to be included in those departmental processes that assessed and categorized jobs. Treasury Board insisted that these were management prerogatives.

The stalled negotiations moved on to conciliation. The board's unanimous report of 11 July included hundreds of pages of suggestions on procedural matters. However, it made no recommendation on wages, which led the CPU to reject the report. It felt that the absence of a recommendation on wages favoured the government, for Treasury Board could simply wait for a mediated settlement. When the CPU then called for a strike to begin on 18 July, the government imposed an embargo on mail. Mediation began on 15 July, headed by Judge René Lippé. Treasury Board finally made its first wage offer on 17 July: 4 per cent retroactive to the previous August and a further 2 per cent starting in March. This fifteen-cent-an-hour offer was a far cry from the seventy-five cents sought by the CPU, but it was consistent with other public-sector offers of the time (eight other agreements had been signed that were in the 6–7 per cent range). The government had set a 6 per cent wage guideline for itself, as part of its anti-inflation program.

On 18 July, the CPU reversed its decision and accepted the conciliation board report as the basis for negotiations. The report had included recommendations on air conditioning and modernizing buildings, a better holiday schedule, and premium payments for weekend shifts, among other things. But the CPU held firm on its wage and job classification demands, and the strike began. At the end of July, the government increased its offer to a forty-nine cents, a 19 per cent increase over thirty-eight months (7.5 per cent retroactive to August 1967, 6.5 per cent on October 1968, and 5 per cent on October 1969). As the strike dragged on, the business community pressured the government to end it (the Canadian Manufacturers Association asked that the right to strike be withdrawn). The government's patience began to wear thin; on 7 August, Prime Minster Trudeau scheduled a press conference to announce that Parliament would be recalled to legislate an end to the strike. The press conference was never held. A tentative agreement was reached that day for 15.1 per cent (thirty-nine cents) over twenty-six months, 8.1 per cent (twenty-one cents) retroactive to August 1967 and 7 per cent (18 cents) on October 1968. The value of the settlement was estimated to be $33 million. With regard to working conditions, Justice Montpetit was to report on the extent to which his commission's recommendations had been implemented. The settlement also gave the unions the right to bring a grievance over any job classification.[2]

The 1968 strike was a harbinger of events to come within postal labour relations. First, it demonstrated the extent and depth of labour's militancy. Postal workers went out on strike for the second time in three years and stayed on strike for over three weeks. Moreover, the settlement was approved by only 59.6 per cent of postal workers, suggesting that many postal workers were not content with their lot. Second, the 1968 strike illustrated the new procedural character of postal bargaining. Postal unions negotiated not with postal management, but with the Treasury Board, for whom postal matters fit into a broader picture of government strategies and priorities. In bargaining with postal unions, Treasury Board was motivated by non-postal matters, such as the government's anti-inflation strategy. The postal unions thus found themselves bargaining against the government and its broad policy orientation, necessitating a higher degree of forcefulness than might otherwise have been required. The CPU seemed to be rewarded for its efforts. On 17 July, Treasury Board offered 4 per cent retroactive to August 1967 and a further 2 per cent beginning 1 March; in the final settlement, the CPU gained 8.1 per cent retroactive to August 1967, and 7 per cent on October 1968. On wages and other matters, it seemed obvious to the postal unions that its members had "paid" to strike. Third, the strike was not simply about monetary matters. Job classifications, grievable issues, and grievance procedures would become the stuff of collective bargaining over the next decade. *How* labour relations were carried out would be as important as their substance.

The architects of the postal reform agenda recognized that labour's changed circumstances presented a serious challenge to postal policy. Kierans admitted that labour had been treated shabbily in terms of wages, working conditions and management practices. He lauded the effort and commitment of postal workers but admitted that this praise "would be meaningless if it were not accompanied by a resolve to improve their working conditions, enhance employee job satisfaction, and open up opportunities." After a tour of the Toronto Post Office, Kierans stated, "It is a terrible thing to admit that only by next summer will we have air conditioning in the post office terminals ... The most undeserved image is that of the postal worker in the public mind ... The handicaps under which they work are a lack of proper facilities and of modernization." While anticipating that collective bargaining would improve their wages and working conditions, he was sympathetic with the unions' dissatisfaction in negotiating with Treasury Board — a condition that studies concluded had also hamstrung postal management. The "attitude in the Post Office isn't good," concluded Kierans; "management and labour just aren't working together and the service is suffering ... I am worried about the attitude of senior management [which] too often doesn't know how to handle people."[3]

The Financial Challenge

Labour's new position in the postal equation affected the POD's financial position. The latter had already undergone a substantial and surprising transformation when the new postal accounting system was introduced. Previously, the postal accounts reported postal surpluses in thirteen of twenty post-war years. Any annual postal deficits were trivial: less than 1 per cent of expenditures in three years and 1-2 per cent in three other years. The old accounting sytem presented a picture of a financially healthy Post Office accumulating $80 million in net surpluses in the two decades after the war. The new accounting system suggested the reverse. Table 3 illustrates how the post-war postal balance was almost perpetually in deficit. There were no surpluses after 1948, and the overall deficit between 1946 and 1965 was $258.6 million. This recast financial picture led the POD to raise postal prices, but, as Table 3 shows, the deficit continued to grow in the mid-1960s: to $11.5 million in 1965, $30.7 million in 1966, $47.8 million in 1967, $67.2 million in 1968, and $88.2 million in 1968-69. During the latter the deficit comprised 23.5 per cent of postal revenues.

This financial deterioration had two obvious sources. First, the postal strikes of 1965 and 1968 constrained postal volumes, as Table 1 indicates. Volumes declined by almost 2 per cent in 1965-66, by nearly 1 per cent in 1968-69, and again by 3 per cent in 1969-70 and by 5.4 per cent in 1970-71. The changed and uncertain postal environment was bad for business. The second factor was the rise in wages associated with unionization. Labour costs as a proportion of postal expenditures had typically been fairly low, despite the POD's labour intensity and limited mechanization. As Table 4 indicates, labour comprised but 52 per cent of postal costs at the end of World War II. This proportion rose over the course of the 1960s, and not simply as a result of growth in the labour force. From 1961-62 to 1967-68, postal volumes and employment grew at the same rate, by 18 per cent; but labour costs rose to almost 70 per cent of postal expenditures. Postal deficits were then blamed on rising wages. As Kierans reported in parliamentary committee, "The fact that people have become unionized and feel that there is a great deal of lost ground to catch up has resulted in a rapidly rising curve of this cost."[4] As will be seen, this view would fuel the drive to mechanization.

A third and less widely recognized factor seriously affected the postal budgetary balance. Kierans noted that "to an increasing extent we are being superceded by other systems of communication, telephone, teletype machines, telegraph, television, radio and satellites ... Nearly all of the important innovations in communications are taking place outside the Post Office."[5] Indeed, a white paper later pointed out that it was no longer realistic to consider the POD a monopoly. Following a number of consultancy studies that confirmed this situation, Kierans declared: "We have until 1975 to put our house in order. This is when we can expect the big breakthrough in many technical advances now on the drawing board. The Post Office must be ready to compete by then. If it isn't, we'll lose out to the new systems." Growth in technological competition also constrained direct POD revenue, forcing it to be cautious about raising prices to mitigate the deficit. In a departmental background paper to a proposed price increase, Deputy PMG Sinclair explained that "in view of the rapid growth of competitive delivery services, we believe that an improved level of postal service would be necessary to prevent further traffic erosion in the face of rate increases"[6] The POD had lost business to private couriers, small delivery operations, internal self-delivery systems, and electronic and mass media communication – despite the fact that the price of stamps had not risen as fast as the Consumer Price Index. The latter had doubled since 1945, whereas the price of a first-class stamp had increased by only 50 per cent.[7]

The POD thus found itself positioned between a rock and a hard place. Rising wages and improved working conditions had increased expenditures; and any increase in postal volumes would further increase expenditures, as more sorters and delivers and expanded postal facilities would be needed. From the other side, increased competition as well as strikes and postal uncertainty limited expansion of volumes and revenues. Indeed, these could no longer be taken for granted. The POD had to contain its wage costs and/or increase its business – or it faced the prospect of a perpetual and growing deficit.

The Political Challenge

The POD was limited in its capacity to address the labour, financial, and competitive challenges of the late 1960s, owing to its political setting and the character of its postal constituency. It functioned in three postal worlds: the *executive* world of postal administration, the *political* world of postal legitimacy, and the *operative* world of postal workers and users. Each world had changed recently, seriously affecting the POD's capacity to deal with it.

Within the executive world, the POD had suffered from low political and bureaucratic status, exacerbated by the rise of alternative systems of communications via which the state could pursue its national goals. The 1965 strike and the Montpetit report increased the political saliency of postal matters, but the ensuing notoriety and attention were a mixed blessing for the POD. Although these events created momentum in favour of new postal policy, they also created high postal expectations and put postal constituencies on their guard.

PMG Eric Kierans was the first high-profile MP or minister assigned to the POD in the post-war period. He brought a wide range of experiences, talents, and leadership possibilities to the POD. But his appointment, although it appeared to express a strategic logic and a setting of political priorities, was accidental. His entry into the cabinet seems to have been an afterthought, and his assignment to the PMG portfolio was not well considered.[8] Kierans would have no more political support on postal matters in cabinet than any of his predecessors had. Other departments retained the political authority to make postal decisions: Treasury Board would negotiate contracts, Finance would approve financial plans and actions, Public Works would build facilities and maintain buildings.[9] The government, cabinet ministers and the major postal users persisted in seeing the position of PMG as an "honorific position" that of a cheerleader whose main responsibility was in public relations.[10]

Within this narrow political terrain, the PMG functioned in a similarly constrained bureaucratic and administrative environment. Low on the bureacratic totem pole, the POD had little status or authority with which to compete for resources or power. The postal administration remained over-centralized, overfocused on operational details, and underexperienced in commercial and technological matters, and offered the PMG little in the way of strategic or planning support. Indeed, it was suspicious and sceptical about innovative plans or initiatives. As we saw earlier, POD management was recruited disproportionately from miliary ranks, and its attitude and organizational view were paternalistic, traditional, and intolerant. The authority of this approach was rocked by the 1965 strike, criticized and ridiculed by the Montpetit report, and jolted again by the 1968 strike. The morale of postal management was low. It confronted a new generation of postal workers, who were now unionized and no longer willing to accept low wages, poor working conditions, and the illegitimate exercise of discipline and authority.

Thus, the executive world of postal administration had little capacity to address the challenges faced by the postal system. The political world of postal legitimacy also constrained possible POD responses to its challenges. The House of Commons and Opposition postal critics stood vigilant against deteriorating postal service, rising prices, or any sign that the POD's social goals were being usurped by economic ones. Price rises or substantial service changes required the approval of the House of Commons, which could block such moves or demand *quid pro quos* in exchange for support, or simply embarass the government sufficently that it withdrew its proposals. Opposition postal critics insisted on the maintenance of low prices and universal and efficient postal service, even if this resulted in postal deficits, which were seen as an acceptable subsidy of a public good. The parliamentary defence of the interests of mail users acted as a substantial constraint on developments in postal policy. For example, low postal prices produced insufficient revenues to modernize the POD and pay postal workers decent wages.

Parliament was naturally allied with the public in perpetuating the postal *status quo*. The mass of postal users remained unorganized, but this did not diminish their effective political influence in the House of Commons. For example, rural MPs defended the interests of rural postal users, who benefitted from the uneconomical rural route system and the extensive network of rural post offices. Similarly, urban MPs defended the interests of urban postal users, who wanted to maintain low prices and a daily, efficient, and door-to-door delivery system. That only 25 per cent of the mail was sent by "ordinary Canadians" was not widely recognized. The rest was generated by a few hundred large users, who used the postal service to distribute magazines, bills, statements, and so on. These major mail users also remained relatively unorganized, but their interests were perpetually defended in the House of Commons, albeit indirectly, by MPs defending low prices and a universal and accessible postal system and expressing little concern over postal deficits. The result was a substantial subsidy for business mailers, the major users and beneficiaries of the postal service and its deficit. The large users also looked after themselves directly, by visiting the POD or by communicating with the minister. Second-class mailers and receipients were particularly effective in this regard, but the interests of postal users in general constrained the articulation and pursuit of postal alternatives.

The final postal constituency group was labour. It had become a formidable force in the late 1960s, allowed to organize as a union by the PSSRA and made increasingly radical and confident by the strikes of 1965 and 1968. Postal workers still commanded a reservoir of public and parliamentary good will, based on their exploitation in the past as well as on the perception that they were hard-working and reliable. Postal policy could no more ignore the postal unions than they could ignore the major mail users.

The POD thus faced postal challenges with a limited capacity for action. It remained politically isolated, with little political or administrative power or authority. Its administration was old-fashioned, technologically and managerially backward, and demoralized by the labour developments of the mid-1960s. It functioned in an uncertain political arena. The legitimacy of its actions was determined by parliamentarians, whose views were more in tune with those of postal users than of postal administrators. Postal users benefitted in substantial and calculable ways from traditional postal policies, and they were not anxious to have political innovations dissolve these benefits. Labour had become a formidable force, unionized, experienced, and with an intense sense of mission. In sum, the POD was politically and administratively weak and lacked the backing of postal political constituencies.

The Reform Strategy: Philosophy and Vision

Kierans' reform strategy foreshadowed the orientation that would be embraced by Canada Post almost two decades later: a hard-nosed, practical, and business-oriented strategy, that did not genuflect before the altar of postal romanticism or traditionalism. The strategy responded exclusively to two considerations: the POD's deteriorating financial situation and its loss of competitiveness. It promised to push postal policy to the economic end of the postal spectrum and far away from the social side, where the POD had been located since Confederation. The strategy included five major ingredients:

- reconceptualization of the POD as part of the broader communications industry
- balanced budgets through a user-pay policy
- increased productivity through mechanization
- regeneration and transformation of management
- redirection of the POD on a commercial course.

The POD had traditionally been conceived as a world unto itself; Kierans presented a new vision of the postal system, as part of the broader economic and communications environment. The former view may have made sense when the POD was the "only game in town" or the dominant one, but technological developments had made it only one of an increasing number of communications players. The government could now abandon the postal functions to other technologies. Or, as Kierans wanted, it could encourage the POD to rise to the technological challenge of competing in this market:

We may have to undertake major changes in structure to mold the Post Office into all the other mediums of communication — telegraph, telephone, telex and television, facsimile, video-phones, data transmission, and on up to communication by satellite. All of these are waves of the future. It is my intention that the Post Office Department should ride these waves and not be submerged by them.[11]

The POD was in a competitive battle and had to initiate "rapid and radical changes ... if it is, almost literally, to survive."[12]

For the POD to survive, it had to be placed on a more solid financial footing. Kierans was especially frank about this: "We intend to do everything possible to reduce the deficit and balance the budget within a few years."[13] This was a considerable ambition, given the size of the POD's deficit — rapidly approaching $100 million. Various tactics were adopted, but they were all based on the same strategy: "The philosophy is simply that you have to charge the costs to the users and not to the taxpayers."[14] This marked a sea change in how the POD financed its various services. It had freely admitted to "cross-subsidizing" various classes of services and activities; for example, losses on second-class mail were subsidized by surpluses on first-class mail, and losses on rural delivery were financed by surpluses on urban mail. And overall postal losses were paid for by taxpayers, an implicit national tax to finance a national public service.

Kierans rejected the idea that taxpayers should subsidize postal users: "Do you want your business community to be subsidized by the general taxpayer?"[15] He also rejected the idea of one class of mail or service subsidizing another. Broadly speaking, the price of a postal product or service was to cover its costs. This reflected a governmental decision reached by Treasury Board on 28 April 1966:

It should be departmental policy wherever economically and administratively feasible to charge for all goods supplied or services rendered to the public, including those now supplied free, unless there are provisions for specific exemptions.

Where this was not possible, it was proposed that the government target specific subsidies for each of the postal services that could not pay for themselves. These might include postal delivery in remote areas ($3.5-5 million estimated cost), second-class mail ($33 million deficit in 1970-71), and even home delivery (estimated cost of $140 million).[16] This pay-as-you-go philosophy included the goal of making a postal profit:

The primary economic objective of the Post Office is aimed at maintaining an economic balance for the whole of the services rendered to the public. Yet, it would appear quite in keeping with its role as a public utility that the Post Office should aim at a reasonable profit so as to be able to help finance investments designed to improve its services in the public interest.[17]

The reform strategy thus envisioned increased postal prices to put the postal system on a firmer financial footing.

This financial goal could not be attained exclusively by a new pricing policy, as rising prices were limited by competitive pressures, popular responses, and competing government goals such as containing inflation.[18] Budgetary goals could also be attained by keeping costs down (via improved productivity and efficiency) and by increasing postal business and revenues (by improved service). Both cutting costs and increasing service required postal modernization and mechanization.[19] There had been little movement on this front in the post-war period; technology had developed everywhere in the communications world save at the Post Office. Kierans' view was that the POD had never been given "the capital equipment or the advanced mechanization to handle the tremendous problems [of volume] ... We are at the stage now where the provinces were 15 or 20 years ago if they hadn't built the great auto routes."[20] Thus, the postal reform strategy would accelerate postal mechanization to exploit economies of scale, reduce unit labour costs, and improve postal services.

The fourth ingredient in the reform strategy was regeneration of postal management. Senior postal administrators worked their way through the ranks to find themselves managing a complex, billion-dollar operation, but they had little to no education or technological or market experience. They were administrators rather than managers, focusing primarily on production processes to the neglect of commercial and market issues. Seventy per cent of postal management had no more than a high-school education; only 13 per cent had a university degree, and over half were above fifty-five years of age. They had little commercial experience, a critical weakness in the increasingly competitive communications environment. They had no background or preparation in human relations management, an important weakness once postal workers had unionized. A consultant concluded that "the quality of the senior management group is the most significant consideration before the Post Office today."[21] The situation required an injection of new administrative blood — from the private sector.

Finally, Kierans maintained that the POD had to become more oriented to market realities and developments. The reform strategy aimed to create "an organization that is responsible to the needs of its customers, alert to the realities of the competitive environment, and produces efficient service at the lowest possible cost."[22] Kierans believed that the POD should act as much as possible like a private company, organizing itself on business lines and developing the same strategies and sensibilities as a private-sector firm. He wanted the POD to diversify its operations, to develop new postal products and services to meet competitive challenges. This could involve the purchase of existing firms or technologies. It would certainly require the reorganization of the POD, to privilege marketing and commercial activities over production and processing ones.

The Reform Strategy: The Policies

The postal strategy was given effect in a number of policies to be outlined in this section. Their impact — including the various political responses to them — is considered in the following section.

The policy process was driven by a set of private-sector consultancy studies of conditions in the POD, commissioned by Kierans in the fall of 1968. In conjunction with the department, six consulting firms produced fifteen studies over the next twelve months. For example, a marketing task force analyzed the POD's commercial strengths and weaknesses and suggested ways to extend its retail market reach.[23] The penultimate study, *A Blueprint for Change*, set the logic and framework for postal policies over the next decade. This was an extremely well considered and thorough study, both in its analysis of postal challenges and in its presentations of policy solutions. Indeed, many of its ideas and recommendations were acted on in the following years.[24] It presented all the key postal themes: the imperative to innovate to compete with the new communications technology and to deal with increasing postal complexity associated with urbanization; to mechanize, lest growing volumes increase labour costs and exacerbate the deficit; to decentralize postal authority; to recruit a commercially oriented management to steer the POD through the market.[25]

The policies that comprised the reform package can be divided into two areas: measures to balance the budget and measures to make the POD more commercial and competitive.

Balancing the Budget

The postal deficit was addressed in three ways: by increasing postal rates, rationalizing postal services, and initiating productivity improvements.

Introduced on 8 October 1968, Bill C-116 raised postal prices. This legislation was similar to that which PMG Côté failed to pass in 1967. It abolished the drop rate, thereby increasing the price charged for the delivery of "local" mail. It also increased the first-class mail rate to six cents, the first postal price increase since 1954: "Those were the days of the five cent telephone call and the five cent cup of coffee," said Kierans; "we are now in the era of the ten cent telephone call and ... the fifteen cent cup of coffee. Yet we remain in the era of the five cent stamp." The price increase was intended to stem the growth of the deficit and to financing the postal modernization program: "Are we to bring the Post Office into the modern era as a living, changing force, or are we to turn back the clock to 1951 and 1954 and condemn the department to exist in the strait-jacket of outmoded rates, regulations and procedures?"[26]

The price increase followed the pay-as-you-go or user-fee philosophy, which Kierans had firmly embraced. Each class of mail or service would pay for itself. The rate increase transformed the $29 million deficit on first-class mail into a $12 million surplus. Similarly, changes in third-class rates reduced that deficit from $30 million to $1.5 million. (Second-class rates are discussed separately below). Kierans tried to neutralize any political fallout by noting that the price increase would cost the average Canadian family about two dollars a year in increased postal charges.

The POD had planned to increase postal prices again in 1970, but Prime Minister Trudeau announced in February of that year that planned price and service charge increases in the public sector would be delayed for anti-inflation purposes.[27] Postal policy was once again being determined by the broader governmental agenda. The planned price increase was thus delayed for a year, by which time the POD had posted a record-breaking deficit of $100 million. The April 1971 price increase included a two-year phase-in for the increase in the first-class rate, whose price would rise to seven cents in July 1971 and to eight cents in January 1972. The deficit was forecast to rise to $114 million in the absence of any rate increase.[28]

With respect to second-class mail rates, Kierans accepted the long-standing Canadian tradition of subsidizing the dissemination of information. But he was also aware that the UK had just eliminated preferential treatment of second-class mail. His aim was to make this subidy clearer, more specific in the way it was financed, and justified on its own terms; he criticized it for being hidden, autocratically set with no public input, and distributed haphazardly and unfairly. The subsidy forced the POD "to play God with the publishing industry." If this policy was to be continued, he argued, the subsidy should not be buried or hidden within the POD's accounts. The government should transfer the funds to the POD as a targeted subsidy.[29] The subsidy was extraordinarily large — $54 million in 1969-70 (it had totalled $300 million over the last decade). The POD recovered only 20 per cent of the costs of distributing second-class mail and only 10 per cent in the case of newspapers. Kierans proposed that second-class rates be raised so that at least 50 per cent of costs would be recovered. Despite the rate increase, the second-class deficit remained at a substantial level, $39 million; this suggested the extent to which Kierans felt that political caution had to prevail.

Complementing the price increases were a series of postal service changes, announced on 27 September 1968. These were designed to eliminate "unnecessary" or expensive postal services. First, post offices were to be closed on Saturdays and Saturday mail delivery would be eliminated, even in rural areas. Given that 80 per cent of mail was business mail, a five-day postal week seemed sensible. Second, a number of rural routes and rural post offices would be closed, at an estimated savings of $13 million and fifteen hundred jobs. Kierans aimed to close down two thousand rural post offices; five hundred had already been closed by the time of his announcement. "Our approach to the building of Post Offices was political, not for social or economic purposes. They were built as winter work projects, built when there was no need for them, but for the political interests of the MP."[30] Third, the postal savings bank was closed, as it was not being used by the public. Finally, a freeze was imposed on the extension of letter carrier service, a policy that continued through 1971.

Over and above price increases and rationalization of services, productivity measures were introduced to improve the budgetary situation. The elimination of Saturday service and the freeze on extending letter carrier routes were designed to increase productivity in the delivery of mail; but as well, a "straight-through" mail delivery system was introduced.[31] Letter carriers were directed to stay out on their routes straight through the lunch period, without returning to their post offices. The POD estimated that this would save $2 million a year.[32] In 1969 it also introduced a number of changes in local transportation arrangements, which reflected the change to a five-day delivery system and the end of the practice of setting cost-plus contracts.

With regard to mail sorting, a $100-million mechanization and modernization program was introduced in 1969: thirty mechanized postal plants were to be established across the country. A Blueprint for Change had maintained that postal costs could be reduced by 20 per cent over the short term if sorting was mechanized. It also recommended the system of "marked mail" for optical character recognition; if the POD used that system in the ten largest-volume plants, annual savings would be in the $6-8 million range.[33] The POD pursued the mechanization proposal with enthusiasm. Two Ziptronic letter-sorting machines were purchased in 1969 for evaluation. A twelve-operator, 277-separation Burroughs letter-sorting machine was installed in Winnipeg in 1970. In February 1970, Kierans presented the Sampson Belair study on the postal code and announced the introduction of a national postal code, with testing to begin in Ottawa in April 1971. The mechanization plan unfolded so quickly that PMG Côté declared in June 1971 that Canada would soon have the fastest, most mechanized postal system in the world. The coding and sorting machines were purchased by December 1971, and were delivered to Ottawa, where the system would be tested, in January 1972. By this time, coding had been completed in Ottawa, Manitoba, Saskatchewan, and Alberta. At the same time, the POD launched a modernization program, to build new facilities and renovate existing ones. Between 1969 and 1975, 100 additions were made and 473 new buildings were constructed.[34]

A More Commercial Orientation

Kierans pushed the POD in a more commercial direction, proceeding on four fronts: he reorganized and decentralized the POD and recast it within the wider technological world in the Department of Communications; he injected private-sector managers into it; he encouraged a market orientation and the diversification of the POD's product lines; and he recommended that the POD be transformed into a Crown corporation.

The consultancy studies confirmed that the POD was overcentralized and that too many operating decisions were made in Ottawa. This inhibited initiative and discouraged decision making in the field. A Blueprint for Change recommended that the POD become far more decentralized. A pilot project was undertaken in Ontario and was so successful that the POD was quickly transformed into four decentralized regional operations, each with its own general manager, and with wide accountability and real authority.

The regionalization program was fully in place by 1972. Postal headquarters concentrated less on operational details than on marketing, finance, and business planning. New organizational units were developed, including Marketing, Engineering, Coding and Mechanization, Organization and Development, and Finance.[35]

The POD was simultaneously connected to the wider communications market by being placed within the Department of Communications. Bill 173 created a Ministry of Communications, combining a new Department of Communications and the POD. Each would have its own deputy minister. The initiative was the brainchild of Michael Pitfield and was sanctioned by Prime Minister Trudeau. It aimed to connect the POD with the revolutionary changes taking place in communications; it appeared to have great significance, but amounted to little.[36]

To rejuvenate the Post Office, Kierans recruited commercially oriented senior managers from the private sector, or the "golden 50," as they came to be known. They included James Corkery of Canadian General Electric, John Ubering of Southam, Garth Campbell from CNR, Jack Prescott from American Air Filter, Larry Sperling from Consumers Distributor, and John Mackay from IT&T. Another hundred or so were recruited at lower levels of management.[37] The new senior managers headed up the new postal units, such as Marketing, and Finance and Engineering, and introduced a number of innovations.

Kierans tried to project to the market a new image of the POD as a modern communications business. He encouraged the diversification of postal products and services to create this image. The marketing task force had suggested a retail expansion into travellers cheques, gift certificates, postcards, and writing materials;, advertising in postal lobbies and on stamp books;, photocopying and duplication services, information and computer services;, and facsimile transmission service. Many possibilities were mooted at this time, including the introduction of a European-style Giro banking system, automated money systems, and expansion into electronic mail and telecommunications. A Marketing Branch was established in 1969, reporting to the new associate deputy minister of finance and marketing. This branch was responsible for postal rates, mail classification, and customer sales and service. It had the responsibility of keeping the POD in closer contact with, and more responsive to, customers. It developed a variety of new products and services, including new incentive-pricing policies, the aerogram, a small packet service, expanded philatelic sales, and the "all up" airmail service. In March 1971 it opened a new-style postal outlet in Toronto's Fairview Mall offering a full range of postal products as well as government information, coin sets, and other products. The Marketing Branch also developed a new kind of mail called "assured mail." This service was introduced in February 1971 in Toronto and was expanded into forty-two cities over the next year. It was introduced to renew the expectation that the POD could provide reliable service. Finally, the Telepost system was introduced in October 1971, which service combined CNCP's telex system with regular first-class mail delivery.[38]

At the heart of these commercial policies was the aim of transforming the POD into a market-sensitive business operation, capable of responding quickly to market and technological developments and able to pay its own way. There were, though, serious institutional limits to the commercialization of the POD. It was caught between the ideals of a corporate orientation and the political necessities of life as a department. Kierans thus proposed to his cabinet colleagues that the POD be transformed into a Crown corporation.

The idea of a postal Crown corporation built up considerable momentum in the late 1960s and early 1970s. The Montpetit and Anderson reports had encouraged the government to give the idea serious consideration, and the consultancy reports also supported the idea. A Blueprint for Change concluded that "from these studies emerged the overpowering conclusion that the Post Office as a Crown Corporation could better fulfill its role ... It cannot operate effectively as a department of government" if it is to realize its goals of providing good service at a reasonable cost in a self-sufficient financial environment.[39] An unpublished white paper on Crown corporation status for the POD drew a similar conclusion: "Corporate status is really the only means to achieve any semblance of business management in the true sense."[40]

The rationale behind the proposed postal transformation will be explored in fuller detail in Chapter 6. Broadly, there were four reasons presented by supporters of a postal Crown corporation. First, the Post Office did not perform like a conventional department of government, because it carried out service functions, had a high degree of market contact with the public, and was required to have a commercial orientation. This feature demanded a degree of corporate flexibility that its departmental form and its place within the government did not allow. Second, its financial requirements were complex and extensive but, as a department of government, it was tied to the annual appropriations process. It could not set its own prices, control the flow of its financial resources, or count on using its surpluses. This discouraged initiative, disallowed reasonable forward planning, and hampered attempts to raise the capital required to invest in new techologies and activities. Third, the Post Office was really an industry and had a large, well-organized industrial labour force. The departmental form did not lend itself to good industrial relations. Collective bargaining was carried on by another government department whose broad white-collar orientation contrasted with the blue-collar postal scene. Negotiations took place under the narrow PSSRA labour regime, which did not allow negotiation over critical staffing and mechanization issues that were negotiable in the private sector under the Canadian Labour Code. Recruitment of staff and managers was also cumbersome in the departmental setting. Fourth, a number of other important activities were carried out by other departments, such as construction and maintenance of buildings. In sum, adherents of the idea argued that a postal Crown corporation could put itself on a more successful commercial and competitive footing, innovate technologically, balance its books, and engage in more reasonable and progressive labour relations.[41]

A consultancy study on the feasibility of transforming the POD into a Crown corporation was quickly followed by a white paper outlining the implications and details of this proposed transformation. A cabinet committee recommended that the POD be transformed into a Crown corporation, a recommendation later accepted by cabinet. There was minimal cabinet discussion or division, and little controversy was generated. It was widely anticipated in 1969 and early 1970 that the government would soon announce the change, a view not discouraged by PMG Kierans in his public statements.[42] The idea was given further momentum in 1970 when the United States set up its own postal corporation, the United States Postal Service.

Policy Results and Outcomes

The postal reform strategy comprised the most radical change in postal philosophy since Confederation. The resulting policies were the most extensive and varied since 1867. Policy results did not, however, match policy expectations. Many initiatives were constrained by the political process and were either not implemented or were undermined. Other actions generated unforeseen consequences and new policy problems. In aggressively pursuing such an ambitious postal agenda, Kierans managed to alienate most postal and political constituencies, and he became increasingly isolated politically. The postal reform agenda collapsed under its own weight and Kierans himself resigned.

The Politics of Postal Reform

The postal reform package exacerbated the traditional tension between the POD's economic and social goals. At the heart of this intensified conflict was parliamentary opposition to the ideal of the balanced budget. Kierans was accused of destroying a century of postal history. "All of a sudden after 100 years or more the Post Office Department must operate in the black and there is something immoral or illegal about subsidizing postal service," complained the NDP's Orlikow. A balanced budget imperative discriminated against postal users, argued Macquarrie: "I think we must look at the basic assumption ... that the department must pay its own way; why should it? ... Is there some unwritten law ... which says that the users of the mails must balance the Post Office budget but that the users of the airways, the sea lanes or the rail lines need not do so?" According to Benjamin, the user-pay philosophy would destroy the POD's public purpose: "The Minister is attempting to use so-called private enterprise efficiency methods in respect of an instrument that is basically a social enterprise designed to render service." The decline in the quality of postal services and morale, postal strikes and disruptions (see below), and skewered postal priorities seemed in the eyes of many MPs to confirm this view. The Opposition contrasted government's financing of communications with its postal funding cuts: Kierans was characterized as the man who "put Canada in the space age in the statosphere and slowed down the mail on the ground."[43]

Opposition criticism of the balanced budget, user-pay approach was directed particularly to two policy initiatives: postal rationalizations in rural areas and increased second-class mail rates.

Political reaction to rural postal rationalization was a metaphor for the fate of the postal reform agenda. Of the price and service changes introduced in the fall of 1968, rural changes generated the most intense reaction. Rural MPs claimed that Kierans' initiatives had a disproportionately large and negative impact on rural areas: "If anyone deserves a real subsidy it is the people who live and have pioneeered in the rural areas," claimed the NDP's Harding. Conservative postal critic Walter Dinsdale accused Kierans of being too city oriented, postal policy having "lost contact with the vital needs of the rural community." These policies would undermine the rural way of life and lead to the disappearance of rural communities. There was considerable and well-organized political opposition to the termination of six-day delivery and the planned closing of two thousand post offices. MPs besieged Kierans, asking that their ridings be exempted. A parliamentary petition was circulated urging the government to reconsider the postal changes in rural areas (thirty-five backbench Liberals signed the petition). Kierans was criticized mercilessly for weeks in the House of Commons. The media was also highly critical. The *Globe and Mail* mocked Kierans with an editorial entitled "Anything to Save a Buck"; it contrasted the POD's service cuts with the price increases imposed in all postal categories: "In a just society anything is possible."[44]

The government eventually withdrew a number of initiatives. First, six-day rural delivery was reintroduced in communities with less than two thousanad points of call, that is, in areas with no letter carrier service (this was done mainly to ensure Saturday delivery of local papers). Kierans admitted that this change reflected political pressure, pure and simple. He planned to reintroduce the policy at a later and quieter moment.[45] Second, rural post office closings were halted, also as a result of political pressure. Once he became PMG, Jean-Pierre Côté stated that no rural post offices were to be closed for reasons of economy after October 1970. He himself believed that many of the postal closings did not make economic sense, so he terminated the program.[46] Each year some post offices opened and others closed. There were around 200 annual post office closings in the post-war period, and a net result of 1,000 closings in the decade before Kierans became PMG (see

Table 6). The net closings in the Kierans era were well above average: 372 in 1969, 875 in 1970, and 575 in 1971, double the number of closings in the previous decade. The policy of rural postal closings was then discontinued, and over the next decade there was a net closing of but 290 post offices. The political reaction to postal closings effectively confined the long-term possibility of rationalizing the network of post offices.

A second target of opposition and public criticism was the price increase on second-class mail, which was thought to discriminate against rural areas and the print media, and intensified the debate over the POD's social versus its economic functions. Rural MPs insisted that increasing second-class rates would harm local newspapers and periodicals, cutting off the rural community's access to news and information. Opposition MPs also decried the policy's discrimination against the printed word and its privileging of electronic media. "We spend millions in trying to establish a national radio and television network," stated Macquarrie, "but what of other media?" The publisher of *Le Devoir*, Claude Ryan, claimed that the policy change would increase his paper's postal charges by 275 per cent. Maclean-Hunter announced that its postal bill had increased by $1 million; it closed a number of small magazines and increased its advertising rates by 10–15 per cent. The Committee For Fair Postal Rates, which included the Canadian Labour Congress, the Canadian Farm Association, newspaper and periodicals associations, was formed and held a conference in Ottawa in November 1968. It accused the government of killing small magazines and newspapers. Ironically, the major beneficiaries of the second-class subsidy had been the large American publications like *Time* and *Readers Digest*, a fact that muddied analysis of the issue at the time. The Davey Committee on Mass Media argued that the rate increases undermined "the freest possible flow of printed information and opinion," which is "vital to the national unity of Canada." Comparing the second- class mail subsidy of $24 million to the $166 million assigned to the CBC, the committee concluded that "we can think of no better way to invest $24 million." It also noted that POD officials had given the committee the impression that "the department would be happy to be relieved of the newspaper distribution burden altogether."[47]

This intense reaction to the second-class changes politicized to a great extent all of the other postal initiatives, constraining the evolution of new postal policy. Publishers and newspapers exerted substantial pressures on Kierans, often to a hysterical extent. Newspaper editorials across the country decried Kierans' attempt to balance the postal books on the backs of the press. A further irony was that the second-class price increase hardly dented the deficit, which remained at $39 million. Postal charges still recovered only 80 per cent of the costs of delivering daily newspapers, 13 per cent of the costs of delivering weekly newspapers, and 33 per cent of the costs of delivering magazines. The enormity of the post-price-increase deficit illustrated the size of the subsidy, as well as how anticipated reactions to these proposed increases constrained policy initiatives in the first place.[48]

Kierans was unsuccessful in selling the idea that price increases and service rationalizations were required to put the POD on the right track:

In September when I said that we were going to put the Post Office on a more efficient basis, to reduce costs, and to attempt to balance the budget, there was not a newspaper in the country that did not hail the Postmaster General as the ideal man for the job. But ... when the details of the budget were published ... nearly every newspaper in the country ... turned the other way. The attitude was, "Balance the budget, yes. Who, me? Never."[49]

Opposition reaction to rural postal changes and second-class mail increases demonstrated the continuing impact that Parliament had in the area of postal policy. Kierans underestimated this, rushing ahead without considering parliamentary or political tactics. He was frustrated by the intricate parliamentary process that surrounded postal policy and that he felt had led to the POD's financial predicament:

Members of this house on many previous occasions have refused to accept their responsibility, either when they were in power or in opposition. The 1951 bill was emasculated, and between 1957 and 1962 no bill came forward. A bill was withdrawn in 1964, and another defeated in 1967.[50]

The parliamentary opposition insisted on its right to criticize his policies and to reject or alter them. It was highly critical of the "casual" fashion in which Kierans introduced his 1968 changes. Although these did not require regulation, the opposition argued that there should have been more consultation and that Parliament should have been allowed to scrutinize them. The government's action was characterized as "jam[ming] legislation down the throats of the opposition," and there were widespread calls to send the policies to committee for further scrutiny. Even without this action, the process of increasing postal prices in 1968 was gruelling: second reading took four days, and another two days were spent in committee of the whole.[51]

The politics of postal reform resulted in the delegitimation of Kierans' strategy. Some of his policies were initiated, but others were withdrawn or undermined. More importantly, the political process wore down the reform agenda and built up a substantial body of political resentment against the policy changes. This isolated Kierans and the reform approach, built up a matrix of interests against the policies, and dissipated the momentum for postal reform.

Policy Reform and Labour

Two dimensions of the postal reform strategy affected labour relations in the Post Office. First, the strategy rejected the "cheap-labour" policy utilized throughout the post-war period: postal workers would no be required to subsidize the government or postal users. However, price increases were required to pay for improved wages and working conditions; Kierans introduced these increases, with the political consequences noted above. Second, the strategy aimed to increase productivity and efficiency, in order to increase the POD's competitiveness and its financial viability. The pursuit of this goal generated disruptive policy results and outcomes, particularly on the labour front. There were three major labour difficulties in the brief Kierans era: the straight-through dispute, the Lapalme truckers problem in Montreal, and the rotating strikes of 1970. These difficulties alienated labour even further from POD management and the government, and intensified labour's historical sense of grievance.

The 'straight-through' dispute arose at the beginning of the reform period, polarizing labour and management's positions early in the Kierans era. As discussed above, Saturday mail delivery was eliminated in September 1968 to save costs. The postal unions supported this move, for it eliminated the unpopular swing shift, but they were not consulted about it before it was announced; this was the source of the dispute. If the same amount of mail could be delivered in fewer shifts, then postal productivity would increase, but as well, some reorganization of the pattern of mail delivery would be required. Mail carriers had traditionally organized their deliveries around a lunch break, which they would take back at their home or local post office. The travel time to their routes from the post office and back was considered to be paid company time, as was the wash-up time before lunch at the end of their shift. The POD proposed to have mail carriers stay out on their routes over the lunch period in order to save travel time; it also proposed to eliminate wash-up time. The postal unions, not having been consulted about these changes, charged that the collective agreement was being broken. Negotiations were held between the unions and Kierans, but the new system when into effect as planned, despite widespread political criticism. Wildcat action then broke out in Hamilton, Welland, and Toronto in late February and early March, and spread to sixteen centres in three provinces. The wash-up issue was resolved when an adjudicator ruled that postal workers should have a paid five-minute wash-up time at the end of each shift. But the lunchtime controversy dragged on and on before being sent on 10 March to a special panel of adjudicators. In its 4 July 1969 report, the Martin Committee ruled that the POD had violated the collective agreement by introducing the straight-through system without consultation. It did not order the POD to undo the change, but it was brutally critical of how the POD had proceeded:

It is quite clear that ... management's conduct has resulted in creating unrest, the undermining of morale, and the development of hostlities between the parties ... An assessment of employer attitudes ... shows that the employer position is characterized by arrogance and high-handedness ... There is lacking a genuine desire to work in the atmosphere of mutual respect and understanding. Hostility, vindictivness, and possibly distrust, appear to frustrate every opportunity for effective inter-relationship. It would appear that senior officials in the Post Office Department have not as yet reconciled themselves to operating the postal facilities within a progressive collective bargaining atmosphere.[52]

The Opposition accused Kierans of poisoning morale and labour relations and called for his resignation. Kierans acknowledged that a mistake may have been made in changing mail delivery without prior consultation. But he was unrepentant about the change itself; reverting to the system of carriers lunching at their post offices would cost the POD as much as $2 million a year.[53]

For the postal unions, the straight-through issue was as much about trust, consultation, and implementation procedures as it was about the substance of the issue. The right to have lunch and to wash up in decent facilities, and the time to travel to these facilities, was not one of the most pressing labour relations issues at the time, but to the unions it symbolized the fact that postal management had not learned much from the 1965 and 1968 strikes and the Montpetit report. It appeared to them that postal management planned to proceed as it had in the past, pursuing the reform strategy without considering postal workers' needs or views. Unlike in the past, though, postal workers were now unionized and aggressive and would pursue their intersts firmly, even if this meant disrupting postal operations.[54]

A far more dramatic and far-reaching incident was *"Les Gars de Lapalme"* dispute (this infamous event has been well chronicled elsewhere).[55] The dispute arose in the context of the POD's efforts to reduce transportation costs. For example, the task of collecting mail from street boxes had been contracted out to private firms. The Lapalme dispute centred on the Montreal contract, which, like others, had been set on a cost-plus arrangement. Rod Service Ltd. had held the $3 million contract since 1952. When the POD moved from six- to five-day city mail delivery, Rod Service gave up the contract, as it did not feel that it could make a profit. The POD at first decided to collect the Montreal mail itself, but the Rod truckers — unionized, well paid, and highly organized — threatened industrial action. The contract was then assigned to G. Lapalme Inc. for the 1969–70 postal year. Lapalme hired the nearly four hundred Rod Service workers at their existing wage levels. Kierans was extremely unhappy with this and similar arrangements, which he felt were too expensive and susceptible to labour disruption. He went to cabinet and proposed to open transportation contracts to competitive bidding. He warned that there would probably be political and labour fallout; on 24 September 1969 cabinet nonetheless approved his proposal.

Lapalme did not participate in the new process, because its workers refused to accept the wage cuts required to make its bid competitive. The Montreal transportation work was awarded to five companies in contracts that would save the POD between $1.5 and $2 million a year and would result in more efficient service. None of the companies was obliged to hire the Lapalme workers, who would lose their jobs once the Lapalme contract expired. The issue then became a moral one: Did the Lapalme workers have a claim to be treated as postal employees, even though they had worked for private operators and were not affiliated with any of the postal unions? Did the POD have an obligation to employ these workers, 278 of whom had worked indirectly for the POD for over five years? Indeed, the POD had acted as an intermediary between Rod Services and the drivers in 1966, tacitly ratifying that agreement. Similarly, a POD representative was assigned to be present during the 1968 negotiations.

The dispute turned nasty even before the Lapalme contract concluded at the end of March 1970. There were rotating strikes, slowdowns, and a certain degree of violence and destruction. The POD started hiring replacement workers in early March, which only exacerbated the situation. The media was relatively sympathetic to the Lapalme workers and portrayed the POD as callously abandoning what were, in effect, its own workers. The cabinet was also sensitive to this view. It decided on 16 March to instruct the five companies to hire the Lapalme drivers, on the basis of seniority. This would require a return to the cost-plus arrangements, to allow the five companies to make financial ends meet. Kierans was furious, as the arrangement reverted to the costly situation that he had tried to reform. He submitted his resignation on 17 March, but Prime Minister Trudeau did not accept it, instead, proposing to delay implementing the cabinet decision until a one-person arbitration committee presented its findings. Kierans reluctantly agreed. A week later. Justice Carl Goldenberg ruled that the POD had a moral obligation to direct the new companies to hire the Lapalme workers: "This was a serious omission. Although the Post Office was not their direct employer, its change of policy would directly affect the livelihood of the Lapalme employees." Goldenberg also concluded that the five newly signed contracts were dubious in the extreme, as they were based on wage rates and attitudes to labour that were certain to generate industrial disputes. He recommended that the new transportation contracts be cancelled and directed the POD to take over the Montreal transportation activities and to hire the Lapalme workers as postal employees.[56]

The government accepted Goldenberg's recommendations, and entered into negotiations with the Lapalme drivers. It offered full-time jobs to 257 of the 450 Lapalme workers at 77–95 per cent of existing wage rates; severance pay was offered to the remaining drivers. The government revised its offer to 330 jobs at a higher wage level, in the face of renewed disputes and violence. The Lapalme affair became increasingly messy, wrapped up in issues of union jurisdiction, Quebec nationalism, and seniority rights and job security. After its last offer was rejected, the government finally decided to hire its own drivers. For the next two years, *les gars de Lapalme* protested the government's actions and demonstrated on Parliament Hill.

At the heart of the Lapalme affair was a dispute between two visions and rights. The POD was anxious to improve productivity and efficiency, even if this involved disrupting existing labour arrangements. Once the new transportation contracts were in place, the POD insisted that private companies should have the right to employ the workers they wanted at wage rates they negotiated. This challenged the "rights" and conditions of workers, who would be displaced or would be offered lower wages. In short, the POD openly privileged the principles of productivity and management rights, exacerbating an already unstable labour relations scene. It was publicly and self-consciously hard-line in this dispute, despite contrary media and public opinion. It did not want to signal to its own unions that the POD would compromise in the face of concerted union activity.[57] Like the straight-through dispute, the Lapalme affair was a local issue that had tremendous symbolic resonance. As it dragged on and on, it soured the mood of labour relations and weakened what little trust existed between management and labour at this critical moment in the POD's evolution.

The most widespread labour disruption occurred during contract negotiations in 1970. The two major ingredients in the dispute were complicated by external factors. First, postal issues were again subsumed by the wider government agenda. Bargaining over wages was affected by the government's six-and-five anti-inflation program, which limited the size of the government's wage offer. This exacerbated negotiations, particularly as the six-and-five program characterized unions as being responsible for inflation. Second, the postal unions negotiated to have some say in the POD's mechanization plan; postal management and the government refused. The PSSRA excluded from negotiations issues such as the introduction of new technology, job classification and security, the use of part-time and casual employees, and the determination of working conditions, which were considered to be management's prerogatives. But these were precisely the central issues of labour-management relations in the 1970s, and their exclusion from negotiations frustrated the postal unions.

Negotiations unfolded in a pattern that would be reproduced with dispiriting regularity throughout the decade.[58] Talks broke off in early March 1970 after months of unsuccessful negotiations. The stumbling blocks were wage rates and management rights to determine technological change. A conciliation board was set up 26 March, headed by Judge René Lippé. The board failed to reach a consensus agreement in its 4 May report, with the government and union representatives posting separate reports. On wages, Lippé proposed twenty cents, ten cents, and twenty cents over three years. The Council of Postal Unions asked for thirty-cent-an-hour in each of two years; Treasury Board offered a three-year deal with increases of sixteen cents, ten cents and fifteen cents. With regard to technological change, Lippé invoked PSSRA 86(3):

> No report of a conciliation board shall contain any recommendation concerning the standards, procedures or processes governing the appointment, appraisal, promotion, demotion, transfer, layoff or release of employees.[59]

The CPU rejected the report and, after a series of temporary work stoppages, set a strike date of 19 May. Postal union president Joe Davidson declared that since "automation is coming, now is the time to stand and fight." The postal unions then initiated a new strategy of "'rotating strikes,'", beginning on 26 May in Winnipeg and continuing until 4 September: instead of calling out all its members in a national strike, it organized strikes in one or a number of regions or centres at a time, chosen on a rotating basis. This tactic was tremendously disruptive for the POD but did not require that all workers come out on strike and lose their income. The POD could not plan its activities, not knowing which or how many postal centres would be affected on a given day or for how long. PMG Kierans threatened to close down those parts of the system affected by the rotating strikes, for example, the smaller post offices in the region affected by the rotating strikes. In an escalating game of tit for tat, a number of postal shut-downs matched the rotating strikes. Strikes and lock-outs closed down half the postal service on 24 July.[60]

Treasury Board applied for mediation in late May, but the efforts of mediator A.W.R. Carrothers collapsed on 2 June. The situation dragged on through the summer, until the government made a new offer on 12 August. Thomas O'Connor was named mediator on 19 August. On 24 August, the CPU called off the rotating strikes for five days in an effort to impove the negotiating atmosphere. On 3 September an agreement was reached in principle, following a formula put forward by O'Connor. There would be a fifty-five cent wage increase over thirty months, a level exactly midway between the conciliation offer and the CPU's original demand. With other benefits the government declared the package to be worth 6.8 per cent, the unions 7.2 per cent.[61] On the issue of technological change, the postal unions won a form of job security and the promise of advance consultation. A letter by PMG Kierans was appended to the contract:

> The planned modernization program will not result in layoffs of present full-time employees during the life of the present agreement pro-

vided that employees will accept relocation, reassignment and retraining. This will not be done without consultation nor at the expense of present employees.[62]

The 1970 dispute was extremely costly for the POD, in more ways than one. First, the wage and benefits package amounted to $25 million, raising costs and increasing the pressure to either improve productivity and competitiveness or raise prices. Second, the disruption affected postal revenues by as much as $30 million according to some estimates. Postal customers, unwilling to tolerate the uncertainty caused by the rotating strikes, took their business elsewhere.[63] As Table 1 indicates, postal volumes declined in each of 1968-69, 1969-70, and 1970-71, the last year by 5.4 per cent. The implications for revenue of these declines were mitigated only by price increases, which did not improve the POD's competitive position. Third, the disruption exacerbated already tense labour-management relations. The Opposition and the media blamed Kierans and postal management for this and other disruptions. The single-minded drive to efficiency and a balanced budget, the unilateralism of the POD's policy approach, and lack of sensitivity to labour's job security concerns were seen to have caused the 1970 labour dispute: "If we are close to a strike it is because of the stubborness and incompetence of not only ... Kierans ... but of the ministers responsible. Although the minister has inerited a bad situation, he has done everything possible to make it worse."[64] Relentless parliamentary and media scrutiny of the government's handling of labour relations isolated Kierans and postal management from mainstream public and political opinion. It also to a great extent legitimized labour's claims and strengthened its historical sense of grievance.

This sense of grievance deepened after the strike. Regardless of assurances, there was little POD consultation with the unions on mechanization throughout the rest of 1970 and 1971. By this time, the government had already ordered coding and sorting machines for the Ottawa post office. The scale of the modernization and mechanization project increased far beyond unions' expectations: the estimated $96 million plan expanded to $200 million in the early 1970s. Limited consultation and secret postal planning led to an indictment of the POD in a December 1971 report by Carleton professor Richard Vandenberg (commissioned by the LCUC).[65]

Mechanization would be the core postal issue in the 1970s. For the POD, it was a critical means of cutting costs, improving productivity, and increasing competiveness. For the postal unions, mechanization represented a threat to jobs, wages, and working conditions. The 1970 strike and its aftermath illustrated the polarization around mechanization and its importance for healthy labour-management relations. It also suggested, however, the extent to which the POD lacked the institutional capacity to manage the mechanization issue in a way that maintained harmony with labour.

In conjunction with the Lapalme and straight-through disputes, the 1970 strike illustrated how the postal reform strategy had serious consequences for labour-management relations. By the end of the Kierans era, postal workers had become increasingly radicalized and even further alienated from postal management and the government.

The Demise of the Crown Corporation Idea

Of all the fatalities of the postal reform era, perhaps the most consequential was the decision to shelve the plan to transform the POD into a Crown corporation. Cabinet had adopted the Crown corporation approach in the fall of 1968, at which time there was little or no political controversy or opposition within cabinet. However, the senior bureaucracy was not especially keen. There was substantial resistance particularly from the Privy Council Office (PCO) and the Public Service Alliance. Senior PCO and Treasury Board officials insisted that Kierans and the POD required operational "back up" to the formal cabinet decision. A PCO committee was established to detail the ramifications of the decision and to set up the legislative framework for the transformation. That committee consisted of seven deputy ministers only one of whom had any real interest in the matter. Nine months and $750,000 later, the committee reported, and restated the obvious.[66]

The political situation had, however, changed dramatically in the interim. The postal setting had become far more uncertain and unsettled: price and service changes had created considerable political fall-out; the Lapalme dispute had been violent and disruptive, and had to be resolved in cabinet; wildcat action over the straight-through delivery decision had been disobliging politically. It was well into 1970 when the committee reported, and a white paper had been prepared — the political time had passed and political will had dissipated. Kierans had alienated most of his cabinet colleagues in the straight-through, Lapalme, and 1970 strike disputes. Many felt he had tried to do too much too quickly and that he had not been sufficiently politically sensitive to the concerns of those affected by these changes. He was blamed for the political fall-out associated with the rural postal closings, labour problems, and price increases, which caused political grief to ministers and MPs alike. Prime Minister Trudeau himself became hesitant about the idea of making the POD a Crown corporation. He was apprehensive that it would become a political football, constraining other initiatives if debated for months in the House of Commons. The plan was shelved in the fall and was conspicuous by its absence from the October 1970 Throne Speech. The white paper was never released.[67]

Soon after his reappointment, PMG Côté told a legislative committee that "it is still government policy to look at [the Crown corporation idea] and study it very deeply before any changes come about."[68] This statement signalled that, almost three years after the cabinet had approved it, the idea had been buried. Indeed, neither Côté nor André Ouellet nor Bryce Mackasey nor J.J. Blais nor Gilles Lamontagne — no PMG or government — would give the idea serious consideration for the next seven years. The idea of a postal Crown corporation would not re-emerge on the political agenda until Prime Minister Trudeau's unilateral declaration on the matter in 1978.

The postal reform era ended with the shelving of the idea of a postal Crown corporation and Kierans' resignation as PMG in April 1971. Prime Minister Trudeau was exasperated by the many postal controversies and invited Jean-Pierre Côté to head the portfolio for the second time. Trudeau exhorted him to recreate the halcyon days when postal life was quiet and postal matters were not debated perpetually within cabinet.[69] Backbench MPs hailed the administrative change as a sign that appointments, post offices, and services were to be matters of political discussion and calculation once again.[70]

Other policy initiatives of the reform period did not survive long. The freeze on extending door-to-door delivery ended in 1972. The assured mail delivery system was unsuccessful and was dropped in the mid-1970s.[71] The extended range of materials sold in the new-style postal outlets drew criticism from the auditor general and the Public Accounts Committee, and the experiment was ended. The POD was later removed from the Ministry of Communications umbrella. But, Kierans' organizational changes and recruiting initiatives had some staying power. The private-sector people fit in fairly well, according to PMG Côté. A few of the more aggressive consultants on efficiency matters were bad for morale and were let go. By and large, though, much of the consultancy work initiated by Kierans did not have great impact. What little Côté read of it he found to be uninteresting and unlikely to improve postal life, so the consultancy material was not pursued to any great extent.[72]

Conclusion

The POD and the postal agenda were changed in a number of ways during the Kierans era. An infusion of private-sector managers steered the POD in an increasingly commercial direction and their talents and values would inform postal developents for a generation. The POD undertook a number of marketing initiatives, which built up commercial momentum. It was decentralized into regional groupings, which allowed a range of operational decisions to be made in the field. Postal prices were increased, services were rationalized, and a number of post offices were closed — to considerable financial effect. A long-overdue postal modernization and mechanization program was put in motion. A variety of consultancy studies gave a sense of postal challenges and opportunities, particularly with respect to the POD's competitive and commercial situation. Kierans intensified the political spotlight on postal matters, which were debated more clearly and coherently.

The 1965 strike, the Montpetit report, and the advent of the PSSRA created an opportune moment for postal transformation in the late 1960s and early 1970s. As a Crown corporation, the Post Office might have found itself in a stronger position to modernize and mechanize, improve labour relations, and increase competiveness and commercialization. Kierans' reform strategy did not, however, transform the POD; indeed, the POD reverted to a number of traditional tendencies for the remainder of the 1970s. It persisted as a department, which constrained even the positive accomplishments noted above. The opportunity for reform and for transformation into a Crown corporation was fumbled politically. This may not have been Kierans' responsibility. He was insensitive politically, and blinkered in the procedural and political manner in which he proceeded, but this may very well have been necessary. As Kierans himself characterized it, "I'm guilty of waking a sleeping, drugged giant, drugged by nonsense of 100 years of policies."[73] Moreover, much of the process was out of his hands. Other departments continued to influence and determine postal policy: Treasury Board negotiated contracts, the government determined pricing policy, the PSSRA skewed the labour policy process, and the PCO influenced the legislative process.

There were four reasons why the postal reform agenda succeeded as little as it did: it was too ambitious, the ideological context was inappropriate, there was insufficient private-sector support, and cabinet backing was lacking.

The postal agenda was extraordinarily wide and extensive. Management was weak, with limited skills, and so had to be rejuvenated. New, commercially oriented administrators were required. The organizational structure had to be recast to allow new ideas and iniative. Labour relations were a shambles, built on mistrust and a long and bitter history. The POD's finances were shaky and uncertain, and it had no control over its pricing or revenues and no capacity to plan or raise resources for capital investment. Its physical plant was old and decrepit and its technology primitive. The POD existed in a parliamentary fishbowl, constrained by a series of deeply held social expectations about what it should and should not do. All of these issues leaned on each other, so that a reform strategy had to attack them all simultaneously. This was an overloaded agenda even in the best of times and circumstances, which these were not.

Second, while there was considerable feeling that the POD had to be changed, the ideological context for effecting these changes was not supportive. It is useful in this regard to note the striking similarities between the Kierans stategy of the late 1960s and the CPC strategy of the mid-1980s, as well as the different ideological contexts surrounding these strategies. The idelogical context in the latter period was far more supportive: the prevailing neo-conservative political mood allowed, indeed encouraged, Canada Post to initiate and pursue balanced budgeting, contracting out, privatization, service rationalizations, and other measures. In contrast, the post-war's progressive liberal ideology was still relatively strong, and the Trudeau government aimed to create the just society, a far distance from the neo-conservative agenda. Kierans' attempt to shift the postal focus from social to economic priorities lacked sufficient political resonance; when political troubles or controversy arose, there was no ideological framework or environment to protect him and his approach. For example, the Lapalme affair would not have raised the same level of moral concern, media criticism, or cabinet panic in the mid-1980s as it did in Kierans' era. Similarly, rationalization of rural services and cuts in postal subsidies could be carried out with fewer inhibitions in the 1980s. The drive for competitiveness of the late 1980s allowed policy ruptures; no such agenda or mood of crisis bolstered Kierans' efforts.

Third, the postal strategy lacked sufficient interest group backing to carry it in the face of political reaction. It provided no large benefit to any group, and so provided no reason for any group to champion it. Everyone appeared to agree about the necessity of modernizing the POD and putting it on a more solid footing; but once in place, the stategy alienated all groups and interests. For example, no group supported price increases. Large users benefitted from the postal deficit, which subsizied their postal bill, and although small or ordinary users would benefit financially from a declining postal deficit, the subsidy was so small in per capita terms that cutting the deficit could hardly induce mass support. In any event, the saving was neutralized by postal rationalizations and cuts in service. The parliamentary opposition and even government backbenchers viewed the reform policies as against both the national interest and, more importantly, their constituencies' interests. MPs were inundated by complaints from users, constituents, postal workers, and business. Media support was alienated by cutting the second-class mail subsidy. The one group that could have carried the reform agenda — labour — was alienated by the reform strategy, particularly its organizational changes and mechanization. Management and ministerial behaviour during labour disputes further undercut labour support.

Finally, the cabinet could have backed Kierans, particularly on the critical issue of transforming the POD into a Crown corporation. This transformation might have created organizational and political space and momentum to allow simultaneous pursuit of a number of potentially controversial reforms. But the cabinet wanted protection from the POD. It did not want to be bothered by postal matters, which were not considered to be important. As the reform package was implemented, the cabinet found itself having to protect Kierans from the implications of those reforms. Because the reform package lacked political support, the cabinet did the practical thing: it cut the string on Kierans. The POD then reverted to its traditional, business-as-usual stance for the rest of the decade.

Chapter Five

THE POLITICS OF POSTAL NEGLECT: MECHANIZATION, LABOUR, AND THE DECLINE OF THE DEPARTMENT IN THE 1970s

K ierans' resignation in the spring of 1971 brought the postal reform era to an end. Regardless of its merit and political tactics, the reform strategy had placed postal matters in clear focus and had presented a concrete plan of action. In the following decade, postal matters became unfocused and no clear plan or strategy emerged. What followed was an extended period of policy floundering and *ad hoc* responses to periodic crises. The events of this decade weakened the POD's capacity to confront the future.

This chapter examines the decade between Kierans' resignation and the advent of Canada Post Corporation in 1981. It will consider how the POD re-embraced its traditional orientation, that is postal matters were to be "endured" rather than creatively managed. The authority of the POD sunk further, aided by the rapid arrival and departure of seven PMGs, which encouraged *ad hoc* policy and the strategy of minimizing problems rather than maximizing postal possibilities.

The chapter also explores the implications of the decision to mechanize postal operations. Once established in the Kierans era, mechanization was pursued relentlessly and was the decade's only consistent postal policy. The scale, cost, and consequences of mechanization were all enormous, which made governments' neglect of postal matters particularly consequential. But once adopted, the mechanization policy was pursued in an unmanaged fashion. It took on a life of its own and produced many unintended consequences. Mechanization revolutionized postal operations without a corresponding institutional change. This was especially evident in the area of labour relations; there were five major labour disturbances in this decade, each related to the mechanization program.

Third, the chapter will investigate how the POD suffered a crisis of identity in this period. Ravaged by constant labour disputes, disrupted by the size and scale of mechanization, powerless in the face of other departments' interference, neglected at the highest policy levels, and ridiculed as chaotic by the public and the media, the POD became incapable of carrying out its responsibilities.

The chapter begins with an outline of the ongoing challenges confronting the POD. It then sketches the insubstantial postal vision and strategy that informed governmental policies in the 1970s. These postal policies are analyzed and their outcomes and consequences evaluated, particularly with respect to labour relations and the functioning and morale of the POD. The chapter concludes with an explanation of the causes and consequences of the politics of postal neglect.

Political Context and Postal Challenges

The POD's existence was threatened by ongoing heavy volumes, competition and financial challenges. And it had to take on these challenges in an uncongenial political setting.

The level of postal activity presented two conflicting challenges. As noted earlier, the post-war boom generated increasing postal volumes. As Table 1 indicates, volumes doubled from 1947-48 to 1967-68, to five billion pieces a year. Processing fifteen to twenty million pieces each working day was a considerable technical challenge as well as an inducement to mechanize. Although the absolute volume was high, the pace of growth declined in the late 1960s and 1970s. Postal activity decreased in each of 1968-69, 1969-70, and 1970-71; it took until 1973-74 to regain the level reached in 1967-68. Overall, the volume growth over 1968-81 was only 62 per cent of the growth over 1955-68.[1]

The overall weakening of postal growth manifested itself differently within the various classes of mail. First-class mail increased by about 50 per cent from 1968 to 1981. However, this was only 78 per cent of its overall growth in the previous thirteen years.[2] Its pace of expansion decelerated in the late 1970s: it grew by only 4 per cent between 1976-77 and 1980-81. Volume performances in the other classes of mail were even worse. Parcel post collapsed, from eighty-five million pieces to fifty-four million pieces. Second-class mail declined by 23 per cent and third-class mail by 43 per cent.

This poor performance reflected one contingent factor and one permanent one. With respect to the former, volumes declined when there were labour disputes, as in 1968-69, 1970-71, 1971-72, 1975-76, 1977-78, 1980-81. As PMG Blais stated, "With every stoppage of work, the Post Office loses more business to private couriers, telephone networks, computerized messenger services and the long distance telephone." For example, postal disruptions created the market opportunity which the courier business filled. There were eighty-five private messenger services in Toronto alone in 1973. As postal officials noted, "Usually the longer the strike is, the more business we'll lose, because people get used to using the couriers." The 1968 strike was three weeks long, and the strikes in 1975 and 1981 were six weeks. Even the Canadian government moved in this direction; a number of departments spent $7 million in courier services in 1977 and 1978. By 1977, the POD estimated that it had lost $60-100 million of business to the couriers — about 10 per cent of postal revenue at that time. Similarly, fourth-class mail volumes (parcels) collapsed. Despite their higher prices, Canpar, CP Express and Air Canada Courair increased their business as a result of their faster, more reliable service.[3]

The effect of labour disruptions on volume was only one example of the impact of competition on postal business, which occurred both within the "old" technological world of the POD and the new communications markets. The small-parcel business was an example of increasing competition in the traditional, old-technology markets. Private trucking, bus, rail, and air companies offered a competitive alternative to the POD, as did couriers. The POD's parcel and courier service declined by 40 per cent from 1968 to 1977. The late 1970s saw increased use of non-unionized, less expensive private carriers, students, and employees, who hand delivered items such as utilities bills. This raised the spectre of "cream-skimming" in the major urban markets, the POD's competitors "tak[ing] away the most lucrative business [to] leave Canada Post in the unprofitable areas of service." POD reports anticipated increased competition in the traditional mechanical methods of distribution, such as private door-to-door distributors, goods, courier services, newspaper and magazine inserts, and other advertising media.[4]

The new communications technologies provided an even greater competitive threat. A Price Waterhouse study predicted that first-class mail — the POD's most stable product — had an uncertain future because of the changing competitive environment. First-class mail faced no competition for most of the 1800s, the telegraph being its only competitor in the late years of that century. But the telephone emerged as a competitive threat in the early twentieth century, and was followed by the teletype, telex, computers, and satellites. The Price Waterhouse report predicted that first-class volumes would peak in the early 1990s, at which time there would be nine billion communications transactions outside of mail and telephone use. First-class mail's proportion of the information market declined from 17 per cent in 1965 to 13 per cent in 1975, and was predicted to decline to 5 per cent in 1995.[5]

The most obvious competitive source in the 1970s was the long distance telephone call. Less than 4 per cent of households were without phones by 1975, and there were more telephones (fifteen million) than postal points of call (six million). As prices declined, use of long-distance telephone calls grew faster than use of first-class mail: twice as fast between 1949 and 1959; four times as fast between 1959 and 1969, and 1969 and 1979; and seven times as fast between 1979 and 1989. Long-distance calls amounted to only 8 per cent of first-class mail volumes in 1949, but this rose to 17 per cent by 1969, 33 per cent by 1979, and 64 per cent by 1989. Telephone messages had increased from 78.4 per cent of the transactions of the communications market in 1970 to 86.7 per cent in 1975. The Price Waterhouse study predicted that by 1995, long-distance calls would outstrip first-class mail (6 billion calls vs. 4.1 billion letters).

Moreover, the telephone was only one of a variety of electronic systems which could be used in place of the postal system. A 1976 postal study estimated that 30–40 per cent of letter mail could be transmitted electronically without using the mail services. A Post Office out of touch with the electronic future could see its volumes decline to 4.3 billion by the year 2000.[6] A postal study in the early 1970s anticipated that electronic handling of mail by the late 1980s could rise to as high as 10 per cent of first-class mail.[7] By 1978, an internal report estimated that there would be eight billion electronic communications transactions by 1995, one and a half times the current volume of all mail. These electronic communications would include data transmissions, word processing, electronic funds transfer, and facsimile transfers.[8] An internal report in 1978 concluded that "should the Post Office be unable to retain its share of the market through the provision of an effective and competitive service, its very existence will be in question."[9]

Volume developments had obvious financial consequences. These were mitigated to some extent by the more regular postal price increases of this period. There were six such increases between 1968 and 1979, which saw the price of a first-class stamp increase from six cents to seventeen cents. Despite weak volume growth, postal revenues grew by a factor of four between 1968 and 1981, from $375 million to $1.5 billion (see Table 2). For example, although volumes increased by only 10 per cent from 1974-75 to 1980-81, revenues increased by 129 per cent. Despite price increases and substantial revenue growth, the postal budget was in deficit in every year in this period. As Table 3 indicates, the deficit grew to over $500 million on three occasions, and ranged from 12 per cent to 96 per cent of postal revenues. Overall, the POD ran an accumulated deficit of $3.844 billion between 1968 and 1981, an average annual deficit of $275 million. This represented 38.6 per cent of its revenues in this period.[10]

The budgetary situation also reflected a structural problem, which will be explored more fully below. Labour costs in the POD had traditionally been low and well contained. For example, the number of postal employees grew by 18 per cent between 1961 and 1968 (see Table 4). This was exactly the size of postal volume growth in this period. However, from 1968 to 1976 employment grew by 32 per cent at a time when postal volumes grew by only 18 per cent. This asymmetry was due to a number of factors. It reflected the disappointing expansion of postal business through the mid-1970s: anticipated volume growth simply did not materialize. Moreover, the mechanization program had been initiated to meet the anticipated volume expansion, and had two financial consequences in the short term: there were enormous direct and indirect expenses; and two postal systems existed side by side for a time. The new, mechanized system had to be staffed, but the old, manual system had also to be maintained until the new system was entirely in place. The need for a double cohort of postal workers resulted in a rapidly rising labour force and increased labour costs – in a period of disappointingly slow volume growth.

The POD thus confronted a set of substantial technological, competitive, and financial problems. At the same time, the political context worked against it as it confronted these problems. To begin with, after Kierans' departure, seven ministers handled the PMG's portfolio between 1971 and 1981: Jean-Pierre Côté, André Ouellet, Bryce Mackasey, J. J. Blais, Gilles Lamontagne, John Fraser, and André Ouellet again. None of them came to the position with much political experience or authority; and none stayed long enough to have a real impact or to build up sufficient authority to make the POD's case in cabinet. For example, Gilles Lamontagne was rushed into the position soon after being elected as an MP and after a very short stint as a minister without portfolio. He was uninterested in postal matters and not attracted to the position, which by 1978 had become the least appealing ministerial appointment. He did the job conscientiously but with neither imagination nor great initiative, as he had no great vision; he maintained the received cabinet line on the Post Office.[11] PMGs Blais and Côté report that their cabinet colleagues directed them simply to keep postal matters out of their hair. After Kierans' resignation, Trudeau exhorted Côté to reconstruct the "good old days," when postal topics rarely emerged in cabinet.[12] The PMG's position was exclusively and deliberately a short-term assignment. Both Ouellet and Blais report that they were interested in staying longer but were dissuaded from remaining by the prime minister and other cabinet colleagues, who insisted they move on to new positions or else risk ruining their political careers.[13] Indeed, after Kierans' fall from political grace, any politician with ambition would avoid crusades on behalf of the Post Office.

The department itself remained "at the bottom of the totem pole," according to Deputy PMG Corkery. The real decisions affecting it were made by Treasury Board and others. It was considered to be a blue-collar or operations department like Public Works. Indeed, it had the lowest ratio of executives per person years in the 1970s; there were only twenty-five executive officers out of sixty-five thousand employees in 1980. The POD had no status or authority and no political clout in this period.[14]

The politics of the Post Office in Canada were not played out in Parliament in the 1970s. There were increasingly few parliamentary debates in this period, reflecting reforms in the functioning of the House of Commons, which no longer held traditional debates on "supply" matters (these were now examined in parliamentary committees). Moreover, as will be seen below, price increases were handled administratively, outside of parliamentary scrutiny. Parliament's decline as the site of postal politics also reflected the increasing public focus on postal labour negotiations. From 1968 to 1981, there were two CPU, five LCUC, and four CUPW contracts negotiated, as well as countless other smaller contract negotiations and labour disputes.

The POD seemed always to be on strike or nearing one. Labour issues and negotiations consumed POD energy and media and public attention. This led to a widespread and deep anti-labour mood on postal matters, which "simplified" the postal agenda; many came to view the proper course as simply a matter of putting postal workers in their place.[15] However, anti-labour sentiment was also politically distracting: it deflected attention away from the financial, competitive, and administrative challenges at the POD, and it let the government off the political hook for these matters.

Given the PMG's political alienation and the POD's limited authority, the PMG became a type of "lone wolf." Some PMGs arrived on the postal scene convinced that their good will and understanding could be applied to productive ends in dealing with the postal situation. This was observable at the beginning of their terms and during postal negotiations. Deputy PMG Corkery recalls how quickly PMGs became worn down and dispirited by the scale and intractability of postal problems. In the absence of an effective institutional setting or political authority and backing, PMGs were more or less on their own; but an isolated PMG did not have the capacity to "solve" postal problems.[16]

Political Vision and Strategy

The political vision that informed postal policy in this period was not coherent. It combined a number of elements, which were neither synthesized nor thought through to any extent. PMGs and policy makers accepted that postal mechanization was required and acknowledged the competition that the POD faced, but they maintained that the POD should continue to assign equal priority to its social role and the emerging economic and technological imperatives. Among other consequences, the departmental form of the Post Office was maintained and postal policy was formulated and pursued in the traditional ways.

Mechanization was a central ingredient of this period's postal vision. It was a response to two challenges: competition and volume increases. Even if it was the best system in the world, recalls PMG Côté, the Canadian postal system had to be changed because other national postal systems were becoming mechanized and the business community was evolving in this direction. The POD would have to mechanize to remain competitive. Even more compelling, according to various PMGs, was the fact that the POD and its aging plant and equipment could not handle the growth of mail. As PMG Ouellet put it, "The volume of mail has increased too much for us to sort it manually." The expansion of cities and their suburbs generated an expanding and complicated network of street addresses, which also undermined the traditional "brain and brawn" sorting system and the mental capacity of highly qualified and experienced sorters (of which there was a diminishing pool as a result of retirements). The subsequent replacement of this sorting system by the deskilled ABC alphabetical sort impoverished the job.[17]

There was a double rationale behind the decision to mechanize: cutting costs and improving service. J. G. Fultz — the postal administrator charged with mechanization — declared: "We hope to cut down the handling of mail by humans by about two-thirds, putting more capital into the system and mechanizing. This in turn should slow down the need for postal increases and should increase the quality of the service."[18] Postal mechanization aimed to contain labour costs and prices while increasing productivity and service, to keep the POD competitive in the communications market.

PMGs were well aware of the competitive challenges facing the POD. Mackasey expressed concern about "cream skimming"; CUPW threatened to take legal action against the government if it did not move to ban courier services; PMG Blais promised that the POD would be aggressive in the market to stem the tide of couriers.[19] In the wider communications field, Blais was concerned that the POD would lose its chance to exploit the new communication technologies. Speed had become more important than cost, and so Blais wanted the POD to speed up its delivery, even if this meant higher prices. He also suggested that the POD of the future should be involved in the new electronic systems. "I would like to see us . . . shift from a passive to a more active role. Instead of mechanically shuffling paper around the country, the Post Office could be providing more services."[20]

All this seemed to suggest the need to take a different and more businesslike orientation. Ouellet asserted that the POD would have to become more aggressive in order to increase its volumes and revenues to deal with the growing deficit. He reminded business that "it enjoys one of the cheapest postal rates in the world," but added that "we are constantly on the go to improve our services towards these big firms." The POD was aware of business's price sensitivity, and began to anticipate how price changes affected business. Indeed, PMG Lamontagne claimed that "everything is being done to make Canada Post a governmental business, administered as close as possible along the lines of a private business." Worried about losing its major customers, the POD moved to service its business clients with greater care. A number of postal users conference were organized, in October 1972, November 1973, and November 1976. These were attended by the PMG and his deputy and allowed for an exchange of views between businesses, organizations, large and medium-sized postal users, and the POD administration.[21]

During the Kierans era, these technological and competitive concerns led the POD to embrace new strategies and approaches, including a user-pay and balanced budget philosophy and the commercialization of the POD's orientation. However, this no-nonsense market orientation was now replaced by the more traditional philosophy that had informed the POD since 1867, which saw the re-emergence of the POD's social role in an equal partnership with its economic role, as evoked in the following passage from the POD's 1979-80 report:

> The Post Office is perhaps the most talked about of our institutions. . .. Because of their diversified role in providing both services and information, Canada's post offices are a genuine window on the nation. In this way, Canada Post provides a federal presence throughout the country. In many communities . . . the post office with its Maple Leaf flag is the clearest manifestation of the federal government for miles around . . . The Post Office's objective of maintaining a policy of easy and universal access to postal service is in keeping with the redistributive function of Canadian federalism: to share as equitably as possible the costs of service brought about by the demographic disparities in Canada from coast to coast.[22]

This characterization had much to do with the period's concerns over national unity, as the federal government sought to assert its and Canada's identity against the growing tides of provincialism and separatism. It evoked many of the POD's traditional political functions, both as an agent of nation building and national unity and as a redistributive mechanism of social policy. This depiction was distant from Kierans' market vision, which implied an end to redistribution (pay-as-you-go) and the rationalization and closing of post offices. Indeed, underlying this re-emerging vision was the notion that the POD could not balance its budget or be run as a commercial operation. Mackasey asserted that "it is unrealistic to think you can run a Post Office without a subsidy or deficit if we are at all concerned about service." A 1973 POD study expressed scepticism about the department's capacity to balance the budget, given its social and national responsibilities, expensive letter carrier service, job guarantees, and other political expectations. Blais also characterized the POD as an "aspect of public service. . .. There is no way we can function without the Post Office . . . the question is: How much is the taxpayer ready to pay to subsidize the Post Office?" Lamontagne put it even more bluntly:

> It is not the mandate of the Post Office to make a profit. Its mandate is to serve the people of Canada. . .. Because Canada Post has been and must continue to be primarily a public service and an instrument of public communication policy, it still requires subsidization from the Treasury. . .. We are not here to make a profit. We are here first to give a service. . .. If it does not pay . . . to send the mail to the Yukon, I am not going to cut the mail off; I have to send it. It is my duty.

Postal discourse in the 1970s reasserted the social obligations and goals of the POD, even as its economic and technological imperatives mounted. The former were not to be sacrificed to commercial objectives or to the goal of a balanced budget; rather, the POD was directed to balance its economic and social goals. This was summed up in the 1977–78 POD report:

> Within the framework of government operations, Canada Post has held a unique position. It is a hybrid of business and service, with elements of both. It provides a service and charges for the service just as a commercial enterprise in the private sector, except that it must function under the very severe limitation of not being allowed to choose its markets. [Social obligations] place constraints on the operation that no Canadian business experiences.

Postal events of the 1970s were enveloped within an uneasy and unstable balance of social and economic goals. As a 1978 internal report stated, "The Post Office must reconcile conflicting aims, perceptions and expectations regarding its purpose. There has been no satisfactory resolution of its role as a public service and the essentially commercial nature of its activities."[23]

The idea of transforming the POD into a Crown corporation was shelved for a decade, as a result of the postal vision of the 1970s. Smothered politically by cabinet and seven PMGs, the POD reports of 1972 to 1980 mention nothing about this policy option — which was the central topic of postal discussions in the late 1960s and early 1970s. The politics behind this development will be examined fully in the next chapter. Simply put here, the idea of a postal Crown corporation did not fit into the postal vision embraced at the time, for it was too closely identified with Kierans' reform strategy. Politically, the transformation to Crown corporation status simply looked dangerous to the PMGs of the time. Ouellet feared that the postal Crown corporation would be obsessed with economics and balancing the books to the neglect of service and social goals. Most PMGs agreed with Blais that even if the POD became Crown corporation, "there is no way that the public will stop thinking of the Post Office as a government agency. . .. There always has been and will continue to be a great deal of public identification with the Post Office being a Department of the Public Service." PMGs were also affected by the new corporate postal service in the United States, which was experiencing a number of financial and operational difficulties.[24] In sum, the continuing concern with the POD's social functions inhibited its development into a Crown corporation. The Post Office would confront its financial, technological, labour, and competitive challenges as a department of government.

Postal Policies

Instead of Kierans' broad strategy of raising prices and rationalizing services, the POD emphasized increasing sales (commercialization and diversification) and increasing productivity (mechanization). These policy areas will be outlined in this section; their impact, and responses to them, will be considered in the next.

Price and Service Changes

Postal prices were increased regularly during the Kierans era, to six cents in 1968, to seven cents in 1971, and to eight cents in 1972, reflecting a pay-as-you-go philosophy and a balanced budget orientation. The political fallout from these and other actions led to the abandonment of the philosophy and the goal. There were no further price increases until 1976 — despite relentlessly rising labour, fuel, and transportation costs. The uncertain politics of postal price increases — to be played out in an unreceptive parliamentary environment — made PMGs cautious, and eager to assure the public that postal prices would not rise. Released from the shackles of the balanced budget goal, PMGs put off the financial day of reckoning for as long as they could.[25]

The Consumer Price Index rose by 7.6 per cent in 1973, 10.9 per cent in 1974, and 10.8 per cent in 1975. But the price of a first-class stamp remained at eight cents. The POD proclaimed that "no country in the world provides less expensive postage than Canada."[26] Low rates were designed to maintain and increase postal volumes, but competition and labour disruptions neutralized this strategy. PMG Blais reported in 1977 that volumes fell one billion pieces below expectations — a shortfall.[27] Low prices, rising costs, and disappointing volumes resulted in serious deterioration of the POD's financial situation. Table 3 shows that the deficit doubled from $77 million in 1971-72 to $177 million in 1973-74, and then tripled to $546 million in 1975-76. This represented 50 per cent of postal revenues.

The deficit provided a substantial subsidy to postal users, and was a tremendous target for political criticism. Finally, in 1976, the government increased postal prices to reduce the deficit. In May 1976, PMG Mackasey announced a two-stage first-class price increase, to ten cents in September 1976 and to twelve cents in March 1977. Parliamentary reaction was predictably negative, centring on the inflationary impact of the price increase and its inappropriateness given deteriorating postal services.[28]

Price increases were desperately needed; but the parliamentary process was cumbersome and politically embarrassing, leading PMG Blais to direct his officials to find some way of increasing prices in an extra-parliamentary way. Basing his argument on an obscure part of the Financial Administration

Act (section 13), Blais convinced cabinet that price increases could be passed through order in council.[29] The price of a first-class stamp was subsequently increased to twelve cents in 1977, fourteen cents in 1978, and seventeen cents in 1979 — without parliamentary approval. The Opposition was incensed at this usurping of its authority. The joint parliamentary committee on regulations concluded that the government's action was illegal, a conclusion endorsed by the House of Commons. The government was also taken to court over its actions.[30] Nonetheless, the Liberal government persisted with this approach until it lost the 1979 election.[31]

The price experience of other classes of mail was similar. There were no serious second-class rate changes from 1968 until 1977, when, in conjunction with PMG Blais' extra-parliamentary strategy, there was a 20 per cent increase in 1977 and a 25 per cent increase in 1978. Nonetheless, there was an $880 million deficit on second-class mail from 1968-69 to 1978-79.[32] A long-building consensus suggested that the second-class subsidy should be spelled out and targeted as a distinct policy objective with a separate funding source. The POD and Secretary of State signed a memorandum of agreement in late 1978, in which the latter would provide the POD with $135 million in subsidies for the delivery of periodical publications. This figure was the estimated difference between the POD's costs and the second-class revenues it received.[33]

Table 3 shows that price increases alleviated but did not solve the problem of the deficit. Save for during 1979-80, the deficit as a proportion of postal revenues remained over 30 per cent. The accumulated deficit was $3.5 billion between 1972 and 1981. A 1978 POD study found that over the previous five years, the revenue per piece of mail rose by only 26 per cent while costs rose by 92 per cent.[34]

Outside of the price area, there were some examples of service rationalizations. A fee was introduced in 1976 for the Notice of Change of Address to the Postmaster. The POD announced that in 1977 it was eliminating its re-addressing service (which had but a 30 per cent success rate). And charges for Parcel Post were altered in 1976 to reflect the distance travelled; this was the first departure in Canadian postal history from the principle of a universal postal charge.

Generally, rationalization of postal services slowed considerably after Kierans' initiatives. The quintessential example was rural post offices. PMG Côté concluded that the savings generated by rural postal closings were so small that they weren't worth the resulting political disruption. PMG Ouellet promised to maintain the network of thirty-nine hundred rural post offices, despite its contribution to the postal deficit. "This is a price we have to pay in a large country like ours," he suggested; "to give the same service to every Canadian we have to pay a little extra. Generally speaking, I think the public is ready to pay the little extra." PMG Blais did not pursue his officials' recommendations to cut the rural network, fearing a loss of political credibility. Despite its own recommendations, the POD was not especially motivated to insist on rural postal closings. The PMG would probably duck any resulting political fallout, exposing the POD itself to the political reaction from MPs and the media.[35] Post offices opened and closed, but Table 6 demonstrates that the post office network stayed intact. There were 8,564 post offices in 1972, a level that increased to 8,710 in 1974 before slowly declining to 8,275 in 1981. This represented a modest 3.4 per cent decrease over the ten-year period.

Door-to-door mail delivery followed a similar pattern. Expansion of this service was frozen by Kierans to limit costs, but was "unfrozen" in 1972. A freeze was reimposed in 1975 as part of the government's anti-inflation program. A document leaked in 1978 suggested that the POD planned to eliminate 2,670 letter carriers by a reduction in door-to-door service. The alternative mode of delivery — group mail boxes — had been introduced as an experiment in new suburban areas. Alternate day delivery was also mooted. PMG Blais disassociated himself from the report and alternative approaches, declaring that home delivery was an essential service. The prospect of limited home delivery generated considerable political reaction, particularly in areas hard hit by the policy (e.g., suburbs). According to Blais, it was the issue raised most often in caucus (he himself tried to get home delivery for his riding of Sturgeon Falls in northern Ontario). In response to considerable political pressure from cabinet and caucus, Lamontagne lifted the freeze in March 1979 to extend service to all communities whose population was at least 150,000. This expanded letter carrier service to another 160,000 addresses at a cost of $15 million. Asked if the impending May election was a factor in this decision, Lamontagne replied: "Well let's be honest, it didn't harm it . . . whatever we do these days is because of the election." This decision did not emanate from postal management. It swallowed the increased costs, recognizing the political pressures on the PMG.[36] Despite periodic freezes, home deliveries rose in the 1970s. In the period 1960–61 to 1970–71, the number of addresses served increased by 47 per cent from 3 million to 4.4 million (see Table 6); the increase in the following decade was roughly comparable — 44 per cent, to 6.34 million.

Ironically, while service rationalization was being halted, the POD was criticized for not providing adequate postal service. Indeed, there was a broad consensus that postal service had declined, if not deteriorated badly.[37]

Commercial Orientation

Instead of raising prices and rationalizing service, the government proposed to remedy the POD's competitive and financial difficulties by increasing postal business and productivity. The latter involved mechanization, which will be explored in the following section; the former involved diversification, to be examined in this one

Rejecting a price increase in 1973, PMG Ouellet presented aggressive marketing and product diversification as revenue-generating tactics to get the POD's deficit under control. Similarly, PMG Blais declared, "I would like to see us shift from a passive to a more active role." This orientation also reflected concerns about increased competition.[38] The new POD Marketing Department, formed under Kierans' administration, searched actively for new products and opportunities, albeit not always successfully. Assured Mail was introduced and guaranteed next-day delivery; the program was dropped quietly in July 1979 after generating more confusion than revenue.[39] Other innovations were more successful. The POD introduced Telepost in 1972, which combined CN/CP telex with first-class mail delivery. This was expanded into Intelpost (International Electronic Post) in 1980. In conjunction with CNCP Telecommunication and Teleglobe Canada, the POD began sending mail by satellite between Toronto and London. It was the first postal system in the world to offer such a service, by 1984 offered to twenty-four countries. In October 1974, the POD introduced a certified mail service. In January 1979, Priority Post offered overnight service between major cities. The latter was especially successful, responding to businesses' increasing need for rapid delivery in situations where price was a secondary consideration. This service was expanded to small and medium-sized cities in 1980.

These were significant but relatively modest developments, reflecting the fact that diversification was constrained by political and ideological factors. For example, the POD located post offices in commercial settings, such as Toronto's Fairview Mall, in order to increase retail activities. The Department of Public Works complained about the high rents for these locations. This "forced" the POD to expand into other product lines to generate sufficient revenue to pay the rent. The POD was already interested in increasing retail sales in its post offices. It had sold postal-related products such as string, wrapping paper, and tape, as well as coin sets from the Mint, postal products, stamp albums, and Canadiana such as Canadian flag lapels and native headbands. These minor commercial initiatives were assaulted from all quarters. The auditor general criticized the POD's retail activities, for which it had no mandate under the Post Office Act. The retail strategy was then savaged at the Public Accounts Committee hearings in 1975. MP Blackburn attacked the POD for selling lapel pins at a cheaper price than a gift shop owner in his constituency: "I would like to know why Canada Post was in that business? Was it to make a profit? Was it to undercut small boutique owners and gift shop operators?" Deputy PMG Mackay admitted that "it was recognized shortly afterwards, from the uproar created by some of the private entrepreneurs, that this might be cutting into the business, hence our withdrawal from the sale of those sorts of items . . . maybe not enough consideration was given to the impact this might have on the private sector." Mackay insisted that the products were introduced for the convenience of customers, rather than as a means to generate profits or reduce its deficit.

Using tortured logic, he claimed that the POD was simply trying to bring in more customers: "Indirectly, yes, it was not to try to reduce the deficit but to earn more revenue which in turn would reduce the deficit." MP Schumacher characterized the public market reaction to postal diversification when he insisted that "the Post Office should be concerning itself with the movement of the mail first . . . before it launches into any other activity it should solve the problems of moving mail." The episode ended with Mackay promising that, other than Mint sets, no non-postal items would henceforth be sold.[40]

The diversification strategy was built on an internal contradiction. The POD was encouraged to become more commercially oriented, in order to generate more revenue to keep prices and the deficit down. But commercialization and diversification were constrained by private-sector reactions and cries of "unfair competition." The mid-1970s diversification experiment ended abruptly, upon direction from the private sector, parliamentary committees, and cabinet.[41]

Other ambitious projects were halted. PMG Blais and his officials mooted the idea of using the POD's retail presence to offer one-stop banking services. This was vetoed by the Department of Finance.[42] The POD was directed to stay away from the burgeoning field of telecommunications. A Price Waterhouse study anticipated this issue, suggesting that the POD consider offering electronic services, but warning of

> the question of whether expansion in the uses of services offered by CP would be politically acceptable . . . resistance must be expected from those opposed in principle to the growth of the public sector, and from the telephone companies and suppliers of other competing information transfer services.

This reaction was not long in coming. The Ministry of Communications commissioned the Clyne Committee to produce recommendations on the telecommunications future and its impact on Canadian sovereignty. The committee insisted that the POD stay out of this sector, as it had the potential to destabilize the industry. Later, the Conservatives' Ritchie Report also recommended that the POD be directed to stay out of the telecommunications field. PMG Blais broached this issue with his cabinet colleague Jeanne Sauvé at the Ministry of Communication, suggesting that their departments work together in the modern telecommunications world. Her initial reaction was positive, but then her senior officials vetoed the idea, arguing that it was evident that the private sector did not want the POD to be involved.[43]

The diversification strategy promised to improve the POD's financial situation, without price increases or service cuts; but private-sector and political reactions rendered it a chimera.

Mechanization

The second dominant element of postal policy during this period was increasing productivity through mechanization, a fascinating, complicated, and tragic story that demands a fuller and more technically informed exposition than can be offered here.[44] This section outlines the process of mechanization; its implications are analyzed in the following section.

The origins of mechanization lie in the late 1950s and early 1960s, when its nuances and challenges were first discussed. The realization of a mechanized postal system was related to decisions taken in the late 1960s and early 1970s. The key policy decision was to choose which mechanized system to use. Samson, Belair, Riddell, and Stead were commissioned to evaluate the technological options available at the time, and recommended that a system of "marked mail" be used. Their report was tabled in the House of Commons in February 1970 and was accepted later by the POD and cabinet.

In the marked mail system, all addresses are translated into a national postal code system. The mailer places both the address and the appropriate postal code on the envelope. This postal code can then be "translated" into a machine-readable binary code on the envelope, by a sorting operator or by a computer. The code is printed on the envelope, allowing for mass sorting and directing later on "downstream." The sorting can be done by an operator or by an optical character recognition (OCR) machine, which "reads" the postal code and sorts and directs it. The mechanized system would work as follows. Once the mail arrived at a postal station, it would be moved to a "culling" station to remove oversized, undersized, and unacceptable articles. A culler-facer-canceller (CFC) teases out non-standard or overly thick mail, then faces the remaining mail up so that the stamp can be located and cancelled. Stacked on coded trays, this mail is processed by the OCR, which locates and reads the postal code and applies a coloured bar code. This code activates the letter-sorting machines, which sort the mail. Addresses that cannot be identified by the OCR are sent to operators, who key in the code. The remaining pieces are sorted by hand.

The marked mail system had technological and financial advantages, but specific implications. An envelope would have to be read just one time in order to be coded, making the system inexpensive to operate (10 per cent of the U.S. cost).[45] However, a marked mail system required a postal code system and OCR machines — neither of which existed. A national postal code system would have to be developed, and some sort of pre-sorting and letter-sorting machines would be required as an interim technological step while the OCRs were developed. Once adopted, the marked mail system would have to be applied quickly to attain national coverage so that mail coded in one part of the country could be read in all other parts of the country. Until then, productivity gains would not be realized.

The mechanization process unfolded on two tracks. First, a national postal code system was created. Kierans announced that the first coding would be released on 1 April 1971. The POD worked with its large-volume users to create the postal code system, holding fourteen meetings with over six hundred users. The original code and schedule of implementation suggested by consultants was rejected by the major users; a revised format was designed and finalized by July 1970. The POD aimed to add the code to addresses that the major users had in their computers; it decided early on to code customer lists free of charge, to accelerate the use of the postal code. Ottawa was chosen as the pilot city for coding, and the Ottawa post office received its coding system on 31 October 1970. The official start-up of the code took place on 1 April 1971. Once a city was coded, the POD moved on to code the province. The entire country was covered by the now-familiar six-character code by early November 1973. The code's use did not increase as quickly as had been anticipated. An April deadline had been set for its use, but public utilization was low through early 1975 (even the federal government's usage was only 45 per cent at the time). Since the new machines required an 80 per cent code utilization rate to run efficiently, the government considered legislating mandatory use of the postal code. This would have been a public relations and operational fiasco, so a voluntary approach was used, supplemented by mass advertising and exhortation. The POD reported in 1975–76 that the postal code was used in 55 per cent of mail volumes; in 1976–77 it reported that this had risen to 66 per cent. The media saw these figures as wishful thinking, and put use at no higher than 50 per cent at this time.[46]

The second track of implementation of the marked mail system was mechanization. While waiting for the OCRs to be developed, the POD purchased a number of pre-sorting and letter-sorting machines from IT&T in late 1971 and early 1972 and was able to handle mail mechanically by April 1972. This was a complicated process, inasmuch as the POD was ordering a generation of equipment that would soon be supplanted by the next generation. Tenders were called for the OCRs in May 1972. In March 1973 Treasury Board approved the purchase of thirty-three OCRs from Leigh for $12.5 million. The first of the machines arrived in March 1974. Meanwhile, the Ottawa plant in Alta Vista was becoming Canada's first mechanized postal plant. Letter-sorting machines were first used in August 1972, and PMG Ouellet started up the first Canadian-built postal machine in July 1973. The system was fully in place by February 1974, with forty-eight coding desks and four LSMs. The strategy was to open new plants in the smaller centres first. Nine facilities had letter sorters by 1974–75, including Winnipeg, Regina, and Calgary. The Toronto plants were to open in 1975–76 (actual opening, 1977) and Montreal in 1978–79 (actual, 1980). Nineteen of thirty plants had mechanical sorters by 1976–77, twenty-six of them by 1977–78, and twenty-eight of them by 1978–79.

The mechanization of the Canadian postal system was a complicated undertaking and its evolution was not without incident. Some problems were of the POD's making, but the central feature of mechanization was the speed with which it was carried out. No postal system in the world mechanized its operations as quickly as did the Canadian POD. The rationale for this pace was simple. There would be no productivity until the entire system was in place, with mail coded in one postal centre able to be read in any other centre. Until then, manual and mechanized sorting systems would operate side by side — a complicated and expensive prospect.[47] There may have been a technical misunderstanding of this on the part of politicians. Kierans' view was that the new machines would be added on one at a time, as postal volumes increased. Similarly, Côté did not anticipate that the mechanized system would require new and larger postal plants to be constructed all at once.[48]

Politically, mechanization was embraced. The POD proposed to cabinet that the postal system be mechanized, using the marked mail system. As growing mail volumes required more workers (whose wages were rising), the POD argued that mechanization could cope with volumes while keeping (labour) costs under control. It also maintained that the marked mail system could be initiated and implemented with minimal transition costs and quick productivity pay-offs. The proposal was strongly supported by Treasury Board, and cabinet approved the mechanization plan with little to no political struggle. This is perhaps the most astonishing feature of the story. The costs of mechanization and modernization were enormous, but financing was assigned without incident, in stark contrast to the POD's treatment in the past, when it was constantly starved for funding. Treasury Board was convinced that now was the time to mechanize and made the money available. As well, this was an era in which government officials believed that spending money could solve any problem. Finally, government felt that mechanization would solve the POD's bedeviling labour problems.[49] There were nonetheless ebbs and flows to the financing of mechanization, which had important consequences. Mechanization was carried out simultaneously with the modernization of postal facilities, for two reasons. First, postal plant was old and decrepit, and various consultants declared that the POD had to modernize its facilities. Second, the mechanization process required the construction of larger plants, to house the new sorting equipment and to deal with increasing volumes. Cabinet also approved the Major Area Postal Plants project and Treasury Board approved the funding. Twenty-two new facilities were initiated in 1973, and the process would continue across Canada through the 1970s. But the financing of the expansion of the plants was not completely in the POD's control. For example, Treasury Board directed the POD to consolidate the planned letter and parcel plants in Toronto, in order to cut costs. This resulted in the construction of the enormous and infamous Gateway facility, constructed on a seventy-acre site near the airport. The south-central plant in Toronto was twice as large as planned, as the North Toronto plant was never built. The pace of change was also accelerated by the POD's own needs. For example, in order to avoid the freeze in work conditions that comes under contract negotiations, the POD rushed the move from the old Toronto plants into the new ones — with some consequences when the new machines could not handle peak loads.[50]

The mechanization program apparently cost $1 billion, far above its original $150–200 million financing. The billion-dollar figure is misleading, however, as it includes the costs of the major buildings program. Parts of the latter would have ensued regardless of mechanization, as volumes were increasing and postal plants were outdated. According to the 1977–78 POD report, $900 million was spent on new equipment and facilities from 1972–73 to 1977–78. At this time, the mechanization program was considered more than 80 per cent complete.[51]

The pace of mechanization conflicted with the principle of consultation. As will be explored more fully below, the postal unions were consulted to a certain extent about mechanization. The cabinet and PMG assured postal workers that "no one in the Post Office is expected to lose his job because of automation or mechanization." PMG Kierans appended a letter to the 1970 contract in this regard: "The planned modernization program will not result in layoffs of present fulltime employees during the life of the present agreement provided that employees will accept relocation, reassignment and retraining." Mechanization was also promoted as offering increased job satisfaction and decreased drudgery and routine. Assurances were given throughout the mechanization process that, as PMG Mackasey put it, "our number one priority is to assure the inside worker that he has nothing to fear from the introduction of automation."[52] The unions appeared unprepared for the size and scope of mechanization, which was not fully appreciated in the early 1970s. The nature of the technology was not fully understood; the unions seemed surprised when they discovered that mail could be read automatically by these machines.[53]

Perhaps of greater consequence was the management style of consultation, which left much to be desired. The mechanization project was carried out by J. G. Fultz, whose attitudes towards unions and workers bordered on contempt. He openly characterized the young and radical workers as "hippies" and "malcontents." Other postal managers were openly provocative in their anti-union views.[54] The nature of the technology and its implications were not understood and were poorly explained. Assured by management of a slow and incremental process, the unions felt steamrollered when the POD felt compelled to apply the system "all at once." Postal management presented their mechanization plans in broad, general, and benign terms while working as hard as possible to get the full system in place as fast as possible. The unions were not given the full details, logic, or timetable of the mechanization plan. They reacted with suspicion and dragged their feet to slow down the mechanization program. Whereas postal management assumed mechanization would be in the interests of all, the unions perceived it as a threat and sought a greater say in its implementation and greater access to its benefits.

Policy Results and Implications

Postal politics in the 1970s were grim and chaotic, largely owing to policy decisions and policy inactivity. The most dramatic results were on the labour front, where labour-management relations degenerated into endless guerrilla warfare. The POD's financial and competitive situation did not improve, because the benefits of mechanization were a long time coming. Chaos on the labour front, the continuing deterioration of the POD's financial picture, and political attitudes and policies towards the POD resulted in a serious deterioration of postal morale. Each of these factors will be examined in turn.

The Economics of Mechanization

The mechanization process took almost a decade to complete. The new system was not in place until 1980 and not functioning to capacity until 1982 or 1983. It is impossible here to say whether the system could have been made operative sooner or more effectively. It is evident, though, that automation did not improve postal productivity in the 1970s. Ironically, the labour force expanded substantially, despite the *raison d'être* of mechanization — to use less labour — and the postal unions' fear of job losses. Increased employment was inevitable over the short term, because two labour forces were required in this period: one to run the automated system and one to run the old, "manual" system. The latter was required for two reasons. First, until the mechanized system was fully in place, a substantial amount of mail had to be processed manually. Second, a large proportion of the mail remained "unreadable" by machines, because it was uncoded, handwritten, oversized, and so on.

The POD thus carried a double cohort of labour. As Table 4 indicates, full-time employment rose from 37,051 in 1970-71 to 53,243 in 1977-78 — an increase of 44 per cent (total employment rose by a similar amount). But mail volumes — both first-class and total volumes — rose by only 33 per cent. Despite investment of hundreds of millions of dollars in labour-saving mechanization, the growth of the labour supply outpaced that of volume by one third. Even as the expensive mechanization program unfolded, labour costs rose as a proportion of total postal expenditures, from 60 per cent in 1970 to 76 per cent in 1980 (see Table 4). Productivity declined by 8 per cent between 1971 and 1977.[55]

These facts perplexed politicians and gave ammunition to postal critics. During committee hearings in 1979, Deputy PMG Corkery explained that productivity gains could not be realized until the mechanization program was completed: "It is only in the last three months where we have got the total system talking to itself, and it is from here on in that we will start to see it progressively improved."[56] This all-or-nothing nature of the system was not widely appreciated in the early stages of mechanization. There were two other factors that contributed to the lag in productivity improvements. First, volumes were lower than anticipated because of increased competition and constant labour disruptions. This meant that the system was under-utilized. Second, Treasury Board's generous funding at the start of the process resulted in the construction of facilities that were only partially used. These facilities and their size and capacity reflected the availability of resources rather than actual need. As late as 1977, only two plants were in full operation, much of the mechanical equipment was not in use, and the final plants were not yet constructed. Again, the result was that the system was seriously under-utilized.[57]

Mechanization and Labour

A broad consensus emerged in the mid-1970s — and has persisted — that the mechanization process had been fumbled, and badly. The view is not that mechanization should not have taken place, or that the marked mail system should not have been chosen, or that it did not increase Canadian postal capacity. Rather, it is thought that the specific character of the mechanization process — and its scale and pace — did irreparable damage to labour relations and to the institution of the Post Office. Amongst many others, CPC president Warren characterized the mechanization program as one of the worst things done in Canada. The Ritchie report concluded that, on balance, the mechanization program should not have taken place.[58]

Neither postal officials nor government leaders acknowledged this at the time. Committed to mechanization, they understood the grim logic that the process had to proceed as quickly as possible if mechanization was to pay off. Negative reaction emanated from the unions, as well as from the Opposition and media, which saw that mechanization seriously undermined postal morale. A major complaint was that there had been insufficient consultation about mechanization and its implications. Conservative postal critic Dinsdale observed that "one of the reasons there are less than ideal conditions amongst postal employees is because of the way that the whole process of automation and mechanization has proceeded." Postal chaos could have been avoided, he maintained, if the Canadian POD had been as consultative in applying mechanization as postal officials had been in the United States and the United Kingdom. Deteriorating labour-management relations and worker frustration were the result of "too much haste in proceeding towards mechanization," as well as postal management's paternalistic and authoritarian perspective and approach. Opposition criticism culminated in Ronald Ritchie's report to Conservative leader Joe Clark, which concluded that the mechanization process had been an ill-considered gamble that had proceeded too far and too quickly.[59]

One consequence of the poorly planned and ill-managed rush to mechanization was the creation of horrendous working conditions. Postal officials were aware that, optimally, plant size should be kept below seven hundred workers. The POD directed Fultz to design plants with a maximum of one thousand employees. Instead, the mechanization program created enormous plants, the size of multiple football fields, with up to four thousand workers under one roof. This reflected the "big is better" thinking of the time, but was also the result of Treasury Board's directing the POD to double up facilities to limit costs. Officials recognized that these plants were too large, but nothing could be done. The media sympathized with workers' complaints: "the union often has good reason for its militancy. . .. Our postal facilities have grown bigger, more centralized, more automated, and postal workers have been called upon to endure more noise, monotony, impersonality and an off-beat work schedule." The Gateway plant in Toronto covered 1.2 million square feet — twenty-five acres under one roof. Parts of the plant produced ear-splitting noise up to eighty-nine decibels (the sound of a subway). The Ritchie report concluded that "these huge installations could scarcely be better designed to encourage all of the negative effects of large scale depersonalization."[60] These plants created an uncontrollable management situation; as President Warren observed, paramilitary routines were required to keep the plants operating, which even further undermined morale.[61]

As the mechanization process unfolded, PMGs themselves expressed concern about its implications. PMG Blais admitted in 1976 that disputes about mechanization could have been handled better and that the postal unions were taken advantage of during the early stages of consultation. Blais concluded that the mechanization process had been too ambitious and had been implemented too quickly.[62] PMG Ouellet also concluded that mechanization had been overly rushed and that the POD had been ill-prepared for it and its implications. The huge plants created a series of management problems, for which no one was prepared.[63]

Labour Negotiations in the 1970s

Mechanization exacerbated labour–management relations and increased worker militancy.[64] Lack of consultation, authoritarian management decisions, oversized and noisy plants and working conditions, and other problems gave the unions numerous issues to fight over. Mechanization and its impact was the central bargaining issue of the period.

Ironically, mechanization was not a negotiable item under the PSSRA. The act prohibited bargaining over technological change, training, lay-offs, and classification of work, which were considered to be management rights and not negotiable. But they were also the vital labour–management issues of the day. Thus, bargaining was a charade. The unions ignored the PSSRA and bargained over these non-negotiable issues; Treasury Board and the POD shrugged their shoulders and hid behind the act.[65]

Postal management and the government used the PSSRA as a shield. There were discussions about mechanization; but when push came to shove, the PSSRA was used in an offensive fashion by management. This tactic was a metaphor for managerial attitudes towards the postal unions, which were broadly anti-labour. Indeed, PMG Mackasey admitted as much:

> The government . . . has been anything but a model employer. . ..
> Inadequate compensation, work places that are a disgrace, uneven
> managerial policy, regimentation that at times bordered on a military
> mentality . . . resulted in a slow but steady reduction in morale, in
> pride of association and in inevitable hostility on the part of the
> workers.[66]

Management hostility towards workers was a cause for alarm. The Arnot-Mullington report was commissioned by Treasury Board for various reasons, including concern about management's antipathy to the unions. Mullington recounts the startling anti-union, McCarthyistic views of senior managers: postal workers were seen to be hippies and freaks, and operations personnel provocatively expressed their contempt for them. Deputy PMG Corkery admitted that managers recruited in an earlier era were terribly anti-union. Both postal management and the government exploited the public's anti-union attitude when it was to their advantage.[67] This attitude reached its nadir in the late 1970s. PMG Lamontagne, who later became minister of defence, was cheerfully anti-union and cynical about its positions. This reflected caucus opinion, particularly that of Ontario members, who were feeling the heat about constant labour disruptions. Lamontagne wanted to fire postal workers during the 1978 strike; he claimed that firing five hundred key "trouble makers" would end the POD's problems. His senior officials were also unsympathetic to the unions. After his appointment, officials briefed him on industrial relations in a paper which dripped with sarcasm and antipathy towards union positions.[68]

Treasury Board negotiated postal contracts that, given management's attitudes, may have been for the good. It did complicate matters, though. An internal POD report put it bluntly: "The present personnel policies of government established by the PSC and the Treasury Board are not always appropriate for a quasi-commercial activity such as the Post Office."[69] The conciliator in the 1972 negotiations noted that management . . . is hampered . . . because it must consider the impact of any decisions on the remaining employees in the Public Service and, in addition, management, which has the responsibility of operating the Post Office, does not effectively control the labour relations with its own employees. . .. In these negotiations one felt that each time the employer was required to reach a decision that it was looking over its shoulder at the remaining government employees. This was an impediment to sound negotiations with respect to the needs and problems of the Post Office and its employees.[70]

Treasury Board's negotiating position was set by cabinet and was driven by finance rather than policy. It often made eleventh-hour compromises on non-monetary issues to reach a deal. These did not affect its monetary guidelines, but had consequences for working conditions and practices. For example, the use of casuals and the organization of work were "costless" matters for Treasury Board, but had financial consequences for the operation of the POD. After negotiations, management tried to win back these matters, worsening labour-management relations.[71] Treasury Board's bargaining positions were set by the government's overall economic strategy; if the latter was oriented to fighting inflation, postal workers' wage interests would be "sacrificed" to this larger goal. Similarly, as the long post-war economic expansion came to an end, unemployment began to rise. Postal workers expressed anxiety about job security, but this issue was outside the bounds of bargaining, because of the terms of the PSSRA and governments' broader employment and budgetary policies.

Negotiations in this period were dispiriting and hopelessly unsuccessful. The parties were incapable of bargaining, and hardly tried. The countless conciliators of the time commented on this. "The climate of labour-management relations did not seem to be very good . . . this unhealthy climate deteriorated still further." Both parties have "inherited the frustration, mistrust and. . .the attitude of contempt which seems to have characterized the parties and the general climate of relations since early 1968." Negotiations were in a "lamentable state," the parties not having negotiated and not seeming to know how to communicate with each other. Each awaited the conciliation process as a substitute for negotiations. They met but four times before giving up: "The parties distrust each other, refuse to talk to each other and refuse to negotiate seriously." Neither side really seemed to know the other's position. The "climate was not very conducive to true conciliation . . . no real negotiations had taken place," owing to the fact that "the most complete distrust exists between the parties, each one accusing the other of bad faith."[72] The two sides were incapable of resolving differences by themselves. Settlements were reached by third-party outsiders or imposed by governments. Neither side built up a negotiating capacity or a culture of collaboration.

FIGURE 1

Work Disruptions: Person Days Lost

1970	13,248.2	1976	5,528.4
1971	3,913.6	1977	13,680.0
1972	2,313.9	1978	161,968.0
1973	7,392.8	1979	620.0
1974	174,604.0	1980	5,975.0
1975	786,667.0	1981	663,350.0

FIGURE 2

Grievances

	Lodged	*Adjudicated*
1974	1,338	96
1975	1,676	227
1976	3,408	457
1977	9,732	384

One other development should be noted here. The Council of Postal Unions had been the bargaining agent for both the inside workers (CUPW) and the letter carriers (LCUC) since unionization. After the 1974 contract, CUPW voted to disassociate itself from the CPU and applied to the PSSRB for independent negotiating authority. The PSSRB concluded that two separate unions would improve the representation of the postal workers. CUPW and LCUC negotiated separate contracts from 1975 on. Negotiations with LCUC ran smoothly; no letter carrier strikes occurred in this period. Technological change did not affect carriers to the same extent as it affected sorters. For the latter, mechanization transformed conditions of work, affected levels of pay, and created anxiety about future employment. For example, mechanization saw the POD use numerous "casual" workers, to staff the "twin" mechanical and manual systems. Expenditures on casuals grew by 181 per cent from 1970-75, compared to 68 per cent for full-time workers; CUPW estimated that 20 per cent of labour expenditures were on casuals and overtime in 1973-74.[73] Casuals were perceived by CUPW as a threat to job security. As well, mechanization raised concerns about health and safety: half of the disabling injuries in the public service in 1979 occurred in the Post Office.[74] These concerns were at the heart of relations between CUPW and the POD. The LCUC's moderate image led to CUPW's being portrayed as the "villain," which further alienated CUPW from postal management and the government.

The deterioration in labour-management relations took two primary forms: strikes and grievances. As the table above indicates, the latter grew rapidly, reflecting the guerrilla warfare that followed the operationalization of mechanization and contracts. Health and safety, job classification, the organization of work, the use of part-time and casual labour, and disciplinary procedures were fought out daily. Dismissals in the POD were higher than in other government areas. Of the total workers released for incapacity or incompetence between 1976 and 1980, 48 per cent were postal workers. In the first six months of 1979, 589 federal firings took place, 219 of which were in the POD.[75] The application of mechanization increased radicalism, which in turn increased the intensity of discipline. There were no letter carrier strikes, but there were four strikes involving CUPW in 1974, 1975, 1978, and 1981, which the table below shows involved a considerable amount of lost time.

I will eschew detailed analysis of negotiations in this period[76] and instead focus on the difficulties confronted in negotiations, how these difficulties were managed, and the government's role in negotiations. The remainder of this section highlights the labour difficulties generated by mechanization and their implications for postal policy.

Negotiations in 1972 were a paradigm of negotiations throughout the 1970s. Talks began in February and broke down in August. Postal workers wanted more money than Treasury Board was offering.[77] More importantly, the CPU sought job security and assurances that the classification scheme would not destroy the seniority system and cut wages. In establishing a conciliation board, PSSRB Chair Finkelman suggested that the board examine the issue of job security, even though this was not really within the its terms of reference.[78] It reported on 14 December, with economic recommendations favouring the unions (the government representative dissented).[79] The report proposed that the POD operate a form of industrial democracy, to deal with the issue of job security. Wage security should be guaranteed for employees, even if automation changed the character of their jobs. The board urged labour to be given a say in applying the new technology. Since "the introduction of technological change is a matter of mutual interest," it recommended the creation of a "manpower" Committee composed of four representatives of the CPU, four representatives of the POD, and an independent advisor. The committee would be authorized to discuss technological change, job descriptions, wages in redesigned jobs, the use of casuals, dispersion of the postal machines, and deployment of the workforce. The government representative on the board dissented, asserting that the board had no jurisdiction to make such a recommendation.[80] The CPU negotiating committee rejected the conciliation report (6-4), but the membership in turn narrowly accepted the report (52 per cent). After weeks of silence, Treasury

Board accepted the report on 15 January 1973. A tentative deal was struck on 24 January and was confirmed by postal workers by a 72 per cent vote on 15 February.[81]

These negotiations indicated the extent to which bargaining was constrained under the PSSRA. Indeed, it was unclear whether what had been proposed could be legally acted upon. There were prospects for a more collaborative approach to mechanization; but there was no sense that the conciliation board had the authority to make this recommendation, and no guarantee that its "industrial democracy" model was in fact legal.

These negotiations set the scene for the "coder" dispute, which shaped the contours of labour–management relations for the rest of the decade. The dispute was hardly earth shattering in its significance, but it dragged on for thirty months. In the process, it disrupted postal operations and alienated labour still further from postal management and the government.[82]

The dispute started when the new coding desks arrived at the Alta Vista plant in 1972. Operating the desks required little skill; the job would be fairly boring. Treasury Board had the authority to classify this new job, which it set at PO1 — the lowest level on the scale — without consulting the union. The PO1 rate was $2.94 an hour, 20 per cent less than the PO4 level of an experienced clerk and 50 per cent lower than the wage of the postal worker who sorted the mail manually. Not surprisingly, no one from inside the union applied for the lower-paying and boring job. In the union's eyes, reclassification and the creation of the coder position undermined the government's promise that mechanization would not cut wages or eliminate jobs. The union lodged a complaint at the PSSRB, which noted that while management held classification rights, Treasury Board should have made greater efforts to consult. It directed Treasury Board to negotiate a mutually satisfactory pay rate for the coder position. But there were no mechanisms at the POD for this sort of discussion. The anticipated manpower committee had not been formed; despite being recommended in December 1972, it would not meet until April 1974. Thus, Treasury Board did not pursue consultation with any alacrity. Wildcat actions developed; a "boycott the postal code" was organized in Montreal; and suspensions, sympathy walkouts, and injunctions proliferated. These disruptions spread to forty-five cities in April 1974. CUPW president Davidson announced that he would recommend an illegal nation-wide strike unless the coding dispute and related matters were resolved. The dispute was costing the POD $500,000 a day.[83]

The coder dispute symbolized a mélange of union concerns about mechanization, insufficient consultation, the non-functioning of the promised manpower committee, and reclassification. PMG Ouellet assured postal workers that "permanent employees . . . have no reason to fear being kicked out, laid off, or being forced to work at lower rates." In April, he named Eric Taylor to mediate the dispute. He recommended to a hastily formed manpower committee that the coders be classified at PO4. Negotiations continued throughout the summer and fall, with interim compromises cooling off the dispute. A final solution was reached in December, to fudge classification by having the job description include worker knowledge. Coders would do other tasks, to increase the skill level of the job; the job could thus be ranked higher. No employees would be left at the PO1 rank.[84]

The bitter coder dispute led to a further deterioration in labour-management relations. The absence of institutional machinery was critical, allowing the dispute to drag on longer than it should have. The issue was set by Treasury Board's responsibility in the matter of pay and classification. This undermined the POD's capacity to manage technological change. Senior officials felt that the dispute could have been avoided. Deputy PMG Sinclair stated that "we would have been quite happy to have the coders classified at a fairly high sorter level. The additional dollars compared to the size of the mechanization program were infinitesimal. But being in the public service, you were a slave to the classification system."[85] Future deputy PMG Corkery argued that the issue could have been resolved, but the POD was boxed in by Treasury Board, who would not budge on the issue.[86]

The inside and outside workers negotiated separate contracts from 1975 on. Each followed a different trajectory, mainly because the mechanization process did not pose as great a threat to the letter carriers as it did to the inside workers. The LCUC bargained hard and fairly successfully, but its negotiating agenda was not nearly as ambitious or as politically or ideologically charged as CUPW's. Relations between LCUC and Treasury Board and postal management were thus not as stressful. Negotiations proceeded relatively "smoothly," centring mainly on monetary matters. Settlements were reached without strike action in 1975, 1977, 1978, 1980, and 1981.

Negotiations in 1975 were not without incident; in late April up to one quarter of carriers were off the job (the Montreal carriers defied the union after a settlement was reached). The settlement included a cost-of-living allowance, which set a precedent in the federal public service, and reflected to a considerable extent the direct involvement of PMG Mackasey.[87] The 1977 negotiations proceeded more smoothly. Two weeks of conciliation concluded successfully in mid-August. The one-year agreement included an 8 per cent wage increase, extension of weekend premiums and injury leave to part-time workers, and four weeks of vacation after thirteen years of service.[88]

The 1978 negotiation process was constrained by two non-postal government policies. First, the Anti-Inflation Board ruled that nineteen cents an hour of LCUC's cost-of-living agreement was beyond the legislated wage limit. Second, Bill C-28 amended the PSSRA, directing arbitrators to consider private-sector wage levels and settlements when making salary recommendations ("comparability"). The LCUC felt that its past moderation was being ignored by a government determined to show its anti-inflation firmness. The union was given a strike mandate on 14 September, and rotating strikes began on 22 September. They were called off on 25 September, when PMG

Ouellet became directly involved in negotiations. A letter was attached to the agreement addressing LCUC concerns about mechanization. The POD would not restructure delivery routes for the life of the contract, even when the introduction of machinery reduced route times.[89]

The 1980 LCUC contract was the first to be reached without resort to a strike or third-party involvement. A one-year settlement focused on job security and protection from inflation. There was again substantial political involvement in the process, with Prime Minister Clark, PMG Fraser, and Treasury Board president Stevens intervening to alter earlier Treasury Board positions.[90] Treasury Board then insisted on exclusive control of negotiations in 1980-81, which were very tough. LCUC vice president William Findlay described the negotiations as "the worst I've ever sat on." Treasury Board aimed to remove the cost-of-living allowance clause and to change job security provisions. But in the end, the contract perpetuated the *status quo*.[91]

Negotiations with LCUC were characterized by four features. First, they were settled with a high degree of political involvement. Second, political goals such as the government's anti-inflation targets shaped the negotiation process. Third, the mechanization issue had an increasing impact, particularly with regard to job security. Finally, settlements were fairly generous and were reached with a modicum of labour disruption.

Negotiations with CUPW were of a different character. The first process in 1975 led to a bitter strike, for CUPW sensed that this might be its last opportunity to influence how the mechanization program was implemented.[92] Asked if his union enjoyed public support, CUPW president Joe Davidson gave the memorable reply: "At the moment I'm becoming a little frustrated, and I say this, maybe I shouldn't say it, if the public doesn't see the justice of our cause then to hell with the public." Early bargaining was fruitless, marked by periodic work slow-downs, vicious name calling, and accusations of unfair bargaining. There were three main issues in dispute. First, CUPW and Treasury Board were over two dollars an hour apart on wages. Second, CUPW wanted to limit the use of casual workers; Treasury Board insisted that management be allowed to staff according to its needs. Third, CUPW demanded a greater say in the mechanization program; postal management insisted this was its exclusive responsibility.[93] A conciliator was appointed in mid-June but gave up by the end of the month. Negotiations dragged on over the summer. A new conciliation board was established in September.[94]

The conciliation report made two critical recommendations regarding technological change. First, it asserted that "the decision to proceed with technological change belongs to the employer." But, second, it introduced the principle that "neither an employee, nor a group of employees, must suffer an injustice or wrong or be deprived of any of their rights . . . as a result of automation." The employer should be *obliged to redress any wrong that might result from the exercise of that right.*[95] The Moisan report assuaged

CUPW's concerns, but a strike vote received 69 per cent support. A national postal strike began on 21 October and lasted a record forty-two days. Anticipating a long strike, PMG Mackasey argued that it would be better to resolve the many issues in this way than to have a number of small strikes. The minister's firmness on the wage question was underlined when the government imposed a system of wage and price controls in October. Agreements signed after 14 October would have to adhere to guidelines set by the Anti-Inflation Board. In late November, Mackasey met with CUPW and CLC officials, using former associate deputy minister Bernard Wilson as a go-between. A remarkable number of issues remained on the table: weekend premiums, shift differentials, a cost-of-living allowance, reduction of wage differentials, limits on casuals, improvements in overtime allocation, improved benefits for injuries, and transfer rights. Mackasey proposed to write a letter appended to the contract to the effect that if technological changes improved productivity, some of the benefits would be passed on to postal workers by shortening the work week.[96]

A tentative settlement was reached on 30 November. It was accepted by CUPW members on 2 December by the slightest of margins, 662 votes (of 14,591 votes cast). CUPW did not gain wage improvements, but it did make a number of gains. Some were not obvious or appreciated; for example, part-time workers would now climb the pay scale after two years' employment (previously they remained at the starting rate). Other gains were more obvious, such as clause 39, which limited the use of casuals in insisting that regular and part-time workers be used in predictable circumstances.[97] CUPW's key accomplishment was article 29 on technological change. The Canada Labour Code clause on technological change was injected into the postal contract (this was precisely the clause that the PSSRA disallowed), promising to eliminate the adverse employment effects of mechanization. It required the POD to give ninety days' advance notice before introducing a technological change, which was defined as equipment or methods that affected more than one worker. The POD would be required to provide a detailed description of what was proposed. Constructive and meaningful consultations between the two parties would then have to follow. If agreement or compromise could not be reached, or grievances developed, then the issue would go to a "special adjudication committee." CUPW president Davidson hailed article 29 as a pioneering break-through: "We have won what is probably the best contract language on technological change in North America if not the world." However, the language in the clause was very broad and general, and each side could try to use the clause to its own advantage. Moreover, the proposed process rested on the good faith of the POD, as the union had no right to strike over its implementation.[98]

Any strike casts long shadows on the memories and attitudes of the players involved; a forty-two-day strike cast especially long shadows, and union attitudes towards postal management and the government hardened.

Each side demonstrated an incapacity to negotiate with the other. The intractability of mechanization issues exposed the continuing absence of adequate institutional mechanisms to engineer and manage postal modernization. Oddly, the Anti-Inflation Board ruled that the settlement was too high; the government rejected this ruling on the next day.[99] Estimates were that the strike had cost leading postal users $275 million. On the other hand, private couriers, Bell telephone, and the banks benefitted immensely; POD volumes and revenues plummeted. CUPW itself did not escape undamaged. The media portrayed it as the villain of the episode, and public opinion turned distinctly anti-union during and after the strike.[100]

The protracted and painful 1975 strike should have settled the question of technological change. Instead, the issue continued to be rehearsed through the remainder of the decade. The POD had been surprised when the government agreed to article 29; management felt that this undercut its authority and capacity to implement the mechanization program. Deputy PMG Mackay and senior management disliked the clause's generality and its inclusive features. In a classic example of undoing what had been negotiated by others, the POD moved to limit article 29's potential impact. Indeed, management proceeded with mechanization as if the clause did not exist. First, the POD generally insisted that the clause was not legally binding, as it contravened the PSSRA. Moreover, it defined "'technological change'" in the narrowest of terms, asserting that if a change did not involve a new piece of equipment or technique that had never been used somewhere before, then it was not a technological change. If a new piece of equipment had been used somewhere previously, article 29 would not apply. Given that all the new machines and techniques had been used somewhere by 1975, on this reading article 29 was more or less useless.[101]

This issue came to a head in May 1976. CUPW applied for a restraining order to prevent the implementation of proposed changes at St. John's (and changes about to be initiated in Windsor and London). The POD maintained that the equipment to be introduced in Newfoundland had already been used in Calgary; thus, no notification or bargaining was required. At the May hearings, CUPW won a small moral victory but lost the war. Adjudicator E. B. Joliffe ruled that the POD had violated the contract by not giving proper notice and more detailed information and by not offering more meaningful consultation. However, he could not do anything about the POD's actions. Article 29 did not set out any penalties for this sort of behaviour. Indeed, he noted "that there are no words in Article 29 . . . providing that a technological change shall not be implemented until after the procedures established therein are exhausted." Joliffe also maintained that the union had not demonstrated that "irreparable harm" would be done if the machinery was introduced. Finally, even if article 29 had been contravened, he noted that adjudicators have no power to penalize management under the PSSRA.[102]

Article 29 had thus quickly become a dead issue. Frustrated by this disappointing development, CUPW organized a series of illegal rotating strikes in fall 1976 and the summer and fall of 1977, to slow down the implementation of technological change. It launched further grievances, adjudications, and court cases. The government then took CUPW to court to stop its illegal strikes. All the while, the POD insisted that article 29 was in conflict with the PSSRA and that the latter should prevail — ensuring that technological change would be an exclusive managerial concern.[103]

PMG Blais finally halted this two-year internecine warfare. When first appointed, he agreed with his officials' view of how the mechanization process was unfolding. But he was less convinced that the POD was acting properly, the more he learned about the situation. Ultimately, he concluded that what his department was doing constituted technological change. "I read the contract, I looked at the circumstances that were at issue, and I said, 'There's no question in my mind. These are technological changes' . . . there was resistance, but once the arguments were advanced, my officials accepted."[104] However, by this time — well into 1977 — the POD had moved the mechanization program along to a great extent. The technological parade had essentially passed the unions by.

Contract talks in 1977–78 returned to the scene of the 1975 negotiations, to clarify the Article 29 clause on technological change. Talks in May 1977 broke off after one day. This set the stage for a miserable summer punctuated by illegal walk-outs, union protests over management's communications with postal workers, the acclamation of Jean-Claude Parrot as CUPW president, and the advent of mass advertising campaigns. CUPW promoted the idea of a postal corporation in an ad campaign: "A Crown Corporation Will Deliver." The government launched its own $350,000 campaign in August, appealing for public support for the POD: "Canada's mail system has taken about all the knocks it can handle. . .. There is nothing wrong that discussion and reason can't put right."[105]

Three weeks of failed talks in October set the scene for the longest conciliation hearings in Canadian labour history. CUPW's demands centred on putting teeth into article 29. Over and above the issues of technological change, job classification, and the organization of work, it made demands regarding work measurement and surveillance, grievance procedures, casuals, workers, a shorter work week, and improved benefits.[106] Governmental proceedings were based on the view that PMG Mackasey had given everything away in 1975, so that the "unworkable" and "unacceptable" deal had to be undone. PMG Lamontagne declared four non-negotiable negotiating positions: the POD would proceed with technological change; it would contract out work; it would use casual and temporary workers to meet peak demands; and it would measure work performance.[107]

The Courtemanche conciliation board's 5 October report was not favourable to CUPW on salary, work week, part-time work, and other matters.

Courtemanche agreed with his predecessor Moisan that technological change is the employer's right and that management has the duty to redress its adverse effects. The mechanisms put in place to the latter end did not seem to be working: "This is largely due to the parties not having given it a chance to work. The parties should realize that they have been leading a path which could soon lead to disaster."[108]

Perceiving that the report rolled back the 1975 contract, CUPW called a national strike, to begin on 17 October. The government wanted to avoid a strike during a possible federal election.[109] Labour Minister Ouellet and his associate deputy minister, William Kelly, at the eleventh hour unsuccessfully attempted to head off the strike. There was a split in cabinet over PMG Lamontagne's call to introduce back-to-work legislation immediately. Prime Minister Trudeau backed Lamontagne, and a consensus eventually developed.[110] Bill C-8 legislated CUPW back to work on 17 October, the very day it could begin a strike. Ouellet maintained that the choice was "either to allow the strike to continue with no hope of settlement . . . or legislate an end to the work stoppage."[111] The bill was unfavourable to CUPW: it imposed binding arbitration on rather narrow grounds, automation issues were not to be considered, and wage increases were limited by the 6 per cent anti-inflation guidelines. The legislation also imposed harsh penalties if the union did not comply with the order: workers could be fined $100 a day, union officials $250 a day, and CUPW $1,000 a day. The union could be decertified and the strikers dismissed. The government and CUPW then began a war of nerves. After unsuccessfully suing to have the legislation declared invalid, CUPW recommended that its members continue to exercise their right to strike until a new contract was in place. A week-long illegal strike began on 18 October. Defiance of the government legislation was extensive. On 19 October, only seventeen Montreal and eighty-one Toronto postal employees arrived at work. On 22 October, there were no workers at the Gateway plant in Toronto and only sixteen at the south-central plant. The strike ended when a court order obliged CUPW president Parrot to retract any previous strike calls he had made and to order his postal workers back to work.[112] This was an extraordinary episode. It showed the depth of CUPW's radicalism and unity as well as the government's determination. The government later laid charges against the postal unions' leaders; Parrot was given a three-month prison sentence for defying Parliament. After appeals up to the Supreme Court, he was sent to jail on 29 January 1980.[113]

As Glasbeek and Mandel have argued, the government's treatment of Parrot and CUPW was especially harsh and its withdrawal of the right to strike fundamentally unfair. The legislation was passed before the strike started, while there was no evidence of an emergency. Moreover, the government had played both sides of the fence. At the start of negotiations, the POD had informed the government that CUPW could not muster the support for a strike.[114] The government thus negotiated accordingly. When the POD analysis turned out to be wrong — after essentially useless negotiations — the government then withdrew the right to strike. Further, the severity of Bill C-8's penalties seemed out of proportion to the situation. The PSSRA already provided for penalties. The government contrived the requirement that Parrot rescind his earlier statements in order to assign CUPW the responsibility of getting the postal workers back to work. The government thereby forced Parrot to speak against his conscience.[115]

The 1977 negotiations concluded anticlimactically in April 1979, when Tremblay issued the binding agreement. Former Chief Justice of the Quebec Court of Appeal, Tremblay had no previous labour or postal experience. The arbitration worked to CUPW's disadvantage, which, given the legislated end to the strike and Parrot's prison sentence, was a bitter pill to swallow. Tremblay rejected most of CUPW's monetary demands and its positions on casuals, work measurement, and surveillance.[116] He also rejected the union's demand for a veto on technological change: "It is generally recognized that the introduction of technological changes in the Post Office is the responsibility and prerogative of the employer and that he alone is to decide when the introduction is to be carried out."[117]

The government made a strike-free settlement a political priority in 1980, for it wanted a smooth transition to the postal Crown corporation. Legislation was already being drafted to this end and would be introduced in July 1980. The government was thus determined that Treasury Board would not be the lead agent in negotiations; this responsibility was assigned to PMG Ouellet, who was given a broad mandate and large purse by cabinet in order to reach a contract agreement without a lengthy and costly strike. The government also wanted to mend its fences with the labour movement. Indeed, CLC president McDermott was deeply involved in negotiations with PMG Ouellet and CUPW president Parrot. These events combined to ensure a smooth and generous road to settlement.[118]

CUPW aimed to negotiate back what it had lost or not attained in the 1977–78 arbitration. It placed an incredible ninety-eight items on the table, including job security, a reduced work week, overtime at doubletime, increased shift premiums, better vacations and benefits, a higher proportion of day jobs, a decline in the number of part-time jobs, an end to monitoring and measurement, and protection against inflation. On these and most other issues, the POD negotiated for the *status quo*.[119] Negotiations headed to conciliation in April, and the Jutras report was issued in mid-May that formed the basis of the ensuing settlement, struck a week later. The majority report was unusually pro-union on wages, protection from inflation, full-time jobs, and job security.[120] After three days of intensive negotiations among Ouellet, Parrot, and McDermott, a one-year settlement was reached and eventually ratified by 90 per cent of CUPW's members. The settlement included a wage increase of 8 per cent, a 1979 cost-of-living allowance of seventy-nine cents an hour, improved procedures to expedite grievances, and enhanced overtime and shift premiums. A paid lunch hour and a reduction in the work week to 37.5 hours were "financed" by a productivity agreement, with CUPW guaranteeing 40 hours of output in the reduced hours. POD backed down on insisting on work measurement.

Thus occurred the first strike-free settlement with CUPW in fifteen years. The essential factor was that the political winds had changed since 1977–78. The settlement was a generous one; Treasury Board costed it at $36 million. Ouellet said it comprised a 10.4 per cent increase. But opposition spokesperson Stevens insisted that the agreement had cost the government between 24 and 27 per cent.[121]

The 1980 contract was for only one year, as it was to be the last contract signed by the POD. This would provide the new postal Crown corporation with a relatively clean contractural slate. But the transition to corporate form took longer than anticipated, and another contract had to be negotiated under departmental conditions. The key players in the early 1980s – PMG Ouellet and CPC president Michael Warren – were not involved in these negotiations. Cabinet kept Ouellet away from the bargaining process, seeing him as having given away the shop in 1980. CUPW asked for Warren to be involved, but he declined unless given full negotiating authority. Cabinet considered the idea but stayed with Treasury Board as its negotiating agent.[122] This "farewell" negotiation between Treasury Board and CUPW followed the dispiriting pattern of the past and led to a six-week strike, from 30 June to 10 August 1981. Two months later, the Post Office Department became Canada Post Corporation.

Negotiations began months after the previous contract had ended. Seven futile bargaining meetings led to collapse. A conciliation board was struck in February.[123] CUPW had a long list of demands in economic and non-economic areas[124] – including a maternity leave program (43 per cent of its members were women). It proposed that the POD make up the difference between a member's regular salary and the weekly payment financed by the six-month unpaid maternity leave provision of UIC. Treasury Board balked at setting a precedent for the rest of the civil service. The conciliation board reported in 19 June, splitting three ways. Chair Jasmin favoured the *status quo* recommendations, given the imminent transition to the Crown corporation form, but he recommended paid maternity leave as a social right. He proposed a scheme whereby the POD would pay the two weeks of salary before UIC payments started and would top up UIC payments to full salary.[125]

Treasury Board rejected most of the Jasmin report. CUPW produced an unprecedented 84 per cent strike vote on 24 June; after talks broke off on 26 June, a national strike began on 29 June.[126] Treasury Board was stubborn, determined to keep CUPW's contract comparable to those in the private sector. A $100,000 advertising campaign tried to sway union and public opinion.[127] Treasury Board was perceived to have fumbled the negotiations. Opposition leader Clark supported CUPW and asserted that Treasury Board had deliberately provoked the strike. The strike split the cabinet. "Hard-liners" — including Finance Minister MacEachen — wanted to avoid being seen as "giving in" to a militant union, which would set a bad example for other unions.[128] The cost difference between the two sides' proposals was insubstantial; the C. D. Howe Institute estimate was $2 million. The cost of implementing the Jasmin recommendations would involve but a 2 per cent increase in costs. For example, as only 1 per cent of postal workers might take maternity leave each year, this provision would cost the POD about two cents per worker per hour. The government was also embarrassed politically when it was discovered that the POD's Priority Post service continued to operate during the strike.

On the other hand, the POD was losing $4.2 million a day as the strike dragged on. Business opposed the strike vigorously. The Canadian Direct Marketing Association (CDMA) estimated that $9 million a day was being lost and ten thousand lay-offs had resulted.[129] In response to claims that the strike was causing bankruptcies, PMG Ouellet retorted that "I can't accept that businessmen have to rely on the Post Office to make a living. If they do they better find other ways." This led to private-sector calls for Ouellet's resignation, a legislated end to the strike, and the removal of the strike weapon in the public sector.[130]

The parties accepted mediation in mid-July.[131] After seventeen days of mediation with Chief Justice Alan Gold of the Quebec Provincial Court, a tentative settlement was reached on 6 August. It included seventeen weeks of maternity leave at 93 per cent of salary. This was unprecedented, as were path-breaking health and safety provisions in the contract, which were stronger than those afforded workers under the Canada Labour Code. Wage increases were limited to seventy cents an hour, and Treasury Board got the two-year contract it wanted; but these measures could have been attained weeks earlier and hardly seemed worth the costs of a six-week strike. Postal officials priced the settlement at $150 million. The Canadian Federation of Independent Business claimed that its members had lost $3 billion in business. The POD itself lost $158 million in revenues, $47 million net.[132] This had been a costly and unnecessary strike, which the government had lost.

Labour disruptions were the central feature of the Canadian postal experience of the 1970s. This fact had enormous consequences for the POD's financial and competitive position as well as for labour and management morale. Given the scale and pace of mechanization, a certain amount of industrial disruption was perhaps unavoidable. Nonetheless, political decisions and strategies exacerbated the labour–management environment. Governments were schizophrenic in their involvement in negotiations. On some occasions their offensive, hard-line position provoked and encouraged strike action. On other occasions, they determined that a settlement should be reached and offered generous compensation and benefits. This ambivalence unsettled the process, but more importantly, it told the unions that they were negotiating with the government and not with the POD. Governments determined if and when a settlement took place and what its terms would be. This made the bargaining process a meaningless charade of name calling and accusations, and alienated postal workers even further from the POD.

The POD was in a hopelessly untenable situation. Treasury Board determined contract settlements, which the POD would then have to live with. Where these were not bearable, the POD would move to undermine the contract — which served only to anger the unions. The government's insistence on maintaining the departmental form of the Post Office constrained meaningful discussion of technological change. Institutional change lagged behind the operational changes brought by mechanization; this was the most serious lacuna of postal policy in this period.

The Demoralization of the POD

The morale and capacity of the POD were sapped by strikes and mechanization. By the end of the 1970s, management was dispirited and lacked any sense of identity or purpose. Its members were incapable of carrying out their responsibilities creatively or effectively. This state of affairs was the government's responsibility. Its neglect of the POD placed the latter in an impossibly difficult position at a time of tremendous stress and strain.

First, the POD remained in awkward power-sharing arrangements with other departments. A report by the associate deputy minister to the PMG (the Ubering report) catalogued the ways in which these arrangements created problems for the POD:

> The Post Office Act states that the Postmaster General shall administer, superintend and manage the Post Office. This seems to be a simple enough authority, but a number of other acts have superimposed effects on the operation of the Post Office so as to give certain authorities to other Ministers of government or to limit severely the ability of the Postmaster General (and through him the Department) in dealing with problems.

This situation could have been resolved: the government could have increased the POD's authority in these areas, through legislative and regulatory amendments, or could have considered making the POD over into a Crown corporation. The government pursued neither action, and the POD was left to flounder in policy limbo at a time when its buildings, purchases, staffing, managerial, financial, and organizational needs were being transformed by the mechanization process. It could not address these changes authoritatively or on its own terms. Treasury Board negotiated contracts, whose terms and conditions often caused operational and labour problems. Not being familiar with the requirements of a blue-collar industrial operation, it often signed away matters dealing with the organization of work, and postal managers were left to undo these arrangements or manage them as best as they could, which increased tensions between postal management and workers. The POD had little authority in the area of new buildings, relocation of equipment, purchase of supplies and materials — all affected by mechanization. Facilities maintenance was a Public Works responsibility. The planning of buildings was set by the priorities of Treasury Board and Public Works. Postal managers confronted horrendous managerial and disciplinary problems in plants like Gateway in Toronto, whose size and design were not of its making. Supply and Services controlled POD purchasing, and bad publicity and deteriorating labour relations ensued. Ubering characterized Supply and Services as a "pregnant elephant, slow, stodgy, continually growing, and difficult to convince that it must change its ways." The POD had no authority to recruit talented and experienced managers. It had to rely on the PSC, whose procedures were bureaucratic and slow.[133] In any event, Treasury Board refused to approve the needed expansion of senior management, as a result of periodic bouts of restraint. The POD was always first in line for budgetary and staffing cuts.[134]

The 1970s was a time of transition and modernization. But the POD had little authority to manage this change. If the POD floundered, this was the responsibility of the government which showed no interest in managing or synthesizing the various component parts of postal policy. A government study in 1978 concluded that "it is almost impossible with various departments having authority over various aspects of postal operations to hold the Postmaster General or his departmental executive properly accountable."[135]

Second, government policies exacerbated unsettled labour-management relations. Treasury Board policies and the rigid application of the PSSRA created a messy labour situation. Governments' on-again, off-again predilection for eleventh-hour bargaining interventions led the unions to wait for the "real" negotiations and battles with the government. The labour situation was all-consuming. A joint Post Office/Treasury Board study (the Arnot-Mullington report) found that neither the PMG nor senior postal officials had time for postal policy; they were always confronted by short-run "emergencies" and labour–management crises. Senior management's time and energy were consumed in firefighting, which disallowed forward planning, the setting of priorities, imaginative thinking and initiatives, or even basic departmental management. Middle managers saw senior officials concentrating on labour and political matters to the neglect of departmental concerns, which was bad for morale.[136] Third, government policy undermined the morale of officials. A 1975 environmental study (the Hay report) found a consistent, homogeneous negative view of the organizational climate. The respondents see no area of Canada Post's climate as being "average" or "positive" . . . the results have no parallel in Hay's experience . . . Canada Post has the lowest climate profile of any organization for which we have carried out such an analysis.[137]

The discovery of "low morale" was not terribly surprising; but "the sources of the problems were more extensive than was foreseen." Postal managers felt that they were poorly paid and lacked mobility, and that the POD offered minimal resources for human resource development. They complained that they had no authority, that initiative was not rewarded, and that there was no demand for performance. Headquarters still ruled supreme over the field, which had no say in postal policy. Managers felt besieged by public criticism and the chaos of labour relations. Arnot-Mullington concluded that the key factor was lack of political articulation of the POD's goals: "Managers at all levels of the organization complained that there had been a failure to provide the Post Office with clear objectives." POD objectives were unclear and inconsistent, and submerged in short-term political requirements and *ad hoc* reactions. The government's negligence had caused considerable confusion about postal objectives. Postal managers felt caught up in the tension between the POD's service goals and the requirement to keep costs and revenues in some sort of balance.[138]

Fourth, governments abandoned the POD to its own devices at critical moments and in critical ways. For example, after insisting on controlling the deficit, the government did not initiate a postal price increase between 1972 and 1976. This caused considerable financial uncertainty and anxiety. The POD saw its financial needs sacrificed to governmental desire to avoid political embarrassment. As the postal deficit rose, the POD's options were constrained and its public image assaulted. Similarly, the POD was directed to act more like a commercial operation; however, as soon as it acted in this way, the small-business sector complained about unfair competition. Sensitive to charges of being "anti-business," the government allowed its commercial overtures to dissipate. While PMGs hid away to avoid the political controversy, the POD was left in the embarrassing position of having to withdraw its commercial initiatives.[139] It was portrayed as the villain in contract bargaining, while governments made a last-moment entrance to sweeten the pot and get a contract. The morning after, postal managers would confront postal workers whose view was that the former had tried to deny them available improvements.

Fifth, governments continued to rank the POD as a low-level ministerial assignment. Junior or insubstantial appointments were made, for short terms. Rapid ministerial turnover (seven PMGs in the 1970s) undermined ministerial continuity and leadership. Postal policy suffered, and managers floundered, unaware of where the government wanted the POD to go.

Sixth, the government shelved the idea of a postal Crown corporation. Numerous reports had catalogued the benefits of so transforming. The Jutras, Moisan, and Tremblay conciliation board reports urged the government to move the POD in this direction, to create a better framework for labour-management relations, particularly in the area of technological change. The Ubering, Arnot-Mullington, and Darling-Ubering-Kelly reports suggested that only a Crown corporation setting would give the Post Office sufficient authority to do an effective job. But the government did not make this a political priority. Nothing pushed the idea onto the agenda, and no PMG took the initiative, remembering the political damage Kierans had experienced in introducing postal reforms.[140]

Thus, as a result of governmental and policy negligence, the POD remained becalmed in a sea of organizational and policy confusion and deteriorating morale.

Conclusion

The politics of postal neglect in the 1970s replayed the traditional politics of the post-war Post Office, but its results were perhaps more obvious and more consequential. The political negligence of the earlier period rested on ignorance; the negligence of the 1970s could not be excused in this way. The strikes of the late 1960s and early 1970s, the Montpetit report, and the consultancy studies of the Kierans period had alerted the government to the pressing problems facing the POD. This made governments' subsequent behaviour all the more irresponsible. The lack of policy attention in this period did incalculable damage and closed down a series of future postal possibilities.

Policy makers shelved Kierans' postal reform strategy and tied the POD's fate to a single policy: mechanization. The POD was one of the last Canadian institutions to be mechanized, and this was done all at once. To use economics terminology, the pent-up demand for technology was met by a huge (over-)supply of machines. The earlier condition reflected political negligence; the latter action reflected a vision of the time, that technology was a panacea, that social and economic problems could be solved by applying enormous resources and a huge injection of modern technology. The mechanization program was presented as a simple, comprehensive solution to what ailed the POD, from bad labour relations to the postal deficit. A decade later, the mechanization program was more or less completed; in record time, Canada had developed one of the most modern postal systems in the world. This was no small accomplishment: it had required tremendous determination, imagination, and skill. But it had far-reaching implications.

Mechanization swamped the postal policy agenda. It consumed an enormous amount of resources, in both direct and indirect costs — such as training, maintenance, and carrying a double cohort of workers. It undermined labour–management relations. The pace of its implementation limited proper consultation and the adequate management of unintended consequences. The POD was ill prepared for new problems in areas like job classification, the use of casual and part-time workers, and health and safety. The resulting labour grievances threatened to overwhelm it. Mechanization drew postal management and the government into an unhealthy relationship with the postal workers. It caused serious strikes and work disruptions, which harmed managerial morale and cut postal business. And it overwhelmed the capacity of the POD's institutional structure.

It failed to solve many of the challenges that had led to it in the first place. It did help in coping with rising postal volumes; the new plants and machines had enormous capacity. But the POD's business and financial challenges were not solved. The Darling-Ubering-Kelly report concluded that the POD's economic situation remained grim. Expenditures had grown at an increasing rate almost doubling over the previous five years. This reflected mechanization, higher fuel prices, urbanization, and rising wages and benefits. But postal revenues had expended at a decreasing rate, because of increased competition, the loss of volumes associated with regular strike activity, and the political and competitive constraints on postal price increases (which had increased by only 26 per cent over the previous five years). Moreover, productivity declined by 8 per cent between 1971 and 1977 as a result of two factors: lower-than-anticipated volume increases (causing under-utilization of mechanized sorting operations) and the need to carry two labour forces in the transition from a manual to a mechanized system.[141]

Mechanization and its consequences monopolized the postal agenda to the neglect of other matters. Competitiveness and the new technology were given lip service. Commercial initiatives were limited and constrained by ideological reactions, which the government did not neutralize. The POD's institutional setting persisted. Its capacity to act was inhibited by its having to share postal authority with a myriad of other departments, which had their own priorities. The vexing question of the relationship between the POD's social and economic goals went unconsidered in the 1970s. The relationship between the POD and the government remained informed by the same pressures and concerns that had dominated postal policy since Confederation. The only change was the decision to increase first-class prices by order-in-council, without parliamentary approval. This created increased fiscal flexibility for the POD, but the approach was challenged legally and had an uncertain future. The postal *status quo* prevailed on most fronts, which is why the decade unfolded as chaotically and as ineffectively for the POD as it did.

No one group "benefitted" from the contours of postal policy in this period. Mechanization and postal policy did not enjoy the active support of any particular social group, which explains to a degree why postal policy was unsuccessful. The public enjoyed uneven postal services, regular disruptions in service, rising prices, and an enormous deficit that had to be financed through tax revenues. The large postal users benefitted because their postal services were subsidized by this deficit, but they also experienced regular postal interruptions, lost business, uncertain service, and the short-term chaos induced by the change from a manual to a mechanized system. Postal workers won a certain degree of inflation protection and realized unprecedented contract gains in health and safety, maternity leave, and paid lunch hours; nonetheless, their real wage gains were limited, they did not win effective protection from technological change, they were continuously frustrated in bargaining with Treasury Board and under the PSSRA, and what gains they did make required weeks of strikes. Postal management endured a miserable time. Shell-shocked by mechanization and vicious labour–management relations, it suffered from crippled morale and most postal officials hid their identities when they ventured into social settings. Political leaders and bureaucrats benefitted to the extent that their interests lay in perpetuating the *status quo,* but this was a perverse benefit, if a benefit at all. There was no governmental interest to any real extent. Postal goals and responsibilities were too widely dispersed. The government accumulated over $2 billion in postal deficits in this period. Bureaucrats and departments successfully protected their territories, with the Crown corporation idea shelved. The department with the greatest responsibility outside the POD —Treasury Board — had a mixed experience. Its authority ebbed and flowed, with cabinet and PMGs imposing their authority on occasion. Budgetary and negotiating targets were rarely hit.

In short, postal policy in the 1970s was incoherent. Its lack of political or structural logic reflected and implied that there were no postal "winners" in this period, a fact obvious to all postal observers at the time. The postal policy process was tilting in all directions, buffeted by the complex social and economic forces surrounding it. Ironically, this irrational state of affairs was dealt with peremptorily by Prime Minister Trudeau in 1978. A well-known advocate of reason and rational planning, he announced — out of the blue, with no forewarning and no cabinet consultation — that the Post Office was to become a Crown corporation.

Chapter Six

CROWNING THE POST OFFICE

The idea of transforming the POD into a crown corporation germinated for a considerable time. From the moment the postal crisis took public shape in the mid-1960s, a postal corporation was mooted as a possible strategic solution to what ailed the Canadian postal system. The Glassco Commission (1963), the Montpetit Commission and the Anderson report (1965), the *Blueprint for Change* study (1969), the unreleased White Paper on the Post Office (1970), the Arnot-Mullington and the Ubering reports (1975), and the Darling-Kelly-Ubering report (1978) all recommended that serious consideration be given to transforming the POD into a Crown corporation.

This support was not surprising. Canadian governments had persistently found the Crown corporation a useful instrument, particularly during the 1960s and 1970s. Moreover, Crown corporations already abounded in the transportation and communication industries, precisely those sectors of the economy in which the Post Office operated. And there was increasing recognition that the POD's retail services and commercial activities required that it be unleashed from day-to-day government control.

What was surprising was the political lethargy governments demonstrated in acting on these recommendations. An equivalent postal transformation to the corporate form had taken place in the United Kingdom in 1969 and in the United States in 1971; but political leaders in Canada dithered for over a decade about the idea. Crisis mounted upon crisis through the 1970s until finally, in summer 1978, Prime Minister Trudeau made a unilateral declaration of postal independence. However, it took another three years to put this announcement into practice, a metaphor for postal politics in the 1970s. This was the first time in Canadian history that a department of government had become a Crown corporation. The transformation confronted political constraints and interests, which explain the length of the process and the eventual shape of the new postal Crown.

A postal Crown emerged out of two cross-pressures. First, the POD's deteriorating financial and competitive positions encouraged a more commercial orientation, as did fundamental changes taking place in the economy. As the post-war economic boom ran out of steam, the rate of growth declined and public deficits rose. This encouraged governments to cut spending, control the public sector, and adapt a more commercial and market-oriented policy orientation. The Crowning of the POD was part of this strategy. The second pressure conflicted with this commercial impulse. Canada Post Corporation was created at the end of the halcyon period of Canadian Crown corporations. A number of spectacular Crown corporation failures and misadventures in the 1970s raised political suspicions and led to demands for increased public control of their activities. Thus, Canada Post Corporation was formed under twin and contradictory impulses: to be commercially oriented yet politically controlled. The advent of CPC was in another sense not timed propitiously: its formation came after the accumulation of a mountain of problems and at a time of great economic uncertainty.

This chapter explores these developments and evaluates how the Canada Post Corporation Act reflected the twin expectations of commercialization and political control. It first reviews the rationale behind the Crown corporation instrument and Canadian affection for its use. It then explains the politics of delay, including the failed initiative of 1978, and examines the vision informing the idea of a postal Crown corporation, particularly the expectations of the postal community. The legislative controversies surrounding Crowning are examined. Finally, the chapter presents an accounting of who "won" and "lost" in the process, concluding with an evaluation of CPC's capacity and prospects.

Crown Corporations in Canadian History

Canadian governments have persistently demonstrated what Langford terms an "ardour" for using Crown corporations to public policy ends. This affection has been shared by wide segments of the public. The phenomenon is often presented as a defining characteristic of the Canadian political culture, reflecting Canadian willingness to use the state for economic purposes. But this view can be overstated. Canada has embraced the Crown corporation option to a greater extent than, say, the United States and Japan; but it has used that instrument less frequently than France, Austria, and the United Kingdom.[1] Moreover, the privatization process in the Mulroney era has been relatively extensive and widely accepted.

The earliest use of Crown corporations was in the late nineteenth and early twentieth centuries, when the instrument was used regularly to nation-building ends. The CNR was an example of this first wave of Crown corporations in infrastructure developments.[2] Two further waves followed. The period 1930-60 saw Crown corporations used for crisis management and stabilization purposes (viz., the Depression and World War II). The third wave occurred between 1960 and 1980. This was the boom era in the creation of Crown corporations: of all Crown corporations existing in the early 1980s, 58 per cent of them had been created in this period. Only 15 per cent were from the pre-1940 era. These third-generation Crowns were different from those created in the earlier waves: "While many of the early enterprises were monopolies, corporations established in the recent period have generally had to contend with the challenge[s] ... of a competitive market environment." Typically, they performed in the market, producing goods and services for the consumer at prices reflecting market values. There were sixty-one of these "commercial" Crown corporations at the end of the 1970s, comprising over half of all Crown corporations. These commercial Crown corporations were disproportionately grouped in areas such as electric power, transportation, communications and industry, trade, and commerce. They held $53.5 billion in assets, and $15 billion in revenues, and had 183,000 employees. As will be seen, they were part of Canadian governments' response to structural and international changes then taking place in the economy. These are the Crown corporations to be discussed here.[3]

Case studies of Crown corporations suggest an array of rationales for their creation.[4] This is not surprising, given the different environments in which they were formed. Ideological and partisan politics have been of varying importance. Policy goals have ranged from the protection of employment and national development to ensuring cultural identity and piloting new technologies. One can establish theoretical reasons, but in each case there were also specific political causes for their creation.[5] In broad terms, "Ideology can be important but ... for the major Crowns, the choice of using a Crown corporation more often represented an instrument of last resort for the achievement of enduring and important public policy goals."[6]

While owned by the government, these corporations were allowed a high degree of autonomy to engage in commercial activities in the market. A hybrid form of organization, they combine public ownership and control with corporate organization and performance. A Crown corporation is different from a department of government. The government delegates it a degree of autonomy and authority, to allow it to act in a politically impartial way. It is organized on decentralized corporate as opposed to hierarchical departmental lines. Although motivated by public policy goals, the Crown corporation is directed to behave like a private-sector corporation and to attain efficiency, commercial, and profit goals. Nonetheless, the Crown corporation is different from a private corporation. The government is its sole shareholder: It has created the corporation and defines its *raison d'être* and public purpose. After creating it, the government may issue directives to the Crown corporation.[7]

Governments use Crown corporations when they believe that instrument is most likely to realize certain policy goals. Other policy instruments — such as regulation, taxation, and spending   can be wrapped up in bureaucratic considerations that can be counterproductive where policy has a commercial character. In the departmental setting, policies are subject to daily political scrutiny, pressure, and potential interference, for they are subject to the financial goals and priorities of the government. The Crown corporation form frees policy from short-term political and governmental pressures, allowing risk taking and consideration of longer term commercial possibilities. The Crown corporation also offers possibilities for managerial improvement. Quality personnel are more easily attracted to the corporate as opposed to the departmental setting (e.g., operating styles and salary levels are more alluring). Labour relations are carried out under a more flexible regime, free of the comparability constraints within the civil service. Pricing, purchasing, and financing can be pursued on commercial grounds, independent of government priorities or the political needs of the moment.

In short, "the proponents of government enterprise viewed [the Crown corporation] as combining the advantages of the public and the private sectors," particularly where public policy has a commercial character. Crown corporations can be liberated from departmental and bureaucratic controls to act in a commercial way. While the government retains ultimate authority to articulate goals and ensure corporate accountability, these goals are pursued using private-sector techniques.[8]

The attitude of Canadian governments towards Crown corporations has been schizophrenic: attracted to their potential as a policy tool but also fearful of the political consequences of their use. For, once created, Crown corporations seek to maximize their autonomy and to limit government control. Driven by market and profit logic, their actions can conflict with and undermine governments' public policy goals.[9] Governments are "in love with the corporate form as an instrument of public policy ... [but] frightened by the possibly dire consequences of its independent action [and] the impact on their capacity to govern. . .. What they cherish for its potential for independent, innovative management, they paradoxically despise because it is outside of their complete control."[10]

The Crown corporation thus embraces an internal tension. It is directed to behave like a private-sector firm, and so will be motivated by goals different from those of government. There will thus be an inevitable tension between the "corporate side's" drive for independence and the "Crown side's" desire to realize public goals. This tension has not gone unrecognized by governments or proponents of this instrument, who anticipate that it will act as a creative force:

> The theory of the autonomous public corporation is based upon the optimistic assumption that a balance can be struck between managerial autonomy, executive direction, and parliamentary scrutiny. . .. While freed from the nagging irritants of departmental, financial and personnel procedures, and theoretically immune from partisan interventions into its routine operations, the Crown corporation operates within a web of government control and influences.[11]

These features of Crown corporation existence were played out in the 1970s. Global economic imperatives compelled governments to give policies a more commercial slant. Crown corporations were created and directed to this end. There was, at the same time, substantial public and political revolt against the state, the proliferation of bureaucracy, and the rise in taxes and deficits. Amongst the calls for a diminished state role in the economy was the demand for increased public scrutiny of Crown corporations. This was also the result of the odd and unsuccessful behavior of certain such corporations.

The origins of what is now called globalization occurred in the late 1960s and early 1970s, at the end of the long post-war boom. This saw domestic economies and their industries increasingly subject to conditions and decisions made internationally, under conditions of increasingly intense global competition. Globalization undermined the policy approach upon which governments' post-war strategies and consensus were constructed. The combination of domestic Keynesian economic management and construction of the welfare state seemed inadequate to changed economic circumstances dominated by international factors and far-reaching technological change. Governments faced two broad policy options: they could either extend their role in the economy in a far more specific and directed way, to control and regulate these international and technological factors; or they could pursue the neoconservative agenda, withdrawing from the economy to allow the market to generate technological and international competitiveness.[12] Many governments, the Canadian included, first pursued the former option. This had particular implications for the use of Crown corporations. As Laux and Molot describe it, "By the late 1960s governments in all advanced capitalist countries, faced with a relative loss of control over domestic economic development in an increasingly transnational world economy, sought to reassert control through renewed intervention, including the use of state investment and state enterprise." The proliferation of Crown corporations in the 1960s and 1970s was one of the Canadian government's post-Keynesian responses to changes taking place in the world economy. Crown corporations were used as an instrument to increase domestic and state control over the direction of economic development. These public corporations were not created under the same circumstances or with the same powers or rationale as those of the nation-building era:

> state enterprises and state investment [were reoriented] towards competitive and profitable industries. ... state enterprises underwent a trend to commercialization ... as part of a broader international realignment. The norms governing public enterprise shifted accordingly to emphasize "business logic" ... . to give primary attention to financial results.[13]

Thus, Crown corporations in Canada in the 1960s and 1970s were directed to act more like private firms, to ensure Canadian competitiveness, and to make a profit. The latter was required to assist in the elimination of government debts.

This imperative to commercialization, an uninhibited expression of the corporate dimension of Canada's state enterprises, inevitably confronted their Crown dimension: "The ... trend to commercialization exacerbates traditional tensions between autonomy and control. . .. Once state enterprises are required to compete or to produce for profit, their managers tend to seek greater autonomy." In the process, the government loses its ability to direct the Crown to public policy ends: "The relative autonomy of state enterprises, most pronounced in commercial enterprises with a profit mandate operating in competitive markets, inhibits the ability of the government to use such corporations as vehicles for policy."[14]

Concern about lost political control developed almost immediately in the 1970s. A series of controversies led to calls for scrutiny of Crown corporations and increased control over their activities, obstructing the impulse to commercialization. This counteracting force manifested itself on two levels. First, there was concern about the growth of the state and the bureaucracy, the ballooning deficit, and the proliferation of Crown corporations. The last became an issue unto itself: the commercialization mandate resulted in diversification, and this increased proliferation generated a sense of loss of control and accountability. Second, there were specific concerns about the activities of a number of Crown corporations. A series of spectacular and well-publicized financial losses and questionable commercial practices led to full-scale public enquiries into Air Canada, de Havilland, Atomic Energy of Canada Limited, and Polysar. The 1976 auditor-general's report, various Public Accounts Committee studies, the Lambert report (1979), and the 1977 Privy Council Office *Blue Paper* all portrayed a chaotic scene, characterized by serious financial losses, inefficiencies, poor policy co-ordination between the government and the Crowns, questionable managerial practices, and uncertainty about how many Crown corporations existed. The reports also found few mechanisms to ensure Crown corporation accountability to their public goals and objectives, and called for greater government authority and increased political control over Crown corporations.[15]

This maelstrom of discontent led to Bill C-24, which changed the "Part X" provisions of the Financial Administration Act (FAA), under which Crown corporations functioned. The government and Parliament were assigned new mechanisms and processes to assert their authority over Crown corporations, including the power to issue directives; cabinet approval of Crown corporation sale or subsidiary purchase; clarification of the role of the boards of Crown corporations; requirements to provide increased information about corporate plans and results; annual approval of capital budgets by Finance and Treasury Board; annual submission of multi-year corporate plans and borrowing requirements for approval; comprehensive audits by the auditor-general; and improved mechanisms for reporting to Parliament, including automatic review of annual reports by standing committee.[16]

Crown corporations are now overseen by the Crown Corporation Directorate (CCD) of the Department of Finance and Treasury Board. A dozen bureaucratic analysts are responsible for the forty or so Crown corporations that function under this part of the FAA. The CCD reports to the assistant deputy minister, Finance, and the deputy secretary of the Treasury Board, connecting the Crowns to the government in a two-way flow of information and analysis. This process culminates in the annual presentation of a multi-year plan and capital budget (to be approved by both the responsible minister and Treasury Board) and an annual report (which is sent to the appropriate standing committee of Parliament).[17]

The 1970s "freeing" of Crown corporations to allow a more commercial orientation thus had the opposite result: a political counter-reaction against Crown corporate autonomy led to increased political scrutiny and control. The issue of "how to structure decision-making processes to ensure public accountability and responsibility while allowing for commercial independence"[18] was intensified.

A new and radical resolution of this tension arose in the mid-1980s. The privatization approach took the commercialization and political control trends to their logical conclusion. The move to privatization was based on the following perception, as enunciated by the Economic Council of Canada:

> Rather than having combined private-sector efficiency with democratic controls, public enterprises have at times reflected the shortcomings of an entity that was neither subject to the discipline of the capital market nor open to the light provided by legislative scrutiny.[19]

It was then argued that commercialization and democratization could be attained via privatization. A private firm could act more like a private firm than any public corporation could ever manage, regardless of how much autonomy the latter was given.

Privatization was part of the alternative post-Keynesian option noted above, intended to address globalization and competitiveness. State enterprises were characterized as a drain on public resources and an impediment to private-sector efficiency and growth. Their deficits needed to be eliminated. Their labour practices and wage rates appeared to be overly generous. Their "service" functions looked to be indulgent. Their overall orientation was too political and not sufficiently commercial. Their inefficiency hampered competitiveness and their presence in the market inhibited opportunities for other businesses. Thus, their elimination would increase the global competitiveness of the entire economy. Advocates of privatization also maintained that adequate public accountability would always be impossible to attain without a degree of political control, which would undermine commercial behaviour. This view reflected the ideological concern that the state had grown too large, and that the bureaucracy and Crown corporations could not be managed democratically. Reducing the bureaucracy, deregulation, and privatization were considered to be "democratizing" actions. This case for privatization of Crown corporations on commercial and democratic grounds built up considerable momentum.[20] The Conservatives established a private-sector task force study on privatization in 1983, and the Mulroney government made privatization a policy priority in the 1985 budget. A Ministry of State for Privatization and Regulatory Affairs, a cabinet committee, and a secretariat were established. From 1984 to 1991, the government privatized or dissolved more than twenty Crown corporations, reducing the number of Crown employees by eighty thousand. Major privatizations have included de Havilland, Canadair, Teleglobe, Eldorado Nuclear, Air Canada, and Petro-Canada.[21]

Canada Post was thus formed at a complex historical juncture for Crown corporations. It was encouraged to act in a commercial manner to improve Canada's international competitiveness. There was also increased political concern that it was not adequately democratically accountable. CPC's formation and early evolution thus took place under the ever-extending shadow of privatization.

The Politics of Delay: Governmental and Bureaucratic Factors

The United States Postal Corporation was formed in 1971, despite considerable resistance to the idea of a postal corporation. Numerous groups felt that they benefitted from its departmental form and hence supported the *status quo*. Postal unions felt that their interests could be maintained via their influence in Congress. Postal users benefitted from the deficits that subsidized prices. The idea of a public postal corporation thus had to be sold to the major postal players.[22] The Canadian situation was unlike that in the United States, where the idea of a postal Crown corporation did not have to be sold to the postal community; outside of immediate government circles, no postal constituency was opposed. Only political lethargy and dithering delayed postal transformation.

Postal union support for the idea dated from 1949, at which time the CPEA (predecessor of CUPW) proposed transforming the POD into a Crown corporation. The 1965 convention of postal workers again proposed a postal Crown corporation. The CPU supported the idea in dozens of submissions before the Montpetit Royal Commission, and union support persisted through the 1970s. CUPW campaigned in the mid-1970s on the slogan that "A postal Crown can deliver." Conciliation reports of the 1970s indicated union support for the idea, with which conciliators also agreed.[23]

"Expert" support began in the 1960s. The Glassco Commission on government organization (1962) encouraged the government to give the Post Office autonomy, particularly financial freedom. It supported a postal Crown on "logical grounds." The Anderson report — which settled the 1965 strike — argued that industrial relations would improve under the Crown corporation form:

Reforms needed in working conditions and work rules in the postal service are not necessarily the same as those needed in the other branches of the civil service. Under a Crown corporation organization, such matters ... could be best adjusted to meet the special character of the Post Office employment, unrestricted by an obligation to take into account the needs of quite different classes of civil servants.

A Blueprint for Change reiterated this argument in 1969:

As a Crown corporation, the Post Office should have full authority to bargain with the unions representing its employees. It should not be required to seek the approval of any government agency before concluding an agreement with the unions.

This report synthesized the many consultancy reports commissioned by PMG Kierans in 1968:

From these studies emerged the overpowering conclusion that the Post Office as a Crown corporation could better fulfill its role in the future.... It cannot operate effectively as a department of government.

This position was endorsed by the Conservative opposition.[24]

While the idea of a postal Crown corporation was well articulated, political circumstances were not propitious. Minority governments (1963-68) worried about being defeated or over-extended politically if they initiated such a policy innovation. Moreover, the POD lacked political authority within the bureaucracy, and the senior administration was cool to the idea. Deputy PMG W. A. Wilson (1961-68) was a particularly weak deputy. Thus, the Crown corporation idea received little political attention through most of the 1960s. Matters went no further than a preliminary study of the possibility of making the POD a Crown corporation.[25]

The rise and fall of the idea of a postal Crown corporation during the Kierans' era has already been detailed (Chapter 4). Political ineptness and uncertain labour conditions conspired to remove the issue from the policy agenda, even after cabinet had approved the idea in the fall of 1968. Two governmental factors were most telling in delaying the idea. First, the senior bureaucracy remained cool to the idea. After the cabinet decision, it delayed the issue by insisting on another study. By the time that study was concluded and released, political circumstances had become less conducive to postal transformation. Second, Prime Minister Trudeau feared that the process of transformation would tie up the legislative agenda, to the neglect of higher policy priorities. Thus, the Crown corporation idea was delayed by bureaucratic and political interests and considerations. In June 1971, PMG Côté reported that the idea was still being studied and a statement would be made. But no announcement was forthcoming one way or the other.[26]

This pattern continued in the early 1970s. Officials were distracted by other postal events, such as deteriorating labour-management relations, which often took on significant political dimensions. For example, the Lapalme truckers dispute became entwined with the FLQ crisis. Ministers spent an enormous amount of time on this feature of postal politics, and the Crown corporation idea was pushed into the political background.[27]

Expert opinion continued to support the POD's transformation into a Crown corporation. Most of the analysis of the Arnot-Mullington report (1975) suggested that this was the organizational form the Post Office should take. The Ubering report (1975) demonstrated the extent to which the departmental form constrained the POD's effective operation. The Conservative Party's Richie report (1978) concluded that the departmental form was not conducive to postal efficiency and effectiveness, and called for the creation of a Crown corporation. The Darling-Ubering-Kelly report (1978) inquired into the consequences of converting the POD to a Crown corporation. Directed to report on the merits of various organizational forms the Post Office might take, its conclusions were in tune with the arguments for a postal Crown. Conciliation reports in the 1970s validated the union view that industrial relations could be improved within a postal Crown corporation. The Conservative opposition supported the idea of a Crown corporation throughout the 1970s. A postal users' conference in 1978 also supported the idea, in order to give postal management more freedom to operate.[28]

Even as opinion in favour built up, the idea failed to take on priority policy status. Cabinet never pushed or encouraged PMGs in this direction, partly due to the ambivalence, if not antipathy, of the senior civil service. Supportive of the idea in theory, they were in no hurry to transform the POD into a Crown corporation; this would diminish its authority and resources. PCO officials worried about being bypassed in postal matters once postal authority was handed to "outsiders." Moreover, the auditor-general had begun to complain about proliferation of Crown corporations, and officials were wary about creating another one.[29]

PMGs through the 1970s demonstrated no enthusiasm for the idea. None of them made it his policy priority, so the Crown corporation idea never worked its way onto the policy agenda. PMG Ouellet was concerned that a postal Crown would neglect political and social goals in pursuing business ones. He and subsequent PMGs were not anxious to jump into a potential political frying pan, Kierans' fate after initiating the postal reform agenda. A wary Ouellet concluded that the government should at most move slowly and cautiously. PMG Blais was similarly anxious about the disruption and political chaos that transformation of the POD might bring, particularly in unsettled times. He felt that a period of labour stability was first required. Blais stifled discussion, sceptical of the extent to which a postal corporation could be distanced politically to act in a commercial way: "There would be a certain greater flexibility, but there is no way the public will stop thinking of the Post Office as a government agency."[30]

Postal officials were thus not encouraged by their ministers to look at the Crown corporation idea, or to plan or think through its consequences. The deputy minister at the time — J. A. Mackay — was an outsider who had been recruited by Kierans from the private sector. He had little clout to wield in articulating the idea of a postal Crown corporation within the senior bureaucracy. As a result, postal management gave no consideration to the idea through to the late 1970s. Indeed, POD reports through the 1970s note nothing on this issue.[31] By the late 1970s, then, the idea of a postal Crown corporation had apparently faded away. Ministers were not anxious to rock the boat, and expressed scepticism about the viability of the idea. Moreover, they and their cabinet colleagues had other priorities to pursue. Senior bureaucratic officials were wary of the idea. These were the postal constituencies that delayed the pursuit of the idea, despite the support of the postal unions, interest groups, the opposition parties, the media, and experts.

Out of the blue, Prime Minister Trudeau crossed the Rubicon. In a television address on 1 August 1978, he declared, "The situation in the Post Office is intolerable and has been for some time. Canadians are losing their patience. They are increasingly fed up. So am I." He announced that his government would transform the POD into a Crown corporation.[32] This change in policy was as sudden as it was unanticipated. POD officials were not working on the idea at the time. Senior bureaucrats were lukewarm towards the idea. There was no ongoing study of the idea taking place. Indeed, neither PMG Lamontagne nor Finance Minister Chrétien were aware of the decision before it was announced.[33]

This decision was not atypical of Trudeau's policy style in major matters (e.g., wage and price controls in 1975, the National Energy Policy in 1980). The postal decision reflected considerations that were not exclusively, or even primarily, related to the needs of the Post Office itself. Indeed, this decision was the *reductio ad absurdum* of the POD's mode of operation: it did not emanate from the Post Office and was not based on the POD's needs and calculations.

The 1970s saw economic policy shift to a focus on the market as a result of concerns about structural changes and global competition. This policy shift included downsizing government and its involvement in the economy. Trudeau's fiscal orientation tilted this way in the summer of 1978, under two direct influences. First, his principal secretary, Jim Coutts, had directly observed the Proposition 13 tax revolt in California. Returning to Ottawa, Coutts reported to Trudeau on the anti-tax, anti-government movement that foreshadowed neoconservativism and the Reagan election victory. Second, these impressions were confirmed later that summer at a meeting of the

Group of Seven heads of state. The neoconservative view, as propounded by the German prime minister, dominated discussions. Immediately upon his return from Europe, Trudeau made his televised announcement of spending cuts and program containments to limit the deficit — including the change in postal policy. This policy promised to eliminate responsibility for the postal deficit (over $1 billion in 1976–78) and to cut the size of the civil service by over fifty thousand postal employees. None of this had been rehearsed with either PMG Lamontagne or Finance Minister Chrétien; and the POD's needs and objectives were considered at best indirectly.[34]

Given no forewarning, the POD did not have legislative proposals or design models in hand to turn itself into a Crown corporation. The government formalized this policy in the October Throne Speech, and Crown corporation legislation was introduced in December. In the intervening months, the POD negotiated contracts with both LCUC and CUPW. The former organized rotating strikes in September before a contract was settled in October. The latter was legislated back to work later that month and carried out a week-long illegal strike. The POD thus did not have much time or energy to consider the Crown corporation legislation. Indeed, the PCO and the Department of Justice drove the legislative process; the POD was only marginally involved.[35] Bill C-27 died on the order paper when Parliament was dissolved for the 1979 election. The legislation would not be reintroduced until July 1980, after the rise and fall of the Conservative government and another election. Politics thus continued to conspire to delay the introduction of the postal Crown.

Bill C-27 contained one particularly intriguing strategic feature. Clause 34 proposed the creation of a department of government called the Post Office Secretariat. Comprising the PMG, a deputy PMG, and a group of officials, it would "coordinate, promote and recommend national policies and programs with respect to postal services ... [and] promote the establishment, development and efficiency of ... postal services." The postal Crown corporation would thus be politically "overseen" by the Post Office Secretariat. This was an odd but not surprising idea. The legislation emanated from the PCO, which had never been keen about dissolving the POD; the secretariat proposal was designed to perpetuate its postal influence. It feared what ultimately developed: a situation in which the head of the corporation bypassed the bureaucracy to deal directly with the responsible minister. The secretariat would have required the new corporation to go through traditional bureaucratic channels.

This proposal demonstrated the continuing postal authority of the senior bureaucracy, as well as the weak position of both the PMG and the POD. The latter was not terribly keen on the idea of a secretariat, which it viewed as an impossible mix of departmental and corporate forms. It went along with the idea because it felt that anything was better than the existing arrangement. PMG Lamontagne thought the idea was foolish, as he saw no need to have a department once the corporation was created. He went along to get the legislative ball rolling, and because as a new and inexperienced minister, he did not have sufficient authority to challenge a PCO plan. Thus, clause 36 appeared at first reading.[36] The secretariat was universally opposed when the legislation appeared. A *Financial Post* headline summarized the consensus about the secretariat: "Post Office to remain under political thumb."[37] It is unlikely that the secretariat idea would have survived had Bill C-27 been pursued. Indeed, it did not reappear in Bill C-42 in 1980. But the secretariat incident suggested the continuing influential role played by the senior bureaucracy in shaping the fate of the Canadian postal system.

The Crown Corporation Vision

The idea of a postal Crown corporation was informed by a clear and optimistic vision, which had been well articulated and well honed over the previous decade in numerous studies, reports, and debates. The ingredients of this vision — repeated like a mantra in legislative debates during 1980–81 — generated no significant controversy or debate as the Canada Post Corporation was being formed. There was near-universal agreement that the corporate form of postal organization would be far more effective than the departmental form. As to what the postal Crown corporation would accomplish, there was broad agreement on the financial, labor, managerial, and commercial dimensions to this Crown vision.[38]

First, there was a consensus that the postal Crown would stem the POD's financial deterioration. A financially autonomous Crown corporation would have the authority to set postal rates strategically, based on its needs and its assessment of the market. Under departmental conditions, postal prices were shaped by political considerations and priorities, which made price increases difficult to effect. The under-pricing of postal products had been a substantial contributor to the POD's deficit. The Post Office would operate in an improved investment climate once budget was under control. The postal Crown corporation would also have quicker access to resources and easier procedures to pursue its financial requirements. And its financial situation would improve as a result of improved labour relations, increased managerial autonomy, and a commercial orientation.

Second, there was universal agreement that labour–management relations *would* improve under a Crown corporation regime. The PSSRA had constrained the development of healthy industrial relations at the POD in the 1960s and 1970s and disallowed bargaining in a variety of critical areas. A Crown corporation would come under the jurisdiction of the Canada Labour Code, which offered far greater bargaining latitude, particularly in areas such as technological change. Moreover, postal employees would no longer be members of the civil service. This would end the constraining practice of having to ensure comparability of wages and conditions between postal workers and civil servants. Postal unions would no longer bargain with Treasury Board, whose interests were broader than postal ones. Negotiations would probably improve because those directly involved — postal workers and management — would bargain directly with each other.

Third, advocates of a postal Crown anticipated improved managerial capacity. Postal managers would be given the autonomy to make decisions, pursue them, and be held accountable for them. Postal authority would no longer be shared with other departments. From labour relations to financial planning, from purchases and expenditures to recruiting personnel and managers, the Post Office would now be managed directly to postal goals and based on postal considerations — not government or civil service or political ones. Post Office management would have an incentive to pursue the best possible decisions for the organization. Managerial instability associated with high ministerial turnover would come to an end. The corporation would be guided by a permanent board of directors, who would hire a corporate president and managerial team with longer term managerial contracts and incentives geared to performance.

Fourth, an autonomous postal corporation would be better placed to act like a commercial entity and rise to competitive challenges. The departmental form had been ill suited to an organization that bought and sold products and services in the market place and processed thousands of business transactions each day. Free of political and bureaucratic constraints, the new Post Office could behave like a private corporation. Liberated from a hierarchical, centralized departmental form, it could be organized as a flexible, responsive, decentralized, market-oriented corporate entity. Its values and motives would be increasingly shaped by market pressures and requirements, which would improve its performance in areas ranging from cost cutting to technological innovation. It would be capable of making rapid changes and adjustments in response to market changes and competition. This would lead it to an increasingly competitive and commercially oriented perspective. Because it would make decisions on business and market grounds, not on political ones, a market-oriented organization and management would be better positioned to turn around the postal financial situation.

The Crown vision was shared by most groups in the postal community. The postal unions were keen because a Crown corporation offered freer collective bargaining, away from the restrictions of the PSSRA, and labour would deal directly with the real, day-to-day postal decision makers. The large postal users were also supportive, anticipating labour peace and stability to the postal scene. An autonomous postal corporation was likely be more sensitive to their market needs and behave more like a rational, efficient business operation. They were also keen to see the postal deficit eliminated (this was an ideological rather than a practical concern, as they benefitted from the deficit). A postal Crown offered the general public the prospect of a more stable postal scene and a more efficient and effective postal corporation, maintaining and improving postal services. Postal management was anxious to be free of government control and departmental rules and regulations. It wanted the autonomy to manage the Post Office more efficiently and effectively. Finally, the government had numerous reasons for supporting the postal Crown, which promised to relieve it of a political irritant and embarrassment. The government was harassed by postal concerns, from bad labour–management relations to lost letters, from rising postal prices to deterioration in postal services. It was held responsible for these issues, over which it had little effective control. The prospect of eliminating a $500 million to $1 billion a year postal deficit was financially enticing, given the government's own fiscal problems. At the same time, it would retain authority for setting the Post Office's broad policy goals. It would be able to intervene or hide behind Crown corporation autonomy when it was to its political advantage.

As the above portrait suggests, the Crown vision had more economic dimensions to it than social ones. This feature was inescapable, inasmuch as the government was Crowning an existing public entity rather than a private company. In the latter situation, arguments for a Crown corporation rest on the social motivations for creating a state enterprise; the economic side of the equation is already in place in the private company. In the former situation, the social aspects already existed, as the Post Office functioned as a department of government. The economic aspects were thus in the forefront of discussions. This had the effect of creating a one-dimensional vision and one-sided and asymmetrical debate. The traditional idea of a Crown corporation – the idea of a balanced relationship between public goals and their pursuit through the corporate instrument – was not fully or energetically articulated.

The logic of this situation dovetailed with the economic realities of the day. The POD was experiencing serious financial and competitive difficulties. The government itself was facing a deficit and was trying to fend off the economic decline threatened by increasing international competition. There was thus a practical, political urgency to this focus on economics. The bottom line was the hopeful, indeed optimistic, vision that a postal corporation could improve both the Post Office's and the government's economic position as well as contribute to the competitiveness of the Canadian economy.

The Politics of Postal Transformation

The broad consensus around the postal Crown vision translated into all-party support for the idea. There were, however, numerous and serious disagreements over how to realize the idea. It took nine months to pass Bill C-42 – the act creating the Canada Post Corporation. This extended legislative process was not anticipated by the government and postal observers. It reflected the nature of postal pressures and expectations at the time, and also foreshadowed the experiences the Post Office would have as a Crown corporation.

First, there was a high degree of participation in the pre-legislative process. Critics of Bill C-27 claimed that there had been insufficient public consultation in preparing the 1978 legislation, particularly of the postal unions.[39] Given the legislation's objective of making the Post Office more commercially oriented, it made a great deal of sense to seek the advice of those with whom the postal Crown would be dealing. The Conservative government initiated a consultation process with labour groups in 1979. Senior officials from the POD, the Department of Labour, and the PCO met regularly with CLC president Shirley Carr and representatives of the postal unions.[40] This process was extended after the Liberals were elected in 1980. A small tripartite committee was established under the umbrella of the CLC, comprising government, union, and POD officials. PMG Ouellet insisted on the unions' involvement, because they were key supporters of a postal Crown corporation:. "I wanted them to feel that it was a piece [of legislation] they would be satisfied with." This committee wrote drafts of the legislation in the CLC boardroom; these drafts were then passed on to the Department of Justice. The major mail users were consulted simultaneously by postal officials, who passed on users' and management's advice. This "balanced" the results of consultations with the postal unions. The legislation was negotiated directly between PMG Ouellet and the postal unions, but the latter did not win every issue, as will be seen below. The CPC's first president, Michael Warren, was not involved in this process.[41]

Second, the legislative process was politically and ideologically intense and drawn out. This turn of events was surprising given the broad consensus surrounding the proposal. The bill was given first reading on 17 July 1980. After further consultations, second reading began in late October, only to be delayed again until late November. Second reading was uneventful, with only fourteen speakers none of whom was a substantial political figure. The leadership of the political parties was not divided over the legislation. Hansard records but forty pages of debate. One participant complained that there were seldom more than ten MPs present for the debate. The bill went to committee, where the political and ideological battle began. Foreshadowing future postal politics, this battle was initiated by backbench Conservative MPs such as John Gamble, Bill Kembling, and Don Blenkarn. They took highly ideological and principled stands on fundamental questions, such as the Post Office's monopoly. Their arguments reflected the burgeoning neo-conservative attitude of the time, one highly suspicious of monopolies and government activity in the economy. The leadership of the Conservatives took a far more sanguine position. Postal spokesperson and former PMG John Fraser was supportive and, although critical about particular issues, was one of the most active in seeing the bill through the legislative process. Bill C-42 did not emerge from the committee until April 1981, at which time it had been influenced by the backbenchers' concerns. Canada Post Corporation came into existence on 16 October 1981.[42]

Third, the postal community made extensive use of the legislative process to articulate its concerns and objectives. This highly participatory affair brought out numerous interests and organizations, indicating the continuing ubiquitousness of the postal system and the extended social and economic web in which it functioned. From the financial and retail community to the telecommunications and transportation industries; from the print and visual media to advertisers and publishers; from governments and business organizations to labour and consumer groups — most sectors of the economy and society continued to be affected by the postal system and wanted to shape its future operations as a Crown corporation.[43] Nearly two hundred groups, organizations, and individuals pressed their concerns at the legislative hearings, reflecting as well the increasing influence of interest groups in the political process of the 1980s.

Fourth, there was insubstantial media coverage of the process. The media was distracted by labor negotiations in 1980 and 1981, which included a CUPW strike in the summer of 1981. Substantial attention was paid to the recruitment of CPC's first president, the glamorous Michael Warren.[44] And a Royal Commission study of security problems in the POD (the Marin report) was released in January 1981. Save for scrutiny of the Post Office's monopoly, or exclusive privilege, the transformation of the POD into Canada Post Corporation went widely unnoticed.

Before I examine Bill C-42's completed form, I will look at the major controversies in the legislative process. These included the definition of a letter, the postal monopoly, the Post Office's role in telecommunications, the question of a balanced budget, postal pricing and regulation, the right to strike, and the composition of the board.

The Post Office's monopoly on first-class mail was debated fiercely. PMG Ouellet proposed to maintain this monopoly "so as to have a guaranteed source of revenue to ensure the universality of services." The original wording of the legislation gave CPC the "exclusive privilege of collecting, conveying and delivering letters within Canada," where "conveying" was defined as "any physical, electronic, optical or other means to transmit mail." The broad principle of the exclusive privilege was debated only superficially. Concerns were raised on two, more focused issues: Who would define a letter? and Should the Post Office be given a privileged position in the telecommunications industry?[45]

The original legislation reflected a tacit agreement among postal officials, government authorities, and the postal unions to define the postal monopoly in broad and loose terms. For the unions, the broader the definition, the more business would come the Post Office's way, providing jobs, security, and improved economic prospects. What was at stake was the elimination of private couriers and a postal presence in telecommunications, both of which were seen as threatening the Post Office's viability. Postal officials appreciated that the way in which a letter was defined would also define CPC's future territorial boundaries in the highly technological and rapidly changing communications market. Postal and government officials also confronted the practical question of how to create an operational definition. Legal advisers suggested it was not possible to define a letter clearly and cleanly and encouraged Ouellet and Corkery to support a broad definition. As Corkery put it, "My guess is that there will never be a definition," as it was too hard to cover all circumstances.[46] While promising not to extend the Post Office's monopoly, Ouellet refused to offer a precise definition of a letter, maintaining that precision would straitjacket the Post Office's future and its capacity to respond to technological and market changes. He tried to clarify matters by saying what a letter was not; he limited the Post Office's exclusive privilege by proposing a list of exemptions to the postal monopoly. This list included newspapers, magazines, books, catalogues, householder or resident items, advertising matter, greeting cards, and electronically or optically transmitted material.

Despite these assurances and limitations, there was broad concern that the legislation was designed to extend the postal monopoly into new territory. The Standing Committee on Regulation and Other Statutory Instruments was "seriously concerned by the power given to the Corporation to define, by regulation, the word 'letter' and, hence, the extent of its own monopoly." This authority was seen to be "inappropriate to a parliamentary democracy." The committee worried that the legislation authorized CPC to define by regulation a term — mailable matter — that was already defined in the enabling statute. Co-chair of the Standing Joint Committee on Regulation Perrin Beatty argued that the bill was a "frightening example of government by regulation" that could put numerous Canadian companies out of business. Provincial governments protested the ostensible extension of the postal monopoly into new areas, as did editorial opinion. The business community expressed concern about the Post Office's future business and monopoly practices.[47]

Opposition MPs predicted postal intrusion into the private sector, and various industries anticipated the extension of the postal monopoly into their territories. For example, the Canadian Telecommunications Industry worried that the definition of a letter might give the Post Office undefined grants of enabling power in the electronic and telecommunications areas. The Canadian Trucking Association demanded a clearer definition of "goods," to know where the definition of a letter ended and the competitive goods and parcels sector began. The Canadian Bankers Association worried about postal involvement in electronic funds transfer and any competitive advantages the Post Office might gain. The courier and parcel delivery industries were apprehensive about time-sensitive material like laboratory tests, pharmacy prescriptions, vaccines, and legal, financial and accounting data.

Utilities and other companies worried about whether they would be allowed to deliver their bills. MPs reported concerns that hand delivery of birthday and greeting cards would become illegal.[48]

The most heated aspect of this debate concerned the Post Office's role in the telecommunications industry. Post Offices and telecommunications were often twinned in a state monopoly in Europe, a development that the private sector feared might occur in Canada. This scenario was certainly mentioned positively by many groups in the early stages of discussion, resulting in a number of very intense meetings with the PMG. The unions and the postal bureaucracy were close allies on this matter, as the entry of the Post Office into the telecommunications area would increase postal jobs and influence. Dr. Maurice Levy, a former technical adviser to the Post Office, argued at committee hearings that if electronic mail was excluded from the exclusive privilege, "it [would] mean the gradual death of the Post Office." The legislation itself directed the Post Office to be in the forefront of technological change and innovation.

Despite the union–bureaucratic alliance, the extension of the postal monopoly into the telecommunications area could not withstand the social, economic, and ideological pressures of the early 1980s. Opposition MPs voiced private-sector concerns that the proposed definition of a letter would allow the Post Office a monopoly in the telecommunications industry, a market already well served by various private telecommunications carriers. "The government could be giving the Post Office the right to put the telecommunications industry in Canada out of business," worried future PMG Perrin Beatty. "We are not after the telecommunications world," retorted Ouellet. "Everything that is in the air and electronic would be competitive." Nonetheless, he ruled out the proposition that all things electronic would not be considered letters: "I would not want to deprive the Post Offices of expanding in this area of communication. This is the future." Despite these assurances, the business community attacked the government vigorously. The Canadian Manufacturers Association adopted an extreme position, arguing that the legislation should disallow the Post Office from participating in this field. This position was tempered by other firms and organizations, which, broadly speaking, did not want to see the Post Office granted any special privileges or monopoly powers in the telecommunications sector. Business was willing to allow the Post Office into this field, but only on a competitive basis.[49]

The issue of private courier services was played out in similar terms. The regularity of strikes and labour disruptions had created a market for courier services, a flourishing industry by 1980. Postal officials and unions wanted the industry to be curtailed if not eliminated, for it had gained a considerable portion of the business mail market. The unions claimed that the industry was undermining the Post Office's financial viability, as couriers "skimmed" business in the dense, lucrative urban markets. They asked for a two-year phase-out of the industry. When the postal legislation first appeared, business feared that clause defining a letter would allow the Post Office to limit the activities of courier firms. The Canadian Bankers Association insisted that the courier system be protected to allow same-day transfer of cheques. The Canadian Trucking Association, the Canadian Manufacturers Association, the Canadian Business Equipment Manufacturing Association, and courier companies such as Loomis argued that "the exclusive privilege should not be extended to time sensitive material and information." PMG Ouellet was sympathetic to the analysis and concerns of the unions. He offered to consider curtailing couriers, but on condition that the unions give up their right to strike. Otherwise, the proposal to eliminate couriers would be unacceptable in the business community. This the postal unions would not countenance, and so the couriers and time-sensitive mail business was safe from postal "incursion."[50]

Although the monopoly and telecommunications issues dominated the legislative process, a number of other concerns raised important issues and led to changes in the legislation. For example, the original legislation proposed third-party regulation of postal price and service changes. PMG Ouellet maintained that as "the Corporation will have [a] monopoly ... [t]his procedure is [necessary] to protect the interest of the people and to establish the necessary arm's length relationship." Postal proposals were to be published in the *Canada Gazette*, and CPC would make formal representations to the Canadian Transportation Commission (CTC). Regulatory hearings would offer input from the public and the postal community. The CTC would approve or disapprove the request for the price or service changes, a decision to then be confirmed or overturned by the governor-in-council.

This approach was supported by numerous groups.[51] Many others requested a more strenuous and formal regulatory process than the one proposed in the legislation, and still others insisted on a broader regulatory mandate and greater opportunities to appeal decisions. There was, however, considerable Conservative opposition to the idea of regulation, an expression of the anti-state, anti-regulatory mood that was congealing as neoconservatism. Blenkarn objected to the complicated regulatory process "where there is a necessity for people objecting to have lawyers present, present briefs and go through hearings." Why bother with this process, the Opposition asked, if the government could still approve or reject the CTC's decision? "The government cannot absolve itself from its responsibilities," Blenkarn claimed. "The way the bill is drawn, you are responsible for it." Ouellet did not deny this: "What Mr. Blenkarn says is pure political life." Nor were postal officials keen on the idea. They saw it as an expensive and time-consuming process that did not guarantee approval of rate and service proposals. There was also great uncertainty as to who should regulate the Post Office. Some groups, like the Canadian Chamber of Commerce, wanted the CRTC to regulate it, as the former had more experience in the communications and high technology area. But the CRTC had a very heavy workload. The CTC had time, but not much experience of activities beyond the POD's more narrow transportation ones. Designing and initiating a new regulatory body would be expensive and time consuming; and there was concern that the regulatory process might constrain the Post Office from acting in a commercial, market-oriented way. Finally, the postal unions were split, a number of them concluding that regulation would undermine their political leverage over Parliament and cabinet.[52]

The original legislation directed the CPC to attain "financial self-sufficiency" while providing "basic customary services." These important, controversial, and contradictory goals were not given precise definition. The legislation implied that CPC should balance its budget, but no time frame was provided, nor did the legislation suggest how CPC should realize this goal. Ouellet and his officials hinted that prices had to rise if the deficit was to be eliminated. A time frame for balancing the budget was suggested only late in the legislative process. Before a Senate committee in April 1981, Ouellet stated that "we have in mind to gear the corporation to achieve that objective within the next three to four years." The NDP's Orlikow asserted that postal self-sufficiency doomed Canadians to deteriorating services. The Canadian Direct Marketing Association considered the balanced budget target to be unreasonable. Other business groups such as the Canadian Chamber of Commerce welcomed the objective, but insisted that the legislation spell out the means to be used. Overall, the balanced budget goal did not generate intense debate, despite its consequences for postal services.[53]

With respect to postal services, Ouellet stated that the legislation was framed to ensure that CPC would continue to provide the level and extent of services to which Canadians had become accustomed. He assuaged anxieties that the new postal corporation would cut services in rural and remote areas:

> In villages and small towns across Canada, the Post Office remains one of the most frequently visited places. . ... The Post Office has over the years become a much needed resource centre. . ... the Post Office is a meeting place for all and creates a bond between members of the community. It is a unifying force which gives one the feeling of belonging. . ... in many places the Post Office Department was the only representative of the Canadian government. In many villages, the Canadian flag floats at the end of the pole in front of the Post Office and may be the only sign of the federal presence. . ... We urge the Crown corporation to maintain and reflect a corporate identity as an institution of the government of Canada.

The Opposition characterized this as rhetorical and empty political posturing. It argued that the service goal would be undermined once CPC acted to balance its budget. It wanted the government to spell out in the legislation the precise meaning of "basic customer service," to include home delivery to communities of a certain size, the maintenance of rural post offices, and the provision in the suburbs and rural areas of postal services equivalent to those provided in urban services. The postal unions placed intense pressure on the government to specify that the provision of postal services was the primary goal of the Post Office — a higher priority than goals such as financial self-sufficiency. Other groups pursued their particular interests in this area. For example, the Canadian Daily Newspaper Association argued that the legislation should guarantee daily service to all the rural routes in Canada.[54]

Two final issues are worth noting. Business groups such as the Canadian Chamber of Commerce, the Canadian Business Press, and the Magazine Association of Canada wanted the legislation to define the Post Office as an essential service in order to eliminate the postal unions' right to strike. Others made less draconian proposals for a system of binding arbitration. Ouellet maintained that these proposals were "unrealistic," given that the government could not restrain illegal strikes.[55] He proposed instead to give the postal unions increased responsibility, by appointing labour representatives to the board. The postal unions were told in pre-legislation discussions that they would be assigned three places on the Board. The issue was discussed in only general terms during the hearings. Labour representation on the board was not specified in the legislation, for doing so had created a problem in the United Kingdom when the postal unions quit the board and their places could not be filled. Ouellet wanted to make the board broadly representative of all postal constituencies. A small, seven-person board was proposed, in order to avoid political appointments. Most groups considered this number to be too small, as it would not allow a broad cross-section of postal users to be appointed. Various groups encouraged the government to name representatives of postal users — particularly themselves — to the board.[56] The Canadian Labour Congress, for instance, proposed that various such interests be appointed, including representatives from smaller communities.[57]

Policy Results: The Canada Post Corporation Act

Bill C-42 repealed the Post Office Act in order to establish the Canada Post Corporation. It received royal assent on 23 April 1981, and CPC came into existence on 16 October 1981. Bill C-42 was similar to Bill C-27 with some important exceptions, noted in the elaboration of the act that follows. Bill C-42 transferred to Canada Post Corporation postal power, authority, and responsibilities previously assigned to the POD; set CPC's goals and objectives; and established the procedures CPC was to follow in pursuing its responsibilities and goals.

Goals

Section 5 of the act set out the goals of the corporation. It was directed to collect, move, and deliver the mail while considering a number of criteria and objectives.

First, CPC was directed to be mindful of "the need to conduct its operations on a self-sustaining financial basis." No time frame was specified for balancing the budget, nor was "self-sustaining" defined: would it require simply a balance or an operating margin for investment and expansion? The government first introduced the CPC as a "Schedule C" Crown corporation, planning to reschedule it later as Schedule D — a corporation financially independent of the government.[58]

Second, CPC was to pursue financial self-sufficiency "while providing a standard of service that will meet the needs of the people of Canada and that is similar with respect to communities of the same size" (Section 5[2]c). This "service" goal was assigned equal status with the goal of a balanced budget. But the level of service to be attained or particular characteristics of service were not specified. The phrase "similar with respect to communities of the same size" was added during the legislative process, to ensure continued postal services in rural areas. This "comparability" clause involved a significant change from Bill C-27.[59]

A third goal specified in the legislation was the improvement of labour-management relations. CPC was to "utiliz[e] the human resources of the Corporation in a manner that will both attain the objects of the Corporation and ensure the commitment and dedication of its employees to the attainment of those objects." This goal was given equal status with the service and financial goals.

Fourth, the act settled the issue of postal involvement in the telecommunications and high-technology markets: it drew the CPC's attention to "the desirability of improving and extending its products and services in the light of developments in the field of communications." Its exclusive privilege would not be extended into these markets, but it was not denied the opportunity for involvement.[60]

Organization

The idea of a postal secretariat was dropped. A minister responsible for Canada Post Corporation would be held accountable for CPC in Parliament. The minister was not assigned a staff or a department, and his or her role was left implicit in the act. A nine-person board of directors would "direct and manage the affairs" of CPC.[61] Its composition was not specified; no positions were designated to postal unions, user groups, or community representatives. The chair of the board, the directors, and the president of CPC would be appointed by the government. The vice presidents of the corporation would be appointed by the board but approved by the government. There were no fixed terms for either the chair or the president. CPC was authorized to hire staff and set the terms and conditions of their employment. With certain exceptions — for example, in the provision of pensions — CPC employees would not be considered part of the public service, which allowed labour relations to be conducted outside the terms of the PSSRA.

Exclusive Privilege

Sections 14 and 15 transferred the POD's exclusive privilege to CPC. The act assigned to CPC "the sole and exclusive privilege of collecting, transmitting and delivering letters to the addressee thereof within Canada,"[62] and defined a letter indirectly, by elaborating what kinds of mail would not be covered by CPC's exclusive privilege. For example, "letters" did not include newspapers, magazines, books, catalogues, or goods. Other exceptions included:

- Letters carried "incidentally" to a friend's address (hand delivering of birthday cards and so on)
- "Letters in the course of transmission by any electronic or optical means" (electronic mail, telecommunications, facsimiles)
- Inter-office mail, documents issued by a court of justice (commissions, affidavits, writs, processes or proceedings), delivery notices carried without renumeration, and other idiosyncratic categories
- "Letters of an urgent nature that are transmitted by a messenger for a fee at least equal to an amount that is three times the regular rate of postage payable for delivery in Canada of similarly addressed letters weighing fifty grams" (courier services)

Outside of these exceptions, everything was a letter and the exclusive privilege prevailed. Three of the above exceptions were additions to those outlined in the earlier Bill C-27: inter-office, electronic, and time-sensitive mail. This settled two major matters. First, CPC's "monopoly" was not to be extended to electronic mail. Second, the courier industry would remain intact as a competitive market. First-class mail was "protected" by insistence that time-sensitive service had to be at least three times more expensive. Courier services and telecommunications were highly political issues and these exceptions to exclusive privilege were made under competing pressures. The minister wanted the Post Office to advance into telecommunications and electronic mail, as did postal management and the unions. He was also sympathetic to the view that private couriers should be constrained or eliminated. But neither objective was politically feasible. POD and union behaviour in the past inspired no confidence that CPC could at the moment perform in these areas effectively. The minister instead directed the postal unions and CPC to improve postal operations and "earn" the right to expansion of services.[63]

Powers and Procedures

Sections 16 and 17 of the act specified the legal powers assigned to CPC — such as the power to determine what is a letter, the conditions under which the mail is to be transmitted, the rates for this transmission, and the opening and closing of postal offices and routes — and the means by which it could exercise these powers. The procedure for price and regulation changes was altered during the legislative process. Third-party regulation was proposed both in Bill C-27 and in the first draft of Bill C-42: CPC's price and regulation proposals would be scrutinized at public hearings of the Canadian Transportation Committee. A more "traditional" approach was adopted instead: CPC would publicize its price and regulation proposals in the *Canada Gazette,* to afford "a reasonable opportunity ... to interested persons to make representations to the Minister." Sixty days later, the minister would recommend to the governor-in-council whether to accept, alter, or reject the proposals; the latter had sixty days to accept or reject the minister's recommendation. This "gazetting" system was intended to allow public input on postal changes in a relatively informal way. Ultimate authority for price and regulatory changes remained with the government.[64]

Relations With The Government

As already noted, the government set the Corporation's goals in the legislation. It had the authority to name the chair, the directors of the board, and the corporation's president, and to approve the appointment of vice presidents. It had authority over CPC rate and regulation changes. But the government did not rest content here: other parts of the act further extended its authority over CPC. Section 20 specified a "directive" power whereby CPC had to "comply with such directions as the Governor in Council or the Minister may from time to time give it." Section 21 specified that CPC could not acquire shares or companies without government approval. Section 28 forbade CPC to borrow, take on debt, or sell property without the approval of the minister of Finance. That minister could lend money to CPC up to a maximum of $500 million. Section 29 established a mechanism for the government to absorb deficits incurred in the postal operation. Section 31 provided for an annual audit by two auditors appointed by the government. Section 33 directed CPC to present an annual report to the minister, to be presented to Parliament and referred to the standing committee on transportation. Government authority in postal matters thus continued to be substantial.

Winners and Losers

The transformation of the POD into CPC was a fluid political process. To begin with, this was the first time a department had been transformed into a Crown corporation, so there was no model or tradition to guide the process of Crowning. But, second, this "open-ended-ness" reflected the conflicting pressures of the time. There was a sense of urgency to the view that economic policy — and Crown corporations — had to become more commercially oriented. At the same time, it was widely thought that Crown corporations should become more accountable. How these pressures were to be resolved was an open question. Third, postal discussions had taken on an anything-goes character, as a result of the crises and disruptions of the 1970s. Fourth, the constituency groups of the postal community were tremendously interested in what shape the postal corporation would take, and so participated energetically in the legislative process. Thus, the ultimate legislative shape and direction of CPC was very much up for grabs. Who were the winners and losers as the act was passed in April 1981?

Labour

The postal unions were afforded considerable input, working closely with the PMG and officials in drafting the legislation. This was an accomplishment in itself, and set a precedent for the future. They played a less central role in the legislative process, as one fish in a sea of interest groups. Nonetheless, the postal unions emerged from the process with a number of substantial accomplishments. First, they would bargain under the Canada Labour Code, a far freer regime than the restrictive PSSRA. Bargaining would be conducted directly with the management of the corporation, as opposed to indirectly with Treasury Board. Second, labour–management relations were given special status, cited as one of the three major objectives of the corporation. Third, the rights of their membership survived the transition to the corporate regime. The bargaining units were maintained, as were pension rights. All parties agreed that the planned merging of the bargaining units would have required too much change all at once. An agreement was reached to maintain the *status quo* for one more round of negotiations. Fourth, the postal unions had not been keen about third-party regulation. The regulatory process could have worked against them if the regulatory board became dominated by businesspeople and outsiders. The unions sensed that regulation might have inhibited CPC's aggressiveness as well as its capacity to raise prices to get needed revenue. They also felt that the existing system afforded them the opportunity to make a greater political impact. Fifth, they retained the right to strike, despite pressure from business for its elimination.[65]

In other areas, it was not evident that postal workers had been successful. First, the unions considered that section 5(2) identified service as the primary goal of CPC, with precedence over financial and labour relations objectives.[66] The phrasing of the service commitment was soft and general and, predictably, did not stand up to subsequent attacks. Deputy PMG Corkery and CPC president Warren maintain that this phrasing was a political "gesture" to the unions, not a concrete or specific policy directive.[67] A balanced-budget orientation had in the past conspired against service and union goals, and the section 5 objective of financial self-sufficiency was designed with this purpose in mind.

Second, the unions pressed to have the Post Office assigned more authority in the area of electronic mail. The act did not assign this authority to CPC, but neither did it disallow postal involvement in the area. Third, time-sensitive mail was another case of minimizing losses rather than maximizing gains. The unions recognized that it was not possible politically to eliminate the courier business. Unhappy that the act protected private couriers, they felt that CPC could take on the couriers in a competitive setting. Fourth, the unions did not obtain a very specific definition of "letter," which would have offered protection to the Post Office. (However, the approach used in the legislation provided substantial room to manoeuvre in the future.)[68]

The net balance of the postal unions' political influence was unclear. In the previous departmental setting, they had various political avenues for exerting pressure in Parliament. The act distanced CPC from the parliamentary process, suggesting that the unions would operate in a less political and more commercial environment. Depending on circumstances and skill, this might work to their advantage. Overall, though, the corporate setting diminished the political resources of the unions.[69]

Major Mail Users

The major mail users had a considerable impact on the legislative process, but their successes, while extensive, were not complete. They focused their attention on the definition of a letter, the CPC's role in telecommunications, and the containment of the postal monopoly.

The legislation protecting the courier industry from the postal monopoly was obviously a victory for the courier industry, and for the part of the commercial world that had come to rely on courier service during postal disruptions. The legislation gave CPC no special privileges in the telecommunications and high technology communications markets; it was simply directed to remain alive to technological developments. The definition of a letter remained an unfinished battle. Business wanted a narrow and constraining definition, but the government instead decided to list exceptions to the exclusive privilege.[70] This list addressed the concerns raised by business, but business remained apprehensive that CPC could expand in the future.

The continuation of the right to strike was a loss to certain business groups. What was more important to the major users, however, was the prospect of labour–management stability, which the new CLC labour regime promised. The section 5(2) statement on customary services was a minor victory for the periodical and newspaper associations, which wanted the second-class mail prerogatives to be maintained. Major users favoured a more formal and precise regulatory process for price and regulation changes, and so the abandonment of the CTC approach was a loss of sorts. The issue, however, had little salience at the legislative hearings. The alternative, gazetting system was obviously more "political" and less "neutral," but business influences this process as much as postal unions and the public.

Business wanted its interests represented directly on the board. Although the government rejected this approach as being too constraining, there were expectations that business interests would be adequately represented. In general, the major users benefitted from the creation of a de-politicized, commercially oriented corporation. This afforded them opportunities to make direct commercial arrangements and deal with the Post Office in a business-like manner. It promised an efficient communications network, which would increase productivity and competitiveness.

The General Public

Ordinary postal users were not well represented during the legislative process; rural constituencies, the suburbs, home-owners, or other postal constituencies outside of the major users and the unions had no formal presence. They were implicitly represented by others, such as unions and politicians. For example, the definition of exclusive privilege excluded hand-delivered greeting cards, a public concern pursued by politicians. Similarly, section 5(2) was changed to include a clause maintaining customary postal services, to guarantee consistent coast-to-coast service. This addressed the anxieties of rural and small-town residents. Maintenance of door-to-door mail delivery, regular delivery, and subsidization of second-class and other types of mail and services was implicit in this clause. However, the clause was also very broad and general; a more precise service clause would have better served the general public's interests. The balanced-budget objective seemed contrary to the interests of small postal users, as postal deficits subsidized the costs of postal services; but these deficits were paid for in taxes. Third-party regulation offered the prospect of "formalizing" the corporation's goals and responsibilities, and could have been used by public groups to press their cases and make the corporation live up to the service clause.[71] Instead, the gazetting system offered mixed possibilities for the general public. Price and regulation changes would ultimately end on the minister's desk. In this loose political setting, anything could happen. Public groups could exploit the political process for their purposes, but it was just as likely that business groups would exert inordinate influence. In broad terms, though, the general public would benefit from increased postal stability and a more commercial and efficient Post Office.

Postal Management

While remaining in the shadows, postal management played a central role in legislative consultations. It was happy with the results, although it would have supported any change from the departmental form.[72] There was nothing in the legislation that was irksome to postal managers. Some wanted to see recertification of the postal bargaining units, but this was not seriously considered. Management realized its longstanding ambition to bargain directly with the unions. It was delighted that third-party regulation was dropped, as that strategy appeared to be a formal, expensive, and time-consuming process that did not guarantee the desired outcome. The budget goal was desirable, as it gave management specific financial direction and promised to limit political intrusions. The service clause was worrisome as a future policy constraint, but it appeared to be empty and to have little authority. Postal management, although it pressed to limit couriers and extend CPC powers in technological areas, realized that neither was politically viable, and in any case, it felt that the corporation could become competitive in both areas. Broadly speaking, postal management was happy with the autonomy it had been assigned in the corporate form, but it was wary about the degree of authority retained by the government.[73] Future president Michael Warren was not terribly concerned about the legislation in any case: "I never felt it was what it said. . .. we just throw the ... legislation away, because this was for public consumption." Issues outside the legislation were often more important to postal management. For example, the implicit assumption that there would be labour representation on the board of directors worried it. As a further example, a verbal agreement was struck with Prime Minister Trudeau, Michael Pittfield, and André Ouellet that the latter would remain as minister responsible for Canada Post Corporation for Warren's full term; this was to guarantee Warren a degree of political stability and continuity and access to a senior minister of the government.[74]

The Government

The government appeared to be the big winner in creating Canada Post. It proclaimed that it had undertaken the biggest postal initiative since Confederation — an initiative that made almost everybody happy. This is a cheerful state of affairs for a government. Labour was happy to deal directly with postal management and had been flattered by its legislative involvement. Despite the strike in 1981, the postal unions were optimistic and open-minded, which augured well for industrial peace.[75] Business was happy with the idea of a commercially oriented Post Office free of political interference, limited in its monopoly reach, and directed to balance its budget. Political constituencies appeared happy with the prospect of maintained and improved postal services, fewer disruptive labour disputes, and less tax support of a self-sufficient, debt-free Post Office.

The only losers were the bureaucracy, Parliament, and MPs opposed to a continued postal monopoly. The bureaucracy saw its forces depleted by fifty thousand workers and its postal authority diminished. MPs' capacity to influence the Post Office would decline as it became commercialized and distanced. Backbench Tory MPs failed in their efforts to eliminate the Post Office's monopoly and force more competition.

The government seemed to have obtained the best of both worlds. It was rid of a political nuisance: the labour-troubled, debt-ridden, complaint-gen-erating Post Office, whose problems now belonged to the "autonomous" corporate management. The government claimed to have cut the bureaucracy by tens of thousands; the postal deficit would be placed in a different ac-counting column; and in any event, the autonomous corporation would be sure to act more efficiently. The government would now be insulated from the expectations that the departmental Post Office had in the past brought to it. At the same time, the government retained authority over the corpo-ration, which could be used advantageously. It retained patronage appoint-ments: nine board members and the chair, the corporation president and vice presidents. It had stamped its vision of the Post Office onto the legis-lation. It had the authority to audit the corporation's books and receive an annual report, which it could comment on and criticize. It could issue directives to the corporation to pursue certain policies or drop others. It held ultimate authority over price and regulation changes.

This last point clearly illustrates how the government emerged with con-siderable postal authority even after Crowning the POD. It had been expected that, once the POD was made into a Crown corporation, its monopoly powers would have to be regulated.[76] This regulation would distance the corporation from politics and the government — a prime reason for Crown-ing the Post Office. Third-party regulation was proposed in both Bill C-27 and the first version of Bill C-42. The government would lose its postal authority under such conditions. This strategy was dropped for a number of reasons. It was felt that it would be simply too much to introduce third-party regulation simultaneously with the transformation to corporate form. The anti-regulation feeling at the time suggested that this approach was too bureaucratic, undemocratic, formal, and expensive. There was uncertainty as to which agency should regulate Canada Post. The CTC had the time but experience only in transportation, not in communications; the CRTC had the appropriate technological experience but was already heavily burdened; a new agency would require substantial organization expenses and a long start-up period. But the key issue was, Who ultimately would be held accountable for price and regulation changes? The cabinet would approve changes, so the government would be involved.[77] Thus, a more traditional but "open" system was developed, the gazetting system, which offered obvious political advantages to the government. After the rates or regulation announcement had been made, the public could express its feelings. If there was no reaction, the government could approve the rate increase and state that this was the corporation's decision. But if public reaction was negative, the government could delay, cut, or reject the increase and appear as the protector of the public interest.[78]

Conclusion

Bill C-42 created the Canada Post Corporation, which at its birth in October 1981 was one of Canada's largest companies. It had fixed assets of $1.5 billion dollars, 29 sorting plants, 3,500 vehicles, 1.6 million lock boxes, 22,000 owned properties, 1,100 leased properties, 2,100 sub-post office agreements, more branch offices than the Canadian banks, and 62,000 employees.

CPC was born in inauspicious circumstances that shaped its character and limited its capacity. First, it inherited a daunting array of problems and challenges. Labour-management relations were poisonous, the legacy of countless strikes and disturbances in the previous fifteen years. CPC faced thousands of unresolved grievances, associated mainly with the mechanization program of the 1970s. Its agenda was complicated by a labour force too large for postal volumes, as a result of carrying a double cohort of labour through the mechanization program. It confronted collective agreements and work practices that were not of its making. The situation with management was hardly more promising. Management's morale had been broken by government neglect, the mechanization program, and guerrilla warfare with labour. There was also universal agreement that the mechanization program had created a set of plants that were vastly oversized, dehumanizing, and unmanageable. The corporation inherited serious financial and competitive difficulties. The deficit for 1980-81 was $487 million — 32 per cent of postal revenues. Competitive challenges abounded, from couriers, shippers, and delivery alternatives in the traditional sectors to the telephone, telecommunications, and other electronic communications in high-tech areas. First-class mail volumes — the lifeblood of the postal operation — stagnated in the late 1970s, and in 1981-82 were only 4 per cent higher than in 1973-74.

The second circumstance that shaped CPC's character and capacity was the cross-pressures under which it was formed. Governments across the Western world were experiencing a fiscal and ideological crisis as a result of the tapering off of the post-war boom. Economic growth slowed and governments confronted deficits. Many chose to cut programs and employees and to give their economic policies a more commercial orientation. The POD was dissolved to this end — taking 60,000 employees and a half billion dollars off the government's operational books. The Canada Post Corporation was born, and was directed to act commercially and increase its productivity and competitiveness. At the same time, though, there was growing political suspicion of Crown corporations. They were seen to have proliferated out of democratic control, incurring debts, misbehaving, and not carrying out their public mandate. Governments moved to increase public scrutiny and control of Crown corporations — precisely at the time when CPC was formed. This process culminated in the 1984 revisions to the Financial Arrangements Act, which made government relations with Crown corporations more precise, specific, and authoritative.

The prospects for Canada Post Corporation's success were highly uncertain. It was given a commercial mandate and the autonomy to confront the formidable array of postal problems in a corporate manner. But it was not given *carte blanche* to do so. Canadian governments' traditional ambivalence about Crown corporations was reproduced in Bill C-42. A Crown corporation was formed enthusiastically, but the government refused to let the Post Office leave its political home completely. Government authority was retained via the power of appointment (the board and its chair, the president and vice presidents); the directive power; price and regulation authority; the setting of postal goals and objectives in the enabling legislation; and scrutiny of the annual corporate report. The government's involvement in postal affairs increased in 1984, when amendments to the Financial Administration Act required the corporation to submit annually a five-year plan for approval.

Traditional governmental ambivalence saw the creation of an autonomous, market-driven *corporation,* but one existing within a *governmental* web. And the constraints on CPC's commercial orientation extended beyond this formal relationship. First, the legislation directed CPC to maintain customary services. This had obvious non-commercial implications. The legislation did not elaborate on what constituted customary services; the government would eventually have to decide what this meant. The legislation did not specify the "trade-offs" between service and fiscal goals, the time frame for reaching the target of a balanced budget, or the specific postal services that could be considered for elimination. Instead, it reproduced and strengthened public expectations about the services that Canada Post should continue to deliver. The government would eventually have to decide how to resolve the tension between these economic and social goals — as it had been doing since 1867.

The legislation placed a second constraint on CPC's commercial orientation. The government bowed to business and ideological opposition to giving the postal corporation authority to expand into new technological and market activities. These were not disallowed, but the legislation did not assist CPC in dealing with the competitive challenges that had been ignored over the previous decade. The courier industry was left intact to skim a considerable amount of postal business from profitable urban markets. Exceptions to the exclusive privilege allowed a number of alternative and highly competitive forms of delivering mail. The legislation "encouraged" CPC to be mindful of technological developments, but it entered the technological race from far behind and without any legislative or financial assistance. Indeed, while CPC was directed to act "commercially," it was not given much incentive or authority to do so. When it acted like a private-sector operator, reaction was swift, and it lacked adequate authority and political protection to resist ideological and private-sector attacks. In short, CPC faced a market constraint on its commercial orientation as substantial as the service constraint.

The Canada Post Corporation Act faithfully reproduced Canadian governments' longstanding optimism that a Crown corporation could happily and creatively balance commercial behaviour with the attainment of political goals. CPC was directed to act commercially; balance its books; solve labour problems; maintain customary postal services; follow political directives; and remain subject to political decisions. How it proceeded to manage the unresolved tensions between commercial and political responsibilities is the subject of the following chapters.

Chapter Seven

CANADA POST AND THE LIBERAL GOVERNMENT,

1981–1984

C anada Post Corporation's first years provided a test case of whether a postal corporation could successfully balance the economic and social responsibilities assigned to it. CPC operated between 1981 and 1984 under the Liberal government that had created it. The Liberal vision was that the postal Crown was both a commercial business operation and a public institution with social goals. From Confederation to 1981, postal politics had been shaped by the trade-off between economic and social forces; the Liberals reproduced this tension in the Canada Post Corporation Act, even as the POD was transformed into an "autonomous" corporation. CPC was directed to balance its budget as well as to maintain customary services and improve labour–management relations. This was a difficult if not impossible task, especially given the POD's legacy of declining competitiveness, massive deficits, bitter industrial relations, inhuman postal plants, and high public expectations.

CPC continued to function in a political milieu, despite its increased autonomy. First, the act granted the government considerable postal authority. Second, the legislation left dangling the precise meaning of CPC's commercial and social goals and the character of the trade-off between them. The Liberals optimistically assigned CPC the task of juggling these balls better than the POD had done in the past. However, it was inevitable that goals and trade-offs would be determined by the government. The political contours of the postal scene remained largely unchanged. Like the POD before it, CPC would be required to balance political necessity with commercial imperatives.

The circumstances in which the CPC would have to pull off this balancing act seemed propitious. First, the major postal players were well cast. André Ouellet, the minister responsible for CPC, and CPC president Michael Warren were both widely experienced in government. They were pragmatists who, while alive to economic realities, were not consumed with ideological passion or a blind faith in the market. They were sensitive to political circumstances and the play of social expectations. Second, this was a period of postal calm, the result of a number of contingent factors. The six-and-five anti-inflation program put off labour negotiations until 1984, so CPC did not have to endure destabilizing contractual negotiations. An unusually large price increase in 1982 kept CPC financially afloat, creating the illusion of financial improvement (despite the business implications of the early 1980s recession). Canada Post's first report and five-year plan did not appear until 1984, so there were few targets for postal critics' fire. Scrutiny of postal matters eased as public attention shifted to other matters once the CPC act was passed; a honeymoon period began. As Parliament's postal role dwindled, postal politics took the form of elite accommodation among the major postal players outside of public view. This increased CPC's operating space. Media coverage was limited and positive, the result of Warren's superb public relations vision of a humane postal corporation heroically balancing social and economic goals to resolve the postal problem. Finally, the administrative scene remained stable. In contrast with PMGs in the 1960s and 1970s, whose tenure was brief, Warren and Ouellet stayed on until the 1984 election. These were good conditions in which to test CPC's balancing act.

Unfortunately, a number of events demonstrated that disequilibrium still ruled at the Post Office. The 1982 battle over the definition of a letter, the fallout from price increases, and the reaction to CPC's diversification efforts demonstrated that the tension between social and economic goals had not been resolved. Ideological, business, and interest group reaction to postal initiatives indicated the extent and strength of the constraints on CPC. These pressures were not played out exclusively through CPC, but rather were resolved by the government — typically to CPC's disadvantage. Despite its increased autonomy, the corporation remained dependent on the government in numerous areas, because of the persistence of the deficit, the reproduction of public expectations about customary postal service and labour expectations about jobs and working conditions, and the Liberal government's penchant for using its postal authority to political ends. CPC enjoyed the worst of two worlds: its commercial autonomy was constrained while its social responsibilities were maintained.

The test period ended with the summer 1984 election of a Conservative government. Within a year, Warren departed and the postal balancing act was terminated. Economic goals were given priority over social ones: CPC's commercial autonomy was expanded and its social responsibilities limited. In this chapter I explore the limits to, and consequences of, the early balancing act. I first review the postal vision that inspired CPC during this period. I then review the policies initiated to realize its social and economic objectives, following up with an evaluation of the political and economic consequences of these actions. A concluding section assesses the political results of CPC's performance in this period.

Political Setting and Postal Vision

The government set the character of the new postal regime in two ways. First, it injected its expectations into the legislation that created CPC, directing it to balance commercial and social goals. Second, it appointed the key personnel to implement its expectations, including the president, the board, and its chair.

The government chose Michael Warren for the position of president from a short list of candidates presented by an executive search firm in February 1981.[1] This looked to be an inspired choice. Warren fit the vision that the government had imposed on CPC's legislative mandate. Described as the "ultimate golden civil servant," Warren was an imposing and attractive figure. Tall, handsome, and extremely articulate, he had held a number of senior bureaucratic appointments in Ontario under Conservative governments. He became the general manager of the Toronto Transit Commission in 1975 where, by all accounts, his term had been very successful. He subsequently became the interim manager of the Canadian National Exhibition. On 1 April 1981, he was hired as a special adviser to PMG Ouellet, and waited for the Crown corporation legislation to be passed to become CPC's first president.[2]

Ouellet chose Warren for a number of reasons. He did not want to make an internal appointment, and so he looked for someone from outside immediate government and postal circles, someone with knowledge and experience of government that did not limit his or her managerial and business talent and experience. Thus, an obvious candidate, Deputy PMG Jim Corkery, was not a serious contender, even though he was short-listed. Corkery had both private- and public-sector experience, as well as immense postal experience and operational knowledge; but his long and hard experience working with the postal unions during the gruesome 1970s made it unlikely that he could establish the kind of rapport with labour that Ouellet sought. Moreover, the public relations impact of the move to a Crown corporation would be limited if CPC appeared on the scene with the same POD officials at its top. CUPW very much welcomed the appointment of Warren and thought that they could work with him. Public response to Warren's appointment also was positive.[3]

Ouellet and Warren met frequently before the appointment. Warren asked Ouellet to draw up a one-page statement of CPC's purpose to ensure that his and Ouellet's postal visions were in harmony. Warren was keen to avoid an unstable political environment, with postal ministers coming and going and CPC exposed to political winds of change. An understanding was reached with Prime Minister Trudeau and Privy Council head Michael Pittfield that Ouellet would remain as PMG throughout Warren's time as president. Warren understood that Ouellet was more experienced, powerful, and senior than any replacement might be. He wanted CPC to remain in a strong position in its relations with the government. Ouellet subsequently retained responsibility for Canada Post even after becoming minister of Labour.[4]

The relationship between Ouellet and Warren was fluid but intense. Arguments and disagreements were not uncommon, and Ouellet often made decisions that were not in Warren's favour. An early disagreement occurred even before CPC began to operate. Ouellet named René Marin as chair of the board. Marin was familiar with the functioning of the Post Office and its problems, having chaired a royal commission on the security and investigation services within it.[5] The postal unions were not excited about this appointment, nor was Warren. The appointment called for a full-time chair, and this suggested to Warren that the government wanted its representative to be directly involved in CPC's operations and decisions. Warren preferred a part-time, less intrusive chair. This anxiety was exacerbated by a second concern, that Marin was not a businessman; he would not bring commercial experiences or sympathies to the job. Nor was he from the civil service (he was a judge); he did not offer political experiences or skills that might have been useful to Warren. Ouellet persisted, seeing Marin's "public-sector" orientation as balancing Warren's more "commercial" orientation. The appointment also balanced an English Canadian president with a French Canadian chair, a strategy also held to in the vice presidential appointments.[6]

Warren was also unhappy when Ouellet named two labour representatives to the board. Neither Ron Lang nor Henri Lorrain were from the postal unions, but Warren was not keen on CPC's first years' including an experiment in industrial democracy. Ouellet again persisted, as he wanted the board to represent business, labour, and postal users in CPC's "balanced" pursuit of its social, economic, and labour goals. The general public was to be represented by Lynda Sorenson, a Liberal from the Northwest Territories and a member of the Consumers Association of Canada. Business representatives included George Cohon of McDonald's, Clarence Beaudoin of Bombardier and Montreal Trust, and Derek Oland of Moosehead.[7] The attempt to strike a regional balance also influenced the choice of board members.[8]

These top appointments reflected the postal vision that motivated CPC's first years. Officials saw CPC as a "self-supporting social business" and "a socially responsible and economically viable organization." CPC would sign "business-like but people-caring contracts." Its legislative mandate came down to three primary goals: financial self-sufficiency, maintenance of customer service, and improved labour–management relations. These were repeated like a mantra during CPC's early years. "At first blush," Marin admitted, these appear to be "irreconcilable objectives," and "satisfying them [will be] a balancing act of delicate but monumental proportions." But, he maintained, "we can pull them together and manage them as being mutually self-supporting rather than conflicting goals." This optimism irradiated CPC's first business plan in 1983–84: "Our three basic objectives are closely interrelated, and progress can only be made by keeping a balance among all three."[9]

Despite the non-hierarchical presentation of this triumvirate of goals, commercialization of the Post Office was the *sine qua non* of CPC's first years. A marketing report prepared for Warren gave a sense of urgency to this task. To survive, CPC had to change the image that it projected to the public: "CP suffers from a relatively poor image . . . the perceived negative influence of unions and politicians and government agencies contributes to the poor image . . .. Canadian's beliefs in the myths of free enterprise come through clearly in this survey. CP should emphasize its new business-like approach to postal services and its willingness to compete."[10]

Thus, one of the corporation's first objectives was to convince the public and the market that CPC was now a customer-driven commercial institution. It promised to be competitive and to follow a commercial and market-driven agenda — not one set by the government or the postal unions.[11] Its considerable efforts to this are discussed below; the immediate results were heartening. The 1983 Canadian Trend Report indicated that CPC's image had improved, because it now gave the impression that it was "business-like." Any lingering weakness in this area was due to the public impression of continuing government interference and labour influence. These would have to be minimized, if not eliminated.[12]

The need to project a commercial orientation was underpinned by CPC's understanding of market conditions. The information/communications market expanded 115 per cent in the 1970s, triple the rate of economic growth. Mail volumes also expanded faster than the rate of economic growth, but not as quickly as other sectors or as fast as in the past. Table 1 indicates that postal volumes grew by only 41 per cent (first-class by 43 per cent). This was 38 per cent lower than in the previous dozen years. A 1981 study by Price Waterhouse demonstrated that postal service was being left behind in the communications market because of its declining competitiveness and importance. This was particularly noticeable in comparison with long-distance telephone usage. As Table 9 shows, long-distance calls grew twice as fast as first-class mail between 1949 and 1959, four times as fast between 1959 and 1969 and between 1969 and 1979, and seven times as fast between 1979 and 1989. Long-distance calls grew from 8 per cent of first-class mail in 1949 to 44 per cent in 1979 (and 64 per cent in 1989). First-class mail's share of the information market fell from 17 per cent in 1965 to 13 per cent in 1975 (to 5 per cent in 1985). Mail's diminishing competitiveness was a function of a number of factors. Its high demand for labour and energy generated a high cost structure; its technology provided a slow service; its constrained and uniform rate structure inhibited business opportunities; and its susceptibility to competition made its volume and revenue prospects uncertain. Rising postal costs and prices could push the Post Office out of the competitive race, to be left with the low-priority, isolated, marginal, and unprofitable parts of the market.[13]

An understanding of the competitive situation underlay CPC's actions and dominated its early annual reports and plans. Warren argued that "we are far more vulnerable to competition than people realize — from currently available communications and distribution services."[14] CPC derived only 60 per cent of its revenue from its exclusive privilege over first-class mail; the other 40 per cent was in competitive markets, where it was faring poorly (for example, parcel volumes had collapsed to 1940s levels.) Within the first-class "monopoly" CPC faced real technological competition. This pointed it in the commercial, customer-oriented direction that was the basis of its corporate vision. Addressing the issue of sluggish volumes and rising competition, the first annual corporate report of 1982-83 rejected the Price-Waterhouse scenario of the Post Office becoming a service of last resort: "Rather than adapt its system to shrinking volumes, Canada Post sought to expand the flow of mail."[15] The customer-driven strategy was a survival one, to sustain and expand CPC's volumes in a competitive environment.

Warren thus spent a considerable amount of time and energy in CPC's early years doing public relations work. He travelled the country articulating the new CPC vision, selling the image of a Canada Post anxious to please customers and keen to attain new clients. At the same time, he chanted the CPC mantra that its new business orientation was tempered by its social and labour-management goals. This required him to market CPC's plans to an eclectic array of constituency groups, to sell its vision to each of its stakeholders. All the while, he noted, "We are subjected as an organization to the most minute and ongoing examination of our activities, probably more so than any other organizations and institutions in this country."[16]

Postal Actions

Less than a month after CPC came into existence, the federal budget of 12 November 1981 directed it to balance its books by the 1985-86 fiscal year.[17] This placed CPC's financial goal at the centre of its plans and actions. The privileging of this goal was not entirely surprising, as key reason for Crowning the POD was to relieve the federal government's budgetary problem by cutting its spending on the Post Office.

What was surprising to many was the establishment of a formal timetable to reach a balanced postal budget. The balanced budget goal and its timetable had not been discussed to any great extent in the legislative debates of 1980 and early 1981, nor in meetings between the government and the postal unions. Ouellet had been anxious to delay discussion of it, as it was an obvious potential source of political conflict. Moreover, as Ouellet put it, not much more could be accomplished than to agree to disagree with the postal unions on this matter.[18] But once the CPC legislation was passed, the issue moved from Ouellet's domain to the government's — where the postal deficit was an element in the government's wider financial planning. The government then insisted on a timetable for deficit reduction, to which Ouellet reluctantly agreed. The postal unions and political opposition expressed genuine surprise,[19] maintaining that this would undermine the goal of maintaining customary postal service.[20]

Nonetheless, the timetable for self-sufficiency that was set was an early CPC "victory," for Treasury Board and the Priorities and Planning Committee wanted it to balance its books in *two* years. This would have required an increase in first-class postal rates from seventeen cents to fifty-four cents (an immediate balance would have required a sixty-four-cent stamp). Early relations between Warren and Treasury Board were quite hostile as a result. "Negotiations" between CPC and the government led to a compromise in late 1981, to balance the books by the end of the first five-year plan in 1985–86.[21]

The directive to balance the budget was the government's first straight-forward signal to CPC of how it should proceed. It moulded all of CPC's activities, putting the budget goal in the foreground of all planning and decisions. Indeed, one can organize all of CPC's policies in this period according to how they contributed to meeting the balanced-budget timetable. There were four ways in which CPC could meet the schedule. On the expenditure side, it could restrain its costs and try to improve productivity, or it could cut or rationalize services. On the revenue side, it could raise prices or try to increase postal business and volumes. As we will see, the first three had serious limits, which led CPC to concentrate on the fourth.

Generally, CPC pursued a two-step financial strategy: first, a large increase in prices immediately after Crowning, which would substantially reduce the deficit; and second, non-price and longer-run strategies, such as increasing productivity and reducing costs, which would eliminate the remainder of the deficit.[22] On 25 September 1981 — three weeks before CPC came into formal existence — a general, across-the-board price increase was announced, which would increase postal revenue by an estimated $500 million. The price of a first-class stamp was increased 75 per cent from seventeen cents to thirty cents. Overseas mail and third-class prices doubled. The enormity of the price increase reflected a number of factors. First, there was a "catch-up" character to the increase: prices had not changed in the previous two years, and postal services had been seriously underpriced for the last two decades. It was estimated that the deficit would rise to $1 billion if prices did not increase for another year. Second, the increase reflected a change in philo sophical orientation, away from taxpayer support for postal services (via the deficit) to a user-pay principle. The thirty-cent price involved a guess as to what the market would bear; there was little "scientific" basis for the price chosen, for CPC lacked detailed financial or other information. Third, political considerations loomed large. CPC's first years provided a honeymoon period, a one-time opportunity for such an unpopular and enormous increase.[23] Indeed, neither Ouellet nor Warren wanted to make the announcement and take the blame alone; they announced the increase jointly.[24] A further two-cent price increase was introduced a year later.

CPC announced in its first report (1982–83) that the second price increase would be its final resort to this budget-balancing tactic: "In the next phase of the turnaround, Canada Post will shift the bulk of the financial burden from customers and the taxpayers to the Corporation itself." CPC concluded that further price increases would be counterproductive: "Many of Canada Post's products and services are at the edge of price tolerance," explained Warren. "We would be in danger of pricing ourselves out of some markets if we instituted the previously planned pricing strategy for the 1984-88 period." CPC announced an indefinite price freeze in September 1983 and backed away from a planned price increase in October 1984. Postal prices were not increased until 1985.[25] The price-increase approach to a balanced budget quickly reached its limit, for competitive reasons, particularly given CPC's weakened monopoly position.

Another way to balance the budget was to reduce costs to cut expenditures. Numerous such initiatives were undertaken, some of them symbolic, as in May 1982, when Warren introduced a policy of executive wage restraint (salary increases were limited to 5 per cent).[26] Other actions were more substantial. On the capital side, expenditures between 1982-83 and 1985-86 were limited to $214 million, which was $82 million less than depreciation. This lower pace of capital spending may have reflected Warren's scepticism about the mechanization process, which he felt had been a catastrophic mistake; he considered selling plants like Gateway, which he saw as a dehumanizing and unproductive white elephant.[27] On the labour side, there were three programs to reduce expenditures. First, Warren insisted in 1982 that unless productivity was raised and a business-like approach was taken to reducing the deficit, fifteen hundred jobs might have to be cut. He promised no lay-offs for the time being, and a policy of attrition was pursued to eliminate three thousand jobs between 1981 and 1984. This included the elimination of eleven hundred mail-sorting jobs in 1980-81 and another seven hundred over the following three years. Wicket jobs were also eliminated by replacing postal stations with sub-post offices (see below). Less expensive part-time workers were used to an increasing extent.[28] Second, CPC claimed that the level of absenteeism was double the private-sector rate in comparable areas. A program to reduce absenteeism was introduced, to increase productivity and save $100 million. The 1984-85 report noted $10 million had been saved by lowering the absenteeism rate by 1.24 days per year.[29] Third, Warren tried to address the issue of wages and productivity: "While Canada Post's wages and benefits are among the highest in the message and parcel delivery industry, a major problem is that our output per employee is significantly lower." But negotiation over wages and productivity was not possible while contracts were frozen by the six-and-five program. In its earlier 1981 negotiations with the LCUC, a fairly generous settlement was ostensibly financed by a productivity agreement. LCUC members gained an inflation-proof wage increase, the first dental plan in the federal public service, and a wage and cost-of-living-allowance increase of 12 per cent.[30] Overall, though, Table 4 indicates that labour costs as a share of overall costs fell only modestly, from 75.4 per cent in 1980-81 to 74.4 per cent in 1984-85.

There were limits to the cost-cutting approach to deficit reduction. For example, controlling executive salaries hampered CPC's capacity to attract quality private-sector managers, another CPC objective. Limiting capital expenditures would run down plant and equipment, lowering productivity over the long term. Cost-cutting efforts on the labour front were in tension with CPC's responsibility to improve labour–management relations. Serious cost cutting — in the form of either lay-offs or wage renegotiation — would weaken CPC's capacity to pursue this goal. And CPC was very sensitive in this area; it consulted with labour on major policy issues and on the construction of the business plan,[31] as well as placing two labour representatives on the Board.[32] It used attrition rather than lay-offs to reduce the labour force. Its wage settlements in 1981 and 1985 were too generous to help in reducing the deficit. Warren later admitted that CPC's deficit could not be resolved until wages, benefits, and performance conformed to private-sector levels.[33]

A third approach to reducing the postal deficit involved cutting or rationalizing postal services to decrease expenses. Warren early on suggested that there would be substantial initiatives of this sort. Asked what was involved in maintaining "basic customary service," he replied that this could involve a mix of improving services in the aggregate while initiating specific service cuts. "I believe basic customary service . . . is a phrase which is a moving concept . . .. If it is anything else, it means a mandate to make no changes."[34] But CPC initiated relatively few service cuts in this period. The most notable was the August 1982 decision to terminate Saturday mail delivery in the rural areas. Overall, CPC actually introduced more service improvements than cuts in this period, although the quality of service may have suffered with the decline in the number of postal workers and post offices. The Priority Post system was expanded, service testing was introduced, the freeze on expanding home delivery was lifted, special Christmas rates were offered, and new services were introduced. At most, Warren prepared the way for future service changes. For example, he marketed the idea of community (group) mailboxes even as 170 new letter carrier routes were approved in February 1982 and 365,000 more addresses received home delivery between 1981 and 1985.[35] Warren insisted that universal door-to-door delivery conflicted with and would have to bow to the goal of financial self-sufficiency. CPC introduced the first community boxes in 1984, and declared that it was considering ending home delivery in new subdivisions: servicing an address through a community box cost it $28, compared to $113 per home delivery address. "The question becomes," claimed Warren, "do you give Cadillac service to 50,000 homes and businesses or Volkswagen service to 200,000?" Indeed, in its submission to the Marchment Committee, CPC predicted that "costs will eventually cause door-to-door delivery to follow the path of dairy and bakery industries."[36] CPC documents indicate that it was also considering a variety of other service rationalizations, including post office closings, fee for delivery, franchising, and contracting out of trucking and transportation.[37]

Service rationalization to reduce the deficit confronted severe constraints in the form of CPC's legislative responsibility to maintain customary postal service. "The Post Office has been run almost as a social service up until 3 or 4 years ago," Warren observed. "People take it as an inalienable right that they should have letter carrier service as soon as they move into their house in the country even though the sod is not down yet. It's a Canadian ethic." The idea of a "right" to door-to-door delivery had to be neutralized if the deficit was to be controlled.[38] At this stage, though, neither the public nor the government accepted that this right should be abandoned. As a result, this and other cost-saving service cuts could not be pursued with any great devotion.

The first three budget-reducing options encountered great obstacles. Price increases were constrained by competition in the market; cost cutting was constrained by productivity concerns and the objective of improving labour–management relations; and service rationalization was constrained by social expectations and CPC's responsibility to maintain customary postal services. Some of these limits could be overcome, but only through government initiatives, and the Liberal government was not inclined, for example, to jettison the service or labour goals or increase CPC's power in the market. Thus, CPC looked to a fourth tactic to balance its budget: expansion of postal business and volumes. This approach did not appear at first glance to suffer the same sorts of restraints as the other tactics. Indeed, it appeared to be in harmony with CPC's triumvirate of goals, particularly in symbolic terms. CPC initiatives to increase business could have employment-generating implications, which would ease pressure to cut jobs and reduce labour expenditures and would contribute to improved labour–management relations. Business initiatives could also increase the products and services offered to CPC's customers, thereby also improving its commercial and entrepreneurial image.[39] Increasing business thus became the centrepiece of CPC strategy in this period, to reduce the deficit, provide and improve customary postal services, and maintain the postal labour force and pay its wage bill.

Over and above its public relations aspects, the volume expansion strategy had a wide array of elements. First, Warren assembled a new postal management team, recruiting fifteen private-sector senior managers and releasing most of the old POD management, who were considered to be insufficiently commercially oriented. This move was intended to inject strong corporate and commercial elements into CPC from the private sector. The government and the board gave Warren a free hand to this end.[40] CPC then "launched one of the largest internal management training programs in Canada . . . to enhance our ability to manage the turnaround of the Corporation." Its internal structure was revamped to create project-oriented management teams and increased managerial accountability. A Business Development Division was established, to exploit CPC's delivery and retail network, to protect it from competition, and to increase volumes.[41]

Second, CPC introduced a twelve-point service improvement plan, to highlight its increased reliability, commercial orientation, and focus on the customer. It expanded sales and marketing efforts and pushed vigorously into ad mail. It promoted and improved product lines like Priority Post and Telepost. Priority Post was expanded in 1983 to random, non-contract users and by 1984 extended to five hundred cities and eighteen countries. Changes to parcel post ranged from proof of delivery to increased ceilings on COD. The Incentives Rates Program diversified CPC's rate structure, offering postal discounts to major users and resulting in a range of nine different rates over and above the basic first-class rate. There were experiments with precoded mail and parcel pick-up. All these initiatives were designed to attract and expand business volumes by creating an image of a dynamic, competitive, and modern commercial organization. Business reaction was favourable: CPC was characterized as a "reborn" commercial player in the communications market.[42] CPC also introduced a new definition of a letter to protect its first-class volumes from competitors, particularly in the area of bill delivery.

Third, CPC introduced testing systems to increase its service achievements and improve its image as a reliable communications service. For the first time in the history of the Post Office, testing reports on first-class mail movement were issued to the public on a regular basis. An internal evaluation system tested the delivery rates of forty thousand pieces of mail a month. CPC claimed that national on-time delivery rose from 70 per cent in October 1981 to 89 per cent in 1982–83. Regular performance reports were subsequently released, with as much publicity as possible. This was supplemented in 1983 by the Customer Co-Operative Testing Service, in which postal customers themselves measured the mail performance that they experienced. Stung by suspicions that these tests were biased, CPC later hired an independent research organization to test sixty thousand pieces of mail a month, which were delivered to houses in thirty Canadian centres.[43]

Fourth, CPC (via a task force) created new products to generate increased business and revenues. This was important for CPC's future, as first-class mail was a "mature" product with little growth potential. Alternative activities proposed included selling traveller's cheques, lottery tickets, and packaging material in postal outlets; managing the federal government's sports pool; offering electronic mail; using letter carriers to read meters; and offering banking and catalogue services in remote areas.[44] CPC aggressively created and distributed advertising material, particularly newspaper inserts. It entered an electronic mail venture with Trans Canada Telephone System. It invested in its e-mail capacity, expanding Intelpost and Envoypost (a next-day message delivery system). It created an electronic bulk mail capacity, with a national electronic printing and delivery service, and public access to e-mail networks.[45]

There were two especially noteworthy retail initiatives. The Consumers Post program was introduced in February 1984. This was an experimental project, in which CPC would act as a modified sales outlet for Consumers Distributors. A ninety-day pilot project was established in eight CPC outlets in Quebec and Ontario, where Consumers Distributors had no presence. Customers placed a Consumers Distributors order for a product at a postal outlet, and returned within three days to collect the item. CPC was willing to consider similar arrangements with other retail and marketing organizations, such as banks.[46] As well, CPC experimented with a number of new kinds of retail outlets to increase postal business. In February 1984, the Retail Outlet Experiment was announced. Six former sub-post offices were converted to retail outlets, to be staffed by CPC personnel.[47] Further, five "New Directions" retail outlets were to be opened in large shopping or major retail office centres through the mid-1980s. These outlets featured a customer-oriented layout: self-service shelves filled with new products like toy mail trucks, mail box banks, and promotional material on postal services.

These retail experiments were featured in contracts signed by CUPW in the mid-1980s (the 1985 contract specified that a total of nineteen New Directions outlets and nine more retail outlets were to be in operation by October 1986).[48] The diversification strategy dovetailed with CUPW's "Job Creation through Service Expansion" strategy, introduced in 1982 (this was the origin of labour's "alternate plan"). The six-and-five program disallowed bargaining, so the postal unions had time to experiment.[49] They supported these and other initiatives as a way of saving the Post Office through expanding it.[50]

In sum, constraints on increasing prices, rationalizing services, and cutting costs led CPC to emphasize initiatives to increase business volumes as the way to balance the budget. The tactic was critical, as it was a way of buying time until CPC could improve its productivity. It was also a way of building consensus on postal matters, as each constituency group could conceivably benefit from this approach: labour in the form of job maintenance and expansion; the public and business via new, improved postal services; and the government by a smaller deficit. Hence, Warren expended considerable effort in marketing this approach to all members of the postal community. The approach was also a way of avoiding more Draconian measures, such as service rationalizations, post office closings, lay-offs, and wage cuts. Indeed, if the business volume strategy failed, CPC's juggling act would be over: it would be unable to balance its budget without undermining its social goals. The government and CPC would confront a choice. If balancing the budget remained the top policy priority, CPC would have to initiate cost cutting and service rationalizations with serious and disruptive implications for its labour and service goals; or the pursuit of the labour and service goals would require abandonment of the balanced budget goal. Either approach would require a serious reconceptualization of CPC.

Policy Reactions

The four budget-balancing tactics generated a combination of political, ideological, market, and interest group reactions. These responses constricted CPC's capacity to use these tools and undermined its efforts to improve its budgetary situation.

To begin with, the privileging of the balanced budget over social goals was controversial in itself. There was nothing in the legislation establishing CPC that gave any guidance on how long it should take to attain self-sufficiency; the timetable was imposed on CPC by the Liberal government. CPC did not want to be saddled with a publicly posted time frame for self-sufficiency, which created an inflexible planning situation and set CPC up for embarrassment and ridicule if it was unsuccessful. CPC managed to negotiate an extension of the timetable before it was publicly announced, from two years to five years (i.e., by 1985-86). Thereafter, it tried to push the deadline further into the future with each passing year. For example, in its first annual report (1982-83) CPC extended its own expectations of reaching self-sufficiency to 1987-88.

Nonetheless, even a five- or six-year balanced budget plan presented certain policy consequences — especially in the early 1980s recession. The downturn in capital expenditures was a case in point; the normal pace of renewal of plant and equipment was slowed to serve the goal of a balanced budget. The timetable was thoroughly criticized by the opposition parties and postal interest groups. Conservative Stan Darling characterized it as an "insane repayment schedule," and the NDP's Kristiansen ridiculed the government for imposing "unrealistic and stupid restrictions . . . at the same time as demanding service improvements," which "creates an unrealistic pair of handcuffs for Post Office management." The Conservatives' Bud Bradley questioned why CPC could not be subsidized like other Crown corporations: "We could maybe slide the deficit laterally for a year or two. We could maybe allow a longer period for it to be paid off. We could maybe authorize a permanent subsidy program." Opposition critics concluded that the timetable required cuts that would lead to a deterioration in postal service, and the postal unions and postal interests concurred with this view.[51]

Once announced, the balanced budget timetable took on a symbolic quality, representing a challenge to service and labour goals. All CPC's actions were looked upon suspiciously as designed simply to remedy the budget imbalance, and everything negative about the postal condition was blamed on the timetable, from deteriorating service and limited home delivery to rising prices. The timetable seriously weakened the stock of good will that CPC began with in 1981, and put the corporation on the defensive at precisely the moment when it wanted to adopt an offensive and positive posture. This situation was, unfortunately, out of CPC's control, for the time frame had been imposed by the government, and so was non-negotiable. For it was the government that picked up CPC's deficit.

The September 1981 announcement of a 75 per cent increase in the cost of first-class postage generated a swift and savage political and public response. The opposition parties were predictably critical, the Conservatives insisting that the increase was far too much and the NDP complaining that no assurances were given that postal services would improve. The fact was, though, that Parliament no longer played a substantial role in reacting to price proposals. CPC proposals to increase prices were first placed in the *Canada Gazette,* followed by a sixty-day waiting period to allow for public comment and reaction, played out through the minister's office, not via Parliament. Public, and particularly business, reaction far outstripped political reaction in intensity and impact.[52] Fully 9,316 representations were made, from over 5,000 individuals and nearly 3,000 businesses and charities; 769 constituents complained to their MPs; and 51,980 people signed petitions protesting the increase. The protests came mainly from small business, which was not well placed to make use of the lower incentive rates offered to large-volume users at the time of the price increase; they were not able to take advantage of mechanization and coding to the same extent as big business.[53] Almost all CPC's proposed rate increases were ultimately approved by cabinet.[54] This led the Canadian Federation of Independent Business (CFIB) to ask "why they even asked for comments when they had no intention of listening." The intensity of public reaction rattled the nerves of both the government and postal management, who would subsequently be wary about raising postal prices. The reaction to the next year's more modest two cent increase was similar, with business, consumers' groups, the postal unions, and the Opposition claiming that service had not improved enough to warrant the increase. The clash over price increases led groups like the Consumers Association of Canada to demand formal regulation of CPC's rates.[55]

This was as far as CPC would — or could — go on the price front. It lost government support for further price increases until well into 1985. CPC introduced an indefinite prize freeze in September 1983, for a number of reasons. First, the business community needed appeasing, and the price freeze was a symbolic gesture in that direction. Second, there was concern about the competitive implications of further price increases: "We would be in danger of pricing ourselves out of some markets if we instituted the previously planned pricing strategy for the 1984–88 period." Third, the government itself feared further price increases. In October 1984, a planned price increase was delayed for political reasons as well as in anticipation of business reaction.[56] Indeed, the government kept CPC on a "very short leash," according to its chair, René Marin. Although it was obvious that CPC needed the revenue, and Warren's elaborate presentation notwithstanding, the government still said no to a tiny, one-cent increase. The politics of price increases followed a similar pattern in all revenue-producing postal sectors in the early Crown years.[57]

The political fallout from the postal price increases affected CPC's 1982 proposal to redefine the meaning of a letter. This issue had been fudged at the 1980–81 legislative hearings. The business community had demanded a narrow definition of a letter, to limit CPC's exclusive privilege; the POD and the postal unions had wanted a loose, expansive one. The government avoided a divisive decision by introducing a compromise, defining a letter by exceptions to the exclusive privilege. That is, it defined a letter by what it was not. This caused immediate difficulties for the corporation, creating a series of openings for firms and organizations to deliver their own mail. For example, a number of utility companies and municipalities in Ontario began delivering their bills themselves, claiming that notices and bills were not letters, and hence were not subject to the exclusive privilege. Delivery of bills in dense urban markets — an enormous proportion of CPC business — could be done privately at a fraction of the cost of first-class rates. If CPC lost this sort of business, its revenues would drop dramatically and it would lose its financial capacity to service more isolated and less dense markets. A related issue at the time was the practice of "bulking": sending a bundle of correspondence in one package. This practice made private couriers' higher charge more economically tolerable to its users.[58]

On 3 July 1982, CPC proposed a changed definition of "letter" in order to stop these practices. The timing of the proposal could not have been worse. Business resentment lingered after the 1981 postal strike and CPC's massive 1981 price increase. The proposed definition unleashed anti-CPC feeling, generating a backlash and a political controversy far out of proportion to the issue itself. CPC was unprepared for business's closing of ranks around this issue.[59] An *ad hoc* group of sixteen business associations argued that CPC's proposed definition would make many business practices illegal.[60] The number of responses was, however, less than that following the 1981 price increase proposal, reflecting the character of the issue and its focused impact. About three hundred representations were made, all of them negative. They included 100 business interventions, 152 from individuals, 44 from MPs, 76 letters, and 24 briefs.

Ouellet declared in the House of Commons on 22 November that the government had to protect CPC's exclusive privilege as the basis of a universal postal service. As with the price increases, the issue of the definition of "letter" was not played out in Parliament. Indeed, despite Ouellet's assurances to the House, cabinet rejected CPC's proposal the next day, stating that the business community had drawn its attention to the need for further exemptions to the exclusive privilege. The coalition of business associations was elated. They declared that the cabinet decision "restore[d] their confidence" in the regulatory process and in government's willingness to listen to the concerns of business.[61] CPC, business, and the government then devised a mutually acceptable definition, which was proposed on 12 February 1983 and approved by cabinet on 30 May.

The new definition doubled the exemptions to the exclusive privilege, loosening the postal monopoly on delivery of financial documents, invoices, credit card payments, and bulk deliveries. A letter was redefined to mean "one or more messages or information in any form." A new exemption covered "an invoice or other document prepared for delivery to an addressee from information obtained at the location at that address at the time of its delivery." This allowed utility company employees to make up bills on the spot (but not to deliver bills prepared at the office). The exemptions continued to allow bulking (by preserving the notion of payment by weight) and urgent hand-delivery of messages by employees. Items delivered by a friend were exempted. Concerns about CPC's role in electronic mail were allayed by exempting transmission of electronic mail. At the same time, CPC introduced a new set of incentive rates to regain the business of utility companies.[62]

These matters were settled in private between CPC and business outside of either parliamentary or public scrutiny. The Consumers Association of Canada complained that the process had been "unfortunate for consumers": "We don't know what trade-offs were made." This event — and the price increases — raised concerns about postal accountability and demonstrated how postal matters had become detached from traditional parliamentary processes.[63]

In a model of understatement, CPC's 1982-83 report characterized the experience as demonstrating "the need for a revenue base to fund universal mail services balanced against intrusion into competitive markets and the choices in the private sector."[64] This incident illustrated four postal realities. First, it demonstrated how CPC's monopoly continued to weaken. Second, the incident illustrated how business interests acted as a constraint on CPC's capacity to participate in the market and to balance its budget. Third, it demonstrated how Parliament's postal role had declined; CPC had to survive in a context in which the key relationship had become that between business groups and the minister. Fourth, it clarified how the government determined what CPC could and could not do. In this confrontation between CPC and the business community, the government intervened to support business to CPC's disadvantage.

The expectation that CPC provide and improve customary postal service limited the extent to which CPC could pursue service cuts and rationalizations to balance the postal budget. These public expectations were played out in the House of Commons, the scene of ferocious and well-publicized debates on this issue. In an emergency debate in November 1982 on the alleged deterioration in postal services, the government was attacked for not directing CPC to ensure the maintenance of customary postal services. There was widespread consensus that the balanced-budget schedule was too tight and was leading to the deterioration in services. This argument had particular resonance with regard to home delivery of mail, an area where considerable postal savings could be made. Home delivery was considerably more expensive than delivery to group mail boxes, and home delivery of provisions such as milk and bread had ended long ago. Nonetheless, public expectations limited CPC's potential action in this regard. At committee hearings, Warren expressed frustration at Canadians' "tak[ing] it as an inalienable right that they should have letter carrier service as soon as they move into their house in the suburb even though the sod is not down yet." Despite marketing attempts, neither the public nor the government came to accept the idea of the community mailbox during Warren's term — as CPC acknowledged in its 1985 submission to the Marchment Committee. Another delicate area of potential savings was in rural areas. The termination of Saturday rural mail delivery brought criticism from many quarters, including interest associations like the Canadian Federation of Agriculture and the Canadian Daily Newspapers Association. The NDP's Kristiansen commented that rural service cuts are "typical of what happens when you give any city slicker lawyer the responsibility for essential services to rural Canada." Rationalizations such as franchising and rural postal and service closings might have generated savings for CPC; however, "the problems and difficulties which would be presented would be too much for the Corporation to contend with at this time." This had wideranging policy implications. For example, cross-subsidization would need to be maintained, as this would be the only way to keep the rural network in place.[65]

Public reaction also led CPC to withdraw deficit-reducing proposals when they were actually presented. The construction of CPC's first five-year plan was influenced in this way. A draft version was leaked in October 1983. It contained proposals for staff and service cutbacks, including alternate-day delivery, closure of postal stations and rural routes, levying of fees for postal services, cuts in the rural network, and contracting out. There was an enormous public outcry, particularly from the postal unions which led a public campaign against the plan. As part of this campaign, CUPW exhorted the public to mail Christmas cards with only ten-cent postage (the unions promised to process and deliver mail with insufficient postage).[66] CUPW produced an alternative "Job Creation through Service Expansion" plan of new services, increased hours, and expanded retail activities. In the final plan, CPC dropped most proposals for service cutbacks and added initiatives to increase services and diversify its products.

The government chose not to intervene to back CPC's plans to rationalize services. It left CPC alone to face public and union reaction to emotional issues like post office closings and limited home delivery. CPC was not given the authority to pursue these service rationalizations: its plans were either dropped or pursued half-heartedly. The government's inaction maintained public expectations about provision of postal services, a serious constraint on CPC's actions.

CPC's diversification policy met a similar fate. This strategy was critical to its future, as a way to balance the budget without cutting wages, workers and services. It initiated a number of new programs and began an aggressive retail expansion, to create jobs, improve customer service, increase revenues, and generate a positive commercial image. These initiatives met a wall of negative reaction and business protest. For example, CPC's efforts to increase its third-class mail revenues were criticized by the Canadian Community Newspaper Association and members of the Quebec Chamber of Commerce who maintained that CPC was too aggressive in pursuit of "their" market for the distribution of ad inserts.[67] The government directed CPC to rein in these efforts. Similarly, with regard to initiatives in fax, e-mail, and new communications technologies, CPC chair Marin recounted that "no one wanted to see our face on this." For example, the banks did not want CPC to enter the electronic funds transfer market. CPC was discouraged whenever it asked for government support in this area.[68]

Generally, the government frowned upon revenue-generating schemes. Some of Warren's ambitious ideas did not receive board approval (e.g., investing in MCI, buying out Loomis couriers). Even when board support was forthcoming, Warren was not backed by the government.[69] The most dramatic case was the Consumers Post affair. CPC established a test network in eight markets, acting as mail-order outlet for Consumers Distributors, where the latter had no presence. Merchants in these markets petitioned the government to kill the project, claiming that it competed unfairly with them. In parliamentary committee hearings, MPs accused CPC of "getting into other private enterprises within the Canada Post to make bucks" and of having "the audacity to go so far in competing with the private sector." CPC was told to stick to the "principle that your corporation should not compete with the private sector." The CFIB declared that Canada Post's "unwarranted intrusion into commercial activities is a blatant misuse of the corporation's public resources"; 87 per cent of its members were against the Consumers Post initiative, because it was subsidized, unfair competition. The Consumers Association of Canada worried that the project was financed by first-class mail revenue.[70]

CPC was surprised at the vehemence of business reaction. It had not anticipated that it would be accused of unfair competition and had no effective counter.[71] After the period ended in May 1984, the Liberal government directed CPC to put the Consumers Post experiment on hold. The project was killed in October by the incoming Conservative government. Prime Minister Mulroney had earlier referred to Consumers Post and other diversification activities as "ill-considered schemes to generate greater revenue."[72] The small business community had made clear to the Conservatives that CPC should not be involved in competitive retail activities. An October 1984 survey reported the business view that CPC should not compete with private business as long as it was subsidized (i.e., in a deficit position).[73] Indeed, an earlier study had predicted this response: "Initiatives which are not directly related to fulfilling this mandate [viz., delivering the mail] will not be viewed positively, even though they might be business-like to the extent they turn a profit for the Corporation." As MP Towers put it, "I would rather see you do the things you do best, and that is deliver mail."[74]

The Liberal government chose not to back CPC's initiatives to extend its commercial activities. This seemed surprising, given that the purpose of Crowning had been to commercialize the post office. The government did not deem the diversification strategy to be bad in itself; however, in practice it had consequences for private business, consequences that had not been foreseen or understood by the Liberal government. The reason the government gave CPC for limiting its commercial activities was ironic: their view was that CPC should not have diversified until it had improved basic postal services and balanced its books. This would protect it (and the government) from business complaints that diversification was subsidized by the postal deficit.[75] However, CPC's capacity to balance its books was a function of its being allowed to act commercially; it was not evident that it could attain financial self-sufficiency without doing so. In order to become more commercial, CPC had first to pay off the deficit; and in order to pay off the deficit it essentially had to become more commercial. As Stanley Hartt (conciliator in the 1984–85 CUPW negotiations) noted, "Canada Post is not free to implement such a system when the howls of protest come to the attention of the political authorities which control its destiny."[76]

Reactions to CPC policies demonstrated that CPC faced a formidable interest group alliance, in which consumer groups, postal unions, and business associations formed an unusual coalition against its initiatives. Postal unions and small business jointly opposed service cuts; large-volume users and consumers groups fought the alleged monopoly-strengthening redefinition of a letter; consumer groups and postal unions united against price increases and a pricing system that appeared to favour big business.[77] Reaction to the 1981 price increase and the attempted redefinition of a letter forced Warren to spend an inordinate amount of time selling, brokering, and negotiating CPC's plans. He went on the road for two years, complete with slides, graphs, and visual aids, selling CPC plans to customers, small business, unions, and consumer groups, all the while pleading for patience and understanding.[78]

CPC's most powerful constituencies were the large-volume mail users and the postal unions. The general public, or ordinary users, were not organized at this time. Their views and expectations were expressed and often confirmed through MPs and the parliamentary process, the locale for symbolic postal politics. As service cuts were moderate, formal interest groups and associations had not yet coalesced around issues such as rural mail delivery and community mailboxes; this would occur later.

Business groups were stimulated to organize around postal issues when the POD was Crowned. They were a formidable presence during the legislative hearings, and once CPC was formed, it often solicited business approval before acting. This was evident when an informal collection of business associations attacked its proposal to change the definition of a letter and subsequently participated directly in determining an acceptable definition. Later, twenty-six professional and business groups came together to lobby against price increases, service changes, and unfair competition.[79] Business's postal presence was formalized in 1983 with the formation of the National Association of Major Mail Users (NAMMU). Its membership consisted of postal users who mailed at least one million first-class units a year. Its purpose was "to unite major users of domestic first class mail for purposes of expressing and developing their policy, professional, economic and technological interests and of representing them to the Canada Post Corporation." At its founding, its fifty members generated $200 million in postal business a year.[80]

NAMMU and CPC enjoyed a symbiotic relationship. CPC tried to establish closer links with its large-volume users, the top five hundred of whom generated 35 per cent of postal revenues. CPC initiated joint efforts to increase efficiency and maximize the benefits of mechanization; the resulting savings would be "shared" between the two (e.g., via incentive rates). This strategy was also pursued with regard to large-volume users of third-class mail.[81] At the same time, CPC played a critical role for these groups. "For our members," NAMMU stated, "the postal services by the Corporation are the principal communication vehicles in providing information to clients and associates . . . for some of our members the Corporation's services are the foundations upon which business is conducted." Business was very much dependent on CPC, as alternatives were neither satisfactory nor readily available. A 1981 business seminar explored alternatives to the Post Office and concluded that there was no other affordable option. Maclean-Hunter and other users experimented with an alternative distribution system, with no great success. Studies suggested that an alternative system would be more expensive and less effective than the postal service.[82]

NAMMU aimed to formalize its relationship with CPC in a "joint standing committee, consisting of representatives from both organizations, with a mandate to discuss issues of mutual concern." It hoped to develop a simpler, "deregulated" rate and policy environment, whereby large-volume users could enter into one-on-one contractual arrangements with CPC (which would result in cheaper rates reflecting their higher volumes).[83] Although the relationship was not formalized, interaction increased steadily. NAMMU proposals were initiated, particularly in the area of individual contracts and incentive rates.

CPC tried to build a similar relationship with its unions. Broadly speaking, it led a charmed existence in the area of labour relations. The six-and-five program froze contracts for a number of years. Labour supported Crowning the POD and wanted the postal corporation to be successful. Warren's management style encouraged personal contact, which labour appreciated.[84] CPC declared that major decisions would not be taken without prior consultation. A Personnel and Labour Relations Department was established, and labour took up its representation on the board. New training courses were introduced to improve supervisors' relations with workers. A health and occupational safety program was created. A committee cleared the backlog of grievances; 25,636 of 28,517 were handled (23,401 were fully or partially sustained and 2,235 were denied). Disruption was minimal; only 149 person-days were lost in 1982 and 183 in 1983.[85]

Nonetheless, labour–management tensions developed, focusing on the corporate slant to CPC's plans. The unions felt "'tricked'" when the balanced-budget timetable was introduced. As CPC sought to reduce its deficit, the unions waged a rearguard action against service cuts, elimination of jobs, and changes in working conditions. For example, CPC's absenteeism program was characterized by LCUC as "the most vicious anti-union document put out by any company" and was actively resisted. LCUC found CPC confrontational in interpreting contract language, as it pared costs and streamlined its operations.[86] CUPW was outraged when asked to "productivity bargain," as it had explicitly and persistently rejected this approach. It refused to agree to rollbacks in one area in order to obtain gains in a different area, another Warren suggestion regarding wicket positions. CUPW concluded that job losses were financing the budget-balancing efforts. In 1980–81, eleven hundred mail-sorting jobs were eliminated, and another seven hundred positions were lost in the next three years. CUPW membership fell from 24,476 in 1978 to 23,392 by 1982. CPC cut staff by cutting services and replacing postal stations with sub-post offices. In October 1982, it announced plans to open nineteen sub-post offices and to extend services at another twenty-eight. Warren also twinned the idea of postal price restraint with the need to cut jobs. Jobs were the key issue in the 1984–85 CUPW negotiations.[87]

These tensions eventually focused on the 1983–84 business plan. CPC's budget plan included service and cost cuts, including staff cutbacks; a speeded-up work pace; restrictions on the use of sick leave; use of part-time labour; wicket closings; contracting out; post office closings; and alternate-day delivery. The plan proposed to eliminate 2,525 person-years by 1985, mainly through attrition and productivity increases. "It must be clearly indicated to the unions," CPC declared, "that layoffs will and must take place if attrition measures do not succeed."[88] On 4 November 1984, the CLC, CUPW, LCUC, and UCPE held a joint press conference to denounce the CPC's plan and declare that any honeymoon was now over. The unions rejected a balanced budget at the cost of diminished postal service, cuts in jobs, and deteriorating working conditions. The unions' alternative was to increase postal revenues through business-generating initiatives. The Christmas card protest, mentioned above, encouraged Canadians to mail their cards with only a ten-cent stamp. The Canadian Labour Relations Board ordered CUPW to drop the protest, but not before the unions' points were thoroughly aired.[89]

Labour's well-orchestrated reaction led CPC to pause. Its plan eventually de-emphasized cost-cutting measures and replaced them with revenue-increasing initiatives.

Once the six-and-five program expired, CPC negotiated eight collective agreements in 1984-85, covering 75 per cent of its staff. These negotiations were strike free, and CPC pointed to the longest continuous period of postal labour stability since 1968. The contracts perpetuated labour peace, but none of them contributed significantly to deficit reduction. This was not surprising, given pent-up union demands accumulated through the years of frozen contracts. For example, the UCPE was given a 95 per cent strike mandate to attain a national pay scale, job security, and benefits parity with CUPW.[90] In LCUC negotiations, CPC gained flexibility in the way mail — particularly ad mail — was delivered and in rearranging the organization of work; but LCUC gained a 3 per cent wage increase, the cost-of-living escalator lost during the six-and-five program, improvements in benefits (including meal payments and medical insurance payments), and job security.[91]

CPC's negotiations with CUPW were the most intriguing in demonstrating the character of its plans and unions' reaction thereto, as well as the tension between balancing the budget and improving labour relations. CPC maintained that if a balanced budget was to be attained without job losses, wage increases had to be minimized and productivity improved. The idea was wage levels comparable to those in the private sector. "If we are going to be competitive in the years ahead and we're going to put our customers first and respond to the market place," said Warren, "then we're going to have to contain in relative terms the kind of wage increases that postal workers get." CPC proposed a modest 2.9 per cent wage increase (a thirty-eight-cent-an-hour increase) and bargained to gain "amendments to working rules that hinder us from getting the world-class service we want," through more efficient ways of operating, flexibility in scheduling, and increased use of part-time and casual workers.[92]

Given that two thousand jobs had been lost since 1981 — at a time of increasing volumes — CUPW claimed that productivity had already increased substantially. It called for a thirty-two-hour week as a way of sharing the benefits of technology; job security; and eighty-five-cent and ninety-cent hourly wage increases in a two-year contract. It demanded the elimination of contracting out and early retirement incentives. Most importantly, it called for a job creation program, to stem CPC's plans to eliminate another three thousand jobs through attrition.[93]

A settlement was reached only after stalled negotiations went to conciliation, headed by Montreal labour lawyer Stanley Hartt, a close friend of
Prime Minister Mulroney (the negotiations began before the 1984 election
but were concluded after it). Hartt's recommendations appeased both sides.
He accepted CPC's reading of its declining competitive situation and so
judged its modest wage offer to be reasonable. He also approved CPC's
strategy of reducing staff through attrition and rejected CUPW's demand
for a reduced work week. But he ruled that the remaining inside workers
were entitled to a no-layoff guarantee, and he supported CUPW's proposal
to produce jobs through revenue-producing initiatives. In return, CPC gained
increased flexibility in matching remaining personnel with existing jobs. In
the context of the wage-dampening impact of the early 1980s recession,
CUPW traded off wage gains for job security and job creation, including:

- guaranteed jobs for CUPW members, including protection from
  transfers beyond a radius of forty kilometres
- extension of the retail outlet experiment to 1986, under the conditions of the February 1984 agreement
- an increase in New Direction outlets from five to nineteen
- re-evaluation of the sub-post office conversion experiment in July
  1985, with fifty-three to be closed in the interim and more if the
  experiment was successful
- a letter attached to the contract promising to explore new employment opportunities, such as extended hours; bulk e-mail; sale of licences and transit tickets; payment of bills; and new projects and
  products
- a limit of forty-five hundred on the number of part-time workers[94]

In return, CPC made a number of gains: a two-year 2.9 per cent wage
settlement limited future labour costs; it gained flexibility in using part-time
and casual labour; and it also gained an increase in the number of part-timers
to forty-five hundred from the existing four thousand. In this, Hartt rejected
CUPW's proposal to cap the number of part-time workers at a fixed percentage of full-time workers.[95]

Both sides were happy with the settlement. CUPW acquired some job
guarantees and a diversification promise. CPC moderated the wage package,
acquired some productivity benefits, and gained two years of labour peace.
However, the settlement did not move CPC closer to a balanced budget.
First, jobs could not be cut to balance the budget; second, diversification
legitimized the idea of a certain kind of post office. CPC bought time, but
by reproducing the policy ball-juggling act.

The 1985 CUPW contract put off the day of reckoning. It did not seriously deal with the level and character of staffing, work deployment, and

private-sector wage and benefits comparability. Warren insisted that CPC could not successfully cut its labour costs on its own. It needed government assistance to deal with what he characterized as CPC's "dark side" — the postal unions. Collective agreements would have to be rewritten to reduce unit costs if CPC was to become competitive. Cutting wages, reducing staff, and altering working conditions required parliamentary involvement. These actions would probably precipitate a vigorous response from the unions, who would strike and wage war on the Post Office in a desperate fight for survival. The state's authority was required to contain the violence and destruction that would result, to see through this necessary means of attaining competitiveness.[96]

CPC faced formidable opponents in balancing the budget, improving labour relations, and maintaining customary postal service. Business organizations limited its commercial activities, and the large-volume users exercised a considerable amount of effective influence. Postal unions stood between CPC and the increased productivity and lower unit costs required to remain competitive and balance the budget. The public's postal expectations curtailed service rationalizations. CPC required the government's help in overcoming these constraints on its actions, help that, during the Liberal administration, was not forthcoming.

Policy Results

CPC's financial and volume performance did not improve to any great extent for two reasons: the early 1980s were recessionary years, dampening postal business and revenues; and strategies to balance the budget were constrained by market, social, ideological, and political forces.

Postal volumes stagnated in this period. Table 1 shows that total volume grew by a modest 14 per cent between 1979-80 and 1984-85. Net of the increase in unaddressed third-class mail, though, postal volumes actually *decreased* by 1.7 per cent. The key issue was the performance of first-class mail. Its level in 1984-85 was more or less the same as in 1979-80. It declined in three years: 1980-81, 1981-82, and 1983-84. Indeed, first-class volume — the Post Office's most crucial revenue source — was but 13 per cent higher than a decade earlier. This suggested that the first-class mail market had matured and would grow no larger in the technologically sophisticated and competitive communications market. It fell from 66 per cent of overall volumes in 1975-76 to 54 per cent in 1984-85. CPC attributed its sluggish volume growth to the economic recession, the residual effects of the 1981 strike, the large price increase of 1981-82, and steadily increasing competition.[97] Its efforts to increase volumes and business had little success, save in doubling the volume of unaddressed third-class mail. CPC had become the largest advertising medium in the country after newspapers, which became an issue in itself, inasmuch as the proliferation of ad mail ("junk" mail) was widely criticized. This class of mail produced little revenue, but its growth allowed CPC to keep other prices at a reasonable level.[98]

Sluggish volume growth translated into disappointing revenue expansion. Price increases produced an enormous $728 million revenue expansion between 1980-81 and 1982-83, reducing the deficit from $487 million to $291 million. Over two-thirds of the deficit reduction was the result of price increases — which had reached their competitive limit. Indeed, CPC recognized that the remaining reduction in the deficit would have to be pursued through other means.[99] In the following years — when there was no price increase — the reality of sluggish volume growth showed through. Revenues grew moderately by a total of 10 per cent. The deficit thus persisted. Although it declined to $291 million by 1982-83, it rebounded to $300 million in 1983-84 and increased to $395 million in 1984-85. The latter amount represented 16 per cent of postal revenues (admittedly half of the 32 per cent level in 1980-81). The government picked up $1.3 billion in postal deficits between 1981-82 and 1984-85.

The persistence of the deficit reflected limited business expansion and moderate containment of costs. While CPC volumes grew by 12 per cent between 1980-81 and 1984-85, its expenditures increased by 44 per cent — despite frozen wages and a decline in the level of employment. CPC's biggest success was in containing capital expenses, which amounted to a modest $214 million between 1982-83 and 1985-86, $82 million less than depreciation. But this minor victory would soon go sour, as plant and equipment became run down, dampening productivity. Labour costs were contained to an extent, a result of the six-and-five program and of attrition. As a percentage of total postal costs, labour costs fell only marginally, from 75.4 per cent in 1980-81 to 74.4 per cent in 1984-85. The labour force remained stable at around sixty two thousand, and the level of full time employees fell modestly.

Conclusion

The Canada Post juggling act had not produced great results by the time the Conservatives were elected in 1984. The postal situation in 1984-85 was substantially similar to that which CPC faced at its birth — with a postal deficit in the $300–$400 million range. Prospects for deficit elimination were not good, as the obvious and easy cost containments had been carried out: job attrition, a modest increase in the use of part-time workers, no replacement of capital, moderate decreases in absenteeism, minor service rationalization. More substantial cost reduction would undermine CPC's service and labour goals. Cutting labour costs would require lay-offs, more part-time and casual labour, increased workloads, decreased absenteeism, and cuts in wages and benefits. None of these could be carried out without a serious confrontation with labour. CPC shied away from this kind of confrontation in the

1984-85 CUPW settlement. Similarly, rationalization of postal services would undermine CPC's responsibility to maintain customary services and would lead to a strong reaction from rural communities, small business, suburbanites, and parliamentarians, which CPC avoided in the 1983-84 business plan. Price increases remained constrained by the market and politics, as did the strategy of expanding business through diversification. Business was unwilling to allow CPC market space, as the definition of a letter and the Consumers Post cases indicated.

CPC thus faced a matrix of interests ready to coalesce against it on any issue. Whether an issue provoked labour, popular, or business reaction, the government chose not to intervene to support CPC's efforts. Rather, it directed CPC to pursue a different course of action. The government did not want a confrontation with the postal unions in 1984-85; that Stanley Hartt was appointed conciliator in the 1985 CUPW dispute suggests the extent to which even the newly elected Conservative government wanted a settlement. The government did not want a confrontation with suburban homeowners, rural citizens, and small business, so CPC rolled back its proposals for service rationalization. In the process, the government legitimized and strengthened labour and service expectations of CPC. The government listened to the business community in the definition of a letter and Consumer Post cases. In the process, CPC was placed in a contradictory position. The government weakened CPC's monopoly powers but limited the extent to which it could participate in the market. All the while, CPC was directed to reduce the postal deficit. This was an impossible situation.

The persistence of CPC's deficit had critical implications: it weakened CPC's efforts to project an image of a sound, commercial, and competitive business operation, and seriously limited its political autonomy. For as long as it paid the deficit, the government could tell CPC what to do: he who pays the piper calls the tune. The persistence of the deficit also suggested to the government that CPC had not yet "earned" the right to autonomy that comes with "delivering the goods." Third, the lack of improvement in CPC's financial position would alarm any new government and suggest to it that the attempt to juggle social and commercial ends had not been successful. Indeed, this was precisely the conclusion reached in 1984 by the newly elected Conservative government.

Chapter Eight:

THE RECONCEPTUALIZATION OF CANADA POST, 1984-86

The election of the Conservatives in September 1984 dramatically changed the political context in which postal policy was determined. The Mulroney government reconceptualized Canada Post's character and purpose and transformed its functioning and performance. The new postal policy reflected the Conservatives' broad strategic response to international economic developments. The challenge of globalization led governments in the 1980s to consider ways of increasing national economic competitiveness. The Liberals had been inclined to extend state power, to increase national control over economic circumstances; numerous Crown corporations were created in the 1970s to this end. The Conservatives responded differently, proposing to cut government spending, taxes, and the deficit and to roll back the state presence in the economy, on the theory that such measures would create more space, incentive, and opportunity for private economic activity, thereby encouraging efficiency, competitiveness, and growth. The privatization of Crown corporations was an important element of this neo-conservative strategy.

The Conservative government was thus disinclined to follow Liberal postal policy. While they had accepted the need to commercialize the Post Office to increase competitiveness and reduce the deficit, the Liberals continued to attempt to balance social and economic goals. This traditional postal juggling act had no political or ideological resonance for the Conservative government. It saw the postal deficit as a metaphor for what ailed the economy: bad business practices, inefficiency and uncompetitiveness, indulgent labour relations and wages, and unreasonable social expectations about public services. The Conservative government initiated a sharp break with the tradition of the Crown corporation and with the immediate postal policy past. It rejected the heroic notion of the Crown corporation as balancing act, in which public enterprises pursued commercial and social aims simultaneously. The Conservatives privileged CPC's economic goals over its social ones, and delegitimized the Post Office's public service function.

The reconceptualization of Canada Post was by no means an easy task. It required a sustained act of political will and took two years, from the autumn 1984 election until a radical postal strategy was tabled in the House of Commons in November 1986. The latter was set out in the 1986-87 business plan, which has directed CPC's functioning and decisions ever since. The postal transformation involved two conscious, well-considered government interventions. First, the government reined in what little autonomy CPC enjoyed. It terminated CPC's diversification initiatives and rejected Michael Warren's last five-year plan. Second, it initiated and dominated a process of reconceptualizing CPC's mandate and goals, with the aim of "depoliticizing" the postal function. CPC was gradually allocated increased autonomy by the government, but in a smaller market area with a narrower and more commercial policy focus.

In many ways, the 1986 plan supplanted Bill C-42, the legislation that established Canada Post in 1981. The process that created the 1986 plan was very different from that of 1980-81. The Bill C-42 legislative hearings were open and visible, and all elements of the postal community — including the unions — played influential roles. The legislation that emerged bore the stamp of their interests and concerns. Canada Post enjoyed a high degree of political legitimacy at its origin, because most elements of the postal community felt that the new postal corporation was "theirs." The 1984-86 process was far less visible and open. It was accessible only to invited participants and took place outside of public scrutiny. The postal unions and public interest groups had insignificant influence over the process and its results. The resulting postal mandate and strategy was exclusively commercial and lacked public service objectives, such as improving labour relations or maintaining customary services. The reconceptualized Canada Post enjoyed little legitimacy, as many interests felt that major business users now commanded most of CPC's attention.

The idea of privatizing Canada Post informed this process of postal transformation. This influence was not surprising, given the government's broader economic perspective and its ongoing scrutiny of Crown corporations. Indeed, it was implicit in the new strategy that CPC should be made a private corporation. Although privatization was neither seriously considered nor adopted at this stage, the Conservative government's postal strategy nonetheless constituted a kind of psychological and incremental privatization.

This transformation had considerable political, social, and commercial implications for CPC, the government, business, and the public, which are considered in chapters 9 and 10. This chapter focuses on the process of postal transformation and its broad policy results. After introducing the Conservative government's economic and Crown corporation strategies, I examine how the government in 1984-85 withdrew CPC's authority to devise postal policy, and then investigate the subsequent process of reconceptualizing Canada Post, from the Marchment task force to the construction of the 1986 plan. I then present and characterize the main features of the new postal plan. My objective in this chapter is to delineate the political character of the transformation process and to establish the Conservative government's responsibility for the results of this transformation.

New Political-Economic Context

The Mulroney government was elected in 1984 with the largest electoral majority in Canadian history. This majority allowed it to alter the political agenda in a fundamental way, to establish a new set of political priorities, and to give these priorities concrete legislative effect. The Conservatives maintained that the post-war construction of the welfare state and government management of the economy had constrained initiative, undermined efficiency, inhibited economic growth, and created a bloated public sector with an enormous deficit. The Mulroney government planned to regenerate private enterprise and the market in response to increased global competition, which in its view required rolling back government involvement in social and economic life. This was the context in which postal policy was reformulated.

The broad outlines of and rationale behind the government's economic strategy were first presented in a policy paper in November 1984 and in the May 1985 budget.[1] These pronouncements indicated how the government planned to pursue the neo-conservative economic agenda, and were dominated by two declarations. First, the government declared that deficit reduction, as a necessary condition of economic regeneration, would be the core of its economic policy. It pursued this goal immediately by proposing billions of dollars of reductions in program expenditures and by setting a schedule of deficit reduction. This approach has was pursued thereafter, and was formalized in expenditure reduction plans in the early 1990s. Second, the government assigned primary responsibility for economic regeneration to the private sector. It insisted that governments could not solve economic problems or create economic growth: "We will promote growth and job creation by encouraging private initiative, improving government effectiveness and controlling our national debt."[2] This orientation to the private sector persisted thereafter, and was again formalized in the early 1990s in the Prosperity Initiative and the devolving of staff and training policy to participants in the market.

Thus, deficit reduction and economic growth were the government's central economic objectives. Private enterprise, not the state, was to pull Canada towards increased competitiveness and growth.[3] Numerous social and economic policies were directed to these ends in the late 1980s and early 1990s: the free trade and the North American free trade agreements; reform of the unemployment insurance system; retrenchment of the welfare and social security systems; deregulation of the transportation, energy, financial, and communications sectors; tilting of economic, regional, and industrial policies from a public- to a private-sector approach; expenditure control plans; deficit reduction via operations surpluses; cuts in the size and expense of the public service; restrictive anti-inflation monetary policy; tolerance of high levels of unemployment; diminished progressivity of personal income taxes and increased importance of regressive taxes (e.g., the GST).

The government considered the future of Crown corporations from within this neo-conservative framework. Their privatization could reduce public expenditures (subsidies) and the deficit, create private market opportunities, and increase efficiency, productivity, and competitiveness. Then Conservative leader Mulroney appointed a task force on Crown corporations in 1983, chaired by William Kelly. The committee spent more than a year studying the issue, but did not issue a report. The government quickly signalled its intention to make privatization a policy priority, early after the September election. Sinclair Stevens announced on 30 October that all Canadian Development Investment Corporation assets would be sold within six months, including its holdings in de Havilland, Canadair, Teleglobe, and Eldorado Nuclear. In a November 1984 economic statement, Finance Minister Wilson declared that Crown corporations should be managed more soundly: "We must also consider the appropriateness of our present investment mix and of the support provided by the public treasury. Although each corporation was established to serve what, at the time, might have been very important public policy purposes, we must ask ourselves whether that remains the case."[4] The 1985 budget declared baldly that "Crown corporations with a commercial value but with no ongoing public policy purpose will be sold."[5] The government identified thirteen such Crowns. It created a privatization secretariat and a ministerial task force on privatization, chaired by the president of Treasury Board. In the 1986 budget, Wilson again declared that "as we identify Corporations which do not meet public policy objectives, we will either close them or sell them to the private sector where they can become more competitive, lessen the burden on taxpayers, and provide better service."[6] Later that summer, Barbara McDougall was named minister of state for privatization, and the task force on privatization was converted and enlarged to a full-fledged Cabinet Committee on Privatization, Regulatory Affairs and Operations. Don Mazankowski became privatization minister in April 1988. Early privatizations included Northern Transportation Co. Ltd, Canadian Arsenals Ltd., and de Havilland (1985); CN Route and Canadair (1986); and Teleglobe Canada Ltd. (1987). By the spring of 1991, the government had privatized or dissolved more than twenty Crown corporations, including Eldorado Nuclear, Air Canada, CN Exploration, and Petro-Canada. These privatizations involved more than $5 billion in assets and introduced more than eighty thousand people to unemployment.[7] Where did CPC fit in the Conservatives' privatization plans?

The Conservatives and the End of the Warren Era

CPC president Warren could reasonably have anticipated that the election of the Conservatives would make his life easier. After all, Warren was himself a Conservative who had worked comfortably with Tory governments in Ontario in the 1970s. He anticipated that the Conservatives would make hard decisions and give CPC a clearer sense of direction. By the next summer, however, Warren had lost the confidence of the government and offered his resignation, which was accepted without government protest or tears.[8]

The Conservatives arrived in office without a postal policy or a clear sense of postal direction. Previous Conservative leader Joe Clark commissioned Ronald Ritchie in 1978 to write a report on the POD. That report recommended creation of a postal Crown with a sharper commercial focus, increased contracting out of postal services, a ban on postal strikes, and limits on the POD's forays into fields like telecommunications.[9] Some of these recommendations appeared in the first legislative attempt to Crown the POD in 1978. The Conservatives supported Crowning the POD and would have proceeded to this end had the minority Clark government not fallen. The Conservatives supported the Liberal's CPC legislation in 1980–81. Former PMG Fraser was instrumental in helping the Liberal government pass the legislation, in the face of considerable backbench Conservative opposition. These MPs were the advance guard of neo-conservativism, and were suspicious of the CPC's monopoly powers. They wanted CPC's exclusive privilege to be terminated and fought aggressively to limit its mandate and market. To an extent, they were responsible for the legalization of private couriers as well as for the constraints placed on CPC's entry into the telecommunications market.

Once in office, the Conservatives proceeded slowly on the postal front. Prime Minister Mulroney had not shown interest in postal matters, although he had expressed scepticism about CPC's diversification schemes, which he characterized as "ill-considered." In the pre-election effort to please everyone, he wrote to Glenn Hooper, president of the Postmasters and Postmistresses Association: "The Progressive Conservative Party feels that Canada Post's current program of rapid debt reduction is unrealistic. I can assure you ... that restoring the quality of service will be our top priority with Canada Post."[10]

The policy agenda was crowded in 1984 and 1985, so postal matters did not have much political salience.[11] The government's economic framework was not in place until the 1985 budget, and its Crown corporation strategy was still evolving in 1986 (the government's privatization plan was not outlined until May 1985). There were few postal initiatives in 1984 and 1985. The government watched and to a degree helped as CPC signed relatively benign contracts with CUPW in March 1985 and with LCUC in early 1986.

The slow evolution of postal policy reflected the cautious approach of the minister responsible for Canada Post. Mulroney's choice of Perrin Beatty for this position was a bit odd. Beatty was as surprised as observers at his assignment for he had no previous experience in, and had expressed no interest about, the Post Office. His primary interest was National Revenue, for which portfolio he was also assigned responsibility. He had no clear vision of how he wanted the Post Office to evolve, which made him susceptible to backbench pressures and the expectations of various political constituencies. He relied mainly on common sense and ideological instincts, as well as on private consultants' reports.[12]

Beatty was disturbed that the postal deficit had persisted. Although he had no positive postal vision, he had firm views about the paths CPC should not take. He immediately put Warren's plans on hold. First, he delayed CPC's request for a price increase. This was not without political calculation, especially with regard to the backbench. It also reflected Beatty's view that CPC should reduce its deficit internally rather than via price hikes for users. Second, he directed CPC to end diversification experiments like Consumers Post. This was ominous, for it suggested that the government — its market orientation notwithstanding — would not allow a revenue-increasing approach to balancing the budget. Beatty imposed a classic catch-22 on the Post Office, disallowing market interventions until CPC attained financial self-sufficiency. In this he was again alive to small business, which claimed that CPC's diversification schemes provided unfair competition, and which anticipated increased market possibilities in areas of activity withdrawn from CPC's domain. The government aimed to devise a new postal strategy that spoke to postal constituencies' concerns.[13]

Upon entering office, Beatty asked Warren to present a postal overview and to devise a set of options for CPC's future. Warren responded with a background paper and five policy options presenting a spectrum of possibilities. At one extreme was a dramatically cut-back model of a Post Office of "last resort." At the other extreme were more ambitious plans involving expansion into electronic mail, parcel transfers, and other high-tech communications activities, and addressing high unit costs by cutting labour expenses by 30 per cent.[14]

The two men viewed the decision process entirely differently. Warren felt that the government was dragging its feet to avoid making hard choices — particularly about labour costs and CPC's place in the market. He felt that the government had no postal vision, although it entertained privatization, and was naively disappointed that none of the five options was "easy" or a "no-lose" solution. Warren insisted that Beatty present CPC's analysis and options to cabinet. Because there was little postal consensus and the Post Office was not a priority, cabinet chose not to act. Warren accused Beatty of dithering and of being distracted by his other department, leaving CPC without direction. Beatty delayed specific decisions by initiating another round of consultancy studies.[15]

For his part, Beatty was sceptical about what Warren and CPC presented. Beatty was hard working, competent, and extremely inquisitive — he was not a passive minister who accepted plans and proposals without serious scrutiny. When a report or request was submitted, he bombarded Warren with questions, demands for more information, and deeper justification of CPC's analysis. Warren's five options were scrutinized by government officials, both in Beatty's office and at Treasury Board, who confirmed Beatty's view that CPC was incapable of basing decisions or choices on financial criteria. (After four years as a Crown corporation, CPC lacked hard data about unit costs, prices, productivity, efficiency, and so on.) Beatty was told that none of Warren's options seemed likely to work or to be based on numbers that added up. Both Treasury Board and Beatty's officials concluded that Warren did not have the data to prove his case; that his plans were smoke and mirrors designed to dazzle and impress; and that these plans involved large expenditures on risky ventures in an attempt to put the corporation on an even footing far in the future. This confirmed Beatty's anxiety about Warren's sense of adventure. Beatty was inclined to pursue a narrow balanced-budget approach, with no increased spending unless it contributed immediately to balancing the budget. And so he did not choose one of Warren's options, but initiated management and consultants' studies over the winter.[16]

The fencing between Warren and Beatty continued in the formulation of CPC's business plan. The Financial Administration Act was amended in June 1984 to require Crown corporations to submit annually a five-year plan and capital budget for government approval. The 1985–86 plan was the first CPC plan to be examined under this new regime. It was scrutinized by the Crown Corporations Directorate, which made a recommendation to Treasury Board and the Department of Finance. The process began in late 1984, when CPC submitted as its business plan Warren's fourth option, which involved a massive and ambitious incursion into, and investment in, parcel shipping and electronic mail.[17] Treasury Board reviewed the plan and concluded that it was not achievable. Calculating that costs had been underestimated by between $700 million and $1 billion, Treasury Board reported that the plan would not improve postal service to any great extent and would extend CPC's deficit into the indefinite future. It recommended that the plan as a whole be rejected. As an interim measure, it suggested that the first year be approved. The government accepted this recommendation.[18]

Thus, by the spring of 1985 Canada Post lacked a corporate plan and the government had rejected all its other options, demonstrating total lack of faith in CPC management. On the other hand, the government itself lacked a postal vision to impose on Canada Post. In short, while it did not trust the corporation's plans, it was incapable of imposing a plan of its own. In the spring of 1985, then, the government made a critical decision. Reversing the normal planning flow, it decided to formulate a postal plan by itself. This plan would be presented to Canada Post as a *fait accompli*.

This scenario began to unfold on 10 April 1985, when CPC announced rate hikes as part of the interim 1985–86 business plan. The increase was greeted negatively in all quarters — from postal unions and users to businesspeople and Conservative MPs. The latter group articulated the concerns of small business and social constituencies, whose support underpinned the Conservatives' electoral success. Despite these enormous pressures, the government approved the proposal reluctantly on 24 June, after a perfunctory review process characterized as a "farce" by NDP critic Cyril Keeper. The government admitted that changes in postal service did not warrant a price hike; it approved the hike because, quite simply, CPC needed the money. It would have to pay for any increase in the budgetary shortfall, and this would exacerbate its own deficit situation. However, the government provided a *quid pro quo* to pacify its backbench and the business community. It announced that a private-sector committee would examine the postal situation and advise the government on CPC's future plans.[19]

The decision to set up the private-sector study reflected a combination of factors: the government's lack of a postal vision, Beatty's postal inexperience and uncertainty, the strength of the Conservative backbench and its political constituencies, the government's business and ideological orientation, and the government's lack of confidence in CPC's administration and its (Liberal-appointed) board. Warren was predictably upset by the move, as it demonstrated a total lack of confidence in his judgement and administration. Significantly, the CPC board did not criticize the decision.[20]

The government's loss of confidence in Warren was further signalled when it reinstated Ad Varma. Varma was a productivity specialist, fired for accusing the CPC of fudging its testing procedures. His case was taken up by Conservative MPs when in opposition, who defended Varma as a way of attacking Canada Post. After the election, Beatty had to respond to backbench pressures that Varma be reinstated and that his case be examined — despite the fact that, even in the minister's office, Varma was considered to be an oddball whose claims were at most dubious and whose demands could never fully be satisfied. Nonetheless, the politics of the backbench drove the issue out of the government's control, and the government reinstated Varma. This annoyed Warren, as it once again undermined his authority. By the time a consulting firm concluded that only one of Varma's nine charges could be substantiated, Warren had long since resigned.[21]

Warren's resignation stemmed from a number of factors. The government's continuing display of non-confidence was a substantial concern; but it was not altogether unexpected. Warren had been appointed by a Liberal government, and incoming governments are often suspicious of inherited appointees. Moreover, the deficit situation was never satisfactorily explained and CPC's plans seemed to be hopelessly optimistic. The government's scepticism was exacerbated, from Warren's position, by its unwillingness to make a quick decision about how CPC should proceed. This left Warren dangling and open to attacks by backbench Conservatives. And the government continued to make decisions that undermined his authority. This was not an acceptable situation; he resigned, disappointed and frustrated.

Warren's departure simplified matters for the government. While not very active in 1984–85, it had achieved one crucial objective: it withdrew any remaining postal authority from CPC, particularly by hastening Warren's departure. The government faced few constraints and could now consider CPC's future on its own terms.

Reconceptualizing Canada Post

The reconceptualization of Canada Post required two steps. First the previous approach to postal matters had to be delegitimized; and then the government had to construct a coherent postal alternative. With respect to the former, the traditional postal juggling act had to be shown to be an impossible and indulgent fantasy. All postal policy options other than strictly commercial ones were to be undermined, especially the revenue-generating diversification approach. In order for the campaign to be effective, the weaknesses of non-commercial options had to be demonstrated "objectively" by someone or some body other than the government. This was the rationale behind the formation of the private-sector review. And while delegitimizing one approach, the government had to produce a credible and compelling alternative; this had to respond to globalization imperatives and fit the Conservatives' ideological and political agenda. This was the goal of the 1986 five-year plan. Each of these steps, delegitimization followed by construction of an alternative, will be examined in turn.

The Marchment Report

On 20 June 1985, Beatty announced the formation of a private-sector review to examine Canada Post and its future:

> Nearly four years have passed since the Canada Post Corporation was formed. In that period considerable progress has been made in converting the former postal department to a corporate enterprise. However, the period has also seen rapid social, economic and technological change. In light of this changing environment a review of the Corporation's mandate is required in order to bring the corporation into the twenty-first century.

The Review Committee on the Mandate and Productivity of Canada Post Corporation was to assess CPC's legislative mandate and its policies and practices, and to estimate the future requirements for Canada's postal system. It was directed to examine:

- the optimum scope, quality, and level of services to be expected over the next fifteen years
- the existence of possible statutory or institutional constraints on the postal system
- the question of exclusive privilege

- the role of the private sector in the postal system, and whether and how Canada Post should compete with or complement the private sector
- CPC's productivity performance, and the means to improve its use of plant, labour, and capital equipment
- the issue of who should bear the financial burden of the postal service and whether there should be third-party regulation of Canada Post.[22]

The five-member committee was appointed on 16 July 1985. Alan Marchment was named chair;[23] he was president and chief executive officer of Traders Group Limited and Guaranty Trust Limited. The other members were Louis R. Comeau (president and CEO of Nova Scotia Power) Alix Granger (investment manager with F.H. Deacon-Hodgson) Fred McNeil (chair and president of Bank of Montreal, 1975-81; chair of Dome Canada), and Julien Major (retired past vice president of the Canadian Labour Congress). The committee was balanced regionally (Ontario, Maritimes, British Columbia, Alberta, and Quebec, respectively), but was unabashedly business oriented, with only a minority labour voice and no public-interest representation. The committee was expected to hold cross-country hearings and to report to the government in early autumn.

The government's action was linked to political and ideological considerations, as well as being a device to retain the support of the Conservative backbench and its small business and neo-conservative electoral constituencies. Conservative MPs had informed the government that they would not support the 1985 postal price increase without two guarantees: that CPC clean up its financial act and that they get some sort of input into CPC. The Marchment Committee would be that input. Moreover, given that Warren's postal options had been rejected and that the government did not have an alternative strategy in hand, the Marchment report would provide a blueprint for CPC's future. The private-sector committee was likely to devise a plan consistent with the government's political and ideological orientations.[24]

The appointment of the Marchment Committee generated mixed reactions. The business community supported the review process, as did Conservative backbenchers. Both were confident that the committee would criticize Canada Post, recommend that Warren be fired, and insist that postal management be put in its place. While hoping that the process would be valuable, former PMG Ouellet summed up opposition concerns that it was politicallly motivated: "If it's going to satisfy some Tory backbenchers' need to exercise their frustrations, I don't think it will be useful." The postal unions did not take the exercise seriously; they thought the process was designed to splice the government's neo-conservative agenda onto the postal agenda. The Marchment Committee was predictably unimpressed by labour's input into the process. It found itself accused of being too business oriented and lacking credentials, and considered the unions' presentations to be polemical and insufficiently constructive. The CPC Board supported the exercise, while Warren did not (Warren resigned on 25 July, three days after the committee was named). The committee was as unimpressed by CPC's input as it was with labour's. It found CPC to be unbusinesslike in its presentations and unable to provide sufficiently disaggregated data to document claims in a solid cost-benefit way.[25]

The committee met in late July to plan its work and establish a ten-person secretariat. It commissioned studies on topics such as third-party regulation, the legal mandate of the corporation, and the requirements to achieve financial self-sufficiency. It also commissioned polls to survey public and business views. It held hearings in eight cities over the remainder of the summer, meeting with union and CPC personnel in each location, as well as with their national officials in Ottawa. All meetings were held in private; confidentiality was chosen to generate frank and open discussion.[26] The committee completed its task within three months. It presented its final report in November to Michel Côté, the newly appointed minister responsible for Canada Post.

The private character of the process, the predominance of corporate representation, and the quick pace of the review suggested to many that the process was a "quick and dirty" study. That is, it was designed to give the government a weapon in dealing with CPC, to allow it to appease the business community and Conservative backbenchers, and to give it a coherent, alternate postal vision.[27] If these were its ends, the process was a success: the Report was highly critical of CPC, delegitimized Warren's options and approaches, and recommended that Canada Post adopt a far more commercial orientation.

The Marchment Committee presented a short, straightforward report on 18 November 1985. It packed a broad analysis and forty-three recommendations into fifty-three pages. The report analyzed the challenges facing CPC, criticized CPC's management and performance, and presented recommendations in four areas: CPC's scope and mandate, cost and productivity improvements, political and organizational changes, and financial self-sufficiency and privatization.

The committee was brutally critical of CPC management. Although it granted that the Post Office had progressed somewhat after becoming a Crown corporation, the committee concluded that "real achievments are not so readily apparent." It dismissed CPC's 1985–86 corporate plan and its focus on parcel revitalization and a massive investment in e-mail, claiming that "neither of these schemes as outlined ... can withstand serious analysis." Members commented on the sloppiness, generality, and lack of professionalism evident during CPC's presentation. Committee member Alix Granger noted that "management had an extremely confrontational attitude and they had twice as much management as they needed."[28]

The committee characterized CPC's problems as "massive, if not unresolvable":

[Canada Post is] one of the greatest management challenges in Canada today. It is confronted by serious financial difficulties, has one of the worst labour relations climates in the country and faces intense competition from couriers and burgeoning technology. At the same time, it operates in the full glare of public interest and suffers from political intervention.

Committee member Grainger reported that "we came away thinking it was basically hopeless." First, CPC's volume trends had not changed since 1968; postal business had not kept pace with population growth. Canadians used the mail service only infrequently, about ninety times on average per year. Rapid service by private couriers had taken away parcel and message business. New technology allowed high-volume electronic communication. The public perceived postal service as unreliable and inadequate compared to the standards set by its competitors. Second, weak volume growth created financial difficulties, but none of CPC's options for eliminating the deficit was promising. Price increases were limited by public reaction and lost business; expanding services was unlikely to succeed or to generate sufficient revenue to recoup costs; cost cutting was constrained by expectations and contractual obligations. Third, postal difficulties were exacerbated by labour-management relations. The committee was "disturbed by the vehemence and animosity" between labour and management; it had "never seen labour relations in any jurisdiction that are as acrimonious as those that exist between CPC management and the postal unions. They are poisonous to the point of the potential destruction of the enterprise ... The relationship is more reminiscent of a class war than any kind of mutual objectives." Fourth, postal productivity had fallen, despite huge investments in plant and equipment. From 1963 to 1984 processed mail volumes had increased by 25 per cent, while constant dollar operating costs (excluding personnel costs) had risen 75 per cent and constant dollar personnel costs had tripled. "The sharp drop in efficiency of mail processing which coincided with the new equipment suggests that, if this were the only variable, continuation of manual sorting operations might have yielded a higher level of productivity." Indeed, the committee felt that the new plants should not have been built. It suggested starting over and building made-to-measure plants for CPC's big users.[29]

Despite its grim analysis, the committee made a series of recommendations to improve postal circumstances. These recommendations delegitimized Canada Post's past activities and existing plans, and pointed it in a new direction.

First, the committee recommended that CPC limit its activities to delivering the mail: the "primary goal of the Corporation ... [should] be the provision of a consistently reliable service ... Canada Post should give priority to the development and marketing of present services." This recommendation flew in the face of the arguments of both Canada Post and the postal unions. CPC argued that if it was not allowed to expand into new market areas, it would become a declining industry reduced to providing only skeletal services. CPC wanted to adopt an agressive approach to increase business, as a way of covering costs and improving service; it proposed that it invest substantially to regain lost postal business (particularly parcels) and to gain an entry into e-mail and other technological innovations.[30] The postal unions also proposed that CPC increase its revenues through diversification of services and long-term investment in technological improvements such as e-mail.[31] NAMMU was alarmed at the prospect of an expanded and diversified CPC mandate:

> The Association would like to warn the Corporation of the pitfalls of attempting to diversify its activities to non-related areas ... Nothing should reduce Canada Post's capability to perform its current postal services, fulfill its mandate and to serve the needs of its customers for a fast and efficient nationwide postal service.[32]

The Marchment Committee sided with NAMMU on the question of CPC's mandate and the scope of its activity. It doubted that expanding services would balance the budget; in the short run, the approach would not increase revenue sufficiently to cover costs. The committee did not feel that the government should subsidize postal expansion by picking up CPC's deficit:

> Should the Post Office be entering a field already or potentially well served by the private sector, particularly if to do so requires the investment of major public funds or continued subsidization? .. if the Post Office remains dependent upon federal subsidies, should it be allowed to compete with other Canadian companies for a share of these other markets?

It rejected CPC's 1985–86 five-year plan proposal to revitalize parcel post ($191 million over 5 years) and expand into e-mail ($791 million): "Neither of these schemes as outlined in the corporate plan can withstand serious analysis." The committee recommended that CPC not be allowed to enter new fields or carry out major capital investments until it had balanced its books. It acknowledged CPC's perplexing position in this regard:

As it faces the uncertainties of the future market place, it is required to produce a product which is becoming less essential as time goes on. In such an environment, a private sector company would seek to diversify, thereby reducing its reliance on its most vulnerable product lines. The Post Office, however, exists to provide a relatively specific service ... and has no mandate in law or in fact to diversify into unrelated business ventures.

The committee nonetheless insisted that CPC should give priority to the development and marketing of present services, and that it should not be distracted by other ventures until it improved its performance in pursuing its basic activities. The committee perceived CPC to be but one of a number of players in the communications field: "Canadians do not look to Canada Post Corporation to supply all their communications needs."[33]

Second, the committee recommended a number of potentially disruptive measures to reduce costs and increase productivity in order to balance the budget. CPC's submission noted that it had inherited contracts containing clauses that "in comparison with contracts in other industries were restrictive, and total compensation levels that were higher than in comparable and competitive industries." It maintained that it needed to downsize its labour force, negotiate more flexible work rules, and contract out work and services. It proposed using community mailboxes and private retail outlets to cut delivery costs. CPC concluded that the government would have to sanction these controversial initiatives.[34] The postal unions proposed to take CPC in the opposite direction, by providing adequate staffing in all postal areas, guaranteed door-to-door mail delivery for all communities with two thousand or more points of call, expansion of postal hours and services, and the diversification of CPC activities into new retail and technological activities.[35]

The Marchment Committee embraced CPC's approach and proposed a number of cost-cutting and productivity-improving measures: expansion of sub-post offices; contracting out services; expanded letter delivery via alternate-day service or group boxes; relaxation of delivery standards to two days for local mail, three days for intra-regional mail, and four days for national mail; and increased use of part-time and casual workers. It made benign labour recommendations suggesting simply that the parties work "to eliminate restrictive clauses impeding the achievement of efficiency in operations."[36]

Third, in the Marchment Committee's view "the corporation need[ed] greater insulation from political and governmental interference." The government had directed the committee to examine third-party regulation of the postal service. The postal unions favoured the existing gazetting process. Regulation would diminish direct "political responsibility" for postal matters, which the unions felt would be to their disadvantage.[37] Canada Post supported the idea, but reported that it needed two years to become "ready" for regulation.[38] NAMMU rejected the idea, favouring a deregulated environment where CPC and large-volume postal users could strike "total service" agreements.[39]

The Marchment Committee made two major institutional recommendations. First, it resisted NAMMU's arguments, recommending that CPC be regulated by an independent third party whose decisions could not be overturned by cabinet. This was designed to remove postal questions from the political arena. Second, the committee proposed a private-sector and American model for the board of directors, to grant the board more independence and authority. The committee believed that the government remained too involved in Canada Post, from its appointments to its responses to constituents' pressures. It recommended that the membership and roles of the board be recast: experienced senior executives should be recruited to fill board positions, with CPC management accountable to the board, not to the government. The board should be given authority to hire and fire senior management, including the president. The committee recommended that a clearer statement of postal goals be drawn up; once given to the board to implement, these would allow the government to withdraw from the postal scene.[40]

Fourth, the Marchment Committee directed Canada Post to become financially self-sufficient and to balance its books by 1990. The committee was unimpressed by CPC's financial accomplishments and modest reduction of the budget deficit, for, first, a large part of the reduction in the deficit was the result of the huge price increase in 1981, a one-time event; and second, costs had been controlled mainly by restraining capital spending, running down CPC's asset base. Neither tactic could be repeated. If the deficit persisted by 1990, "then this committee recommends that the Post Office monopoly be phased out ... the corporation should not be guaranteed that the [exclusive] privilege will stay in place indefinitely if service improvement and financial self-sufficiency are not achieved." No-one was keen on withdrawing the exclusive privilege from Canada Post. Even NAMMU supported its maintenance, for without it, "Canada Post could not provide an efficient, nationwide service. Fragmented suppliers would not be able to perform effectively for some categories of mail." The committee itself concluded that "a complete elimination of the monopoly in Canada would not appear desirable. CPC would be reduced to the carrier of last resort." Polls indicated that over 50 per cent of Canadians wanted the Post Office to remain publicly owned (31 per cent supported privatization).[41]

The Marchment report altered postal discourse and redirected the postal system. To the surprise of its chair, half of the committee's recommendations were implemented right away; most of the others were pursued at a later time.[42] The report had two broad consequences.

First, it delegitimized Warren's and the unions' strategy of increasing revenue through postal expansion and diversification. This strategy promised to balance the budget without sacrificing other postal goals, because increased revenue would allow service and labour cuts to be avoided. The strategy required expanding CPC's mandate and extending its place in the market. The Marchment Committee rejected this approach as economically unsound, utopian, and potentially counterproductive. It concluded that the strategy required government subsidization and would generate unfair competition — both of which were unacceptable politically. The committee instead recommended that CPC be constrained from diversifying and entering new markets. It proposed that CPC be set on a narrow, traditional, mail-processing and -delivery course. This was the approach that the government had hoped the Marchment Ccommittee would embrace.

Second, the report undermined the idea of a potential equilibrium among CPC's economic, social, and labour goals. It gave momentum to the cost-cutting, service-rationalizing, and labour-downsizing measures that became the core of the 1986 plan. Its recommendations for community mailboxes, slower but reliable mail delivery, service rationalizations, and contracting out of retail services were telling, especially given its concern for maintaining and improving postal service. It told the Canadian public that there was a trade-off between a balanced budget and service goals: "Compromises are necessary if the Post Office is to become more efficient and minimize the drain on the public purse and the pocket books of its users." The report lowered and intensified public postal expectations at the same time: lowered expectations that CPC could do everything without financial consequence and increased expectations that CPC would do the simple things — like delivering the mail — reliably and efficiently. The report presented the need to downsize the labour force, cut wages and benefits, increase use of part-time and casual workers, and create more flexible working conditions. It gave priority to commercial and budget-balancing objectives over service and labour goals.

The government accepted the Marchment report's analysis and vision, which became the heart of the 1986 CPC five-year plan. One set of its recommendations, however, was not accepted: the proposals for distancing the government from Canada Post. The government did not introduce independent third-party regulation. Nor did it strengthen the CPC board and give it full authority over postal management and policy. The government chose instead to retain its full postal authority to regulate Canada Post and to hire and fire management. It wanted to determine postal policy for itself, which it proceeded to do in the formulation of the 1986 corporate plan.

Formulating the 1986 Corporate Plan

The Marchment report fed into an ongoing policy process that produced the new CPC plan in 1986. The report was critical, but a number of government policies and initiatives in 1985 and 1986 also gave direction to this process. Within the broad neo-conservative orientation presented in an economic policy statement in late 1984 and in the 1985 budget, the government declared that a Crown corporation should be privatized if it was not fulfilling a particular mandate or public purpose. The government also laid out exacting standards for the Crown corporations that continued to exist. This policy had two objectives. First, privatization of Crown corporations or an increase in the remaining Crowns' operating efficiency would improve the efficiency and competitiveness of the economy. Second, government coffers would benefit, either from receipts of funds generated through the sale of Crown corporation assets or from reduced financial demands made by fewer and more efficient Crowns.

The 26 February 1986 budget presented an important decision in this regard. It acknowledged that CPC would not balance its budget within the time frame set by the Liberal government:

> The Marchment Committee has recommended another five years to reach the break-even point. This is not acceptable. Following discussions with the President of Canada Post, the government has requested a new operating plan to improve productivity so that the Corporation will reduce its operating deficit to zero by the end of 1987-88.[43]

The new budget time frame then appeared as the central feature of the 1985-86 CPC report. It noted that this goal required substantial changes in how CPC operated:

> Postal services in Canada have not evolved to the same extent as other service industries in the private sector that have developed to meet changing technology, demographics and increasing labour costs. If consumers want their postal services to be as effective as other service industries, the Corporation must have the same freedom to adopt practices already introduced and generally accepted in the private sector. Canada Post employees and their unions should also be prepared to accept the norms of the private sector in terms of productivity and service if the Corporation is to continue as a viable business and a secure source of employment in the years ahead.[44]

CPC's increasing resort to euphemisms notwithstanding, the Opposition and the postal unions knew how it would have to proceed to address the budget guideline. The opposition claimed that it required service cuts, layoffs, and higher postal prices.[45] If "communications, trains and industries are subsidized", enquired NDP postal critic Keeper, "why not the Post Office? ...paying a reasonable subsidy to the Post Office for certain services is a legitimate activity for the government."[46] The unions anticipated price increases, service cuts, and confrontation. The balance among service, labour, and financial goals tipped in favour of the last, which was considered a surrogate for turning CPC into a public service for big business.[47]

The Opposition demanded that the plan be formulated in an open way, to give input to groups who were most likely to lose in the balanced-budget drive.[48] The floor of the House of Commons was as close as MPs and their constituents would come to the formulation of the plan. The CLC and the postal unions attempted to influence the formal planning process, but had to do so from the outside. They ran an advertisement campaign ("Canada Post: It Can Deliver") to incite public opinion to pressure the government to devise a public-service postal plan. Newspaper ads were run, one million pamphlets were distributed with mail-back cards attached, and endorsements were accumulated from community groups and municipalities. The campaign asked that CPC's legislative responsibility to maintain basic customary service not be sacrificed to a balanced budget.[49] Unlike in the 1980–81 legislative hearings, neither the postal unions nor opposition MPs nor public groups were involved in the creation of the 1986 corporate plan. These groups did not influence the process or have an impact on the final plan. Its formulation took place within the government, in a closed and secret fashion, and the result was determined exclusively by the government.

The revision of the Financial Administration Act in 1984 set new conditions and processes for Crown corporations' relations with the government. They were directed to submit annually to the government a five-year plan and capital budget. The governor-in-council would approve the corporate plan, after Treasury Board scrutiny and recommendation. After some early institutional changes, a Crown Corporations Directorate (CCD) of Treasury Board and the Department of Finance evaluated Crown corporations' plans. The CCD acted as the intermediary between the Crown corporations and the central agencies, advising the Crowns on government thinking and objectives while offering them a liaison with the central agencies. A policy analyst was assigned responsibility for one or more Crown corporations, and made recommendations to the deputy secretary of the Treasury Board and the assistant deputy minister of the Department of Finance. Typically, the management of a Crown corporation devised the plan, which was submitted to the corporation's board for approval. It was passed on to the responsible minister for his or her signature, then submitted to the government to be scrutinized by the CCD analyst. The analyst initiated recommendations up the hierarchy until approval was given by the government.

The uncertain and changing situation in 1986 led the CPC plan to be formulated in an atypical way, the opposite of the process just described. After Warren's 1985–86 plan was rejected, the planning process was initiated and directed by Treasury Board and the minister of Finance, not Canada Post. Its management was but one element of a collective enterprise, comprising the CCD analyst, various government departments, and Treasury Board. This working group was directed by the government to devise ways to save money and improve postal service. Options were judged by three criteria: their contribution to cost savings and balancing the postal budget, and their contribution to the improvement of service, and their ideological and political resonance. On the last point, the working group had a clear sense of the government's preferences. For example, they were aware that the government had called a halt to Consumer's Post and considered postal expansion in the market and diversification schemes to be too costly and politically nonviable. The working group also recognized that the government was unwilling to extend any financial support to Canada Post or to approve price increases higher than changes in the cost of living. Their understanding of the governmental view narrowed the range of possible options. The Marchment report arrived in the middle of this process and clarified certain issues and options. The working group accumulated thirty options, which were distilled into a dozen ideas in a presentation to cabinet. Three broad options were presented: the *status quo*, slow, incremental change; or accelerated change. Cabinet chose actions that centred on the last option, comprising the upper end of the continuum of "radical" changes. Privatization was raised in cabinet, which was only natural given the privatization process that the government had set in motion. The steering committee concluded that the privatization option was a non-starter: CPC's deficit, labour problems, poor service record, and bad image would make it all but impossible to find a buyer.[50]

CPC president Donald Lander played a limited role. He was acting president through much of this process, and was still a relative outsider, so he possessed little authority.[51] He admitted in committee hearings that "I do not have a direction in relation to the plan ... the plan is being assembled by several government departments, not the Post Office itself." The government plan was presented to the CPC board; this reversed the normal planning process of the board presenting the plan to the government. The board had been bypassed and had no option but to accept the plan and its postal logic. The change in direction was more or less welcomed by the board, for it had come to see that CPC's first four years had been devoted almost exclusively to *ad hoc* actions to put out brushfires. Some features of the plan were distasteful to the board, such as the limitations set on home delivery, but these were swallowed as part of the entire package — which had been determined by the shareholder.[52]

The 1986 corporate planning process was closed, secret, and governmentally driven and directed, with no public or union involvement.[53] Canada Post itself intervened only from the margins. The government alone shaped and determined the critical 1986 corporate plan at each stage of its evolution. First, it rejected all of Warren's options and withdrew CPC's authority to produce its corporate plan. Second, it directed a private-sector committee to devise an exclusively commercial direction for CPC. The committee delegitimized Warren's and the unions' approach — the closest thing to a public-interest approach at the time. This neutralized the CPC's service and labour goals — which existed in legislation. Third, the government set a fiscal time frame for balancing the budget, knowing that this would require the corporation to cut services and labour and other costs. Fourth, it organized an internal steering committee to devise the formal plan, which comprised service and cost cuts to meet the two-year balanced-budget goal. At each stage, the government exercised a monopoly on postal authority, and consciously determined the policy and planning results. CPC functioned much like a minor department of government, with its policies overdetermined by budgetary constraints and directives from the cabinet and the central agencies.

Finally, the government appointed new leadership to put the plan into effect. First, Caldwell and Associates set up a search for a permanent presidential appointment. Responding to accusations that the appointment would be based on patronage, Prime Minister Mulroney quipped, "If we wanted to do a favour to a friend we wouldn't make him Chairman of Canada Post." There were a number of high-quality candidates for the job, including existing and former deputy ministers as well as senior managers from the private sector, such as Robert Bandeen (CNR) and Gil Bennett (Canadair). The strongest internal candidate was Donald Lander, who let it be known that he wanted to be considered for the position. He had a strong private-sector background in the car industry (Chrysler and De Lorean, among others). Warren hired him in 1984 to be the tough, operations-oriented senior executive. He quickly became Warren's second-in-comand. The government and the board were keen to keep Lander as chief operating officer, but feared losing him if another person was recruited as CEO. And there was considerable sense in hiring a postal "insider" who could quickly begin operationalizing the government's plan. Don Lander was appointed CPC president on 17 February 1986, in a low-key announcement that foreshadowed Lander's style of operation. He had no political experience and little feel or empathy for the political process. But politics was not to be his responsibility; the government would deal with any consequences of the new plan, and as far as possible protect or insulate Lander from political pressures.[54]

Government appointments also changed the composition and orientation of the board. First, Sylvain Cloutier replaced René Marin as chair in October 1986, increasing its economic or business orientation. Marin, a judge, had been an ideal chair in the early 1980s, with the right sensibilities and background to assist CPC's delicate balancing act between economic and social goals. Cloutier was a civil servant with a background in accounting and economics, who had been deputy minister of several departments, including Treasury Board, National Revenue, Defence, and Transportation. He had also been board chair and president of the Export Development Corporation and director of the Federal Business Development Bank.

A second board development was the termination of labour participation. The government ousted labour representative Ron Lang from the board in June 1986 and replaced him with a businessman. This followed a messy period in which Lang sued CPC for not providing him with adequate information as the 1986 plan was being developed. Board appointments in this period included J.J. Chernoff (Cominco), Anne Chippendale (Encor Energy Corporation), W. Dalton (sales executive from Newfoundland), A.E. Downs (a Saskatchewan chartered accountant from Burrough, Weber), D.J. Scanlon (Arbour Capital), O. Tropea (retired deputy chair of Bell Canada) and T.E. Yates (Setay Holdings). They gave the board an exclusively business flavour, with no representation of labour, postal users, or the public interest.

Finally, the hapless Michel Côté was replaced by Harvie Andre in February 1987 as minister responsible for Canada Post.[55] Côté was plagued by bad luck and misfortune in his cabinet career (he had been the minister in charge of the Bill C-22 legislation on pharmaceutical drug patents). The implementation of the corporate plan required a tough, thick-skinned, skilled, and experienced politician to protect and insulate CPC from the inevitable political reaction to the plan. Harvie Andre subsequently played this role in an assertive, combative, and effective fashion. The Andre-Lander partnership worked exceedingly well. It gave postal policy and activity a stable political and managerial context, and a coherent and consistent ideological and commercial direction. Continuity and stability have also been maintained at the Crown Corporation Directorate, where David Salie remained as policy analyst for CPC. CCD policy analysts normally change position every two or three years, so Salie's stint has been unusually long. He participated in the construction of the 1986 plan. His postal vision was shaped by that experience and its results, and coincided closely with that of Andre and Lander.

The 1986-87 to 1990-91 Corporate Plan

Canada Post's 1986-87 to 1990-91 business plan was presented to cabinet in September 1986, approved on 17 October, and tabled in the House of Commons on 5 November. The plan redefined CPC's existence and shaped the contours of its evolution. Neither the government nor CPC has subsequently tampered with the plan's strategy. The next critical plan — 1989-90 to 1993-94 — extended and deepened its predecessor's logic. The 1986 plan resolved the lingering policy uncertainties and political compromises that had beset the 1981 Canada Post Corporation Act. It gave concrete meaning to CPC's various goals and their relation to each other. A firm financial target was set within a short-term time frame. Service changes were sketched out, clarifying, if not redefining, the meaning of "customary postal service." The labour-management goal was all but ignored, labour becoming simply another cost input. The plan characterized the Canadian Post Office of the future by setting out what CPC would *not* do, specifying its technological, communications, amd market roles, and indicating how it would carry out the limited responsibilities it was assigned. Management determined its operational or detailed features, but the plan's strategy and goals were set by cabinet.

The full plan was not released; like subsequent corporate plans, it remains secret because it contains "commercially sensitive material." A synopsis of it was tabled in the House of Commons, and can be fleshed out with the help of leaked documents as well as the statements and testimony of CPC and government officials. The plan can be characterized as a commercially oriented strategy to balance the budget quickly, through a number of service cuts and cost-cutting measures, including the virtual elimination of the retail network.

First, the plan proposed to reduce the deficit to $132 million in 1986 and to $60 million in 1987; to balance the budget in 1988; and to generate a $53 million surplus in 1989. This was to be accomplished through cuts in service, productivity improvements, increases in efficiency — and an immediate increase in postal rates: a 9 per cent increase in commercial rates and a two-cent increase in first-class mail to thirty-six cents. Future price increases would be regular and automatic, and tied to changes in the cost of living (Lander predicted accurately in hearings that the price of a first-class stamp would rise to forty cents by 1991). The price of publications mail, northern mail, and mail for the blind would also increase; subsidies for these categories of "social" mail would decline 25 per cent to $191 million by 1992, following the recommendation of the Nielson Task Force on Program Review to end the concessionary postal rate subsidy.[56]

A second tactic to improve CPC's financial situation was the widely anticipated decision to limit expansion of home delivery of mail through expansion of the community mailbox program (originally dubbed "supermailboxes"). All new urban growth areas would be serviced by community mailboxes, not by home delivery (existing door-to-door service, however, would be maintained). This policy had been adopted in the U.S. in 1978. The boxes would be located no further than two hundred yards from any address. Moreover, mail delivery to 100,000 rural clients would be transferred to community boxes installed at major intersections, as would delivery for a further 400,000 users of green mailboxes. The plan estimated that 120,000 Canadians would receive their mail in this fashion by the end of 1986. CPC was adding on 150,000 new addresses a year, and planned to service 66 per cent of these by community mailboxes (about 50 per cent of addresses received home delivery at this time). At less than a third of the cost of home delivery, the community mailbox program could save CPC up to $45 million a year by decade's end. The plan suggested that the program simultaneously improve postal service. Community boxes were "more conveniently located and more generally accessible," given changing demography and life-styles.

The plan also introduced a new set of delivery standards, following the recommendations of the Marchment report: two days for local mail, three days for intra-regional mail, and four days for national mail (next-day delivery was quietly dropped). This new standard would simplify operations and ease cost pressures. Independent, third-party assessment of CPC's delivery performance would gauge its success in meeting these standards, by June 1987.

The third ingredient in the plan's budget strategy was the rationalization of rural services. Hard-headed analysts considered the rural network to be over-developed and a contributor to the deficit. Yet social expectations and political considerations weighed against changes to the rural system. The 1986 plan proposed a number of significant changes. First, it proposed to eliminate a number of rural routes by combining them into larger, more economically viable ones. Second, laneway service was to be eliminated for about 100,000 rural customers. Third, the network of rural post offices was to be rationalized. The plan proposed to "privatize" 3,500 rural post offices, by turning them over to private contractors over a ten-year period. A further 1,500 rural post offices with less than seventy-five customers were to be amalgamated; and another 1,700 were to be amalgamated, eliminated, or replaced by community mailboxes. As the plan was being developed during 1986, 72 rural post offices had already been closed.

Fourth, the plan assigned the private sector a greater postal role. Canada Post's retail network was to be replaced by a private one: The plan proposed to "significantly expand on the current involvement of the private sector in the provision of counter services, including the adoption of franchising and other arrangements." As noted, the majority of rural post offices were to be privatized, as were urban counter services. Many large urban stations were closed in 1986, and the plan listed a further 734 urban offices to be closed.[57] CPC would realize substantial savings by off-loading its overhead retail costs to the private sector, and could then concentrate on picking up, sorting, and delivering the mail, thereby, the plan claimed, improving postal service. Given changes in business patterns, life-style, and demographics, the private retail network offered convenient access (near to people's workplaces) as well as longer and more convenient hours. The retail strategy was raised by Lander and CPC during the planning process. The steering committee responded positively and gave it a high priority.[58] The plan proposed to contract out work and other postal functions, as a way of lowering costs. Following the Neilson report, CPC had already contracted out the cleaning of its facilities, lowering cleaning costs from $8–12 an hour to the minimum wage, a savings of about $3 million a year.

Fifth, the plan proposed to reduce labour costs. First, labour contracts would be renegotiated to attain "required operational flexibility," primarily through productivity bargaining. Wages and benefits would be made comparable to those in the private sector. Second, the labour force would be reduced by 14 per cent from 61,186 to 53,116 by 1991, in a variety of ways: cuts in service, privatization of the retail network, containment of expanding home delivery, elimination of rural routes, reduced absenteeism (from seventeen to thirteen days a year), and increased mechanization. The last proposal marked the advent of the second wave of postal mechanization. Underinvestment in plant and equipment in the early 1980s exacerbated an already serious situation: "At the time of incorporation, Canada Post inherited an asset base consisting of many facilities which were obsolete, expensive to operate, ill-suited to the requirements of the Corporation, poorly located, or surplus to its needs." In a ten year plan to renovate and rationalize facilities and upgrade equipment, the government promised equity contributions of $103 million in 1986–87 and $161 million in 1987–88, for expenditures not generated from CPC's cash flow. By 1988–89, capital expenditures would be financed through internal means.

Conspicuously absent from the plan were initiatives to extend CPC's activities in the market. While the plan aimed to increase revenues, this was not to be pursued via diversification of products and services. Nor was it to be attained through aggressive intervention into the new, technologically sophisticated communications markets. Rather, CPC hoped to attract increased business by becoming more reliable, efficient, and aggressive in its traditional postal activities of picking up, sorting, and delivering mail. The plan announced a program of recruiting new private-sector managers, injecting a "corporate culture" to make CPC more aggressive in its pursuit of markets.

Reaction to the 1986 plan, considered in more detail in the following chapters, can be briefly described as initially mixed. NAMMU was broadly and enthusiastically supportive, particularly of the emphasis on sound business practices and increased reliability as well as the rejection of diversification. The opposition parties and the unions criticized the balanced-budget focus for generating inequity, by creating two classes of postal users. The unions claimed that the plan aimed to make CPC profitable and easier to privatize. Minister Côté lauded the plan's "delicate balance between providing postal service and balancing the budget." He agreed that the only way to do this — while maintaining some semblance of a postal service — was to expand the role of the private sector in the postal system. This had the added advantage of creating business opportunities for postal employees, for example in franchising. "Canada Post will be encouraging its own employees in these positions to accept the entrepreneurial challenge and use their experience at working with such a franchise." Conservative backbencher Pauline Bowes praised the expanded opportunities the plan provided for small business.[59]

Conclusion

By the end of 1986, CPC's character and purpose had been reconceptualized and postal policy took a new direction. In formulating the 1986 plan, the Conservatives rejected and delegitimized the reasoning behind the creation of a postal Crown corporation as well as the traditional Canadian approach to the Post Office. No longer was CPC responsible for juggling social and economic goals in some sort of equilibrium. Of the trio of goals set in 1981, the government directed CPC to attend only to balancing the budget and to eschew the service and labour goals. The plan proposed to change customary postal services dramatically, with many traditional postal functions to be performed outside of the public sector by private firms. The goal of improving labour management relations was all but ignored. The retail rationalization, absenteeism, and productivity strategies threatened workers' jobs and incomes.

The public-service or public-purpose rationale behind the Crown corporation all but dissolved with the construction of the 1986 plan, reflecting the constrained process that had generated the plan. The public was not consulted during its formulation. No parliamentary or legislative hearings were held, even though the changes imposed by the plan seemed to defy CPC's legislative mandate. The idea of a balance between corporate and Crown objectives was transformed into an identification of Crown with corporate objectives. This was not displeasing to the business community, which would benefit from the more efficient functioning of a commercially oriented and market-sensitive postal service. The government unleashed Canada Post to act like a private corporation. Franchising and contracting out, user-pay pricing, rationalization of service, elimination of social objectives, a focus on financial self-sufficiency, recruitment of private-sector managers — these comprised a private-sector postal orientation. As Lander characterized it in committee hearings:

> The operation of Canada Post Corporation ... is bringing about a form of ... privatization, albeit the owner is still the Canadian government and its people. But with the methodologies in which we are now approaching Canada Post, trying to bring in the values that are inherent in other corporations, I believe that is a form of privatization in its relationship to its responsibilities, its measurement of its assets, and its return on those investments that heretofore under a department was not possible ... the corporation ... is evolving into a private, corporate-value entity ... the cultural change ... is to a private corporation.[60]

CPC was to act like a private corporation, but the government limited its activities to picking up, processing, and delivering mail. It disallowed CPC's entering other economic areas, so as not to offend, or compete with, the business community. Political and ideological factors thus determined CPC's fate and future, demonstrating the government's continuing postal authority.

The 1986 plan steered Canada Post into an inevitable series of confrontations with the public and its unions. Changes to customary postal services would upset smaller postal users and the rural community. The retail rationalization, absenteeism, productivity, and mechanization strategies threatened postal workers' jobs and income; the unions would defend their interests. It was transparently obvious to the government that the plan would generate public reaction as well as confrontation with the unions. Canada Post would be placed under tremendous pressure to compromise or back away from controversial policies. The government nonetheless directed Canada Post to generate these confrontations, giving assurances that it would defend and support CPC when difficulties emerged.

Chapter Nine

THE PRIVATIZATION OF CANADA POST

Once the 1986 business plan was in place, Canada Post's *Crown* motives came to be dominated by *corporate* rationales. Public-purpose functions became trivial as the agenda grew increasingly market oriented. To the extent that CPC pursued the plan, the government granted it increased autonomy. Public scrutiny of postal activities lessened to the point of elimination. With this increased authority, Canada Post began to evolve into a private-sector corporation.

The 1986 plan did not "privatize" Canada Post in any formal sense; it encouraged and sanctioned CPC to strategize, calculate, and function like a private-sector corporation. The goal of a balanced budget — recast by the government in 1989 to mean a 14-15 per cent return on equity — was a proxy to this end. CPC could become market competitive and make a profit only if it behaved like a private-sector company. It was thus required to act like a private corporation in practice, if not in law.

The balanced budget goal contained three imperatives. First, competitiveness in the high-tech communications market demanded high speed and low price — so CPC needed to modernize its plant and equipment. This would be expensive and would require substantial internally generated postal surpluses, given governments' deficit problems. Second, CPC's ability to attract business was constrained by the fact that it did not project a business image, particularly given its perpetual deficit. Balancing the budget was a necessary (albeit insufficient) condition for attracting increased business. Third, the government would not support CPC's diversification plans in new market areas as long as the latter carried a deficit, for CPC's private-sector competitors would claim that the government was subsidizing unfair competition. Before it could improve its technological capacity, attract new business, and enter into lucrative new markets, CPC first had to eliminate its deficit. How it pursued this goal — in the process coming to act like a private corporation — is the subject matter of this chapter.

There were two preconditions for balancing the budget, neither of which could be established by CPC itself. First, the government had to release CPC from its legislative responsibility to pursue the other goals set at Crowning in 1981: maintaining and expanding customary postal services and improving labour-management relations. The social or public-purpose constraints on postal profits had to be neutralized, and only the government could do this. Second, there would be social and political reaction against CPC's abandonment of its public-purpose orientation in favour of a private-sector one. CPC, to be able to design and pursue a complex and extensive array of commercial plans, would require continuous political protection from this reaction. Only the government, then, could create the conditions required for transforming the postal function into a commercial one. The government's role in neutralizing public postal goals and restraining reaction to a commercial post office will be the subject matter of chapter 10. This chapter focuses on CPC policy and consequences from 1986 to 1993. It first establishes how the importance of budget balancing and profitability defined CPC's existence and shaped policy choices. Two sections then investigate CPC's revenue-raising tactics and explain cost-cutting and productivity-increasing actions. A concluding section characterizes these policies and evaluates their impact. My purpose in this chapter is to document and characterize CPC policies in this period, to demonstrate the extent to which CPC has been privatized. Chapter 10 then looks at how the government enabled CPC to pursue this strategy.

Balancing the Budget

Balancing its books defined CPC's existence after 1986. The strategic rationale of this approach was exposed starkly in the 1985 Plog report, which concluded that there was "a very strong link between corporate image and willingness to patronize Canada Post Corporation."[1] The consultant's report estimated that CPC's poor corporate image cost the corporation about $300 million in lost business a year (p. 165), representing about 12 per cent of CPC revenues and 75 per cent of its $395 million deficit in 1984-85.

CPC's poor corporate reputation derived from three factors. First, business saw it as unreliable and as providing poor service (p. 41). Second, the market believed that CPC's poor performance reflected union rather than management control of the corporation (pp. 80-81). Third, poor performance was thought to reflect government involvement, which transformed business decisions into political ones (p. 98). There was confusion about whether CPC was an independent Crown corporation or a department of government. The latter identification was costly: "The stronger the (perceived) connection with government, the more Canada Post Corporation is seen as lacking aggressive management, operating at a deficit, and failing to perform well...the less customers associate Canada Post Corporation with government, the more positive their image, and the more likely they are to patronize CPC" (p. 101). Businesses that considered CPC to be part of the government provided only two-thirds as much business as their numbers warranted. If they used CPC's services as much as those who considered CPC to have strong management, postal revenues would increase by 13 per cent (p. 161-62).

To improve its corporate image to attract business activity, CPC had to convince the market that it was a private-sector participant like any other. To project this image, it had to eliminate the perception of union influence, create a perception of reliability and performance, distance itself from the government, and make a profit. This required recasting the three goals set in the 1981 Crown corporation legislation. Improving labour-management relations and maintaining and improving customary postal service were made subservient to the balanced budget goal. Labour's "privileged" position ended in 1986, when labour began to be considered just another "cost ingredient," like raw materials; CPC president Lander characterized management's relations with labour as "no different than the purchasing department interfacing with the suppliers."[2] Union leaders met Lander infrequently and were no longer consulted, in contrast to Warren's open-door policy in which the unions were consulted on all important policy matters.[3] As outlined below, CPC deliberately distanced itself from labour, to demonstrate that labour had no special influence in corporate affairs and to emphasize that management was in charge. Similarly, service goals were directed away from social and national functions towards controlling costs (to keep prices down) and improving the speed and reliability of business mail.

While the service and labour goals were quietly dropped, the balanced budget goal was placed front and centre. This goal had tremendous symbolic resonance in the market. The private sector identified fiscal balance and profitability with sound management and good business practices. A balanced budget also symbolized the nature of CPC's relationship with the government and the corporation's capacity to act like a real business. Postal deficits implied dependence on an interfering government, poor management and inefficiencies, and lack of competitiveness. A balanced budget or profits signalled that the corporation was independent of the government, able to act in true corporate fashion. Hence, private corporations were unlikely to do business with a deficit-ridden corporation. Moreover, in order to generate more business, CPC needed to expand its mandate and participate in new market activities. The same condition held: "Profitability is an important prerequisite to expanding the mandate...the belief that the Post Office is becoming more profitable presupposes strong and aggressive management" (p. 106).

To sum up, the broad strategy was to project an image to the market of being the same as any other private-sector company, struggling to be competitive and balance the books. To do so, the corporation had to distance itself from the postal unions, from the government, and from any hint of public obligations. The new image was expected to increase postal business, easing the task of balancing the budget. CPC's corporate plans indicated that business growth was to contribute substantially to the increased revenues required to balance the budget: 38 per cent of the anticipated financial improvement was to come from business growth in 1987-88 compared to 29 per cent from price increases and 38 per cent from productivity improvements. By the 1991-92 plan, this had increased to 41 per cent, compared to 19 per cent via price increases and 40 per cent via increased efficiency.[4]

The February 1986 federal budget directed CPC to balance its budget in two years: "Following discussions with the President of Canada Post, the government has requested a new operating plan...so that the Corporation will reduce its operating deficit to zero by the end of fiscal 1987-88."[5] CPC accepted the directive confidently in its 1985-86 annual report (it had already cut the deficit to $210 million in 1985-86).[6] This target became the basis of the 1986-87 to 1990-91 corporate plan, which proposed cuts in deficit appropriations from $132 million in 1986-87, to $30 million in 1987-88, and to zero thereafter. It also proposed to cut equity contributions from the government to $103 million in 1986-87 and to $161 million in 1987-88; the capital program in 1988-89 and thereafter would be funded predominantly from internally generated cash flows.[7] CPC posted lower deficits of $129 million in 1986-87 and $30 million in 1987-88, and in 1988-89, announced a profit of $96 million. This was the first postal profit in thirty years, and the first year in which CPC would not seek appropriations from the government.[8] The plan proposed that operations be financed entirely through internally generated funds or through borrowing.[9]

The government reconceptualized the meaning of "budget balance" in that year. It rescheduled Canada Post under the Financial Administration Act as a Schedule III(2) Crown corporation, the category assigned to Crown corporations that function in a competitive market environment and that are not dependent on government appropriations. This rescheduling formalized CPC's existence as a quasi-private corporation financially independent of the government. The April 1989 federal budget directed CPC to increase its rate of return on equity to 14-15 per cent by 1993-94 and required it to pay the government $300 million in dividends over the next five years. There was a strong market rationale behind this directive. The government's view was that if CPC was operating on a commercial basis, it should establish appropriate financial targets and pay dividends to its shareholder (the government).[10] These targets were based on a commissioned study (Warburg and Dominion Securities) that concluded that if CPC was to be a self-sustaining corporation, it would have to have access to debt and equity capital in order to make investments. These investors would compare CPC's financial performance to that of similar corporations in the market, such as the express delivery companies and the communications and transportation industries in the regulated sector. In order to borrow money, Canada Post would have to match the financial performance of firms in these sectors, such as a return on equity of 14-15 per cent and an operating profit of 6-7 per cent. These considerations were the basis of the 1989 budget directive.[11]

This directive informed the 1989-90 to 1993-94 corporate plan, which deepened the logic of the 1986 plan. Its core was to "realize a level of profitability that supports future growth and provides a fair return on investment" (p. 7). The plan established financial criteria for judging CPC's progress towards financial self-sufficiency and generating a return on equity similar to that within the private sector. Equity targets were set: 6 per cent for 1988-89, 1989-90, and 1990-91; 7 per cent in 1991-92; 11 per cent in 1992-93; and 14 per cent in 1993-94. The plan also established a dividend payout ratio of 35-40 per cent of earnings to provide a reasonable rate of return to the shareholder while providing enough financial resources for the capital investment required for CPC to remain technologically competitive.[12] CPC thus internalized the logic and expectations of the market like any other private-sector corporation.

As we will see below, the setting of profit targets was politically controversial, flying in the face of traditional notions of the Post Office as a public service. It is worth noting the government's and the corporation's response to this criticism, in order to clarify the rationale behind this policy. There were three basic reasons why the balanced budget definition was expanded to a more ambitious profit target. First, the minister responsible for CPC — Harvie Andre — maintained that anything less than the attainment of a normal level of profit was tantamount to allowing the corporation a subsidy, which was to be avoided for both economic and political reasons.[13] Second, as CPC president Lander put it, most corporations pay dividends, so CPC should pay dividends as well: "otherwise, we will be deemed or seen to be not a 'fair competitor' in vying for customer business."[14] Third, there was an urgent sense that CPC had to respond to the competitive pressures associated with new communication technologies, such as telecommunications, e-mail, fax, computers, and electronic funds transfers. A five-year $2.5-billion capital plan was presented in the 1989 plan to this end. Since the government was disinclined to pump funds into Canada Post, the corporation had to raise these funds internally or borrow them on the financial markets. In either case, balancing its books was insufficient, for, as Lander argued, "Businesses that do not offer a return on investment or fail to finance their capital needs through other means do not stay in business for long. Just breaking even means that in the long run you go broke."[15] Expanding self-sufficiency to include recovery of the cost of capital was an idea supported in major reports by the Consumer and Corporate Affairs Committee and by the Postal Services Review Committee, which both agreed that the profit targets would raise CPC's efficiency, impose corporate discipline, provide for capital expansion, and ensure fair competition.[16]

Canada Post reported a $149 million profit in 1989-90, a return on equity of 10.9 per cent. CPC paid a dividend of $60 million to the government, as the first instalment of the $300 million in dividends it planned to pay over a five-year period.[17] Like other companies, Canada Post was subsequently affected by the extended recession of the early 1990s, which began in the second quarter of 1990. Profits fell to $14 million in 1990-91, and the dividend paid to the government was only $5.7 million. A loss of $128 million was announced in 1991-92, blamed on weaker than expected economic growth as well as on the labour disruption that year. No dividend was paid. The target of a 14–15 per cent return on equity was put off until 1996–97. While CPC returned to a profit position in 1992–93 ($25 million), the corporate plan did not anticipate that the 14–15 per cent target would be reached over the next five years.[18]

CPC's primary objective since 1986 has been to balance the budget and increase profits. It pursued a "balanced" approach to this end, combining price increases, business growth, and productivity improvements. This involved two general policy means. First, it attempted to increase revenues to cover its costs and make a profit. The projection of a corporate image to the market was a key ingredient of this strategy, to raise revenues through increased postal volumes and revenues. Second, it sought to contain and cut its costs. This included downgrading the goals of improving labour-management relations and maintaining and improving customary postal services in order to cut costs and improve productivity. These approaches to balancing the budget will be examined in turn.

Raising Revenues

Two approaches were used to increase revenues: CPC raised prices and sold real estate, and it undertook initiatives to increase business.

Raising Prices and Selling Property

The price of a first-class stamp has increased annually since 1986. The 1986 corporate plan announced a two-cent increase, (for political reasons to be discussed below). Cabinet approved the increase in March 1987, and the price of a first-class stamp rose from thirty-four to thirty-six cents — an increase of about 6 per cent (see Table 5). Commercial rates were increased by about 9 per cent. Prices were subsequently increased annually, in a predictable and modest pattern. There were successive annual one-cent increases through 1992, interrupted only by a two-cent increase in 1991. This took the price of a first-class stamp to forty-three cents in 1993 — plus GST (the government rejected a two-cent request in 1989).[19] Since 1982, letter rate price increases have amounted to two-thirds of the rise in the Consumer Price Index.[20] In 1991–92, the price of a first-class stamp in Canada was the second lowest in the industrial world, after the United States, gauged by the amount of time required for an average worker to earn the price of that stamp.[21]

First-class mail is the most important source of postal revenues, so its rate is critical. There have been initiatives in other mail categories. Canada Post has embraced the user-pay or pay-as-you-go price philosophy introduced by PMG Kierans in the late 1960s. Postal rates have been set to reflect the costs of providing services, and a more complex system of mail categories has been developed to this end. This system fine-tunes postal prices to the service being provided. In the late 1980s, CPC replaced the traditional categorization — first-class (letters), second class (newspapers and periodicals), third class (advertising material), fourth class (parcels) — by a wider classification scheme based on criteria such as speed, service, and security. For example, first-class mail changed to comprise four subproducts, electronic, express, priority, and regular, each offering a different mix of price, speed, service, and security. Moreover, various incentives were offered to large-volume and frequent mail users, who qualified for significant price discounts if their mail was coded and presorted. The user-pay approach had the effect of increasing prices in various categories and in the provision of services. For example, charges for postal money orders, insurance, second-class mail, rental of postal boxes, and change of address notices were increased regularly and often quite substantially.

CPC also increased revenues by selling real estate. Overseen by a vice-president in charge of real estate, this was a natural strategy given the changes in CPC's strategic orientation. Given CPC's plans to off-load retail operations, for example, numerous of its buildings became too large or unnecessary for its operations. Technology, transportation, demographic, and locational changes encouraged CPC to transfer sorting operations from downtown to suburban and industrial areas.[22] CPC thus owned much valuable real estate that was not integral to its operation. CPC president Lander indicated that the sale of disposal assets would finance much of CPC's capital expansion. Canada Post announced in 1988–89 that it had disposed of $51 million in fixed assets, for a net gain of $29 million (representing 30 per cent of CPC's announced profit of $96 million that year). Next year, it sold two blocks of land and buildings in Toronto for $112 million (for 75 per cent of its announced profit of $149 million that year). CPC admitted that this tactic would decline in financial importance over time, but estimated that it would generate earnings of $363 million by 1994–95. The centrality of the sale of real estate to CPC's financial progress became evident the following year. CPC reported in 1990–91 that its profits had fallen to $14 million, partially because the weak economy delayed the planned sale of $50 million in real estate.

There were limits to these "direct" means of increasing revenue to balance the budget. Competition and communications alternatives limited the extent to which postal prices could be increased; and price increases could become self-defeating if volumes declined as a result. There were also political limits to price rises, which generate public and business reaction that the government has to absorb. If CPC relied too much on price increases to reduce the deficit, the government would be less impressed with CPC's managerial and commercial capacity and less willing to grant it autonomy. Finally, Canada Post would sooner or later run out of excess real estate to sell.[23]

Increasing Postal Business

CPC's second revenue-increasing tactic was to increase business, in three inter-related ways. It tried to improve its corporate image within the market; it altered and expanded its product line to attract business and exploit new markets; and it undertook a substantial capital investment plan, to improve its competitiveness in the sophisticated communications market.

The Plog report concluded that CPC's corporate reputation was a real market constraint: its poor image "costs the Corporation many millions of dollars each year, and severely handicaps its efforts to compete vigorously in areas where alternative services are available" (p. 32). To make up the estimated $300 million a year in lost business,[24] CPC would, hypothetically, have to increase the price of a first-class stamp by seven and a half cents.

CPC initiated a number of measures to improve its corporate image, such as increasing the reliability and performance of its services and improving its product line, which will be explored below. The central initiative was to project to the market that it was a competent, commercially oriented and customer-sensitive *business*. CPC adapted itself to think and act like a private business, not like an institution tied to the public sector or to public service. Within this new paradigm, public issues are transformed into customer and market issues.[25] CPC fairly easily convinced itself of its corporate status, but had to persuade the business community to consider it in these new terms. It attempted to do this in seven ways.

First, it had to demonstrate to potential customers that it was a business corporation just like them, just as able to deliver a competitive and competent service. To do this, it had to convince customers that it was not "part of the government," that it was not subsidized and propped up in a manner that refused to penalize inefficiencies, bad management, and lack of productivity. Thus, the vital importance for Canada Post of balancing the budget and making a profit — the defining characteristic of a successful business, for profits suggest capable management, good products and services, and an efficient and productive operation. Customers were unlikely to deal with a business perceived to have weak management and poor products and services, as was suggested by the persistence of the deficit and government subsidies.

Thus, Canada Post found itself in a catch-22: it had to reduce the deficit and make a profit in order to increase postal business sufficiently to reduce the deficit and make a profit. At a parliamentary hearing, President Lander was asked why Canada Post insisted on making a profit (which required a variety of cuts and price increases). He replied:

> If we are going to compete...we have to make sure we are operating on a competitive basis. If other companies have to pay [dividends], then that is a cost to that company, and similarly our corporation should have costs. Otherwise, I believe we run the risk of not being

seen as a full-fledged corporation and as such I believe that that opens up a Pandora's box as to not being good or fair competition.[26]

Second, CPC initiated closer contact with business, in physical terms and in terms of what the market saw it doing, to increase business contacts as well as to project its new corporate image. One instance of this strategy was CPC's rental of a box at Skydome, which received considerable scrutiny and criticism. CPC shared the rental of the box for one year, at a cost of $200,000, an ostensible indulgence at a time of high unemployment and allegedly declining postal service.[27] But this move had strategic significance, as group vice-president William Kennedy explained:

> We like to see and understand our customers...We like to be seen and work with business...One of the things we have analyzed in the past has been the corporation's anonymity...[the] faceless people in Ottawa and Toronto...One of the things we are doing overtly right now is pulling back from advertising and promotion in newspapers and television into event participation...where we get our people...to participate with other people in other domains, so they can see us, use us and understand our system, and we can explain that. The Skybox is an experiment.[28]

The Skybox rental was only one aspect of CPC's attempt to be in contact with business people and other businesses, to do "business" things, and be associated with the things that businesses do, and to meet potential customers and explain and demonstrate what CPC is all about. There were a host of others: it entered into a number of sponsorships and promotions with private businesses such as McDonald's, which sponsored "Stamp Months."[29] The association with McDonald's had a marketing value in itself, raised a quarter of a million dollars, and marketed stamp collecting to children.[30] CPC helped in Petro-Canada's Olympic "Share the Flame Campaign." In one mailing, ten million pieces of unaddressed admail were distributed — the largest single mailing ever. In total, CPC delivered over 39 million pieces of unaddressed admail related to the Winter Olympics. CPC has sponsored the Canadian Football league, the Molson Indy, and the Canada Games, where officials could be seen with and talking to business people. Priority Courier was a sponsor of the 1992 Olympics in Albertville and Barcelona, where it was Canada's official courier. CPC also co-sponsored an Olympics promotion with Kraft Foods. As official mail service sponsor to the XV Commonwealth Games, CPC assisted the Games to promote tickets, products, and sponsors and provided expertise to assist with marketing and revenue generation. It has done high-profile advertising, such as on the sideboards in the rinks of all the Canadian teams in the National Hockey League.[31]

Third, Canada Post tried to convince the media to treat it as a business.[32] Newspaper coverage was the second most important source of the business community's negative image of the Post Office (after personal experience).[33] Newspapers traditionally covered the Post Office as a political spectator sport, filling space on slow and unexciting days with accounts of late and lost mail, postal incompetence and inefficiencies, gross examples of political interference, the horrors of antagonistic labour-management relations, and unjust price increases and unacceptable postal deficits. This coverage reminded the business community that the Post Office was part of the government, and hence inefficient, incompetent, and not to be used. CPC wanted to be covered, not on the front pages as a political entity, but in the business section as a corporation. Even if problems were being reported, they would be written about by business writers, who could be kept informed of CPC's corporate developments. This issue was seen as so substantial that CPC considered moving its corporate headquarters away from Ottawa, and the political coverage it received there, to Toronto, centre of the national business media. This did not happen, but CPC's press conferences and releases are often held or made public in Toronto, where writers are thought to be less "political" and Ottawa-focused, and more likely to cover the event as a business story. CPC developed a substantial Media Relations Office, to track media coverage and intervene to neutralize negative or misleading coverage. Critical characterizations are responded to, to ensure that CPC is perceived as competent and businesslike and not part of the government. All major CPC events and issues are required to have an approved communications plan before they are pursued or released. Media strategy has become part of the planning process and has affected basic decisions themselves.[34]

This strategy has been quite successful. Coverage of postal matters has declined substantially since 1985 (save at strike time). For CPC, no news is good news, as it fosters its claim to be just another business. As well, the news coverage of Canada Post has shifted to the business section. For example, coverage of the 1990-91 and 1991-92 annual reports was minimal, despite the fact that CPC's profits collapsed and a deficit was generated, and was buried fairly deep in the business section or given only seconds of air time. The modest accomplishments of the 1992-93 report were barely noted, the media focusing instead on CPC's purchase of Purolator at the time.[35] During the 1991 postal strike, CPC concentrated its efforts on the Toronto press, to draw out business angles on the strike. It strove to identify itself with the business community: "Our Business is Your Business," claimed its ads, which went on to present CPC's case, that it was trying to make a "responsible settlement considering the current economy" with the "flexibility to put our customers first." Media coverage tended to play these business rather than political angles.[36] Coverage has also focused increasingly on CPC's business "turn-around" or its "high-tech" features.[37]

Fourth, a Business and Community Affairs Office nurtures personal and institutional contacts with business. It interacts regularly with 25-30 business groups and lobbies and periodically with another 100 groups. CPC has joined a number of associations, such as the Canadian Manufacturers' Association, and the Canadian Direct Marketing Association. The Business and Community Affairs Office interacts with this "postal community," to neutralize negative postal images and to troubleshoot when problems arise. It keeps that community well informed so that it comprehends what CPC is doing. For example, response to the two-cent price increase in 1991 was relatively controlled — compared to past reactions to similar policies — because the Business and Community Affairs Office had explained the rationale behind the increase. These efforts are not simply altruistic, for the positive relationships created increase the likelihood that the postal system will be used.[38] The relationship is particularly intimate with regard to the National Association of Major Mail Users (NAMMU), whose executive meets regularly with senior management at Canada Post to rehearse its members' needs. CPC responded to NAMMU overtures to set up one-on-one contracts with individual users; details, costs, schedules, and other aspects are tailored to the particular client.[39] Relations are also nurtured in other ways. For example, at an Annual Supplier Awards evening that is well-publicized in the media, CPC makes awards of excellence to twelve companies and awards of distinction to forty others that provide CPC with materials, services, equipment, and so on. These suppliers might in turn become postal users.[40] Postal customers themselves make the annual Heritage Club and Silver and Golden Postmark Awards to long-serving and outstanding CPC employees.

CPC has expended considerable energy in attracting business. For example, it provides a free information and advice service for small and medium-sized companies who want better communication with their customers or who would like to become involved in direct marketing and advertising. Magazines such as *Business Access* and *Canadian Connexion* offer advice and suggestions. CPC has helped develop the direct marketing industry in Canada, and has formed a good working relationship and partnership with the Canadian Direct Marketing Association. It sees itself as contributing to Canada's competitiveness, particularly in sharing ideas with business on how to do direct marketing.[41] It has also increased its presence in the wider community. It won the 1991 Corporate Humanist Award for its literacy program, which included issuing a commemorative stamp, developing an international literacy symbol, making financial contributions to literacy groups, sponsoring a television special, and initiating its Workplace Integrated Skills Program. In association with the CRB Foundation and Power Corporation, CPC produced fourteen Heritage Minutes for television and produced and distributed an associated Heritage Post newsletter to be used in the classroom.

Fifth, the National Control Centre (NCC) that oversees CPC's operations has been marketed widely as a symbol of Canada Post's modernity, technological competence, and connection to high-tech communications. For example, the joint government-CPC announcement of the Employee Share Ownership Plan in April 1992 was made at the NCC; Lander informed the watching media that the NCC "symbolizes the progress that Canada Post Corporation has made...[and] the future of Canada Post, a company that will continue to apply the best technology...to meet the needs of our customers into the 21st century."[42] On the top floor of headquarters at the Sir Alexander Campbell Building, the NCC combines Star Trek with Barnum and Bailey. In one part is a large oval-shaped room, where the CPC president and top executives meet daily at 8:30 a.m. to review the previous day's activities and remedy any problems. On the other side, behind moveable panels, is the control room, staffed by two to three technicians and a director, monitoring all of Canada Post's operations. The electronically wired M.C. hosts the morning meeting and takes the group through a rapid-fire presentation. A beeper sounds to start the presentation, the lights dim, and the show begins with a cross-Canada weather update. Each CPC section reports and updates the past day or week, pointing out weekly, monthly, and yearly trends and targets while highlighting accomplishments or difficulties. All aspects of the postal operation are reviewed; from broad volume, distribution, transportation, and operations activities to specific sectors like Priority Post, parcels, and "trouble" areas like admail (for environmental concerns). Significant problems or anomalies are noted and often questioned by the president, sending a chill over the meeting and the promise of fast remedial action. The spectacle proceeds briskly and ends at 9:10 a.m.

The control monitoring room is dominated by electronic maps: a huge Canadian one and various smaller regional and area screens and monitors. This is CPC's central nervous system, wired into similar rooms in each of CPC's operating divisions. If a problem develops, the entire system is aware of it and can react in a coherent manner. If a truck breaks down between cities, the driver's call is fed through the cities, to get the truck repaired and to avoid late delivery of the mail. The destination city is informed, with consequences for staffing or delivery schedules. Depending on the deadlines, the mail on the truck — which has been identified and recorded centrally — might be shifted to air transport to meet deadlines, with the upstream system and destination then informed. The NCC has its own generator and wiring system. The engineering of the entire system is mapped together, so that the Centre knows the organization and operation of all CPC's plants, routes, and locations. The system is totally integrated, from the manufacturing plant, through engineering, transportation, and delivery, for all cities. Maps follow the progress of the corporation's six hundred mail vehicles, and the system is directly linked to airline information. The truck network will soon be integrated to the NCC via onboard computers communicating to Ottawa by satellite. The system is unique and extraordinarily sophisticated, and is being marketed abroad. The NCC is featured in CPC's marketing and advertising, and customers, potential business users, and observers are encouraged to visit it. It has projected a new image of Canada Post: as technologically sophisticated, customer oriented, and in command of its operations.[43]

Sixth, and related to the NCC strategy, CPC attempted to create an image of a reliable operator performing at a high standard. The Plog report demonstrated that "of all the factors affecting evaluations of Canada Post Corporation and willingness to use its services, performance is clearly the most important" (p. 41). CPC tried to neutralize business's perception of a service shortfall in a number of ways. First, the NCC demonstrated that Canada Post knew what it was doing, and was using all technological means to improve service. Second, CPC created attainable expectations of what "good service" meant. It accepted the Marchment committee's delivery standards: two days for local mail, three days for intra-provincial mail, and four days for national mail. This reflected CPC's studies that postal users were concerned less with speed than with reliability and dependability. "Time-sensitive" mail was reconceptualized as courier mail and charged a higher price (which surveys had suggested was an acceptable strategy). CPC committed itself to a higher level of performance, within the modest 2/3/4 delivery system. Third, it initiated an independent testing system to track its performance in this area. Up to 1986, measurement and testing systems were not audited. CPC announced in 1986 that "a new measurement system more closely representing the experience of average mail users, and run by an independent external organization, is being developed and will be introduced in 1986-87."[44] Tenders were called for an independent audit. Clarkson Gordon won the contract, which provided for quarterly service reports whose results were widely advertised. An independent audit of "good performance" was intended to project an image of reliability to the market. In 1988, for example, Clarkson Gordon reported that CPC's service was improving, with 92 per cent of local mail, 94 per cent of intercity mail, and 96 per cent of national mail being delivered on time. Similar results were released at regular intervals. In 1991-92 and 1992-93, CPC's annual reports declared a delivery success rate of 98 per cent, as determined by auditors.[45] CPC also implemented a new dress code and wardrobe in April 1992 as a "visible symbol to customers of the corporation's move to a more business-oriented company, committed to service."[46] In 1990-91, CPC joined the Better Business Bureau, which acts as an impartial mediator in resolving disputes between Canada Post and its customers. Postal service customer councils have been established in each of CPC's divisions.

Finally, CPC tried to distance itself from government and the postal unions, to establish that management rather than politicians or union leaders drove the postal operation. Many if not most of CPC's actions contributed in some way to this strategy. CPC's dealings with the postal unions will be explored in some detail later; in broad terms, it attempted to dismiss the unions' claims for special treatment or special status and negotiated hard with the postal unions in all areas, from absenteeism and productivity to wages and discipline. This tactic was designed to project the idea that CPC management was in control and could "handle" its unions. Similarly, CPC tried to distance itself from the government, both by eliminating its financial dependence thereon and by developing a corporate identity that contained no reference to its political existence. CPC adopted a new corporate identity in March 1989, centring on a new corporate logo, a stylized design of a piece of mail in motion. Nothing in the design or related material made any reference to CPC's Crown existence.

CPC's second means of increasing business was to alter its product line and explore new markets. The increasing importance of this strategy was highlighted in the 1990-91 to 1994-95 plan, where CPC shifted its capital expenditure focus from plant and equipment to its product and service line.[47]

CPC first considered that it served three markets — communications (letters and time-sensitive material), advertising (admail and publications mail), and physical distribution (parcels) — and reconceptualized its product lines within these markets. Within the communications market, it transformed the four-class structure, categorizing products according to customers' price and service needs. This allowed CPC to fragment the product structure in order to explore "market niches." The entire operation moved towards a system of individual, one-to-one contracts (particularly with large-volume users). Letter-mail was broken down into four categories — regular, express, priority, and electronic — to offer customers a matrix of speed and price options. New products were introduced along these strategic lines, such as Special Letter and Special Occasion envelopes (in 1989). These offered a service similar to that of couriers, but at a lower price ($1.95 for a standard envelope). The envelopes were prepaid, offered guaranteed service (via a money-back guarantee), and could be introduced into the delivery stream from any point, even from a collection box. CPC subsequently has offered customized contracts for the use of these new products (e.g., delivery of tickets for Air Canada).

The 1981 CPC Act perpetuated the existence of private couriers, which represented serious competition and an enormous financial loss for CPC. "Traditional" mail had diminished in importance for customers whose communications needs were time sensitive, given new technological developments. Priority Post (now Priority Courier) was thus made a policy priority. It has been the featured product and service in CPC's mass advertising campaigns, such as during the Olympics. In 1978-79, the Post Office sent 100,000 expedited units; this figure rose to 900,000 in 1981-82 and 3.3 million in 1983-84 (5 per cent of the expedited volumes in that year). In 1989-90 dedicated facilities were opened in the Montreal and Ottawa airports. Courier products have their own processing stream to increase speed and efficiency. Priority Post is now located at Pearson Airport in Toronto. A computerized track and trace system was wedded to Priority Post, allowing customers to be informed of courier items through bar coding and personal computers. This produced a new product category — trace mail — which offers five options: security registered, registered, signature, confirmation, and proof of delivery. Customers are offered a matrix of options, trading off security and price.[48] The Priority Post system expanded internationally in 1985, and in 1988-89 was linked up to the "Eagle" network to offer next-day delivery in many American cities. CPC offered courier service to 66 countries in the late 1980s and 120 by 1991. It entered into a joint venture with four other government postal authorities (Germany, Sweden, France, Netherlands) and Australia-based TNT Ltd., to start a $1 billion-a-year international courier company called GD Express Worldwide, an organization offering world-wide time-certain deliveries.[49] Within Canada, CPC has developed a thirty-four-dealer national network to service medium and small-sized businesses,[50] and claimed in 1991-92 that Priority Courier attained a 99.2 per cent on-time delivery record. This market is a highly competitive and lucrative one, somewhat over-serviced and facing a competitive shake-out of a number of companies, all of whom were seriously affected by the recession.[51] Indeed, in June 1993 CPC announced that it was buying a 75 per cent stake in Purolator Courier for $55 million. This made CPC the largest courier operator in the country, with perhaps over half the $1.4 billion market.[52]

Incentives were introduced to keep regular mail products competitive. Discounts were offered at Christmas time to large- volume mailers. In 1986-87, a five-cent discount was available for Christmas cards addressed in machine-readable form. In co-operation with the greeting card industry, in 1987-88 CPC introduced the Greetmore program; consumers received discounts for using specially designed, machine-readable envelopes. CPC entered the coupon market in 1991, offering "inflation fighter coupons" to offset the 5 per cent rate increase that was to come into effect in January 1992.[53] With respect to large-volume users, CPC designed an incentive system that rewarded customers for placing correct addresses and postal codes on their mail. The lettermail ENCODE rate offers large savings for placing special bar codes on mail to make automatic sorting easier. A high percentage of regular mail has become incentive mail, with about 25,000 large mail customers using this system. The government has decreased its support of second-class mail (to be discussed in chapter 10); CPC has developed two new commercial products in this area, Canadian publications mail and international publications mail.

CPC has attempted to deal with changes of address, a major service issue: in 1991 4.4 million Canadians moved in 1991 (20 per cent of the population) and 120,750 businesses filed change-of-address forms. A mobile population annually costs CPC about $150 million in redirects and mistakes. It introduced a new system for mail addressing and redirection in 1990–91, establishing thirteen centralized redirection centres that, using computerized change of address labels, were designed to redirect mail faster, more efficiently, and with fewer errors. CPC also tightened its "return to sender" policy, to weed out people who did not pay the $12.50 charge to have their mail forwarded.[54]

Within the advertising market, CPC has aggressively pursued the third-class or admail market, which it sees as a tremendous growth area. Direct marketing is a $7.8 billion market in Canada, yet is vastly underdeveloped compared to that in the U.S. CPC has increased its market share by offering companies advice and services, as well as magazines such as *Canadian Connexion* and *Business Access* and sophisticated demographic databanks. It offers a wide array of services at various costs, for various markets. Working closely with the Canadian Direct Marketing Association, it produced a new admail kit, including a video and a manual. Two new products were developed. Admail Plus allows a customer to send CPC a direct mail letter, a response form, and a mailing list in machine-readable form. CPC develops the format, sorts the mailing list into postal code sequence, and transmits the material electronically across the country to whichever of the eight production sites is nearest the address. There the material is printed, folded, inserted into envelopes, and deposited into the mail stream. Lettermail Plus is a similar system used for sending out invoices, statements, and financial documents. The electronic system speeds the process up by two days. This service as attracted various large-volume customers such as Zellers, with whom CPC signed a record contract to distribute between 175 million and 210 million units in 1991–92.

Within the physical distribution market, CPC tried to stop the erosion of volumes and revenues in fourth-class or parcel mail. New product lines were developed to offer a broader range of options and services to potential customers. Commercial ground parcel service (begun in 1988–89) offers five-day-a-week parcel pick-up for postal customers who send at least twenty-five parcels a week. Commercial air parcel service also offers two-day delivery service by air to most cities. An expedited parcel service was introduced in 1989–90, offering one- and two-day ground service for local and regional delivery and two-day national air service. A proof-of-delivery option was introduced, and parcel delivery has been integrated into the track-and-trace system. A computerized shipping system is being developed, to be installed at customer locations. CPC has a special experimental relationship with Sears to do its local delivery, and a CPC agent has an office at Sears.

Two characteristics of this product differentiation strategy are of crucial importance. First, it did not embrace the diversification strategy articulated by Michael Warren and the postal unions in the early 1980s. All of the products outlined above focused on picking up and delivering mail; they were variants of basic postal or letter products, differentiated in order to find a niche in markets where letters faced traditional or new competition. None of them involved an expansion of CPC's retail operation, which was being privatized (see below). Second, the strategy saw CPC products become increasingly deregulated. As the exclusive privilege extended only to first-class mail, only first-class prices were regulated; the prices of other classes of mail were set by the Post Office itself. CPC's differentiation strategy within the old third- and fourth-class categories was market driven and pursued in a nonregulatory environment. But the differentiation strategy also pushed CPC into a nonregulated mode of operation within the first-class or lettermail category. Special lettermail was introduced as a nonregulated product; CPC set its price and service conditions in response to market information. Priority Post operates in an nonregulated environment. Most incentive rates were simply declared by the corporation (although the relative size of the incentive rate was determined by the regulated first-class price). CPC and large-volume users struck one-on-one deals regarding price, standards, schedules, and guarantees, an approach favoured by NAMMU, which pressed for deregulation of the postal service in favour of "total service contracts."[55] CPC deregulated various services, including counter parcels, money orders, incentive letter mail, and electronic mail.

Canada Post's third approach to increasing business was to improve competitiveness in the communications market, in two interrelated ways. First, within its traditional array of services and products, it elevated its service capacity to levels comparable to those of the new communications technologies. Second, it adapted its products or developed new ones to compete directly with the services offered by the new communications technologies. Both of these moves required CPC to upgrade its plant, equipment, and technological capacity.

CPC's plant and equipment were deteriorating because maintenance and improvement expenditures had been sacrificed in the early 1980s attempt to balance the budget. In the period 1982-83 to 1985-86, capital expenditures were only once greater than capital depreciation; overall, depreciation was $296 million and capital expenditures $214 million.[56] The plant and equipment adopted during the 1970s drive to mechanization was now technologically obsolete. Other parts of the capital stock were badly located or no longer adequate to the tasks at hand.[57] These shortcomings had serious competitive and financial implications, and threatened CPC's effort to project the image of a serious, modern, and technologically sophisticated communications business.

CPC announced in 1986-87 that it "has determined that fundamental changes must be made to revitalize the asset base," and embarked on an ambitious capital investment plan. Its purpose was to renovate, rationalize, and upgrade postal facilities; test new technology and introduce a new generation of technological equipment; replace out-of-date letter-sorting equipment; and shift mail processing out of the city core to less expensive and more useful locations.[58] A ten-year project of $200 million a year in capital investment was announced in 1987–88. With depreciation, it was anticipated that CPC would invest $370 million a year over the five-year plan, a figure that rose to $500 million a year in the next plan. The early 1990s recession moderated expectations somewhat, and plans presented lower expenditure levels.[59] Nonetheless, between 1987 and 1991 CPC's investment projects amounted to $1.55 billion (an average of $387 million a year). Recent plans push capital expenditure plans higher and higher, with the 1993–94 to 1997–98 plan proposing $2 billion in capital investment (including $1.5 billion in capital assets).[60] This investment was directed to a number of areas: over 150 systems engineers improved the distribution system (cutting the number of handling steps in half); uniform operating standards and procedures were introduced; more timely and adequate reporting systems were developed; industrial engineering developed uniform standards and procedures to operate an integrated system; and delivery commitments were colour-coded to provide visual monitoring. The NCC was developed as a state-of-the-art monitoring system to integrate the network of plants and transportation links.

Some of the new equipment replaced the previous generation of optical character readers (OCRs) and letter-sorting machines (LSMs). The older OCRs were capable of processing 22,000 pieces per machine per hour using 60 stackers. The new generation of MLOCRs (multi-line optical character readers) process 32,500 pieces per hour — 10,000 pieces an hour faster, or a 45 per cent increase in capacity. These machines are capable of 1,152 separations, increasing dramatically the capacity to fine-tune the sorting procedure. The machines have multi-line reading capacity: they can read up to four lines of address and the postal code and cross-check to make sure the code is consistent with the address. If something is wrong, the machine bar codes the address correctly. These machines should improve "read rates," reduce errors, and speed the mail through the system. By 1992–93 implementation of MLOCRs in mechanized plants was over 80 per cent complete, and retrofitting of earlier equipment was completed in the summer of 1993.

Similar results are expected from streamlining mail processing and the twin mailbox program. Introduced in 150 communities in 1990–91, the former processes only local mail locally, with the remainder forwarded to the large sorting plants for mechanical sorting. This eliminated one more step in the sorting process. In May 1992, 125 more communities received the twin boxes, at an expected savings of 450,000 hours of work and $11 million a year (about 200 full-time jobs).[61] The boxes also increased the amount of mail that was processed mechanically. In 1991, 67 per cent of the mail was handled by the big mechanical plants, 16 per cent by smaller mechanical sites, and between 6 and 8 per cent by hand. The twin box program is designed to lower the last two figures to near zero. (Presently, 87 per cent of mail is coded).[62]

There were forty-four MLOCRs in place by 1992. The existing LSMs processed 16,500 pieces of mail per hour, whereas the new machines process 20,300 to 25,000 pieces per hour (an increase in capacity of 23 to 50 per cent). Video encoding systems (VES) will replace the current group desk suites (GDS) for the manual coding. When the MLOCR cannot read an address, the envelope is recalled from the sorting stream and its televised image appears on the coder's video screen. The operator properly codes the envelope, which is returned to the sorting process. Coders will no longer be required to be in the same physical space as the mail itself (they could even be in another country). These developments are designed to increase productivity, speed, and accuracy and cut maintenance, errors, and costs.[63]

These mechanical changes occurred within the broad strategy of integrating computer and equipment technology in mail processing. CPC has organized a $20 million project to this end, run by its vice-president of information technology and strategic development, Dr. Kenneth Tucker.[64] The PARADIGM project — so named with the idea of breaking down old paradigms — employs a fictitious a town called Paraville (located in a building in Gloucester, a suburb of Ottawa) in which CPC experiments with the application of electronic and computer technologies to the organization of the postal service. The aim is to better integrate its cost, revenue, and processing information to maximize efficiency of operation and rates of return. It integrates the three functions by information flows, to make a letter's point of entry into the system a piece of information that connects to everything else. Bar-coding allows this, as it can contain limitless amounts of information that can be read, stored, and operationalized simultaneously, from a letter's entry into the system until its delivery. Because it makes a letter technologically similar to a telephone call, the system knows at any given moment how many letters are being mailed, how long they take for delivery, when they are made, from where to whom, at what cost, and so on.

Various applications are envisioned. Letters could be introduced into the system through machines similar to automatic teller machines. Various buttons offer information on addresses, codes, and services for purchase. All is bar-coded at this point, and the information is automatically recorded centrally. This information is distributed downstream, for pick-up, transportation, and delivery schedules. Letter sorting can be better organized by front-loading destination information, to design and redesign optimal routes by an accordion-like expanding and contracting according to volume. This would save the one-and-a-half hours that letter carriers use to sort routes, and the routes themselves would be designed more efficiently. The sorting place could be eliminated; it could now be in the plant or at the letter carrier's house. The same type of strategy could maximize the sorting plants' capacity, with increased information via bar-coding not just of letters but also trays, mono-units, container trucks, and so on. On the delivery side, letter carriers read the bar-code as they deliver the mail, feeding the information back into the central system, recording, and transmitting information at each step.

All of this unfolds against the backdrop of an increasingly sophisticated information communications market, containing competitive alternatives like the telephone, fax, and e-mail. By the early 1980s, the number of long-distance telephone calls outstripped the number of first-class letters. There are presently millions of fax machines in North America, over 250,000 in Quebec and Ontario alone. By 1992, there were over 2 billion fax transmissions in Canada (compared to 4.5 billion first-class letters), and faxes were expanding by 30 per cent compound per year. By 1995, electronic transmissions, fund transfers, and faxes will number close to 10 billion in Canada — double the existing volume of first-class mail. About 50 per cent of Canadians now pay telephone, utility, and credit bills through their banks, and Ottawa is encouraging the direct deposit of social support cheques. In all of this, the technological competition confronting the Post Office is obvious and overwhelming, as table 8 suggests. From 1984 to 1987, electronic mail doubled its market share to 11.5 per cent, while lettermail fell from 53.6 per cent to 46.8 per cent.[65] In the same period, the data communications market grew by 198 per cent, e-mail by 90 per cent, and fax by 41 per cent; postal revenue grew by 36 per cent and first-class mail by 26 per cent.[66]

This evidence should be interpreted with caution. First, some of these technologies have increased rather than displaced communication. Faxes need to be confirmed, or the original copy of an order and statement must still be sent, or mail is sent in response. And, faxes seemed to have displaced as many phone calls as letters, if not more. Many people prefer to deal with mail, or are wary of technological communications. Finally, e-mail and other devices tend to be intra-organizationally used, and have not displaced external communication by mail.[67]

Second, Canada Post enjoys some competitive advantages within this technological environment. Although the new technologies are more sophisticated than postal ones, they basically act as one-to-one communication. But although it has expanded massively, only 4 per cent of communication is electronic to electronic. Indeed, despite the preponderance of business mail, 53 per cent of all mail is still delivered to the public. There is thus room on the market for "old-fashioned" modes of communications, or variants on them. The Post Office retains two comparative advantages: the one-to-many mode of communication and the seam between the old and the new technology. Hence, CPC's focus on hybrid services, combining electronic and physical communications, such as Omnimail, to be launched in 1993–94. This is the umbrella name for a number of electronic mail products. CPC softwear provides the link from computer to computer, from electronic input to hard-copy delivery, and provides delivery to electronic mailboxes or fax machines. Customers will be able to use their personal computers to prepare and send electronic mail and fax to hard-copy mail. For example, the Omni service provides a one-stop shopping choice of communicating with many businesses or individuals, whether through fax, e-mail, or hard copy. Customers often need a variety of delivery services, from first-class mail through electronic communication. It is inefficient to have to shop around for each mode. If a business wants to communicate a letter or material to a number of customers in the fastest way possible, it can lease an Omni line into the Post Office and transmit a mailing list and the hard copy. CPC is developing directories that include not only postal addresses and codes, but e-mail and fax numbers. The latter runs the mailing list through its information banks. This allows it to see which individuals and customers have fax or e-mail numbers, or neither. With respect to the two former cases, the information will then be sent directly via these modes. If neither fax nor e-mail is possible, the material can be transmitted electronically to the appropriate postal centre, where it will be printed, stuffed, addressed, and entered into the local mail stream or picked up. In this way, Canada Post can take advantage of its position on the border among all these technologies. For companies that don't want to buy fax machines or install electronic mail, or cannot afford the new technologies but want access to them, Canada Post can offer all the technological services.[68]

A good example of the meeting of old and new technologies is volume electronic mail (VEM). Organizations and businesses can send their message and large-volume mailing lists to Canada Post, which then sends the message electronically to its eight bulk mail production sites across Canada. There, the message is laser-printed, folded, stuffed, addressed, and entered into the local mail stream to reach the various addresses on the mailing list in that area. Volumes were already 22 million by 1991-92, and CPC expects this soon to increase to over 54 million units. These new computer-information-based technologies are being applied to all facets of the mail-processing operation, from optimizing the use of space in trucks and organizing trucking routes, to assisting large-volume users in managing addresses in their databanks, to organizing the postal plants themselves.

Finally, CPC's technological expertise has created a market for it to exploit. Canada Post Systems Management Limited (CPSML) was created as a subsidiary to market its expertise, technologies, and systems to other postal administrations around the world. It offers to design operational information systems, optimized organization of postal routes, and specifications for mechanical and automated equipment. CPSML has signed eighteen international contracts, including a $5 million contract with New Zealand Post. Eight marketing agreements were signed in 1992-93 to create marketing/teaming alliances with other technological companies, to extend CPC's global reach.[69]

CPC has also quietly expanded its electronic mail capacity. By 1985-86, it had expanded its Intelpost system — a domestic and international fax service, whereby faxes enter the local mail stream — to over fifty centres in

Canada and fifty countries around the world. In 1986–87, customers were given direct access to fax machines at a number of CPC outlets. By 1990, Intelpost could be accessed in 540 places in Canada to transmit messages to sixty-four countries. CPC has also constructed a telecommunications system to transmit digital information coast to coast, with a voice interface.

In sum, CPC's actions on the revenue-generating front saw it think, strategize, and act more and more like a private-sector operator. This culminated in a corporate reorganization in 1993, which saw its operations division split off from its marketing/sales operations. The result was increasing centralized control of mail processing and delivery and decentralization of customer sales and service. As will be seen in chapter 10, CPC's expansion into new areas was politically sanctioned by the government, despite some business complaints about unfair competition. Reaction was relatively mute and limited to one or two markets. CPC was "allowed" to enter new areas because it had eliminated its deficit and started to make profits. The government sanctioned its growth as a result of these financial improvements and because — broadly speaking — business was not complaining about increased CPC activity. Both the government and the market were happy that CPC was acting like a private-sector corporation.

Cutting Costs

Chapter 10 will demonstrate that CPC's revenue-increasing strategies had fairly benign social and political implications. However, cost-cutting measures generated intense political controversy and struggle. CPC proceeded on two fronts to increase productivity while keeping prices competitive. It rationalized its services and initiated ways to process and deliver the mail more cheaply, and it reduced the labour share of total costs.

Rationalizing Services

Rationalizing postal operations had two aims: it could save money to help eliminate the deficit, and it could improve postal service and CPC's image. The latter was a real concern. The Plog report had presented a market perception of a "service shortfall" that limited business.[70] CPC rationalized its postal operations in four ways: by de-emphasizing door-to-door delivery and expanding the use of group mailboxes; by rationalizing the rural postal network; by transforming much of its retail network into private outlets; and by contracting out activities to the private sector.

First, delivery costs rose relentlessly as population growth generated new families and businesses — and new addresses, new postal routes, more delivery personnel, and longer transportation networks. Total addresses climbed to over 10 million by 1985 and reached nearly 12 million by 1992–93. Door-to-door delivery, only one of various delivery modes, accounted for about half of the addresses served; despite this, the "principle" and expectation of home delivery is strong in Canada, particularly within the middle class, which comprises a considerable proportion of the 150,000 new addresses added each year. But home delivery is expensive, three times more costly than delivery via group boxes. If it gave in to expectations, CPC could anticipate substantial increases in delivery costs, in perpetuity. For this reason the United States eliminated home delivery in new neighbourhoods in 1978.

Canadian governments and the Post Office had long mooted alternatives before 1986. Delivery every second and even every third day was contemplated in the late 1970s and early 1980s.[71] There was some experimentation with group or community mailboxes in the latter stages of the Warren era. Neighbourhood postal shelters or sites contained multiple mailboxes for the various addresses, as well as slots for outgoing mail and larger compartments for parcel pick-up. The site covered a certain area of addresses within a neighbourhood, so that any address fell within two hundred yards of the community mailbox.

This approach was an integral feature of the 1986-87 corporate plan, and the government approved introduction of community mailboxes on a wide and far-reaching scale in June 1986. The approach focused on new addresses; home delivery would continue to be provided where that service already existed. In servicing new addresses, "Canada Post sought to use the method of delivery that was both convenient and cost-effective. Letter carrier service, the most costly, was extended only to fill in new addresses on existing routes, and other new growth was handled primarily with group and community mailboxes."[72] As early as 1985-86, 13.8 per cent of new addresses were serviced by community boxes, and 37.4 per cent moved from general delivery to group mailboxes. Thirty-five per cent of additional addresses were serviced via community in 1986-87, and the next year 150,000 more community mailbox addresses were added. By 1988-89, 405,000 addresses were serviced by community mailboxes, compared to 5.7 million home deliveries. Another 402,000 community addresses were planned for the end of 1992-93.

This system had obvious cost advantages. A corporate study demonstrated that the annual cost of home delivery was $120 per household, compared to $40 by community mailbox, so that transforming all 3.6 million addresses not serviced by home delivery service would cost $1.3 billion in conversion costs plus an extra $417 million annual operating costs.[73] However, there was no expectation that home delivery be universal, and it was widely accepted that home delivery be offered only in areas with more than two thousand points of call. On this basis, expanding to home delivery would cost CPC $540 million over the first five years and $160 million annually thereafter.[74] Regardless of the precise figures, "Canada Post believes that the increase in rates required to support the extension of door-to-door service would not be tolerated by its customers."[75] By 1990-91, there were 27,400 community mailbox sites servicing 712,000 addresses; the corporate plan indicated that another 6,000 sites were to be added that year, serving another 157,000 addresses. Assuming a modest $60 per address annual savings in this mode of delivery, CPC had saved at least $50 million a year in delivery costs by introducing the community mailbox system. By 1991, 7 per cent of addresses were serviced by community mailboxes. CPC planned to increase this to 12 per cent by 1996. The proportion of addresses receiving home delivery declined from 48 per cent in 1983 to 43 per cent in 1991 (with a figure of 40 per cent planned for 1996).[76]

CPC also claimed that community mailboxes improved the quality of postal service. Given changes in demographics and life-styles, community mailboxes were "more conveniently located and more generally accessible." Increasing numbers of working women made it unlikely someone would be at home when the mail was delivered. CPC presented the community box as reasonable, as a place to be visited on the way to or from work, and convenient as well. Unlike the home delivery system, it was capable of delivering parcels when no one was at home. The community box was seen as an improvement over green mailboxes and over picking mail up at the nearest post office.

Second, CPC rationalized the rural postal network to cut costs. This move had also long been contemplated, but the likely political consequences scared off most PMGs. The 1986–87 corporate plan proposed a ten-year plan to transform the network of 5,200 post offices in the rural areas to a private network. The largest 3,500 were to be transformed into private post offices, with the double benefit of reducing operating costs and improving service. The private post offices would have longer operating hours, operate seven days a week, offer a fuller range of services, and be more conveniently located. This tactic would not involve postal "closures" in a technical sense, but a "conversion" or relocated to a private office, typically in a commercial operation. The remaining 1,700 or so rural post offices would be amalgamated, closed, or see their customers serviced by community boxes.[77] At the same time, about 100,000 customers receiving lot line service would be transferred to community mailboxes, as would another 400,000 who were being serviced by green group boxes. Even before the 1986–87 plan was approved in the first six months of 1986, CPC closed 72 rural post offices and eliminated 50 rural routes. It estimated that these rural changes, in conjunction with the urban changes outlined below, would save it $1 billion over the decade.[78] CPC has initiated new arrangements in the North as well, entering into partnerships with bands and municipal councils for postal facilities run by Natives. In the Yukon, a bank and CPC have arrive at an arrangement whereby an employee works half the day for the bank and the other half for CPC in shared facilities.[79]

The rationalization of the rural network did not take place as quickly as planned. As of May 1992, 1,245 federally operated post offices had been closed. About 1,000 were replaced by retail postal outlets in the private sector, but another 250 communities have been left with only outdoor boxes. The demise of another 353 was imminent: 208 continued to operate in areas where a retail post office had been opened, thereby ensuring that their days were numbered, and another 145 federal post offices were under review. Thus, by 1992 about 30 per cent of the rural network had been changed or was in the process of being changed.[80]

CPC's third means of cutting costs was to privatize the urban retail network. It drew the strategic conclusion in 1986 that it should get out of the retail business and concentrate on the pick-up and delivery of mail. This view killed the strategy of diversification, devised by Michael Warren to avoid cost cutting in the service and labour areas. The unions favoured this approach, as initiatives like New Directions postal outlets and Consumers Post promised to maintain or even expand counter jobs. Increased revenues and a postal surplus were to result from the sale of postal and postal-related products — from e-mail services and new postal products to stationery, greeting cards, licences, lottery tickets, and transportation tickets to bill-paying and other services.

The Conservatives and Lander were unconvinced of the merits of this strategy, which they characterized in a negative way. Future prime minister Brian Mulroney referred to "ventures into ill-conceived schemes to generate greater revenue."[81] Harvie Andre asserted that the diversification actions of the early 1980s "failed, and failed miserably."[82] The Plog report noted that two-thirds of the market wanted CPC to stick to traditional postal activities.[83] The Breedon research study of CUPW's diversification schemes concluded that "the 'bottom line' is that expansion of counter services is not in the best interests of the corporation, is not in step with what the market indicates is the prime mission of the corporation, and would only serve to aggravate an already bad image problem."[84] Lander presented an alternative retail vision:

> The postal product line alone is not sufficient to sustain a retail outlet. Some people have suggested that the Post Office should add non-postal products to our line, most of which are already stocked by other merchants. It makes more business sense to add our product line to that of an existing store than for us to get into other areas of the retailing business. Our main experience is in collecting, processing and delivering the mail.[85]

CPC concluded that it should put retail operators out of business, that the financial obligations required to pursue a diversification strategy were beyond its capabilities, and that the retail side of its business could be better done by others.[86]

It thus chose to privatize its retail operations, by "significantly expand[ing] on the current involvement of the private sector in the provision of counter services, including the adopting of franchising and other arrangements."[87] The 1986 corporate plan proposed to close the 734 existing urban offices over a ten-year period.[88] Existing post offices would be closed or transformed into private-sector retail outlets and new postal outlets would be offered as franchises, to create 971 full-service franchises and 9,250 stamp counters.[89] The transformation began in April 1987, when Canada Post sold its first franchise to Shelly Manly, owner of a Shoppers' Drug Mart in Fairview Mall, Toronto. Fifty more franchised outlets were planned in the next year, but this plan was caught up in, and delayed by, legal problems (to be examined in the next chapter). CPC developed tactics to avoid the legal problem of successor rights, by opening second outlets beside existing ones. These would compete for a year, and then the CPC outlet could be closed.[90] The transformation of the retail network did not take place as quickly as anticipated, although 300-350 conversions were taking place annually by the early 1990s. At the same time, the number of points of sale for CPC products increased each year, to 18,200 in 1991–92 (75 per cent of which were private outlets).

CPC chose this approach for a number of reasons. There were considerable savings in defraying overhead costs. CPC's wage structure was high, as counter jobs were held by experienced inside workers, who were high on the union scale. Clerks in the private sector would be paid minimum wage, cutting the cost of a counter operation to 30 per cent of CPC's costs. In conjunction with the rationalization of the rural network, privatization would, CPC hoped, save $1.3 billion over a ten-year period, in both labour and capital costs.

Moreover, CPC's retail outlets were not money-makers. The locations were often not chosen on the basis of market need or business patterns, and demographic and urban changes had since exacerbated this weakness. Many outlets were in the old downtown locations, where parking was difficult to find, time of operations was inconvenient, or urban density had shifted.[91] The costs of running many of these old outlets were greater than the revenue they generated. Franchising and privatizing was to increase access to service in a cost-effective way. The net impact of the strategy was to increase the number of outlets for postal business. Hundreds of new postal outlets opened each year, with nearly 19,000 retail outlets by 1992–93. These included 2,200 franchised outlets, making CPC the largest franchise organization in Canada.[92]

Lastly, CPC believed that assigning the retailing of postal products to the private sector would increase postal business. A study showed that 75 per cent of total post offices operated by CPC generated only 66 per cent of postal revenue; the private sector's 25 per cent of outlets generated 34 per cent of revenue. This suggested that postal products would be better marketed if retailed by private business. And sales would increase once the quality of postal service improved, which this move anticipated. As Lander put it, "Who knows better than local businesses about providing good retail service to the local community?"[93]

A fourth cost-cutting strategy was contracting out. The cleaning of Canada Post facilities has been contracted out since April 1986 to private firms who hire women and immigrant workers at minimum wage; previously, employees of the Department of Public Works were paid eight to twelve dollars an hour. The Nielson Task Force report estimated annual savings of $3 million a year in contracting out the two hundred department cleaning jobs.[94] Maintenance of the new generation of OCRs, LSMs, and group desk suites has also been contracted out, as has data processing, some payroll functions, computer and vehicle maintenance, admail delivery, and most of the parcel business. The pre-sort incentives given to major mail users are a variant of contracting out: customers are given discounts to code their mail and deliver it to CPC in order, which saves CPC an enormous amount of time, effort, and labour and allows it to cut its costs substantially. CPC has financed the construction of its new $90 million corporate headquarters in a similar way (in itself, consolidating its seven Ottawa offices in one site will save CPC $5 million annually). Rather than call for tenders, it invited developers to make offers. Perez Corporation won the competition and a ninety-nine-year lease on the land. Perez will construct and own the building, for which it will receive $13 million in rent for the first five years.

Cutting Labour Costs

As part of the drive to eliminate its deficit and make a profit, CPC had to reduce its labour costs, which comprised 74.4 per cent of its expenditures in 1985–86. Indeed, CPC plans to lower this figure to 50 per cent.[95] Various revenue-raising and service-rationalizing policies cut labour costs. Privatizing the retail network and contracting out eliminated jobs and put downward pressure on wages, as expensive unionized jobs were replaced by minimum-wage non-union jobs in the private sector. In addition, the next generation of sorting equipment increased productivity and minimized labour inputs.

There was a revenue-generating dimension to the labour strategy. The Plog report had presented the market perception that labour enjoyed a "privileged" position within CPC, and that this was bad for business. The public saw overpaid postal workers dominating management, weakening the corporation and making it ineffective. "The Canadian public places a substantial portion of the blame for the relatively poor quality of postal services directly in the hands of the postal unions," the report declared; "The perception of union rather than management control of Canada Post Corporation negatively impacts on revenue, image and support for expanding the CPC mandate."[96] The implication was that if CPC aggressively disciplined labour and brought its labour costs under control, business would increase. CPC took various initiatives to this end. Labour representation on the board of directors was abruptly terminated in 1986. Warren's open door, consultative, and "understanding" approach was replaced by a hard-nosed business approach to the unions, in which labour was to be just another input cost. CPC cut wages and increased workloads, to project a stronger business image. Management disciplined and fired what it considered to be lazy or inefficient workers and initiated policies to reduce absenteeism. This aggressive approach to discipline and productivity led to a spectacular increase in grievances, of which, by the early 1990s, there were over 130,000 outstanding.[97]

CPC's initiative to merge the postal unions was also designed to improve its corporate image. It asked the Canadian Labour Relations Board (CLRB) in May 1985 to review its existing twenty-eight bargaining units, the number of which made contract negotiations confusing and expensive. Eleventh-hour contract settlements and periodic strikes created the impression of labour-management chaos and perpetual work stoppages. This was obviously bad for business, as customers were unlikely to give business to a company about to go on strike. It was also very bad for CPC's business image. The CLRB responded positively, ordering a revamping of the bargaining structure in an attempt to make life more reasonable for Canada Post, to reduce the likelihood of industrial unrest, and to increase CPC's operational efficiency.[98]. It ordered consolidation into four units: a supervisory unit of low-level managers (then mainly in the Association of Postal Officials of Canada); the rural postal staff; a white-collar unit of clerical workers and administrators (then mainly in PSAC); and an operational unit, comprising letter carriers, inside workers, blue-collar workers, electricians, and so on. LCUC and CUPW would have to merge and, given their different histories, traditions, and interests, this could not be realized smoothly. An unsuccessful voluntary merger was followed by a winner-take-all election, which process seriously weakened the effectiveness of the postal unions in the late 1980s and early 1990s. CUPW emerged as the union for operational workers, which was not what CPC had anticipated (it might have preferred the more moderate LCUC as the dominant union). Regardless, as Lander put it, "There will now be only one round of negotiations...regardless of the outcome...the Canadian public and our business partners will not be subject to the same media attention that accompanies three separate protracted sets of negotiations."[99]

A central feature of the 1986 corporate plan was the elimination of 8,700 jobs in the following five years. The plan projected a 14 per cent downsizing in employment by 1991, from 61,886 to 53,116. Moreover, an increasing proportion of the workforce was to consist of part-time and casual workers.

The part-time issue was particularly contentious. CPC, to be successful, had to reach the service standards anticipated by the market, at a competitive price. It thus had to process the mail as quickly as possible at the lowest possible cost. This had inevitable and controversial implications: night work and part-time labour.

Over 80 per cent of CPC's volumes comprise business mail, which is typically sent out at the end of the work day to be delivered during the following day. The vast percentage of processing would thus have to done be at night, and the bulk of processing jobs would continue to be night jobs, for otherwise sorting would wait until the following day, adding a day to the delivery standard. The quantitative measure of success in this regard is the "in process" figure — the amount of mail in the plants at 7 a.m. In the early 1980s, this figure was in the 30-35 million unit range — a day's worth of mail remained to be processed from the previous day. The number fell to 12-14 million units by the end of the decade and to 7 million units in 1991. In the early 1990s, typically 28-29 million units were mailed each day. A substantial part of the sorting work would have to be done by part-time or casual labour, giving CPC enough flexibility to meet surges in volumes without committing itself to the cost of full-time employment. The objective was to fine-tune the workforce to adjust to surges and declines in volumes, right down to the plant and the shift level, and so avoid excess overtime or perpetual overstaffing. This fine-tuning would increase productivity by cutting down the cost per piece of mail processed. Labour usage had to be better planned, absenteeism cut, and part-time and casual labour used on a stand-by basis.[100]

There were already 2,000 fewer postal sorters in 1987 than in the early 1980s: between 1984 and 1987, 1,085 full-time sorting jobs were eliminated, while part-time workers increased by over 500. Full-time jobs fell from 40,626 in 1984 to 37,052 in 1989, a 9 per cent drop, and part-time jobs increased from 4,883 to 6,001, to 16 per cent of the labour complement. Overall, there were 2,943 fewer full-time jobs at the end of the decade than when the POD was Crowned. In the process, salaries and benefits fell from 74.4 per cent of expenditures in 1985-86 to 68 per cent in 1990-91; the 1989-90 plan called for a drop to 58.8 per cent by 1993-94. Accelerated attrition and job buy-outs were announced in 1990-91, to cut full-time employment by a further 3,555 jobs (part-time work would increase by over 300). In 1991-92, hours paid declined by 5 per cent and total employment declined by 3 per cent.

Overall, postal volumes increased by 40 per cent over the 1980s while total labour usage declined by 45 per cent (see Tables 1, 4). In this regard, 1990-91 was typical, with an increase of 90,000 points of call but a decline in letter-carrier years of 300. Postal volumes increased by 19.2 per cent but employment fell by 1947 person years, or 5.4 per cent. By the early 1990s, the workforce had shrunk to mid-1970s levels, but postal volumes had doubled. Table 4 indicates that processing productivity increased by 24 per cent between 1988-89 and 1992-93, to 334 pieces of mail per hour (this is anticipated to rise to 430 pieces by 1997-98). Delivery productivity increased by 13 per cent to 54 points of delivery per hour. In this period, full-time employment declined by over 10,000 (18.4 per cent) from 54,731 employees to 44,683. Part-time employment increased from 14 per cent to 19 per cent of the work force. Finally, CPC employees have been encouraged to take early retirement. CPC spent $342 million in employee termination benefits in 1990–91, and the 1992–93 plan forecast a further $1.9 billion in expenditures to this end.

Contract negotiations also aimed at cutting labour costs and downsizing the labour force. The 1987 and 1990–91 negotiations are examined in chapter 10; discussion here will focus on CPC's efforts to use negotiations to further the 1986–87 and 1989–90 plans. First, as the 1986 plan phrased it, CPC sought to "negotiate changes in contracts with unions to attain required operational flexibility." That is, CPC wanted to weaken or end job-security provisions, particularly with regard to technological change and conditions of work, to ease the introduction of new machinery and equipment and part-time and casual labour. Second, CPC looked "to continue to move corporate wages and benefits toward comparability with the private sector."[101] Lander set the tone for contract negotiations in these two areas:

> If consumers want their postal services to be as effective as other service industries, the Corporation must have the same freedom to adopt practices...generally accepted in the private sector. Canada Post employees and their unions should also be prepared to accept the norms of the private sector in terms of productivity and service if the corporation is to continue as a viable business and a secure source of employment in the years ahead.[102]

This view was repeated in the 1986–87 report: "The Marchment Report confirmed the Corporation's own analysis that Canada Post's wage and benefit levels are higher than those of comparable businesses, and that our labour contracts contain a number of restrictions that inhibit the effective management of the Corporation."[103] CPC looked to the "negotiation of labour contracts with the operational flexibilities required to manage the business in a cost-effective manner and in a competitive market place; the negotiation of the flexibility to downsize the operation through layoff or selective buyout...[and for] remuneration to be brought in line with the private sector over the plan period." Moreover, "increased emphasis will be placed on relating remuneration to individual performance against predetermined, fair and readily measurable standards." CPC expected this course to save it $4.5 billion over the next decade.[104]

CPC looked for numerous employment concessions in the 1987 negotiations with LCUC. First, it aimed to end the system of job security and to remove lay-off prohibitions from all of its collective agreements. It maintained that it needed flexibility to deal with "surplus" labour, particularly if it was allowed to introduce new work rules (see below). And it wanted authority to initiate lay-offs where relocation or retraining was impossible. Second, CPC sought the freedom to use non-union contractors to deliver mail, particularly third-class mail or admail. Third, it looked to significant changes in work practices, including extended routes and increased work-loads. These changes required a reduction in the work "values" assigned to functions other than actual delivery, such as meal and wash-up periods. CPC wanted carriers to stay on their routes over lunch rather than return to their postal installations. It proposed lifting the ban on letter carriers' using pri-vate vehicles for travel to and from work with mail (this would require all new carriers to own a vehicle). Fourth, it wanted to remove the restrictions on the number of part-time and casual workers it could use, particularly in replacing workers who were absent or on vacation. Community mailboxes also featured in these negotiations, for, in conjunction with the limits placed on home delivery, this policy would have obvious employment implications. LCUC in turn negotiated to extend door-to-door delivery to all communities having more than two thousand points of call.[105]

These negotiations were unsuccessful, resulting in nineteen days of rotat-ing strikes in the summer of 1987. CPC did gain greater management flexi-bility in some areas, but was broadly unsuccessful in obtaining concessions in job security or work conditions. Among other gains, however, it won the right to use casual workers to replace those whose scheduled absence was greater than five days (previously, twenty days).[106]

The employment issue loomed especially large in the 1987 CUPW nego-tiations. Franchising and privatizing the retail network had enormous em-ployment and job security implications for inside workers, as did the intro-duction of the new generation of machinery and equipment. CPC sought the right to lay off surplus employees, use more casual and part-time workers, weaken the technological change clauses, and increase the use of work meas-urement. CUPW reacted more assertively than LCUC, having already con-fronted decreasing employment brought on by subcontracting, precoding by the large mail users, and increased use of part-time and casual workers. It wanted job-security provisions maintained; employment levels increased via a variety of tactics, including a prohibition on contracting out and a variety of job-creation initiatives; and use of part-time and casual workers limited, to increase the number of full-time jobs. CPC responded that it was not in the job-creation business and looked to rationalize its labour force, through lay-offs or by buying out certain jobs where attrition, retirement, and trans-fers were not enough to increase efficiency. It also negotiated for greater flexibility in using part-time and casual labour at any time and for longer periods.[107]

The negotiations were unsuccessful and, after seventeen days of various forms of strike action, CUPW was legislated back to work on 19 October 1987. A mediated settlement was imposed on both sides the following July.

CUPW's no-layoff guarantee was preserved, as were the technological change clauses. This was balanced by granting CPC more operational flexibility. The settlement imposed no formal obstacles on privatizing the retail chain and affirmed CPC's right to contract out work. It also assigned CPC more flexibility to use casual and part-time workers, although the latter was to be capped at 4,200.[108]

Employment was again central to the 1990–91 negotiations, the first to take place since the LCUC/CUPW merger and the setting of profit targets in the 1989 corporate plan. The latter anticipated a decline in the labour share of costs from 71.6 per cent to 58.8 per cent by 1993. Even as business increased by 50 per cent, the existing level of labour expenditures would be frozen. The postal labour force had to be downsized, through franchising, contracting out, labour-saving technologies, and part-time strategies. Job security and employment were at the heart of the negotiations and subsequent strike. CUPW president Parrot characterized the process as "a fight against cheap labour...against eliminating jobs in the community...part-time work and casual work is not good for our economy....We've got people that want jobs, decent jobs."[109] CUPW looked for job security and initiatives and diversification to create jobs. CPC negotiated for flexibility and the right to contract out, to introduce the new sorting equipment, and to privatize the retail chain.

Five major issues were at play. First, CPC wanted to alter the technological change clauses to facilitate introduction of new sorting equipment (to allow it to displace surplus workers or to lay them off when no replacement positions were available). CUPW wanted no change and limits on the displacement of workers. Second, CPC wanted to subcontract without constraint, to initiate technological and operational changes. CUPW aimed to ban subcontracting, franchising, and postal closures and to start a job-creation program. Third, CPC wanted greater flexibility in using part-time employees to meet volume fluctuation. It agreed to eliminate casual workers but wanted a new category of "flexible part-time employees," who would be guaranteed eight hundred hours of work a year. This required raising the cap on part-time workers. CUPW wanted to limit the ratio of part-time to full-time employees and regroup part-time positions to create full-time jobs.[110] A fourth issue was the delivery of admail. In 1987, CPC and LCUC agreed to make additional admail delivery voluntary, through a vote in each local. In 59 per cent of locals the decision was not to deliver the additional admail, particularly non-standard pieces. This number rose to 90 per cent in May 1991. Admail delivery was contracted out at rates far below union rates, even on weekends. CUPW now wanted admail delivery back, as it was a growing market likely to provide jobs over the long run. CPC was loath to lose competitiveness and wanted to keep labour costs low, especially on weekends. Fifth, CUPW wanted to reverse the 1987 agreement on the voluntary use of vehicles on delivery routes. (About one thousand carriers had taken up the option.) CPC wanted to expand this strategy, as it promised to reduce the number of carriers by cutting route times and the number of routes required.[111]

Negotiations were again unsuccessful, despite mediation efforts by Chief Justice Alan Gold of the Quebec Superior Court. The government introduced legislation to pre-empt a postal strike, which ended after two hours on 28 October 1991. The dispute was assigned to André Bérgeron for arbitration on 19 December 1991. CUPW and CPC each feared a lengthy arbitration (CUPW feared imposed rollbacks and CPC erosion of business). They returned to negotiation in June and July, successfully. CUPW retained job security for its members through the life of the five-year contract, until January 1995. There would be a "one-shot" opportunity to fill vacant positions, and changes to the way admail was handled, including no more "opting out."[112] These measures suggested the extent to which CPC desired corporate stability, in order to project a business image to the market.

Although remuneration was important in CPC's cost-cutting plans, it was not as central to these negotiations as employment. It was often dealt with indirectly. Franchising was a remuneration issue as much as an employment one, for salaries in the franchised operations would be lower. Depending on circumstances and location, those working in the private operation might be the same as in the old post office. Part-time, casual labour and contracted labour also placed downward pressure on wages.

CPC bargained directly in negotiations to reduce its labour bill. It proposed a two-tiered wage system in the 1987 LCUC negotiations: new carriers would receive wages 25 per cent less than existing rates. Overall, it looked to freeze wages in the first year and offered 2.5 per cent in the second year. The settlement saw carriers receive 5.5 per cent over thirty-one months: 3 per cent on 1 August and 3 per cent a year later. Instead of receiving a wage increase retroactive to the termination of the previous contract, workers were paid a lump sum of $500. The increase was assigned only to workers at the top of the scale; newer workers' wages were essentially frozen.[113]

Monetary issues did not play a central role in the 1987 CUPW negotiations,[114] but were more important in 1990–91, particularly for CUPW. It claimed that workers had received no real wage increases for the previous decade. Specific proposals came only late in the negotiations. CPC offered a five-year package: a lump sum payment of $3,000 for the first two years (back pay); 9 per cent effective August 1991; and 2.25 per cent in each of 1992 and 1993. CUPW looked for a three-year contract retroactive to August 1989, with 7.9 per cent, 7 per cent, and 6.5 per cent increases. Later, CPC offered a 12.5 per cent four-year deal, with a lump sum payment of $3,600, 5.4 per cent retroactive to August 1989, 4.25 per cent retroactive to August 1990, and then 6 per cent and 3.2 per cent.[115] After the government imposed an arbitration process, CPC and CUPW negotiated a 3.34 per cent average annualized increase in a five-year settlement that extended to January 1995.[116]

The length and substance of the settlement again indicated the degree to which Canada Post desired stability as a goal in itself: only in this way could it project a businesslike image to the market.

Over and above cutting jobs and wages, CPC attempted to lower its labour bill through disciplinary strategies such as cutting absenteeism. This issue had as much symbolic resonance as financial significance, and engendered the longest and most heated discussions at parliamentary committee hearings and in business submissions, consultants' and expert reports, and parliamentary and corporate statements. CPC's rate of absenteeism in 1985 was 17 days, apparently higher than the industrial average (CPC's level had actually been higher earlier in the decade, at 19.1 days in 1983-84). CPC wanted to reduce this number to 13 days; a well-publicized effort would improve its corporate image. Unfortunately, not a terrible amount of care was taken to understand why the level of absenteeism was high. Objective observers implicated postal shift work, a high proportion of which was on nights. This has been proven to have disruptive physical and mental consequences, as does repetitive and monotonous work in large plants.

The National Attendance Strategy (devised in 1983) was intensified after 1985 in the form of the Attendance Management Program. Absenteeism was reduced to 15.5 days in 1986-87, its lowest level in a decade, and fell to 13.1 lost days per full-time employee. CPC aims to reduce total days lost to 9 days.[117] Improved attendance was sometimes induced through programs that offered TVs and microwaves for perfect attendance records over the summer. However, CPC's strategies tended to be aggressive. The Cossette arbitration report (1988) commended CPC's efforts to promote regular attendance, but Cossette concluded that "the least I can say about the national strategy for improving attendance is that in too many cases, application of the strategy has given rise to clear errors in judgement and real injustices that are tantamount to abuse."[118] A Liberal party inquiry (1989) investigated a number of well-publicized cases, including the suicide of a thirty-five-year old London letter carrier, Peter Lemay. He had allegedly been harassed for absenteeism due to illness and, after unsuccessful attempts to regain his job after an accident, he took his life.[119] The Standing Committee on Consumer and Corporate Affairs commended CPC's efforts, but acknowledged union complaints about harassment and asked CPC to administer its program "in a reasonable, fair and consistent manner and with respect for the dignity of its employees."[120] The Lapointe report (1991) noted that matters had gotten worse since 1988. The Attendance Management Program had "thrown oil on the fire" and "[given] rise to all types of abuse," resulting in a torrent of grievances.[121]

These aggressive disciplinary actions were not isolated. CPC's strategy was to take advantage of opportunities to discipline workers, to demonstrate that management — not labour unions — was in charge. It fired workers at three times the rate in the federal public service and most private-sector workplaces.

During 1981–84 it fired five workers a month; during 1991 it fired fifty-nine workers a month. Only 39 per cent of its firings were justified (compared to 63 per cent of Air Canada's firings). The early 1990s saw increasing harassment and intimidation, from scrutiny of all sick leave to disciplinary hearings for trivial matters. CPC also chose to challenge all cases CUPW brought before the Workmen's Compensation Board.[122]

Results and Conclusion

From 1986 to 1993, CPC raised its revenues, increased its productivity, and cut its costs to balance its budget and make a profit. In this section I review its mixed successes.

Table 1 indicates that volumes grew by 35 per cent from 7.7 billion in 1985–86 to 10.4 billion in 1992–93 (around 5 per cent on average per year). These figures were affected by negotiations and industrial unrest: volumes declined in 1987–88 (by 1.6 per cent) and weakened in 1991–92 (only 3.1 per cent growth). Thus CPC's labour strategy had a negative effect, with the 1991 strike affecting postal business substantially. Business was also affected by the recession of the early 1990s. Disaggregating total volumes demonstrates that CPC's greatest attainment was expanding in the direct mail and admail markets. Third-class volumes rose to over 5 billion units in this period. Addressed admail increased by 96 per cent and unaddressed admail by 89 per cent, to comprise 50 per cent of CPC's volumes in 1992–93. CPC held its position in the highly competitive parcel market, with volumes remaining over 100 million units in the early 1990s.[123] Publications mail (to be examined in the next chapter) remained relatively stable, but declined by 5.3 per cent in 1992–93, reflecting declining subsidies.

The prospects for lettermail were not bright. Lettermail did not disappear, despite competing communications technologies. Relative to its position in the late 1970s and early 1980s, lettermail had improved, and looked stable. Between 1974–75 and 1984–85, first-class volumes expanded by only 12 per cent; in 1985–86 alone they expanded 6 per cent. Nonetheless, overall growth was modest, less than 6 per cent between 1985–86 and 1991–92 (9 per cent to 1990–91). First-class volumes were susceptible to contract uncertainty; volume growth was negligible in 1987 and declined by 3.2 per cent in 1990–91. The recession of the early 1990s also affected volumes. The reality is that first-class volumes have decreasing importance within CPC's business profile. First-class mail's share of volumes was 63 per cent in the 1970s, 56 per cent in the 1980s, and fell to 45 per cent in 1991–92 (in the new vernacular, the communications market fell to 43 per cent of volume in 1992–93 from 54 per cent in 1988–89). Priority Courier was a bright spot, more than holding its own in the competitive time-sensitive market. Volumes grew by 36 per cent in 1988–89, 33 per cent in 1989–90, and 18 per cent in 1990–91.

Flux in volume did not translate into flux in *revenue* owing to the postal price structure. First-class mail prices did not increase as fast as the Consumer Price Index in this period. A first-class stamp was thirty-four cents in 1985 and forty-two cents in 1992, an increase of 23.5 per cent. The price structure outside of the exclusive privilege was more flexible. Changes were varied and often higher, but competitive pressures loomed large. Table 2 shows that postal revenues grew 42 per cent from $2.76 billion in 1985-86 to $3.9 billion in 1992-93 (volumes increased by 35 per cent). Postal revenue as a proportion of GNP fell by 3.4 per cent, from 0.58 per cent in 1985-86 to 0.56 per cent in 1991-92.

First-class mail comprised a substantial part of revenues, despite its diminished proportion of postal volumes, generating 52 per cent of CPC's revenues in 1990-91 compared to 60 per cent in 1984-85 (again, in the new vernacular, the communications market comprised 58 per cent in 1988-89 and 54 per cent in 1992-93). First-class mail revenue grew by 22 per cent to 1991-92 (26 per cent to 1990-91), even though it did not grow in volume. Revenue from parcels more than doubled, from $154 million in 1985-86 to $425 million in 1991-92 — at which time it comprised over 11 per cent of CPC's revenues. Despite admail's impressive volumes, its revenue growth was moderate, the result of its lower price structure. In 1985-86, it generated $268 million of business, about 10 per cent of CPC's revenues. This increased by about 92 per cent to $514 million in 1991-92, about 14 per cent of CPC's revenues compared to 48 per cent of its volumes (in the new vernacular, the advertising market grew in revenue by 15 per cent compared to 58 per cent in volume between 1988-89 and 1992-93; its revenue represented 20 per cent of total postal revenue, compared to 55 per cent of volumes).

As regards expenditures, CPC has cut its relative and absolute labour costs substantially. As a proportion of total costs, CPC's labour costs are far below those of the United States or the United Kingdom. Table 4 indicates that this fell from over 75 per cent in the early 1980s to 68 per cent by 1990-91. CPC plans to lower this figure to the 50-55 per cent range, reflecting a number of factors.

First, full-time employment has dropped substantially, and CPC gained the flexibility to use more part-time labour. Between 1988-89 and 1992-93 alone, more than ten thousand full-time positions were cut as overall employment declined 15 per cent. The percentage of part-time employees grew from 16.5 per cent in 1984-85 to 24 per cent in 1992-93. The employee complement in the 1990s was at a level similar to that of the mid-1970s, while postal volumes had increased by over 80 per cent.

These employment figures point to a second factor, initiatives to increase sorting and delivery productivity. The 1992 settlement indicated CPC's understanding that cutting wages and jobs eventually causes industrial disruption, which can harm its corporate image. It has thus increasingly switched

FIGURE 1

Five-Year Projections From 1993-94 Plan

(millions of dollars)

	93/4	94/5	95/6	96/7	97/8
Revenue	4070	4190	4383	4578	4766
Costs	4027	4027	4141	4306	4476
Net Income	35	45	65	90	115
Return on Equity	3%	3%	5%	6%	7%

emphasis to productivity increases. For example, absenteeism was cut substantially to an annual average of around thirteen days (down from over twenty days), nine of which were paid (around the national average). Infrastructural costs were cut dramatically when retail activities were shifted to the market. Over 1,000 rural post offices have been closed, and 300–350 post offices a year have been privatized. Cleaning, maintenance, delivery, and sorting functions have been contracted out to be performed by cheaper labour; and 33 per cent of mail is now presorted, which has improved accuracy as well. Over 700,000 addresses were serviced by community mailboxes by 1991-92 (7 per cent of the total number of addresses; this is to rise to 13 per cent by 1996). Expensive home delivery has fallen from 48 per cent of the total number of addresses served to 43 per cent in 1990-91, and will fall to 40 per cent by 1996. Finally, CPC improved its sorting capacity, with labour-saving consequences. It has introduced the new generation of sorting equipment and has made capital investments of $1.7 billion between 1986-87 and 1990-91. Capital investments will comprise nearly $1.5 billion over the next five years.

Productivity has increased as a result. Table 4 indicates that mail processed per hour paid increased by 47 per cent from 227 pieces in 1984-85 to 334 pieces by 1991-92. Points of call made per hour paid increased by 2 per cent from 43.9 to 53.7. Savings were substantial, as was service improvement. CPC plans to increase productivity by around 5 per cent a year to 430 pieces of mail processed per hour by 1997-98.

CPC's financial situation has improved as a result of creating business, cutting costs, and increasing productivity. Table 3 indicates that its $395 million deficit in 1984-85 fell to $210 million in 1985-86, $129 million in 1986-87, and $30 million in 1987-88. CPC made a $96 million profit in 1988-89, a 6 per cent return on equity. Its best year was 1989-90, when it realized a 10.9 per cent return on equity of $149 million profit (it paid a $60 million dividend to the government). Profits fell to $14 million in

1990-91 (a 1 per cent return on equity).[124] CPC made profits totalling $259 million over these three years. The deepening recession and the 1991 industrial dispute saw a return to deficits. Revenues weakened sharply, to $227 million less than what had been planned for the year. CPC lost $128 million in 1991-92 (3.4 per cent of revenues, 11 per cent negative return on equity). The picture improved in 1992-93, with a $26 million profit. CPC's profit expectations have been lowered considerably. In its 1992-93 plan, it anticipated $800 million in profits over the next five years. The next year, this was lowered even further, to $350 million. Both reflect diminishing expectations of growth, down from the earlier plan's anticipated $5.1 billion by 1996-97 to the later plan's $4.77 billion by 1997-98.

Chapter 10 discusses how CPC's financial picture became controversial in itself. Finances had been presented in overly optimistic terms. Indeed, CPC's profits were seen to be illusory, a result of a number of factors: deferred termination expenditures, no interest charged on capital, amortization of extraordinary restructuring costs; funds CPC had on deposit in the government's Consolidated Revenue Fund, interest income, and income from the sale of properties.[125] CPC admitted that real estate proceeds were likely to decline.[126] Its profit figures were as important for their symbolic value as for their financial accuracy. But the latter should not be trivialized, inasmuch as the elimination of the deficit has also ended CPC's financial dependence on the government, which — struggling to bring its own finances into balance — is asked neither to absorb the Post Office deficit nor to finance CPC's capital improvements.

At the same time, attainment of modest profits has allowed CPC to project an improved image of itself to the business community, as efficient, competitive, and well managed. Business concern over service has been greatly assuaged; independent reporting by Ernst and Young suggests that CPC met its 2/3/4 delivery standards 98 per cent of the time in 1991-92, up from 85 per cent in the mid-1980s.[127] CPC's making a profit was greeted positively by most segments of the business community, particularly major users (the claims of the exceptions — especially competitors — will be examined in chapter 10). When CPC's $149 million in profits was announced, *Reader's Digest* (whose president headed NAMMU) had 149 pink flamingos placed outside CPC headquarters as a tribute. The business press responded enthusiastically to CPC's activities. For example, *Canadian Business*'s flattering November 1990 article ("Toast to the Post") asserted that "after decades as an object of ridicule and vilification, the post office has actually turned itself around and is behaving like a real company."[128] An unflattering (and poorly informed) article in *The Globe and Mail* was challenged by John Gustafson of the CDMA, who rushed to CPC's defence, claiming that "the increasing productivity and efficiencies by Canada Post Corporation have been evident for some time."[129] When *The Globe and Mail* inaugurated *The Change Page* ("Managing in the New World Economy"), its first article featured CPC:

"The Post Office and the Power of Information" portrayed the corporation as a high-tech communications corporation, adapting new technologies to increase its competitiveness and capacity to serve its customers.[130]

Business's happiness with CPC's performance had three effects. First, the perception of CPC as a successful and competent operation probably increased postal business. Second, not being subsidized by the government strengthened CPC's bid to be allowed to enter new markets to generate postal business. Third, CPC's making a profit and keeping business happy pleased the government, which was then more willing to extend CPC's autonomy and provide more support to CPC's efforts to become a commercial business operation.

CPC had by 1993 transformed itself considerably, from a Crown corporation motivated by public goals into a private operation motivated by commercial goals. The 1986 plan established the primacy of corporate and commercial values, which were instituted by a recruited private-sector management team. Cost-recovery pricing replaced cross-subsidization. Retail activities were franchised or privatized. Various activities and functions devolved to the private sector. The centrality of home delivery was reduced. Labour-management relations were placed on an equal footing with the purchase of goods. CPC rolled back labour's monetary gains and improvements in conditions of work to comparability with those in the private sector. It focused its commercial attention on large-volume users, entering into one-on-one contractual obligations. It socialized with businesses and entered into joint sponsorship and marketing arrangements. CPC aimed to make a private-sector level of profits, to compete with other private companies in equity markets. Profit targets required competitiveness, which altered the way CPC organized itself, set objectives and priorities, and made decisions. Numerous products were deregulated, and CPC injected itself further into the logic of competitive markets. It even bought out one of its competitors, Purolator Couriers.

In sum, CPC acted very much like a private-sector corporation from 1986 to 1993, despite the fact that it was still owned by the Canadian people and remained answerable to its shareholder, the government. As this chapter suggests, CPC was given a considerable amount of space in which to function like a private, commercial operation. To the extent that CPC balanced its budget, generated profits, and made the private sector happy, the government increased its support and granted CPC more autonomy. The government played a substantial role both in encouraging CPC in a commercial direction and in lessening its public obligations. It also protected CPC from the inevitable reactions to its market reorientation, as we shall see in the next chapter.

Chapter Ten

THE POLITICS OF PRIVATIZATION

Once the 1986 business plan was in place, the Mulroney government assumed a hands-off stance concerning postal matters, ostensibly to allow CPC to pursue a commercial course without political interference. Although there is an element of truth in this, the political reality was more complex. The Mulroney government's postal role after 1986 was by no means passive: it played the critical role in determining the recent evolution of Canada's postal system.

First, the government set CPC's course in 1986 and appointed the management team to pursue this course. Even if the government had subsequently done nothing, it would have played a significant postal role, now adopting a hands-off position towards a policy that it created and that was implemented by its appointees. Second, the government retained considerable postal authority after 1986, approving postal price and regulatory proposals, scrutinizing annual reports and updates of CPC's five-year business plan, and appointing the board and senior management. The government approved CPC's actions and performance three or four times a year. Third, the government remained the major target of public reaction to postal matters. The implementation of the business plan provoked widespread and intense reaction. The government acted as shock absorber, buffering CPC from public, union, market, and political reaction and insulating it from public scrutiny and complaint. When necessary, it used its political authority to impose postal policy. This support provided CPC with the stability to stay the course in implementing the plan. Fourth, the government allowed the ideal of a postal public purpose to be smothered by commercial concerns, from CPC's national and rural functions to its role in distributing information. The government allowed CPC to attach lesser importance to two of the three goals set for the postal Crown: maintenance and expansion of customary postal services and improved labour-management relations. Fifth, that the government gave CPC increased autonomy to compete in the market did not imply government abdication of postal authority, for the government left Canada Post alone only because it was pleased with its eliminating the postal deficit and because business action had been positive. Had CPC's actions been less to the government's liking, the latter would likely have intervened to assert its interests. The corporation's autonomy remained an "autonomy on parole."[1]

The government actively supported the commercial strategy analyzed in chapter 9. This chapter completes the analysis, explaining how the government supported the privatization of the postal service while assisting CPC in implementing the plan. The chapter has four sections. First, it analyzes the supportive political environment that allowed an ostensible "depoliticization" of the Post Office. This section considers government appointments, the role of Treasury Board and the board of directors, the declining role of Parliament and public scrutiny of the Post Office, and the asymmetrical impact of postal interest groups. Second, the chapter explains how the government role delegitimized traditional public service functions, such as the rural system and provision of subsidized service for "social" mail like newspapers and periodicals. Third, it examines government assistance in CPC's critical struggles with the postal unions. A concluding section presents the 1989 Postal Services Review Committee incident as a metaphor for the political support given to Canada Post in this period.

The New Political Environment

When postal matters were raised in the House of Commons, Harvie Andre replied, typically, as follows:

> When Canada Post was made a Crown Corporation by the actions of the previous [i.e., Liberal] government, it was for the purpose of restricting and eliminating possible political interference with the management of the Post Office. We have been adhering to that principle, which we thought was quite properly elucidated by the Liberal government of the day.[2]

Andre often asserted that the government respected CPC's autonomy and would not inject political calculations into postal policy. This position was contrasted with that of earlier political regimes, when political interference caused inefficiency, postal deficits, and decline in postal service and competitiveness. Andre declared that the politics had been taken out of the Post Office, and would remain at a distance because "given [CPC's] tremendous track record...I am not about to go second guessing the management and saying they should do this and that."[3] Members of Parliament in turn complained about the dissipation of their influence in postal matters. During a lethargic, predictable, and insubstantial postal debate in May 1991, an exasperated Tory MP, Greg Thompson, claimed that "Members of Parliament have just about zero clout when it comes to Canada Post, as everyone here will nod their head, just about zero, a big fat zero."[4]

"Non-interference" and the diminished role of MPs reflected conscious political decisions. CPC enjoyed increasing autonomy precisely because its actions fulfilled government expectations of what it should be doing. Andre's view that "the corporation is on the right course" was not the result of guesswork on CPC's part: the government had given it a very specific idea of what the right course was. Nor was the declining postal influence of MPs other than a political decision. The Post Office had not been depoliticized; rather, its politics were removed from Parliament and relocated elsewhere.

Indeed, Andre was disingenuous in citing the principle of political non-interference in refusing to comment on or accept responsibility for CPC actions and postal controversies, for these were generated by the commercialization of the postal function, which the government determined via three political decisions. First, the 1986 plan was politically driven, written in a top-down way and presented *by* the government *to* the corporation (see chapter 8). Corporate suggestions — like the elimination of CPC's retail network — were accepted and approved by the government. Second, the government accelerated the drive to commercialization in its 1986 budget, presenting CPC with a two-year deadline to balance its budget (three years faster than the Marchment Committee schedule). Third, the government intensified this commercial orientation in 1989, reconceptualizing a balanced budget as a 14–15 per cent return on equity, a goal to be reached within five years.

These directives determined CPC's commercial purpose and course of action. Their consequences were substantial — and were the government's responsibility. Once this orientation was set, the government reconstructed the political context to allow CPC to get on with its job. This recast environment had a number of ingredients: a slender government postal bureaucracy, a stable and supportive ministerial environment, a symbiotic relationship between the minister and the CPC president, a supportive and passive board of directors, a predictable and sympathetic Treasury Board review, a "soft" regulatory environment, diminished parliamentary and public scrutiny, and a privileged role for major mail users. In combination, these elements created policy and political predictability, ensured the persistence of commercial goals, and limited outside interference in the pursuit of these goals. A postal policy community developed, comprising the minister, the CPC president, Treasury Board, and the major mail users. The closed environment insulated CPC from those outside of this community, such as Parliament, the public, and groups that saw themselves less effectively served by the new orientation.

Direct governmental presence in the Post Office ended in 1981, when the POD became a Crown corporation and the postal bureaucracy became Canada Post. The position of minister responsible for Canada Post was established to create a link with the government. A rather insubstantial office, it has no interests, ambitions, or resources to "control" CPC or compete with it for attention or results. After the Conservatives' election in 1984, the office comprised only two people, and this declined to one after 1988.[5] The government's postal bureaucracy is in CPC; the minister's office considers the senior CPC people to be its staff. It calls on Treasury Board for technical expertise and assistance and on other departments when necessary, such as Labour at times of industrial disputes and Communications and

Native Affairs regarding postal subsidies.[6] The government thus oversees CPC in an insubstantial and fragmented way. There was no core governmental or political bureaucracy on postal matters, outside of Gary Billyard in the minister's office and David Salie at Treasury Board. The government pulled together extensive postal expertise and personnel only once, in the construction of the 1986 plan. Once this plan was set, the "political" arm of the Post Office shrank again. This reflected Andre's objective of letting CPC use its expertise to get on with the task.[7]

The government's relationship with CPC is primarily via the minister, which fact has been of advantage to CPC. Harvie Andre's stint as minister responsible for Canada Post between 1987 and 1993 was the longest continuous term as PMG or postal minister in the post-war period, which gave CPC a stable and predictable political environment without policy U-turns even in the face of intense criticism. Andre was extremely loyal, retaining CPC responsibilities even as his ministerial duties changed. A senior cabinet minister with strong ties to Prime Minister Mulroney, he enjoyed political autonomy over postal matters and represented and defended CPC's interests in cabinet, to effect.

His postal influence extended to critical areas, especially postal appointments. (The minister appoints the president of the corporation.) In 1985 Michel Côté appointed Donald Lander; Lander subsequently developed a close relationship with Andre, who admired Lander's toughness, drive, and sense of purpose. They saw eye to eye on CPC's direction, sharing a postal vision that privileged commercial goals over public ones. The government demonstrated its support for Lander on a number of occasions. In June 1990, Andre reappointed Lander, then sixty-four years old, to a second term as CPC president.[8] In 1992 Lander was named to the Order of Canada, and he later became chairman of the board and chief executive officer. He was replaced as president by one of CPC's group vice presidents, Georges Clermont.[9]

Andre used his appointment powers to shape the relationship among the board of directors, the CPC president, and the government. As we saw in chapter 8, the Marchment Committee recommended that the board be given more authority to act like a private-sector board; it suggested that the board hire and fire the CPC president.[10] This was one of the few Marchment recommendations the government did not pursue; it decided instead to further decrease the board's already insubstantial role to allow the corporation to bypass it. The minister was reinstated as the political head of the corporation, with the president functioning as in-field deputy. The political content of the board was diminished in two ways; labour representation was eliminated in 1986, and Andre's appointments were almost exclusively from the business community, ensuring the board's commercial orientation.[11] But, Andre did not recruit directors from the fields of communications, advertising, and transportation to connect CPC to the wider business community or confront CPC with new ideas and values. Rather, recruits have been from business, law, land development, natural resources, banking and insurance, and so on; and none of them were high fliers who might want to run the corporation. The board, constructed from middle-ranking business people with no connection to the postal world and no postal ambitions, gave Lander room to manoeuvre without having to look over his shoulder. The government made CPC a management-run company.[12]

This moulding of CPC's contours has been especially evident in the appointment of the chair of the board. The second chair, Sylvain Cloutier, was unhealthy during his tenure and died in February 1991 before the end of his term. His successor, Roger Beaulieu, was appointed three months later, the 1990-91 planning process thus occurring without a board chair. Beaulieu's appointment was sanctioned by Andre but was not actually made by him. In accord with the Canadian tradition of balancing French Canadian with English Canadian appointments, a French Canadian had to follow Don Lander. Beaulieu was recruited by Benôit Bouchard acting as minister in charge of Quebec appointments (Beaulieu was a Conservative party member and friendly with senior party people in Quebec, including Prime Minister Mulroney). Beaulieu never met or talked with Harvie Andre before he was appointed,[13] which indicates the extent to which the board had lost any policy function in representing the government or the public in the corporation. Nonetheless, Beaulieu's appointment fit the emerging purpose of the board determined by the government. Beaulieu was from the business world, predisposed to CPC's commercial orientation and extremely comfortable with its focus on profit maximization. He had been a member of the Quebec government's committee on privatization and thought the evolution of CPC into a private company was simply a matter of time.[14] Second, Beaulieu took the position on a part-time basis for a modest fee (maximum $35,000); Cloutier's had been a full-time position.[15] None of Beaulieu's business experience connected him to CPC's operational worlds. As an outsider and part-timer, he understood that his role was not to give CPC a new direction; if the government had wanted more assertive board involvement in the corporation's affairs, it would not have chosen him. To Beaulieu, his appointment was confirmation that the government was happy with the performance of CPC and its management. Thus, he declared that "Lander won't have to worry too much about me looking over his shoulder."[16]

The board's role, in short, became purely symbolic and legitimizing. CPC's key authoritative relationship is directly with the minister. This strategy was taken to a logical conclusion in late 1992 when Donald Lander was chosen chair of the board and chief operating officer after Beaulieu's death.

A similar process has evolved in the two key formal procedural relationships between CPC and the government: the annual approval of the corporate five-year plan, and approval of price and regulatory changes.

The FAA was amended in 1984 to oblige Canada Post to submit an updated five-year business plan and capital budget to the government for approval. This amendment had two purposes: to increase Crown corporations' accountability to the government and to give them a glimpse of what the government expected of them. The procedure of drawing up CPC's corporate plan was reviewed in an earlier chapter, as was the relationship between the corporation and the Crown Corporation Directorate (CCD) of Treasury Board and the Department of Finance. Briefly, Treasury Board approves CPC's capital and operating budget, and the governor-in-council, on the recommendation of Treasury Board, approves the corporate plan. There is two-way communication. CPC submits preliminary plans to the CCD analyst, who prepares briefing notes for circulation up through the chain of command. Most working knowledge of postal matters rests at the analyst's level, but the flow of information works up to the minister, whose policy reactions are fed into the process. When CPC proposes a policy change, the minister is briefed and his or her reaction given. CPC's planning process begins in the summer and fall; a framework is approved in principle by the board in October. The plan comes to board meetings in December or January, and approval is given in January or February. The plan is submitted for ministerial approval sixty days before the fiscal year begins, that is, by 1 February. Informal discussions are held before this; a draft is typically reviewed in December.[17]

The planning process, despite its formal, legal status, operates in a relatively informal manner. On most operational and technical issues, CPC encounters very little interference from the government. As its autonomy increases, CPC increasingly finds the process to be a nuisance: it agrees, grudgingly, that the corporate plan should be approved by the shareholder, but feels that everyone on the bureaucratic and government side agrees with what it has been doing.[18] The checks and balances process has become predictable and non-threatening. Treasury Board brings limited resources and personnel to the process; there are eleven or twelve analysts for the forty or so Crown corporations subject to this process. Each analyst is responsible for one or more of the major commercial Crowns. Analysts are rotated every two to three years to subject the Crowns to new questions and fresh ideas. CPC has been an exception to this pattern: the CCD analyst responsible for CPC has remained in this position since February 1985, which longevity reflects both personal preference and government contentment. David Salie was present at the creation, when the 1986 corporate plan was drawn up. And he supports the broad orientation of that plan and the elevation of commercial goals to policy predominance. As a result, Treasury Board and the CCD have maintained a consistent, supportive approach to the analysis and evaluation of CPC's plans. Salie has built up an impressive degree of postal knowledge and contacts, and CPC feels comfortable with him. He remains independent of the corporation and often critical of certain of its activities, but inevitably, there has developed a symbiosis of attitudes. Salie considers CPC to be a "winner" and very much identifies with its accomplishments and ambitions.

The government's decision to retain Salie in this position had two critical implications. It provided CPC with a stable environment for the pursuit of its commercial goals; and it signalled to CPC to stay on the same track. If the government wanted a fundamental rethinking of CPC, it would have moved a new analyst into Salie's position. Instead, the planning process has evolved into an informal and benign affair. The checks and balances are relatively insubstantial, ensuring that the ministerial-presidential relationship remains the predominant or critical operational one.

The Canada Post Corporation Act assigned to the minister the authority to approve price and regulatory changes. The long-standing intention to introduce third-party postal regulation of the postal Crown was not pursued, for reasons reviewed in the previous chapter.[19] Instead, a gazetting system was introduced: CPC's price and regulation proposals were published in the *Canada Gazette*, and the public had sixty days to convey its reaction to the minister, who would recommend to the governor-in-council that the proposal be accepted or rejected. The governor-in-council then had sixty days to accept or reject the minister's advice. Enormous public response was commonplace; for example, the 1981 price increase proposals generated 5,460 letters, 2,269 business and charitable briefs, and 50,000 signatures on petitions.

Third-party postal regulation returned to the policy agenda after the 1984 election. The Conservatives felt that pricing decisions remained subject to political pressure and were insufficiently informed by market considerations. The Marchment Committee recommended that CPC's rate and regulation proposals be overseen by an independent regulatory body not subject to cabinet overrule.[20] The government did not pursue this recommendation; the issue remained on the policy table and was studied in a variety of contexts.[21] Andre was sympathetic to the claim that the regulation of Canada Post remained too political:

> We moved to a Crown corporation to get away from political interference, as in the 1970s. But as a Crown corporation and a monopoly delivering a public service, there is no opportunity for people to express their concerns about the Post Office...except through the political process...The public still feel that they should be able to ask their member of parliament to redress their concerns...[he or she] approached the minister responsible, and you are back in the old situation.[22]

He was concerned that the gazetting process gave the misleading impression that politics — even the floor of the House of Commons — was the site where postal prices were set. This would, of course, project a bad business image of politics interfering with pricing decisions. Andre established a government study team to examine third-party regulation of CPC,[23] which reported that the gazetting system provided insufficient opportunities for public participation and that the political setting for price and service approval complicated life for postal managers. It noted that, despite the varying approaches used by other countries, "the presence of...independent review mechanisms, as forums for public participation and a channel for public complaints...appear to reduce the need for political involvement and generate pressure on the postal companies to improve performance" (p. 9). It presented two models for the government to consider: an *advisory* board and a *regulatory* agency. The former could be a low-cost, limited-resource organization with only consultation authority, or it could carry out detailed investigations. It would make recommendations rather than decisions. A regulatory agency would make decisions that, subject to judicial and other appeal provisions, would be final. It would hold hearings at which extensive and detailed evidence would be required to substantiate or critique proposed postal changes (pp. 14–18).[24]

After public consultations, the government decided in June 1988 to create an advisory body, the Postal Services Review Board (PSRB). It enacted an interim Postal Services Review Committee (PSRC) to influence the coming planning year. Headed by Alan Marchment, the PSRC would review CPC rate and service proposals. After these proposals were published, public hearings would be held. Public responses to CPC proposals would be to the PSRC, no longer to the minister. The PSRC would make recommendations to CPC, outlining its reasons for supporting or rejecting CPC's proposals. The PSRC recommendations and CPC's reply would be forwarded to the minister, who would bring the matter to the governor-in-council for final approval.

An analysis of how this regulatory mechanism worked will be undertaken below. At this point, one can make a number of observations about the character of the regulatory environment that this approach created. The government was embarrassed by the fact that, as Andre put it, "Canada Post is unique among the major providers of major public services that enjoy a monopoly in this country, as it is not subject to any kind of outside review."[25] However, the review mechanism chosen by Andre was an advisory and not a regulatory one, generating only advice and recommendations rather than binding decisions. The government retained ultimate authority over price and service decisions.

The government adopted this approach for a variety of reasons. Its costs would be far cheaper (apparently $3 million vs. $15 million for a formal regulatory approach). The approach would be easier to put into place and be less formal, easing public accessibility.[26] The government was not interested in coercing a monopoly into acting more like a competitive firm, the traditional reason for establishing a regulatory regime. Andre and the government were happy with CPC's performance and saw no reason to alter its course. Nor was the PSRC created to force CPC to operate differently. The government aimed for a regulatory process sensitive to CPC's economic needs and realities, one that would not damage productivity, efficiency, and competitiveness. Finally, the government was wary about delegating authority. It did not want to create an independent postal authority over which it exerted no influence.

This regulatory experiment did not work as planned; the government eliminated the PSRC in the February 1990 budget. But the PSRC contributed to the political environment that the government created in this period. The gazetting system's "political" approach to rate setting created a bad market impression and perpetuated public postal expectations. The government distanced itself and the political process from postal decisions, but in a way that ensured the persuit of its interests. Public participation was increased, in arenas other than from parliamentary and political processes. The informal review process perpetuated the government's ultimate authority over key postal decisions. This again suggested that the government was happy with CPC's performance, but also that it wanted to retain the power to ensure that CPC stuck to its commercial path. Like the Treasury Board planning process and the board of directors, the regulatory process did not contain countervailing authority to control CPC's behaviour.

The PSRC exercise was symbolic, but demonstrated how Parliament's postal role had declined. MPs traditionally exerted postal influence by raising issues in the House of Commons, generating pressure in parliamentary committees, and using their access to the PMG or minister to defend their constituents' postal interests. It was not unusual in the 1950s, 1960s, 1970s, and even the early 1980s to see Opposition leaders participating in lively postal debates, which were held regularly, with wide media coverage. Influence of Parliament and MPs began to wane in the late 1970s, when the Liberal government bypassed the House of Commons by initiating a postal price increase through an order-in-council. The site of postal debates shifted from the House of Commons to committee rooms; but MPs still had the role of articulating the public interest in postal matters.

When the POD became a Crown corporation, the role of MPs declined still further. Parliament and MPs were assigned no particular postal role. For example, the planning process was between CPC and Treasury Board, and the corporate plan remained secret for competitive reasons (only a summary is released). Policy directives were issued directly to CPC or via the minister to the president. Price and service matters were approved outside of the parliamentary process, either directly between the minister's office and CPC or in the new, "distanced" regulatory review. The only postal role assigned to Parliament was to receive the corporation's annual report and to review it in committee. Even this role has been trivialized: the 1991-92 annual report was not tabled directly by the minister in the House of Commons, but rather was handed by Andre to the clerk of the Commons, during Boris Yeltsin's address to the joint session of Parliament.

Parliamentary committee hearings on postal matters have declined in effectiveness. Parliamentarians last made an impact in 1986-87, at the time of the release of the new corporate plan. The proposed price increase and cuts in rural service led to a backbench Conservative revolt. Caucus was divided on postal matters. Many felt that postal losses should be eliminated not through price increases, but through cuts and increased efficiency. Others felt that the Post Office should maintain and extend services. Rural MPs panicked over the loss of post offices in their constituencies.[27] Backbenchers complained incessantly in caucus, unwilling to take political responsibility for the plan in their ridings. Annoyed by how postal matters were dominating caucus discussions and distracting attention from other matters, Prime Minister Mulroney delayed the proposed price increase and directed the Standing Committee on Government Operations to review the corporate plan. This was the backbench MPs' quid pro quo for ending another potential revolt and political embarrassment.[28] There was no legal reason to send the plan to the committee (the plan was a Treasury Board matter), but the move pushed the issue out of caucus and diverted reaction to the plan away from the government and towards the parliamentary committee. That committee (the Holtmann Committee) generated some all-party recommendations critical of the corporate plan.[29] This process let MPs have a kick at the plan and let off some steam; the recommendations led them to feel that they had influenced postal matters. But the recommendations had no binding force; they were accepted in principle but by and large ignored in practice.[30]

So ended the House of Commons' influence over the Post Office. The Holtmann Committee hearings were gruelling, far-reaching, and thorough; President Lander was grilled fiercely for four days. The hearings and recommendations were widely publicized. The government accepted the recommendations and made the appropriate promises in late 1986 and early 1987.[31] The hearings continued well into 1987, and later reports issued further recommendations. Recent committee hearings have been non-events, ignored or at most tolerated by CPC and the government. In 1989, the Liberal party held its own postal hearings in response to alleged CPC "scandals." Despite early publicity, the hearings fizzled out and were ignored.[32] The Standing Committee on Consumer and Corporate Affairs and Government Operations (the Turner Committee) held extensive, well-publicized hearings in 1989-90 in response to the introduction of the 1989-90 plan. It issued a thorough report with dozens and dozens of constructive and, at times, controversial recommendations.[33] The government simply took the report under advisement. This infuriated Garth Turner, who felt that the government should have given his report fuller consideration and some policy responses. The government's response signalled to Canada Post that it could ignore the report — which it did.[34] Parliamentary committee review of CPC reports has become unimportant and ineffective. For example, the 1991 hearings were tame and inconsequential, and Lander had a remarkably easy time.[35] Ironically, even as the process moderates, CPC resents having to appear at the committee hearings. As will be seen below, CPC no longer considers MPs or politicians to require special attention, but rather to be just another group of opinion leaders.

For MPs, the situation has developed in similar fashion. Up to the mid-1980s, the way to influence postal policy was through the minister or in the House of Commons. Since that time, the government has convinced MPs that such efforts are futile and should be channelled elsewhere. There was considerable caucus pressure on Harvie Andre in the mid-1980s to change CPC's policies. Andre toughed it out and absorbed these pressures and criticisms, to allow CPC to stay its commercial course. Andre's office took initiatives to explain postal policy and to convince MPs of the merits of CPC's actions. In his first two years as minister responsible for Canada Post, Andre's office sent out fifty-three memos to MPs, about one each fortnight. His office received two or three calls from MPs on postal matters a *day* and countless letters each week. Andre replied to them all. As will be seen presently, CPC has subsequently built up a political relations branch, and the minister's office simply sends calls and letters over to CPC. That office now receives barely one or two calls and a handful of letters from MPs each month from MPs. Caucus influence has in turn declined substantially since 1987.[36] The former high-profile postal observer MP Felix Holtmann received only one or two letters a year on postal matters. Not only do MPs no longer direct their attention to the minister's office, the public also has stopped raising issues there. Since 1987, the number of representations made in response to the gazetting of rate proposals has never exceeded seventy-five. Twenty-four representations were made in response to the June 1991 proposal, and nine in 1992.[37] Opposition MPs such as the Liberals' Robert Nault claimed that this reflected the fact that Canadians now consider it futile to raise these issues with the government or CPC.[38]

CPC created its own departments to deal directly with MPs and the public. A Government Relations Branch proactively communicates with MPs in order to "manage" postal information. MPs are well informed of CPC's policies so that they can explain them to their constituents. Government Relations briefs parliamentary committee members on the annual report and postal critics and MPs when a price rise proposal is imminent. It sends four to six memos a year to all MPs, explaining major postal events. All enquiries to the minister's office are directed to Government Relations. But there are fewer of them owing to Government Relations' proactive strategy and MPs' sense that they have no postal influence.[39] A Community Relations Branch performs the same function with interest groups and the public.

Within Parliament itself, postal matters have declined in salience. They crop up in the House of Commons at times of crisis like strikes, albeit to limited effect. Parliament's response to postal developments has become irregular, lethargic, and predictable. This was foreshadowed earlier, for example, in 1984–85, when there were only fourteen postal citations, all inconsequential, in Hansard at a time of tremendous postal strain. In late 1991 – when CPC had a high profile – postal matters were raised on only a dozen occasions (most dealing with individual post office closings). MPs have been ineffectual and increasingly silent in the House of Commons since the backbench reaction to the 1986 plan. Postal questions have become infrequent, with MPs realizing that the government will always protect CPC from their enquiries. Even price increases, which generated intense debates a decade earlier, pass almost unnoticed in the 1990s. The 1988 election saw postal issues like rural closings and community mailboxes have some impact, but the salience of postal issues subsequently plummeted. There was periodic debate on rural closings, second-class mail, and cuts in northern subsidies, and some heated debate over the 1989 profit targets. But passion burned out quickly.[40] Political interventions tended towards grandstanding or cheap shots to embarrass CPC – enquiries about Lander's salary, questioning of the Skybox rental, insistence that the Canadian flag be displayed in post offices.[41] This pettiness reflected MPs' powerlessness and decreased their legitimacy in CPC's eyes. MPs insisted that the postal function revert to one of public service, not an exclusively commercial one, but the latter policy was set by the minister and the government and was not open to discussion in the House of Commons. MPs have no special role in the commercial world of CPC. The position of Opposition postal critic has been passed on to junior and less experienced MPs, as more senior people – such as the Liberals' Don Boudria – concluded that there was little to be gained in the effort.

The government has thus diminished Parliament's role in assessing and influencing postal policy. It redirected criticisms from the political process to CPC itself. In this sense, the Post Office has been depoliticized, as there is little political access for citizens and MPs. Moreover, MPs have no special status in dealing with CPC, which prefers to deal with issues on its terms, as customer-related or business matters, rather than via political discourse. Politicians are treated no differently from others – as representatives of consumer interests and opinion leaders.[42] This is a second way in which the government depoliticized postal matters: by allowing CPC to transform public service matters into commercial terms.

For postal users, the decline of parliamentary postal influence had far from benign implications. Indeed, the result was a policy that benefited certain groups and disadvantaged others. Groups attuned to the new commercial orientation have easy access to CPC, uncluttered by government obstacles. The government's hands-off approach to postal policy has favoured the large postal users, which do not need political access, as they already have direct access to CPC. But those groups critical of CPC's commercial operation have a difficult time, with no political access or means of intervening in the postal world. In short, the decline of Parliament's postal role disadvantaged smaller users and community groups.

Particular or local postal pressure groups critical of CPC have seen their effectiveness wane since 1986. CPC has been relatively unsympathetic to their claims as it went about implementing the 1986 plan and rationalizing the postal system. As parliamentary influence weakened, groups like Rural Dignity of Canada (RDC), a rural pressure group, found themselves policy outsiders, alienated from both CPC and the government. These organizations are run on a volunteer basis and often headed by women.[43] They lacked institutional continuity and sufficient resources to affect policy. They have had to resort to extra-parliamentary and court actions, because the parliamentary process is no longer effective. RDC was unable to influence policy despite the efforts of sympathetic MPs. Because some of its funding comes from the Canadian Postmasters and Assistants Association, the government categorized RDC as a front for the postal unions, self-interested and hence illegitimate.[44] Despite the intensity and weight of rural reaction in communities across the country, the government maintained its policy of non-interference, which allowed CPC to wait for the issue to run out of steam,[45] which it did, fading from the political spotlight. Rural postal closings, reaction to which was reviewed daily at the National Control Centre in the mid-1980s, is no longer automatically on the agenda.[46] Groups like RAM (Residents Against Mailboxes) and Citizens United for Equitable Postal Service tapped into suburban discontent about supermailboxes,[47] but they too were unable to penetrate the policy process, having as their avenue of appeal only Parliament and sympathetic MPs. The issue had some play in the 1988 election but was swamped by the debate over free trade. Protected by the government, CPC simply waited out the issue, which faded away — as did RAM and other groups.

The postal unions have also been ineffective in influencing the broad contours of postal policy. CUPW is a policy outsider, with no relationship with CPC (outside of formal processes) and no political access. It has no ongoing relationship with the minister's office, nor with Treasury Board, nor with the various "social" branches of CPC, nor with senior CPC management.[49] Its policy dealings are limited to working with postal critics and the Opposition caucuses and in committee processes. These avenues are ineffective; labour rightly concludes that it exerts no influence over postal policy making. Some labour leaders maintain that this lack of policy input was an inevitable consequence of Crowning the Post Office.[50]

The policy process became particularly asymmetrical at the national level. There are strong national business associations, such as the National Association of Major Mail Users (NAMMU), but there is no equivalent national association that speaks for the public interest in postal matters, or on behalf of citizens and ordinary users. Parliament might have played this role, but the government chose to neuter it. CUPW has periodically joined forces with Action Canada on postal matters, spearheading a coalition of groups that includes seniors' associations, farm groups, women's organizations, anti-poverty groups, and handicapped groups. But the government considers CUPW to be an illegitimate policy player, and so its association with Action Canada has been the kiss of death for that group. This has made the postal policy process distinctly one-sided.

Groups like the large-volume postal users, by contrast, do not need to use Parliament to influence postal policy. CPC takes pains to improve services to these groups to retain their substantial business (of the over 80 per cent of postal volumes that is business mail, about 60 per cent emanates from the large users). There has also been a natural identity of vision between CPC and the large users: CPC's efforts to cut costs, rationalize its operations, and increase efficiency mimic the behaviour of these businesses — and directly serve their interests directly (in efficiency and lower costs).[50] CPC has responded to business needs, offering various incentives for volume use and discounts for pre-sorting mail. The spin-off policies from mechanization benefit the large-volume users to a far greater extent than others. And CPC has created close relationships with its large customers, like those among private firms in the business world (see previous chapter).

Perhaps more important, large-volume users have access to CPC that other groups have not. CPC institutionalized relations with its major customers in a variety of ways. A Business and Community Affairs branch meets regularly with twenty-five to thirty groups, among them the Better Business Bureau, Chamber of Commerce, Consumers' Association of Canada, Retail Council of Canada, and the Canadian Manufacturers' Association. It also meets periodically with one hundred or so other groups. This postal community functions in an intimate relationship with CPC, outside of government circles. All groups have a postal "front person," who works directly with CPC agents. Business and Community Affairs anticipates and solves groups' problems, relaying their concerns and views to the appropriate individual or office within the corporation.[51]

CPC has developed particularly close relationships with certain groups. CPC helped the Gift Packages and Greeting Cards Association of Canada boost Christmas card mailings through its Greetmore program, offering card users discounts for using machine-readable addresses.[52] It worked with business groups on the size of envelopes and use of postal codes. A joint technical committee — including CPC, NAMMU, CDMA, and the Canadian Business Forms Association — worked to standardize the address format. CPC dropped plans to reduce the standard envelope size for first-class mail after the publishing and printing industry claimed that the reduction would have cost it $300 million.[53] And CPC works with the Canadian Direct Marketing Association of which it is a member; the two recently forged a partnership to expand the $8 billion direct mail industry in Canada.[54] CPC's Environmental Affairs group formed a working committee including representatives of the Retail Council of Canada, the Canadian Pulp and Paper Industry, and the Canadian Printing Associations to develop a strategic response to the environmental concerns raised by expansion of the direct marketing industry.[55]

The most impressive relationship is between NAMMU and CPC. The National Association of Major Mail Users was formed in 1983 by fifty major mail users who posted a minimum of one million first-class units a year. By the late 1980s, it comprised one hundred businesses and institutions who annually generated over $600 million of postal business. NAMMU issues regular submissions and reports to the government and CPC, laying out members' concerns and suggestions for improving postal policy. NAMMU members consider themselves to be the mainstay of the postal system, and expect to be treated accordingly. They also expect to be afforded an authoritative voice in postal policy making. Their expectations are met on both counts. Special consultative committees at the national and local levels discuss technical issues such as address accuracy, code accessing the mechanized system, and delivery. Proposals such as rate increases are rehearsed with NAMMU before being gazetted. NAMMU strongly supported CPC's 1986 corporate plan and its 1989 update; in lauding CPC's accomplishments loudly and publicly, it helped build the case for increased CPC autonomy. It encouraged the government to reschedule CPC under the FAA to make it a commercial Crown free of political interference, which the government did in 1989. At the same time, it supported the retention of CPC's exclusive privilege, without which "CPC could not provide an efficient, nationwide service. Fragmented suppliers would not be able to perform effectively for some categories of mail."[56] NAMMU and CPC enjoy a symbiotic relationship. NAMMU members rely heavily on CPC in the conduct of their business, because CPC has the only national distribution network capable of handling hard-copy exchange economically and reliably.[57] NAMMU had put forth a variety of suggestions that have not been pursued,[58] but CPC has changed its policy to reflect NAMMU's concerns. For example, it disaggregated the rate structure to allow big users to negotiate their contracts, prices, services, and standards with CPC in an unregulated setting.[59]

Not all business groups have automatic influence over postal policy or have been part of NAMMU's business consensus. The Canadian Federation of Independent Business has squabbled ceaselessly with CPC over various matters. Periodicals and newspapers associations endured frustrations about the transformation of second-class mail. Groups like the Canadian Community Newspapers Association have accused CPC of stealing admail through manipulation of mail regulations.[60]

The most dramatic example of a business group that exists outside the policy community is the Coalition of Canada Post Competitors. The coalition, formed in June 1991, includes private courier companies and newspaper associations. It accused CPC of predatory pricing (i.e., prices set below cost) through cross-subsidization via its first-class monopoly, claiming that this gave CPC an unfair competitive advantage in a number of markets, including the courier business and the distribution of flyers and catalogues. The coalition also accused CPC of using questionable financial and accounting methods to inflate its profit figures[61] to give the erroneous impression that it had become a competent firm, no longer subsidized by the government, with the right to enter new markets. The coalition demanded formal third-party regulation of CPC, full disclosure of information, limiting of CPC to door-to-door delivery, and reopening of closed community post offices.[62]

The government received the coalition's reports and statements, declared that its analysis was wrong, and concluded that the market should sort out the issue. The government also supported CPC's purchase of Purolator despite intense criticism from courier companies.[63] The coalition's efforts are in some quarters viewed as a strategy to favour large private communications corporations and to disadvantage CPC. For example, some believe, the coalition exploited rural and suburban resentment about service cuts, for reopening rural post offices and extending home delivery would increase CPC's costs and decrease its competitiveness — to the obvious advantage of coalition members. Increased regulation, a narrower focus of activities, and higher prices would again hamper CPC, which fact these private firms could then exploit.[64]

In sum, the government created a postal environment that has allowed CPC to pursue its commercial goals. The essence of postal policy is manifested in the relationship between the minister and the CPC president. Other political angles — such as Treasury Board review of the corporate plan, the board of directors' representation of shareholders' interests, Parliament's representation of the national interest — are all insubstantial to various degrees, and have little impact on postal policy. The government has a direct pipeline into the setting of postal policy, and CPC's agenda has remained uncluttered and uncomplicated by the political process. This political environment has insulated CPC from postal critics and eased large mail users' access to CPC. Postal policy has been shaped within the postal community, consisting in a triangular relationship among the minister, senior management of the corporation, and major postal users. All others have been outsiders. This political environment allowed CPC to pursue its objectives in an unencumbered, predictable, and stable way.

Delegitimizing the Public Service Function

The Post Office remains a critical component of the communications and transportation infrastructure of the Canadian economy, but at the same time has provided a variety of public services that had both commercial and non-commercial dimensions to them. For example, development of a national network of post offices ensured a government presence in all parts of the country, but also created a universal distribution network; subsidies of second-class mail allowed wider distribution of information, accelerating commercial growth. Nonetheless, these activities were motivated primarily by concern for equity, nation building, and education. Public service activities co-existed in an uneasy, if not contradictory, relationship with the Post Office's more obviously commercial goals.

The 1986 corporate plan focused all but exclusively on commercial goals, confronting only one of the three goals assigned to CPC in 1981 — the goal of a balanced budget. Public-service functions were mentioned only in relation to cuts in government funds for postal services delivered at less than cost; funding was to drop from $254 million in 1986-87 to $191 million in 1990-91. As Table 7 indicates, payments made by the government on behalf of postal users fell to less than $150 million by 1992-93.

In commercializing the postal system, the government determined to negate its public service functions. It had a self-interested stake in this decision, for it paid for subsidies; their elimination would ease its deficit problems. From CPC's perspective, a variety of postal activities did not appear to contribute directly to the recovering of costs: home delivery, the rural postal network, and its retail arm. These postal features had served the national interest in some way or other, by linking Canadians together in a universal communications system. But new technologies offered alternate means to this end, and there were other, cheaper ways for the Post Office to pursue that goal. Moreover, many of these activities projected a bad image. For example, retail and banking chains had pulled out of villages and small towns, and home delivery of bread and milk had long ceased. Maintaining the rural network and home delivery contributed to CPC's unbusinesslike image.

Thus, Canada Post eliminated the postal role as public service, assisted by the government in two ways. First, where the government was responsible for particular public services, it cut funding and tried to eliminate those services. In the next section we examine two such services: second-class mail and shipping of parcels to the North. Second, where CPC was directly responsible for public services, the government delegitimized them and insulated CPC from the political reaction that followed. Below we examine three of these activities: the rural postal network, home delivery, and the retail network.[65]

Second Class Mail

The Canadian government has offered a concessionary postal rate subsidy (CPRS) since before Confederation, whereby it purchased from the Post Office a reduced rate (second-class mail) for newspapers and periodicals. Newspapers were delivered free of charge in 1855. Low rates were set at Confederation and then abolished in 1882 to encourage the dissemination of information. The level of the subsidy and second-class rates varied over the next century, depending on governments' sense of whether the program's cost was reasonable. In 1966, the government limited the subsidy and redefined the terms and conditions for qualification; almost half of registered publications lost their second-class status. Rates were increased in 1969, when the second-class subsidy accounted for 40 per cent of the postal deficit. They were increased again in the 1970s to stem costs, but the subsidy rose to $88 million by the end of the decade. It was transformed into an industrial subsidy in 1978, when the POD and the Secretary of State agreed that the POD would be paid a fee for providing this service. This arrangement was transferred to the Department of Communication in 1980. The subsidy was split into two in 1983: the "publishers" subsidy — the actual funding of the concessionary rates — was assigned to the Department of Communication, and the other, larger part — an infrastructure grant — was taken out of the consolidated revenue fund and assigned to the Post Office. The subsidy totalled $225 million in 1985: $55 million to the former and $170 million to the latter. Publishers mailed their products at approximately 25 per cent of costs.[66] This lesser rate was crucial in the Canadian market, where the newsstands are dominated by American publications and play an insubstantial role in distribution.[67] The program provided perhaps the largest subsidy to any cultural industry in the country, with the objective of creating an informed, better-educated population, of increasing access to Canadian culture, and of ensuring the existence of a financially sound publishing industry.[68]

After the election of the Conservatives in 1984, it was widely anticipated that the program would be cut, if not eliminated. The program was examined by the Neilson Task Force on Program Review, as well as in a series of consultancy studies for the Department of Communications. Their conclusions augured poorly: over and above the declining importance of print (versus radio and television) as a medium, the reports gave strong evidence that the program was not realizing its original goals. It remained important in rural areas (e.g., in distribution of community newspapers) as well as for small-circulation and educational/cultural publications. But major publishers benefited disproportionately; the groups that really needed the help were not adequately targeted. Elimination of the program would damage the magazine industry and weaken its competitive position, given the absence of distribution alternatives; the entire newspaper industry would survive, although overall circulation and the number of papers would decrease, substantially so in the case of smaller dailies and rural weeklies. The consensus was that a major part of the program could be cut (that part absorbed by larger publications) but that it should be retained for rural weeklies and small dailies.[69]

The 1986 plan cut the second-class subsidy from $220 million to $160 million. This element of the plan fell prey to political reaction. The publishing industry launched a furious attack on the cut in committee hearings, prompting the Holtman Committee to observe that it would impose

> an onerous financial burden on the publishers of such items, many of whom would be forced out of business...For many rural Canadians, the weekly newspaper represents the single most important source of information about events in the individual's area — a communications link of considerable magnitude.

The committee recommended that subsidies for weekly newspapers not be reduced and that the second-class system be simplified and made fairer.[70]

A year later, in response to furious lobbying and outrage that religious and rural weeklies were to lose their subsidy, Communications Minister Flora MacDonald announced that the $220 million postal subsidy for periodicals would continue for at least another five years. The industry would have to absorb rising postal costs and inflation (estimated to be 12 per cent in 1990).[71] This five-year promise lasted a year: the April 1989 federal budget cut the subsidy by $10 million in 1989–90 and $45 million in subsequent years, assigning the subsidy only to publications that needed help. CPC compiled a registry of those who benefited from the subsidy, to be passed on to the Department of Communications.[72] The publishing industry claimed that the cuts would put many out of business (the profits of the *entire* magazine industry amounted to less than $45 million). The policy was savaged by the industry and by the Opposition, which saw a link with the Free Trade Agreement, accusing the government of cutting cultural subsidies to appease the Americans.[73]

The policy was extended later that year when the government announced the elimination of the remaining $175-million second-class system and its replacement by a $110-million system of direct grants ($25 million directed to books and $85 million to magazines and periodicals).[74] The new system would affect various magazines and newspapers differently.[75] CPPA president Lorraine Flyer responded, "We are shocked. We weren't consulted. We don't know the details of the replacement program for a 100-year-old subsidy."[76] The Liberals and the NDP insisted that the existing program remain in place.[77] The industry strongly opposed the idea of targeted grants: over and above the problem of government discretion, publishers would not be able to plan their distribution costs. The industry asserted that there was no alternative to CPC's distribution system. The Canadian Magazine Publishers

Association declared that "Canada Post is our lifeline. Without it we could not serve our readers. We could not survive." Maclean-Hunter reported that "in our vast country, we cannot serve and reach our readers through the retail system, if at all. The postal service is the logical, practical and most efficient way for Canadian publishers to reach their readers."[78]

The first rate increases under the new regime were gazetted in December 1990. Community newspapers fought the increase when they saw that it would double postal rates (there were cases of 237 per cent and 680 per cent increases). In March 1991 the government eased the pain by delaying the phase-in for a year and by allocating an extra $6 million (over three years) in adjustment subventions for weekly newspapers. At the end of this period, however, full commercial rates would be paid.[79]

Despite strong industry and community reaction, the government persisted with plans to eliminate the second-class subsidy. This took no small amount of political courage, given that the affected industry had considerable communications influence. The government effectively halved its support, from $220 million to $110 million, and this will not rise to cover future inflation and cost increases. Eventually, all publications will be charged market rates; they will then compete for direct grants. The government urged publishers to find alternative ways to distribute their publications and to increase their efficiency to absorb the price increases. CPC favoured cancelling the system and commercializing publication rates, with postal prices reflecting real costs and market competition. It was annoyed when publishers and the public assigned it responsibility for increased prices, as well as for the perception that it was being subsidized by the government.[80] The government absorbed most of the political reaction over this development. Predictably, second-class volumes fell by 10 per cent from 1986 to 1992, to comprise less than 6 per cent of mail volumes (in the new vernacular, publications mail fell by 5.3 per cent in 1992-93).

Northern Air Stage Parcel Subsidy

Another public service postal function that fell prey to deficit reduction was the northern air stage parcel subsidy — the policy of subsidizing parcel distribution to Northern communities. This provided parcel delivery of perishable objects and foodstuffs to northern communities lacking access to year-round surface transportation. Communities sign an agreement with CPC, which contracts with airlines to deliver the goods. Deliveries do not typically pass through CPC's hands, but go from suppliers to air carriers to communities. The postage paid is less than the shipping cost; the difference is made up by the subsidy. The origins and mechanisms of this program are unclear, as its history has never been written. Even line responsibility for the program was hazy, as no department was responsible, in either a policy or financial sense. (More recently, the subsidy became an annual appropriation from Parliament to the minister responsible for CPC.[81]) The service was first offered in the late 1960s in northern Quebec, and was expanded in ad hoc fashion thereafter. This growth was eventually checked as the program's costs spiralled. Its reach was never extensive, being limited to four regions: the Baffin region, eastern James Bay and northern Quebec, northern Ontario, and northern Saskatchewan. By 1989, CPC had shipped 17 million kilos of goods to the north through the subsidy program, more than 50 per cent of which was perishable items. Postal charges covered 40 per cent of costs; the rest — $17 million — was covered by the subsidy.[82]

CPC embraced a new pricing philosophy in its 1986 plan, that price should reflect the cost of service provision, particularly as the air stage subsidy did not in fact cover CPC's costs. The government initiated two changes in line with the new corporate philosophy. It made the subsidy more explicit, setting it at $19 million for 1986-87. And, to reduce its expenditures and commercialize all postal rates, the government proposed to cut the subsidy by $1 million a year until it disappeared (the year 2006). As Harvie Andre explained,

> As part of the overall budgetary exercise we went through in trying to bring down a $38 billion deficit, the government said that as a policy they would be reducing the subsidy by $1 million a year...and Canada Post should recover whatever is necessary by raising the rates in keeping with the policy they were directed to follow...in terms of what Canada Post is doing, they are simply following a directive given by the government.[83]

There was no price adjustment in the following three years to make up for the cut in the subsidy. CPC claimed that it was awaiting the government's instructions on what pricing policy to pursue.[84] Air stage parcel rates increased in incremental steps by 20 per cent to the Baffin region, 64 per cent to Quebec, and 37 per cent to Ontario,[85] but these rises reflected increased transportation costs, not adjustments to the declining subsidy.

These changes unfolded in a quiet, informal way, with no public or political reaction, even though the subsidy had already fallen to $16 million. Then, in April 1989, the government sent clearer signals to CPC on how to proceed. On 10 October 1989, the corporation announced a 32 per cent rate increase for air shipment of food and other commodities to the North, effective 13 November 1989. Reaction in the House of Commons over the remainder of the year was intense. MP Reginald Blair complained that "Canada Post is sacrificing the welfare of those living in remote areas for the sake of profit making...It is the government's intention to cut its deficit on the backs of those who can least afford it."[86] Public protests led the government to initiate consultations. A 2 November meeting in Ottawa was attended by MPs from the North, northern and native representatives, and

DIAND, Health and Welfare, and CPC officials. The government agreed to delay the new policy, and CPC put off its price increase for three months, until the end of January 1990 (the group at the 2 November meeting had asked for a one-year moratorium) to allow an interdepartmental task force to study the issue and make recommendations on the future of the subsidy. Over the next three months, the task force had difficulty getting started, partially because no one agency, such as CPC or DIAND, wanted to play the lead role. Moreover, the government did not issue clear directives for action to the parties involved. All the while, pressure built in the House of Commons. MP Jack Iyerak Anawak (Nunatsiaq) insisted that "people will not be able to feed their families properly. These will be the results of the callous and heartless government position."[87]

The three-month extension brought no policy developments. CPC went ahead with the planned price increases, which averaged 32 per cent and, for example, raised the price of bread in Kuujjuaq from $1.74 to $2.12 and a litre of milk from $2.09 to $2.49.[88] There was angry reaction in the North. Public meetings were held in Yellowknife, Iqualuit, Thunder Bay, Val d'Or and elsewhere. In response, the government on 19 January 1990 announced a 5 per cent cut in the freeze imposed on the subsidy program until February 1991. CPC in turn decreased its proposed price increases to 25 per cent. At the same time, the government announced the formation of an interdepartmental study group, chaired by DIAND with representatives from other government departments and agencies such as Health and Welfare, Transportation Canada, Treasury Board, and Canada Post. It was to consult with air stage communities and review the implications of cutting the subsidy. Its report, issued on 17 May, concluded that despite certain flaws the existing system was efficient and effective and should be retained: "By reducing merchants' transportation costs, the air stage subsidy has been an effective means of keeping the prices of foods and other goods in remote communities lower than they would otherwise be" (p. 59). The fiscal benefits of further cuts in the subsidy would be illusory, for "the costs of social assistance, health care and isolated post allowances for government employees will escalate." It opted for a more focused program that concentrated exclusively on nutritional as opposed to junk food and that applied a more uniform rate structure over all areas of the North.[89] The government accepted its recommendations in August 1991. The subsidy would remain at its existing level of $15 million; it would apply to a restricted range of products, mainly nutritional food supplies; and it would be extended to all isolated communities with no year-round surface transportation.[90]

This affair was a politically messy one that ended in a compromise. Ironically, the CPC remained saddled with a program it didn't want to administer.[91] The government wanted to end the program and to let postal rates to the North reflect market costs; and CPC agreed. The government managed to pursue only one part of this policy for three years — the cutting

of the subsidy. But during this period, CPC absorbed the financial implications of the program change. When it was allowed to increase prices to
reflect the cut in subsidy, political reaction was unleashed against it. This
was unfair to CPC, inasmuch as the price increases reflected a change in
government policy. Nonetheless, the government stepped in to manage the
reaction (albeit clumsily). The ensuing process allowed all those affected to
mull over the possible consequences of the elimination of the subsidy. The
resulting compromise became more palatable to those affected, despite its
limits. The perpetuation of the $15 million subsidy was but a minor victory,
as a 20 per cent cut in funding had already been attained. And as future
funding is unlikely to reflect increased transportation costs and inflation,
with each passing year the subsidy will inexorably decline. Further, in expanding the program to more communities, the government spread the benefits of the subsidy more thinly. Slowly and steadily, then, the subsidized
transportation cost will converge on market rates

The Rural Postal System

Nowhere was the government's buffering and legitimizing role more important and more effective than in the rationalization of the rural postal network. The 1986 plan proposed to turn over 3,500 rural post offices to private
contractors over a ten-year period and to amalgamate, eliminate, or replace
with community mailboxes another 1,700.[92] Laneway delivery would be eliminated for 100,000 rural customers. By May 1992, 1,245 federally operated
post offices had been closed; 1,000 of these were replaced by private retail
outlets, but 250 were left with only outdoor boxes. The demise of a further
353 was imminent; another 208 post offices continued to operate where a
retail post office had been opened, so their days were numbered; and 145
federal post offices were under review. Thus, by 1992 30 per cent of the
rural network had been or was in the process of being changed by 1992.

Rural rationalization was the most intense and lively non-labour issue in
the commercial strategy, and it consumed more political attention in the
House of Commons and in the media than any other issue. It generated a
battle between a modern-day David and Goliath: CPC and the rural community, whose postal visions diverged radically. The corporate and government vision was strictly economic. It viewed the rural postal network as a
legacy of political patronage and electoral machinations. The irrationality of
this inheritance was exacerbated by changing demographics, as the population moved from rural to urban areas, along with the banks and commercial
retail outlets. Only the Post Office remained in these locales, serving a dwin-
dling population. The corporate and government view was that rural postal
service could be provided in private-sector locations with longer hours at a
fraction of the existing cost. The Post Office did not have responsibility for

the national and social functions that these rural post offices ostensibly served.[93]

To postal supporters, closing the rural network made neither economic nor social sense. One-third of Canada's population lived in over 9,000 small cities, towns, and villages, the smallest 5,000 of which were integrated into the wider community through the postal system. Their continued viability depended on the postal communications network, which also provided local employment, a national presence at the local level, and a social institution that was woven into the fabric of the community. The viability of these communities was important in a wider sense. One-third of all Canada's seniors, for example, live in towns and villages of less than 10,000 people, in humane circumstances and in an independent and economical fashion. For such people, the closure of a post office is the closure of a social life-line.

CPC and the government thus translated the rural issue into one of economics, the market, and efficiency, whereas opponents talked in communitarian, non-market, and social terms. The reaction against the rural element of the 1986 corporate plan was intense and persistent, and was played out dramatically in the House of Commons and the media, demonstrating the extent to which the issue had deep political roots and consequences. If Canada Post was to see through its rural plans, it could not do so on its own; it would require the government's assistance.

A backbench revolt forced the government to send the 1986 corporate plan to a parliamentary committee, which after intense debate produced critical recommendations. These, informed by negative reactions to the rural closings, saw the issue as a red herring, for rural costs were a fraction of urban costs — they were simply, in the committee's view, an easier political target. The committee argued that "the proposed changes are unacceptable to rural Canadians...[they] reinforce the existing perception that rural Canadians are considered second-class citizens by Canada Post" (see p. 6). An early report, released 15 December, included a number of procedural recommendations to ensure that CPC applied its strategy in a more subtle way and with more precise procedural guidelines. It recommended that "the present pattern of rural mail delivery not be changed" and that "Canada Post not implement wholesale closures of rural post offices."[94] The principle of franchising in rural areas was not rejected. Before the recommendations were reviewed by cabinet, Prime Minister Mulroney all but promised to respect the committee recommendations and to block the rural cuts: "First and foremost must be the interest and welfare of Canadian citizens, particularly in rural areas. There shall be no second-class citizens in this country...[regarding] postal services or otherwise."[95] The minister responsible for CPC, Michel Côté, then declared that the pattern of rural postal service would continue until at least the next corporate plan: "Canada Post does not intend to conduct wholesale closures of rural post offices and in fact has no plans to close any offices at this time." This position was reiterated on 29 January

1987 and later on 10 March 1987 by the new minister, Harvie Andre. Rural lot line service would be continued and charges for the delivery of small weekly newspapers would not be substantially increased. This all appeared to be good news for the rural community.[96]

Opposition and interest-group pressure forced the reopening of hearings, which began again in February and March 1987.[97] By this time the Nova Scotia legislature had condemned the rural closings and Newfoundland, P.E.I., New Brunswick, Saskatchewan, Manitoba, and Ontario followed suit over the next year. The CPAA demonstrated to the committee that the rural system was efficient and inexpensive and that any savings would be small. Rural Dignity argued that rural postal closings would result in the death of many rural communities and in a lost opportunity for rural economic development. Another unanimous committee report (23 March) expressed "serious concerns regarding Canada Post's planned closure of small rural post offices":

> Your Committee views the monetary benefits accruing from such a move as being quite limited. Canada Post is not going to solve its fiscal problems by closing rural post offices or by changing rural postal service...the corporation should look elsewhere for savings in its operating budget.

The committee criticized CPC's procedures, insisting that communities be given a role in determining their postal service:

> Your Committee is appalled by the heavy-handed approach taken...in [CPC's] attempts to close certain rural offices. In many cases consultation was totally lacking...no closure of a rural post office, or change in postal service, [should] be undertaken without meaningful consultation and the *consent* of the community affected.[98]

These recommendations were stronger than the government had anticipated, because the committee's chair, Holtmann, was keen to attain a unanimous report. The word "consent," for example, used at the NDP's urging, seemed to give communities a veto power. Cabinet accepted what were merely recommendations, with no legal force. Putting them to work was a different matter, as will be seen below. The government believed that, once the storm blew over, rural matters would be sorted out as they were implemented.[99]

Ironically, these political pressures removed rural closures from the political arena. In the wake of the committee's recommendations that the process be fair and reasonable, the process took on a formal consultative character. The committee recommended that no change be made without meaningful consultation; that advance notification of change be distributed to the community; that the consultation period last at least ninety days; and that discussions be held not only on the CPC proposal, but also on alternatives proposed by the community. These procedures were followed, with predictable consequences: the arena for rural issues shifted from Ottawa and the media to an obscure and "formalized" local process; at the same time, CPC was sheltered from charges of procedural misbehaviour.

The major change from the pre-Holtmann period was that CPC improved its PR methods. The final decision — taken by CPC — rarely involved continued operation of a rural post office that the corporation wanted closed or transformed and the community wanted maintained. The rural issue was driven at this time by Rural Dignity of Canada,[100] a kind of citizens' assembly for rural Canada, with its board including representatives from municipalities, regional groups, rural route carriers, postmasters, seniors, the disabled, farm organizations, and women's groups. It is funded mainly by the CPAA (from whom it receives 80 per cent of its budget) but in 1987–88 received a $2,500 grant from a CLC postal umbrella group. It also received support from provincial governments, the postal unions, and social service, women's, fish and farm, veterans, disabled, and regional groups.

RDC propelled the rural issue into the political spotlight by informing MPs, the media, and local groups and by channelling constituency reaction back to MPs and Parliament.[101] The government lost control of the agenda in late 1986 and early 1987 and had to respond to the rural issue as defined by RDC. It successfully intervened in the committee hearings, where it also encouraged and assisted others.[102] But RDC's apparent success in 1986–87 was misleading. The government had not yet taken up the position that CPC was totally independent and that the government would not interfere in its affairs. The Holtmann Committee experience was RDC's last policy success via institutional channels. Parliament's postal role subsequently declined, so that rural issues were persistently raised to no effect.[103] RDC had no political access to postal policy making, as the government considered it to be a self-interested, illegitimate spokesperson on postal matters. For example, during RDC's 1988 coast-to-coast tour on behalf of rural post offices, Andre called RDC representatives liars who were spreading false information about rural postal closings. CPC also considered RDC to be a self-interested group and froze it out of postal policy circles.[104] The parliamentary committee process became less effective. Hearings in 1988 centred on the rural issue, but they were predictable and without spark. The Turner Committee hearings in 1989-90 criticized CPC's procedures and its inadequate consultation, but the government simply ignored the report.[105] MPs' influence on postal policy was negligible. Conservative MPs raised the rural issue in caucus, but Andre absorbed the heat and insisted that CPC be allowed to get on with its job.[105]

Indeed, the government took the offensive in defending CPC's rural conversion plan, making it futile to raise the issue in Parliament. For example, when leaked documents indicated the massive scale of rural postal closings,

Andre trivialized them as simply one of many "planning" documents.[106] He frequently declared that the public "liked" what CPC was doing — extending postal hours to a private-sector schedule of fourteen to sixteen hours a day, seven days a week. He insisted that the public supported privatization of rural retail outlets, which would actually increase the number of outlets: "The customers like it. It is the unions that do not like it."[107] CPC took a similar approach. In June 1989 it ran a controversial ad in which sixty-four local rural politicians endorsed CPC actions: "People in my community are benefiting from this new postal service. It's good for the community." This resulted in a stream of complaints, from a number of the signatories themselves as well as Conservative MPs.[108] Nonetheless, the government backed CPC's marketing actions.

Rural postal closings had a disproportionate impact on women, who comprised 80 per cent of rural postal workers. The National Action Committee on the Status of Women passed a resolution against the privatization of postal service, but Andre insisted that privatization would create new jobs.[109] When petitions were issued or questions raised, the government parroted its policy of non-interference. For example, a number of questions regarding postal closings in May 1991 led Andre to reply that the matter was none of the government's business, as the 1981 Crowning of the Post Office was designed to keep politics out of that institution. In any event, he argued, surveys indicated that 90 per cent of people are happy with the changes.[110] Despite the intensity and range of local communities' efforts to save their post offices, the government chose not to intervene, even in the face of entreaties by Conservative MPs and cabinet ministers.[111] This inertia was particularly controversial in the context of the Holtmann Committee's recommendation that changes not be carried out without the "consent" of the community. The government insisted that "consent" involved giving the community the opportunity for input and a fair hearing — not a veto: the final decision, after consultations, belonged to Canada Post. The government's posture wore down rural opponents, who gave up their attempts to influence MPs, the minister's office, and Parliament.

The declining impact of traditional lobbying efforts led rural groups to take extra-parliamentary initiatives. RDC, for example, engaged in a kind of a guerrilla theatre campaign designed to embarrass CPC, kindle protests against government policy, and buttress the morale of groups fighting closings. Its most elaborate action was the spring 1988 "Coast to Coast for Rural Post" campaign, under the auspices of which two trucks crossed Canada from east and west, raising public awareness and collecting 250,000 cards and letters of protest. When it hears about impending postal closings, RDC provides communities with an action kit, background information, tactical suggestions, media advice, and so on. RDC works with local committees, even attending "consultation" meetings with CPC. Because they cannot match CPC's advertising and communications budgets and its army of consultants and operatives, they are forced to rely on unusual and emotional tactics to make their case.[112] These intense and imaginative initiatives slowed the process of rural closings, but they also alienated rural groups even further from the postal policy community. Real successes were rare.

Rural constituencies and RDC also used the judicial process, once legislative avenues became useless. Six rural communities took CPC to court in October 1987, arguing that it had no right to close post offices without cabinet approval. The case was lost. In late 1990 four communities — Arran, Saskatchewan; Falmouth, Nova Scotia; and Meductic and Aroostook, New Brunswick — took CPC to Federal Court with the help of the Public Interest Advisory Centre. Three issues were raised: that CPC had breached the Canada Post Act in not providing basic customary postal service; that CPC's actions were unfair under section 15 of the Charter (equal benefit of the law); and that CPC had violated procedural fairness. Judge Leonard Martin ruled against the communities (and ordered them to pay court charges). He distinguished the "having regard to" phrase from the "absolute" duty to maintain basic customary service, and concluded that there was no substantial difference between a private postal outlet and the federal office. An appeal was lost in January 1992.

The rural rationalization program rolled on, despite fierce reaction from the rural community, parliamentary committees, the media, and even Conservative MPs. The government ensured that reactions would not have political effect. This was especially critical in the case of the Postal Services Review Committee (PSRC), discussed below. This advisory body was to make independent recommendations on CPC price and regulation changes. In July 1989 it submitted a number of recommendations in response to CPC proposals. The committee noted that "some postal users...have been undeniably disadvantaged by the rural conversion program." Many rural communities were without postal service; residents had to travel — sometimes as far as fifty-eight kilometres — to get postal counter service. Sixty-six communities representing 3,500 households had been substantially affected in this way. The PSRC concluded that improved services to these rural communities would not undermine CPC's financial goals.[113] It recommended that CPC's price increase and a number of regulatory proposals be contingent on improving postal services to these sixty-six rural communities.

This was an opportunity for the government to alleviate the pain of rural rationalization, which had led to intense local dissatisfaction. What was more, the opportunity presented itself in a manner that could not lead to accusations of political interference, for the recommendations came from a non-partisan third party. But the government chose to reject the recommendation and disbanded the PSRC in the next budget. It consciously defended CPC's rural policies and refused to direct CPC to assist communities that had been disadvantaged by the rural conversion plan.

The rural conversion plan was such a politically troublesome issue in the mid-to-late 1980s that it was discussed daily at CPC's NCC morning meetings. In the early 1990s, it remained a sensitive but increasingly marginal issue that was no longer automatically on the agenda at NCC meetings. Rural conversion is no longer raised as frequently in the minister's office, among MPs, or at the CPC liaison offices,[114] vindicating the government's decision to absorb political criticism and stonewall opposition. Critics became worn down by the process and gave up trying to influence postal policy through the political process. The key historical moment was the 1988 federal election. If the rural issue had spun out of control, the government might have been prepared to intervene and change the plan for political reasons. But CPC ran a massive ad campaign to neutralize the effects of a (much more modest) RDC campaign, and the free trade issue deflected attention from the postal arena. The rural conversion plan survived the 1988 election, by which time the issue had been defused and depoliticized. The matter is now dealt with on CPC's terms as a business and commercial issue, and not on political terms as a social and public-service issue. CPC treats rural conversions as a public relations or customer-driven issue: despite its long link to Canada's history and national and economic development, the rural issue is treated no differently than any other commercial consideration. The corporation does not consider itself to be in the business of "history;"[115] and it was the government that allowed it to get out of that business.

Community Mailboxes

The government actively supported CPC's community mailbox program. The 1986 plan determined that new postal addresses – particularly in suburban areas – would be serviced mainly by community mailboxes. By 1991, there were 27,400 community mailbox sites servicing 712,000 addresses, about 7 per cent of total addresses. CPC planned to increase this to 12 per cent by 1996, by which time only 40 per cent of addresses would be serviced by home delivery. But Canadians considered home delivery to be a natural right, and felt ill-treated when not provided with it. Public reaction was sufficiently substantial and well-organized to threaten to undermine the policy, requiring the government's active intervention.

Public reaction to community mailboxes predated the 1986 plan. In February 1986, eighty Thornhill, Ontario, residents circled the post office to protest lack of home delivery in their area.[116] Public reaction provoked the NDP to organize cross-Canada hearings in July 1986. Citizens complained to Cyril Keeper that the boxes were inaccessible to the handicapped and an inconvenience for seniors; were unsightly and generated graffiti and litter; were dangerous for mothers with children; would be inaccessible in winter; provided serious security problems; and would lower property values and deter the sale of new homes. "Canadians consider group and community mailboxes a cutback in service and feel that they are being discriminated against by the Post Office," reported Keeper; Canadians were upset about "being treated as second-class citizens. What galled people the most was paying equal taxes for unequal service." Newer communities such as Kanata near Ottawa had 30 per cent home delivery. There was concern that this was the first step in ending home service altogether.[117]

When the 1986 plan was announced MPs were immediately swamped by complaints, which were rehearsed in the Holtmann Committee. The consensus was that this was an equity issue, with the policy creating two classes of citizens. MPs from the suburbs led the attack, reiterating the points raised in the Keeper report.[118] To make matters worse, technical glitches in the installation of the mailboxes resulted in improperly aligned doors, upside-down lock bars, and keys that opened more than one box at the same location.[119] The Holtmann Committee's December report recommended that installations be delayed until technical difficulties were resolved and that the mailboxes be redesigned to ease access for the physically handicapped. The report approved the "concept" of the community mailbox as a useful strategy for balancing the postal budget, but wanted to ensure the provision of "satisfactory" methods of mail delivery.[120] The committee's third report concluded that the community boxes were "not satisfactory," especially for the elderly, the handicapped, and the disabled, and in winter. The committee was also concerned that CPC was introducing the community mailboxes arbitrarily and was generating obvious inequities. Nonetheless, it accepted CPC's argument that traditional home delivery was too costly, and as an alternative, recommended that home delivery in new areas be contracted out to private contractors, who would tender for postal routes as in rural route delivery.[121]

The issue was pursued vigorously by the Opposition parties, who accused the government of allowing CPC to neglect its service obligations.[122] Liberal leader Turner argued that "when we became a country at Confederation the first two duties of the Government were...to protect the realm and defend the country and...to deliver the mail." He characterized supermailboxes as a "farce" and home delivery as an essential service, which the Liberals would reinstate if elected.[123] NDP leader Broadbent also pledged to scrap the community mailboxes and to extend home delivery to all new urban areas.[124] The pressure group Residents Against Mailboxes planned to join forces with the Opposition parties, which saw home delivery as an important election issue in 1988.[125] While politicians staked out their political ground at the national level, local communities took direct action. For example, the city of Nepean launched a legal challenge, contending that the community mailbox plan violated the Canada Post Corporation Act provisions to maintain basic customary service.[126] The court rejected Nepean's contention, asserting that there was nothing in the act that "imposes a duty to provide door-to-door delivery as part of a 'basic customary service.'" The court distinguished between "having regard" to these basic customary services and actually having the obligation to provide them.[127] This judgement later became the basis for court rulings against the rural challenge to CPC's plan (see p. 324 this chapter).

Property owners followed a different strategy. After CPC placed a community mailbox in front of Karen Feshauner's Winnipeg house, she applied for a property tax rebate. City councillors accepted her claim that this had decreased her property's value and awarded her a fifty-dollar-a-year rebate.[128] Two property owners in Pickering, Ontario, applied for a reduction in property taxes in 1987. Although neither could see the community mailbox from their homes, they claimed that it was a "nuisance," which diminished their privacy and entertainment. The decision recognized a $2,000 reduction to their property's market value. The Ministry of Revenue appealed the decision, and the case went to the Ontario Municipal Board, where the appeal was lost. The OMB did not declare that community mailboxes reduced property values, but did conclude that they were a nuisance. The province granted an estimated two to three thousand homeowners a 5 per cent tax cut in the 1988 tax year and the Town of Pickering prepared to sue the federal government for lost revenue. CPC then hired Central Ontario Appraisals to study the community mailbox's price on home resale prices; three thousand case studies demonstrated no price impact.[129] Following the Pickering case, the City of Calgary reviewed the impact of community mailboxes. Ten complaints were received in May 1987, only one of which was upheld. Although a study indicated no decline in property values, it also demonstrated that property owners faced inconveniences, such as increased noise, litter, a decline in appearance, invasion of privacy, and parking problems. Calgary council recognized the nuisance factor of community mailboxes by awarding a 3 per cent tax allowance beginning in the 1989 tax year. The Scarborough, Ontario, council voted to refuse community mailboxes, fearing that CPC would not maintain them. In response, CPC threatened to put addresses in new Scarborough subdivisions on general delivery and green mailboxes. The council caved in and accepted community boxes.[130] The Association of Municipalities of Ontario assailed the community mailbox approach, because locational and maintenance problems created unfair burdens for municipalities.[131] LCUC president Bob McGarry, at this time a member of the CPC board, sought an injunction against CPC on the ground that community mailboxes violated legislative guarantees of equal postal service in communities of equal size.[132]

The Keeper and Holtman reports, the personal interventions by Turner and Broadbent, organized pressure by Residents Against Mailboxes and Citizens United for Equitable Postal Service, municipal court actions, the prospect of community mailboxes as an election issue in 1988 — together, this constituted a formidable public attack on the community mailbox strategy. The government might have gained political advantage by directing CPC to moderate its delivery strategy. Instead, it stonewalled opposition and absorbed the political fallout, insulating CPC and allowing it to implement the community mailbox strategy.

The government proffered three policy arguments to neutralize public complaints. First, it transformed the controversy into an economic one. In reply to Opposition leader Turner's claim that home delivery was a public service, Prime Minister Mulroney insisted that CPC had the "responsibility...to conduct this service at reasonable cost in the most efficient way considering the expenditure of taxpayers' money."[133] Andre claimed that universal door-to-door service would cost $1.4 billion over the next four years, increase annual operating costs by over $400 million, and raise the price of a first-class stamp to sixty cents.[134] based on a commissioned report on the costs of expanding home delivery. The $1.4 billion figure was sheer hyperbole: it was the cost of providing home delivery to every single Canadian address, even in villages and rural areas. A more realistic figure would have been $540 million over five years and $160 million annually thereafter, the cost of replacing existing group or community mailboxes in urban areas and providing home delivery in suburban areas to communities with more than 2,000 points of call. But the government continued to use the $1.4 billion figure to load the debate in CPC's favour.[135] Andre took the argument one step further, arguing that the delivery of mail to community mailboxes should be contracted out.[136]

Second, the government presented community mailboxes as a "modern" and commonsensical response to social and life style changes. Andre noted that home delivery of milk and bread had long ceased; that the prevalence of working mothers meant that often no one was home to receive parcels; and that an increasing proportion of the population lived in suburbs, where there were no sidewalks and everyone drove. Hence, it made sense for people to pick up and mail letters and parcels at community mailboxes as they drove to and from work and shopping. He accused the Opposition of perpetuating a 1940s and 1950s mythology, and claimed that in any event, a majority of Canadians never received home delivery (this was a slight exaggeration; as around 55 per cent of Canadians received home delivery in the late 1980s).[137] Treasury Board president Doug Lewis ridiculed Opposition complaints, claiming that he needed to go to the post office only once a week to collect his bills: "Everyone pays his bills once or twice a month. What is this need for door-to-door delivery all about...Why do I need a postman to make five trips a week for me?"[138]

Third, the government responded to arguments that the strategy resulted in service inequities by appealing to what was customary in an area. Andre replied (in the case of Ottawa):

You make the point that Orleans gets treated differently from the Glebe...that is true, because the Glebe is an older district that histori-cally received it.[139]

This line of reasoning denied claims that new suburban areas should receive postal service similar to existing ones.

The government was given an opportunity to moderate the policy when the PSRC reflected on the community mailbox program in its 1989 delib-erations, observing that it often involved

> service change[s] that result in clearly inequitable service for a portion of Canada Post's customers. The Committee heard during the public consultations of obvious inequity in service to customers within the same urban community. These situations should be rectified. In addi-tion, alternatives...including an extension of door-to-door delivery should be explored by Canada Post.[140]

PSRC chairman Marchment stated that "800,000 of our points of call could be made for about $42 million...there are an awful lot of people that could be better served at a minimal cost, and we feel that Canada Post can afford that cost."[141]

This was a golden opportunity for the government to fine-tune the com-munity mailbox program. Had it accepted the PSRC's advice it could not have been accused of "political interference," because it was following the counsel of a non-partisan third party. However, the government was annoyed that the PSRC had reintroduced the issue, which had died away after its unsuccessful raising in the 1988 election: it categorically rejected the PSRC's recommendations. Andre later rejected the PSRC's recommendation to ex-tend home delivery, defending CPC's efforts to cut costs.[142]

CPC now manages the community mailbox policy like other issues, as a commercial or service issue.[143] The early political fallout was partially due to the newness of the program and the unprepared, scatter-gun way in which CPC implemented it. Procedures have since been rationalized and formalized. CPC's Bureau of Municipal Relations works closely with the Federation of Canadian Municipalities (FCM) and their postal task force subcommittee (formed in 1989) to establish criteria, standards, and procedures to be fol-lowed in introducing a community mailbox. A memo of understanding with the FCM lays out mechanisms for consultation, advice-giving, procedures, costs, and so on. The Bureau of Municipal Relations also works with fifteen provincial municipal associations.[144]

In sum, the community mailbox issue has been rationalized, depoliticized, and has become a matter of routine, reflecting government's efforts to defuse the issue by absorbing protests until critics ran out of energy. When it became clear that the government would not intervene to change CPC's plans, political criticism and pressure gradually dissipated.

Franchising

Of all the labour-management tensions that plagued CPC after 1986, its decision to privatize the retail operation generated the most intense union reaction. The 1986 plan proposed to expand the private sector's postal role, particularly in the provision of counter services. The plan listed 734 urban post offices to be replaced by private-sector outlets over a decade. Two benefits were anticipated: privatization of the retail operation would substantially cut its overhead costs, and customer service would be improved, for private-sector operations would be more conveniently located and accessible, offer longer business hours, and — given their sensitivity to the market — offer better customer service. But this strategy would undo the gains that the postal unions had negotiated during the Warren years. CPC and the unions had devised ways to maintain and create more "good" jobs, through initiatives like Consumers' Post and New Directions outlets. Privatizing CPC's retail arm was seen to be a cheap labour strategy and an attack on union jobs, among which postal wicket jobs were much sought after, as they involved day shifts in reasonable working conditions.

As discussed earlier, privatizing the retail operation was a CPC initiative. Concluding that its comparative advantage did not lie on the retail side, CPC proposed to let the private-sector market its retail services. The government accepted the principle, which became an integral feature of the 1986 plan. Government support has not wavered since, despite intense union and public reaction. The government's support for franchising has not been as clearly articulated as it was for rural rationalization and community mailboxes, but it has been just as firm. The 1987 and 1991 CUPW strikes centred on franchising, and the government actively supported CPC during the strikes, which enabled CPC to pursue its franchising plans.

The process of franchising has been more protracted than was anticipated, for it became entangled in complicated legal and political manoeuvrings that played themselves out in negotiations and in the 1987 postal strike (the government's role in the latter is examined below). Generally speaking, state support for franchising during negotiations resulted in postal strikes and the imposition of settlements that legitimized and validated the franchising strategy. The judicial system played a critical role in allowing CPC to proceed with its franchising plans.

At first, the franchising question was obscured by the issues of rural rationalization and community mailboxes. The Holtmann Committee, for example, did not examine the franchising issue to any great extent.[145] Reaction developed once CPC sold its first franchise in April 1987. Postal unions, women's groups, anti-poverty organizations, and Opposition politicians denounced franchising, which they saw as leading to job insecurity and a low-wage ghetto, especially for women. The Opposition attributed the 1987 CUPW strike to franchising's impact on postal jobs and wages.[146] CUPW initiated a $2 million campaign against franchising, contracting out, and privatization. Ten regional co-ordinators mobilized union members, informed the public, and met with community groups. A job-creating alternative was presented in a booklet, *Canada Post – It Can Deliver*. Sub-post offices were boycotted and private post offices were leafleted. Questionnaires were sent to all MPs, forcing them to take a position on the issue.[147] CUPW organized a boycott against Becker's stores, which had accepted over two dozen postal stations; Becker's agreed not to accept any more or extend the services offered by existing ones.[148] A National Action Committee on the Status of Women study illustrated how privatization hurt women, who were shifted from unionized to non-unionized jobs.[149] Unlike the rural rationalization and community mailbox issues – which faded from sight after the 1988 election – franchising continued to provoke reaction through the parliamentary hearings in 1989–90.[150]

The government, however, refused to acknowledge the logic or legitimacy of opposition to franchising, which was seen as a common-sense matter of economics. Andre characterized union reaction as self-interested (as wanting to maximize the number of union jobs) and attacked the unions as "the most reactionary forces at the moment...opposed to every change."[151] He cited a 1987–88 conciliation report that, within the private sector, provision of counter service accounted for only 20 per cent of postal costs, compared to 70 per cent within Canada Post.[152] It is "absurd to have some of the most experienced people doing what is an entry-level job," he claimed. "It's a job that teenagers do – that's what it is – operating retail counters. And so for efficiency we just can't really carry on with maintaining these counter jobs to give this bargaining unit a place for their senior people to go."[153] Thus, the government made it absolutely clear that it supported CPC's franchising plans, and that it had no intention of directing CPC to change them. This helped CPC proceed with its retail privatization.

The legal process surrounding franchising was more complex, but acted to the same effect. Canada Post sold its first franchise in April 1987 to Shelley Manly, owner of a Shoppers Drug Mart in Fairview Mall in Toronto.[154] The Shoppers postal franchise was fully staffed by drugstore clerks, who were paid $5.50 an hour (compared to a CPC postal wicket clerk's wage of $13.42). CPC planned to sell fifty more outlets in the next year.[155] CUPW picketed the store and took its complaint against CPC to the Canadian Labour Relations Board (CLRB), where the franchising plan was given a jolt. The CLRB ordered Shoppers to pay its clerks union wages and benefits as set out in the CUPW contract, which made the franchise an unattractive financial proposition. The CLRB ruled that Shoppers was a "dealership" rather than a sub-post office, because the franchise was granted exclusive territory to become a unique part of CPC's business (CPC received a franchise fee and a percentage of sales):

> The franchise agreement gave Manley-Shoppers more than just the right to sell stamps and other Canada Post Corporation products. The agreement gave Manley-Shoppers the right, in a given territory, to be the personification of Canada Post Corporation.

This gave CUPW the same "successor rights" under the Canada Labour Code as when any business is sold. The decision was upheld in the Federal Court of Appeal.[156] In a related decision, CPC was ordered to give CUPW more information and provide more "constructive consultation" before franchising.[157]

Although the Shoppers decision threatened CPC's franchising plans, it had no effect on the "principle" of franchising, as the decision was confined to one particular outlet. CPC dodged the imposition of successor rights by franchising in areas where a CPC outlet existed, to avoid assigning exclusive jurisdiction. The old CPC outlet would later be closed or moved, once its revenues had been cut by competition from the private franchise. For example, Postal Station C in Winnipeg was closed two months after a franchise was awarded to Nieman's pharmacy; a similar development resulted from an agreement with the Rideau pharmacy in Ottawa. This time Canada Post won against those who challenged its strategy in court. As Judy Fudge put it:

> The fact that Canada Post had embarked on a policy of opening private-sector retail postal outlets in competition with corporate outlets did not fall within the narrower scope of the successor rights because there was no direct impact on bargaining unit jobs — there was no immediate closure of a postal station. The long-term impact of this policy was a matter for negotiations, not successor rights.[158]

The CLRB later confirmed that franchises were not bound by union contracts if CPC had not reduced its own business in the area (by shutting a postal station), thus distinguishing this strategy from that of the 1987 Shoppers case.[159]

Legal developments paralleled negotiations. The conciliator in the 1987 CUPW negotiations, Claude Foisy, agreed with CPC's view that its franchising strategy was necessary for competitive reasons:

> The role of Canada Post is not to provide jobs for Canadians or increase the income of bargaining unit members as a form of social assistance. It must operate in an efficient and cost-effective manner, otherwise its spending would be unlimited.[160]

Foisy insisted that the union be consulted and that alternative employment be assigned to members affected by franchising, but also asserted that job creation was a management prerogative and that CPC could franchise its retail operation. Franchising was not equivalent to subcontracting work that belongs to the union, because so many retail outlets were already in private hands. Foisy limited the relevance of the Shoppers ruling to that case, and saw franchising as potentially unacceptable only insofar as it might jeopardize jobs in existing CPC outlets. He distinguished between the opening of sub-post offices and franchises that co-exist with offices operated by CUPW members, and the closure of existing post offices purely on economic grounds. This allowed CPC to proceed in a direction very different from that proposed in the Hartt conciliation report, with its validation of CUPW's job concerns and emphasis on job creation

The conciliation report failed to create a settlement. After a short strike, an arbitrator was directed by the government to take "cognizance" of the Foisy report in his deliberations. This made the franchising decision a foregone conclusion. The Cossette report presented no obstacles to CPC's privatization plans, but job security was balanced with contracting out. Cossette rejected CUPW's demand that contracting out be outlawed, saying he had no right to tell management how to do its job. The price of increased operational flexibility was solid job-security provisions.[161]

Political decisions and the character of the negotiations process "legalized" the issue of franchising, removing it from the political agenda and depoliticizing what had been a controversial issue. Fudge points out that CUPW has been able to delay the closing of existing CPC outlets but not able to stop the opening of new ones. It has used legal tactics to stall matters, by challenging individual instances of franchising on successor grounds and on the consultation provisions.[162] The franchising issue remains fertile legal ground; however, the wider political battle has been won by CPC, political and legal support for which has allowed it to implement its franchising plans.

In sum, the government encouraged and assisted Canada Post in transforming the Post Office from a public service into a commercial institution. This transformation required CPC to fly in the face of public expectations and postal service goals, which it could not have done on its own. The Conservative government assertively lowered the public's postal expectations and delegitimized the Post Office's public service role, allowing CPC room to implement the 1986 corporate plan.

The Government and Labour-Management Relations

Cutting labour costs and changing labour's role in CPC were central to the 1986 plan, which proposed to balance the budget in two ways. First, contracts would be negotiated to make wages and benefits comparable to those in the private sector. Second, 8,700 positions would be eliminated — 14 per cent of postal jobs — through privatization, community mailboxes, mechanization, and reduced services. Moreover, CPC aimed to project a different image of labour-management relationship to the market, one of management control. Thus, the plan aimed to cut labour costs, increase productivity, and roll back labour's "privileges" and authority.

Implementation of these features of the plan required governmental assistance. Lower wages and benefits, the loss of thousands of jobs, and deterioration of working conditions would inevitably generate a negative union reaction, which could undermine efforts to implement the plan. Second, the Canada Post Corporation Act directed CPC to keep in mind "the desirability of utilizing the human resources of the corporation in a manner that will attain the objects of the corporation and ensure the commitment and dedication of its employees to the attainment of those objects." The corporate plan did not acknowledge, let alone meet, this legislative objective.

CPC needed the government's assistance to cut its labour costs and to focus exclusively on commercial objectives. And despite its professed "hands-off" policy, the government assisted CPC willingly. This fact suggested to the unions that CPC remained part of the government web. Negotiations with CPC were supposedly between labour and management alone, but the unions saw themselves negotiating with the state. This made the 1987 and 1990–91 negotiations pitched political battles over the corporate plan and the future of the postal service.

The broad contours of these labour-management relations and postal negotiations differed from those of the Warren era. During the latter there was mutual willingness to collaborate in resolving the problems that beset industrial relations in the 1960s and 1970s. The government legitimized the union role by assigning unions real authority in the new Crown corporation: a voice in writing the legislation, seats on the board of directors, and legislative guarantees in the mandate. Labour negotiated directly with CPC, whose top management came to the table with the authority to negotiate. Warren and the unions developed an open and productive relationship and established an effective working dialogue.

All of this changed after the 1984 election, as the new government created a labour regime contoured to the neoconservative agenda. It sought rollbacks and concessions from public-sector employees on work rules, job security, and wages, to set an example of toughness and restraint for the private sector to emulate. Where negotiations failed, it introduced back-to-work legislation, imposing settlements on its employees. The Ports Operations Act dealt with dockworkers in 1986, and Bill C-85 legislated railroad workers back to work in 1987, introducing tremendous penalties to deter union disobedience.[163] Within this broader context, the government withdrew the postal unions' authority, ending labour representation on the board and ignoring the labour goal in CPC's mandate. The government succeeded in characterizing postal workers as overpaid, underworked, non-productive public employees who caused the public deficit and Canada's declining economic competitiveness. This attitude penetrated CPC management. CPC president Lander did not speak directly with the postal unions; relations with labour were simply assigned to the appropriate division of the corporation. Labour was treated in a "special" way, but like any other input. CPC's top people appeared less frequently at the negotiations table, and CPC negotiators appeared to have less authority than in the past. They dragged out negotiations, suggesting that the government retained ultimate strategic decision-making power. Negotiations were designed to roll back the gains made by postal workers in the past and to undermine the authority and strength of the postal unions. The persistent threat of back-to-work legislation took the soul out of negotiations.[164]

It was ironic that postal unions felt obliged to bargain directly with the government, as this was the precise opposite of what Crowning was supposed to have brought about. As Claude Foisy put in in his 1987 CUPW conciliation report, "The union regards Canada Post as a government agency...its positions are directed more often than not to the Government of Canada." The parties went through the motions of negotiating, but they "did not really enter into direct discussions."[165] Both waited for the government to decide how to resolve significant matters of principle. Yet the 1986 plan had been intended to further distance the corporation from the government in commercial operations. Predictably, after five years without a postal strike, CPC endured two postal strikes during the year following the plan's introduction. The business plan was government inspired and government directed. After 1986, then, the postal unions negotiated and battled against the government.

LCUC 1987

The government's role in the changed labour environment became clear during the summer 1987 negotiations with LCUC and CUPW. In these, the first negotiations since the introduction of the 1986 plan, there was much at stake for CPC and the unions; for labour, thousands of jobs, hard-fought wage and benefit gains, and future conditions of work; for the corporation, the capacity to balance its budget and to become commercial and competitive. Negotiations focused less on particular items than on the overall logic informing the plan. The unions refused to accept commercialization of the postal system and defended the Post Office as a public service. The corporation negotiated to end its public service character, by prioritizing corporate and commercial values and objectives. This conflict of visions made negotiations a zero-sum game, in which one side's gain was the other side's loss. The nature of the 1986 plan gave the 1987 negotiations an "union-busting" character. Faced with a choice between CPC and the postal unions, the government chose to throw its weight behind the former. Despite professions of non-involvement, it aggressively helped CPC to confront its unions.

The government began its aggressive involvement with the LCUC negotiations, which led to the first mail strike since 1981 (nineteen days of rotating strikes, 16 June–5 July). The character of the 1986 plan is well-illustrated by the fact that it pushed LCUC into a strike for the first time since that union won the right to strike two decades earlier — and LCUC did not have a strike fund. Perceived as a "moderate" union (in comparison to CUPW), LCUC had bargained shrewdly to maximize its members' benefits. It had been neither disposed nor compelled to use the strike weapon, mainly because it had not confronted the technologically induced challenges to job security and working conditions that CUPW had faced.

The details of the negotiations have been presented earlier (in the previous chapter). Briefly, CPC warned that negotiations would be tough and controversial and that the country might have to suffer a strike to allow it to pursue its plan.[166] It intended to continue providing postal service during a strike, a first in Canadian postal history. The government approved the principle of continuing service. Harvie Andre, recently appointed minister responsible for CPC, permitted CPC to use replacement workers in exercising its legal right to carry out its social responsibility.[167] CPC launched a national campaign to recruit drivers, carriers, and sorters (although in the advertising it was not mentioned by name).[168] The extent to which the cabinet approved this strategy remains unclear:

> If I'd have said no, he [Lander] wouldn't have gone ahead with it. We never did sort of put that down into a cabinet document that I took to my colleagues and said "Look, do I have the authorization to authorize the Post Office to do that...We never really had a debate about the propriety of using replacement workers or any of that. The issue really was based on the question, are we going to ensure that the mail continues to be delivered, to continue to operate. The few occasions it came up, that answer was sufficient to handle the situation.[169]

Stalemated negotiations proceeded to conciliation, and a report was issued on 8 June. Conciliator Kenneth Swan observed that "the provision of postal service in this country is an intensely political exercise," made more so when the government obliged CPC to balance its budget earlier than planned. Negotiations had a zero-sum character because the plan forced the parties into irreconcilable positions: "There are matters upon which a formal recommendation in favour of one party or the other, or even of a compromise between them, would simply inflame rather than assist the parties." He warned that using non-union workers to move the mail during a strike would lead to violence.[170] Swan's report was ignored.

Rotating strikes began on 16 June in Montreal and Calgary and spread to Toronto, Vancouver, Quebec City, Trois-Rivières, and various cities in Atlantic Canada on 18 June. CUPW workers were sent home from two Toronto plants because there was so little mail to sort; replacement workers had little or nothing to do. CPC seemed unprepared for resistance and for trouble on the picket-lines, where tensions rose and violence erupted. It had difficulty getting vehicles and replacements past picket lines, and many replacement workers quit, citing lack of security. Uncontrollable incidents inflamed tensions: a tractor-trailer was sent through the linked arms of strikers in Prince George, B.C. By 23 June the strike had spread across the country, and disruptions increased. There were more than one hundred arrests and fifty firings. The government insisted that the parties return to the negotiation table, despite widespread calls for mediation. CPC took out newspaper ads outlining its position and defending its hiring of replacement workers. By 25 June, mail volumes had declined by 20 per cent according to CPC, by 60 per cent according to LCUC. On 28 June the associate deputy minister of labour, William Kelly, was named mediator; CPC promised to stop hiring replacement workers and LCUC promised to reduce pickets and not resume the strike in Toronto. Rotating strikes ended by 1 July, with carriers working nearly everywhere. As mediation dragged on, the strike resumed in Sudbury, Toronto, and Quebec City.[171]

All the while, reaction against the strike and the government's role in it grew. The Opposition blamed the strike on the 1986 plan, with Opposition leader Turner insisting that "the Prime Minister has provoked a strike of the letter carriers...by limiting the manoeuvrability of Canada Post to negotiate in terms of what it can settle for." Andre denied this responsibility: "It is simply false for anyone to claim that it is an artificial fiscal discipline that this government has imposed which is the cause of difficulties in resolving this particular negotiation." He maintained that the government had maintained a hands-off policy once CPC had been given its broad program and business directives.[172] Turner also blamed the government for causing the picket-line violence by approving CPC's use of replacement workers: The government was "playing with fire because the Post Office is using the unemployed in an attempt to break the strike."[173] This claim generated further and widespread criticism. The government was accused of exploiting unemployment in keeping the mail moving by tapping into the readily available pool of workers. There were reports that welfare recipients were being offered a choice of working as replacement workers or losing their benefits. Even Tory MPs expressed disagreement with the use of replacement workers, and Louis Plamondon and Robert Layton joined picket lines to show support, with the former declaring that the replacement policy was "reactionary, antidemocratic and totally deplorable."[174] Harvie Andre continued to back CPC's use of replacement workers as its legal right and obligation.[175]

Surprisingly, a negotiated settlement was signed on 5 July. The terms of the settlement were similar to those of the agreement that had expired six months earlier. CPC acquired few of its objectives; why then did it settle and on such terms? The strike and its organization had involved enormous political miscalculations. First, neither CPC nor the government anticipated the letter carriers' popularity with the public, which trusted their sense of grievance. Second, the use of replacement workers made postal service expensive and unreliable, which was bad for business; and it led to widespread violence and security problems, which CPC was incapable of controlling. These developments created an enormous public-relations problem. As the strike dragged on, the public blamed the government for the postal mess. *The Globe and Mail* reported that this strike seemed to be the most unpopular one ever, and that public discontent had shifted to CPC and the government. Despite the government's declarations of non-involvement, the public saw the strike as a dispute between it and the union.[176] The government encouraged the settlement, once it became clear that the strike was hurting its political popularity as well as CPC's image.

As for the strike's financial consequences, a memo prepared for Treasury Board president de Cotret revealed that CPC had lost $20–30 million with little return: "The contract appears to provide the corporation with only minor concessions on contract flexibility...and would appear to yield only small cost savings."[177] It was later reported that a considerable part of CPC's "extraordinary restructuring costs" of $190 million in the budget reflected the expenses of this and the CUPW strike.[178]

The strike was a clear victory for LCUC.[179] However, CPC gained by demonstrating to the market its willingness to confront the postal unions in its efforts to become competitive. It miscalculated the difficulty of maintaining postal services under strike conditions, but most of the strike's consequences were blamed on the government. *The Financial Post*, for instance, blamed the government for the inconsequential settlement, accusing it of a failure of will and a loss of nerve. Its insistence that the government should have stuck it out to break the strike[180] demonstrated the view that CPC could not take on the unions on its own — government assistance was needed.

CUPW 1987

The LCUC strike prompted CPC and the government to pursue a different strategy in negotiations with CUPW. These negotiations, details of which are provided in the previous chapter, centred on CPC's plans to reduce costs by laying off full-time workers, using more part-time and casual labour, and franchising. The latter came to symbolize the essence of these negotiations, and whether the Post Office would provide a public or a commercial service. These two competing visions did not allow an easy compromise: either the two parties would fight to the death over their visions, or the government would impose one vision on a public corporation in which it was the sole shareholder. CUPW saw negotiations as futile, and CPC as simply enduring the process while waiting for the government to intervene in its favour. This is exactly what the government did. Negotiations were carried out in public and took on the character of a public-relations campaign. CUPW tried to influence public opinion to pressure the government. A $500,000 ad campaign decried privatization, the cheap labour strategy, and the elimination of a public service. As rotating strikes were about to begin, CUPW held a news conference with women's groups and anti-poverty organizations to denounce franchising and its implications for women and poverty. In a full-page advertisement, the CLC, Catholic bishops, women's organizations, and anti-poverty groups urged the prime minister to instruct CPC to cancel its franchising plans.[181] Conversely, CDC, in a $1 million ad campaign, tried to convince the public that franchising was essential to creation of a modern, commercial postal service. It declared its willingness "to look at any adverse effects franchising may have on people...but we can't put into a collective agreement how we're going to do our business." It was useless talking to CUPW "unless we were prepared to hand over to union leaders the power to dictate the future of Canada Post." It pronounced that franchising was a one-billion-dollar battle, a statement which had a certain public-relations resonance, even if it was wildly inaccurate.[182]

Negotiations were also influenced by the prospect of a bloody battle on the picket lines. CPC threw down the gauntlet by declaring its willingness to endure a potentially violent strike through which it would continue to deliver the mail. It again hired replacement workers to keep the mail moving. It also hired security guards to protect the processing plants, erected eight-foot-high fences around some sorting plants, rented fleets of buses to move the mail in and out of plants, and constructed special helicopter pads to move the mail over picket lines.[183] These plans and actions were seen as provocation, prompting CDMA spokesperson Terrence Belgue to declare, "I think Canada Post simply wants to break the union."[184] The government sanctioned these plans, while professing non-interference. Andre declared that the government intended to let negotiations take their course, that CPC was an independent corporation, and that strikes were a legal and sometimes normal part of business life. He approved CPC's hiring of replacement workers, insisting that CPC had a social obligation to deliver the mail.[185]

In late September, Claude Foisy's conciliation report asserted that the conflict was over "matters of principle and rarely on the practical application of the proposed clauses" (there were 120 on the table — none resolved). "As long as the parties maintain their extreme positions, all we can do is let them engage in a clash of Titans." He declared that CPC had the right to pursue its franchising plans, but proposed a compromise on the job security of postal clerks affected by franchising.[186]

CUPW initiated rotating strikes after the Foisy report was released, beginning 30 September. It chose rotating strikes to avoid back-to-work legislation, as it was widely anticipated that the government would intervene quickly to end an all-out strike. Labour Minister Cadieux asked his ADM William Kelly to investigate whether a negotiated settlement was possible without a long strike; the latter reported that this was highly unlikely. Rotating strikes started and stopped, and negotiations resumed from time to time. By 5 October, 4,500 workers were off the job, and Cadieux warned CUPW and CPC, "If the parties are incapable of resolving this dispute through collective bargaining, the Government will lift this responsibility from your shoulders." Talks broke down again on 7 October, and CUPW called for a mediator. CPC retorted that this would be useless, and Andre saw it as another delaying tactic. After a week or so of industrial action, the strike had been non-eventful and at most a minor irritant. There had been no major problems on the picket lines, and mail volumes remained close to normal.[187]

Nonetheless, on 8 October, eight days after the start of rotating strikes, the government moved decisively. As *The Globe and Mail* aptly put it, the "Government Applied Iron Fist to End Strike." Bill C-86 (Postal Services Continuation Act) was to end a strike that had never really began. Ironically, it provoked CUPW to escalate the rotating strikes, which extended for the first time to the crucial Toronto plants. The strike became nationwide by 9 October. Picket-line violence began, as CPC started to bring in replacement workers. Helicopters shuttled workers and mail in and out of plants. Bill C-86 received third reading on 15 October and, eighteen days after the strike began, CUPW members were ordered back to work.[188]

The legislation was controversial for both its timing and its content. It was essentially pre-emptive, introduced before the strike escalated into a serious matter. CUPW, by pursuing a low-key campaign, had hoped precisely to avoid such legislation. The Opposition insisted that there was no "national emergency," the usual stimulus to such Draconian measures. The strike was rotating and peaceful, and CUPW's demands were only "normal" in the face of the job-eliminating, wage-cutting implications of franchising.[189] Cadieux, in response, pointed to Kelly's assessment that there was no hope for a negotiated settlement, and insisted the issue had "the potential for disorder on a national scale." Andre agreed with both points.[190] This seemed odd, given the government's patience in the LCUC strike. But the government did not want to re-enact that futile process, which had embarrassed it and cost CPC a great deal of money.

The legislation's content was also controversial. It created a "mediator-arbitrator" to arbitrate an imposed settlement if ninety days of mediated negotiations proved unsuccessful. This person was directed to give "due cognizance" to the conciliation report, which directive seemed designed to determine the outcome, as Foisy asserted CPC's right to pursue its franchising plans. The Opposition accused the government of legislatively imposing CPC's business and franchising plans on the unions.[191] The legislation also provided sanctions that appeared excessive: enormous daily fines for disobeying the back-to-work order; of $1,000 for individuals, $50,000 for union leaders, and $100,000 for the union. The bill also imposed a five-year ban on holding union office for members convicted of a violation against the order. The legislation assigned CUPW the responsibility of getting postal workers back to work and focused sanctions on the union and its leaders. The Opposition and civil libertarians saw these provisions as harsh, inhumane, and perhaps a violation of the Charter of Rights.[192]

The Opposition refused to cooperate in passing Bill C-86 — it took a week to pass this "emergency" legislation — and in return for speeding final passage wrested two concessions from the government. The mediator-arbitrator was instructed to pay only "cognizance" to the Foisy report, rather than "due cognizance;" and the bill came into effect a day after royal assent, to allow a cooling-off period before workers were forced back to work.

Government actions in the 1987 CUPW strike supported CPC's effort to pursue its business and franchising plans. The government did not intervene to alter or manage the franchising issue, which was at the heart of the dispute. Instead, it insisted on CPC's right to pursue this objective. Andre was belligerently anti-union in the process.[193] Arbitration predictably asserted CPC's right to privatize. However, the 1987 CUPW strike put the lie to the idea of political non-interference in CPC affairs.

CUPW 1989-1992

LCUC and CUPW no longer held separate negotiations with CPC after 1987, for in 1988 the CLRB directed them to merge with a number of smaller associations. CUPW won the right to represent all these postal unions in an election in January 1989. All but one of their collective agreements expired by July 1989, and contract talks began in August 1989. These negotiations were complex, as seven different contracts had to be amalgamated into one agreement.[194] Negotiations unfolded slowly, and the government did not try to accelerate the process. By the time Andre Courchesne was appointed conciliator on 25 September, twenty-seven bargaining meetings had been held. Another seventy-eight were held over the following year. CUPW concluded in August 1990 that the conciliation process had been exhausted and that it was being denied rights under the Canada Labour Code. It asked to skip the conciliation commissioner stage and force the conciliator to report. This would move CUPW to a strike position (negotiators had been given an 82.6 per cent strike vote).[195] Labour Minister Corbeil refused CUPW's request, arguing that Courchesne should be given more time to deal with this "highly unusual situation." However, Courchesne later withdrew from his role, concluding that all conventional avenues for negotiation had been exhausted. At this point, Corbeil could order a new round of conciliation — fourteen months into negotiations — or grant CUPW a legal position to strike. He chose the former, and appointed Marc Lapointe as conciliator.[196]

This seemed to CUPW to manipulate the process to CPC's advantage. As negotiations dragged on, CPC continued to implement changes such as franchising, which, once in effect, would be all but impossible to negotiate. As they had in 1987, CUPW and CPC negotiated over two different visions of Canada Post's future. The corporate agenda was given greater urgency by the government's directive that CPC attain a 14-15 per cent return on equity; this intensified CPC's efforts to cut labour costs and to privatize. These were the central issues for CUPW: the future of postal workers, of the postal service, and of the wider Canadian economy itself. "This is a fight against cheap labour", claimed CUPW president Parrot. "It is a fight against eliminating jobs in the community for the profits of the few." It was also a fight for a vision of a public-service Post Office, with improved services, from expanded door-to-door delivery to diversification of postal activities and the retail operation.[197]

The conciliation report was issued in August 1991, two years after negotiations began. Lapointe organized fifty-four meetings with the parties, held hearings in four cities, and visited four mechanized facilities. He concluded that "conciliation" was not possible in any meaningful sense, making a "political" solution inevitable, for several reasons. First, CUPW and CPC despised each other, making working together all but impossible:

> The renewal of this collective agreement at Canada Post Corporation constitutes the mother of all battles...The parties are not speaking, they are hurling abuse at each other. They communicate through intermediaries. At times, we felt like [we were] witnessing a dialogue of the deaf. [Relations] have deteriorated to the point of contempt, if not palpable hatred, and distrust has reached new heights.

Second, their competing visions generated disagreements on an extraordinarily wide range of issues. CUPW brought 250 demands to the table, and management brought more than 60: "There have never been nearly as many points of contention."[198] Third, the process existed in the shadow of politics. The government had directed CPC to make a profit, and so it introduced business approaches to downsizing the labour force. CUPW in turn appealed to public opinion and the government to protect jobs at a time of high unemployment:

> The corporation has moved to the offensive in the collective bargaining process...and the Union has tried every possible means to protect the status quo...Increasingly, Canada Post wants to act as a private business,

while CUPW wants it to continue to act like an operation devoted to...the public service...The parties are headed in opposite directions.[199]

Conciliation narrowed 360 issues down to 29, nine of which were major.[200] There was fundamental disagreement over job security, and so the Lapointe report made no recommendation on the matter: "In such circumstances, where no compromise is acceptable by either party, it becomes imprudent if not dangerous to favour the position of either one."[201] This tack annoyed CUPW, which saw job security as the central issue. "It is our security for the future. At the same time it means a better future for a lot of people," declared Parrot; "part-time work and casual work are not good for our economy...We've got people that want jobs, decent jobs." CPC retorted that its mandate "was not to create 1000s of jobs in the postal system", which would increase prices and the deficit. It refused to negotiate its business plan, likened CUPW to the Soviet Union, and described CUPW's jobs vision as being as outdated as the dinosaur. It claimed that CUPW's demands would cost over $2 billion, an overstated figure that was later withdrawn but remained widely quoted. Finance Minister Mazankowski then claimed that CUPW's demands would result in a one-dollar stamp.[202]

Rotating strikes began on 24 August in eight cities, and half of CUPW was picketing by 26 August. By 5 September, CUPW had pulled out of 469 postal centres and postal volumes in Toronto had dropped to 30 per cent. CPC tried to maintain postal service. Management-level employees were brought into plants to keep the sorting machines working, and were given Diners Club and American Express cards to charge living expenses of up to $200 a day in their new occupations. Helicopters moved people and Priority Courier mail in and out of plants. CPC applied for injunctions to limit picketing, asking for a total ban on all pickets in Toronto, where violence had developed; the court banned pickets at three Toronto processing plants.[203]

CPC announced an alternative delivery system on 28 August. Depots were set up for residential mail pick-up in malls, warehouses, and rented centres staffed by outside contractors and open six days a week from 9 a.m. to 8 p.m. Full-page newspaper ads gave descriptions of service, locations, and instructions. This surprising and expensive development was not as successful as hoped for, given its ambitious scale, and there were bound to be glitches. Indeed, with the Labour Day weekend looming, the system collapsed. As temperatures rose to 30 degrees in major cities, long line-ups of seniors baked in the sun and collapsed waiting for their pension cheques — which were often not available at that particular depot. This led CUPW and CPC to fling charges and counter-charges of holding seniors ransom via their pension cheques. The two eventually reached an agreement to deliver the cheques, by the first Saturday mail delivery in more than a decade.[204]

On 3 September, Labour Minister Marcel Danis made his move. After a two-hour meeting of cabinet's labour subcommittee, he announced that the government would appoint a mediator as a last step before imposing back-to-work legislation. Three days later, he named the well-respected and experienced Alan Gold to the task. Gold was chief justice of Quebec and had mediated the Oka crisis as well a Post Office dispute in 1980. At Gold's insistence, CPC reinstated the expired collective agreement and CUPW went back to work. Postal service resumed on 6 September, and mediation began on 11 September,[205] dragging on for weeks. Holding on through false rumours, alarms, and threats, Gold finally gave up on 23 October, reporting that both sides remained far apart despite giving mediation their "best efforts." Danis then introduced legislation to ban a strike and impose binding arbitration. Both sides declared that they were close enough to a deal to continue negotiating without Gold; both seemed positive and anxious to avoid an imposed settlement. Danis gave them the weekend to reach a settlement. Negotiations collapsed on 27 October, and Danis introduced postal services continuation legislation, known as Bill C-40.[206]

CUPW resumed the strike on 28 October, to protest the back- to-work legislation as well as CPC's decision to withdraw all agreements and offers made over the six weeks of mediation. The legislation was modified to some extent in committee under opposition and union pressure to direct the arbitrator to build on progress made during mediation. CUPW was promised an upfront wage advance — including retroactive pay — that would unfreeze pay levels from when the contract expired in 1989.[207] The legislation became law on 29 October, and CUPW called off its strike after two hours.[208] Strangely, the issue simply disappeared from the public stage for two months, until André Bérgeron was appointed arbitrator 19 December.[209]

Why did the weekend negotiations fail, given that most items — including wages — had been signed off?[210] CPC has been silent about what happened, but CUPW claimed that CPC returned to the table with formal contract language undoing what had been approved or agreed to in principle. This suggests a government role in the collapse of the talks. Job creation and job security were clearly the stumbling blocks: offering job security or new jobs would project a bad business image at a time when the unemployment rate was over 10 per cent. The government would also be placed in an awkward position. Its fiscal and monetary policies had generated high levels of unemployment, presented as necessary to increase Canada's competitiveness. The conciliator had chosen to avoid making a recommendation on job security, so the government could not blame a third party for imposing job security on CPC. Mediation had come to some employment-generation issues — including keeping 80 per cent of CPC outlets open; the government may have become nervous about sending business the wrong signals on employment matters at Canada Post.[211]

As in 1987, the government did not adopt a hands-off policy in labour negotiations. Again as in 1987, however, its actions undercut the CPC's image as just another business pursuing commercial objectives in the market. The government and CPC faced a vexing choice, for the contractual benefits of using government authority projected a bad business image to the market. This dilemma was inevitable, given what was at stake in negotiations. As CPC chairman Beaulieu put it, the strike was not surprising given the confrontation between such different postal visions. The union battle was in the end with the government, not with CPC, whose options have been limited by the government.[212] Moreover, strikes are bad for business. Lander blamed CPC's 1991–92 loss on the strike. Postal business declined in anticipation of, during, and after the strike. As well, expenses rose for security, rental of vehicles, hiring of replacement staff, alternate delivery, and living expenses (the union claimed that these amounted to $200 million in the 1991–92 strike).[213]

The arbitration process began in January 1992 and promised to last until at least the spring of 1993, at which time negotiations would have to start all over again. The process was also dangerously uncertain for both sides. The union feared rollbacks; it was not clear that the arbitrator would accept items agreed to under Gold's mediation. For CPC, a drawn-out arbitration created instability, resulted in erosion of business, and made it look incapable of managing its affairs. Thus, the two sides decided to try to settle the dispute between themselves, and held discussions between 22 June and 4 July. A tentative settlement was reached on 6 July, and was supported by 82 per cent of CUPW members in a ratification vote.[214]

The negotiated settlement had significant benefits for Canada Post. First, it is in force until 31 January 1995, and provides CPC with a period of stability during which to extend its business. Second, it was settled without third-party intervention, and so signals to the market CPC's increased capacity to manage its industrial relations. Third, the deal suggests the creation of what Harold Dunstan, vice president of human resources, called "the beginnings of a more responsible, cooperative and productive labour-management relationship." There was some speculation in this regard that CUPW had moved into a "post-Parrot" era. Parrot had been elected a vice president of the CLC during negotiations, and the presidency of CUPW had been taken up by Darrell Tingley. But the changed environment in which negotiations took place was probably more influential than the relative input of Tingley and Parrot. Increased competition in the communications market, the early 1990s recession, and globalization and neoconservatism had encouraged even CUPW to think in business terms, and from CPC's perspective:

We understand that Canada Post, to survive, has to be competitive. There are a number of people out there in the field of transmission of messages...the old traditional way of delivering communications in Canada has changed...they obviously need some influx of profits...to remain competitive. So this [contract] gives them some stability, a period of time to go out and get into the fields of new communications and to compete with the private sector...we have realized as well that if Canada Post...goes bankrupt then there's a whole whack of employees that are out of work. So obviously we have an interest in...mak[ing] sure that they are a viable operation.[215]

Since 1986, then, the Mulroney government helped CPC negotiate with the postal unions over implementation of the plan. It allowed negotiations to drag on, enabling CPC to implement more and more features of its business plan. CPC tended to bargain in a half-hearted way, knowing that the government would eventually step in to sort things out. The government sanctioned CPC's use of controversial and expensive strike instruments, including replacement workers and the alternate delivery system. When negotiations broke down or threatened to harm CPC, the government intervened to end the process and force postal workers back on the job. It used back-to-work legislation to nip strikes in the bud, effectively eliminating postal workers' right to strike, and thereby supported CPC's efforts to demonstrate that it, not the postal unions, was in charge. It smiled on CPC's attempts to confront the postal unions, to cut labour costs and employment, increase workload and productivity, eliminate "perks" and advantages, and roll back postal unions' authority and the gains made over the last two decades. The government's persistent support increased CPC's capacity to deal with CUPW on corporate terms — which eventually paid off in the 1992 settlement.

Conclusion: The PSRC Incident

An event that clearly illustrated the government's role in implementing the 1986 plan was the Postal Services Review Committee episode. As discussed in the previous chapter, the PSRC was established as an independent agency to advise the government on CPC's rate and regulation proposals. Third-party review was initiated to further distance Canada Post from the government and to limit political interference in postal matters. The intent was to strengthen CPC's business image as an entity independent of the government.

The character of the PSRC reflected the Conservatives' broader neoconservative orientation. Ironically, third-party regulation was introduced precisely when an "anti-regulation" view had come to prominence on both economic and political grounds. The government believed regulation inhibited competitiveness, enterprise, and growth, and that delegation of power to regulatory bodies undermined political accountability. It developed a regulatory reform strategy to contain delegated power, increase public participation in an impartial regulatory process, and make regulation sensitive to the market needs of the regulated.[216] This was termed "smarter" regulation, and resulted in regulatory reform in the financial institutions and transportation sectors, and dismantling of the National Energy Program and the Foreign Investment Review Agency.

The decision to establish a postal *advisory* rather than a *regulatory* body reflected this philosophy. The Conservatives did not consider CPC to be a monopoly requiring regulatory direction to competitive or public-purpose ends. It was pleased with CPC's performance in the market, and instead wanted to increase public participation in the postal policy process in an apolitical way. As Andre put it:

> There is no opportunity for people to express their concerns about the Post Office...except through the political process...their member of parliament [then] approaches the minister responsible and you are back in the old situation....Let us have these things looked at in a non-partisan, more logical, rational, sane fashion [to] get away from that kind of silly stuff and be a little more rational.[217]

The government wanted an impartial scrutiny that provided increased market freedom for CPC. This would legitimate CPC's activities while reinforcing the government's professed hands-off position. The approach was favoured by NAMMU, which wanted a deregulatory environment in which customers and CPC constructed individual contracts and service agreements.[218]

The review process was straightforward. CPC proposals were to be published in the *Canada Gazette* and sent to the PSRC. It would organize hearings, giving 30 days' notice. Within 120 days of the proposal, the PSRC would hold hearings and make recommendations to CPC, with a rationale and financial implications. In making its assessment, the PSRC was to consider the "public interest," defined as provision of satisfactory service, efficient and competitive operation, fair and reasonable rates, fair competition with other like services, financial self-sufficiency, and fulfilling the section 5 mandate under the Canada Post Corporation Act. CPC would then respond to the PSRC recommendations, and both recommendations and response would go to the governor-in-council for an ultimate decision.

Public reactions to CPC proposals were directed not to the minister, but to an independent body, whose members' political independence was fostered by giving them five-year terms, reinforced by drawing them from neither the postal industry nor the federal government.[219] But the PSRC was given little real authority. First, 120 days is not a lot of time for the review process. Second, the committee could only request, and not demand, that CPC provide information and documentation. Third, the agency would make recommendations, not decisions; the government retained ultimate authority. (But, as Andre put it, "It would be a brave minister who would not follow the board's recommendations."[220])

The new regulatory process was set in motion only once. On 22 July 1989, CPC proposed a set of rate and regulation changes in the *Canada Gazette*. These included a one-cent increase in first-class mail, the elimination of certain services (such as certified and registered mail), the deregulation of some products (such as money orders, counter parcels, incentive letter mail, Christmas greeting cards), and minor regulatory changes.[221] Many proposals aimed to improve CPC's competitiveness in the fast-changing and technologically innovative communications market. The PSRC then advertised that hearings would be held across Canada in August and September. CPC submitted three volumes of material in support of its application. This material was made public, but most was already available in published CPC documents. The essence of CPC's case was made in two small sections, or five pages.[222] It argued that the rate increase was less than the rate of increase in the consumer price index, and that the regulation proposals were justified on competitive grounds.

Twenty-three presentations were made during the twenty hours of public hearings held in seven cities over eight days. The PSRC received seventeen written briefs and fifty-six letters; eleven other letters were written to CPC. Interventions were made by associations for the blind, postal unions, the Alberta branch of the CAC, the Federal Superannuates Association, three business users (UPS, *Reader's Digest*, the *Hudson Gazette*), four individuals, Liberal postal critic Don Boudria, and Canada Post. The range of representation and presentation was limited. Many presentations spoke to broader postal issues, not to the proposals themselves. Most were against the price increase, pointing to the alleged deterioration of postal service and to CPC's profits. The service proposals raised concerns about privatization and the potential for cross-subsidization. The consensus was that CPC's policies favoured major over small or ordinary users and that CPC had provided insufficient information or rationale to justify its proposals.

The hearings made a substantial impact on the PSRC. Although it accepted CPC's profit targets and praised its accomplishments, it questioned whether service had been rolled back too far in the interests of cutting costs and increasing efficiency. In two areas — community mailboxes and rural rationalization — numerous postal users were seriously disadvantaged by declining postal services. The PSRC directed CPC to balance its objectives: "As [CPC] moves towards the goal of financial self-sufficiency, service should not be sacrificed in order to achieve the status of a commercial enterprise concerned solely (or primarily) with financial self-sufficiency." It criticized CPC for attending too closely to its major customers to the neglect of the small or ordinary user: "It is quite normal for private-sector corporations to concentrate on providing superior service to their major customers. The difference with Canada Post, however, is that it has a mandate and, for a large part of its business, a monopoly to serve all of its users." The PSRC recommended that the rate increase be granted conditional on CPC's making efforts to "improve service to households and small business customers while, at the same time, continuing on its course towards financial self-sufficiency."[223]

The PSRC submitted twenty-seven other recommendations. Eight of nine CPC proposals for product deregulation were rejected because the products were not delivered in a competitive market; all of the proposals for product or service elimination were rejected; and five of eight other minor regulation proposals were accepted. In sum, the PSRC recommended acceptance of six of the twenty-two regulation proposals. It also recommended that special letter mail be regulated.[224] CPC concurred with only a few of the minor recommendations and rejected the rest.[225]

This was not the sort of result the government had envisioned when it established the review process. It had expected this informal, advisory review process to be benign. The PSRC and CPC were to develop a smooth working relationship, approving CPC plans in a manner that would increase their public legitimacy. This scenario failed to develop for a number of reasons.[226]

First, CPC was far from happy about the PSRC and regulation, as it had little to gain and much to lose.[227] And it had the power to disrupt the process, which it proceeded to do. The process was inherently asymmetrical because of the paucity of public involvement (by 1989, public antipathy to CPC had become mute and regularized, and the public had little organizational capacity to make an impact), which allowed CPC to go on the offensive, challenging the PSRC's authority, vetting its every move, and generally being unhelpful and belligerent. This fractiousness was especially apparent with regard to information. The PSRC considered insufficient the three volumes of material that CPC provided in support of its application, and made two hundred requests for more information. These requests were embarrassing to CPC, which did not have all the disaggregated cost, benefit, and price information the PSRC believed it needed to make informed judgements about the proposals.[228] CPC maintained that the requests were unmanageable, outside the committee's mandate, and potentially damaging to its competitive position (see below).[229] In short, CPC refused to provide the information. As there was no other source of it, the PSRC found it impossible to judge whether the CPC proposals met the public interest. It recommended that in future processes CPC be obliged to respond to PSRC requests for information.[230]

Second, CPC maintained that the PSRC did not appreciate the competition it faced, as but one player in a complex communications sector, including courier companies, the fax process, and the telecommunications industry. It was a hybrid entity, half monopoly (in its exclusive-privilege domain) and half competitive (50 per cent of its revenues were earned in competitive markets). Yet the PSRC proposed to regulate it as if it were a "real" monopoly, while not regulating its competitors. The PSRC was determining where it could behave competitively, thereby constraining it in the quixotic and competitive communications market. Hence also CPC's unwillingness to provide information, which might advantage its competitors. It preferred to be unregulated, to participate in the largely unregulated communications market; but the purpose of the PSRC was to regulate CPC. Costly recommendations to improve rural services and home delivery could only impair its competitive position.

Third, the review process exposed who held postal authority. The relationship between the PSRC and CPC was designed to be benign, with the PSRC sanctioning CPC's activities as in the public interest. This would allow CPC to become more like a private company. The PSRC, however, considered CPC to be a public corporation. It took to heart its mandate to consider the public interest, rethinking the relationship between the Post Office's social and economic goals. This approach resurrected all the postal pressures and contradictions that had existed since 1981: between the major business users and ordinary, small users; between rural and urban needs; between the suburbs and established inner-city areas; between the competing postal visions of a public service and commercial entity; between profits and service. These tensions had been "resolved" by policy decisions after 1986: the freeze on extending home delivery, rationalization of the rural network, the priority given to major mail users, the commercial goal of attaining a 14–15 per cent return on equity, and delegitimation of public service goals. CPC had set these postal policies, which were sanctioned by the government. The PSRC had the temerity to resurrect them for a new round of scrutiny and debate. Costly policy recommendations would hurt CPC's profit and competitive position, have market implications, and oblige it to behave like a *public* rather than a *private* corporation. The PSRC sought to assert its public authority, demanding more information, questioning how CPC was functioning, and directing that CPC pursue a more balanced set of objectives. It even sought to regulate an unregulated product (special letter mail), which was not part of CPC's proposals. None of this was acceptable to Canada Post. It had struggled to delegitimize public service goals and to be allowed to act like a private firm, unencumbered by political or regulatory interference. It did not want these matters debated again.

The government was placed in an awkward position. It had created the review process to distance itself from the Post Office, increase public participation, and protect CPC's market orientation from political interference. However, as Alan Marchment concluded, the review process "didn't go where the government wanted to go."[231]

The government was thus obliged, ironically, to intervene directly to protect the corporation from the PSRC. Two days after CPC submitted its response to the PSRC, the cabinet accepted all but two (minor) CPC proposals. In the process, it rejected the PSRC report and validated CPC's vision of the postal world.[232] First, it accepted CPC's evaluation of the competitive nature of the communications market in which it functioned; it thus appeared to the government that regulation was unworkable and harmful. Second, it validated CPC's self-image as a private communications corporation that, if it was to be commercially competitive, should not be encumbered by public-service goals or regulatory processes. The government once again supported the delegitimation of public-service postal goals. Third, it agreed that pursuing PSRC's recommendations would weaken CPC's financial position. Finally, the government accepted CPC's analysis that it was its competitors (like UPS) who wanted postal regulation, to disadvantage CPC. UPS had used the regulatory process in the United States to burden the postal service with perpetual hearings and disclosure processes, to UPS's eventual advantage.[233] In short, the government accepted CPC's proposals, indeed had never intended to challenge or alter CPC's behaviour in the first place.[234]

The February 1990 federal budget eliminated the PSRC; legislation to create it would not be reintroduced.[235] This flew in the face of the Standing Committee on Consumer and Corporate Affairs, which recommended the creation of an "independent third-party regulatory agency with decision-making power...and the legal authority to compel Canada Post to provide all information necessary to conduct an effective review."[236] Andre maintained in its hearings that "the question...of phasing out the committee came down to a budgetary question," of about $3.6 million and eighteen jobs. Noting that the process generated little participation, he concluded that "the cost...of the Postal Services Review Committee just does not seem to be justified given the public interest."[237]

The financial issue was, however, a red herring: the review generated no costs for the government. A budget was set in the normal way, with Consumer and Corporate Affairs as the lead agency, and an invoice was sent to Canada Post, which paid the costs of the review agency. The rationale was that regulation was a cost of postal service to be borne by users, not by taxpayers.[238] Moreover, low public participation confirmed only that CPC had successfully moved postal matters off the front pages and to the business section, as well as the public's belief that it could no longer influence postal matters (attested by the government's nonresponse to reaction against rural closings, community mailboxes, cuts in second-class subsidies, franchising, and so on).

Why did the government's commitment to postal regulation dissolve so quickly? Regulation was not adopted as a coercive instrument, to force a monopoly to behave like a competitive firm. Indeed, as mentioned above, the government was pleased with CPC's efforts to commercialize. It had tried to create a noncoercive or "quasi-regulatory" instrument to generate a kind of "symbolic scrutiny," to protect CPC from political pressures as it performed in the market. The government was not interested in making the regulatory process more coercive, as Marchment had anticipated;[239] precisely the reverse was true. The government placed no alternative regulatory institution in the PSRC's place. It preferred an institutional vacuum, to allow CPC to pursue its commercial course unencumbered by regulatory demands.[240]

This complete absence of third-party regulation of a public postal corporation is unique in the industrial world. But we should not conclude that CPC became "unregulated," for the gazetting system was reintroduced; reactions to CPC proposals are submitted to the minister, who accepts or rejects them. This system is all but unused by the public. No more than seventy-five responses have been made to any CPC proposal since 1987. There were only twenty-four responses in 1991 and ten responses in 1992 to CPC's price proposals.[241] The government accepted the proposals more or less automatically.

Lack of formal institutional regulation or direct government intervention, rather than attesting that CPC was not regulated, instead demonstrated how CPC had acted as the government expected. To the extent that it delivered the goods (e.g., making a profit), the government was willing to assign it a great deal of autonomy — but only autonomy "on parole." This authority could be withdrawn and the minister's authority used if CPC failed to satisfy the government's expectations.

The PSRC episode confirmed the government's willingness to support CPC's actions, to increase CPC's autonomy and independence, and to minimize social expectations and public-service obligations — as long as the government perceived that Canada Post was realizing the commercial mission that the government had set for it.

CONCLUSION

A substantial part of Canada Post's 1986 corporate plan was implemented by the early 1990s, by which time CPC had become a
commercially oriented business focused on increasing its competitiveness in the communications market. The government encouraged this
transformation and assisted CPC by delegitimizing the public-service dimension of the postal service and insulating CPC from criticism. It assigned
CPC an increasing degree of freedom to act like a private corporation. It
was widely anticipated that the Conservative government was preparing CPC
for sale to private purchasers. This did not appear imminent in 1993 as the
Conservatives faced the electorate, and even less so now, given the election
result.

In this chapter I ask whether the expectations surrounding the Crowning
of the POD have been realized. Many commercial goals set in 1981 were
attained, and social or public goals have been abandoned. Simultaneously,
many enduring postal themes, originating in the eighteenth century, have
persisted. The latter suggests why the Conservative government was reluctant
to sell CPC, even as two dozen Crown corporations were privatized between
1984 and 1991. I conclude by examining the privatization issue, reviewing
the government's attitudes toward selling Canada Post, and analyzing why
this final step in the commercialization of the postal system has not been
taken.

The Crown Corporation Decision

Chapter 6 outlined how Canada Post was created under cross-pressures. The
Post Office was Crowned to encourage commercialization and competitiveness, but there was insistence that Crown corporations be subject to more
public accountability. Occasionally, these cross-pressures constrained CPC's
behaviour, as when the government disallowed Warren's plan to expand
CPC's retail presence in the market. These commercial and political pressures
eventually converged: since 1984 the government's postal expectations have
been exclusively commercial. Broadly, political accountability declined as
CPC increased its commercial and competitive success, and the government
then simply left CPC alone. The two are inextricable parts of the same
process: the government asserted commercial postal objectives, which increased its authority over the Post Office, but increased autonomy was a
precondition of commercialization of the Post Office. CPC gained ever more

autonomy as it behaved increasingly commercially and then insisted on greater autonomy in order to extend its commercial accomplishments. The result has been a hyper-commercial postal operation with little operational interference from the government or the political system.

It was optimistically anticipated that, as a *Crown* corporation, CPC would be able to juggle social and economic goals in some sort of equilibrium. However, it was created in circumstances that privileged economic over social goals. A *public* postal system already existed — in the form of the POD. The unprecedented transition from department to corporation focused mainly on corporate concerns, giving momentum to the commercial over the social side of the postal equation. Three other historical circumstances encouraged asymmetry. First, debt-ridden itself, the government aimed to lessen the financial obligations borne in the late 1970s when the POD presented it with enormous deficits. One of the top postal objectives would be to balance the postal books. Second, there was a consensus that the postal system had to respond to new technological and competitive challenges if it was to survive. Third, globalization and neoconservativism were the predominant visions of the 1980s. This again privileged economic over social goals, and even the postal system would have to learn new rules of behaviour and play its role in the communications infrastructure to ensure the competitiveness of the Canadian economy.

In short, political and economic circumstances ensured that social goals did not compete with economic ones. One can conclude, broadly, that the latter have been realized. A commercial ethos pervades CPC, shaping its behaviour. It thinks, strategizes, behaves, and defends itself as a commercial rather than a government or public-sector organization. CPC recruited its top management in this spirit, organized its business operations on corporate lines, injected itself into the communications market, eliminated noncommercial products, forged commercial and corporate alliances in the market, projected a business image to the market, distanced itself physically and psychologically from the government, and transformed its products, institutions, and goals into market values and terms. Those keen to see the commercialization of the Post Office have seen their dreams realized.[1]

These results are debatable in quantitative and strategic business terms, and remain to be evaluated by analysts. CPC has, by and large, eliminated its deficit and its financial dependence on the government — although there are lingering doubts about whether this reflects accounting skills more than market accomplishments. Profits weakened in the early 1990s, and CPC again ran a deficit in 1991-92, but many communications corporations suffered during the long recession of the early 1990s. The broad political and legislative objective of stemming the Post Office's financial deterioration has effectively been realized.

A complementary objective was that Canada Post adapt to the new communications technologies. Chapter 8 reviewed its strategy for increasing its technological sophistication — capital expenditure and technological plans — since the mid-1980s. Media reports and the attitudes of its major clients suggest that CPC has entered the technological race, even if it may not be leading it. Concerns persist about the technological obsolescence of the Post Office, that the letter will be eliminated by the fax, e-mail, and the telephone. Competition from alternate communication technologies is remarkably broad and intense, but the postal system seems poised to survive into the next century. There will continue to be market demand for traditional services like letter delivery which remains a cheap, convenient, and — controversies aside — fairly reliable product. Moreover, despite government and market constraints, CPC entered the new technological world in a substantial way — on competitive rather than monopolistic terms. Both the market and the government have validated CPC's technological moves. CPC has been allowed to find a market niche as an all-purpose communications organization, offering a full range of communications possibilities to a wide array of potential clients. Precisely how competitive CPC has become, and whether it has advanced sufficiently in technological development, will be determined by market results over the next decade or two.

The financial, commercial, and technological objectives of Crowning the Post Office have thus been broadly, if not deeply, realized. This reflects the attainment of a second objective — the distancing of the postal operation from the political realm. The view was that the Post Office's departmental existence within the government made it susceptible to short-run political, bureaucratic, noncommercial pressures. It was hoped that these pressures could be neutralized in a Crown setting, allowing the Post Office to develop a longer, commercial perspective; and this has been broadly attained. CPC experiences little to no operational pressure from the political realm. Traditional postal issues have been translated into commercial or service ones, which CPC handles in business terms. It has been able to take the long view in rural changes, postal delivery, contracting out and privatization, despite intense short-term political scrutiny and criticism that could have resulted in back-tracking. These policies were pursued in incremental fashion over a number of years, until complete. The institutional setting has been transformed to this purpose: politicians, Parliament, the bureaucracy and even the CPC board have little postal influence. Postal management was given a stable and predictable environment, both within its own ranks and in its relations with the minister, which allowed the long-run, commercial orientation to take root. However, the depoliticization of postal matters required an expression of political authority — by a government committed to commercial postal objectives — which suggests the fragility of this achievement. The depoliticization of the postal function requires continuous political will, and can be reversed with the election of a government with a different agenda. The likelihood of policy changes in the new Liberal regime will be examined below.

Nonetheless, the expectation that CPC would become a depoliticized commercial operation has largely been realized, with implications for the Crown side of the postal equation. The dominance of corporate objectives has been extensive, as a result of political decisions to abandon other postal objectives and public goals.

There was considerable optimism that industrial relations would improve in the Crown corporation setting. Labour and management would negotiate directly and on a full range of matters, unconstrained by government needs and priorities and the constraints of public-sector existence. Labour itself was assigned a special role in the new postal Crown. It helped draft the legislation, which provided it with a number of "guarantees" and a role in running CPC. But the strength of commercial and competitive goals transformed labour issues into commercial considerations and eliminated its "special" role. Labour costs were cut by downsizing, increasing productivity, contracting out and privatizing, and making wages and working conditions comparable to those in the private sector. These policies were pursued relentlessly, with government support and encouragement, regardless of the inevitable political fallout and impact on labour-management relations. CPC also pursued these policies to project to the market a business-like image of a corporation struggling to keep its costs in line and not getting pushed around by its unions. The violent 1987 strikes, the inability to reach contract settlements through normal processes, the deterioration of relations within plants, and the accumulation of tens of thousands of grievances testify that the goal of improved labour-management relations has not been reached, the unexpected settlement in 1992 notwithstanding. The long-term impact of the latter remains to be seen — as both labour and management seem to have used it to buy time.

The pursuit of commercial goals had serious implications for postal service. It was anticipated in 1981 that traditional services would be maintained, as a better-run postal operation would expand and improve postal services. This goal has not been realized in terms of traditional conceptions of postal service. Other analysts must take up the technical question of CPC's claims to have improved postal efficiency. For example, its 98–99 per cent on-time delivery ratings reflect both an easier target (the 2/3/4-day standard) as well as a procedure that — although performed by an outside party — remains open to critical scrutiny. CPC has opted for predictability and reliability over pure speed in letter-mail delivery, and this objective has been realized. There is no reason to doubt its large-volume clients' claims that CPC has improved its efficiency and service; however, the service expectations of ordinary users and small business have been rather less successfully realized. CPC has cut costs in a number of areas by devising alternate methods of delivery and service, and regardless of its claims, the rural rationalization, community mailbox, second-class mail, and privatization programs have not been overwhelmingly popular with the public and small business. Large parts of the Canadian community have concluded that postal service has deteriorated. However, many service cuts or alterations saved modest amounts of resources over the short term, but over the longer term these savings are likely to be quite substantial. Just as important, these actions project to the market a business-like image of a corporation modernizing and changing with the times. The public character of postal issues — such as second-class mail, rural post offices, and door-to-door delivery — has been transformed into commercial, or client, terms. This is not to suggest that CPC has no public profile — it is keen to connect with the public and do service, as in its literacy campaign and its joint sponsorship of events. But these community services have a public character unrelated to postal services. Its literacy campaign is unrelated to the issue of door-to-door service, in the same way that McDonald's community efforts are unrelated to the price or quality of a hamburger. Even traditional nation-building goals have been translated into commercial objectives. CPC feels it has a patriotic duty to increase Canada's international competitiveness, which would strengthen Canada as a nation.

The Crown corporate experience of the postal system has seen a successful assertion and implementation of commercial and competitive values. In this sense, CPC has realized the expectations that surrounded its creation. The ascendency of these values also smothered the articulation of social values and objectives. The CPC experience suggests that a Crown corporation can function much like a private corporation; but it also suggests that balancing social and economic aims within a Crown corporation is a utopian objective, leading at most to a precarious equilibrium.

Enduring Themes

The creation and development of CPC transformed Canada's postal system. The commercial system neutralized a number of enduring postal themes (see chapters 1 and 2) but a number of these did continue to endure. I will now review each of these developments.

The most dramatic transformation concerns the Post Office's political disengagement. This development reflected uncontrollable as well as conscious political and corporate factors. The postal system has become far less central to everyday life than previously: the phone call has increasingly replaced the birthday card, the fax has replaced the letter, bills and payments are serviced automatically through direct deposit arrangements or at automated teller machines, corporate and personal communications increasingly arrive via e-mail and computer networks, and private courier and trucking operations deliver time-sensitive parcels. CPC remains one of Canada's larger business operations and a substantial presence in the communications market, but looms less large in a broader context. At the same time, conscious efforts have been made to remove postal matters from the political spotlight.

Postal scrutiny has been made marginal, for institutional reasons noted below. CPC's media strategy pushed postal matters onto the business pages. The merger of the postal unions made publicity-generating negotiations less frequent: CPC is in the spotlight at times of strikes or upheavals, but coverage of the 1991 negotiations indicated how the Post Office has lost its special place in the public imagination. The 1992 settlement and the announcement of CPC's 1991–92 corporate losses received little public and media attention. This has played to CPC's commercial advantage.

CPC's altered profile reflects the changed institutional setting in which it operates. The advent of the postal Crown accelerated the decline of politicians' postal influence and authority. Changes to the FAA make the government no longer directly responsible for postal finances; thus, there is no call for parliamentary scrutiny of the Post Office. The Conservative government stonewalled public and Opposition complaints about postal matters. The public resigned itself to the view that public pressure and reaction cannot influence postal policy. In conjunction with being shifted to the business pages, postal matters unfold in a low-key and nonpolitical way. These developments did not eliminate political influence on the Post Office; rather, they narrowed and focused the relationship between politics and the Post Office. Postal policy is shaped between the minister and the CPC president in a quiet way, behind the scenes, outside of the public and political spotlight.

These political developments coincided with the asymmetrical manner in which interests affect postal matters. The influence of the general public declined with the waning of parliamentary and politicians' influence. Ordinary citizens have little to no access to the arenas in which postal policy is shaped. Previously, the public responded as citizens to the POD as a public corporation. The public now interacts with a commercial Post Office as consumers. Public-service goals have been translated into commercial ones, and Canadians are said to have benefited from this development: with the postal deficit eliminated, taxpayers no longer subsidize the large-volume mail users. But the system is geared to the needs of those large-volume users; the small user reaps few benefits from the new postal technology and does not receive the discounts offered the major users.

The major mail users have been the major beneficiaries of the POD's transition to Crown corporation. The elimination of the deficit harmed them in the first instance, as the deficit was a taxpayers' subsidy to the mail system. However, they have benefited enormously from CPC's modernization efforts and its sophisticated mechanized system. The major users access the system under different conditions, receiving discounts for making their mail machine-readable and for pre-sorting it. Regular price increases have a far greater impact on the small business user and the general public than on the large-volume users. These uneven results reflect the capacity of the major users to organize and influence postal policy. Unlike smaller users and the general public, NAMMU has a close and permanent working relationship with Canada Post, a relationship uncluttered by governmental or public intrusions. The major mail users deal with CPC strictly on a commercial and private basis, and to positive effect. The "public interest" in postal matters is defined by CPC and its large customers.

Postal matters have traditionally reflected a balance between economic and social factors. The Post Office carried a substantial economic responsibility, aiding in the development of the Canadian economy by providing an efficient and expanding communications infrastructure. This "accumulation" function has been juggled with a "legitimation" function: the Post Office was assigned various social responsibilities, from assisting national integration and national unity to promoting literacy and Canadian culture and providing cheap mass communication. Since 1981, the balance has shifted primarily, if not exclusively, to the former function. CPC has been directed to strengthen Canada's communications infrastructure, to make Canadian companies more competitive in the globalized economy. The large mail users have been the major beneficiaries of this orientation, not surprisingly, as they exerted the most influence over the government and the corporation to this end. Since 1981, postal policy has fit an elite or Marxist model of the world to a greater extent than a pluralist or state-centred one. Nonbusiness pressure groups have had no access to the policy process and little influence on postal policy. Parliament and the state bureaucracy have, in turn, been distanced from the corporation, which has been strictly management run since the late 1980s.

Labour issues continue to loom large in the postal world, but the transition to a postal Crown has changed matters. First, the postal unions lost access to the political process and influence on postal policy because of the declining postal role of Parliament and politicians and the Post Office's diminished importance to Canadian life. Second, the predominance of commercial objectives made labour simply another factor of production, no longer accorded the special privileges in the operation of the corporation given to it in 1981. The transition to Crown-corporation form has not much changed bottom-line matters, as labour still feels it is negotiating with the government over postal policy. But it has no effective institutional access to this end. The unanticipated 1992 contract settlement — concluded outside of the arbitration process — may be a signal that the unions have resigned themselves to the commercial realities of the 1990s.

The asymmetry of postal influence and the elite-driven quality of postal policy reflected two enduring postal themes not affected by the transition to Crown corporation form. First, ideological circumstances continue to determine the character of postal policy. The Post Office has evolved through various stages of development, as the broad political orientations of governments steered postal policy in certain directions. For example, it followed nation-building directives in the late-nineteenth and early-twentieth centuries, even as deficits accumulated. The behaviour of the Post Office and the conditions of postal work changed during the Keynesian welfare-state period of the 1960s and early 1970s, as wages increased and the postal deficit soared. CPC's early days were marked by vacillation between commercial and public goals, which reflected the Liberals' political orientation in the early 1980s. The emergence of neoconservatism — suspicious of public goods and political interference in the market — reconceptualized the Post Office and transformed postal concepts and goals. Wages were to be cut, the deficit eliminated, services contained, and commercialization increased: these were the expectations that governed the corporation after 1984. The postal story might have been very different had CPC been created in the late 1960s, at a time of more buoyant economic conditions, a bountiful public treasury, and a different ideological regime.

Geography, competition, and technological change are continuing influences, but international pressures have taken on new significance. Despite changes in transportation and communication, Canada remains an immensely large and sprawling country with a small population base and bad weather conditions for much of the year. This continues to constrain postal speed and efficiency in a number of ways. The postal system has since 1981 been especially influenced by technological change, which has had enormous consequences for capital funding, profit maximization, shared market deals and possible takeovers, conditions of work, and labour relations. Moreover, it has made the corporation susceptible to competition both within its own markets and from complementary markets. The character of technological change, the intensity of competition, and the funding and financial aspects of these realities will continue to be central to the Canadian postal experience and the discourse surrounding it. Indeed, these persistent features — along with new international competition from foreign couriers and "trans-border mailing" — underpin the prevailing ideological context that shapes postal policy. They also constrain what might appear to be the next stage in the evolution of the Canadian postal system — privatization.

The Privatization Decision

Since 1985 the government and CPC have negotiated the degree of independence that the latter should enjoy. This process has not been antagonistic, inasmuch as both have a vested interest in CPC's commercial success. Nonetheless, governmental support of CPC's goals and efforts has not been without political cost. The government gives up some power each time it assigns CPC more autonomy; and it expends political capital whenever it defends CPC from public criticism or scrutiny. For these and other reasons, CPC has had to prove itself to the government, to earn each increase in its commercial autonomy. By the early 1990s, the government had assigned Canada Post substantial autonomy, basically because it approved of what

CPC had been doing. Hence, it defended CPC's purchase of Purolator Courier despite market scepticism about the wisdom of the takeover, although Michael Warren's plan eight years earlier to buy out a private courier company was rejected. Having strived for and now tasted this freedom, CPC has sought to defend and increase its autonomy. It resists the idea of public scrutiny of its activities and enters the public arena only grudgingly, when necessary (e.g., in the annual planning and parliamentary review processes).

Why, then, does CPC continue to be *Crown* corporation? Its Crown functions — the public purpose — have been largely eliminated; the Crown process — public scrutiny — has become increasingly perfunctory. Why didn't the Mulroney government privatize the postal system?

The question is particularly pressing given that government's predilection for privatization. Privatization was a central component of its neoconservative economic agenda. In October 1984, Sinclair Stevens announced the sale of the Canadian Development Investment Corporation, which took place in the summer of 1985. Privatization was made a priority in the 1985 budget, which set out working principles to this end. A Ministry of State for Privatization and Regulatory Affairs was created in June 1986 (with Barbara McDougall as first minister), and a cabinet committee and secretariat were established. In 1985, Canadian Arsenals and de Havilland were sold, as was Canadair in 1986. From 1984 to 1991, the government privatized or dissolved over twenty Crown corporations, reducing the number of employees by 80,000. Other privatizations included Teleglobe, Eldorado Nuclear, Air Canada, and PetroCanada.[2]

What of CPC? There was some evidence during the first term (1984–88) that it would be sold, a sort of "incremental" build-up of events. First, there was a "state-of-mind" privatization, beginning in 1985 with Lander's appointment and the construction of the 1986 corporate plan. Commercial values were introduced into CPC. As Lander characterized it in 1986:

> The operation of the Canada Post Corporation...in putting this particular entity into a corporation, is bringing about a form of...privatization...with the methodologies in which we are now approaching Canada Post, trying to bring in the values that are inherent in other corporations, I believe that this is a form of privatization in relationship to its responsibilities, its measurement of its assets, and its return on those investments...the corporation is evolving into a private, corporate-value entity...the cultural change [involved] is to a private corporation.[3]

This change was implemented by recruiting private-sector managers into senior positions, as well as by transforming the board of directors into an exclusively business-oriented entity.[4]

The second stage was "piece-meal" privatization. Formal privatization was not considered in constructing the 1986 plan. It was raised in cabinet but was never taken seriously, owing to CPC's poor reputation and its still-large deficit, which made a sale unlikely.[5] The 1986 corporate plan was an exclusively commercial one, pursuing policies that a private corporation would adopt in the circumstances. These policies had a piece-meal privatization quality to them. CPC franchised counter services and transformed rural post offices (the privatization of the retail network); it contracted out functions (delivery and sorting of parcels, equipment, and vehicle maintenance, cleaning, some payroll functions, computer services); it introduced a user-pay pricing system; and it devolved postal functions to the private sector (e.g., pre-sorting of mail). CPC was also released from many public-service functions, and allowed to act like a private corporation. Responsibility for the rural network was decreased; subsidies for "social" mail (e.g., second-class mail) were recategorized or cut, as were programs such as support for parcel shipment to the North; the centrality of home delivery was lessened; the physical presence of the post office in the community was all but terminated; any lingering responsibility for improving labour-management relations was eliminated; the level of wages and working conditions was to be driven by comparability with the private sector, whose downsizing efforts would also be imitated. These policy actions freed CPC to concentrate on its major mail users. Like any actor in the private sector, CPC gave these customers privileged treatment ranging from one-on-one arrangements outside the regulatory environment to partnerships with business through sponsorships and joint marketing deals.

These steps suggested that privatization was well on the way. The Opposition concluded that CPC wanted to make a profit, to ready itself for privatization ("fattened for sale"),[6] and the media began to rehearse the possibilities for a private postal system.[7] Up to 1988, in any event, the government poured cold water over the idea. In a clear response to questions about possible privatization, Barbara McDougall, minister of state (privatization), declared that such a move was unlikely:

> It would only take me three and a half minutes to decide not to, because it takes a buyer as well as a seller, and I would not have to go very far as I know there are not a lot of buyers....The only way anybody in the private sector...can afford to produce the quality of service is to increase the price; and you would have to pay somebody to take it off their hands for them to provide the service....As soon as you privatize it, the buyer is going to say this is unprofitable...and goodbye rural routes except at a dollar a letter.[8]

Traditional political and practical economic concerns persuaded the government not to privatize CPC at this time.

The momentum for privatizing CPC accelerated after the 1988 Conservative re-election. Guarded in the past, officials began to talk openly about privatization. Andre declared, "I have an open mind about privatization, especially if local and regional service was retained." "I'm not working on a proposal....But people are suggesting it."[9] Piece-meal privatization continued. In April 1989 CPC was re-scheduled under the FAA in April 1989 to become a Crown corporation financially independent of the government. The April 1989 budget determined that it should generate a level of profits comparable to those of a similar-sized corporation in its sector. CPC was directed to make a 14–15 per cent return on equity and to pay the government $300 million in dividends over the next five years. Finally, the government rejected the PSRC's recommendations concerning CPC's 1990 rate proposal. This ensured CPC would enjoy a loose, deregulated postal environment in which to pursue its commercial activities.

These political decisions appeared to indicate that privatization was imminent. The right-wing Fraser Institute organized a conference to address this matter, ("Canada Post Privatization: A Postal Reform Option?"), and Harvie Andre endorsed the idea in a keynote address.[10] He later revealed that consultants were studying the possibility of selling CPC to the private sector: "Given that the Post Office is making a profit, it's only logical to look at what would be the ramifications [of selling it]."[11] On the eve of the Turner committee's examination of the issue, Andre again declared his support for privatization, because "a private sector company is more efficient."[12] He pointed to the telephone industry as a modern, low-price, and universal private service:

> Should we look at this model in relation to postal services? What happens when a Crown corporation outgrows the conditions that made its establishment necessary? What happens when a Crown corporation can meet its responsibilities to provide the goods and services required to protect the public interest and, at the same time, through good management and growth in markets also can create an attractive investment opportunity in the private sector? Does the government have to be in the business of delivering the mail?

At the same time, he noted that "there is no government policy at this point to privatize Canada Post. And I have not asked the government to examine the question. That is why there is no formal involvement by the minister responsible for privatization."[13] The Turner committee recommended that "the government of Canada privatize Canada Post once adequate financial performance, comparable to private-sector levels, has been attained and once the industrial relations climate has been improved."[14] This was seen as paving the way for privatization.[15] Andre then predicted that

CPC could be sold in a few years: "If you put the arguments for and against on the scale...I suspect that they will probably point toward privatization."[16]

CPC quietly avoided pronouncements about privatization, a decision to be made by the government, not it. At the Fraser Institute conference, Lander warned that if the exclusive privilege was eliminated, the private corporation would have to be subsidized to provide postal service in rural and remote areas — or prices would have to rise to cover costs.[17] He later maintained that CPC was not ready for privatization:

> Canada Post is very young as a Crown corporation and is still evolving as a business [and] starting to understand the values of competition. [To] be attractive for privatization is going to require running the company satisfactorily from a service standpoint and making sure we are technologically keeping up to date. We would have to have some record of profit. These values are not there at the present time. I do not see any reason why Canada Post cannot move in that direction. I think it would take a number of years in the three- to five-year time frame.[18]

But CPC would follow the government's lead: "If the shareholders decided tomorrow that was the way we were going to go, we would do our very best to fulfil that direction."[19]

Despite Opposition claims to the contrary,[20] there were no immediate plans to sell CPC. Andre declared in 1990:

> It is still a possibility, although not a probability, in the near turn. I do not think the Post Office is ready, but the government has not made a decision not to privatize it....I am hopeful that if we continue the progress that we have been making, within a reasonable period of time, we will have enough experience and evidence and make the appropriate decision. We are not ready to make an absolute decision.[21]

In October 1991 there was no formal mechanism or process in place to consider the next step towards privatization.[22]

The government took another incremental step towards privatization in the spring of 1992, when it presented Bill C-73, its Employee Share Ownership Plan (an idea first floated in the 1989 budget). This plan allowed employees to purchase up to 10 per cent of the shares of CPC. Andre offered four reasons for the plan: it would improve labour-management co-operation and create a real "partnership" in CPC's efforts to increase its competitiveness. Increased co-operation would in turn accelerate adoption of new technologies. The plan would increase CPC's capacity to compete with firms that had similar plans (23 per cent of companies listed on the Toronto Stock Exchange had such a plan, and seemed to have a higher average rate of productivity). And given a stake in the corporation and its financial results, postal workers would improve service. Overall, the goal was to increase employees' level of co-operation by increasing their interest in CPC's competitiveness and profitability.[23] Andre insisted that this plan would not lead to privatization and that only CPC employees would be allowed to purchase shares. The Opposition and the unions saw it as a first step to privatization, and jeeringly pointed to the earlier promise that Air Canada would not be privatized. The unions complained that the plan side-stepped negotiations, gave workers no voting rights or access to decision-making, and internalized or locked in CPC's need to make profits (lest shares be sold).[24] The legislation was passed in the spring of 1993, and the Gallop firm was commissioned to survey CPC employees in preparation for the design of the program.

The government had transformed CPC into a *de facto* private firm by the early 1990s; why not *de jure* as well? There were three major reasons which prevented the government from taking this final, formal step.

First, there remains considerable doubt about CPC's capacity to function successfully as a private corporation. For example, the unsettled character of its labour-management relations has dampened the prospects of a private sale. For CPC has been unable to reach contract settlements with CUPW in a "normal" process. Until the extraordinary settlement in 1992 (stimulated by the prospect of endless arbitration), the government has been required to end strikes legislatively or to impose arbitration; and if CPC was privatized, this political option would no longer be available. Moreover, existing labour contracts scare off potential buyers, as a profitable postal operation would not be possible unless wages and conditions of work were rolled back to private-sector levels and made open to negotiation. The government might have to legislatively alter conditions of work or labour contracts before a buyer could be found — a daunting prospect. And enormous financial resources would be required to settle the thousands of outstanding grievances that plague labour-management relations.[25] On the business front, potential purchasers might not be willing to buy or operate the less profitable sections of the postal operation, outside of the dense urban markets. A private operator might insist that the unprofitable parts of the postal system be closed, or that prices in these sectors be substantially increased. A two-tier or even multi-tiered postal system would be unattractive to the government as well as the public, for a willing buyer would probably demand substantial subsidies to provide unprofitable services, and so the government would face a long-term fiscal commitment to a private postal system it did not control. Ironically, the longer CPC continues along its present path, the more difficult it will be to privatize it, for it is selling off more and more of its prime real estate and thereby making it less feasible to finance a purchase through asset-stripping. Moreover, franchising and contracting out have created a small-business interest content with the status quo.

Second, the large-volume users are not entirely enthusiastic about a private postal system. In fact, the Fraser Institute's conference on postal privatization revealed that big business was cool to the idea.[26] As NAMMU president Ralph Hancox put it:

> We see a decline in service, an increase in costs and chaos from deregulation and privatization. [For] most major users, "privatization" is not a real issue. No sane person sees the central management and control of a postal system passing from the Crown corporation's hands to that of commercial or private suppliers.[27]

NAMMU has not taken a clear-cut position, for its members, and their interests,[28] are heterogeneous. The lack of a clear, precise message from this crucial quarter has complicated policy matters. NAMMU defends the exclusive privilege, for without it "CPC could not provide an efficient, nationwide service. Fragmented suppliers would not be able to perform effectively for some categories of mail."[29] Private-sector observers like Alan Marchment anticipate that privatization would destroy the national and universal features of the postal system, which benefit all Canadians, including large-volume users. The public system's universality is most attractive and valuable to the latter. "NAMMU members for the most part are totally reliant on Canada Post for the conduct of their business....Canada Post has the only distribution network capable of handling hard copy exchange economically and reliably."[30] Periodical and magazine groups have experimented with their own private delivery networks, but these efforts failed to generate anywhere near the 100 per cent coverage CPC provides — even in small urban settings, only 72 per cent coverage was attained, and the cost of setting up the system was five times what was being paid to CPC. "Canada Post is our lifeline," claimed the Canadian Magazine Publishers Association; "without it we could not survive." And Maclean-Hunter reported:

> Our survey showed that, on the whole, Canada Post has been admirable with respect to the timing and accuracy of deliveries....The cost of delivering alternate delivery systems, even on a collective basis with other publishers, is likely prohibitive, given today's rate structure and because of the infrastructure needed to serve all Canadians....The magazine industry could not viably fulfil its national mandate through an alternate delivery system.[31]

The large-volume users do not want the system fragmented into a set of regional operations, or a set of public and private systems. This would complicate their lives and increase costs and operational problems. They also do not want to be held ransom to what might turn out to become private monopolies. They have been reasonably happy with CPC, which in their view has developed into a reliable and technologically sophisticated communications company. CPC's formal public character has become increasingly less relevant to the ways in which they deal with it. Relations have become less constrained by government or public regulations, allowing one-on-one postal arrangements outside of public scrutiny. CPC also offers advantages not matched by other communications companies: universal service, total delivery coverage, and a range of technological capacities. Even the one lingering weakness — CPC's poor record of generating labour contracts without government intervention — can be viewed positively: it has in practice neutralized the postal unions' strike weapon.

Third, at the moment privatization is not in the interests of either CPC or the government. The former presently enjoys the best of both worlds. Its (albeit limited) monopoly powers have been left unregulated to allow it to pursue a commercial course. When necessary, the government has come to its assistance and protected it. Private-sector reticence inhibited the Conservative government's enthusiasm for the idea, which was manifested in Harvie Andre's countless statements in this spirit.[32] The Chrétien government is even less likely to overcome private-sector doubts about privatization.

How would the government have realized this change? There may be willing buyers,[33] but there are various reasons why selling CPC would be awkward politically (some of them mentioned briefly above, as economic concerns). First is the issue of liability for the thousands of grievances presently in the pipeline. There might also be a buyer's request to do something about CUPW and the existing labour contracts. Both issues could generate an intense conflict with CUPW. Second, although the public-service dimension of the Post Office has been negated, the government would be required to establish some minimum conditions for the continued operation of a universal postal system. Privatization would have to involve the guarantee of universal service and something close to a universal pricing system that approximated the existing price level. This might require subsidizing the private company well into the future; but without these guarantees, there would likely be an enormous political backlash, as prices in outlying regions would probably skyrocket and there would be substantial price increases outside urban markets. As well, postal services might be terminated in parts of the country, making these areas open to exploitation by smaller, more expensive, and less reliable services. Third, the universality of the system would have to be guaranteed, lest the major users complain about system fragmentation. This would complicate the terms and conditions of a possible sale. Fourth, if the privatized CPC retained the exclusive privilege — or was held to service and price guarantees — it would have to be regulated by a third party. Given the PSRC experience, this would be very unattractive to a private CPC and to the government. Regulation would complicate CPC's life and would probably resurrect the issue of the social obligations of CPC and the government. It would also require the provision of detailed cost information, which the corporation is at present not capable of producing.

It is useful to consider the Teleglobe experience in this regard. Before being privatized, Teleglobe was a Crown corporation monopoly. It had been more or less left on its own and was essentially unregulated, because it had been doing a fairly good job in its own way. Once privatized, though, it faced tough rate-of-return regulation — precisely the sort of regulation it did not face as a Crown corporation. As Richard Schultz explains, privatization does not automatically result in diminished political interference or control. It changes the government-corporate relationship, and can actually increase public control over the privatized corporation.[34]

CPC's present situation is similar to that of pre-privatization Teleglobe. As a Crown corporation with certain monopoly powers, it is ostensibly controlled by the government; but, it is more or less unregulated and left alone to follow its commercial and competitive way. From CPC's perspective, privatization would actually be threatening — as formal, third-party regulation would be sure to follow. From the Conservative government's perspective, regulation was an unattractive idea. It was not keen on regulating a corporation that functions in a mercurial and highly competitive market; indeed, regulation would probably be ineffective in such a market. Further, any government would have little interest in expanding a regulatory net to include the privatized CPC's market competitors, such as parcel, couriers, and telecommunications companies. In any case, the benefits of regulation would in such conditions be unlikely to flow to CPC. The Liberal government will confront similar considerations, but in any case seems unlikely to give privatization serious consideration.

In the early 1990s the postal situation seemed to be relatively stable politically. The government and the corporation were mutually supportive, and shared coinciding interests in and visions of existing postal operations and the system's medium-term prospects. Longer-term prospects are more perplexing. The Conservative government was uncertain about the next step in CPC's institutional evolution, waiting to see how CPC developed before taking this decision.[35] In the interim, it supported CPC's efforts and protected it from interference and criticism. The recent change in government will likely disturb this stable equilibrium, but it will not necessarily destroy it. The incoming government will find its options relatively limited, no matter how critical it has been of postal policies and CPC's behaviour. It might attempt to re-inject a sense of public purpose into CPC and to reject profit maximization as the top priority. It might direct CPC to re-open a number of rural post offices and expand door-to-door delivery in new suburban areas — along the lines of the PSRC recommendations. CPC would probably be able to live with these limited changes, if they had moderate financial consequences.

Nonetheless, these modest policy changes — or more dramatic ones — could generate a number of possibly distasteful scenarios. First, senior management might defect from CPC, if they took policy changes as the first step in a reversion to the old-style Post Office, with serious short-term consequences for CPC's business. Second, these actions might create a business crisis of confidence or, at the least, a bad corporate image, resulting in loss of business, decline in volumes, and deterioration in CPC's finances. Third, these government initiatives could resurrect the idea of the Post Office as a public service and re-open the political debate on its function, which would increase public expectations about postal matters and place both the government and CPC in an awkward position. Fourth, all these considerations would raise a fiscal question for the newly elected government. If business volumes declined and a deficit developed, or if the expansion of postal services was targeted and financed by specific public subsidies, or if an avalanche of service requests increased postal costs in a substantial way, then the government would be faced with a large postal bill. Given likely budgetary restraints over the medium term, the government would have to decide whether to devote scarce fiscal resources to the postal system rather than to other policy priorities. It is extremely unlikely that the incoming government will rate postal matters as a high priority, especially given the public's shrinking postal expectations over the last decade. A new government will at most probably initiate token or symbolic changes. It will also confront a highly competitive and technologically changing communications market, in which it will have limited capacity to make effective postal policy.

The foregoing speculation suggests how the Crowning of the Post Office has successfully placed postal matters on a nonpolitical, commercial footing. This experience has transformed the public discourse on, and vision of, postal matters. Under present conditions, CPC's plans or behaviour cannot be questioned to any great effect — without framing the question in economic or business terms. The new government's postal initiatives will be scrutinized and evaluated primarily from a business or commercial perspective. Canada Post is another example of how the public sector and the sense of public purpose have been transformed in the neoconservative era. From the privatization, rationalization, and elimination of air, rail, cultural, and other communication activities to the privatizing and deregulation of large sectors of the economy, the Conservative government reduced the public presence in social and political life and replaced it with commercial processes, values, and visions. The commercialization of Canada Post has been part of this larger process, and postal discourse has changed accordingly.

Some critics of Canada Post advocate a re-introduction of a sense of public purpose within the postal system. This prospect has become doubtful, as any such attempt would confront the hyper-commercial value system that now encloses the Post Office. The resurrection of a more public approach to postal matters could, however, unfold in a number of ways. The Canada

Post Corporation Act could be revisited, to fill the social lacunae left in 1981 and to make public criteria and goals more precise. Public expectations about postal services and other matters could then be specified in a concrete way. This would generate the various political scenarios noted above, as would the reintroduction of third-party regulation. A more radical approach would be to consider privatization of Canada Post, which would remove CPC from the government's protection, to be regulated by a third party. This would require CPC to conform with some standards of public purpose and performance, as defined by the regulatory legislation. At the moment, CPC is regulated partly via competition and partly by the government's sense of what a commercial Post Office should be doing, neither of which guarantees any articulation of the public purpose.

Each of these scenarios illustrates how the exercise of neoconservatism has changed Canadians' policy ideas and expectations, including their views on postal matters. Postal policy and the postal public good have been defined primarily by the large-volume users and postal managers; Canadians have not had much of a say in these matters. There are many postal matters of concern to rural residents, small business people, suburban home-owners, postal workers, CPC competitors, and the general public that are not attended to in this state of affairs. These postal matters continue to be addressed as commercial or consumer concerns, not public ones. However, as a result of the postal experience of the last decade, many Canadians may now have views not dramatically different from those of NAMMU and Donald Lander. They may no longer consider the Post Office to be a public service or the mail to be a public good. They may be willing to accept higher prices in return for fuller postal services. Or, given the choice, they might chose a smaller and leaner public Post Office — perhaps supported by public funds — with the commercial arms of the operation (such as admail) provided by private firms. The experience of the last decade may have "commercialized" their views and expectations of postal matters, and they might now be willing to let the market provide postal and other communications services. This very uncertainty is a good reason to consider all possible ways of opening up postal policy to fuller public discussion. Privatization with third-party regulation could also be considered in this regard. Consideration of this strategy would encourage a fuller public debate about the postal system — a debate presently discouraged by the institutional arrangements within which Canada Post operates.

Postal experience since 1981 has demonstrated that a Crown corporation can embrace commercial values and behave like a private-sector corporation — if encouraged and supported by the government. What remains unclear, and perhaps unlikely, is whether a balance can be struck between the postal Crown's commercial values and broader public or social goals. Any attempt to achieve this balance would require political patience and a willingness to tolerate both the perpetual tension between social and economic goals and the likely economic consequences of this juggling act. However, unless this sense of broader public purpose is injected into Canada Post, there seems to be little reason for its continued existence as a Crown corporation.

TABLES

TABLE 1 - POSTAL VOLUMES
(billions of units by class of mail)

Year Ending	First (1)	First (2)	Second (a) (1)	Third (b) (1)	(a+b) (1)	Fourth (1)	Fourth (1)	Total (1)	Total (2)
1948	1.22		.52			.65	.051	2.44	
1949	1.34	10.4	.59			.72	.056	2.71	11.1
1950	1.37	1.9	.53			.83	.063	2.79	2.9
1951	1.46	7	.49			.88	.061	2.89	3.6
1952	1.48	1.4	.51			.87	.069	2.92	.86
1953	1.59	7.9	.47			.88	.066	3.02	3.4
1954	1.65	3.2	.49			.92	.068	3.13	3.6
1955	1.69	3.2	.52			.96	.07	3.24	3.5
1956	1.75	3.6	.53			.99	.072	3.35	2.8
1957	1.86	5.9	.51			1.09	.076	3.53	5.4
1958	1.99	7.	.52			1.19	.079	3.77	6.8
1959	2.02	1.5	.53			1.23	.089	3.87	2.7
1960	2.13	5.7	.54			1.29	.089	4.04	4.4
1961	2.23	4.9	.53			1.34	.091	4.19	3.7
1962	2.18	-2.2	.59			1.31	.088	4.17	-0.5
1963	2.3	5.3	.56			1.39	.088	4.33	3.8
1964	2.35	2.3	.58			1.46	.091	4.49	3.7
1965	2.5	6.1	.61			1.55	.091	4.75	5.8
1966	2.56	3.2	.62			1.36	.095	4.66	-1.9
1967	2.69	4.5	.68			1.41	.098	4.88	4.7
1968	2.79	3.5	.69			1.38	.096	4.96	1.6
1969	2.53	-9.1	.67			1.38	.085	4.96	
1970	2.70	7	.52			1.21	.080	4.82	-2.8
1971	2.72	0.6	.51			.94	.074	4.56	-5.4
1972	2.7	-0.8	.49			1.15	.082	4.71	3.3
1973	3.14	16.4	.44			1.09	.088	4.75	0.8
1974	3.35	6.6	.45			1.14	.076	5.07	6.7
1975	3.5	4.7	.45			1.22	.073	5.31	4.7
1976	3.24	-7.4	.43			1.14	.062	4.94	-6.9
1977	3.69	13.7	.46			1.52	.066	5.80	17.4
1978	3.61	-2.1	.48			1.74	.066	5.96	2.8
1979	3.73	3.2	.49			1.71	.062	6.06	1.7
1980	3.91	4.9	.50	.80	1.08	1.88	.056	6.41	5.8
1981	3.85	-1.6	.52	.84	1.17	2.01	.054	6.52	1.4
1982	3.48	-9.5	.49	.73	1.22	1.95	.048	6.11	-6.3
1983	3.98	15.0	.52	.66	1.31	1.97	.045	6.61	8.2
1984	3.96	-0.7	.54	.64	1.59	2.23	.045	6.86	3.8
1985	3.97	0.4	.55	.63	2.01	2.64	*.090	7.31	6.6
1986	4.21	6.1	.57	.66	2.09	2.75	.101	7.7	5.4
1987	4.36	3.5	.59	.74	2.08	2.82	.103	7.94	3.1

1988	4.37	0.1	.59	.89	1.81	2.70	.093	7.81	-1.6
1989	4.47	2.3	.58	1.02	2.05	3.07	.090	8.27	5.9
1990	4.58	2.4	.61	1.10	2.64	3.74	.103	9.12	10.3
1991	4.61	0.5	.59	1.17	3.1	4.27	.106	9.66	5.9
1992	4.46	-3.2	.55	1.21	3.56	4.77	.107	9.96	3.1
1993	-0.3				1.29		10.41	4.5	

(1) Number of units (billions)
(2) % change from previous year
(a) addressed (b) unaddressed

*Data series changes

*PostalVolumes 1989-93

	Communications		Advertising		Physical		Total	
	(1)	(2)	(1)	(2)	(1)	(2)	(1)	(2)
1989	4.5	3.6	.141	8.27	5.9			
1990	4.63	2.8	4.3	19.4	.156	10.6	9.12	10.3
1991	4.66	0.6	4.8	11.6	.165	7.1	9.66	5.9
1992	4.49	-3.4	5.29	10.4	.175	6.1	9.96	3.1
1993	4.49	-0.3	5.74	8.5	.180	2.9	10.41	4.5

SOURCE: Postmaster General and Canada Post Corporation, *Annual Reports*

TABLE 2: POSTAL REVENUES
(Millions of dollars by class of mail)

Year Ending	First		Second	Third (a)	(b)	(a+b)	Fourth	Total	
	(1)	(2)	(1)	(1)	(1)	(1)	(1)	(1)	(2)
1968	161.2		9.7				57.5	337	
1969	175.2	8.5	9.8				65.3	375	11.3
1970	213.7	22	14.5				69.2	441	17.6
1971	215.3	0.7	13.8				73.7	433	-1.8
1972	247.2	15	14.2				89.4	504	16.4
1973	321.8	30.2	14.9				101.9	563	11.7
1974	349.5	8.6	15				89.5	591	4.97
1975	358.6	2.6	15				88	617	4.4
1976	338.8	-5.6	15.3				76.4	568	-7.9
1977	454.7	34.2	19.3				97.2	775	36.4
1978	563.3	23.9	22.7				103	946	22.1
1979	659.7	17.1	29				118.5	1108	17.1
1980	834.2	26.5	125.9**	149	55	204	116.4	1483	33.8
1981	820.1	-1.6	134.9	156	59	215	116.8	1530	3.2
1982	880.5	7.3		164	66	230	116.2	1670	9.2
1983	1374	56	269	132	88	220	116	2258	35.1
1984	1477	7.5	275	139	110	249	126	2400	6.3
1985	1504	1.8	278	104	134	238	*217	2500	4.2
1986	1527	10.3	282	123	145	268	270	2758	9.1
1987	1648	7.7	282	129	151	280	301	2970	7.7
1988	1762	5.7	296	183	139	322	296	3139	5.7
1989	1895	8.7	298	218	165	383	324	3411	8.7
1990	1985	5.0	315	246	175	421	365	3580	5
1991	2041	2.8	299	268	187	455	404	3739	4.4
1992	1980	-3.0	307	312	204	516	425	3804	1.7
1993				341	211	552		3909	2.8

(1) revenue (millions)
(2) % change
(a) addressed third class
(b) unaddressed third class

* data series changed
** includes revenue received from Department of Communications

(Millions of dollars)

	Communications		Advertising		Physical		Other	Total	
	(1)	(2)	(1)	(2)	(1)	(2)	(1)	(1)	(2)
1989	1980	678	496	257	3411	8.7			
1990	2087	5.4	711	4.9	547	10.3	235	3580	5.0
1991	2138	2.4	719	1.1	620	13.3	262	3739	4.4
1992	2077	-2.9	768	7.1	673	8.5	286	3804	1.7
1993	2130	2.6	777	0.4	694	2.8	308	3909	2.8

SOURCE: Postmaster General and Canada Post Corporation, Annual Reports

TABLE 3: POSTAL BUDGET BALANCE
(millions of dollars)

Year Ending	Revenues	Expenditures	Balance	(as %Revenues)	Net Income
1946	68	57	11	16	
1947	72.9	64.2	8.8	12	
1948	91.6	81.8	9.8	10.7	
1949	95.9	92.9	2.9	3.1	
1950	101.3	99.4	1.9	2.0	
1951	105.6	106.9	-1.3	-1.2	
1952	122.3	115.6	6.7	5.5	
1953	129.4	122.9	6.5	5.0	
1954	129.9	132.3	-2.5	-1.9	
1955	151.7	144.0	7.7	5.1	
1956	158.7	148.3	10.3	6.5	
1957	167.9	162.0	5.8	3.5	
1958	177.5	177.9	-0.4	-0.2	
1959	183.4	183.6	-0.2	-0.1	
1960	193.7	191.8	1.8	1.0	
1961	202	206.7	-4.7	-2.3	
1962	213.6	214.8	-1.3	-0.6	
1963	222.4	218.8	3.5	1.5	
1964	235.9	241.9	-6.1	-2.6	
1965	263.8	243.7	20.0	7.6	
1966	276	278.8	-2.8	-1.0	
1967	295.5	310.5	-15.0	-5.1	
1968	327.2	347.3	-20.1	-6.1	

new accounting scheme

Year Ending	Revenues	Expenditures	Balance	(as %Revenues)	Net Income
1964	239.7	277.2	-37.5	-15.6	
1965	268	279.6	-11.5	-4.3	
1966	285.1	315.8	-30.7	-10.8	
1967	305.4	353.2	-47.8	-15.7	
1968	337.6	404.2	-67.2	-20.0	
1969	374.9	463.1	-88.2	-23.5	
1970	444.1	497	-52.9	-11.9	
1971	432.9	533.5	-100.6	-23.0	
1972	504.7	581.2	-77	-15.3	
1973	563.1	654.1	-91	-16.2	
1974	591	768	-177	-30	
1975	617.7	938.7	-321	-51.9	
1976	568.2	1114	-546	-96.1	
1977	775	1353	-579	-74.7	
1978	946	1505	-559	-59	

1979	1109	1594	-485	-43.7	
1980*	1483	1762.7	-279.5	-18.8	
1981	1529.8	2017	-487	-31.8	

as Crown Corporation

1982	1669.7	1984.7	-315	-18.9	
1983	2258	2549	-291	-12.9	
1984	2400	2700	-300	-12.5	
1985	2500	2895	-395	-15.8	
1986	2758	2968	-210	-7.6	
1987	2970	3099	-129	-4.4	-129
1988	3139	3169	-30	-1.0	-38
1989	3411	3313	98	2.9	96
1990	3580	3473	107	3.0	149
1991	3739	3664	74.8	2.0	14
1992	3804	3905	-101	-2.7	-128
1993	3909	3827	82	2.1	26

* includes imputed difference of costs over revenues, with regard to Secretary of State publication subsidy received

SOURCE: Post Office Department, Canada Post Corporation, *Annual Reports*

Year Ending	(1)	(2)	(3)	(4)	(5)	(6)	(7)	(8)	(9)
1860					36				
1890					46				
1914					56				
1939					61				
1945					52				
1949			42,000						
1954					61				
1957	35,000								
1960					64				
1964			42,000						
1965					67	11.2			
1968			48,376			45.5			
1970			47,599		60	13.2			
1973			52,207			7.4	17.1		
1974			55,421			176.6	17.3		
1975			60,208		70	788.7	20.8		
1976	50,779	12,862	63,641			5.5	18.1		
1977	52,538	12,224	64,762			13.7	18.2		
1979	53,053	9200	62,253		75	158.4	19.6		
1980	58,819	3607	62,426		76	1.8	19.1		
1981	53,465	9112	62,577		75.4	5.3	18.8	203	41
1982	56,080	7420	63,500			662.2	18.8	209	41
1983	54,407	9131	63,530	130.7	73.2	.2	18.4	213	42
1984	54,372	9031	63,403	132.3	73.2	1.6	19.1	218	43
1985	54,009	8946	62,955	134.4	73.2	5.7	17.9	227	44
1986	52,345	9027	61,372	132.9	74.4	51.9	16.3	233	45
1987	52,760	8880	61,640	131.2	72.3	9.4	15.5	240	47
1988	53,093	9089	62,182	132.2	71.6	1394	14.7	250	47
1989	52,193	8945	61,138	132.1	70.1	253	13.7	270	48
1990	50,522	9802	60,324	130.9	70	2.8	12.5	285	48
1991	*49,046	10114	*59,160	127.8	68	0.2	13.1	302	50
1992	*46,661	10574	*57,240	121.8		1357		320	52
1993	*44,683	10731	*55,414	118.4				334	54

(1) Full Time Employees
(2) Part Time Employees
(3) Total Employees
(4) Total Hours Paid (millions)
(5) Labour expenses as % of total postal expenditures
(6) Work Stoppages: to 1982-3 - person days lost (thousands) after-hours lost (thousands)
(7) Absenteeism - days per year
(8) Pieces of mail processed per hour paid (rounded)
(9) points of call per hour paid (rounded)

* The data series changed regularly in this area, particularly with regard to (1)-(3) and (8)-(9), so that estimates have been made. The 1991 to 1993 employment statistics are from the 1992-3 annual report, which lists full-time employment in 1989 as 54,731 and 52,839 in 1990.

SOURCES: Postmaster General and Canada Post Corporation, *Annual Reports*; Canada Post Corporation, *Corporate Plans*

TABLE 5: POSTAL PRICES

	First Class		Local	Air Mail
pre-1851	18¢ per 1/2 ounce (average)			
1851	5¢ per 1/2 ounce (uniform)			
1868	3¢ per 1/2 ounce		1¢	
1889	3¢ per ounce		1¢	
1899	2¢			
1915	*	3¢	2¢	
1926		2¢		
1928		5¢		
1931	*	3¢	6¢	
1943	*	4¢	3¢	7¢
1951	**	4¢	3¢	7¢
1954		5¢	4¢	
1968		6¢	***	***
1971		7¢		
1972		8¢		
1976		10¢		
1977		12¢		
1978		14¢		
1979		17¢ per 500 grams		
1982		30¢		
1983		32¢		
1985		34¢		
1987		36¢		
1987		37¢		
1988		38¢		
1989		39¢		
1990		40¢		
1991		41¢ (plus GST)		
1992		42¢		
1993		43¢		

*   War Tax of 1¢ added
**   War Tax Corporated
***   local and air mail rates abolished

Year	Number
1817	25
1828	151
1851	601
1861	1775
1867	2333
1871	3943
1875	3054
1881	5935
1891	8061
1901	9834
1911	13,324
1913	*14,178
1921	12,252
1931	12,427
1941	12,477
1951	12,305
1961	11,421
1971	9000
1981	8275

* peak number of post offices
SOURCE: Post Office Department, *Annual Reports*; I.Lee;

TABLE 7: POINTS OF CALL

	(1)	(2)
1912		900
1944-5	2.3	
1947		4887
1957-8	3.7	5476
1960-1	4.1	5600
1966-7	4.9	5561
1977-8	7.5	4991
1981		5024
1985-6	10	
1988-9	11	
1992-3	12	
1997-8	*13.2	

(1) points of call (millions)
(2) rural routes

* estimate from 1993-4 to 1997-8 Corporate Plan
SOURCE: Post Master General and Canada Post Corporation, *Annual Reports*

TABLE 8: POSTAL SUBSIDIES *
(millions of dollars)

1981-2	*87
1982-3	220
1983-4	223
1984-5	226
1985-6	225
1986-7	254
1987-8	252
1988-9	251
1989-90	239.6
1990-1	203.6
1991-2	183.3
1992-3	147.98

* Payments by the government on behalf of postal users, including publications mail, government free mail, literature for the blind, and Northern air stage services.

Source: Canada Post Corporation, *Annual Reports*

TABLE 9: COMMUNICATIONS COMPETITORS

revenue in millions (% change)

	Data Communications Market*	New Information Industry	Postal System Total	First Class
1947		300	775	
1985	356	2100 (700)	2500 (220)	1504
1989	1086 (198)		3411 (36)	1895(26)

*includes Public Data Networks, Enhanced Services, E-mail, Fax

Telephone

	(1)	(2)	(3)	(4)
1939	32			
1949	105	1342	.078	
1959	205 (95)	2035 (50)	.102	1.9
1969	434 (112)	2532 (26)	.17	4.3
1979	121 (179)	3725 (47)	.325	3.8
1989	2847 (135)	4471 (20)	.64	6.8
1949-89	(2611)	(233)		11.2

(1) millions of long distance calls (% change over decade)
(2) millions pieces of first class mail (% change over decade)
(3) ratio — telephone calls: letters
(4) ratio — % change calls: % change letters

SOURCE: Canada Post Corporation, *Annual Reports*; Statistics Canada, *Telephone Statistics*

	(1)	(2)	(3)	(4)	(5)	(6)	(7)
1851-61	33	*341					
1861-71	14	*475					
1851-71	51	*2435					
1871-81	17			67		83(80)	
1881-91	12	95		87			
1891-1901	11	77		36			
1871-1901	55			325		71(00)	
1881-91		244					
1901-11	34	152		167			
1911-21	22			188			
1921-31	18			16			
1901-31	93			789	.55(30)	48(30)	
1931-41	11		72	33	.47(41)		
1941-51	22		161	161			
1931-51	35		348	247	.47(51)		
1951-61	15	20	48	50		37(55)	
1956-61	13	28	24	27	.49(61)	28(61)	1.2(61)
1961-66	10	15	58	37			
1966-71	8	6	51	51		26(69)	1.6(71)
1971-76	7	19	103	31	.45(71)	22(74)	
1976-81	6	19	80	169	.43(81)	19(81)	2.8(81)
1951-81	74	163	1498	+253			
1981-86	4	10	42	80			2.9(86)
1986-89	3	6	29	24	.52(89)		3.7(90)
1981-89	8	16	83	123			

*Quebec/Ontario
+1971-81
(1) % change population
(2) % increase first class mail
(3) % increase GDP
(4) % increase mail revenue
(5) mail revenue as % GDP (actual year end)
(6) mail revenue as % communications revenue (actual year end)
(7) communications as % of GDP

Source:Postmaster General and Canada Post Corporation; *Annual Reports*; Statistics Canada, *Historical Statistics of Canada*, assorted years; Lee, 474ff.

TABLE 11: EARLY POSTAL STATISTICS

	(1)	(2)	(3)	(4)	(5)	(6)	(7)
1827	*19						
1834	103						
1840	405		1.4				
1851	601		2.1				
1861	1775		9.4		.7	.67	4
1867			14				
1869							14
1871	3943	30,039	27	22	1.08	1.27	51
1879							57
1881					1.35	1.88	39
1893	23						

(1) number of post offices
(2) number of miles of routes
(3) letters and cards (millions)
(4) newspapers (millions)
(5) revenues (millions of dollars)
(6) expenditures (millions of dollars)
(7) deficit as % of revenues

* Canadas

SOURCE: Postmaster General, *Annual Report*

NOTES

Notes to the Preface

1   For example, see E. Batstone (et al), *Consent and Efficiency* (Oxford: Basil Blackwell, 1984); K. Conkey, *The Postal Precipice: Can the U.S. Postal Service be Saved?* (Washington: Centre for the Study of Responsive Law, 1983); M.E. Corby, *The Postal Business: A Study in Public Sector Management* (1979); M.J. Daunton, *Royal Mail: The Post Office Since 1849* (London: Athlone Press, 1985); J.L Fleischman (ed), *The Future of the Postal Service* (New York: Praeger, 1983); W.E. Fuller, *The American Mail: Enlarger of the Common Life* (Chicago: University of Chicago Press, 1972); R.J Myers, *The Coming Collapse of the Post Office* (Englewood Cliffs: Prentice-Hall, 1975); I. Senor, *Liberating the Letter: A Proposal to Privatize the Post Office* (London: Institute for Economic Affairs, 1983); R. Sherman (ed), *Perspectives on Postal Services Issues* (Washington: American Enterprise Institute, 1980); J.L. Tierney, *Postal Reorganization* (Boston: Auburn House, 1981); S. Wall and P. Nicholson, *Posts and Telecommunications* (Oxford: Pergammon Press, 1986).

2   David Stewart-Patterson, *Post-Mortem: Why Canada's Mail Won't Move* (Toronto: Macmillan, 1987), is a journalist's view of Canada's postal problems.

L.M. Read, *The Intelligent Citizen's Guide to the Postal Problem* (Ottawa: Carleton University Press, 1988) is an idiosyncratic study, suggesting that the postal malaise reflects the crisis of modernity and the influence of Marxism.

Julie White, *Mail and Female: Women and the Canadian Union of Postal Workers* (Toronto: Thompson Educational Publishing, 1990) analyses women's roles in the post office and CUPW's record in promting women's interests.

Douglas Adie, *The Mail Monopoly: Analysing Canadian Postal Service* (Vancouver: The Fraser Institute, 1990) is a neoconservative study of the post office, written by an expert on the American postal scene.

See also two recent doctoral dissertations, I. Lee, *The Canadian Postal System: Origins, Growth and Decay of the State Postal Function, 1765-1981* (Carleton University, 1989) and T. Langford, *Workers' Attitudes and Bourgeois Hegemony: Investigation of the Political Consciousness of Workers in the 1980s* (McMaster University, 1989).

3   The most interesting and useful studies include: A. Tupper and G.B. Doern (eds), *Privatization, Public Policy and Public Corporations in Canada* (Halifax: The Institute for Research on Public Policy, 1988) and *Public Corporations and Public Policy in Canada* (Montreal: The Institute for Research on Public Policy, 1981); H. Hardin, *The Privatization Putsch* (Halifax: The Institute for Research on Public Policy, 1989) and *A Nation Unaware: The Canadian Economic Culture* (Vancouver: J.J. Douglas Ltd., 1974); J.K Laux and M.A. Molot, *State Capitalism: Public Enterprise in Canada* (Ithaca:

Cornell University Press, 1988); J.R.S. Prichard (ed), *Crown Corporations in Canada* (Toronto: Butterworth's, 1983); W. Stewart, *Uneasy Lies the Head: The Truth About Canada's Crown Corporations* (Don Mills: Collins, 1987); Economic Council of Canada, *Minding the Public's Business* (Ottawa, 1986).

4   The few publications available included A.W. Currie, "The Post Office Since 1867", *Canadian Journal of Economics*, May 1958; J. Davidson and J. Deverell, *Joe Davidson* (Toronto: Lorimer, 1978); B. Laidlaw and B. Curtis, "Inside Postal Workers: The Labour Process, State Policy and the Workers' Response", *Labour/Le Travail*, Fall 1986; G.S. Lowe and H.C. Northcott, *Under Pressure: A Study of Job Stress* (Toronto: Garamond Press, 1986); David MacFarlane, "Moving the Mail", *Saturday Night*, July 1982; B. Osborne and R.M. Pike, "Lowering 'The Walls of Oblivion': The Revolution in Postal Communications in Central Canada, 1851-1911", in D. Akenson (ed), *Canadian Papers in Rural History*, Vol. IV (Ganonoque: Langdale Press, 1984); B. Osborne, "The Canadian National Postal System, 1852-1914", in R. Berry and J. Acheson (eds), *Regionalism and National Identity* (Christchurch: University of Canterbury Press, 1985); W. Smith, *The History of the Post Office in British North America, 1639-1870* (Cambridge University Press, 1920); "Jean-Claude Parrot: An Interview", *Studies in Political Economy*, Summer 1983; P. Vadeboncoeur, *366 Days and as Long as it Takes: Long Live the Lapalme Guys* (Montreal, 1971); M. Wolfe, "The Perennial Canadian Postal Crisis", *Saturday Night*, April 1976.

A number of dissertations had been written, including A. Gonnsen, *Labour Conflict in the Canadian Post Office* (State University of New York at Buffalo: PhD, 1981); B. Leimsner, *The Labour Process and Worker Resistance: A Survey of the Degradation of Work in the Canadian Post Office* (Carleton University, M.A., 1983); P. Noble, *The Post Office and Postal Communication in Canada, 1763-1914* (Queen's University, M.A., 1978); S. Reynolds, *The Struggle Continues: An Analysis of Conflict in the Canadian Post Office* (McMaster University, M.A., 1981).

The best source of information on the Post Office was in Royal Commission and other governmental studies and reports.

5   G. Stevenson, *The Politics of Canada's Airlines* (Toronto: University of Toronto Press, 1987).

J. Lanford's article "Public Administration in the 1980s: moving from rhetoric to analysis", *Canadian Public Administration*, 25/4, Winter 1984 was particularly important.

Notes to introduction

1.   J. Langford, "Public Corporations in the 1980s: Moving from Rhetoric to Analysis," *Canadian Public Administration*, 25, no.4 (1982).

2.   See in particular the articles in A. Tupper & G.B. Doern, eds., *Privitization, Public Policy and Public Corporations in Canada* (Halifax: The Institute for Research on Public Policy, 1988); G. Stevenson, *The Politics of Canada's Airlines* (Toronto: University of Toronto Press, 1987); and J.K. Laux & M.A. Molot, *State Capitalism: Public Enterprise in Canada* (Ithaca: Cornell University Press, 1988).

3. G. Stevenson, "Canadian National Railways and VIA Rail" in Tupper and Doern, p. 45.

4. See A.W. Currie, "The Post Office since 1987," *Canadian Journal of Economics*, May (1958); Ian Lee, "The Canadian Postal System: Origins, Growth and Decay of the State Postal Function, 1765-1981" (Ottawa: Ph.D. Diss., Carleton University, 1989); B. Osborne, "The Canadian National Postal System, 1852-1914" in R. Berry & J. Acheson, eds., *Regionalism and National Identity* (Christchurch: University of Canterbury, 1985); B. Osborne & R. Pike, "Lowering 'the Walls of Oblivion': The Revolution in Postal Communication in Central Canada, 1851-1911" in D. Akenson, ed., *Canadian Papers in Rural History*, vol. 4 (Gananoque, Ontario: Langdale Press, 1984); W. Smith, *The History of the Post Office in British North America, 1639-1870* (Cambridge: Cambridge University Press, 1920). See also Canada Post Corporation, *The History of Canada Post* (Ottawa: CPC, Public Relations Branch, 1981); B. Brown, *The History of Canada Post* (Part of a submission to the Canadian Labour Relations Board) (Ottawa: CPC, Corporate Communications, 1938); R.W. Rapley, *Canada Post Office: A Chronology of Change* (Ottawa: CPC, 1984).

5. Derived from Table 7 and census figures. There were 9,834 post offices in 1901, and Canada's population was 5.4 million. In 1861, there were 1,820 people per post office, a figure that was halved after Confederation to 938 in 1871, and that continued to fall through the remainder of the century: to 595 in 1891, and 549 in 1901. The figure increased thereafter, to 554 in 1911, 718 in 1921, and so on. By 1971, the figure was 2,400 people per post office. If one includes all retail outlets, there were 17,200 outlets in 1990, and a population of 26.7 million for an average of 1552 people.

6. See Canada Post Corporation, *Report*, 1990-91, 1991-92; and *Globe and Mail*, Report on Business Magazine, July 1992. To place these figures and Canada Post's size in perspective, one can note the following. With respect to employment, only BCE (124,000), Camdev (110,000), Imasco (86,863), and CP (78,200) are larger. With respect to revenues, the total revenue of the top eleven hospitality service companies — from McDonald's and Cara through Hilton and St. Hubert — is $3.1 billion, less than Canada Post's $3.8 billion; the thirteen top broadcasting and cable companies generated $3.8 billion in revenues. With respect to assets, Canada Post's level of assets of $2.7 billion is similar to Chrysler ($2.8 billion), Loblaws ($2.4 billion), Abitibi Price and Macmillan Bloedel ($2.8 billion each), and Canadian Airlines ($2.6 billion).

7. In the first year of Canada Post's existence, its president was receiving more mail than the Prime Minister, over five thousand letters a month (Interview with Michael Warren, 9 November 1989). See also David Stewart-Patterson, *Post-Mortem: Why Canada's Mail Won't Move* (Toronto: Macmillan, 1987), p. 227.

8. Canada Post recently chopped the system of categorizing mail into various classes, which was thought to imply — mistakenly — different degrees of quality of service. First-class mail is now called letter mail, second-class mail publications mail, third-class mail ad mail, and fourth-class mail has become parcel mail.

9. The Québec government's Allaire report on the Constitution proposed that postal matters become a shared jurisdiction. This suggestion has not been embraced by the

other provinces and has generated no public or media discussion. Ironically, the provinces ran their own postal service between 1851 and 1867.

10. Canada Post Corporation, *Report*, 1990-91, 1991-92.

11. Canada Post's recent efforts to cut labour costs caused this figure to decline to 68 per cent in 1990-91. The intention is to deflate the proportion towards 50 per cent; see Table 5.

12. For a broad overview of these changes, see Robert Campbell, *Grand Illusions: The Politics of the Keynesian Experience in Canada, 1945-1975* (Peterborough: Broadview Press, 1987) and M. Lamontagne, *Business Cycles in Canada* (Toronto: Lorimer, 1984).

13. Ironically, this priority was informed by "business values." Yet the elimination of the postal deficit would eliminate what was in effect a subsidy to business – the major postal user.

Notes to chapter one

1. The history of the postal service goes back to 2000 B.C. Archaeologists have discovered "letters" of Babylonian and Egyptian monarchs written on tablets of baked clay and delivered in baked clay envelopes. Egyptian couriers carried messages in relays via the canal network. Passages in the Old Testament refer to post-boats and to letters carried by posts on horseback, mules, and camels. King Cyrus, founder of the Persian empire, established post stations at regular intervals along relay routes. The Romans established a similar but more sophisticated system, establishing quarters called "postas" at regular intervals along well-travelled land routes: hence the origin of the word "posts." Their purpose was to keep rulers in contact with the provinces. In the late thirteenth and early fourteenth centuries, merchants' posts were organized; for example, there was a butchers' post, with mail travelling via butchers as they delivered meat. Universities operated postal services in this period, to allow their students to keep up contact with their families; the universities pocketed the profits. The English followed the Roman system in the late fifteenth century; King Charles established horse stops every twenty miles along similar routes. Some cities organized their own messenger systems, and monarchs organized their own independent couriers. From the late fifteenth to the mid-nineteenth century, the House of Thurn and Taxis operated a monopoly postal service in much of Europe, employing over twenty thousand people in the eighteenth century. See Post Office Department, *Postal History* (Ottawa: POD, 1938); Canada Post, *Postal Services Down the Centuries* (Ottawa: PC, 1974).

2. Post Office Department, *Canada Post Office: A Chronology of Change* (Ottawa, April 1984). p. 2. Prepared by R. W. Rapley; hereafter Rapley.

3. Rapley, pp. 2-10; "Postal History," in National Library Archives, File 2743, RG 3; A. W. Currie, "The Post Office Since 1867," *Canadian Journal of Economics*, May 1958; B. Osborne, "The Canadian National Postal System, 1852-1914," in R. Berry and J. Acheson (eds.), *Regionalism and National Identity* (Christchurch: University of Canterbury, 1985); B. Osborne and R. M. Pike, "Lowering 'The Walls of Oblivion': The Revolution in Postal Communications in Central Canada, 1851-1911," in D.

Akenson (ed.), *Canadian Papers in Rural History*, vol. IV (Gananoque, Ontario: Langdale Press, 1984).

4. I. Lee, *The Canadian Postal System: Origins, Growth and Decay of the State Postal Function, 1765-1981.* Ph. D. Thesis, Carleton University, 1989, esp. chap. 2.

5. W. Smith, *The History of the Post Office in British North America, 1639-1870* (Cambridge University Press, 1920) pp. 96-97.

6. In 1834 Toronto had one postman for its nine thousand inhabitants; the latter grew to twenty-one thousand by 1850, but there remained only one postman. See Gordon Donaldson, *Images of Canada: A Nation in Postal Stamps* (Toronto: Grosvenor House, 1990), p. 9.

7. Smith, pp. 122-24.

8. Smith, pp. 100-231; Lee, chap. 2.

9. Post Office Department, *Postal History*, Vol. 2743, file 46, p. 3; Canadian Encyclopedia, "Postal System," H. Griffin, pp. 1459-60; Rapley, p. 4.

10. Lee, p. 117.

11. Canada, New Brunswick, and Nova Scotia produced their own stamps until Confederation. British Columbia, Prince Edward Island, and Newfoundland continued to issue their own stamps until each joined Confederation (Donaldson, p. 10).

12. Canada Post Corporation, *Postal Service*.

13. On the Post Office's role in early Canadian economic development, see Osborne (1984, 1985); Currie.

14. Smith, p. 264 (emphasis added).

15. House of Commons, *Debates*, 4 February 1884.

16. *Annual Report of the Postmaster General* (Ottawa: 1856), p. 6; cited in Lee.

17. Osborne & Pike (1985), p. 3.

18. Lee, p. 116.

19. Canada Post, *Postal Services* (1974); J. Langford & K. Huffman, "Air Canada," in A. Tupper and G. B. Doern (eds.), *Privitization, Public Policy and Public Corporations in Canada* (Halifax: The Institute for Research on Public Policy, 1988), p. 95. See also G. Stevenson, *The Politics of Canada's Airlines* (Toronto: University of Toronto Press, 1987) p. 9.

20. The T. Eaton mail-order service was initiated in 1868, with postal support.

21. Osborne & Pike (1984), p. 219.

22. Lee, p. 130. The railroads charged high rates, advantageous to themselves, with the effect that the Post Office subsidized the financing and extension of the rail system. It served a similar function in the development of the airline system.

23. For example, establishing the Winnipeg-Edmonton route cost $10,000, at a time when postal revenues from all of the Northwest Territories amounted to less than $100. Smith, p. 317.

24. Currie, p. 241; Lee, p. 153.

25. Currie, p. 241.

26. Lee, p. 157.

27. Currie, p. 244.

28. Canada Post, *Postal Services*, pp. 37-38.

29. Lee, p. 127.

30. In 1889, publications issued more frequently than weekly no longer received free distribution. A half cent a pound rate was charged for urban newspapers. Publications issued at least monthly received free transmission within a twenty-mile zone. In 1903, the rate was reduced by half for publications issued at least monthly but less often than weekly and mailed within three hundred miles. In 1908, the half-rate three hundred-mile zone limit was eliminated, the free zone was increased from twenty to forty miles, and the rate was reduced from a half cent to a quarter cent per pound. In 1920, the size of the community in which the periodical was published became a determining factor: the population of the place of publication had to be less than ten thousand and only twenty-five hundred copies could be mailed free of charge — provisions that continued into the 1980s. Rates were tripled to three-quarters of a cent a pound in 1921, doubled to a cent and a half the following year, and reduced to one cent in 1927. Rates were set relative to circulation in 1931, with publications of greater than ten thousand copies levied an extra 50 per cent charge. In 1933, an advertisement surcharge of four cents a pound was added to publications whose advertising content was above 50 per cent. See Department of Communications, *Study of Canadian Concessionary Postal Rate Changes and Periodical Publishers for the Evaluation of the Postal Subsidy Program* (Prepared by Ekos Research Associates) (Ottawa: 16 December 1985).

31. Lee, pp. 18-19, chap. 4.

32. D. K. Adie, *The Mail Monopoly: Analysing Canadian Postal Service* (The Fraser Institute, 1990) pp. 4, 51, 52, 78.

33. Review Committee on the Mandate and Productivity of Canada Post Corporation, *Report* (Ottawa, November 1985); hereafter Marchment report, p. 5. Postmaster General André Ouellet in a 1973 speech to postmasters said:
Everyone knows his post office. It's a building you can't mistake. The only building in town with a flagpole, a sign and a mailbox in front . . . about the only federal building that most people feel at home in. And everyone in little towns and villages knows his postmaster. People know you by your first name. They deal with you person-to-person. They think of you, rightly or wrongly, as their personal link with the government, a little peephole into that great Ottawa beehive . . . The post office is familiar. It cuts the government down to size. It's a reference point in that huge federal landscape. (cited in D. Stewart-Patterson, *Post Mortem: Why Canada's Mail Won't Move* (Toronto: Macmillan, 1987) pp. 12-13.

34. The postal volume is presently about forty million pieces per working day. The record amount processed in one day is sixty-two million.

35. This discussion is taken from an interview with J. Corkery, former deputy PMG and assistant to Michael Warren in the early 1980s.

36. Interview with L. Blanchette, 25 November 1991.

37. Post Office Department, *Annual Report*, 1925, p. 7.

38. These included stamp-cancelling machines for letters, cash registers for prepayment of third-class mail, elevators, gravity feed systems, and conveyor belts for mail bags and parcels. Two punching machines were purchased in 1925 that did the work of

one hundred people in sorting and auditing the mail. Pitney Bowes installed the first postage meter in Eaton's in 1923. Commercial cash registers were introduced to post offices in 1925.

39. Post Office Department, *Canada Post Office: An Organizational History, 1841-1974* (Organization, Planning and Development, October 1975).

40. Currie, p. 246.

41. Interview with L. Blanchette, 25 November 1991. The introduction of the twin-mailbox system—one box for local and one box for non-local mail—is designed to increase this figure, by having a larger proportion of mail processed in the large mechanized plants.

42. See Lee, pp. 18-19, chap. 4.

43. See Adie (1990) for an opposing argument.

44. The National Association of Major Mail Users (NAMMU) has not supported privatization. At a Fraser Institute Conference conference on privatization of Canada Post in 1989, NAMMU's spokesperson, *Readers Digest*'s Ralph Hancox, said: "In the minds of most major users, 'privatization' is not a real issue. No sane person sees the central management and control of a postal system passing from the Crown Corporation's hands to that of commercial or private sector suppliers. We see a decline in service, increase in costs and chaos from deregulation and privatization."

45. Currie, p. 243.

46. Currie, pp. 242-43, 245.

47. POD *Report,* 1944-45; see also Currie, p. 246.

48. Lee, pp. 220ff.

49. Lee, pp. 225-53.

50. Canada Post Corporation, *Labour Relations in the Post Office: A Chronology* (Labour Relations Branch, 1981).

51. Ibid.

52. Interview with Eric Kierans (10 December 1989), who on various occasions depicted the Post Office in the 1950s and 1960s as being carried on the backs of the workers.

53. When this claim was presented to postal worker and past president of the LCUC Bob McGarry in a Dominion Store, he replied that "security can't buy these groceries" (Interview, 14 August 1990).

Notes to chapter two

1. The Liberal Party's Allaire report (1991) listed the Post Office as one of the numerous areas of federal jurisdiction that the Province of Quebec wanted transferred to its jurisdiction.

2. At this time it was connected administratively to the Department of Communications.

3. Interview with PMG J. J. Blais, 14 August 1990.

4. On 26 April 1978, the House of Commons endorsed a joint Senate-House of Commons committee conclusion that the rate increase was illegal. Prime Minister Trudeau

announced the government's plan to make the Post Office a Crown corporation on 1 August 1978.

5. Interviews with Deputy PMG J. Corkery, 22 January 1990; PMG E. Kierans, 10 December, 1989. See D. Stewart-Patterson, *Post Mortem: Why Canada's Mail Won't Move* (Toronto: Macmillan, 1987), pp. 58-59.

6. See Post Office Department, *Canada Post Office: An Organizational History 1841-1974* (Ottawa: POD, 1975).

7. See Kates, Peat, Marwick & Co., *A Blueprint for Change* (Ottawa: 1969).

8. Interview with Deputy PMG J. Corkery, 22 January 1990.

9. Interviews with PMG E. Kierans, 10 December 1989; H. Mullington, 27 June 1990; PMG J. P. Côté, 18 November 1991; PMG G. Lamontagne, 8 February 1992; PMG A. Ouellet, 23 January 1990.

10. Interviews with PMGs J. P. Côté, E. Kierans, A. Ouellet, G. Lamontagne.

11. Judy Lamarsh, cited in J. Swift, *Odd Man Out: The Life and Times of Eric Kierans* (Vancouver: Douglas & McIntyre, 1988), p. 211.

12. Interviews with PMGs J. J. Blais, 14 August 1990, and A. Ouellet.

13. Interview with J. Corkery.

14. There were no female deputy postmasters general. There was one female postmaster general, Ellen Fairclough, for a brief period in the short-lived third Diefenbaker government.

15. Interview with G. Lamontagne.

16. J. Woods & Gordon Limited, *Canada Post Office: Survey of Organization and Administration* (Ottawa: 20 November 1952); Royal Commission on Government Organization, *Report*, V. 3, sec. 17 (Ottawa: 1963); Commission of Inquiry into Increases in Rates of Pay for Civil Servants in Group D, *Final Report* (Ottawa: 1965); Royal Commission on Working Conditions in the Post Office, *Report* (Ottawa: 1966); *A Blueprint for Change*; Commission of Inquiry into Mail Transportation in Montreal, *Report* (Ottawa: 1970); Post Office Department, *Major Organization and Compensation Issues in Canada Post: Report of the Joint Post Office-Treasury Board Secretariat Study Group* (Ottawa: December 1975); Post Office Department, *Considerations which Affect the Choice of Organizational Structure for the Canada Post Office* (Ottawa: 1978); Ronald S. Ritchie, *The Ritchie Report on Canada's Postal Services* (Ottawa: April 1978); Auditor General, *Report* (Ottawa: 1980-81); Commission of Inquiry relating to the Security and Investigation Services Branch within the Post Office Department, *Report* (Ottawa: 1981).

17. G. Bruce Doern & V. Seymour Wilson, *Issues in Canadian Public Policy* (Toronto: Meuthen, 1974), pp. 339-41.

18. Interviews with J. Corkery, J. P. Côté, A. Ouellet, H. Mullington.

19. See Economic Council of Canada, *Minding the Public's Business* (Ottawa: 1986); M. Gordon, *Government in Business* (Montreal: C. D. Howe Institute, 1982); H. Hardin, *A Nation Unaware: The Canadian Economic Culture* (Vancouver: J. J. Douglas, 1974); E. Kirsch, *Crown Corporations as Instruments of Public Policy*, Economic Council of Canada, discussion paper no. 295 (Ottawa: 1985); J. R. S. Prichard, ed., *Crown Corporations in Canada* (Toronto: Butterworths, 1983); W. Stewart, *Uneasy Lies the Head:*

The Truth about Canada's Crown Corporations (Don Mills: Collins, 1987); A. Tupper & G. B. Doern, eds., *Public Corporations and Public Policy in Canada* (Montreal: Institute for Research on Public Policy, 1981); A. Tupper & G. B. Doern, eds., *Privitization, Public Policy and Public Corporations in Canada* (Halifax: Institute for Research on Public Policy, 1988).

20. On the optimism of the Crown corporation idea, see A. Tupper & G. B. Doern (eds.), *Privitization, Public Policy and Public Corporations in Canada* (Halifax: The Institute for Research on Public Policy, 1988) p. 14.

21. Langford, pp. 621-23.

22. Judge René Marin was deputy solicitor general (1977) and headed a royal commission on security in the Post Office (1980). Sylvain Cloutier had a background in accounting and economics, with senior appointments in Treasury Board, National Revenue, National Defence, Transportation, Export Development Corporation, and the Federal Business Development Bank. Roger Beaulieu was senior partner and chair of Martineau, Walker, with a host of directorships, including Pirelli, Monsanto, Laurentian Life Insurance, CARA, Laurentian Group, and Capital Broadcasting Operations.

23. Interview with M. Warren, 9 November 1989; Canadian Labour Congress president Shirley Carr, 27 June 1990; PMG A. Ouellet, 23 January 1990.

24. Interview with CPC board chair Roger Beaulieu, 12 November 1991.

25. Interview with R. Beaulieu, 12 November 1991.

26. According to the minister's office and CPC's Government Relations Department, there were only 30 or so responses to CPC's 1991 proposal to raise prices in 1992. There have been no more than 75 responses to a price proposal since 1987. This is in contrast to the 3,500 submissions in 1986, and the 50,000 signatures on petitions, 5,460 letters, and 2,269 business and organization briefs in 1981.

27. Much of the information in this paragraph is based on an interview (17 October 1991) with Gary Billyard, Harvie Andre's assistant in his capacity as minister responsible for Canada Post Corporation. Until the 1988 election, there were two people performing this function, but thereafter only one. It is not evident why there have been fewer MPs' enquiries and public submissions on price increases. The political opposition claims it is because the public recognizes that their overtures will not be successful; in short, they have given up trying (correspondence with Liberal postal critic Robert Nault).

28. Much of the information in this paragraph is based on a 28 October 1991 interview with David Salie, Crown Corporations Directorate, who has been the analyst for Canada Post Corporation since February 1985.

29. See Standing Committee on Government Operations, *First Report*, 15 December 1986, Minutes of Proceedings and Evidence No. 7.

30. See House of Commons, Standing Committee on Consumer and Corporate Affairs, *Moving the Mail: Canada's Postal Services in the 1990s*. Second report, issue no. 53, 11 April 1990.

31. Interview with Bob Labelle, Director, Government Relations, Canada Post Corporation, 28 November 1991.

32. House of Commons, *Debates*, 31 May 1991.

33. Interview with LCUC president Bob McGarry, 14 August 1990. He maintained that under the departmental form, labour had more political influence via committee hearings and MPs.

34. See W. D. Coleman & G. Skogstad, eds., *Policy Communities and Public Policy in Canada* (Toronto: Copp Clark Pittman, 1990).

Notes to chapter three

1. Franked mail is mail carried by the POD for other government departments, for which no charge is levied. The POD delivered customs notices, collected revenues for many departments, sold UI stamps and radio licences, distributed income tax forms, displayed government notices, and offered postal banking services for no charge.

2. See the discussion of the Royal Commission on Government Organization, *Report*, vol. III, sec. 17 (Ottawa, 1963) p. 322. It estimated that building costs alone saved the POD $25 million a year and the superannuation contribution was another $15 million saving. Franking was estimated as a $6 million annual cost.

3. For example, it was reported that 183 postmen had been bitten by dogs in the first eight months of 1956. MP Bell complained about the "modern art" on stamps, suggesting that the POD was "just like the CBC's ballet dancers . . . out of touch with the people." *Globe and Mail*, 14 August 1956 and 7 March 1957.

4. Jean-Pierre Côté reports that Prime Minister Pearson informed him that there was no particular reason that he was chosen to be PMG, other than that he seemed to have good sense (Interview with Côté, 18 November 1992).

5. Six of the ten PMGs were French Canadians, in an era when a "balanced" Cabinet required a certain quota of French Canadian ministers. They tended not to be assigned to prestigious or important portfolios such as Finance but to be given minor portfolios such as Public Works and the Post Office.

6. Interview with J.P. Côté, 18 November 1991.

7. Lee points to the development of the electronic media in the post-war period as leading to the POD's diminishing stature. See I. Lee, *The Canadian Postal System: Origins, Growth and Decay of the State Postal Function, 1765-1981*. Ph.D. Thesis, Carleton University, 1989, pp. 373, 400, 405-6.

8. A comptroller of the railway service was established, and two Chief Post Office superintendent positions were created. These were simply reactive developments, which tacked new positions onto the existing administrative structure. See Post Office Department, *Canada Post Office: An Organizational History, 1841-1974* (Ottawa: 1975), p. 37.

9. Ibid., p. 8.

10. J. D. Woods & Gordon Limited, *Canada Post Office: Survey of Organization and Administration* (Ottawa: November 1952).

11. See Post Office Department, *Report*, 1952-53.

12. Post Office Department, *Canada Post Office: An Organizational History, 1841-1974* (Organization, Planning and Development, October 1975).

13. See Royal Commission on Government Organization, *Report*, vol. 3, sec. 17 (Ottawa: 1966).

14. A separate position of comptroller was established, and engineering and development was separated from operations and transportation. A formal attempt was made to introduce corporate planning.

15. Royal Commission on Working Conditions in the Post Office, *Report* (Ottawa: 1966), p. 1. (hereafter "Montpetit report").

16. See Hamilton file, box 26, memo to Deputy Postmaster General, file X40.

17. Hamilton file, box 20, file X40, Policy and Recommendations on Post Office. See *Memorandum on Relations between MPs and the Post Office Department*, 19 July 1958, 28 p. See also letter to MPs, 19 August 1958, in file nos. 20-23.

18. See House of Commons, *Debates*, 1942, pp. 4762-66, 4965; 1943, pp. 3819ff; 1950, pp. 4241-45; 1951, pp. 3547ff, 4950-62; 1954, pp. 4739-44, 4764-65; 1960, p. 4288; 1963, pp. 6075-76, 6080ff; *Globe and Mail*, 24 May 1941, 18 June 1943, 31 May 1951.

19. J. White, *Mail and Female: Women and the Canadian Union of Postal Workers* (Toronto: Thompson Educational Publishers, 1990) p. 12.

20. *Globe and Mail*, 24 May 1941.

21. See House of Commons, *Debates*, 1941, pp. 3102-4; 1942, pp. 4666-67; 1944, pp. 2023, 6389; 1945, pp. 2818ff; 1947, pp. 4790-91; 1948, pp. 4772; 1949, pp. 2905-22; 1950, pp. 2333ff, 4195ff; 1951, pp. 3355-58ff; 1952, pp. 928-29, 3068-70, 4212-18; 1953, pp. 1446, 1470, 3381, 3386, 5307; 1954, pp. 4722-67; 1956, p. 7530. PMG Côté introduced Bill 107 to deal with this issue in 1953, and a special committee on the bill was formed and produced an extensive report.

22. See House of Commons, *Debates*, 1941, pp. 3092-3113; 1947, pp. 4790-91; 1951, pp. 3905-6, 4950-62.

23. See Department of Public Works, *Report*, annually from 1957-58 to 1967-68. "In 1957, Cabinet decided to undertake a programme of small post offices as winter works to stimulate the construction industry in areas of low employment" (Department of Public Works, *Project Reports: Design of the Small Post Office* [Ottawa: October 1962].

24. For example, see House of Commons, *Debates*, 1942, p. 4963; 1947, pp. 4790ff; 1948, pp. 4772-73; 1949, pp. 2905-22; 1950, pp. 4195-4219, 4239-45; 1954, pp. 4722-67; 1955, p. 4128; 1957, 5, 6, 7, 8, 14 March; 1960, pp. 4296-97. The Hamilton papers contain an extraordinary number of files and letters pleading for improved services or ministerial attention to special issues or needs: see box 265485. Jean-Pierre Côté recounts how MPs were always collaring him in the House of Commons or phoning his office, pleading for local postal services or improvements (Interview with Côté, 18 November 1991).

25. See R. Campbell, *Grand Illusions: The Politics of the Keynesian Experience in Canada, 1945-75* (Peterborough: Broadview, 1987), ch. 2.

26. Post Office Department, *Report*, 1944-45. pp. 4-5.

27. Cited in Currie, p. 246.

28. Post Office Department, *Report,* 1945-46; 1946-47; 1947-48; 1948-49, p. 6.

29. *Ibid.,* 1954-55, p. 2.

30. House of Commons, *Debates,* 1960, p. 4277; 1961, pp. 3629-30.

31. Post Office Department, *Report,* 1955-56, p. v; and 1967-68; House of Commons, *Debates,* 1957, p. 2714; Rapley.

32. See Debate on Supply, House of Commons, *Debates,* 8 December 1949, p. 2916.

33. *Ibid.,* 5 April 1943, pp. 1850-53.

34. It should be noted that the price for second-, third-, and fourth-class mail could be changed by the minister through regulation, without parliamentary approval. Up to 1968 there was a "drop," or local, rate, that was one cent cheaper. When the price of a first-class stamp is discussed, I am referring to the national or non-local rate. To further confuse matters, from 1928 to 1968 there was a third category of first-class mail — air mail — which was more expensive. This rate was dropped as well in 1968.

35. House of Commons, *Debates,* 8 December 1953, p. 691; 15 January 1954, p. 1145. See Lee, pp. 373, 382-83, 387, 400, 405-6. He notes that twice-daily delivery was eliminated in the year that television arrived.

36. *Ibid.,* pp. 1104-5, 1115-19, 1131, 1148, 1172ff. The Opposition suggested that the rate increase was required mainly to provide a first-class surplus to subsidize second-class mail, which benefitted the large publishing and newspaper operations. This point is examined below.

37. *Ibid.,* pp. 1859-1904, 1912-21.

38. *Ibid.,* 1956, p. 7530; *Globe and Mail,* 8 March 1957.

39. See House of Commons, *Debates,* 1959, p. 6248; 1960, p. 4277.

40. Campbell, ch. 4.

41. See Hamilton papers, 265496, XA-5, especially PCO memo dated 7 April 1959.

42. House of Commons, *Debates,* 1960, p. 3636.

43. See correspondence between PMG Hamilton and Finance Minister Fleming, Hamilton papers, box 265495, file XA2. In the run-up to setting the 1962-63 estimates, the deputy PMG pleaded unsuccessfully with Treasury Board to approve the hiring of ten more time-study officers, to save labour and cut costs as a way of balancing the budget without raising prices.

44. Hamilton papers, box 265494, file X40 (1960-61), memo to deputy PMG.

45. House of Commons, *Debates,* 1964, pp. 2768, 2770, 2771, 2778-90; Post Office Department, *Report,* 1963-64, p. 3.

46. House of Commons, *Debates,* 1967, p. 1098.

47. *Ibid.,* 1967, pp. 1985-86.

48. *Ibid.,* p. 2689.

49. As will be seen below, the Opposition characterized the rate increases as benefitting the large publishing houses, to the detriment of ordinary users. "The principle here is wrong that the little people of the country should have their burdens spelled out in unmistakable terms while we are not nearly so emphatic where strong organizations are concerned" (*ibid.,* pp. 2687-88; 4784-86).

50. The Liberal whips erred in not ensuring that a sufficient number of Liberal MPs came into the House of Commons for the vote (interview with Jean-Pierre Côté, 18 November 1991).

51. The government was very much aware of the deficit-generating consequences of having this price proposal defeated (interview with Jean-Pierre Côté, 18 November 1991).

52. Currie, p. 249.

53. House of Commons, *Debates:* Drope, 8 May 1947, p. 2892; Shaw, 1951, p. 3527; Hatfield, 1951, p. 3561; Drew, 1951, pp. 3896-97; Adamson, 1951, p. 3901; Rinfret, 1951, p. 3903; MacKenzie, 1952, p. 4210; Fairclough 1954, pp. 1104-5; Noseworthy, 1954, pp. 1119-20; Knowles, 1954, p. 1124; Bigg, 1966, p. 5337. *Financial Post*, 9 June 1951; Royal Commission on Government Organization, p. 309.

54. House of Commons, *Debates*, 1954, p. 1145.

55. House of Commons, *Debates*, 1951, p. 3898.

56. See House of Commons, *Debates*, 1945, p. 2815; 1946, p. 470; 1951, p. 4956; 1952, pp. 4207-9; 1953, pp. 5307-10; 1954, pp. 4730-32; 1956, p. 7530; 1957, pp. 1950-51, 1805; 1958, pp. 2715, 2719, 2721, 2742; 1959, pp. 6251ff; 1960, pp. 4285, 4292-93.

57. This issue will be dealt with in considerable detail in Part 3.

58. See House of Commons, *Debates*, 1947, pp. 4800-3; 1948, p. 4793; 1951, pp. 3510ff, 3525, 3530, 3534, 3959-61. See also *Globe and Mail*, 3 June 1947, 22 May 1951, 30 May 1951.

59. The NDP estimated that second-class rates gave *Time* and *Reader's Digest* a subsidy of $600,000 to $900,000 a year. House of Commons, *Debates*, 1964, pp. 2788-90. This estimate rose to $1.5-2 million in 1967. Edith Fowke presented an interesting overview of this issue at the time in "Who Should Pay the Postage?" *Canadian Forum*, July 1954, pp. 79-80.

60. Royal Commission on Government Organization, *Report*, pp. 325-27.

61. *Ibid.* See also Currie, pp. 248-49.

62. House of Commons, *Debates*, 1964, pp. 5631-34. Jean-Pierre Côté and Eric Kierans recount the forceful reaction of the large newspaper and publishing concerns whenever the POD raised or threatened to raise second class rates.

63. House of Commons, *Debates*, 1941, p. 3106; 1948, p. 4773; 1950, pp. 4210, 4213; 1957, p. 1784; 1959, pp. 6258-59; 1960, p. 4295; 1964, pp. 2784-85; 1964, p. 5268; 1967, pp. 1083, 4785; Woods & Gordon Study, 11; Hamilton Papers, box 20, file 20-23; Royal Commission on Government Organization, *Report*, pp. 308, 312, 341-42.

64. House of Commons, *Debates*, 1941, pp. 3098-99; 1945, pp. 2815-16; 1948, p. 4774; 1950, pp. 4210, 4213; 1953, p. 5309; 1954, p. 1149; 1957, pp. 1784, 1805; 1964, p. 2767; 1967, p. 1083. Royal Commission on Government Organization, *Report*, pp. 341-42.

65. Post Office Department, *Report*. 1957-58, p. 5.

66. *Ibid.*

67. Hamilton papers, box 265495, file XA2, Estimates 1957-58 and 1958-59. "Primarily we are not seeking a decrease in manpower but an improvement in our efficiency to allow us to deal without delay with our ever-increasing volume of mail."

68. See Post Office Department, *Report*, 1953-54, 1954-55, 1958-89, 1961-62; House of Commons, *Debates*, 1957, p. 2023; 1958, p. 2717; 1959, p. 6247; 1960, pp. 4280, 4291-92; R.W. Rapley, *Canada Post Office: A Chronology of Change* (Ottawa: April 1984).

69. House of Commons, *Debates*, 1961, p. 3637; see also 1958, p. 2721; 1960, pp. 4291-92.

70. *Ibid.*, 1956, p. 7530; 1959, p. 6251; 1960, pp. 4291-92.

71. See House of Commons, *Debates*, 1941, pp. 3092-93; 1942, pp. 4897-98; 1946, pp. 4391-92; 1948, pp. 4772, 4774-75; 1948, p. 2906; 1950, p. 350; 1951, pp. 3554, 3896-97; 1952, pp. 4204ff; 1959, pp. 6258-59. See also *Globe and Mail*, 19 December 1963, 24 October 1964. The example of toilet facilities was recounted by Jean-Pierre Côté, whose father was an inside worker. For a full cataloguing of the poor working conditions, see the Montpetit Commission report.

72. Post Office Department, *Report*, 1947-48.

73. See House of Commons, *Debates*, 1944, pp. 2012ff; 1945, p. 2816; 1948, pp. 4772, 4778; 1949, p. 2906; 1951, pp. 3543-44; 1951, p. 4956. See *Globe and Mail*, 6 August 1946, 6 February 1954.

74. Interview with Jean-Pierre Côté, 18 November 1991.

75. See *Globe and Mail*, 14 May 1953, 24 October 1964, 19 December 1963. See House of Commons, *Debates*, 1954, p. 4724; 1956, p. 949; 1960, p. 4295; 1960, p. 3637; 1963, pp. 6073, 6088.

76. *Globe and Mail*, 24 July 1965.

77. *Globe and Mail*, 28 July 1965; see also 22 July 1965. "Almost everywhere, postmen enjoy a good public image . . . They are their own best PRs and are respected for the reasonable job they carry out in all weather. In many constituencies, especially rural ones, postmen are looked up to as well-paid men of substance" (*Financial Post*, 31 July 1965).

78. Among other groups and individuals, Canada Post interpreted the 1965 strike in this way. In its submission to the Marchment Postal Review Committee in 1985, it characterized the 1965 strike as a chicken coming home to roost. See Canada Post Corporation, *Presentation by Board of Directors and Management of Canada Post Corporation to Review Committee on Mandate and Productivity* (Ottawa: September 1985), p. 8.

79. Commission of Inquiry into the Increase in Rates of Pay for Civil Servants in Group 'D', *Final Report* (Ottawa: 4 August 1965) (hereafter the Anderson report). Group D was made up largely of postal workers, customs and immigration workers, and certain technicians.

80. Anderson report, pp. 3-4.

81. Montpetit was assisted by Paul Faguy, at the time director general of the Emergency Measures Organization and later deputy PMG (1968-70), and by Romeo Malone, then assistant director of international affairs of the Canadian Labour Congress.

82. Royal Commission on Working Conditions in the Post Office, *Report* (Ottawa: 1966).

83. *Ibid.*, p. 287.

84. The *Globe and Mail* headline introducing the report was "Post office enquiry critical of bosses."

85. Royal Commission on Working Conditions, *Report,* p. 24.

86. *Ibid.,* p. 17.

87. *Ibid.,* p. 22.

88. Interview with the PMG, J. P. Côté, 18 November 1991. He reports that cabinet was not bothered by most of the recommendations, as they did not require large expenditures.

89. See Post Office Department, *Replies to the Recommendations of the Royal Commission on Working Conditions in the Post Office* (Ottawa: 1966).

90. While it supported the idea in the abstract, the commission was ambivalent on wider political grounds: "The universality of the service and traditional public interest militate against the depriving of the Post Office of its constitution as a department of government" (pp. 328, 329).

91. *Ibid.,* pp. 3-4.

92. See Canada Post Corporation, *Presentation by Board of Directors and Management of Canada Post Corporation to Review Committee on Mandate and Productivity* (Ottawa: September 1985).

93. Royal Commission on Working Conditions, *Report,* p. 31. Monpetit urged that the idea be studied thoroughly before proceeding.

94. House of Commons, *Debates,* 1967, p. 112; interview with Deputy PMG J. Corkery (1977-81), 22 January 1990; interview with J. P. Côté, 18 November 1991.

Notes to chapter four

1. See *Globe and Mail,* 15, 16 November 1966; House of Commons, *Debates,* 1966, pp. 9956-57; interview with PMG Côté, 18 November 1991.

2. The CPU also gained time-and-a-half for all work performed after 40 hours (down from 44-48 hours), an increase in holidays from nine to eleven days a year, and an accelerated movement to the maximum salary rate in three years (down from five years). *Globe and Mail,* 16 July to 9 August 1968; Canada Post Corporation, *Work Disruptions History: Report 1965-83*; Canada Post Corporation, *Labour Relations in the Post Office* (Ottawa: Public Relations Branch, May 1981).

3. House of Commons, *Debates,* 1968, p. 14601; Kates, Peat, Marwick & Co., *A Blueprint for Change* (Ottawa: 1969), pp. 1, 79-81; *Financial Post,* 10 May 1969.

4. See Eric Kierans in Standing Committee on Transportation and Communications, *Minutes of Proceedings and Evidence,* 1970, 15:12, 15:72. See also Côté, *ibid.,* 1971, 6:9.

5. House of Commons, *Debates,* 1968, p. 9280.

6. Eric Kierans papers, deputy PMG submission to PMG, re: proposed rate increases for 1971-72 and 1972-73, 10 July 1970, p. 2.

7. See Kierans papers, unpublished White Paper on the Post Office Department; *A Blueprint for Change; Financial Post,* 10 May 1969; S. Shapiro (*et al.*), *Report of the Marketing Task Force* (internal study); see also S. Shapiro and J. A. Barnhill, "The Post Office in the Market Place: A Ten Year Retrospective," in D. N. Thompson (*et al.*), *Macromarketing: The Canadian Perspective* (Chicago: American Marketing Association, 1980). In early 1969, an American company called the Independent Postal

System began performing services in the second-, third-, and fourth-class mail categories, areas in which there was no postal monopoly. In these and other areas the POD worried about cream-skimming, the practice of carrying out business in the dense, lucrative urban markets (the "cream") while leaving the less profitable activity to the Post Office. See *Financial Post,* 1 March 1969.

8. Interview with E. Kierans, 10 December 1989.

9. The POD's problems continued to reflect "factors over which the Post Office has largely no control . . . constraints are placed on the administration of the Post Office which prevented fulfillment of their tasks. . .. The Post Office has had to compete with other departments of government for scarce financial resources." *Blueprint for Change,* pp. 1, 4-5, 7.

10. Interview with E. Kierans. See also D. Stewart-Patterson, p. 137.

11. *Globe and Mail,* 23 January 1969; *Financial Post,* 8 February 1969.

12. House of Commons, *Debates,* 1969, p. 6078.

13. Standing Committee on Transportation and Communication, *Minutes of Proceedings and Evidence,* 1971, 15:13.

14. *Ibid.,* 15:89.

15. *Ibid.,* 1970, 15:85.

16. See *Post Office Manual* in Eric Kierans papers.

17. See Eric Kierans papers, *Post Office Manual,* "Economic Objective of the Post Office Department."

18. See Eric Kierans papers, *Post Office Manual,* departmental financial overview of 1971–72.

19. House of Commons, *Debates,* 1968, p. 1602.

20. Special Senate Committee on Mass Media, *Minutes of Proceedings and Evidence,* 1971, p. 163.

21. *Blueprint for Change,* p. 16.

22. *Ibid.,* p. 10.

23. Shapiro *et al.*

24. Interview with J. Corkery, 22 January 1990.

25. *Blueprint for Change.*

26. House of Commons, *Debates,* 1968, pp. 930, 1604.

27. Kierans explained that "postal charges are becoming quite a heavy item in the cost of corporations . . . if we were to increase the costs by another $50 million or $60 million . . . business would then say that they have $50 million or $60 million more reason and justification for increasing their own prices" (Standing Committee on Transportation and Communication, *Minutes of Proceedings and Evidence,* 1970, 15:27).

28. House of Commons, *Debates,* 1971, p. 6312. Côté engineered this price increase, as Kierans resigned as PMG three days after first reading of the bill.

29. House of Commons, *Debates,* 1968, pp. 68, 929, 1604; Special Senate Committee on Mass Media, *Minutes of Proceedings,* pp. 80ff; *Globe and Mail,* 12 February 1969.

30. House of Commons, *Debates,* 1968, p. 496; *Globe and Mail,* 20 March 1970.

31. The Shapiro study concluded that door-to-door delivery cost $24 an address a year, compared to $18 for rural routes and $7.75 for mailboxes.

32. House of Commons, *Debates*, 1969, p. 256.

33. *Blueprint for Change*, pp. 22, 126.

34. *Globe and Mail*, 20 February 1970, 3 June 1971; Canada Post Corporation, *The History of Canada Post* (Ottawa: CPC Public Relations Branch, May 1981); J.G. Fultz, *Coding and Mechanization 52 Months Later* (Ottawa: POD, August 1974); Rapley.

35. See *Blueprint for Change*, p. 84; Post Office Department, *An Organizational History, 1841-1974* (Ottawa: POD Organizational Planning and Development, October 1975).

36. House of Commons, *Debates*, 1969, p. 6077; interview with E. Kierans, 10 December 1989.

37. *Financial Post*, 10 January 1970; Stewart-Patterson, pp. 4ff; interviews with E. Kierans and J. Corkery, 22 January 1990.

38. See *Financial Post*, 24 January 1970; interviews with E. Kierans and J. Corkery; Shapiro *et al.*

39. *Blueprint for Change*, p. ii.

40. See Kierans papers, *Post Office Manual*, "Reasons for Change in Status."

41. See *Blueprint for Change*, p. 13; *White Paper on Crown Corporation Status* in Kierans papers; *Post Office Manual*, "Reasons for a Change in Status," in Kierans papers.

42. Interview with E. Kierans, 10 December 1989. See also Stewart-Patterson, pp. 139ff; *Globe and Mail*, 28 September 1968, 23 January, 11 December 1969, 19 May 1970; House of Commons, *Debates*, 1968, p. 1604; 1969, p. 6475; Standing Committee on Transportation and Communications, *Minutes of Proceedings and Evidence*, 1970, 15:35.

43. House of Commons, *Debates*, 1968, pp. 931, 2000; 1969, pp. 6405-6, 6618, 8734-35, 8738-39; *Globe and Mail*, 9 October 1968.

44. Interview with E. Kierans; House of Commons, *Debates*, 1968, pp. 6432, 6749; *Globe and Mail*, 28 September, 26 October 1968; *Financial Post*, 12 April 1969; Stewart-Patterson, pp. 132-33, 142-43; Standing Committee on Transportation and Communications, *Minutes of Proceedings and Evidence*, 1970, 15:50, 16:69.

45. House of Commons, *Debates*, 1968, p. 1603, interview with E. Kierans, 10 December 1989.

46. Côté reported that between 11 April 1970 and 9 March 1971, 646 post offices had been closed at a savings of $2 million (Standing Committee on Transportation and Communications, *Minutes of Proceedings and Evidence*, 1970, 15:50, 16:9; 1971, 6:10; House of Commons, *Debates*, 1971, 6749; interview with J. P. Côté, 18 November 1991).

47. House of Commons, *Debates*, 1968, pp. 934, 942, 1611, 1614, 1658-59; *Financial Post*, 28 December 1968; *Globe and Mail*, 12 February 1969; Special Senate Committee on Mass Media, *Report* (Ottawa: 1971), vol. 1, p. 237; vol. 2, p. 465.

48. Interview with E. Kierans, 10 December 1989.

49. House of Commons, *Debates*, 1969, p. 8744.

50. House of Commons, *Debates*, 1968, p. 2015.

51. House of Commons, *Debates*, pp. 1815-16, 1994.

52. W.S. Martin, chief adjudicator, PSSRB report no. 169-2-1, 1969; *Globe and Mail,* 5 July 1989.

53. House of Commons, *Debates,* 1969, pp. 6172-73, 6393, 6407-9, 6415-17, 6430ff, 6518-20, 6557-58; *Globe and Mail,* 8, 25 July 1989.

54. *Globe and Mail,* 9, 10 January, 7 March 1969; House of Commons, *Debates,* 1969, pp. 5569ff.

55. See J. Swift, *Odd Man Out: The Life and Times of Eric Kierans* (Vancouver: Douglas & McIntyre, 1988), chap. 10; D. Stewart-Patterson, pp. 75-84; P. Vadeboncoeur, *366 Days and As Long As It Takes* (Montreal: Confederation of National Trade Unions, 1971); Canada Post, *Labour Relations in the Post Office: A Chronology* (Ottawa, 1981); Minister of Communications, Transportation Branch, *Montreal Transportation Contracts 1938-1970* (Ottawa: November 1970). See also *Globe and Mail,* 21, 26 March 1969, 17, 18, 19, 25, 28 February, 16, 17, 27, 28, 30 March 1970; House of Commons, *Debates,* 1970, pp. 3783-3818.

56. J.Swift, *Odd Man Out: The Life and Times of Eric Kierans,* pp. 224-25.

57. A senior official wrote to Kierans on 11 March 1970: "Any evidence of weakness or compromise will generate confidence for the Council of Postal Unions to adopt an inflexible attitude" (cited in Swift, p. 222).

58. See *Globe and Mail,* 4, 9 March, 8, 18, 21 May, 20 June, 25 July, 5 August 1970.

59. Lippé also rejected the CPU's demand for weekend shift premiums, overtime after eight hours (regardless of the number of hours worked in a week), and the normalization of the pattern of work to a five-day, eight-hour pattern. Public Service Staff Relations Board, *In the Matter of the PSSRA and a Dispute Affecting the Canadian Union of Postal Workers and Her Majesty . . . in respect of the Postal Operators Group* (Ottawa: 1970).

60. *Globe and Mail,* 10, 22 June, 6, 9, 16, 25 July 1970.

61. Letter carriers gained overtime for shifts longer than eight hours, and postal clerks received an increase in shift differentials. There were also improved vacations, advance notice of shift changes, and limitations placed on casuals doing work normally done by members of the bargaining unit.

62. Kierans had already assured postal workers that mechanization would not eliminate jobs. He declared in mid-May that "over the next 5 years the work force of the Post Office will expand by some 5000 people . . . There is no possibility of people who want to work not having work in the Post Office." The PMG tried to place the modernization program in a positive light: "Investment in plant and mechanical facilities . . . will reduce the drudgery and routine of most postal activities . . . improve working conditions . . . [and] provid[e] greater opportunity for job satisfaction" (House of Commons, *Debates,* 1970, p. 7062; *Globe and Mail,* 10 September 1970).

63. *Financial Post,* 11 July 1970; *Globe and Mail,* 9 June, 25 July 1970; Post Office Department, *Report,* 1970-71.

64. House of Commons, *Debates,* 1970, pp. 6343-44, 7222-23, 7225-26, 7234-35, 8678-81; *Globe and Mail,* 23 May, 22 June 1970.

65. Vandenberg suggested that the POD did not consult meaningfully with the postal unions about technological change. This made postal workers paranoid and distrustful of what the POD was planning, and thus inclined to be belligerent in challenging POD initiatives. He recommended that advance consultation be mandatory prior to the adoption of new techniques or mechanical processes, and encouraged the "inclusion in their next agreement of a clause limiting the introduction of automated equipment during the life of the agreement to what is specifically set forth in the agreement" (R.D. Vandenberg, *The Post Office and Its Workers: An Appraisal of Attitudes that Are Destroying a Vital Public Service* [Ottawa: 1971]).

66. Interviews with E. Kierans, H. Mullington, J. Corkery, J. P. Côté.

67. Interview with E. Kierans; Stewart-Patterson, pp. 143-44; *Financial Post,* 17 October 1970.

68. Standing Committee on Transportation and Communications, *Minutes of Proceedings and Evidence,* 1971, 6:29, 18:11.

69. Interview with J. P. Côté.

70. *Financial Post,* 17 October 1970.

71. The service put the POD in conflict with the postal unions, as it required hiring a considerable number of temporary workers. Interview with J. P. Côté.

72. Interview with J. P. Côté.

73. House of Commons, *Debates,* 1970, pp. 7234-35.

Notes to chapter five

1. Postal volumes increased by 30 per cent between 1968 and 1981, compared to 48 per cent in the previous thirteen years.

2. First-class mail grew by 64 per cent between 1955 and 1968.

3. *Globe and Mail,* 3 November 1976, 12 May 1977, 24 October 1978, 12 August 1981; *Financial Post,* 14 May 1977, 7 April 1979; House of Commons, *Debates,* 1973, p. 4579.

4. *Globe and Mail,* 21 December 1978, 31 July 1981. In 1978, the Scarborough PUC used Riteway Distributors, a private carrier, to deliver its bills, at six cents a unit less than the POD charged (*Financial Post,* 14 May, 8 October 1977, 30 September 1978). Post Office Department, *Report,* 1977-78; *The Future of the Postal Service* (Ottawa: POD Market Analysis and Planning Division, August 1973).

5. Price Waterhouse & Associates, *Canada Post and the Information Transfer Market* (Ottawa: 1977).

6. Post Office Department, *The Choices for Tomorrow: Future Options for Operations of the Canada Post Office* (Ottawa: POD Strategic Planning Group, February 1976).

7. *The Future of the Postal Service.*

8. Post Office Department, *Considerations which Affect the Choice of Organizational Structure for the Canada Post Office* (Ottawa: 1978).

9. *Ibid.,* p. 7.

10. For comparative purposes, if one translated these figures into the old accounting system, no deficit appears until 1974-75. The overall deficit for this period still remained substantial: $2.2 billion, or 23 per cent of revenue.

11. Lamontagne took on the position out of loyalty to Prime Minister Trudeau, a school-mate from high-school days. He would have preferred to be at Defence, where he went later (interviews with G. Lamontagne and D. Collenette, 11 November 1991; *Globe and Mail,* 14 February 1980).

12. Interviews with J. J. Blais, 2 February 1992, and J. P. Côté, 18 November 1991.

13. Interviews with J. J. Blais, 14 August 1990, and A. Ouellet, 23 January 1990.

14. Interviews with J. Corkery, 22 January 1990, and H. Mullington, 27 June 1990. See *Globe and Mail,* 19 January 1981.

15. See J. Granatstein, "The Mailed Fist" *Canadian Forum,* April/May 1975, p. 3; M. Wolfe, "The Perennial Canadian Postal Crisis," *Saturday Night,* April 1976.

16. Interview with J. Corkery.

17. Interview with J. P. Côté; A. Ouellet at Standing Committee on Transportation and Communications, *Minutes of Proceedings and Evidence,* 1973, 8:6-7; interview with J. Corkery.

18. Post Office Department, *Report,* 1972-73. *Globe and Mail,* 7 September 1972.

19. B. Mackasey, *What's Behind the Lemming Urge* (Ottawa: POD, 1976); *Globe and Mail,* 27 July, 10 October 1977.

20. Post Office Department, *Report,* 1976-77; *Financial Post,* 23 October 1976; interview with J. J. Blais.

21. House of Commons, *Debates,* 1973, p. 4588; Standing Committee on Transportation and Communication, *Minutes of Proceedings and Evidence,* 1978, 33:7; interview with J. P. Côté; *Globe and Mail,* 27 September 1978.

22. Post Office Department, *Report,* 1979-80, p. 7.

23. Standing Committee on Transportation and Communications, *Minutes of Proceedings and Evidence,* 1974, 1:28; 1978, 33:5; 1979, 1:11; House of Commons, *Debates,* 1977, pp. 5773, 5775; Post Office Department, *Report,* 1977-78; Post Office Department, *The Future of the Postal Service* (1973); *Considerations which Affect the Choice of Structure,* p. 1.

24. Stewart-Patterson, pp. 146, 151, 161-62, 181. House of Commons, *Debates,* 30 June 1977, pp. 7222-23; 1978, p. 6207; Standing Committee on Transportation and Communications, *Minutes of Proceedings and Evidence,* 1977, 14:18; interviews with J. P. Côté, J. J. Blais, A. Ouellet.

25. Standing Committee on Transportation and Communications, *Minutes of Proceedings and Evidence,* 1973, 8:9; *Globe and Mail,* 15 May 1975.

26. On average, Canadians had to work only one minute to earn sufficient income to purchase a first-class stamp; in the United States and West Germany one had to work one and a half minutes, in Japan two and a half minutes, and in Australia and Sweden three minutes to purchase a first-class stamp (Post Office Department, *Report,* 1976-77).

27. House of Commons, *Debates,* 1977, p. 1068; *Globe and Mail,* 22 November 1977.

28. House of Commons, *Debates,* 1976, pp. 13579ff.

29.   Interview with J. J. Blais.

30.   See Standing Joint Committee on Regulation and Other Statutory Instruments; *Globe and Mail,* 12 May 1977, 21 April 1978; House of Commons, *Debates,* 1978, pp. 4937-44.

31.   The short-lived Conservative government returned to the parliamentary process of approval when it introduced Bill C-11 which involved a price increase in 1979. This legislation died on the order table when the 1980 election was called.

32.   Department of Communications, *Study of Canadian Concessionary Postal Changes and Periodical Publishers for the Evaluation of the Postal Subsidy Program* (prepared by Ekos Research Associates) (Ottawa: 16 December 1985).

33.   Post Office Department and Secretary of State Department, *Memorandum of Agreement* (Ottawa: September 1978); Post Office Department, *Report,* 1979-80.

34.   *Considerations which Affect the Choice of Structure.*

35.   Standing Committee on Transportation and Communications, *Minutes of Proceedings and Evidence,* 1973, 8:31; interviews with J. J. Blais, A. Ouellet, J. Corkery.

36.   *Globe and Mail,* 27 January 1978, 17 March 1979; House of Commons, *Debates,* 1978, pp. 4151, 4198-99, 5265; *Financial Post,* 8 February 1975; Standing Committee on Transportation and Communication, *Minutes of Proceedings and Evidence,* 1977, 13:7, 13:22; interview with J. J. Blais and G. Lamontagne.

37.   For example, see *Financial Post,* 8 February 1975; *Globe and Mail,* 22 April, 28 May 1977; House of Commons, *Debates,* 1973, pp. 4577-88; 1976, pp. 13765ff; 1978, pp. 4150-51, 4198-89, 5265; Ronald S. Ritchie, *The Ritchie Report on Canada's Postal Service* (Ottawa: April 1979).

38.   Standing Committee on Transportation and Communications, *Minutes of Proceedings and Evidence,* 1973, 8:9; House of Commons, *Debates,* 1973, p. 4588. Interviews with A. Ouellet and J. J. Blais.

39.   *Globe and Mail,* 31 July 1979; interview with J. P. Côté.

40.   Interview with J. Corkery; Auditor General, *Report,* 1974; Public Accounts Committee, *Minutes of Proceedings and Evidence,* 24:5-22.

41.   Interview with J. Corkery; see also Stewart-Patterson, p. 181.

42.   Interview with J. J. Blais.

43.   Price Waterhouse & Associates, p. 6; Department of Communications, *Telecommunications in Canada: Consultative Committee on the Implications of Telecommunications for Canadian Sovereignty* (Clyne report) (Ottawa: 1979); Ritchie; interview with J. J. Blais.

44.   A good technical overview of how the mechanization program was initiated can be found in J. G. Fultz, *Coding and Mechanization 52 Months Later* (Ottawa: POD, August 1974). Fultz was the POD official responsible for mechanizing the Post Office.

        Much of the presentation in this section is derived from this publication, as well as from interviews with postal officials and PMGs, particularly J. Corkery, J. P. Côté, A. Oullet, H. Mullington, and J. J. Blais.

45.   A hand-writing capacity was rejected at this time as being too expensive. The system also allowed the code to be placed in a relatively wide band at the bottom of the

envelope, which allowed customer latitude (albeit at the cost of the speed and precision that a more precise location would have generated).

46. *Financial Post,* 18 January 1975; *Globe and Mail,* 17 June 1975.

47. Interview with J. Corkery.

48. Interviews with J. Corkery, E. Kierans, J. P. Côté.

49. Interviews with J. P. Côté, J. Corkery, H. Mullington.

50. Interview with J. Corkery; *Financial Post,* 14 May 1977.

51. CUPW released POD documents showing the cost of the program to be $866 million: $100 million on letter-sorting machines, $8.6 million on culler-facer-cancellers, $10 million on optical character recognition machines, $154 million on other machinery, and $411 million for planning and construction of new buildings (Post Office Department, *Report,* 1977-78; *Globe and Mail,* 23 June 1975).

52. Standing Committee on Transportation and Communications, *Minutes of Proceedings and Evidence,* 1973, 1:56; 1974, 1:11-12; House of Commons, *Debates,* 1973, p. 4587; 1977, p. 5572.

53. Interview with J. P. Côté.

54. Interviews with J. Corkery and H. Mullington.

55. *Considerations which Affect the Choice of Structure,* p. 6.

56. Public Accounts Committee, *Minutes of Proceedings and Evidence,* 29 November 1979, p. 24. See also PMG Blais, Standing Committee on Transportation and Communications, *Minutes of Proceedings and Evidence,* 1977, 13, 14.

57. Interviews with H. Mullington and J. Corkery; *Globe and Mail,* 9 April 1977; Ritchie.

58. Interview with M. Warren, 9 November 1989; Ritchie.

59. House of Commons, *Debates,* 1973, p. 4578; 1977, pp. 5765-66, 5768-69; Standing Committee on Transportation and Communications, *Minutes of Proceedings and Evidence,* 1974, 1:11-12; 1977, 13:8, 14:15.

60. *Toronto Star,* 27 May 1978 (see similar articles in *Globe and Mail,* 28 September 1977, 6 May 1978; Ritchie, p.6).

61. Interview with M. Warren.

62. Interview with J. J. Blais.

63. Interview with A. Ouellet.

64. Interviews with M. Warren, H. Mullington, A. Ouellet, J. J. Blais.

65. See J. White, *Mail and Female: Women and the Canadian Union of Postal Workers,* (Toronto: Thompson Educational Publishers, 1990), pp. 75-78.

66. *Globe and Mail,* 25 April 1975.

67. Interviews with H. Mullington and J. Corkery. See also J. Granatstein; M. Wolfe.

68. Interview with D. Collennette; *Globe and Mail,* 18 January 1979. See also Post Office Department, *Industrial Relations in the Post Office: A Briefing Prepared for the Honourable Gilles Lamontagne, Postmaster General* (Ottawa: April 1978).

69. *Considerations which Affect the Choice of Structure.*

70. Public Service Staff Relations Board, *Report of the Conciliation Board in the Dispute Between the Council of Postal Unions and her Majesty in Right of Canada as Represented by the Treasury Board* (Shime Report) (Ottawa: December 1972) pp. 20-21.

71. Interview with J. Corkery.

72. Public Service Staff Relations Board, *Report of the Conciliation Board Established to Investigate and Conciliate the Dispute between the Canadian Union of Postal Workers and the Treasury Board* (Moisan report) (Ottawa: 1975), pp. 4-8; Jasmin, pp. 5, 6; Public Service Staff Relations Board, *Report of the Conciliation Board Established in Connection with the Dispute Between the Canadian Union of Postal Workers and the Treasury Board in Respect of the Postal Operations Group* (Courtemanche report) (Montreal: 1978), p. 2; Public Service Staff Relations Board, *Report of the Conciliation Board in Respect of the Dispute Affecting the Canadian Union of Postal Workers and the Treasury Board* (Jutras report) (Ottawa: 1980), p. 3.

73. White, pp. 137-38.

74. This was an injury rate of 62 per million hours worked (*Ottawa Citizen*, 7 January 1978, 23 January 1980).

75. *Globe and Mail*, 5 January 1980.

76. See White; Canada Post Corporation, *Work Disruptions History: Report 1965-83* (1984) and *Labour Relations in the Post Office: A Chronology* (Ottawa: Labour Relations Branch, 1981).

77. Treasury Board offered a three year package worth about 13 per cent, with rates of pay varying by region. The CPU was looking for sixty-six cents an hour over fifteen months plus a reduction in the work week, an annual demand of 18 per cent.

78. House of Commons, *Debates*, 1973, p. 4581; *Globe and Mail*, 17 June, 29 August, 8, 9, 13 December 1972.

79. It recommended a sixty-five cents an hour wage increase, including $400 retroactive to each employer. It also recommended the granting of five weeks of vacation after twenty-five years of service.

80. *Globe and Mail*, 15, 16, 18, 19 December 1972.

81. There remained some uncertainty about how grievances over job classification would be resolved. This resulted in some wildcat action in early January. Shime proposed that the union be allowed to grieve this issue before an adjudicator. Treasury Board agreed to this procedure (*Globe and Mail*, 19, 20 December 1972, 3-6, 9-11, 16-20, 22, 23, 25, 26 January, 16 February 1973).

82. For an excellent overview of the dispute, see White, chap. 5, from which much of this section is derived.

83. *Globe and Mail*, 12-29 April 1974.

84. Eric Taylor, *Report of Understanding Reached Respecting Modernization and Technological Change* (31 December 1974).

85. Quoted in Stewart-Patterson, p. 54.

86. Interview with J. Corkery.

87. The union looked for a $100-a-week increase and settled for the $68 increase recommended by the conciliation board. The agreement also included a cost-of-living allowance. In the last sixteen months of the contract, carriers would receive an extra one cent for each .4 increase in the Consumer Price Index, up to a maximum of ten-cents an hour in each three-month period. This offered the potential of another forty cents in 1976 and twenty cents in the first half of 1977 (*Globe and Mail*, 9, 12, 15, 17, 18, 22, 23, 25, 26, 29 April, 8 May 1975).

88. *Globe and Mail,* 17 August 1977, 6 January 1978.

89. The LCUC gained a 7.04 per cent wage increase of forty-three cents an hour, about three-cents an hour above Treasury Board's last offer (*Labour Relations in the Post Office; Globe and Mail,* 16 February, 2 May, 27-29, 31 July, 1 August, 15, 20-29 September 1978).

90. On the monetary side, the LCUC received a 9.4 per cent increase, including a cost-of-living escalator that was activated after the CPI rose by 6 per cent. A number of non-monetary issues were also resolved, including increased job security provisions. An interesting wrinkle in negotiations was the issue of coffee breaks. LCUC asked for parity with CUPW, to increase its present ten-minute breaks to fifteen minutes in the morning and afternoon. To do this, the POD would have had to juggle sixteen thousand routes and hire 324 new carriers. Instead, it simply accommodated the coffee breaks by extending the working day by ten minutes, at a cost of $6.8 million (*Labour Relations in the Post Office; Globe and Mail,* 15 February, 11 March, 1 April 1980).

91. Conciliation was chaired by R. D'Esterre and resulted in a three-way split in its 20 February report. The LCUC sought ninety-cents an hour, Treasury Board offered sixty cents, D'Esterre recommended sixty-five cents. A deal was struck at seventy cents with the cost-of-living allowance clause to be maintained (*Labour Relations in the Post Office; Globe and Mail,* 21 October, 18 December 1980, 21, 27 February, 2, 4, 13 March 1981; Public Service Staff Relations Board, *Report of the Conciliation Board Established to Investigate and Conciliate the Dispute Between the Letter Carriers Union of Canada and the Treasury Board* [D'Esterre report] [Ottawa: 1981]).

92. White, p. 113.

93. With regard to wages, CUPW asked for $3.26 an hour over a one-year contract. Treasury Board offered $1.20 over two and a half years. Moisan recommended that CUPW be given the same wage increase negotiated by LCUC in 1974, a $1.70 increase over thirty months and a cost-of-living allowance clause. He also proposed improved shift differentials and premium pay for weekend work. With respect to casuals, Moisan expressed surprise that this issue remained unsettled from the time it had been raised in the Montpetit report. Its recommendations did not seem to have been implemented. The POD had not launched any plans to limit the unnecessary use of casuals nor to rationalize the crazy system of overtime. Moisan recommended that, as a contractual obligation, these issues be studied by an independent and neutral expert and recommendations reached within ten months.

94. *Financial Post,* 31 May 1975; *Globe and Mail,* 14, 21 April, 7, 16, 23, 24, 26, 27, 29, 30 May, 5 June, 3, 7, 10, 19 July, 8, 9, 11 September 1975.

95. The Moisan report recommended that the POD be required to give advance warning of technological change, to prepare for its impact, to detail the consequences of the change, to consult in conjunction with a third party, and to resort to binding adjudication to resolve disputes. Existing employment, classification, and pay rates were to be guaranteed and retraining and relocation programs established (Moisan report, pp. 25, 27-28, 90-93, 102-121. See also *Globe and Mail,* 7-10 October 1975). In a minority report, the union representative — Irving Gaul — launched a scathing

attack against the POD, describing its attitude as "provocative . . . [it] barely tolerates the existence of the union . . . and [has] systematically refused to negotiate." He noted that while everyone outside the immediate bargaining environment agreed that job security and technological change should be negotiated, the POD hid behind the PSSRA and the issue of management rights. He also accused Moisan of meeting secretly with POD representatives after the conciliation process had ended, and for producing a report biased in favour of the employer (See Minority report to Moisan report, pp. 3-4, 5, 7-8).

96. *Globe and Mail,* 13-17, 20-25, 28-31 October, 1, 5-8, 11-15, 17-21, 24-28, 30 November, 1-3 December 1975; House of Commons, *Debates,* 1975, pp. 9135-80.

97. This led to a decline in expenditures on casuals from 8 per cent of total labour expenditure in 1974-75 to 5 per cent in 1975-76 to 3 per cent in 1980-81 (White, p. 141).

98. See White, p. 176; interview with J. Corkery, 22 January 1990.

99. *Globe and Mail,* 11, 12 December 1975.

100. *Globe and Mail,* 30 October 1977; Granatstein; Wolfe.

101. See White, pp. 177ff.

102. *Ibid.*

103. "Agreement Sabotaged," *Canadian Dimension,* July 1977, pp. 12-13; *Globe and Mail,* 1, 2, 4-6, 8, 9, 15, 18, 23 October 1976.

104. Stewart-Patterson, p. 175; interview with J. J. Blais.

105. Prime Minister Trudeau declared his frustration with the POD in August, and announced that it would be transformed into a Crown corporation. This goal was not pursued for some time, but the announcement contributed to the uncertain mood of the time (*Globe and Mail,* 13 April, 20 May, 7 June, 23 July, 15, 23, 27-30 August, 12 October 1977; Canadian Union of Postal Workers, *A Crown Corporation Will Deliver* [Ottawa: CUPW, 1977]).

106. CUPW demanded an end to work measurement and surveillance at work; improved grievance procedures, for forty-six thousand grievances were now outstanding; a 5 per cent limit to the number of casual workers who could be used in any postal office; a thirty-hour work week, at forty hours' pay; and improved benefits and overtime rates (*Globe and Mail,* 13 April, 24 September, 6, 23, 27, 29 October, 22 November, 8, 14 December 1977, 2, 4 March 1978. See also White).

107. *Globe and Mail,* 2 May, 8 June 1978; interview with G. Lamontagne.

108. Courtemanche rejected the idea of a reduction in the work week and the work day and accepted the Treasury Board salary offer. He recommended that management retain the right to measure and evaluate the work of groups of ten or more postal employees. While supporting the reduction in the use of casuals, he recommended that the POD retain authority and flexibility in the use of part-timers (Courtemanche Report).

109. It had already passed Bill C-45, the Postal Services Operation Act, in April 1978.

110. *Globe and Mail,* 7, 14, 21 April, 7, 9, 11, 13, 14, 16, 17 October 1978; interview with G. Lamontagne.

111. House of Commons, *Debates,* 1978, pp. 190-218.

112. *Globe and Mail,* 17–21, 23–27 October 1978.
113. *Globe and Mail,* 4, 11 April, 8, 9 May, 12, 18, 23, 24 October 1979, 30 January, 11 March 1980.
114. *Globe and Mail,* 4 April 1979.
115. H. J. Glasbeek and M. Mandel, "The Crime and Punishment of Jean-Claude Parrot," *Canadian Forum,* August 1979, pp. 10–14.
116. Postal clerks gained thirty-three cents an hour and mail handlers received twenty-two cents an hour, but the cost-of-living allowance was lowered to stay within Anti-Inflation Board guidelines. CUPW's reaction was that this made real wages 2 per cent less than they were in 1976.
117. Department of Labour, *Report Submitted to the Honorable Minister of Labour by the Mediator-Arbitrator Appointed under the Postal Services Continuation Act and Arbitral Award* (Tremblay report) (Ottawa: 1979). Disputes would be sent to a one-person Special Adjudication Committee, appointed by the head of the PSSRB.
118. *Globe and Mail,* 26 March, 17, 21, 22, 24 May 1980; Stewart-Patterson, p. 186.
119. The part-time issue was increasing in importance. The POD aimed to contain the number of full-time jobs by using more part-time workers in the new mechanized setting. CUPW's demand for greater shift premiums was an attempt to increase the number of day jobs, which were more attractive to CUPW members. (*Globe and Mail,* 30 November 1979, 8 May 1980; *Labour Relations in the Post Office;* White).
120. The report recommended a thirty-minute paid lunch hour, a sixty-six cents an hour wage increase, an improved cost-of-living allowance, major increases in shift and weekend premiums, protection of full-time jobs through greater limitations on overtime and part-time work, double-time wages after two hours of overtime, and improved job security. With respect to increasing the proportion of day jobs, while Jutras felt that this would create an administrative nightmare, he recommended that "the employer accept the principle . . . and try to organize his administration accordingly." He rejected the union's requests to reduce the work week and abolish work measurement and surveillance. With respect to employment guarantees, Jutras recommended following the precedent set in the LCUC contract, whereby the union was offered a written job security guarantee (Jutras Report; *Globe and Mail,* 11 April, 16 May 1980).
121. *Globe and Mail,* 17, 20-22, 24, 27 May, 3, 6 June 1980.
122. Interview with M. Warren.
123. *Globe and Mail,* 13 January, 25 April, 22 May 1981. For a good overview of the process and issues involved, see J. White, chap. 9.
124. CUPW sought a 4 per cent wage catch-up and full cost-of-living allowance protection, amounting to a $1.70-an-hour increase. Treasury Board offered seventy cents. CUPW also looked for the termination of closed circuit TV surveillance, protection from unfair disciplinary action, improved health and safety provisions (especially the right to refuse dangerous work), pre-retirement leave, improved vacations and benefits, and the protection of daytime jobs. Treasury Board rejected the proposals as being too costly, creating inflexibility in the organization of work, and setting standards much

higher than those for other workers in the public or within the private sector (*Globe and Mail*, 25 April 1981).

125. He argued that matters such as protecting day shift jobs and ending work surveillance and shift and weekend work were best studied by the new Crown corporation. He did recommend an improved vacation scheme and some alteration in shift premiums, but accepted Treasury Board's wage offer (albeit with a 6 per cent cost-of-living allowance). He approved the principle of the right to refuse dangerous work and recommended the creation of a joint health and safety committee. (Jasmin Report; *Globe and Mail*, 20, 23 June 1981).

126. Prime Minister Trudeau refused to consider back-to-work legislation and defended the right of public-sector unions to strike (House of Commons, *Debates*, 1981, pp. 11206, 11260, 11452–53).

127. *Globe and Mail* 25-27, 29-30 June, 1, 8, 9, 14 July 1981.

128. House of Commons, *Debates*, 30 June 1981; *Globe and Mail*, 1, 15 July 1981.

129. *Globe and Mail*, 1, 9, 15 July 1981.

130. House of Commons, *Debates*, 1981, pp. 11507ff; *Globe and Mail*, 15, 31 July, 1 August 1981.

131. *Globe and Mail*, 15, 16, 21, 23, 24, 29, 30 July, 7 August 1981.

132. The final contract included provisions for the right to refuse dangerous work, limits on electronic surveillance, shift premiums, and vacation improvements. The wage increase was seventy-cents an hour rather than the requested $1.70. (*Globe and Mail*, 7, 8, 11-13 August, 16 October 1981, 12 February 1982).

133. J. E. Ubering, *Report to the Postmaster General* (Ottawa: 11 August 1975).

134. *Globe and Mail*, 5 January 1977.

135. *Considerations which Affect the Choice of Structure*.

136. Post Office Department, *Major Organization and Compensation Issues in Canada Post: Report of the Joint Post Office-Treasury Board Secretariat Study Group* (Arnot-Mullington report) (Ottawa: December 1975).

137. Hay Associates, *Climate Analysis Report* (Toronto: 1975); Appendix C of Arnot-Mullington report. The study involved extensive interviewing and fifty-five hundred questionnaires.

138. The first and crucial recommendation of the Arnot-Mullington report was that the cabinet should work with the POD to set clear and realistic objectives. This process should then extend to a review and definition of the POD's organizational options in pursuing these objectives. The report recommended setting a break-even goal as the policy priority. This goal should be pursued within the organizational framework of a postal Crown corporation. This would eliminate multiple departmental authority for postal matters (Arnot-Mullington report, vol. 2, pp. 5-6).

139. Encouraged by the government, the POD created a marketing division which, in these circumstances, was bound to be a failure. This led to internal divisions within the POD, where traditional postal managers envied the marketing division's higher (i.e., private-sector-like) salaries and were cynical about and contemptuous of its activities. See Arnot-Mullington report, pp. 42ff.

140. Interviews with J. P. Côté, H. Mullington, J. Corkery, A. Ouellet, J. J. Blais.

141. Darling-Ubering-Kelly report.

Notes to chapter six

1. J. W. Langford, "Public Corporations in the 1980s: moving from rhetoric to analysis," *Canadian Public Administration*, vol. 25, no. 4, p. 619; H. Hardin *A Nation Unaware: The Canadian Economic Culture* (Vancouver: J. J. Douglas, 1974); A. Tupper & G. B. Doern (eds.), *Privitization, Public Policy and Public Corporations in Canada*, (Halifax: The Institute for Research in Public Policy, 1988), pp. 7-9.

2. Privy Council Office, *Crown Corporations: Direction, Control, Accountability* (Ottawa: 1977), pp. 8-9; Economic Council of Canada (hereafter ECC), *Minding the Public's Business* (Ottawa: 1986), pp. 9-11. See also G. Stevenson, "Canadian National Railways and VIA RAIL" in Tupper & Doern.

3. ECC, p. 17; Langford & Huffman, in J. R. S. Prichard, ed., *Crown Corporations in Canada* (Toronto: Butterworths, 1983), pp. 274ff.

4. See the Tupper & Doern volume for an excellent array of case studies.

5. A. Tupper & G. B. Doern (eds.), *Public Corporations and Public Policy* (Montreal: Institute for Research in Public Policy, 1981), pp. 15-17.

6. G. B. Doern & J. Atherton, "The Tories and the Crowns: Restraining and Privatizing in a Political Minefield," in M. J. Prince (ed.), *How Ottawa Spends 1987-88* (Toronto: Methuen, 1987) p. 129.

7. ECC, pp. 4-6.

8. J. K. Laux & M. A. Molot, *State Capitalism: Public Enterprise in Canada* (Ithaca: Cornell University Press, 1988), p. 67; ECC, pp. 5-6, 139; Chandler, chap. 8; Privy Council Office, p. 16.

9. See Stevenson in Tupper & Doern; Laux & Molot, p. 6.

10. Langford (1982), pp. 621, 622-23.

11. Tupper & Doern, *Public Corporations and Public Policy*, p. 14.

12. See R.M. Campbell, *Grand Illusions: The Politics of the Keynesian Experience in Canada* (Peterborough: Broadview, 1987) and "Post-Keynesian Policies in a Post-Schumpeterian World," in *Canadian Journal of Political and Social Theory*, Winter-Spring, Vol. 3. nos. 1, 2 (1984), pp. 72-91.

13. Laux & Molot, pp. viii, 4, 21, 34-5, 72.

14. *Ibid.,* pp. 62, 98.

15. Langford, pp. 623-24ff; ECC, chap. 8; Tupper & Doern, pp. 33ff. See also Privy Council Office.

16. Tupper & Doern, *Privitization, Public Policy and Public Corporation*, pp. 33ff; ECC, chap. 8; Privy Council Office, pp. 22ff.

17. Interview with D. Salie, 28 October 1991.

18. Tupper & Doern, *Privitization, Public Policy and Public Corporation*, p. 33.

19. ECC, p. 139.

20. The drive towards commercialization was an attempt to square this impossible circle. Commercialization was also designed to neutralize the loss of legitimacy experienced

by Crowns in the 1970s, as well as to neutralize concerns about inefficiency and malpractice. See Laux & Molot, pp. 5-6, 72-73.

21. See Department of Finance, *A New Direction for Canada* (Ottawa: 1984), p. 63; House of Commons, *Debates,* 1985, p. 5017; 1986, p. 10982; 1989, p. 9; 1990, p.12; *Budget Papers,* 1985, pp. 26-28; 1986, pp. 26-28; 1990, pp. 5, 83; 1991, pp. 11, 75-77; Tupper & Doern, *Privitization, Public Policy and Public Corporation,* pp. 1-5; G. B. Doern & J. Atherton, "The Tories and the Crowns"; D. Bercuson (*et al.*), *Sacred Trust* (Toronto: Doubleday, 1986), chap. 7; W. T. Stanbury, "Privatization and the Mulroney Government, 1984-88," in J. Gollner & D. Salee, eds., *Canada Under Mulroney* (Montreal: Vehicle Press, 1988); H. Hardin, *The Privatization Putsch* (Halifax: Institute for Research on Public Policy, 1989). In 1992, the government dissolved three dozen agencies and institutes, which included a number of Crown corporations, such as the Economic Council of Canada.

22. J. L. Tierney, *Postal Reorganization* (Boston: Auburn House, 1981), pp. 8ff.

23. See recommendation no. 2 of the Montpetit report, Royal Commission on Working Conditions in the Post Office, *Report* (Ottawa: 1966). See also Canadian Union of Postal Workers pamphlet, *Canada Post: It Can Deliver* (1986); Public Service Staff Relations Board, *Report of the Conciliation Board Established to Investigate and Conciliate the Dispute Between the Canadian Union of Postal Workers and the Treasury Board* (Moisan Report (1975); *Report of the Conciliation Board in Respect of the Dispute Affecting the Canadian Union of Postal Workers and the Treasury Board* (Jutras report, 1980); interview with J. C. Parrot, 20 December 1991. It should be noted that the LCUC was not as sanguine about the prospects of a postal Crown. In an August 1969 submission, it gave an even-handed accounting of the advantages and disadvantages. On the latter, it feared that a balanced-budget approach would squeeze jobs and service, while Crown independence would make the Post Office less vulnerable to parliamentary (political and union) influence. Its view was subsequently confirmed in the eyes of LCUC officials (Interview with B. McGarry, president of LCUC, 14 August 1990).

24. Royal Commission on Government Organization, *Report,* vol. 3, sec. 17 (Ottawa: 1963), pp. 328-29 It should be noted, though, that while the report argued that a postal Crown could be supported on "logical grounds . . . your Commissioners do not consider this the only or even the appropriate solution . . . The universality of the service and traditional public interest militate against the depriving of the Post Office of its constitution as a department of government" (Commission of Inquiry into the Increases in Rates of Pay for Civil Servants in Group 'D', *Final Report* [Ottawa: 4 August 1965], pp. 3, 4; Kates, Peat, Marwick & Co., *Blueprint for Change* [Ottawa: 1969], pp. ii, 2, 13; House of Commons, *Debates,* 1969, 1970, January 1971).

25. Interviews with J. P. Côté and J. Corkery, 22 January 1990; House of Commons, *Debates,* p. 1112.

26. *Globe and Mail,* 3 June 1971; Standing Committee on Transportation and Communication, *Minutes of Proceedings and Evidence,* 1971, 6:29, 18:11.

27. Interview with J. P. Côté.

28. Post Office Department, *Major Organization and Compensation Issues in Canada Post: Report of the Joint Post Office-Treasury Board Secretariat Study Group* (Ottawa: December

1975); Ronald S. Ritchie, *The Ritchie Report on Canada's Postal Services* (Ottawa: April 1978); Post Office Department, *Considerations Which Affect the Choice of Organizational Structure for the Canada Post Office* (Darling-Ubering-Kelly Report, Ottawa, 1978); Moisan Report; Jutras Report; Department of Labour, *Report Submitted to the Honorable Minister of Labour by the Mediator-Arbitrator Appointed under the Postal Services Continuation Act and Arbitral Award* (Tremblay Report, Ottawa, 1979). See also House of Commons, *Debates*, May 1976; *Globe and Mail*, 22 May 1976, 13, 19 May 1977, November 1977.

29. Interviews with J. P. Côté and H. Mullington.

30. Interviews with J. P. Côté, A. Ouellet, J. J. Blais; See Stewart-Patterson, pp. 146, 151, 161-62, 181, 183-84; House of Commons, *Debates*, 1977, pp. 7222-23; 1978, p. 6207; Standing Committee on Transportation and Communication, *Minutes of Proceedings and Evidence*, 1973, 8:33; 1974, 1:26; 1977, 14:18.

31. Interview with J. Corkery.

32. *Globe and Mail*, 2 August 1978.

33. Interviews with J. Corkery, G. Lamontagne, A. Ouellet, H. Mullington. See Stewart-Patterson, pp. 4-5, 184.

34. Interviews with D. Collenette and H. Mullington.

35. Interviews with G. Lamontagne and H. Mullington.

36. Interviews with J. Corkery, D. Collenette, A. Ouellet, G. Lamontagne.

37. *Globe and Mail*, 12 December 1978; *Financial Post*, 23 December 1978; Standing Committee on Transportation and Communication, *Minutes of Proceedings and Evidence*, 5 March 1978, 1:11; House of Commons, *Debates*, 1980, p. 4081. The Conservatives maintained that the proposed two-tier system was cumbersome, would perpetuate political influence in the Post Office, would confuse the lines of accountability, and indicated the extent to which the bureaucracy did not want to lose authority over the Post Office.

38. This discussion is based upon two clear and thorough presentations made during the legislative process, by PMG A. Ouellet (House of Commons, *Debates*, 24 October 1980, pp. 4075-78) and Deputy PMG J. Corkery (Senate, Committee on Transportation and Communications, *Proceedings*, 23 April 1981, 12:9ff).

39. *Globe and Mail*, 12 December 1978.

40. Standing Committee on Transportation and Communication, *Minutes of Proceedings and Evidence*, 27 November 1979, 11:10; correspondence with PMG J. Fraser.

41. Interviews with A. Ouellet, S. Carr, J. C. Parrot, J. Corkery, M. Warren. See Stewart-Patterson, p. 6. The recruitment of Michael Warren trailed the legislative process by a month or two. He talked with the PCO and PMG Ouellet about certain features of the legislation as it took shape; but he essentially confronted a legislative *fait accompli*.

42. Interview with A. Ouellet. See House of Commons, *Debates*, 1980, p. 4926, 9263-64.

43. The following are some of the groups and organizations that appeared before the legislative committee: Canadian Daily Newspapers Association, Canadian Chamber of Commerce, Canadian Business Press, Canadian Periodical Publishers Association, Gift Packaging and Greeting Card Association, Canadian Daily Newspapers Publishers

Association, Canadian Federation of Independent Business, Canadian Trucking Association, Government of Ontario, Government of Alberta, Consumers Association of Canada, Canadian Manufacturers Association, Trans Canada Telephone System, Canadian Telecommunications Carriers Association, Canadian Labour Congress, Canadian Bankers Association, Canadian Chamber of Commerce, Graphic Arts and Industries Association, Loomis Courier Services, Chief Electoral Officer, Retail Council of Canada, Institute of Canadian Advertising and Canadian Institute of Chartered Accountants. Other organizations and groups submitted written briefs to the committee, including: Action Bell Canada, Canadian Business Equipment Manufacturers Association, Canadian Direct Mail Marketing Association, Canadian Industrial Communications Assembly, Magazine Association of Canada, Ontario Trucking Association, Dominion Marine Association, General Motors, Canadian Cable Television Association, United Parcel Services, *Readers Digest* and *Time Magazine*.

44.   Michael Warren was considered to be a "boy wonder" of bureaucratic circles, having recently managed the Toronto transit system as well as the Canadian National Exhibition.

45.   House of Commons, *Debates*, 1980, p. 4077; 1981, p. 9134.

46.   Interviews with A. Ouellet and J. Corkery. See Standing Joint Committee on Regulation and Other Statutory Instruments, *Minutes of Proceedings and Evidence*, 10, 11, 12, 25, 27 November, 5, 11, 12, 14, 17 December 1980; Standing Committee on Miscellaneous Estimates, *Minutes of Proceedings and Evidence*, 16 December 1980, pp. 2-7; 17 December, pp. 55ff; Standing Committee on Transportation and Communication, *Minutes of Proceedings and Evidence*, 12:12.

47.   Standing Committee on Regulation and Other Statutory Instruments, *Minutes of Proceedings and Evidence*, 1980, 17:3, 6; Standing Committee on Miscellaneous Estimates, *Minutes of Proceedings and Evidence*, 16 December 1980, pp. 2-7; House of Commons, *Debates*, pp. 4905, 9038-56; *Globe and Mail*, 2, 13, 16, 24 December 1980, 22 August 1981.

48.   House of Commons, *Debates*, 1980, pp. 4903, 4924-25, 9038-52; Standing Committee on Regulation and Other Statutory Instruments, *Minutes of Proceedings and Evidence*, 4 December, pp. 14-15, 19, 42; 17:4, 5, 8.

49.   Interviews with D. Collenette, A. Ouellet, 23 January 1990, S. Carr, 27 June 1990, J. C. Parrot; Standing Joint Committee on Regulatory and other Statutory Instruments, *Minutes of Proceedings and Evidence*, 25 November 1980, p. 101; 27 November, p. 12, 17; 4 December 1980, p. 4; House of Commons, *Debates*, 1980, pp. 4903-4, 4924-25; Standing Committee on Miscellaneous Estimates, *Minutes of Proceedings and Evidence*, 25 November 1980, p. 32; 27 November 1980, p. 35. Representations were made to this end by the Canadian Bankers Association, the Canadian Chamber of Commerce, the Retail Council of Canada, the Gift Packaging and Greeting Card Association, the Canadian Daily Newspaper Publishers Association, the Canadian Direct Marketing Association, *Readers Digest*, and, of course, the telecommunications industry and the manufacturers of its products. Bell Canada and the Canadian Business Equipment Manufacturers Association insisted that if the Post Office became

involved in the area, it should be obliged to use existing telecommunications technology and equipment.

50. Standing Committee on Miscellaneous Estimates, *Minutes of Proceedings and Evidence,* 4 December 1980, pp. 21-26; 9 December, pp. 73-76, 95-97; 10 December, pp. 21-24; 11 December, pp. 37-39; 16 December, p. 7; *Globe and Mail,* 16 December 1980; Joint Standing Committee on Regulatory and Other Statutory Instruments, *Minutes of Proceedings and Evidence,* 1980, 17:5; 16 December, pp. 2-7; 17 December, pp. 55ff.

51. For example, the Canadian Labour Congress, Loomis Courier Service, the Canadian Chamber of Commerce, and the Consumers Association of Canada.

52. House of Commons, *Debates,* 24 October 1980, pp. 4077-78; Standing Committee on Miscellaneous Estimates, *Minutes of Proceedings and Evidence,* 1980, 16 December, p. 60; 11 December, pp. 38-39; 9 December, pp. 4-6, 12-14, 25-26, 51-54, 73-76; 4 December, p. 50; 9 December, pp. 52-53; 10 December, pp. 2-8; 16 December, p. 59-62; *Globe and Mail,* 11 December 1980; interviews with A. Ouellet, M. Warren, J. Corkery, J. J. Blais. For further background to this issue, see R. M. Campbell, "Symbolic Regulation: Third-Party Regulation of Canada Post," *Canadian Public Policy,* September 1993, vol. XIX:3, pp. 325-335.

53. Standing Committee on Transportation and Communication, *Minutes of Proceedings and Evidence,* 23 April 1981, 12:28; *Globe and Mail,* 11 June 1981; House of Commons, *Debates,* 1980, pp. 4084, 4086; Standing Committee on Miscellaneous Estimates, *Minutes of Proceedings and Evidence,* 4 December 1980, pp. 49-90.

54. House of Commons, *Debates,* 1980, pp. 4077, 4084, 4086, 4170, 9129; interviews with J. Corkery, S. Carr, J. C. Parrot.

55. Standing Committee on Miscellaneous Estimates, *Minutes of Proceedings and Evidence,* 1980, 27 November, p. 39; 4 December, pp. 49-50; 9 December, pp. 4-6.

56. These included the Canadian Business Press, the Canadian Chamber of Commerce, the Canadian Direct Mail Association, the Canadian Periodical Publishers Association, the Gift Packaging and Greeting Card Association, and the Graphic Arts Industries Association.

57. House of Commons, *Debates,* 1980, p. 4077; Standing Committee on Transportation and Communication, *Minutes of Proceedings and Evidence,* 23 April 1981, 12:34-35; Standing Committee on Miscellaneous Estimates, 1980, 4 December, pp. 49-50; 9 December, pp. 4-6, 38; 11 December, pp. 10-11.

58. See A. Ouellet in Standing Committee on Transportation and Communications, *Minutes of Proceedings and Evidence,* 23 April 1981, 12:39.

59. See Miscellaneous Estimates debates, 17 December 1980; House of Commons, *Debates,* 1981, p. 9129; 1980, p. 4077.

60. The act also directed CPC to ensure the security of the mail and to present itself as an agent of the government of Canada.

61. Nine directors was a compromise between the thirteen proposed by Bill C-27 and the seven proposed at first reading.

62. The word "transmitting" was a change from the earlier "conveying." Mailable matter was defined as "any message, information, funds or goods that may be transmitted

by post." In turn, "transmit" was defined to mean "send or convey from one place to another by any physical, electronic, optical or other means."

63. Interviews with A. Ouellet, S. Carr, J. Corkery.

64. The act directed the corporation to set postal rates that were "fair and reasonable and consistent so far as possible with providing a revenue . . . sufficient to defray [its] costs." The act also gave the corporation the authority to vary rates for bulk and pre-sorted mail.

65. Interviews with S. Carr and J. C. Parrot.

66. *Ibid.*

67. Interviews with J. Corkery and M. Warren.

68. Interview with J. C. Parrot.

69. Interview with B. McGarry, president of LCUC.

70. The POD carried out a survey of other countries' postal monopolies and whether they defined "letter." It discovered that all countries surveyed had a monopoly covering letters and correspondence, including business, personal, and government mail. In two thirds of the countries, this monopoly extended to legal documents and negotiable instruments; in five of six, it extended to invoices, bills, and statements of accounts; in half it extended to advertising material and non-advertising printed matter; one of six included periodicals, newspapers, and books. Few countries reported a legal definition of a letter, which, operationally, appeared to be something with an address and a weight limit, frequently five hundred grams or less. See Post Office Department, *Postal Monopoly Questionnaire* (Ottawa: POD Corporate Planning Branch, November 1980).

71. The Consumers Association of Canada criticized the CTC proposal as inadequately formal and biased against ordinary postal users.

72. Interview with J. Corkery.

73. *Ibid.*

74. Interview with M. Warren.

75. Interviews with J. C. Parrot and R. McGarry.

76. For example, see Ritchie report, p. 17, and *Blueprint for Change*, pp. 61-62.

77. Interviews with J. Corkery, M. Warren, A. Ouellet. There was also a practical, financial reason for dropping the idea of third-party regulation. It was apparent that, once Crowned, the Post Office would have to increase its prices substantially to control the deficit. There was fear that third-party regulators would constrain the corporation's capacity to increase prices rapidly at its debut.

78. "The argument that won the day [before Cabinet] was the fact that I was giving my colleagues a buffer zone . . . The increase would be asked by the Corporation, the public would respond. If there was not too much opposition then we agree . . . It's not the government which raised the price of stamps, it's the corporation. If there's a lot of complaints, well then we could always come in as the nice guy to reduce the request" (interview with A. Ouellet).

Notes to chapter seven

1. Ironically, the list included Sylvain Cloutier and Don Lander. They would later be chosen by the Conservative government to be the second chair and president, respectively.
2. Interviews with A. Ouellet, 23 January 1990, and M. Warren, 9 November 1989; *Globe and Mail*, 13 March 1982.
3. Interviews with A. Ouellet and J. C. Parrot, 20 December 1991. The civil service's and Warren's subsequent ruthless dealing with Corkery and other top POD officials surprised and disappointed Ouellet.
4. Interviews with M. Warren, A. Ouellet.
5. Prime Minister Trudeau first raised the possibility of this appointment with Marin, at the time Marin submitted his Royal Commission report.
6. Interviews with M. Warren, R. Marin, 28 October 1991, A. Ouellet; see also D. Stewart-Patterson, *Post-Mortem: Why Canada's Mail Won't Move* (Toronto: Macmillan, 1987) p. 211.
7. Interviews with A. Ouellet, M. Warren; see also Stewart-Patterson, pp. 214-15.
8. Interviews with R. Marin, M. Warren.
9. Canada Post Corporation, *Report*, 1982-83, pp. 2, 22; 1983-84, pp. 3, 5; House of Commons, Standing Committee on Transportation and Communication, *Minutes of Proceedings and Evidence*, vol. 16, 1984-86, p. 96; House of Commons, Public Accounts Committee, *Minutes of Proceedings and Evidence*, vol. 73, 1980-82; Canada Post Corporation, *It's Our Future: The 1983-84 Business Plan* (Ottawa: CPC, 1983).
10. Canada Post Corporation, *Postal Related Habits and Attitudes of the Canadian Public* (Ottawa: CPC Marketing Service Branch, Marketing Directorate, March 1982).
11. See M. Warren in Standing Committee on Transportation and Communication, *Minutes of Proceedings and Evidence*, vol. 16, 1983-4, 24 May 1984, pp. 6-7.
12. Canadian Trend Report, *Labour Relations: A Critical Test for Corporate Management at Canada Post, A Baseline Study, 1981 versus January-October 1983* (Montreal: December 1983).
13. Department of Communications, *Towards a Policy Framework for the Economic Development of the Communications/Information Sector* (prepared by Price Waterhouse for Communications Economics Branch [Montreal: 1981]).
14. *Globe and Mail*, 29 September 1983.
15. Canada Post, *Annual Report*, 1982-83. See also *Annual Report*, 1983-84, p. 7.
16. Interview with M. Warren; Standing Committee on Transportation and Communication, vol. 16, 1984-86, 11 June 1985-86, p. 8.
17. House of Commons, *Debates*, 1981, p. 12725.
18. Interview with A. Ouellet.
19. Interview with R. Marin.
20. Interview with S. Carr, 27 June 1990.
21. Interviews with J. Corkery, 22 January 1990, A. Ouellet, M. Warren.
22. Interview with M. Warren.
23. Interviews with M. Warren, J. Corkery; *Globe and Mail*, 26 September 1981.

24.   Stewart-Patterson, p. 228.

25.   Interview with M. Warren; *Globe and Mail,* 28 September 1983, 14, 15 February, 19 October 1984; Standing Committee on Transportation and Communication, 24 May 1984, pp. 20-21; Canada Post Corporation, *Annual Report,* 1982-83, p. 6; *It's Our Future.*

26.   *Globe and Mail,* 18 May 1982.

27.   See *Globe and Mail,* 9 November 1981; Public Accounts Committee, 16 February 1980-82; Standing Committee on Transportation and Communication, 11 June 1985; interviews with M. Warren, R. Marin.

28.   See 1983-84 business plan and 1982-83 annual report; Review Committee on the Mandate and Productivity of Canada Post Corporation, *Report* (Ottawa: November 1985), p. 7 (hereafter the Marchment report).

29.   See Canada Post Corporation, *Attendance Improvement Task Force* (1983); see also unpublished draft of first five-year plan (1983); *Globe and Mail,* 17 May 1982; J. White, *Mail and Female: Women and the Canadian Union of Postal Workers,* (Toronto: Thompson Educational Publishers, 1990) pp. 173-74; Standing Committee on Transportation and Communication, vol. 16, 1984-86, 11, 13 June 1985; *Canadian Labour,* November-December 1983.

30.   Backgrounder to CPC's Business Plan (1984). Warren's claim that this was a "productivity" deal was overstated, according to B. McGarry, head of the LCUC. He states that Warren was concerned about the perception that this was a "rich" settlement. As a result, he came to the LCUC and said that this was the "spin" he was going to put on it to the media, that the settlement had been paid by saving money here and there. Most of the arrangements were already within Warren's domain as management rights, but LCUC went along with Warren's claim, as they had already received their money (interview with B. McGarry. LCUC president, 14 August 1990).

31.   See Canada Post, *Annual Report,* 1982-83, p. 18; 1983-84, p. 19.

32.   Warren was opposed to labour representation on the board, which he claimed made the environment more difficult for making decisions. There was a bloody battle over Ouellet's later naming of LCUC president B. McGarry to the board. The two previous labour representatives had not been from the Post Office. Warren claimed that the corporation got nothing in return, for example, a no-strike *quid pro quo.*

33.   Interview with M. Warren.

34.   Public Accounts Committee, *Report,* vol. 73, 1980-82, pp. 31-32.

35.   Canada Post, *Annual Report,* 1984-85.

36.   Interview with M. Warren; Standing Committee on Miscellaneous Estimates, vol. 20, 1984-86, 23 May 1985; Standing Committee on Transportation and Communication, vol. 16, 1983-84, 24 May 1984, pp. 13-15 and 11 June 1985, p. 19; *Globe and Mail,* 27 April 1985; CPC submission to the Marchment Committee. Alternate day delivery was studied but never given serious consideration, as it made little sense given that 70 per cent or more of mail was business mail.

37.   See draft of October 1983 five year plan (unreleased); 1984-85 five year plan; *Globe and Mail,* 24 November 1983; Standing Committee on Miscellaneous Estimates, *Min-*

utes of Proceedings and Evidence, 3 May 1985; Standing Committee on Transportation and Communication, 1983-84, 24 May 1984 and 11 June 1985.

38.   *Globe and Mail,* 27 April 1985; interview with M. Warren.

39.   Interview with M. Warren.

40.   *Financial Post,* 12 March 1983. Of the top ten postal bureaucrats, only two "survived" to assume positions on the CPC vice-presidential team. (Stewart-Patterson, p. 2; interview with H. Mullington) Warren's view was that most of the senior POD management had been burned out by the horrible experiences of the 1970s, and that better people were required to deal with the more competitive, technologically sophisticated situation of the 1980s, when expectations were also much higher (interview with M. Warren). There was a melancholy and brutal feature to this change in management, as people with obvious skill and experience were more or less forced out. For example, Deputy Minister Corkery was not informed that the new CPC president was to be recruited from outside the POD and, after entering the competition, found himself playing CEO to Warren as president. This was an unstable situation, which led to Corkery's being forced out. Warren created a team that was very much his, but this left many cruelly disappointed people. Many postal officials felt that since they had been the ones who had fought to make the POD a Crown corporation, they should have been given the first opportunity to make CPC work. On the other hand, there was some logic — political and otherwise — in the idea of beginning a new era with a new management team (interviews with H. Mullington, J. Corkery, R. Marin, A. Ouellet).

41.   Canada Post, *Annual Report,* 1982-83, p. 6; 1983-84, p. 7; *Financial Post,* 2 May 1981, 12 March 1983.

42.   Canada Post, *Annual Report,* 1983-84; *Financial Post,* 15 November 1980, 2 May 1981, 12 March 1983; Public Accounts Committee, 6 March 1984.

43.   Canada Post, *Annual Report,* 1982-83, 1983-84, 1984-85; *Globe and Mail,* 16 February, 16 May 1983, 26, 27 November 1984.

44.   Public Accounts Committee, vol. 73, 1980-82, 15 March 1983, p. 28; 6 March 1984, pp. 24-25. In March 1983, CPC letter carriers read meters in Markham; see *Globe and Mail,* 11 March 1983.

45.   See Canada Post, 1983-84 business plan; *Globe and Mail,* 26 February 1983; CPC submission to the Marchment Committee.

46.   *Globe and Mail,* 28, 29 February 1984.

47.   This was done partially in response to union complaints about CPC's plans to extend the sub-post office network (which in itself was a revenue-generating but job-threatening strategy).

48.   See Canada Post, *Annual Report,* 1984-85, 1985-86; White, pp. 176-77.

49.   Interview with J. C. Parrot.

50.   *Ibid.*

51.   House of Commons, *Debates,* 1982, pp. 20889, 20891, 20898, 20902; Standing Committee on Transportation and Communication, *Minutes of Proceedings and Evidence,* vol. 16, 1983-84, 24 May 1984, p. 18.

52. Businesspeople predicted dire economic consequences if the price increase was ratified. The CFIB claimed that the price increase could have been limited to only twenty-three cents, if proper efforts had been made to improve efficiency. It predicted a sharp rise in business failures. The CDMA predicted a significant drop in the use of third-class mail. The Canadian Manufacturers Association insisted that various exemptions be devised to entice business with lower rates. It was later claimed that the price increase had had a devastating impact on card manufacturers. A small Toronto citizens' group — Voice for Concerned Citizens — published a leaflet urging Canadians to protest the price increase by using twenty-five-cent stamps instead of thirty cent ones.

53. *Globe and Mail,* 26 September, 22 December 1981, 6 January 1982; House of Commons, *Debates,* 1982, p. 29889; Canada Post files.

54. The overwhelmingly negative reaction to the price proposal extended the consultation process, and CPC, unable to wait any longer for government approval, was forced to print a set of interim "A" stamps until approval was finally forthcoming.

55. *Globe and Mail,* 23 October, 1 November 1982, 15 February 1983.

56. *Globe and Mail,* 19 October 1984.

57. *Globe and Mail,* 28 September 1983; interviews with M. Warren and R. Marin; Standing Committee on Transportation and Communication, *Minutes of Proceedings and Evidence,* vol. 16, 24 May 1984, pp. 20-21.

58. *Globe and Mail,* 11, 14, 22 January, 3 February, 28 October 1982.

59. Interviews with M. Warren, A. Ouellet.

60. The Association of Couriers worried that the new definition would put couriers out of business. The Consumers Association of Canada opposed the proposal on the grounds that CPC's monopoly would be strengthened and allow it privileged entry into electronic communications. Other concerns included the proposal's impact on the banking payments clearing system as well as on intra-organizational mail (*Globe and Mail,* 28 August, 13, 16, 28 October, 24 November 1982, 18 January 1983. See also Canada Post Corporation, *Definition of Letter — Summary of the Information Received* [Ottawa; 1982]).

61. House of Commons, *Debates,* 23 November 1982; press release from A. Ouellet's office, 23 November 1982; *Globe and Mail,* 24 November 1982.

62. *Globe and Mail,* 18 January, 12 February, 31 May 1983.

63. *Globe and Mail,* 31 May 1983, 1 November 1982.

64. Canada Post, *Annual Report,* 1982-83, p. 16.

65. House of Commons, *Debates,* 29 July 1982, pp. 19822-28; 23 November 1982, pp. 20889-98; Standing Committee on Transportation and Communication, *Minutes of Proceedings and Evidence,* 24 May 1984, pp. 8-9, 18; 13 June 1985, pp. 7-20; *Globe and Mail,* 21, 23 August 1982; CPC submission to the Marchment Committee.

66. Canada Post, draft of 1983-84 business plan (unreleased, October 1983); *Globe and Mail,* 24, 28, 30 November, 1, 7, 8 December 1983.

67. *Globe and Mail,* 5 May 1983, 14 November 1984.

68. Department of Communications, *Towards a Policy Framework.*

69. Interview with R. Marin.

70.   Standing Committee on Miscellaneous Estimates, *Minutes of Proceedings and Evidence,* vol. 14, 1983–84, pp. 16, 48, 51; Public Accounts Committee, *Minutes of Proceedings and Evidence,* 6 March 1984, pp. 23, 26; Standing Committee on Transportation and Communication, *Minutes of Proceedings and Evidence,* 24 May 1984, pp. 44–47; *Globe and Mail,* 20 April 1983.

71.   Interview with M. Warren.

72.   *Globe and Mail,* 19 May, 19 October 1984; letter from Mulroney to CPAA president G. Hooper, 14 August 1984.

73.   *Globe and Mail,* 22 October 1984.

74.   CPC, *Postal Related Habits and Attitudes;* Standing Committee on Miscellaneous Estimates, *Minutes of Proceedings and Evidence,* vol. 14, 1983–84, p. 16.

75.   Interviews with A. Ouellet, M. Bourque.

76.   Public Service Staff Relations Board, *In the Matter of the Canadian Labour Code and a Dispute Affecting Canada Post Corporation and the Canadian Union of Postal Workers* (Ottawa: 1985), p. 5 (hereafter the Hartt report).

77.   For example, see *Globe and Mail,* 31 January 1983.

78.   Interview with M. Warren.

79.   See *Globe and Mail,* 12 October 1984.

80.   National Association of Major Mail Users, *Report,* (NAMMU, Montreal: 1984) p. 1

81.   Canada Post Corporation, *Report,* 1983–84; see CPC submission to Marchment Committee.

82.   NAMMU, *Report,* 1984, p. 2; *Globe and Mail,* 15 December 1981; *Financial Post,* 31 October 1981, 16 January 1982.

83.   NAMMU, *Report,* 1984, pp. 3, 8, 10, 18, 35.

84.   Interview with J. C. Parrot.

85.   Canada Post Corporation, *Annual Report,* 1982–83, p. 18; 1983–84, p. 19; White, p. 172.

86.   E. Hoogers, "And — At Last — The True Facts About the Post Office," *Canadian Dimension,* October/November 1982, pp. 5–7; *Globe and Mail,* 20 January, 23 May, 10 October 1983, 17 February 1984; interviews with J. C. Parrot, B. McGarry. See also Canada Post, *Attendance Improvement Task Force* (Ottawa: CPC, 1983). The report claimed that absenteeism had cost the corporation $125 million in the last fiscal year, with an absentee rate twice the industrial average.

87.   Interviews with J. C. Parrot, B. McGarry, LCUC president. See also Hoogers; *Globe and Mail,* 20 January, 18 October 1983; Marchment Report, p. 7.

88.   See 1983–84 business plan (draft); White, p.174.

89.   *Globe and Mail,* 5, 29, 30 November, 1, 7, 8 December 1984; interviews with S. Carr, J. C. Parrot, and B. McGarry.

90.   *Globe and Mail,* 8–12 April 1985.

91.   The contract was accepted by only 55 per cent of LCUC members. *Globe and Mail,* 22 June, 18 September, 4, 5, 30 October 1984.

92.   *Globe and Mail,* 13 March, 4 July, 23 September, 20 October 1984.

93.   *Globe and Mail,* 3 September, 22 October 1984, 2, 23, 26 February, 2 March 1985.

94. CUPW also gained a new and fully paid dental plan, hearing-aid and eye-care programs, an extra week of leave in each of the five years preceding retirement, three extra days of leave for night-shift workers, and four weeks of vacation after seven years.

95. Hartt report, 1985; *Globe and Mail,* 7, 8, 10-12 March 1985.

96. Interview with M. Warren.

97. Canada Post, *Annual Report,* 1983-84, p. 28; 1984-85.

98. See Michael Warren in Standing Committee on Miscellaneous Estimates, *Minutes of Proceedings and Evidence,* 23 May 1985, p. 71; Standing Committee on Transportation and Communication, *Minutes of Proceedings and Evidence,* vol. 16, 1984-86, p. 47.

99. *Ibid.,* 1982-83; *Globe and Mail,* 25 February 1984.

Notes to chapter eight

1. M. Wilson, Economic Statement, 8 November 1984, and *A New Direction for Canada* (Ottawa: Department of Finance, November 1984); M. Wilson, *Budget Speech,* 23 May 1985.

2. *Ibid.*

3. For a good overview of the Conservatives' agenda, see the various editions of *How Ottawa Spends* from 1985-92. For example, see Katherine A. Graham, ed., *How Ottawa Spends, 1990-91* (Ottawa: Carleton University Press, 1990), pp. 1-9. See also A. B. Gollner & D. Salee, eds., *Canada Under Mulroney* (Montreal: Vehicule Press, 1988).

4. See Wilson, Economic Statement, 8 November 1984, p. 63.

5. House of Commons, *Debates,* 1985, p. 5017.

6. House of Commons, *Debates,* 1986, p. 10982.

7. For a good overview of these developments, see W. T. Stanbury, "Privatization and the Mulroney Government, 1984-88," in Gollner & Salee, pp. 119-27; and G. Bruce Doern & J. Atherton, "The Tories and the Crowns: Restraining and Privatizing in a Political Minefield," in *How Ottawa Spends, 1987-88,* pp. 129-175.

8. Interviews with R. Marin, 28 October 1991, M. Warren, 9 November 1989; *Globe and Mail,* 26, 27 July, 2, 5 August 1985; Ken MacQueen, "Michael Warren Bows Out," *Maclean's,* 5 August 1985, p. 12; Stewart-Patterson, pp. 253, 259.

9. See Ronald Ritchie, *The Ritchie Report on Canada's Postal Services* (Ottawa: April 1978).

10. The letter was written on 14 August 1984; cited in the postal workers' pamphlet "It Can Deliver," October 1986.

11. Hansard records but a dozen or so references to the Post Office in these years.

12. Interviews with M. Bourque, 27 June 1990, M. Warren.

13. *Globe and Mail,* 19 October 1984.

14. Interviews with M. Warren, M. Bourque.

15. Interview with M. Warren.

16. Interviews with R. Marin, M. Bourque.

17. The plan included various items: the injection of a new "corporate culture," productivity bargaining and increased labour flexibility, a planned 5 per cent increase in productivity through downsizing the labour force by three thousand, a major

campaign against absenteeism, making wages comparable to those in the private sector, a two-cent increase in the price of a first-class stamp, major capital plans to upgrade plant and equipment, and the aggressive development of e-mail and the parcel business.

18. Interviews with D. Salie, 28 October 1991, M. Bourque, 27 June 1990, and M. Warren. The plan presented by CPC also involved some innovative proposals for "off-shore" financing, which would not have appeared as a capital expense on CPC books. This financing would eventually have had to be repaid through postal surpluses. This feature of the plan may not have been within CPC's legal mandate (interviews with various government sources).

19. *Globe and Mail,* 13 March, 10, 11, 17, 22 April, 22 May, 5, 6, 14, 21, 24 June 1985; interview with R. Marin, M. Bourque; House of Commons, *Debates,* 1985, p. 6087.

20. The board's view was that the government was the shareholder, and so could do what it liked. Moreover, it concluded that after a first period of adjustment, the Crown corporation needed another examination to see if its orientation should be redirected (interview with R. Marin).

21. Interviews with M. Bourque and M. Warren; *Globe and Mail,* 10, 13 January, 28 June 1984, 13, 16, 17, 24 April, 23 November 1985; D. Stewart-Patterson, *Post-Mortem: Why Canada's Mail Won't Move* (Toronto: Macmillan, 1987), pp. 257-58. See also Laventhal & Howarth, *An Investigation of the Allegations Made by Postal Clerk A. N. Varma* (Ottawa, October 1985).

22. Review Committee on the Mandate and Productivity of Canada Post Corporation, *Report* (Ottawa: 1985) (hereafter the Marchment report).

23. The government's choice of Marchment appears not to have had a particular logic. He was an experienced businessman, available for the assignment and willing to do a job that many would have shunned. He received a totally unexpected telephone call from Beatty recruiting him for the position. He had no idea why he was chosen, as he had no postal background and had never met Beatty (interviews with A. Marchment, 26 June 1990, M. Bourque).

24. Interview with M. Bourque.

25. *Globe and Mail,* 17, 21 July, 1 August 1985; interviews with J. C. Parrot, A. Marchment, R. Marin.

26. Interview with A. Marchment.

27. Interview with M. Bourque.

28. Marchment report, pp. 6, 9; Marc Clark, "Drawing the Battle Lines" *Maclean's,* 12 October 1987, pp. 10-14.

29. Marchment report, pp. 7, 11, 12, 15, 17, 23, 36, 37; *Maclean's,* 12 October 1987.

30. In a submission to the committee, Canada Post declared that "if [it] is denied the opportunity of future developments in its traditional market areas, the ability to make fundamental changes in current ways in which mail service is provided, and is limited to providing universal hard copy letter mail services, the future can be expected to develop as follows": CPC would spiral downward into a vicious decline, as postal costs would increase and prices would rise; volumes would plummet and the deficit would rise; the quality of postal service would have to be cut; and down-

sizing would generate labour unrest over lost jobs, leading to a further deterioration in service, volumes, and finances (Canada Post Corporation presentation to Marchment Committee, pp. 15, 18-19, 24-25).

31. See brief submitted by CLC, CPAA, CUPW, IBEW, LCUC, and UPCE, 5 September 1985, Ottawa.

32. National Association of Major Mail Users, *Brief to the Review Committee on the Mandate and Productivity of the Canada Post Corporation*, 15 August 1985, p. 22.

33. Marchment report, pp. 9, 11, 12, 42, 44; interview with A. Marchment.

34. "The key issue is the resolution of the cost-service equation. Current service expectations cannot be met if at the same time the Corporation is expected to be self-supporting financially on a consistent basis. Acceptance must be gained for fundamental changes in the way in which universal postal service is provided to Canadians" (Canada Post submission to Marchment Committee, pp. 5, 12-3, 15, 19-20).

35. Joint postal union submission to Marchment Committee.

36. Marchment report, 13, 16, 18-9, 29-30.

37. Joint postal union submission to Marchment Committee, p. 91.

38. CPC submission to Marchment Committee, p. 23. Canada Post still lacked a detailed base of disaggregated cost and price information, which would be required in formal regulatory hearings over proposals to increase postal rates.

39. These would involve customers working closely with CPC on an individual basis, to set rates and obligations based on the real costs and benefits of their specific arrangements. NAMMU claimed that this would create a fairer rate structure for business users, whose present high prices effectively subsidized the "personal" mail user (NAMMU submission to Marchment Committee, pp. 7, 11-13).

40. Marchment report, pp. 23-24, 27-28; interview with A. Marchment.

41. Marchment report, pp. 7, 21, 22.

42. Interview with A. Marchment. See Canada Post, *Summary of Recommendations of Marchment Committee and Actions Taken* (Ottawa: CPC, 1986), pp. 1-6.

43. House of Commons, *Debates*, 1986, pp. 10982, 11011-12.

44. Canada Post Corporation, *Annual Report*, 1985-86, p. 5.

45. House of Commons, *Debates*, 1986, pp. 10997, 13569-95.

46. *Ibid.*, pp. 14212, 14214.

47. *Globe and Mail*, 28 February, 22 March 1986.

48. House of Commons, *Debates*, 1986, p. 14214.

49. See Canadian Labour Congress, *Canada Post: It Can Deliver* (CPC: August 1986).

50. In early March 1987, Minister of State (Privatization) Barbara McDougall responded to a query about privatizing Canada Post: "It would take me three and a half minutes to decide not to, because it takes a buyer as well as a seller, and I would not have to go very far as I know there are not a lot of buyers . . . you would have to pay somebody to take it off your hands for them to provide the service" (Standing Committee on Government Operations, *Minutes of Proceedings and Evidence*, 4 March 1987).

51. Lander was named interim president on 1 August 1985 and president in February 1986.

52. Interview with David L. Salie, Crown Corporation Directorate, Department of Finance and Treasury Board; Standing Committee on Miscellaneous Estimates, *Minutes of Proceedings and Evidence*, 21 May 1986; *Globe and Mail*, 22 May 1986.

53. Interview with J. C. Parrot.

54. Interview with R. Marin. See also Stewart-Patterson, pp. 208, 267-70; *Globe and Mail*, 27 November 1985.

55. *Globe and Mail*, 10 February 1987.

56. See Ministerial Task Force on Program Review, *Report* (Ottawa: August 1985)

57. The plan was to close 20 in 1987-88, 87 in 1988-89, 108 in 1989-90, 98 in 1990-91, 88 in 1991-92, 153 in 1992-93, 120 in 1993-94, 30 in 1994-95, and 30 in 1995-96. The plan also noted that while private-sector outlets represented only 25 per cent of post offices, they generated 34 per cent of postal revenues.

58. Interviews with D. Salie, G. Billyard, 17 October 1991. See also Lander's testimony before the Standing Committee on Government Operations, *Minutes of Proceedings and Evidence*, no. 2, 3, 5, 6.

59. House of Commons, *Debates*, 1986, pp. 1108-12, 1140-41, 1912, 1917, 1938, 13254-55, 13571, 13583, 14213.

60. Standing Committee on Government Operations, *Minutes of Proceedings and Evidence*, 4 December 1986, no. 6, p. 37.

Notes to Chapter nine

1. Canada Post Corporation, *Business Mandate: The Economic Impact of the Corporate Reputation of Canada Post*. Market Research Branch, Marketing and Sales, Plog Research Limited, no. 6646, February 1985 [Hereafter referred to as the *Plog report*].

2. *Financial Times*, 16-22 October 1989.

3. Interview with J.C. Parrot, 20 December 1991.

4. See Canada Post Corporation, *Summary of the 1987/88 to 1991/92 Corporate Plan* and *Summary of the 1991/92 to 1995/96 Corporate Plan*. The 1992/93 to 1996/97 plan noted that price increases would comprise about one-third of future funding requirements (p. 4).

5. House of Commons, *Debates*, 1986, p. 10982.

6. Canada Post Corporation, *Annual Report*, 1985-86.

7. Canada Post Corporation, *Summary of the 1986/87 to 1990/91 Corporate Plan*.

8. Canada Post Corporation, *Annual Report*, 1986-87, 1987-88.

9. Canada Post Corporation, *Summary of 1988/89 to 1992/93 Corporate Plan*, p. 29.

10. House of Commons, *Debates*, 1989, pp. 1060ff; see also Budget Papers, pp. 72-3.

11. See S.G. Warburg, *A Financial Framework for Canada Post Corporation* (August 1989). Other ratios included:
Leverage Ratios: debt-to-equity ratio of 45-65 per cent; cash flow to debt ratio of 30-40 per cent
Liquidity Ratios: current ratio of 0.5-0.7; gross interest coverage 3-5x
Investment Ratios: fixed asset investment rate 10-15 per cent; cash flow to capital expenditures 80-100 per cent

Payout Ratio: dividend payout 35-45 per cent

12. Canada Post Corporation, *Summary of the 1989/90 to 1993/94 Corporate Plan.*

13. House of Commons, Standing Committee on Consumer and Corporate Affairs, *Minutes of Proceedings and Evidence*, 31 October 1989, p. 18.

14. Ibid., 2 November 1989, p. 24.

15. Ibid., 31 October 1989, p. 27.

16. House of Commons, Consumer and Corporate Affairs Committee, *Report*, April 1990; Postal Services Review Committee, *Recommendations to Canada Post Corporation Regarding its Proposed January 1990 Changes to Regulations* (Ottawa: November 1989), pp. 17-20.

17. Canada Post Corporation, *Annual Report*, 1989-90.

18. Canada Post Corporation, *Annual Report*, 1990-91, 1991-92, 1992-93; *Summary of the 1991/92 to 1995/96 Corporate Plan; Summary of the 1992/93 to 1996/97 Corporate Plan; Summary of the 1993/94 to 1997/98 Corporate Plan.* The last corporate plan anticipated a 3 per cent return on equity in 1993-94 rising gradually to 7 per cent in 1997-98.

19. House of Commons, *Debates*, p. 1060ff. This price increase was reviewed by the Postal Services Review Committee, an event examined in chapter 10.

20. In real terms, the price of a stamp declined from 30 cents to 26.3 cents (excluding taxes) between January 1982 and January 1992. Canada Post Corporations, News Release, 26 June 1992.

21. Canada Post Corporation, *Annual Report*, 1991-92, p. 3. In Canada, 1.67 minutes of labour were required to earn the basic letter rate. This compared with 1.55 minutes in the U.S., 2.49 minutes in the U.K., and 2.1 minutes in Australia.

22. For a discussion of this general issue, see *Globe and Mail*, 13 June 1988; *The Toronto Star*, 9 November 1989.

23. The 1992-93 report indicated that there were no substantial gains made in this area.

24. Plog report, p. 32.

25. Interview with W.T. Kennedy, 25 November 1991.

26. House of Commons, Standing Committee on Consumer and Corporate Affairs and Government Operations, *Minutes of Proceedings and Evidence*, no. 4, 20 June 1991.

27. See, for example, House of Commons, *Debates*, 1991, pp. 519, 711-12, 715-16.

28. Ibid.

29. In 1990-91, it issued a souvenir-edition folder containing four collectible stamps featuring mythical Canadian figures, such as the Sasquatch. It produced two million related activity books and fifteen million thirty-nine-cent stamps. For a sponsorship fee of around $250,000, it placed the McDonald's name on all ad material and products, including on the border, or selvage, of the stamps (this was a first). In 1991-92, McDonald's handed out two stamp-related "treats of the week," in association with games and puzzles in which the stamps would be used.

30. *Globe and Mail*, 15 September 1990; Canada Post Corporation, *Annual Report*, 1991-92.

31. This is not done in Toronto, whose rates are considered to be too high.

32. Interview with W.T. Kennedy, 25 November 1991.

33. Plog report, p. 113.

34. Interview with Jack Van Dusen, Director, Media Relations, Canada Post Corporation, 28 November 1991.

35. For example, see *Globe and Mail*, 19 June 1991. The coverage of the 1991-92 loss of $128 billion was spotty and insubstantial, and mainly featured a dispute between CPC and the postal unions as to what caused the loss. The corporation attributed the loss to declining volumes associated with the strike and its aftermath; the unions pointed to the expenses associated with CPC's elaborate efforts to continue delivering the mail during the strike. See, for example, *The Ottawa Citizen*, 20 June 1992; *Montreal Gazette*, 19 June 1992.

36. *Globe and Mail*, 23 August 1991.

37. For example, see the cover story on CPC in *Canadian Business*, November 1990, and the feature story in *Globe and Mail*'s first article (23 June 1992) on its "Change Page: Managing in the New World Economy," which was entitled "The post office and the power of information."

38. Interview with David Newman, director, Community and Business Affairs, Canada Post Corporation, 28 November 1991.

39. See, for example, NAMMU, *1988 Report*, p. 2.

40. See the full-page ad in *Globe and Mail*, 28 November 1991.

41. Interview with W.T. Kennedy, 25 November 1991.

42. Canada Post Corporation, news release, 30 April 1992.

43. See, for example, *Globe and Mail*, 23 June 1992.

44. Canada Post Corporation, *Annual Report*, 1985-88, p. 8.

45. *Globe and Mail*, 24 February, 26 July 1988; 25 January, 26 April, 26 July 1989; 25 April 1990; Canada Post Corporation, *Annual Report*, 1991-92. Ernst and Young reported that between April and June 1992 CPC delivered packages and mail on time between 98 and 99 per cent of the time. CPC reported that 90 per cent of mail met the service standard minus one business day (1992-93 Report). The impact of these reports was undercut in 1991, when it was reported that CPC's contract with the auditor — by now, Ernst and Young — included some intriguing features. Apparently, the $15 million contract can be cancelled at any time; CPC has the right to "kill" any negative reports the auditor might make; and two other "secret" audits are done monthly and quarterly (*The Toronto Star*, 11 October 1990).

46. *Performance*, April/May 1992, vol. 7, no. 1, p. 25.

47. Canada Post Corporation, *The 1990-91 to 1994-95 Corporate Plan* (Ottawa: 1990).

48. Generally speaking, courier customers are most interested in speed and security/traceability, with price as a lesser concern. Hence, CPC's recent emphasis on these two factors.

49. CPC invested $32.4 million in this enterprise in 1991-92.

50. CPC has thirty-four dealers across Canada, at least one in each province. These dealers are given exclusive contracts to service small and medium-sized businesses time-sensitive parcel and envelope needs in particular areas, and can conduct business for Priority Post, Expedited Parcels, and Special Letter. See *Montreal Gazette*, 18 May 1993.

51. For example, Purolator lost $18 million in 1990 after having made only $1 million the previous year. *The Financial Post*, 15 February 1992.

52. For an overview of the courier market and CPC's place in it, see the special insert in *Globe and Mail*, 9 July 1991. See also *The Financial Post*, 19 February 1991; *Globe and Mail*, 30 July 1991. There were a number of reasons why CPC purchased Purolator, including a need to decrease reliance on traditional mail and to become competitive with the large American couriers. Moreover, "this partnership allows [CPC] to learn from, and take advantage of, the innovation and technological expertise that each company brings to the partnership and to thereby better meet consumer needs and successfully compete in an increasingly aggressive marketplace." Purolator would continue to operate as a separate company with separate management. Press reaction was sceptical. See *Globe and Mail*, 6-8 June 1993.

53. Households received a one-dollar coupon valid on the purchase of fifty first-class stamps, which maintained the price of a stamp at forty cents instead of the actual price of forty-two cents.

54. CPC claimed that returns were costing it millions of dollars a year in extra expenses. See *Montreal Gazette*, 10 February 1993. CUPW ridiculed this position in a letter to the editor, *Globe and Mail*, 1 March 1992.

55. NAMMU, *Annual Report*, various years.

56. Canada Post Corporation, *Annual Report*, 1985-86, p. 5.

57. "At the time of incorporation, Canada Post inherited an asset base consisting of many facilities which were obsolete, expensive to operate, ill-suited to the requirements of the Corporation, poorly upgraded, or surplus to needs." See Canada Post Corporation, *1986-87 to 1991-92 Corporate Plan* (Ottawa: p. 12)

58. See also *Financial Times*, 16-22 October 1989; *The Financial Post*, 26 March 1988; *Maclean's*, 9 October 1989. For a full overview, see Don Lander's presentation at the Consumer and Corporate Affairs Committee hearings, 31 October 1989, pp. 33-34.

59. The 1990-91 plan presented a lower than expected $355 million capital budget for 1990-91; the 1991-2 report noted that capital investment was lowered by $174 million, to $95 million.

60. Derived from Canada Post Corporation, assorted years; also data provided by CPC's Corporate Data Reference and Support Centre. The 1993 plan projects a $275 capital budget for 1993-94.

61. See Canada Post, news release, 21 May 1992; *Globe and Mail*, 22 May 1992.

62. Interview with Leo Blanchette, Canada Post Corporation, vice-president, Mail Operations, 25 November 1991. See also *Globe and Mail*, 3 May 1990.

63. CPC has attempted to introduce new clerk categories — "fast coder clerks" — to this end. It proposed a $9.35 an hour rate, far below the $15.86 rate earned by level PO4 clerks.

64. Most of what follows is derived from an interview with Dr. K. Tucker, 25 November 1991.

65. Plog report, p. 6.

66. H.N. Janitsch and R. Schultz, *Exploring the Information Revolution: Telecommunications Issues and Options for Canada* (Toronto: Royal Bank, October 1989); interview with Dr. K. Tucker, 25 November 1991.

67. Interview with David Smith, CPC head of market research, 31 October 1991.

68. The communications market is undergoing some long-term structural change as electronic communications competes with hard copy. Business is the primary generator of Lettermail volumes, and these customers are increasingly exploring the efficiencies of electronic technology to reach all their customers and correspondents regardless of their technological capacities. Canada Post is uniquely positioned to provide the full range of delivery services.
Canada Post Corporation, *Summary of the 1992/93 to 1996/97 Corporate Plan*, p. 4.

69. See Canada Post, *Annual Report*, 1990-91, 1992-93.

70. This was important with regard to that segment of the corporate sector that was *not* using CPC; major mail customers were far more favourable in their assessment of the quality of CPC's service. Plog report, pp. 41-55.

71. See *Globe and Mail*, 14 May 1986; Minister Côté admitted that the government was considering every-third-day delivery. This approach was rejected, because the bulk of mail was business mail, which required faster delivery.

72. See Canada Post Corporation, *Summary of the 1986/87 to 1990/91 Corporate Plan*, p. 2; *Annual Report*, p. 4.

73. See Canada Post Corporation, *Study on Cost of Providing Door-to-Door Delivery* (Ottawa: March 1988).

74. Canada Post Corporation, *Summary of the 1987/88 to 1991/92 Corporate Plan*.

75. Canada Post Corporation, *Summary of the 1989/90 to 1993/94 Corporate Plan*, p. 10.

76. See Canada Post Corporation, *Summary of the 1991/92 to 1995/96 Corporate Plan*.

77. Rural closings and conversions were scheduled to take place as follows: 269 in 1987-88; 300 in 1988-89; 750 in 1989-90; 750 in 1990-91; 750 in 1991-92; 649 in 1992-93; 649 in 1994-95; and 454 in 1995-96.

78. See testimony of Don Lander, House of Commons, Standing Committee on Government Operations, 20 November 1986, pp. 2-18; see also *Globe and Mail*, 9 June 1988, report of the confidential document *10 Year Implementation Schedule – 1987-88 Corporate Plan*. The 1987-88 corporate plan indicated that if the rural plan was not fully implemented by 1996, CPC would move to increase the attrition rate and closures through buy-outs and redeployment.

79. Canada Post Corporation, *Annual Report*, 1991-92.

80. Figures provided by Canadian Postmasters and Assistants Association, *Rural Post Offices: National Statistics* (May 1992).

81. See letter to G. Hooper, Canadian Postmasters and Assistants Association, 14 August 1984, (available in Rural Dignity of Canada Archives).

82. House of Commons, Standing Committee on Government Operations, no. 34, 6 July 1988, p. 25.

83. Plog report, p. 3.

84. Canada Post Corporation, *Report on a Qualitative Research Assessment of CUPW Job Creation Products and Services* (Toronto: Breedon Research, May 1986).

85. House of Commons, Standing Committee on Consumer and Corporate Affairs, 31 October 1989, p. 35.

86. Interview with W.T. Kennedy, 25 November 1991.

87. Canada Post Corporation, *Summary of the 1986/87 to 1990/91 Corporate Plan*, p. 3.

88. See Canada Post, *Corporate Representation – Corporate Plan Review*, 11 March 1987. The ten-year plan of closings was as follows:
20 in 1987-88; 87 in 1988-89; 108 in 1989-90; 98 in 1990-91;
88 in 1991-92; 153 in 1992-93; 120 in 1993-94; and 30 in each of 1994-95 and 1995-96.

89. See *Globe and Mail*, 22 February 1988; the confidential document *Corporate Representation – Corporate Review Plan* was leaked to Canadian Press and reported in *Globe and Mail*, 17 June 1988.

90. For example, Nieman's Pharmacy entered a franchise agreement with CPC in Winnipeg in May 1987; two months later, Postal Station C closed, on 24 July 1987. The same occurred with the Rideau Pharmacy in Ottawa.

91. As Lander put it, "The current outlets were established over a long period of time, and in general have not kept pace with the changing demographics and business patterns throughout Canada." House of Commons, Standing Committee on Government Operations, 20 November 1986, no. 2, p. 9.

92. See Canada Post Corporation, *Summary of the 1987/88 to 1991/92 Corporate Plan*, p. 19; *Annual Report*, 1992-93, pp. 11-12.

93. House of Commons, Standing Committee on Consumer and Corporate Affairs, 31 October 1989.

94. Under a new arrangement, CPC still used some Public Works people, but the department replaced some employees with outside contractors. *Globe and Mail*, 14 March 1985.

95. In spring 1993, the United States Postal Service called for the elimination of 30,000 managerial jobs to cut costs.

96. Plog report, pp. 18, 66, 80.

97. CUPW spends about 25 per cent of its budget handling grievances, about $4.5 million a year. Interview with J.C. Parrot, 20 December 1991.

98. J. Fudge, unpublished manuscript.

99. See speech by Don Lander, Fraser Institute, Conference on Privatization of Canada Post, June 1989, p. 13. See also *Globe and Mail*, 25 April 1986; 12, 24 February, 4 March, 26 September, 7, 14, 21 November 1988; 18, 28 January 1989. *The Financial Post*, 19 January, 12 June 1989; 13 October 1990.

100. Interview with Leo Blanchette, 25 November 1991.

101. Canada Post Corporation, *Summary of the 1986/87 to 1990/91 Corporate Plan*, pp. 4-5.

102. Canada Post Corporation, *Annual Report*, 1985-86, p. 5.

103. Ibid., 1986-87, p. 5.

104. Canada Post Corporation, *Summary of the 1987/88 to 1991/92 Corporate Plan*, pp. 11-12.

105. For a good summary of the issues in these negotiations, see Public Service Staff Relations Board, *In the Matter of the Canadian Labour Code and the Canada Post Corporation and the Letter Carriers Union...on the Matter of a Conciliation Commissioner appointed 23 February 1987* (Ottawa: 1987) [Hereafter referred to as the *Swan report*]. See also *Globe and Mail*, 28 March, 1, 18 April, 9, 15-19 June 1987.

106. *Globe and Mail*, 6, 24 July, 24 September 1987.

107. For a good summary of the issues, see Public Service Staff Relations Board, *Report of the Conciliation Commissioner ... in respect of the Collective Agreement ended 30 September 1986* (Mont-Royal, Quebec: 1987) [Hereafter referred to as the *Foisy report*]. See also *Globe and Mail*, 19, 28 August, 3, 4, 16, 21, 23, 30 September, 10 October 1987; *The Financial Post*, 21 September 1987.

108. Department of Labour, *Report by the Mediator-Arbitrator Appointed Pursuant to an Act to Provide for the Resumption and Continuation of Postal Services* (Ottawa: June 1988) [Hereafter referred to as the *Cossette report*]. See also *Globe and Mail*, 8 July 1988.

109. *The Financial Post*, 26 September 1990; *The Toronto Star*, 23 August 1991.

110. CUPW claimed that the number of part-time jobs had increased by 1,500 (to 7,200) since 1983, while full-time jobs had decreased by 7,600.

111. For a summary of the issues, see Public Service Staff Relations Board, *Report and Recommendation of the Board of Conciliation...concerning the Dispute between the Canada Post Corporation and the Canadian Union of Postal Workers on the Renewal of their Collective Agreement which Expired on July 31st, 1989* (Montreal: 12 August 1991) [Hereafter referred to as the *Lapointe report*]. See also *Globe and Mail*, 23 July, 2, 20, 22, 23 August 1991.

112. All employees hired prior to 27 October 1991 had full job security and could not be transferred beyond forty kilometres. Employees hired into regular positions after 27 October 1991 had full job security as long as they agreed to transfer to vacant positions. See Canada Post Corporation, *Manager*, special issue, August 1992; Canadian Union of Postal Workers, *CUPW Negotiations*, 6 July 1992.

113. *Globe and Mail*, 6 July 1987.

114. CUPW wanted some monetary improvement, while CPC sought to adjust pay scales to levels consistent with those in the private sector. The arbitrator assigned some minor improvements to CUPW — such as improved shift premiums and vacation. The cost-of-living allowance was also retained.

115. *Globe and Mail*, 22, 24 August 1991. See also Lapointe report, pp. 83–86.

116. Wages were increased by 50¢ effective August 1989, 67¢ effective August 1990, 36¢ effective August 1991, 50¢ on August 1992, 37¢ on August 1993, and 42¢ in May 1994. There was also improved vacation leave, funding for union education and child-care programs, and a skill development and service enhancement fund. See Canada Post Corporation, *Manager*, special issue, August 1992; Canadian Union of Postal Workers, *CUPW Negotiations*, 6 July 1992.

117. Data provided by the CPC Corporate Data Reference and Support Centre.

118. Cossette report, p. 30.

119. *Globe and Mail*, 23, 25 March, 7 April 1989.

120. House of Commons, Standing Committee on Consumer and Corporate Affairs, *Report*, April 1990, p. 47.

121. Lapointe report, pp. 63-77.

122. See *Financial Times*, 16-22 October 1989. See also CUPW testimony, House of Commons, Standing Committee on Consumer and Corporate Affairs, 27 November 1989, pp. 17-18.

123. Over-capacity in the parcel delivery industry was signalled by CP Trucks' attempt in spring 1993 to find a buyer or partner for Canpar, which had not made a profit since 1988.

124. The profits on postal operations *per se* were $107 million; the rest of the profits derived from interest income and the sale of two blocks of land and buildings in Toronto.

125. For example, see *Globe and Mail*, 17 June 1989; *Maclean's*, 19 June 1989; *Marketing*, 11 February 1991 (cover story).

126. See Canada Post Corporation, *Annual Report*, 1989-90.

127. Canada Post Corporation, *Summary of the 1992/93 to 1996/97 Corporate Plan*, p. 4.

128. *Canadian Business*, November 1990.

129. *Globe and Mail*, 26 October 1991.

130. *Globe and Mail*, 23 June 1992.

Notes to chapter ten

1. E. Batstone, A. Ferner, M. Terry, *Consent and Efficiency* (Oxford: Basil Blackwell, 1984).

2. House of Commons, *Debates*, 1991, p. 481.

3. House of Commons, *Debates*, 6 June 1991, p. 1283.

4. Ibid., 31 May 1991, pp. 863-930.

5. The two people were Gary Billyard and Roger Pressault; Billyard remained. Ironically, Pressault ran and lost in the 1988 election against Liberal postal critic Don Boudria, and now works in the retail section of the corporation.

6. Interview with Gary Billyard, 17 October 1991.

7. Ibid.

8. The new contract extended until May 1994 and involved a generous salary, in the $250,000 to $310,000 range, plus bonuses (comparable, it was claimed, to salaries assigned to private-sector executives in large corporations).

9. Clermont had been at CPC since 1902. He came to it after a career in law, seven years at Bell Canada, and a number of years at CIP, Inc. See News Release, Office of the Minister Responsible for Canada Post Corporation, 10 December 1992.

10. See Marchment report, pp. 23-24. In an interview with the author (26 June 1990), Marchment continued to take this position, to make the corporation more commercially oriented, and to minimize political interference.

11. The board is also constructed to ensure regional and linguistic balance, with one representative from each of CPC's nine divisions. In June 1992, the board was composed as follows:

Eastern Canada: Kay Le Messurier, principal, CompuCollege School of Business

Western Canada: A.E. Downs, C.A., Burroughs, Weber et al. (Saskatchewan); Judith Romanchuk, senior vice president, BBN James Capel Limited; Bud Smith, president, Mejia Property Inc. (British Columbia)

Ontario: Larry Grossman, lawyer; Peter Cameron, chairman, The Garfield Group; Terry Yates, president, Setay Holdings

Quebec: Micheline Bouchard, vice president, marketing, DMR Group; Pierre Roy, partner, Chartier, Moisan and Associates

Upon vacating his prime ministerial office, Brian Mulroney named Julia Foster — spouse of a prominent Tory fundraiser — to the board, suggesting that it still represented a patronage position.

12. Interviews with G. Billyard, 17 October 1991; R. Beaulieu, 12 November 1991.

13. Interview with Roger Beaulieu, 12 November 1991.

14. Awarded an MBA from Harvard in 1949, Beaulieu was senior partner and chairman of Martineau, Walker Advocates, a law firm specializing in interprovincial and international matters. He held a host of directorships, including in Pirelli, Monsanto, Laurentian Life Insurance, Cara Operations, and Capital Broadcasting. Ibid.

15. Interview with G. Billyard, 17 October 1991.

16. Interview with R. Beaulieu, 12 November 1991.

17. Interviews with David Salie, 20 October 1991; Gary Billyard, 17 October 1991.

18. Interview with W.T. Kennedy. 25 November 1991.

19. For an analysis of the postal regulation issue, see Robert Campbell, "Symbolic Regulation: The Case of Third Party Regulation of Canada Post," *Canadian Public Policy*, XIX, no. 3, September 1993, pp. 325-339.

20. See Marchment Report, pp. 27-28.

21. For example, two study team reports to the Neilson *Task Force on Program Review* (1985) recommended that CPC be subjected to a regulatory process similar to that governing telephone or telegraph couriers. See Task Force on Program Review, *Services and Subsidies to Business* (A Study Team Report) (Ottawa: 1985), p. 526; *Regulatory Programs* (A Study Team Report) (Ottawa: 1985), pp. 590-94.

22. House of Commons, Standing Committee on Government Operations, no. 13, 10 March 1987, p. 19.

23. Consumer and Corporate Affairs, *Third-Party Review of Canada Post Corporation's Rates and Services* (Ottawa: 1988).

24. The advisory approach was supported by NAMMU, the regulatory approach by the Marchment Committee.

25. Consumer and Corporate Affairs, News Release, 27 June 1988.

26. Interview with A. Marchment, 26 June 1990.

27. Interview with B. Domm, 9 December 1991.

28. This was at a time when the government had been forced by seniors' groups to back down over de-indexing of pensions.

29. Interview with F. Holtman, 23 October 1991. Don Mazankowski's response was, "Holy cow, whose side are you on?" Cabinet and various ministers thought the report was too strong and that matters had got out of hand.

30. Interview with F. Holtman, 23 October 1991.

31. See House of Commons, *Debates*, 19 December 1986, pp. 2301-305; 29 January 1987, pp. 2300-302.

32. See *Globe and Mail*, 5, 6, 10, 17, 31 May 1989.

33. House of Commons, Standing Committee on Consumer and Corporate Affairs and Government Operations, *Report* ("Moving the Mail: Canada's Postal System in the 1990s"), 11 April 1990. The committee held twenty-five days of hearings between October 19989 and February 1990 and heard dozens of witnesses and representatives from dozens of organizations.

34. Interview with Gary Billyard, 17 October 1991.

35. House of Commons, Standing Committee on Consumer Affairs and Government Operations, *Minutes of Proceedings and Evidence*, no. 4, 20 June 1991.

36. Interview with G. Billyard, 17 October 1991.

37. Correspondence with D.C. Rowland, corporate manager, Customer Service, Canada Post Corporation, 27 November 1991.

38. Correspondence with Robert Nault, Liberal postal critic, 18 December 1991.

39. Interview with Bob Labelle, director, Government Relations, 28 November 1991.

40. See House of Commons, *Debates*, 1989, p. 3055ff.

41. See House of Commons, *Debates*, 25 October 1991; 18 June 1991, pp. 1910-11.

42. Interview with W.T. Kennedy, 25 November 1991.

43. For example, Rachelle Lecours of Citizens United for Equitable Postal Service, Anne Derrett of RAM, and Cynthia Patterson of RDC.

44. See H. Andre in *The Toronto Star*, 4 June 1988.

45. For a fuller account of the "rural politics" of the Post Office, see Robert Campbell, "Postal Wars," in *The Canadian Forum*, October 1990.

46. Interviews with G. Billyard, 17 October 1991; B. Labelle 28 November 1991.

47. See *The Toronto Star*, 4 June 1998; *Globe and Mail*, 29 April 1987.

48. The minister's office received four to six letters from CUPW president Parrot between 1987 and 1991, typically of a formal, "set-piece" character. Interviews with G. Billyard, 17 October 1991; J.C. Parrot, 20 December 1991.

49. Interviews with G. Bickerton, 9 December 1991; S. Carr, 27 June 1990; B. McGarry, 14 August 1990.

50. The Plog report (pp. 32-34) demonstrated that the big mail users were generally happier with CPC than other groups and had a far different impression of what CPC was doing.

51. Interview with David Newman, 28 November 1991.

52. See *Globe and Mail*, 18 December 1989.

53. See *The Financial Post*, 29 June 1989.

54. See *Globe and Mail*, 5 October 1987; *Canadian Connexions* and *Business Access*, both CPC publications.

55. The group is examining ways of ensuring that distributed materials are recycled; given the need to use recycled materials, much of the advertising material is printed on imported paper because of insufficient domestic supply.

56. NAMMU, 1987 report.

57. NAMMU, 1988 report, p. 18.

58. These include elimination of the postal unions' right to strike and the adoption of binding arbitration; elimination of a formal rate structure; a board comprised of user representatives; performance guarantees; rates set by marginal costs; and elimination of business mail's subsidy of "ordinary" mail (which should be subsidized by parliamentary infrastructure payments).

59. NAMMU also encouraged CPC to franchise the retail sector. It suggested the creation of a technical advisory council, which now exists. It has argued that the corporation's "public" orientation should be limited by business needs. NAMMU's focus on cutting the rate of absenteeism underpinned CPC's commitment to this goal.

60. See Standing Committee on Consumer and Corporate Affairs, 22 November 1989, pp. 4-7.

61. In response to the 1991-92 report, the coalition claimed that CPC's losses were really $320 million.

62. See *The Independent*, August 1991, for the complete text of the coalition's report. See also Glenn Smith of UPS for a presentation of these views at Standing Committee on Consumer and Corporate Affairs and Government Operations, no. 35, 1989-90, pp. 6-12; *Globe and Mail*, 25 June 1991. The coalition pointed to inconsistent trends: (1) despite the early 1990s downturn and extreme competition, CPC had volume growth in 1990-91 in two of the most competitive market areas; couriers (18%) and flyers and catalogues (17%), whereas first-class mail increased by only 0.5 per cent; and (2) from 1980-90, the CPI rose by 78 per cent, first-class rates by 130 per cent, but parcel rates by only 25 per cent. The coalition pointed to what it characterized as dubious corporate accounting practices. For example, CPC chose to amortize its extraordinary restructuring costs (ERC) in 1987-88 on a straight-line basis over five years. But in the 1987-88 report, only $8 million was amortized; $221 million was left in the ERC account. Another $124 million was added to the ERC account the next year, with no explanation of how this was generated. The ERC continued to grow, to $287 million by the end of 1989, despite a $58 million write-off. Profits were in effect the result of heavy deferment of costs, identified as "non-recurring." In 1990, CPC changed its accounting policy, writing off $126 million of restructuring costs against income. In 1990, it decided to no longer amortize its accumulated $287 million ERC, and wrote it off against the retained earnings account, reducing taxpayers' equity in the corporation by that amount. This allowed CPC to reach its profit target. Other practices included the use of the Employers Termination Benefit Fund, which, despite a strategy of amortization over fifteen years, was written off against taxpayers' equity. In interviews with David Salie, Roger Beaulieu, and others, I learned that CPC and the government rejected the coalition's analysis of the accounting system, pointing out that CPC's accounts are scrutinized by an outside, independent auditor. On the issue of CPC's accounting practices — particularly its choice of firms — see S. Cameron, *Globe and Mail*, June/July 1992. She pointed to the unsettling fact that CPC does business with the firm that does its accounting, placing it in a potential conflict of interest.

63. *Globe and Mail*, 5, 8 June 1993.

64. Interview with G. Billyard, 17 October 1991.

65. The issue of third-class or admail could be examined, but it is still unfolding as an issue, and might emerge as *the* predominant "political" issue facing CPC. CPC's expansion into the admail market has raised social concerns about the environmental impact of distributing billions of pieces of unsolicited, unaddressed mail. It has limited responsibility in this regard, inasmuch as it delivers only about 27 per cent of the admail arriving at Canadian households. CPC organized a small Bureau of Environmental Affairs in 1990, which has been developing policy and working with various associations and groups in the direct-mail market. The issue is rehearsed from time to time at the early morning National Control Centre meeting, in the same way that the rural and community mailbox issues were raised in past years. The issue has also been articulated periodically on the national political stage; for example, the Holtmann Committee noted the increasing number of complaints about "junk" mail, and MPs report that this is an issue increasingly raised by constituents. Louise Feltham introduced a private member's bill in October 1991 that would allow an individual to notify CPC that it does not want to receive unsolicited mail. In Montreal, 3 per cent of mailboxes display a non-admail sticker. A controversy arose in spring 1993 in Greenfield Park after a customer refused to accept his admail, and CPC threatened to cut off all his mail. The problem for CPC is that if it respects an individual's wish for no admail, it threatens to undermine the viability of the product. The issue has not yet reached a level requiring political or governmental assistance, but there are regular embarrassments that make the status quo unacceptable, and a policy development appears imminent. Relative to the U.S., Canadian direct marketing is undeveloped and expansion is likely. CPC may be able to use its increasing technological sophistication to fine-tune admail, by asking each address what kind of admail it would like to receive. But this adds a privacy dimension to the environmental problem. The results of a half-million-dollar study recently carried out in Montreal (Dialogue Study) are currently being examined.

66. There are a variety of government and consultancy "histories" of the concessionary rate. See, for example, Ontario Ministry of Citizenship and Culture, *Postal Rates and Consumer Magazine Distribution in Canada*, prepared by McCarthy and McCarthy and Peat Marwick (Toronto: March 1987).

67. For example, in 1984 only 6 per cent of the circulation of Canadian periodicals was via the newsstand. Around 75 per cent was distributed through the postal system.

68. See Department of Communications, *Evaluation of the Postal Subsidy Program* (1986). This study was the culmination and synthesis of a number of consultancy studies commissioned by the Department. For example, see *Report of the Study of Alternative Means of Supporting the Canadian Publishing Industry* (Ottawa: Coopers and Lybrand, January 1986); *Study of the Concessionary Postal Rate Changes and Periodical Publishers for the Evaluation of the Postal Subsidy Program* (Ottawa: Ekos Research Associates, 16 December 1985); *Postal Subsidies Program: Impact on Newspapers: Final Report* (Vancouver: DPA Group, September 1985).

69. For example, see the Woods Gordon study for the Department of Communications: "There is a serious question as to whether the postal rate structure is accomplishing

the goals that it was originally set out to do....The chief difficulty with the postal subsidy program is that it is not easy to target support towards groups of periodicals chosen for support on cultural grounds....The system of 2nd class rates...is no longer an effective instrument whereby the government can pursue any clear, economic communications or cultural goals in the communications industry" (pp.82–83, 155). The study recommended a ten-year phase-out, with the program to be replaced by a targeted subsidy approach with clearly spelled out eligibility criteria. See also Ontario Ministry of Citizenship and Culture study and Department of Communications (1986) on targeting.

70. Standing Committee on Government Operations, *First Report*, 15 December 1986; *Third Report*, 23 June 1987.

71. Rate increases would vary, depending on circulation rates. For publications greater than 10,000 in circulation, the increase would be 75 per cent; for those with less than 10,000 circulation, the increase would be 12 per cent. Weeklies would be exempt from any immediate increase. See *Marketing*, 19 January 1987, 25 April 1988; *Alberta Review*, 16 February 1987; *Globe and Mail*, 15 April 1988.

72. Department of Finance, 27 April 1989 budget, budget papers, p. 22. See also *The Toronto Star*, 8 July 1989; *Globe and Mail*, 9 May 1989; House of Commons, *Debates*, 15 June 1989.

73. See House of Commons, *Debates*, 15 June 1989, p. 2267; *Globe and Mail*, 9 May 1989.

74. For a reaction, see *The Toronto Star*, 16 December 1989.

75. For example, free-circulation magazines would see their rates phased up over the following two years, to reach full commercial rates by 1992; these magazines in turn would not be eligible for the new grant program. For paid subscription magazines, postal rate increases would be limited to the increase in the cost of living until the end of March 1994, at which time full commercial rates would be charged; but by this time the direct grant scheme would have started. Weekly newspapers in areas with less than 10,000 population would continue to be eligible for free delivery for the first 2,500 copies until the end of 1994 (additional copies would be charged the commercial rate); then the new grant system would begin. Daily newspapers would not be eligible for grants, and their postal rates would increase by 25 per cent a year until they reached full commercial rates.

76. *The Toronto Star*, 16 December 1989.

77. See Standing Committee on Consumer and Corporate Affairs and Government Operations, *Report*, April 1990, pp. 70–71ff.

78. See Standing Committee on Consumer and Corporate Affairs, 1990, no. 42, 8-2-1990, p. 29; no. 39, 1-2-1990, p. 25.

79. See House of Commons, *Debates*, 18 December 1980, 1 March 1991, pp. 17845–46, 24 May 1991, 13 June 1991, p. 1641; *Globe and Mail*, 2 March 1991.

80. Interview with W.T. Kennedy, 25 November 1991.

81. See Department of Indian and Northern Affairs and Northern Development, *Food for the North: Report of the Air Stage Subsidy Review* (Ottawa: 1991). Much of the material here is derived from this report.

82. *Food for the North*, pp. 14–16.

83. House of Commons, Standing Committee on Consumer and Corporate Affairs and Government Operations, 31 October 1989, p. 20.

84. See Lander, House of Commons, Standing Committee on Consumer and Corporate Affairs, 31 October 1989, p. 60.

85. *Food for the North*, p. 12.

86. See House of Commons, *Debates*, 20 October 1989, p. 4940; see also 26, 27 October 1989.

87. House of Commons, *Debates*, pp. 6062–63; see also Harvie Andre's response, p. 6510.

88. *Globe and Mail*, 28 December 1989.

89. *Food for the North*, pp. 48, 51, 59.

90. Department of Indian Affairs and Northern Development, *Communiqué* (Ottawa: 12 August 1991).

91. CPC's view is that the government or the bands should be doing this themselves. The program is a charter or air freight program, not a postal one. The flights could be booked and the costs passed on to the appropriate group, with the government paying the difference between total costs and the charges to the bands or communities. CPC feels that it gets nothing from the arrangement but another administrative task. Interview with W.T Kennedy, 25 November 1991.

92. Even as the plan was being developed and discussed during 1986, seventy-two rural post offices were closed and fifty rural routes were eliminated.

93. In October 1987, CPC's director of rural operations, Gilles Hebert, characterized the rural post offices as "relics." All 5,200 could be closed or replaced by private-sector operations that could provide better service at a fraction of the cost. See *Peterborough Examiner*, 22 October 1987.

94. House of Commons, Standing Committee on Government Operations, *Report*, no. 1, 15 December 1986.

95. House of Commons, *Debates*, 1986, p. 1826. Before being elected, Mulroney wrote a letter (14 August 1984) as leader of the Opposition to G. Hooper, national president of the CPAA:

    The Progressive Conservative Party feels that Canada Post's current program of rapid debt reduction is unrealistic...It is not possible for me to promise at this time that a Conservative government will re-instate full rural postal service within a year, or that all laid-off postal workers will be immediately re-hired. I can assure you...that restoring the quality of service will be our top priority with Canada Post. Our party is also committed to rebuilding the economy in rural parts of Canada...postal service is probably more important to the rural areas than to urban centres where alternatives are available.

96. House of Commons, *Debates*, 1986, pp. 2301–305; 29 January 1987. House of Commons, Standing Committee on Government Operations, 10 March 1987, issue no. 13, p. 5. See also *Globe and Mail*, 29 January 1987, where Côté promised to halt rural closings "for the time being."

97. After so many embarrassing revelations, the Conservatives on the committee had used their majority to end the hearings.

98.   House of Commons, Standing Committee on Government Operations, *Report*, no. 2, 23 March 1987, emphasis added; see also *Globe and Mail*, 24 March 1987.

99.   Interview with F. Holtmann, 23 October 1991.

100. For a fuller account of Rural Dignity of Canada and its activities, see Campbell, "Postal Wars." As CPC began to implement its 1986 corporate plan in the rural communities, a Quebec community development group called Operation Dignity organized a meeting in Espirit Saint in December 1986 to organize resistance. This was the origins of RDC. The driving force behind the organization was first Gilles Raymond and then Cynthia Patterson, who in 1987 became its national coordinator.

101. Interview with F. Holtmann, 23 October 1991.

102. See House of Commons, Standing Committee on Government Operations, 5 March 1987, no. 12, p. 4ff.

103. For example, see House of Commons, *Debates*, 1989, pp. 5046, 5056-57, 5152, 6402; 1990, p. 8756; 1991, pp. 331, 481-82, 856-57, 864ff.

104. *Peterborough Examiner*, 28 May 1988; *Globe and Mail*, 6 June 1988. In response to June Callwood's sympathetic article on RDC, André Villeneuve, CPC vice-president of communications, responded that "self-interest groups such as Rural Dignity...have injected an element of fear into the change process and have indulged in misinformation campaigns and scare tactics." *Globe and Mail*, 14 October 1987.

105. House of Commons, Standing Committee on Consumer Affairs and Government Operations, *Report*, April 1990, p. 18. RDC's Cynthia Patterson made a presentation on 5 December 1989.

106. Interview with G. Billyard, 17 October 1991.

107. House of Commons, *Debates*, 1988, pp. 16456-57.

108. House of Commons, *Debates*, 10 June 1988, pp. 16456-57; *Globe and Mail*, 11 March 1987.

109. *Peterborough Examiner*, 23 June 1989. The signatories claimed to have been misled or misinformed.

110. See K. Popaleni, "Shouldering the Burden for Canada Post: Privatization's Impact on Rural Women," *RFR/DRF*, vol. 17, no. 3; Joan Hannant, *Privatizing Postal Services: The Implications for Women* (Ottawa: Canadian Centre for Policy Alternatives, 1989); *Globe and Mail*, 10 June 1988. Over 80 per cent of the postmasters and assistants are women, so rural postal closings is a women's issue. In smaller communities, there are few well-paying jobs for women. The privatization approach threatens women with either the loss of their job or a drastic cut in pay — via a reversal to a mode of payment based on sales commission.

112. House of Commons, *Debates*, 23 May 1991, pp. 481-82. A CPC Decima poll in 1988 indicated 97 per cent satisfaction among rural customers surveyed who had had postal service changes.

113. Health and Welfare minister Perrin Beatty — himself an ex-Canada Post minister — wrote a letter to Lander protesting the closure of the post office in Singhampton in his riding, and its replacement by a retail postal outlet. See *Globe and Mail*, 5 April 1989. This issue dragged on for a considerable time, for months consuming

much of the energy of the minister's office, but CPC's decision was upheld. Interview with G. Billyard, 17 October 1991.

114. See R. Campbell, *Canadian Forum*, October 1990.

115. Postal Services Review Committee, *Recommendations to Canada Post Corporation regarding Its Proposed January 1990 Changes to Regulations* (Ottawa: November 1989), pp. 20-24.

116. Interviews with R. Labelle, 28 November 1991; G. Billyard, 17 October 1991; F. Holtmann, 23 October 1991. There have been symbolic exceptions to the closing down of rural offices, as in the farm community of St. Clément, Quebec, where residents took over and occupied the post office as CPC was set to close it. *Montreal Gazette*, 9 January 1993.

117. Interview with W.T. Kennedy, 25 November 1991.

118. *Globe and Mail*, 17 February 1986. See also questions in House of Commons, *Debates*, 19 March 1985, p. 3169; 18 November 1985, p. 8558.

119. New Democratic Party, *Middle Class Tax Payers as Second Class Citizens: A Report on a Postal Tour of Canadian Suburbs* (Ottawa: July 1986).

120. House of Commons, Standing Committee on Government Operations, 1986, no. 5; no. 6, pp. 6-19.

121. *Globe and Mail*, 5 December 1986.

122. House of Commons, Standing Committee on Government Operations, *First Report*, 15 December 1986. See p. 4 for the approval in principle of community mailboxes.

123. House of Commons, Standing Committee on Government Operations, *Third Report*, 23 June 1987, p. 4.

124. House of Commons, *Debates*, 1988, pp. 14099-14102.

125. House of Commons, *Debates*, 5 December 1986, p. 1698; *Globe and Mail*, 26 May 1987.

126. *Globe and Mail*, 7 October 1988.

127. *Globe and Mail*, 24 April 1988.

128. It asked for a specific ruling with regard to a series of housing developments, which would contain 12,000 people.

129. *Globe and Mail*, 28 November, 13 December 1986.

130. House of Commons, *Debates*, 1986, p. 1698.

131. See *Globe and Mail*, 10 March 1988; D. Forbes-Russell, "Loss in Value: The Super-mailbox Ruling," *Municipal World*, July 1988.

132. *Globe and Mail*, 18 February 1988.

133. *Globe and Mail*, 17 February 1987.

134. *Globe and Mail*, 19 December 1986.

135. House of Commons, *Debates*, 5 December 1986, p. 1698.

136. House of Commons, *Debates*, 1987, pp. 6376-77; 1988, pp. 14103-105.

137. The study was conducted in March 1988 in response to a recommendation by the Marchment Committee. The assumption was that unionized letter carriers would deliver the mail, except in areas with less than 200 addresses, where contractors would be used. The study also assumed that all 3.6 million addresses requiring conversion would be converted. The costs involved were estimated as follows:

1. Urban areas with group or community mailboxes: $259 million over five years, $73 million annually thereafter

2. Suburban areas with more than 200 points of call: $278 million and $88 million

3. Towns with 1-2000 points of call: $278 million and $100 million

4. Small towns with 200-1000 points of call: $403 million and $145 million

5. Areas with less than 200 points of call: $50 million and $10 million

Realistically, only (1) and (2) should have been considered, which would have added only $100-200 million in annual costs.

138. House of Commons, Standing Committee on Consumer and Corporate Affairs and Government Operations, no. 47, 15 March 1990.

139. House of Commons, *Debates*, 1988, pp. 14103-105.

140. Ibid., 1988, pp. 15405-406.

141. House of Commons, Standing Committee on Consumer and Corporate Affairs, no. 47, 15 March 1990.

142. Postal Services Review Committee, *Recommendations to Canada Post Corporation regarding Its Proposed January 1990 Changes to Regulations* (Ottawa: November 1989), pp. 20, 24.

143. Media Tapes and Transcripts Limited, Press Conference, 16 November 1989, p. 7.

144. House of Commons, Standing Committee on Consumer and Corporate Affairs, no. 47, 15 March 1990.

145. Interview with W.T. Kennedy, 25 November 1991.

146. Interview with B. Labelle, 28 November 1991.

147. The committee did note the extent to which privatization would lower wages. Broadly, it was not unsympathetic to CPC's privatization plans. It agreed with the general principle of franchising in rural areas and, in its third report, approved the principle of contracting out of mail delivery in new urban areas as a way of controlling costs. See House of Commons, Standing Committee on Government Operations, *First Report*, 15 December 1986; *Third Report*, 23 June 1987.

148. *Globe and Mail*, 29 September 1987; House of Commons, *Debates*, 1987, pp. 8831, 9387-88, 9550, 9597-98.

149. *Peterborough Examiner*, 16 November 1987; see also J. White, *Mail and Female: Women and the Canadian Union of Postal Workers* (Toronto: Thompson Educational Publishing Ltd., 1990) p. 284; J. Fudge, unpublished ms.

150. *Globe and Mail*, 17 November 1988.

151. *Globe and Mail*, 18 November 1988; see also Hannant, *Privatizing Postal Services*.

152. See House of Commons, Standing Committee on Consumer and Corporate Affairs, 1990, *Report*, pp. 72-73.

153. House of Commons, Standing Committee on Government Operations, 1988, no. 34, pp. 26, 29ff.

154. House of Commons, Standing Committee on Consumer and Corporate Affairs, 31 October 1989, p. 26.

155. Interview with H. Andre, cited in Fudge, unpublished ms.

156. Ironically, although this franchise was central to the events that followed, Manley dropped the franchise agreement a year later. Claiming that he was caught in a war between CPC and CUPW, he closed the franchise on 31 May 1988.

157. Canada Post Corporation, *Annual Report*, 1986-87, p. 10; *Globe and Mail*, 27 April 1987.

158. *Globe and Mail*, 3 September 1987, 30 January, 26 February, 3 June 1988. For a fuller and more technical account of this and other cases and legal dimensions of the franchising issue, see Fudge.

159. *Globe and Mail*, 17 February 1988.

160. See Fudge., unpublished ms.

161. *Globe and Mail*, 7 April 1989.

162. For a good summary of the issues, see Public Service Staff Relations Board, *Report of the Conciliation Commissioner ... in respect of the Collective Agreement ended 30 September 1986 (Mont-Royal, Quebec: 1987)* [Hereafter referred to as the *Foisy report*], pp. 16-30; *Globe and Mail*, 22 September 1987; see also Hartt report, 1985.

163. Department of Labour, *Report by the Mediator-Arbitrator Appointed Pursuant to an Act to Provide for the Resumption and Continuation of Postal Services* (Ottawa: June 1988) [Hereafter referred to as the *Cossette Report*, 1988, pp. 74-78; *Globe and Mail*, 7 July 1988.

164. See Fudge, unpublished ms.

165. For a good overview of this strategy and its logic, see L. Panitch and D. Swartz, *The Assault on Trade Union Freedoms* (Toronto: Garamond, 1988), p. 68ff.

166. Interview with J.C. Parrot, 20 December 1991.

167. Foisy report, p. 2.

168. *Globe and Mail*, 10 November 1986.

169. *Globe and Mail*, 16 May 1987; House of Commons, *Debates*, 25 June 1987, p. 7605, interview with H. Andre in Fudge, unpublished ms., chapter on contracting out.

170. *Globe and Mail*, 28 March, 15 June 1987.

171. Interview with Harvie Andre, in Fudge, unpublished ms.

172. Swan report, 3 June 1987; *Globe and Mail*, 9 June 1987.

173. *Globe and Mail*, 16, 18, 20, 22-27, 29 June; 1, 2, 4, 6 July 1987.

174. *Globe and Mail*, 18 June 1987.

175. House of Commons, *Debates*, 25 June 1987, p. 7605.

176. *Maclean's*, 6 July 1987; *Globe and Mail*, 28 June 1987.

177. House of Commons, *Debates*, 1987, p. 7605.

178. *Globe and Mail*, 27 June 1987.

179. *Globe and Mail*, 24 September 1987.

180. As discerned by the PSRC and reported in *Globe and Mail*, 4 October 1989.

181. For a good overview, see Geoff Bickerton, *Canadian Dimension*, September 1987, pp. 16-17.

182. *The Financial Post*, 13 July 1987.

183. *Globe and Mail*, 19 August, 3, 29 September, 6 October 1987.

184. *Globe and Mail*, 16, 29 September, 2 October 1987.

185. *Globe and Mail*, 16 September, 21 September 1987.

186. *Globe and Mail*, 2 October 1987.

187. House of Commons, *Debates*, 10, 22, 23 September 1987, pp. 8831, 9192.

188. Foisy report, pp. 2, 18-30.

189. *Globe and Mail*, 30 September, 3, 5-8 October 1987.

190. *Globe and Mail*, 9, 10, 12, 14, 16, 17, 19 October 1987.

191. House of Commons, *Debates*, 1987, pp. 9856-7, 9873-4.

192. Ibid., pp. 9852-53, 9855. *Globe and Mail*, 9 October 1987.

193. Ibid., pp. 9856-57, 9894, 9873-74, 9889; Committee of the Whole, pp. 10023-67.

194. House of Commons, *Debates*, 10023-67; *Globe and Mail*, 14, 16 October 1987. See also M.D. Wright, "The Legalization of Labour Relations at Canada Post," *Relations industrielles*, vol. 44, no. 4, 1989, pp. 866-82.

195. See Committee of the Whole, p. 9896ff; and Holtmann Committee hearings, summer 1988, no. 34, pp. 26, 29ff.

196. *The Financial Post*, 4 July 1989.

197. *The Financial Post*, 1, 2 August, 3 October 1989; 2 August 1990; *Peterborough Examiner*, 13 June 1990; *The Toronto Star*, 26 September 1990.

198. *The Financial Post*, 3, 12 October, 1 November 1990.

199. *The Financial Post*, 26 September 1990.

200. In a colourful phrase, CPC vice president of labour relations Harold Dunstan, a balding figure, declared that "I have more chance of growing a full head of hair by noon than there is of ever reaching a collective agreement with the CUPW in the current circumstances." *Globe and Mail*, 4 September 1991.

201. For a summary of the issues, see Public Service Staff Relations Board, *Report and Recommendation of the Board of Conciliation ... concerning the Dispute between the Canada Post Corporation and the Canadian Union of Postal Workers on the Renewal of their Collective Agreement which Expired on July 31st, 1989* (Montreal: 12 August 1991) [Hereafter referred to as the *Lapointe report*], pp. 2-13.

202. These were admail delivery, use of private vehicles by letter carriers, the route measurement system and workload of mail services couriers, seniority and equal opportunity in overtime, equalization of benefits, harassment, a wage insurance scheme for illness, job and wage security, and number of full-time employees.

203. Lapointe report, pp. 81-82. For a useful characterization of CPC's rationale on the issue, see pp. 77-81. CUPW's appointment to the conciliation board — Jacques Desmarais — issued a separate report, critical that no recommendation was made on job security:
    This is the heart of the dispute....The union is seeking to maintain stable, reasonably well-paid jobs rather than precarious, poorly paid jobs such as the ones the employer often creates when privatizing and contracting out its services. (p. 6)

204. *Globe and Mail*, 22, 23, 28 August 1991; *The Toronto Star*, 23, 29 August 1991.

205. *The Toronto Star*, 26, 27, 29 August 1991; *Globe and Mail*, 27, 28, 31 August 1991.

206. CUPW offered to deliver them for free, but CPC insisted on paying $100 a round. *The Toronto Star*, 29, 30 August 1991; *Globe and Mail*, 31 August 1991.

207. *Globe and Mail*, 4, 6, 7 September 1991.

208. *Globe and Mail*, 24, 28 October 1991.

209. House of Commons, *Debates*, pp. 4001, 4072-4, 4142; Legislative Committee H, no. 1, pp. 16-36, 81-98.

210. *Globe and Mail*, 28-30 October; *Montreal Gazette*, 31 October 1991.

211. The arbitrator was to proceed in three stages: he would first discern what Gold had settled, then look to Lapointe's conciliation report, and finally arbitrate on the remaining areas.

212. The only major unresolved issue was grievances.

213. Interviews with W.T. Kennedy, 25 November 1991; J.C. Parrot, 20 December 1991; G. Bickerton, 9 December 1991.

214. Interview with R. Beaulieu, 17 November 1991.

215. *The Ottawa Citizen*, 20 June 1992.

216. Canadian Union of Postal Workers, *CUPW Negotiations*, 6 July 1992.

217. *Globe and Mail*, 8 July 1992; Canada Post Corporation, news release, 7 July 1992; Media Tapes and Transcripts Ltd., press conference, 7 July 1992. There was some dissent within CUPW, particularly in Toronto, over whether the deal adequately resolved the job-security issue. *Globe and Mail*, 14 July 1992.

218. See Office of Privatization and Regulatory Affairs, *Regulatory Reform: Making It Work* (Ottawa: 1988); see also Eric Neilson, House of Commons, *Debates*, 13 February 1986, pp. 19783-4.

219. Standing Committee on Government Operations, 10 March 1987, no. 3, p. 19; 6 July 1998, no. 34, p. 5.

220. "The present structure within which Canada Post relates to its clients is largely a regulatory one. This structure is inappropriate for a customer-driven supplier. NAMMU believes that regulations presently in force should be superseded by a set of guidelines that permit the Corporation to enter into 'total service' agreements with major mail users."
House of Commons, Standing Committee on Consumer and Corporate Affairs and Government Operations, no. 28, 8 November 1989, p. 8. See also NAMMU, *Report*, 1986, p. 6.

221. The Chairman was Alan Marchment, past CEO and chairman of Guaranty Trust Company of Canada. Members were Sally Hall, past president of the Consumers' Association of Canada; Claude Senneville, formerly an executive of SNC Enterprises and member of the National Energy Board; Donald Curren, president of the Nova Scotia Human Rights Commission and board member of the Canadian Paraplegic Association; and Norman Gregory, a British Columbia businessman and community activist.

223. *Peterborough Examiner*, 4 July 1988.

224. For the full set of proposals, see *Canada Gazette*, part 1, 22 July 1989, pp. 3385-3431.

225. See Canada Post Corporation, *Information Provided to the Postal Services Review Committee to Review Canada Post Corporation's Proposed January 1990 Changes to Regulations*, vol. 3 exhibit Q, tabs 5, 6 (Ottawa: 1989).

226. Postal Services Review Committee, *Recommendations to Canada Post Corporation regarding its Proposed January 1990 Changes to Regulations*, November 1989, pp. 20-25.

227. Special lettermail was not part of CPC's package of proposals, but had been introduced as a new product at the same time.

228. Canada Post Corporation, *Response of Canada Post Corporation to the Recommendations of the Postal Services Review Committee Dated November 1989 regarding Canada Post Corporation's Proposed 1990 Changes to Regulations* (Ottawa: 1989).

229. For a fuller theoretical evaluation, see Campbell, "Symbolic Regulation."

230. Interview with G. Billyard, 17 October 1991.

231. Marchment maintains that although the CPC database was better than in 1985, when he previously examined the corporation, "they are still dealing in aggregates...we felt that they should have taken steps to learn the costs and benefits between 1985 and 1988." Interview with A. Marchment. In CPC's submission to the Marchment Committee in 1985, CPC supported the principle of third-party regulation. However, it noted that this process "would also require time for the Corporation to mature — to complete implementation of the performance monitoring, financial and planning systems needed to satisfy the requirements imposed by formal third party review, a process estimated to require 24 months for completion." Canada Post Corporation, *Presentation by Board of Directors and Management of Canada Post Corporation to Review Committee on Mandate and Productivity* (Ottawa: 1985); see paper entitled "Regulatory Process and Rate/Service Determination," p. 23.

232. Canada Post Corporation, *Presentation on Behalf of Canada Post Corporation to Postal Service Review Committee, 12 September 1989* (Ottawa), pp. 11, 14; *Reply by Canada Post Corporation to Documentation Received Subsequent to September 12, 1989* (Ottawa: 3 October 1989), pp. 1-2.

233. PSRC, *Recommendations to Canada Post Corporation*, pp. 10-15. The PSRC reported that the volume, cost, and revenue information supplied was inadequate; that the rationale for specific rate changes and proposals for deregulation were either absent or very general; that no economic evaluation studies of major service changes or of planned investments were submitted; and that indicators of economic efficiency and productivity improvement were inadequate.

234. Interview with A. Marchment, 26 June 1990.

235. See *Canada Gazette*, 3 January 1990.

236. Interview with B. Labelle, 28 November 1991.

237. Interview with G. Billyard, 17 October 1991. For example, the government was never interested in a scenario in which CPC would have to open its books to the PSRC. The feeling was that the PSRC far exceeded its mandate.

238. Department of Finance, *Budget, 20 February 1990*, p. 93.

239. House of Commons, Standing Committee on Consumer and Corporate Affairs and Government Operations, *Report*, 1990, recommendations 22, 28, pp. 36, 41-5.

240. House of Commons, Standing Committee on Consumer and Corporate Affairs and Government Operations, no. 47, pp. 6-7.

241. Interview with Helen Hardy, executive assistant to A. Marchment at the PSRC, 11 July 1990.

242. When he advised Andre in 1988 to try the advisory approach, he thought that "you could always become a regulatory body after, but it's pretty difficult to go backwards.

Therefore, let's try it...if it doesn't work this way, let's go the other way." Interview with A. Marchment, 26 June 1990.

243. When the PSRC was created, there was also a parallel process at the community level. The Postal Service Customer Councils (PSCC) were established to deal with postal issues and complaints of a local nature. They were established in each of CPC's nine operating divisions, comprised of seven to thirteen nominees from municipalities, business, professional groups, and consumer and community groups. Each council had a full-time co-ordinator and an administrative assistant. As of 31 March 1990, 1,227 issues had been brought to the councils, 575 of which became formal complaints; 279 were resolved through fact-finding efforts and/or conciliation. The major source of complaints was mail delivery service. See PSRC, *Annual Report* (Ottawa: 1990), pp. 2–12. After the PSRC was disbanded, the councils languished for six months before a decision was reached to continue with a system of this sort. A consultant was hired to design a system to give these councils some authority and to make them independent of CPC. Coopers and Lybrand made the successful bid to co-ordinate all the councils, which were re-established in February 1991. CPC has an arrangement to use the Better Business Bureau for smaller, operational complaints. The Councils deal with somewhat broader issues. Canada Post sees this system as a kind of self-regulation. Interview with David Newman, 28 November 1991.

244. Correspondence with D.C. Rowland of CPC, corporate manager, Customer Service; interviews with G. Billyard, 17 October 1991; B. Labelle, 28 November 1991.

Notes to conclusion

1   One of the earliest advocates of the creation of a commercial and Crown Post Office was PMG Eric Kierans in the late 1960s; he has expressed admiration of, and support for, CPC's direction and accomplishments since 1985. Interview with Eric Kierans, 10 December 1989.

2   See chapter 6, note 21.

3   Standing Committee on Government Operations, 4 December 1986, no. 6, p. 37.

4   At a conference on privatizing CPC in June 1989, former CPC vice president (1981–86) Keith Joliffe stated that privatization had already taken place internally, as CPC's attitudes gave it a privatized view of the world. See K. Joliffe in Proceedings, Fraser Institute Conference ("Canada Post Privatization: A Postal Reform Option?"), 23 June 1989.

5   Interview with David Salie, 28 October 1991.

6   See House of Commons, *Debates*, 1986, pp. 13571, 13583, 14213.

7   See A. Coyne, "The Last Post," *Saturday Night*, June 1988.

8   House of Commons, Standing Committee on Government Operations, 4 March 1987, no. 11, p. 26.

9   House of Commons, *Debates*, 18 April 1989; *Globe and Mail*, 18 April 1989.

10   See Proceedings, Fraser Institute Conference on Privatization; see also *The Toronto Star*, 18 September 1989.

11   *Globe and Mail*, 9 September 1989.

12   *Globe and Mail,* 23 October 1989.

13   House of Commons, Standing Committee on Consumer Affairs and Government Operations, 31 October 1989, pp. 9, 10, 19–20, 25, 32.

14   See House of Commons, Standing Committee on Consumer and Corporate Affairs and Government Operations, *Report,* 24 April 1990 [Hereafter referred to as the *Turner report*]. The report was entitled "Moving the Mail: Canada's Postal Services in the 1990s." It recommended, though, that the private Post Office retain the exclusive privilege, lest cream-skimming leave it with only rural and money-losing activities: "Removal of the exclusive privilege places the traditional policy of providing service at a standard price to all individuals in all regions of the country at risk" (p. 60).

15   See *Maclean's,* "The Power of Canada Post: Ottawa Prepares to Privatize Canada's New-Look, Profit-Hungry Postal System," 9 October 1989, p. 32.

16   *The Toronto Star,* 25 April 1990.

17   Don Lander, in Proceedings, Fraser Institute Conference on Privatization.

18   House of Commons, Standing Committee on Consumer and Corporate Affairs and Government Operations, no. 47, 13 March 1990.

19   House of Commons, Standing Committee on Consumer and Corporate Affairs and Government Operations, no. 4, 20 June 1991.

20   Political opponents and the postal unions characterized all of these actions as an unrelenting government march towards privatization of Canada Post. CUPW held a conference to counter the Fraser Institute conference, which criticized the decline of CPC as a public service and the commercial prospects of a privatized postal system. The labour unions asserted that privatization would result in a decline in service, loss of jobs, lower wages, and loss of security. The Liberal party opposed the Turner report's recommendations on privatization, stating that "essential public services belong in public hands." The Liberals characterized postal privatization as an extreme act, which even Margaret Thatcher had not carried out. Opponents claimed that privatization would be bad for the rural areas and for labour-management relations. RDC declared that the Turner report "wholeheartedly bows to the Tory god of privatization...and to hell with what the people really want." The CAC warned that a change in ownership was no guarantee that service would improve; indeed, service in rural and remote areas might deteriorate and a two-tier postal service might develop. There was a widespread sense that the government was encouraging CPC to generate increasing revenues and profits, to make it attractive for a private takeover. *Globe and Mail,* 27 November 1989; Turner report, p. 76; House of Commons, *Debates,* 1989, p. 5520; *Globe and Mail,* 25 April 1990; Rural Dignity of Canada, press release, 24 April 1990; N. Murray, "Canada Post: Is Selling It a Solution?" *Canadian Consumer,* 1990, no. 3, p. 50; *Briarpatch,* May 1990, July/August 1991.

21   House of Commons, Standing Committee on Consumer Affairs and Government Operations, 15 March 1990.

22   Interview with G. Billyard, 17 October 1991.

23   See Office of the Minister Responsible for Canada Post Corporation, news release, 30 April 1992. See also House of Commons, *Debates,* 14 May 1992, pp. 10736–40.

24 See CUPW, *Perspective*, March–April 1993, p. 3. CUPW rejected the idea of a "partnership" in the existing postal agenda. Given that a profit-sharing plan could simply have been negotiated, it saw the plan as financially motivated with the aim of imposing stricter financial conditions on CPC. See House of Commons, *Debates*, 14, 15 May, 18 June 1992, pp. 10740-53, 10769-78, 12332-86. The Opposition claimed that the bill was woefully incomplete, as it did not set out criteria for valuation, did not elaborate shareholders' rights or definitions, and provided no dividend formula.

25 Interview with J.C. Parrot, 20 December 1991.

26 *The Toronto Star*, 18 September 1989.

27 Unpublished NAMMU paper presented at Fraser Institute Conference on Privatization.

28 See NAMMU report, 1987, and Standing Committee on Consumer and Corporate Affairs and Government Operations, 8 November 1989, pp. 16, 22, 24.

29 NAMMU report, 1987.

30 NAMMU report, 1988, p. 18.

31 See president of Maclean-Hunter Publishing, Standing Committee on Consumer Affairs and Government Operations, no. 39, 1-2-90, pp. 25-29.

32 "If I had to bet, I would bet that in the next couple of decades you will see Post Offices being privatized all over the world and I would not mind seeing Canada first." House of Commons, *Debates*, 14 May 1992, p. 10746.

33 In an interview with the author, former Canada Post president Michael Warren declared an interest in organizing a group of investors to purchase Canada Post.

34 Richard Schultz, "Privatization, Deregulation and the Changing Role of the State. Lessons from Canada," *Business in the Contemporary World*, Autumn 1990, pp. 25-32.

35 Interview with Gary Billyard, 17 October 1991.

Privatization, 177-8, 231.See Canada Post Corporation

Prescott, Jack, 113

Pressault, Roger, 417

Public Service Staff Relations Act, 13, 46, 47, 58, 67, 94, 100, 114, 122, 150, 154, 155, 158, 165, 169, 194, 196

Public Sector Staff Relations Board, 152, 154

Quebec Chamber of Commerce, 222

Raymond, Gilles, 424

Residents Against Mailboxes (RAM), 69, 309, 326

Retail Council of Canada, 399, 400

Review Committee on the Mandate and Productivity of Canada Post Corporation. See Marchment Report

Richart, C., 7-8

Rinfret, G.E., 55, 84

Ritchie Report, 142, 148, 149, 180, 235

Rowland, D.C., 419, 431

Roy, Pierre, 418

Royal Commissions: Government Organization, 51, 57, 76, 84, 86, 87, 171, 178, 398; Wages, 57, 94, 114, 171, 178; Working Conditions, 57, 87, 89, 95-7, 114, 171, 178; Security, 117

Ryan, Claude, 117

Salie, David, 251, 300, 302, 303

Sauve, Jeanne, 142

Scanlon, D.J., 251

Schultz, Richard, 367

Sears, 272

Senate Committee on Mass Media, 117

Senneville, Claude, 430

Shime Report, 391

Shoppers' Drug Mart, 282, 331

Sinclair, 155

Skybox incident, 265

Smith, Bud, 418

Smith, David, 414

Smith, William 27

Sorenson, Lynda, 208

Sperling, Larry, 113

Standing Committee on Regulation and Other Statutory Instruments, 188

Stevens, Sinclair, 156, 234, 361

Sullivan, John, 55

Swan Report, 336, 416

Taylor, Eric, 154-5

Teleglobe, 367

Telepost, 141

Thompson, Greg, 67, 298

Tingley, Darrell, 345

TNT Limited, 271

Tremblay Report, 161, 167, 394

Tremblay, Rene, 55, 74, 94

Tropea, O., 251

Trudeau, Pierre Elliott, 58, 101, 108, 110, 113, 121, 125-6, 133, 166, 169, 171, 179, 181-2, 207, 388, 393, 395, 402

Tucker, Dr. Kenneth, 275, 414

Turnbull, Walter, 55, 75.79

Turner, Garth, 66, 306. See also Consumer and Corporate Affairs Committee

Turner, John, 326, 337

United States Postal Service, 115, 178

Ubering, John, 113

Ubering report, 164-5, 167, 171, 180

Vandenberg, Richard, 124, 387

van Dusen, Jack, 412

Varma, Ad. See Canada Post Corporation

Villeneuve, Andre, 424

Voice for Concerned Citizens, 405

Warren, Michael, 20, 52, 60, 62, 63, 64, 148, 149, 162, 186, 187, 197, 199, 205, 206, 207, 208, , 209, 210, 10, 211, 216, 218, 223, 225, 234, 236, 239, 241, 249, 250, 272, 281, 399, 403, 404, 434

Wilson, Bernard, 157

Printed by
Ateliers Graphiques Marc Veilleux Inc.
Cap-Saint-Ignace, Québec
in May 1994.